The Active Reader

Strategies for Academic
Reading and Writing

The Active Reader

Strategies for Academic Reading and Writing

Eric Henderson

OXFORD

UNIVERSITY PRESS

OXFORD
UNIVERSITY PRESS

70 Wynford Drive, Don Mills, Ontario M3C 1J9
www.oup.com/ca

Oxford University Press is a department of the University of Oxford.
It furthers the University's objective of excellence in research, scholarship,
and education by publishing worldwide in

Oxford   New York

Auckland   Cape Town   Dar es Salaam   Hong Kong   Karachi
Kuala Lumpur   Madrid   Melbourne   Mexico City   Nairobi
New Delhi   Shanghai   Taipei   Toronto

With offices in

Argentina   Austria   Brazil   Chile   Czech Republic   France   Greece
Guatemala   Hungary   Italy   Japan   Poland   Portugal   Singapore
South Korea   Switzerland   Thailand   Turkey   Ukraine   Vietnam

Oxford is a trade mark of Oxford University Press
in the UK and in certain other countries

Published in Canada
by Oxford University Press

Library and Archives Canada Cataloguing in Publication

Henderson, Eric
The active reader : strategies for academic reading and
writing / Eric Henderson.

Includes bibliographical references and index.
ISBN 978-0-19-542515-4

1. English language—Rhetoric. 2. Academic writing. 3. Report
writing. 4. College readers. I. Title.

PE1408.H385 2007   808'.042   C2007-903532-9

Cover image: Marko Radunovic / iStockPhoto

Cover design: Sherill Chapman

1 2 3 4 – 11 10 09 08

This book is printed on permanent (acid-free) paper ∞.

Printed in Canada

Contents

Preface

Writing as Surviving

The future turns out to be a work-in-progress, not a set of map coordinates but the product of a never-ending argument between the inertia as things-as-they-are and the energy inherent in the hope of things-as-they-might-become.
Lewis Lapham, Editor, *Harper's Magazine*
Convocation Address, Queen's University

All life is problem solving. All organisms are inventors and technicians, good or not so good, successful or not so successful, in solving technical problems. This is how it is among animals—spiders, for example. Human technology solves human problems such as sewage disposal, or the storage and supply of food and water, as, for example, bees already have to do.
Philosopher Karl Popper

The Butterfly Peace Garden in Batticaloa, Sri Lanka, was instituted about a dozen years ago by Canadian artist Paul Hogan to help children traumatized by the Sri Lankan civil war. Batticaloa was virtually destroyed by the tsunami of 2004, but the garden somewhat miraculously survived and is now a refuge for orphans and other victims of that inconceivable tragedy. It reflects a sad but hopeful story of one individual, and then many, confronting a problem and dealing with it in a humbling and human—and above all practical—way. Forty years ago, conventional thinking might have consigned Paul Hogan and his vision to the wasteland of idealism. But in the two generations since counterculture and campus protest, flower children and free speech fracases, it seems that starry-eyed idealist and pragmatic realist have changed places. Or, at least, the frame of reference is different. Perhaps the change is a recent one. No more than six or seven years ago, I watched first-year students tapping hesitantly on keyboards in a computer lab at my university, completing a simple early-term assignment: a short essay on what they considered the major challenge that humans face today. Predictably, I read about dwindling oil supplies, overpopulation, pollution, and the Middle East battleground; a couple of years later, I read a great deal about terrorism. Today, the fruits of their labours are different: their responses are more thoughtful, though seemingly more abstract. Typical problems identified include "our lack of concern for the world around us," "lack of cooperation," "loss of faith in our ability to act," "problems communicating," "flawed human perception," "hatred," "evasion of important issues," "intolerance," "humanity itself," "*we* are the problem." (Interestingly, according to a recent report, Canadians rank religious and ethnic hatred as the number one global concern, well ahead of the next problem, pollution and the environment.)

If this does, indeed, suggest a trend, these students could be called the "new realists." They are willing to confront underlying causes, unlike the idealists of the 1960s who "dropped out," blaming another generation, or the idealists of the 1980s, many of whom were too busy envisioning "the good life" of material success to even think about causes. Certainly, most students today are well aware of the challenges that their generation and future ones face. They also understand the role that communication, especially written communication, will play in meeting these challenges. This book was designed in response to the need both for problem-solvers and for good communicators; the two are intertwined.

One of the sustaining purposes in studying the conventions of academic reading and writing is to direct the human need to explore and learn, to express and create, to discuss and debate, in writing, into useful and fulfilling channels. Although the immediate result might be a level of competence that will help students in their other courses and lead to improved grades, the acquisition of writing and reading skills serves many long-term goals. Language is one of the most powerful tools—possibly the most powerful—for ensuring our survival as individuals, as a society, and as a species. Through the medium of language, we can read about contemporary problems, ask a range of pertinent questions, and propose practical solutions to these problems. *The Active Reader: Strategies for Academic Reading and Writing* seeks to provide student readers, writers, and researchers with the training to question, investigate, analyze, and communicate.

The essays in Part Three, "The Active Reader," focus on problems and solutions. Some problems are writ large: many in the last section, "The challenges of science," concern our survival as a species and the survival of other species whose natural habitats we have destroyed in the name of progress. But they are obviously not the only problems we face. The essays in "The knowledge society" address what could be considered the starting point for enquiry, fundamental questions about the nature, uses, and limits of knowledge. To what extent, for example, is it embedded in and determined by cultural, social, or economic factors?

Of concern to many Canadians is our identity as a nation, the conceptual framework of our racial, cultural, and political selves. The essays in "Defining Canadians: Identity and citizenship" ask such questions as: How do we see ourselves? How do others view us? How can we know more about ourselves? The influence of the media is the subject of essays in the section "Media and image." According to many, the displacement of the printed word began with television and continues with the impact of developing technologies, the influence of which, say some, heralds the Age of the Image. However, these essays suggest that such a formulation may oversimplify the provokingly complex relationship between word and image. Violence, on many levels, pervades our world. The essays in "War and aggression" deal with personal and collective violence, asking questions like: Is human aggression hardwired or is it learned? What are the causes of violence? These are crucial questions, but what unites these different approaches is an often unacknowledged notion: manifestations of violence, from the impulsive act to the institutionalized violence of war and terrorism, can be viewed as learning experiences, opportunities for introspection and analysis.

Besides highlighting various kinds of academic writing and its conventions, the text also includes information on another important form of fact-based prose: journalistic writing aimed at a literate and educated audience. Such writing focuses on issues directly relevant to its readers and their society, often drawing on the latest research. And as instructors have long realized, high-quality essays of this kind can be used not only to engage students and promote discussion but also to develop reading and critical thinking skills. They are often used as models for student writing to demonstrate the variety of rhetorical strategies available to writers—tone and voice and many other linguistic/stylistic choices.

Collectively, the 39 readings, all but one published this century, address a multitude of contemporary problems through a variety of genres—the academic article, the journalistic essay, the editorial, the commentary, and the personal essay. They are drawn from a diversity of disciplines and utilize a range of rhetorical patterns (See "Classification by genre," "Classification by discipline," and "Classification by rhetorical mode/pattern, or style.") A set of questions and activities follows each reading, stressing comprehension and critical analysis as well as engagement through collaborative and written work. Essays similar in content or subject matter are identified by the heading "Related readings" at the end of the questions/activities sections, making possible comparative analyses and other forms of dialogue among essays. Four essays that address problems in Canada's North form a unit at the end of the section "The challenges of science."

Part One, "Academic Reading," introduces students to the conventions of scholarly discourse, beginning with general features of academic essays, then moving to specialized functions and formats. Other forms of non-fictional discourse are also discussed, and the interdependence of academic and journalistic writing underscored. The section "Critical thinking" stresses the need for enquiry, analysis, evaluation, and synthesis in forming conclusions. The specific guidelines and strategies in "Keys for reading challenging essays" can be applied to all the essays in "The active reader" as well as to the kind of cross-disciplinary reading students undertake in other classes. An important principle of *The Active Reader: Strategies for Academic Reading and Writing* is the integration of rhetoric and reader. To this end, many of the essays in Part Three, both academic and journalistic, are used to illustrate material discussed in parts One and Two.

Part Two, "Academic Writing," begins with an overview of the essay. Most students approaching college or university have a grounding in the traditional model of the "five-paragraph" essay. The first chapter offers refinements on this adaptable form but also discusses another common academic assignment, report writing. The sections that follow stress the application of general skills to specific writing tasks, beginning with the argumentative essay. However, with the exception of personal essays, journal writing, and similar activities, most discourse at the post-secondary level requires the student to respond to written texts. The critical response, the critical analysis, and the research essay represent three forms of increasing complexity and sophistication. The research essay, in particular, relies on many of the reading and writing skills discussed in parts One and Two. Today's student faces new challenges in conducting research. A major focus in "Writing research essays" is on locating and identifying useful and credible sources, fully utilizing the electronic resources of the twenty-first-century library.

In parts One and Two and in the appendix, experts, including instructors across the disciplines and writing professionals, offer their perspectives in a feature entitled "The active voice." These essays, on topics ranging from disciplinary writing to research in the digital age, alert students to writing and reading issues of vital concern today. Some of the essays flow seamlessly from the text, while others elaborate on or demonstrate the application of a point mentioned in the text. Many can be treated as mini-essays that can be discussed and analyzed.

The Active Voice
A Journey Inspired

Although it is true that many people on this planet are privileged to take part in interesting adventures and journeys, what concerns me is how people change as a result. This is of particular interest to me after getting back from one of the most inspirational adventures I'd ever been on. My trip to the Arctic with the organization Students on Ice took place in the summer of 2005. This international expedition brought together 65 youth from all over the world for a two-week educational experience whose purpose was to teach us the effects that climate change is having on the Arctic environment.

Even though each day on this expedition had many inspirational or moving moments, one in particular stood out for me. This moment was listening to an elder from a village called Pangnirtung, located on the eastern coast of Baffin Island. Here, we learned of the suffering that the Inuit people were going through as a result of climate change in the area. More specifically, the elder explained how the warming of the area was causing the ice to become thinner and more dangerous to hunt on, and also how it led to increasing unpredictability of the already extreme weather that the town experienced. In addition, we learned the reason why Inuit women's breast milk contained some of the highest numbers of PCBs and other contaminants of any of the world's peoples.

What does a moment like this do to a person? For me, aside from feeling a great deal of grief and sorrow, it reinstated a sense of injustice: it was not the fault of these people that they are having to try to adapt to these changing conditions and circumstances. This is why, upon coming to university, I vowed to bring light to these issues and injustices. I did this in what I thought was the simplest way possible: by doing presentations on my trip, mostly to the local university community. Although many of these presentations were merely to friends of mine, two of them were highly successful. One was at a conference with the BCSEA (BC Sustainable Energy Association) in Victoria, which I had found out about through Guy Dauncey, the director of the organization, who was at a presentation by Elizabeth May, executive director of the Sierra Club of Canada, back in October 2005. The other presentation, which I was grateful to be able to make, was at the Western Division of the Canadian Association of Geographers (WDCAG) Conference in Kamloops, BC. Here, I was actually able to do my presentation in front of about 30 professors and graduate students from across the country.

In hindsight, I realize how fortunate I was to have such a moving learning experience. However, I also realize that an experience such as this can not only inspire one but also work to eliminate apathy in people of my generation. This is why I believe that it should be imperative that youth like me be given this opportunity, regardless of their financial or social status.

Ben Tannenbaum, environmental studies/political science major

ACKNOWLEDGEMENTS

I wish to gratefully acknowledge the editorial staff at Oxford University Press Canada for their enthusiasm and expertise. I would particularly like to thank Eric Sinkins for charting the book's course from the late development stage onwards and Dorothy Turnbull for her meticulous copyediting. I am grateful for the support of my department at the University of Victoria. Lisa Surridge and Colleen Carpenter were among those who helpfully steered me in the direction of possible contributors and contributions to this text. I would also like to thank Robert Miles, at UVic, for his particular support and Anthony Barrett, at UBC, whose guiding hand allowed me to venture, with some confidence, on the thin ice of English etymology.

I am especially indebted to the generosity of those individuals at three Canadian universities who took the time to write essays for the rhetoric section of the text: Bradley Anholt, Anthony Barrett, Rachel Dean, Agustin Del Vento, Jim Henderson, Judith Mitchell, Andrew Rippin, Danielle Russell, Monika Rydygier Smith, Madeline Sonik, and Ben Tannenbaum. Their contributions have enlarged the scope of this book significantly and have imbued it with their knowledge of and passion for their subject.

From its inception to its completion, *The Active Reader: Strategies for Academic Reading and Writing* has been rooted in my teaching life at UVic, particularly the teaching of academic reading and writing to first-year students. I am indebted to the many students who allowed their writing to be represented in this book.

Above all, the support of my family has been a vital and sustaining force in this project, as in every project I undertake.

Classification of Readings

Classification by genre

ACADEMIC ESSAYS (PUBLISHED IN AN ACADEMIC JOURNAL OR BY AN ACADEMIC PRESS)

Barron and Lacombe. "Moral panic and the Nasty Girl" (journal article).

Bryson et al. "Conditions for success? Gender in technology-intensive courses in British Columbia secondary schools" (journal article).

Clark. "Bad borgs?" (excerpt from book chapter).

Ekman et al. "Buddhist and psychological perspectives on emotions and well-being" (journal article).

Fiske et al. "Why ordinary people torture enemy prisoners" (journal article).

Furgal and Seguin. "Climate change, health, and vulnerability in Canadian northern Aboriginal communities" (journal article).

Gidengil et al. "Enhancing democratic citizenship" (excerpt from book chapter).

Gliksman et al. "Heavy drinking on Canadian campuses" (journal article).

James. "Being stigmatized and being sorry: Past injustices and contemporary citizenship" (article in edited book).

Kerr et al. "Safer injection facility use and syringe sharing in injection drug users" (journal article).

Morris. "Enemies of biodiversity" (journal article).

Piantadosi. "The human environment" (book chapter).

Robidoux. "Imagining a Canadian identity through sport: A historical interpretation of lacrosse and hockey" (journal article).

Schwartz et al. "Intended and unintended effects of an eating disorder educational program: Impact of presenter identity" (journal article).

Titchkosky. "Situating disability: Mapping the outer limits" (book chapter).

Wohlgemut. "AIDS, Africa and indifference: A confession" (journal article).

Young. "Universities, governments and industry: Can the essential nature of universities survive the drive to commercialize?" (journal article)

COMMENTARY/EDITORIAL

Binkley. "Wikipedia grows up."

Foster. "Kyoto: Mother of intervention."

Fulford. "A box full of history: TV and our sense of the past."

Henighan. "White curtains."

Horgan. "Can science solve the riddle of existence?"

Iyer. "Canada: Global citizen."

Niedzviecki. "The future's books from nowhere."
Poplak. "Fear and loathing in Toontown."
Posner. "Image world."
Saul. "Anti-Heroism."
Sears. "9/11: The day the world changed."

JOURNALISTIC ESSAYS (GENERAL)

Desai. "In the minds of men."
Ferguson. "How computers make our kids stupid."
Krajick. "In search of the ivory gull."
Thompson. "Game theories."
Unwin. "Dead cooks & clinking sandwiches: The origins of northern humour."

LITERARY/INVESTIGATIVE JOURNALISM AND PERSONAL ESSAY

Cone. "Dozens of words for snow, none for pollution."
Laird. "On thin ice."
Nungak. "Qallunology: An introduction to the Inuit study of white people."
Olding. "Push-me-pull-you."
O'Rourke. "Sulfur Island."
Power. "The poison stream: Sacrificing India's poor on the altar of modernity."

Classification by discipline

Some essays are interdisciplinary in scope and thus have been listed more than once.

ANTHROPOLOGY

Desai. "In the minds of men."

BIOLOGY (INCLUDING ECOLOGY)

Krajick. "In search of the ivory gull."
Morris. "Enemies of biodiversity."
Piantadosi. "The human environment."

COMPUTERS, TECHNOLOGY, AND MATHEMATICS

Clark. "Bad borgs?"
Ferguson. "How computers make our kids stupid."
Piantadosi. "The human environment."
Thompson. "Game theories."

MEDIA AND MEDIA STUDIES

Fulford. "A box full of history: TV and our sense of the past."

Niedzviecki. "The future's books from nowhere."

Poplak. "Fear and loathing in Toontown."

Posner. "Image world."

Schwartz et al. "Intended and unintended effects of an eating disorder educational program: Impact of presenter identity."

MEDICINE, NURSING, AND PUBLIC HEALTH

Furgal and Seguin. "Climate change, health, and vulnerability in Canadian northern Aboriginal communities."

Gliksman et al. "Heavy drinking on Canadian campuses."

Kerr et al. "Safer injection facility use and syringe sharing in injection drug users."

Power. "The poison stream: Sacrificing India's poor on the altar of modernity."

Schwartz et al. "Intended and unintended effects of an eating disorder educational program: Impact of presenter identity."

Wohlgemut. "AIDS, Africa and indifference: A confession."

Young. "Universities, governments and industry: Can the essential nature of universities survive the drive to commercialize?"

POLITICAL SCIENCE

Foster. "Kyoto: Mother of intervention."

Gidengil et al. "Enhancing democratic citizenship."

James. "Being stigmatized and being sorry: Past injustices and contemporary citizenship."

Sears. "9/11: The day the world changed."

PSYCHOLOGY/PSYCHIATRY

Desai. "In the minds of men."

Ekman et al. "Buddhist and psychological perspectives on emotions and well-being."

Fiske et al. "Why ordinary people torture enemy prisoners."

Olding. "Push-me-pull-you."

Schwartz et al. "Intended and unintended effects of an eating disorder educational program: Impact of presenter identity."

Young. "Universities, governments and industry: Can the essential nature of universities survive the drive to commercialize?"

RELIGIOUS STUDIES

Ekman et al. "Buddhist and psychological perspectives on emotions and well-being."

Horgan. "Can science solve the riddle of existence?"

SCIENCE (GENERAL)

Horgan. "Can science solve the riddle of existence?"

SOCIOLOGY

Barron and Lacombe. "Moral panic and the Nasty Girl."

Desai. "In the minds of men."

WOMEN'S STUDIES

Barron and Lacombe. "Moral panic and the Nasty Girl."

Bryson et al. "Conditions for success? Gender in technology-intensive courses in British Columbia secondary schools."

Classification by rhetorical mode/pattern or style

Most essays in "The active reader" employ the problem-solution rhetorical pattern; in addition, virtually all essays use some form of analysis. However, writers utilize other rhetorical patterns to develop their main points. The readings that use such patterns are listed below.

ANALOGY AND METAPHOR

Cone. "Dozens of words for snow, none for pollution."

Foster. "Kyoto: Mother of intervention."

James. "Being stigmatized and being sorry: Past injustices and contemporary citizenship."

Olding. "Push-me-pull-you."

O'Rourke. "Sulfur Island."

Poplak. "Fear and loathing in Toontown."

Power. "The poison stream: Sacrificing India's poor on the altar of modernity."

Titchkosky. "Situating disability: Mapping the outer limits."

ARGUMENT/PERSUASION

Bryson et al. "Conditions for success? Gender in technology-intensive courses in British Columbia secondary schools."

Clark. "Bad borgs?"

Ferguson. "How computers make our kids stupid."

Foster. "Kyoto: Mother of intervention."

Henighan. "White curtains."

Horgan. "Can science solve the riddle of existence?"

Iyer. "Canada: Global citizen."

James. "Being stigmatized and being sorry: Past injustices and contemporary citizenship."

Morris. "Enemies of biodiversity."

Nungak. "Qallunology: An introduction to the Inuit study of white people."

Poplak. "Fear and loathing in Toontown."

Posner. "Image world."

Wohlgemut. "AIDS, Africa and indifference: A confession."

Young. "Universities, governments and industry: Can the essential nature of universities survive the drive to commercialize?"

CAUSE AND EFFECT

Barron and Lacombe. "Moral panic and the Nasty Girl."

Bryson et al. "Conditions for success? Gender in technology-intensive courses in British Columbia secondary schools."

Clark. "Bad borgs?"

Cone. "Dozens of words for snow, none for pollution."

Desai. "In the minds of men."

Ferguson. "How computers make our kids stupid."

Fiske et al. "Why ordinary people torture enemy prisoners."

Foster. "Kyoto: Mother of intervention."

Furgal and Seguin. "Climate change, health, and vulnerability in Canadian northern Aboriginal communities."

Gliksman et al. "Heavy drinking on Canadian campuses."

Horgan. "Can science solve the riddle of existence?"

Kerr et al. "Safer injection facility use and syringe sharing in injection drug users."

Krajick. "In search of the ivory gull."

Laird. "On thin ice."

Morris. "Enemies of biodiversity."

Piantadosi. "The human environment."

Poplak. "Fear and loathing in Toontown."

Posner. "Image world."

Power. "The poison stream: Sacrificing India's poor on the altar of modernity."

Schwartz et al. "Intended and unintended effects of an eating disorder educational program: Impact of presenter identity."

Sears. "9/11: The day the world changed."

Young. "Universities, governments and industry: Can the essential nature of universities survive the drive to commercialize?"

CHRONOLOGY

Robidoux. "Imagining a Canadian identity through sport: A historical interpretation of lacrosse and hockey."

Sears. "9/11: The day the world changed."

Young. "Universities, governments and industry: Can the essential nature of universities survive the drive to commercialize?"

CLASSIFICATION/DIVISION

Clark. "Bad borgs?"

Morris. "Enemies of biodiversity."

Niedzviecki. "The future's books from nowhere."

Nungak. "Qallunology: An introduction to the Inuit study of white people."

Piantadosi. "The human environment."

COMPARISON AND CONTRAST

Barron and Lacombe. "Moral panic and the Nasty Girl."

Bryson et al. "Conditions for success? Gender in technology-intensive courses in British Columbia secondary schools."

Desai. "In the minds of men."

Ekman et al. "Buddhist and psychological perspectives on emotions and well-being."

James. "Being stigmatized and being sorry: Past injustices and contemporary citizenship."

Kerr et al. "Safer injection facility use and syringe sharing in injection drug users."

Krajick. "In search of the ivory gull."

Nungak. "Qallunology: An introduction to the Inuit study of white people."

O'Rourke. "Sulfur Island."

Saul. "Anti-Heroism."

Schwartz et al. "Intended and unintended effects of an eating disorder educational program: Impact of presenter identity."

Sears. "9/11: The day the world changed."

Thompson. "Game theories."

Young. "Universities, governments and industry: Can the essential nature of universities survive the drive to commercialize?"

DEFINITION

Barron and Lacombe. "Moral panic and the Nasty Girl."

Ekman et al. "Buddhist and psychological perspectives on emotions and well-being."

Gliksman et al. "Heavy drinking on Canadian campuses."

James. "Being stigmatized and being sorry: Past injustices and contemporary citizenship."

Kerr et al. "Safer injection facility use and syringe sharing in injection drug users."

Nungak. "Qallunology: An introduction to the Inuit study of white people."

Robidoux. "Imagining a Canadian identity through sport: A historical interpretation of lacrosse and hockey."

Saul. "Anti-Heroism."

Titchkosky. "Situating disability: Mapping the outer limits."

Unwin. "Dead cooks & clinking sandwiches: The origins of northern humour."

Young. "Universities, governments and industry: Can the essential nature of universities survive the drive to commercialize?"

DESCRIPTION

Cone. "Dozens of words for snow, none for pollution."

Ferguson. "How computers make our kids stupid."

Fulford. "A box full of history: TV and our sense of the past."

Laird. "On thin ice."

Olding. "Push-me-pull-you."

O'Rourke. "Sulfur Island."

Power. "The poison stream: Sacrificing India's poor on the altar of modernity."

EXAMPLE/ILLUSTRATION

Foster. "Kyoto: Mother of intervention."
Fulford. "A box full of history: TV and our sense of the past."
Gidengil et al. "Enhancing democratic citizenship."
Iyer. "Canada: Global citizen."
Nungak. "Qallunology: An introduction to the Inuit study of white people."
Piantadosi. "The human environment."
Poplak. "Fear and loathing in Toontown."
Posner. "Image world."
Saul. "Anti-Heroism."
Unwin. "Dead cooks & clinking sandwiches: The origins of northern humour."

HUMOUR/IRONY

Nungak. "Qallunology: An introduction to the Inuit study of white people."
Poplak. "Fear and loathing in Toontown."
Unwin. "Dead cooks & clinking sandwiches: The origins of northern humour."

NARRATION

Cone. "Dozens of words for snow, none for pollution."
Henighan. "White curtains."
Iyer. "Canada: Global citizen."
Olding. "Push-me-pull-you."
O'Rourke. "Sulfur Island."
Power. "The poison stream: Sacrificing India's poor on the altar of modernity."
Thompson. "Game theories."
Titchkosky. "Situating disability: Mapping the outer limits."
Unwin. "Dead cooks & clinking sandwiches: The origins of northern humour."

PART ONE

Academic Reading

As students, you will be introduced to many different kinds of writing during your post-secondary education. The goal usually is to interact with these texts in various ways, such as the following:

- to discuss the issues they raise with your classmates;
- to respond to them in writing, agreeing or disagreeing with the writer;
- to learn the way they are put together and/or the rhetorical strategies used;
- to acquire the specialized knowledge they contain or to become familiar with the procedures through which this knowledge can be acquired;
- to use them as "models" for your own writing, perhaps in preparation for upper-level undergraduate courses.

As you proceed in your program of study, the nature of this interaction will likely increase in complexity. For example, early in the term you might focus on discussing and responding; later, as the texts become more familiar, you may be asked to summarize or analyze them. New skill acquisition invites new challenges. By rising to these challenges early in your college or university career, you will be better prepared for the discipline-specific reading and writing challenges that lie ahead. Inevitably, some of these challenges will present themselves in the form of academic writing, researched and documented studies by experts who seek to advance knowledge in the discipline.

The pages that follow are designed to help you interact with essays that range considerably in their level of difficulty and accessibility. Although the primary focus is on academic essays, written by specialists for specialists, information is included on essays designed for a wider audience, and Part Three, "The Active Reader," includes examples of both specialized (academic) and non-specialized (journalistic) writing because it is often through the latter kind of essay that readers are first exposed to the critical issues of our age. It is therefore important to study and discuss these texts and the strategies they use to convey complex information in a simplified and interesting form for their readers.

The first chapter in Part One provides an introduction to the kinds of reading tasks you perform at the post-secondary level. It attempts to answer the questions: What can you expect when you read academic essays? Who are they written for and how are they written? In what ways is academic writing a distinct genre with its own rules and procedures? How is it similar to other kinds of fact-based prose?

Of course, comprehension skills are required before you can interact with a text. The material in the second chapter is designed to facilitate your understanding of challenging essays, enabling you not only to become familiar with their rules and procedures but also to be able use them in practical ways throughout your college or university career. Questions addressed include: What kinds of thinking does academic reading require of you? What kinds of reading skills are required? What specific strategies can you use to make the reading process easier, increase comprehension of content, and give you the skills to analyze the text and the author's rhetorical strategies?

Chapter 1

An Introduction to Academic Prose

What is academic writing?

For some people, "academic writing" is a euphemism for dense, abstract writing, so highly specialized as to be virtually impenetrable to non-specialists. However, successful academic writing is not intended to baffle the reader; rather, it is customized for an audience familiar with the discipline's formal conventions and modes of discourse, its central ideas, and ways of presenting and analyzing them.

RUDDERS AND RUDIMENTS

Academic writing, then, is not *just* specialized writing for knowledgeable readers. It would likely take a highly knowledgeable reader to follow a set of instructions for assembling an electronic circuit or an aircraft rudder. As well, like academic documents, the assembly document would adhere to certain conventions that make it easy for its audience (intended reader) to understand. For example, the information might be ordered in a numbered sequence, or there might be accompanying illustrations with carefully labelled parts.

Explicit instructions for assembly and implicit "instructions" designed to guide the reader through academic documents take very different forms because the conventions governing each are grounded in different purposes, the one practical and related to the physical world, the other geared toward ideas and analysis—although academic writing has a very practical goal too: the knowledge it generates is designed to be *used*. In most kinds of writing, however, including the writing you will do in many of your courses, **purpose** and **audience** are two key variables that you must think about before you begin writing.

The technical writer must be clear about his or her purpose and audience before beginning to write a set of instructions for assembling an aircraft rudder. Similarly, if the academic writer is not clear on purpose or audience, the reader might feel overwhelmed by unfamiliar terms, procedures, or concepts—or confused by a document that is not laid out as expected. If the document is customized according to its purpose and audience, a knowledgeable reader would respond as expected to this customized design, while the reader who lacked knowledge would quickly realize that the document was not designed for her because she lacked the skills to understand (decode) the language or conceptual framework.

Language and/or problems with discipline-specific concepts and constructs can be barriers to understanding for the uninitiated reader of academic writing. To become a competent reader of an academic document, then, might require working to understand vocabulary, including specialized terms. To become a competent reader could also require a firmer grounding in key concepts. These, in fact, are two of the major challenges presented by academic discourse.

In order to be prepared for the kinds of sophisticated reading tasks that lie ahead, it is necessary to become acquainted with the rudiments of academic discourse: its conventions, its vocabulary, and the critical thinking skills that enable you to respond fully to its challenges. But because all the reading you do at college or university is not designed to train you for a specific vocation—much of it may be to stimulate your interest in a topic, to enable you to discuss important issues with your classmates, or to develop general reading and writing skills—the conventions of journalistic writing and reading are also covered in this chapter.

WHAT ARE CONVENTIONS?

Fortunately, students beginning a commitment to their future as writers and readers usually do not have to deal with highly complex language or concepts, even in academic writing. This is because much academic writing is accessible to a wider audience than students tend to assume; most of the "barriers" of academic discourse are far from insurmountable and can be overcome by paying careful attention to its formal conventions.

You can think of **conventions** (the word means "come together") as a set of implicit instructions. Conventions are recurrent patterns that direct and organize the behaviour of specific groups of people. One reason we follow conventions is to help us communicate with one another. For example, it is a convention in some cultures to bow respectfully when being introduced to a stranger or simple acquaintance. In formal letter-writing, it is conventional to use a form of salutation like "Dear Sir/Madam"; however, in e-mail a more appropriate salutation might be "Hello" or "Hi." A convention must continue to be functional (i.e., serve a specific purpose); otherwise, it may be considered outdated and end up being replaced by a newer, more useful convention.

Academic writing also has its conventions, which vary somewhat from discipline to discipline, just as they vary depending on whether you are writing a formal letter or an e-mail. Conventions help direct the reader and organize the essay. They help him or her respond appropriately and knowledgeably. They also open up an effective channel of communication between writer and reader. The next section focuses on general information applicable to most academic writing as well as several of the more specific conventions of academic writing. This is followed by a section that discusses the conventions of journalistic writing.

General features of academic writing

AUDIENCE: WHO READS ACADEMIC WRITING?

It will come as no surprise that the largest audience for academic writing is scholars, people with knowledge about and interest in the discipline or subject area. However, all writing in academic books and journals is not intended for the same audience. The expert in cell biology will not necessarily speak the same language as his faculty colleague, the expert in theoretical physics. The biologist may be an ardent reader of the academic journal *Cell* while the physicist may bury her nose in every issue of *Communications in Mathematical Physics*. Yet both may faithfully subscribe to scientific journals like *Nature* or *Science* that publish articles of interest in the broad field of science and even, sometimes, in the social sciences. Recently, *Nature* devoted an issue to some of the intersections between science and the humanities.

Academic journals and many academic presses vary in their readership, from highly knowledgeable readers to those with a general knowledge. Examples of the former include researchers in the arts/humanities, the social sciences, and the sciences, along with professionals engaged in specialized work for government or other institutions. They might also include college and university instructors and graduate or advanced undergraduate students. Examples of the latter might include any of the above who are interested but not specialists in subjects covered by the journal. In addition to the divergence from journal to journal, some journals include articles for both specialists and non-specialists in each issue.

In another kind of journal that is not peer-reviewed (see below), the authors may summarize and rewrite technical prose for interested but not highly knowledgeable readers. Such journals are not usually considered academic and may even be sold through retail outlets, unlike academic journals: their stress is less on original research and more on making this research accessible to the literate non-specialist. However, they are usually referred to as "journals," not "magazines," even though they are primarily *interest-centred*, rather than *knowledge-centred*; thus, they are different from consumer *magazines* in which writers often must adopt strategies to attract and maintain the interest of a general reader. (See below, "Where academic writing is found," for different categories of journals and magazines.)

AN EXCHANGE OF IDEAS

The most obvious function of academic journals, particularly those in the social sciences and sciences, is to publish the results of experimentation. However, not all articles in journals are concerned with **original research**. Some review the findings of previous studies and interpret them in light of a specific theory or framework. Depending on the purpose of the author(s), the focus may be on generating new knowledge through experimentation or on modifying the way that future researchers interpret this knowledge. This distinction suggests two basic kinds of academic articles: those that *present* the results of original research and those that *evaluate* or *interpret* the results of others' research on a topic, using these findings to extend knowledge in the field of study. (See "Two common kinds of academic essays," p. 22) Articles may do both, but usually the stress is on one or the other.

What is evident is that academic writing operates as a shared or "open" system, *a medium for the exchange of ideas among informed and interested experts* in order to explore an idea or concept, to answer an important question, to test a hypothesis, or to solve a problem. In spite of the apparent inconsistencies in experimental results and in spite of the many, often rancorous disagreements among experts, it is this common objective to help us better understand ourselves and our world that unites those working in specialized fields. And it is this common objective that gives the lie to the stereotype of the "isolated scholar." Scholars, especially those involved in direct experimentation, seldom work alone; more often, they work in collaborative teams in which breakdowns in communication or a lack of cooperation could endanger the experiment's validity and damage their own credibility.

The aims of academic writing are well summarized by John Fraser, a *Globe and Mail* columnist:

> [T]he best academic publications extend our understanding of who we are in ways that trade publications and magazines and newspapers have largely abandoned. Canada's collective memory, our understanding of our social and economic conditions, aboriginal challenges to national complacency, the actual consequences of de-linking ourselves from the realities of our past . . . all find provocative and highly useful resonances from our academic publishers.

ANALYSIS, SYNTHESIS, AND ACADEMIC WRITING

Another basic feature separates most academic writing from other kinds of specialized writing and from most journalistic writing: the emphasis on **analysis**. When you analyze, you "loosen [something] up," which is literally what the word means. Analysis can be applied to all the disciplines: an earth scientist may literally "loosen up," or break down, the constituents of the soil to determine the concentration of its elements, while a molecular physicist may study the behaviour of atoms in a particle accelerator as they reach very high speeds and begin to "loosen up" and break down into smaller units. A literary analysis could involve breaking down a poem's stanzas or a novel's narrative to study smaller units, such as metre (in a poem) or point of view (in fiction).

Analysis can serve several functions, as suggested by the examples above: in analysis, you separate, break up, or "loosen" a whole in order (1) to closely examine each part individually and/or (2) to investigate the relationships among the parts. Thus, there are various ways that an analysis can proceed—by careful attention to detail, by chronology (a timeline of events), by comparing and contrasting two parts, by dividing and perhaps subdividing a whole, or by applying one criterion to the individual parts (for example, measuring the permeability of different kinds of soils). There are many other methods as well (see "Rhetorical patterns and paragraph development," p. 98).

Critical analysis involves breaking down an idea or a statement, such as a claim, and subjecting it to critical thinking in order to test its validity. In the critical analysis of an argumentative essay, you assess a line of reasoning in order to test each link in the reasoning chain; you probably also test for consistency and coherence. (See "Critical thinking," p. 43.)

As with academic essays, in most research essays you write, you do not just break down; you also synthesize. **Synthesis** is the activity of "putting together." In scientific experiments, the writer(s), in a section titled "results" or "findings," presents the raw data that emerged in the study of a particular phenomenon. However, the data by itself is not meaningful or relevant until it is placed within a larger context—the hypothesis that the experiment was intended to test, for example, or results from similar experiments. In the "discussion" section that follows "results," then, the writer attempts to synthesize his or her findings by connecting them with the hypothesis and/or the results of similar studies.

Some humanities and social science essays may employ a different analysis/synthesis pattern. In these essays, the activities of analysis and synthesis are not confined to distinct sections of the essay but are part of the essay's evolving structure. Other humanities and social science essays may loosely follow the pattern described above, analyzing throughout but focusing on synthesis toward the conclusion of the essay.

Of course, analysis is not unique to academic writing. The media often employ "analysts," and many businesses and governments use consultants who analyze data and give recommendations. Often, however, the more accurate term for the media analyst is "commentator." Commenting implies a personal response, perhaps a subjective approach to a topic (although commentators usually have expertise in their field). Thus, such analysis may be weighted by the writer's opinion, while academic writers, on the other hand, generally avoid directly stating their opinion.

Journalistic writing may include some analysis. Large-circulation newspapers, in fact, sometimes have regular contributors whose function is to analyze significant occurrences in politics, economics, sports, or fashion. But with the exception of the review, the commentary, and many types of literary journalism, the primary goal of most journalistic prose, from hard-facts reporting to investigative journalism, is achieved more through summarizing and explaining than through in-depth analysis.

WHERE ACADEMIC WRITING IS FOUND

Academic writing is published in academic journals and in books published by academic (university) presses. When searching for research sources, you should pay particular attention to *who* publishes the work.

University presses are generally run by non-profit, university-affiliated organizations; they exist primarily to disseminate the relevant research of scholars in diverse fields. Although the decision to publish usually rests with one or more editors, these editors are guided by the comments of "readers," experts in the same subject as the work's author, who evaluate the manuscript. They may recommend rejecting the work, publishing it, or publishing it with designated changes. Although the work may be controversial—for example, if it challenges previous findings or interpretations—you can be confident that it is a credible source. University presses produce **monographs**, the term for a highly specialized scholarly work or treatise in book form.

Trade books, published for profit and usually to appeal to a wider audience than books published by academic presses, may also be reliable academic sources, particularly if they have been commented on favourably by noted authorities. The best way to assess their reliability is by looking for reviews from independent sources. Many journals regularly include book reviews relevant to their content; in fact, some journals are devoted primarily to reviewing current books in their field.

Academic (scholarly) journals are sold by subscription (i.e., they are not sold at retail outlets). College and university libraries subscribe to many of them and make them available to faculty and students in hard-copy versions (i.e., they can be found on library shelves) and/or through electronic databases and indexes. (Do not assume, however, that every article you locate in your library's database is an academic source. Databases often include both scholarly and non-scholarly material.) They are often more current sources than book-length studies because journals publish several times a year—a few publish weekly—and the pre-publication process is quicker than with longer works, so journals can provide "leading-edge" research in rapidly developing fields.

The most reliable academic journals are **peer-reviewed (refereed)**. This means that authorities (peers) in the field have anonymously read the article, assessed it, and determined that it has merit.

For complete information about using research sources, including source reliability, see p. 169.

The following figure summarizes some of the different classifications of academic and non-academic writing. However, the categories are not always clear-cut; for example, some academic journals include material intended for a more general audience. (Note that a **periodical** is a general term for the kind of publication that is issued periodically, at regular or semi-regular intervals.)

In this text, essays written for a prospective audience comprised of scholars, researchers, and professors are referred to as **academic** or **scholarly essays**, whether they are in book or journal format, while essays written for an audience comprised of non-specialists who share certain interests, beliefs, or ideologies are referred to as **journalistic essays**. Articles from mass circulation magazines or newspapers are usually written for an audience with undifferentiated interests and varied knowledge

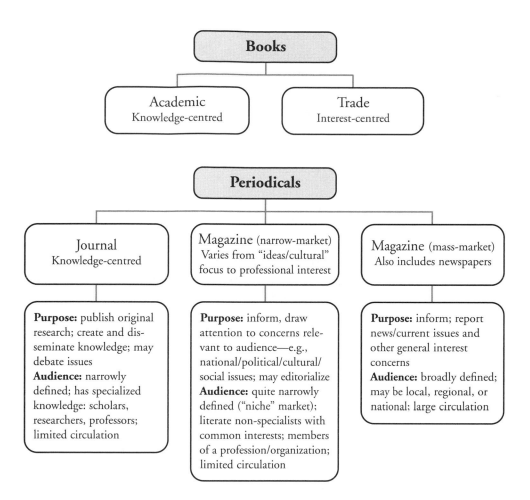

levels; however, specific sections of newspapers and large-circulation magazines could be written for a narrower audience (e.g., the books section, which is part of the more general arts or lifestyles section, or the stock market quotations, part of the business section).

Conventions of academic writing

Some of the conventions of academic writing described below apply more to scholarly journals than to books. However, academic essays on a related topic are often collected in edited volumes and follow formats similar to those described. Although essays in edited books are not preceded by abstracts (see "Abstracts," p. 18), editors often summarize the purpose and content of each essay in the book's introduction and indicate how it contributes to the field of study; each summary functions effectively as an abstract for that particular essay. The sections below on research and on voice/style apply equally to chapters of scholarly books by one or more authors.

AUTHORS

Collaborative research is very common in the sciences and social sciences. This is due to the nature of **empirically based study**, such as experimentation, which relies on direct observation under controlled conditions. Many people may be needed to observe and record the data or to perform statistical operations on the raw data. For example, as is clear from the "contributors" section at the end of "Safer injection facility use and syringe sharing in injection drug users" (p. 432), each author was assigned one or more special responsibilities in the project.

A study's authors may be colleagues from the same institution, or they may conduct their research at different institutions or research centres. In some studies, it is necessary to sample varied populations, in which case the authors may work in different provinces or countries. For example, a 2005 study on national stereotypes published in *Science* lists 65 authors from 43 different countries; interestingly, the complete article is only five pages long! Most academic writing could be considered collaborative, in a sense, because the authors draw heavily on the work of their predecessors in the field.

LENGTH

Academic essays vary in length. It is a truism, however, that good science writing is straightforward and to the point. Empirical studies, in particular, may be quite brief (some as short as two or three pages); others are much longer (see "The Active Voice: How to Write a Scientific Paper," p. 107). Writing in some humanities disciplines, such as philosophy, history, and English, is more discursive (i.e., covers a wide area), partly because of the way that knowledge is defined in these disciplines: writers can be more speculative because knowledge may not be primarily "fact-based." Many fundamental ideas and concepts in these disciplines have been debated for generations, and writers continue to explore new subtleties in and variations on them.

Length is often a function of the depth and detail expected in an academic essay. In addition, many science and social science essays use tables, graphs, charts, and other illustrative matter to summarize and simplify content. In other essays, particularly in the humanities, length may be governed by the need throughout the essay to summarize the work of other researchers and integrate it with the author's own investigations.

RESEARCH

The extensive use of sources is a hallmark of academic writing. The most authoritative research sources for an academic writer are previously published studies on the same or a related topic. Academic writers depend on the writing of scholars and other specialists in their field; however, this does not mean that all academic writing is concerned exclusively with what has been written in academic journals/books or delivered at academic conferences. Nor does academic writing consist solely or even mostly of summaries of other scholars' work. Thus, when you are asked to write a research paper, unless your instructor states otherwise, you too must do much more than summarize.

Most research, whether conducted by scholars or by scholars-in-training—students—involves analysis, which is often centred on first-hand or **primary sources**, *original material in a field of study*. Much research begins with primary source material; for example, it would be logical to study a literary work (primary source) before you looked at what other people had to say about it (secondary source). "Primary," then, means *first in order*, not first in importance, though in some disciplines primary sources may be at least as important as secondary sources. **Secondary sources**, by contrast, comprise *commentary on or interpretation of primary material*.

Kinds of primary sources vary from discipline to discipline. Here are a few examples from various disciplines:

- *Anthropology and archaeology:* artifacts, fossils, original field notes, reports resulting from direct observations.
- *Literature:* poems, plays, fiction, diaries/letters of writers.
- *Fine arts:* sheet music, recordings, photographs, sketches, paintings, sculpture, films.
- *History:* contemporary documents from the period being studied—e.g., newspaper accounts, letters, speeches, photographs, treaties, diaries, autobiographies.
- *Natural sciences:* data from experimentation, field/laboratory notes, original research reports.
- *Sociology:* interviews, questionnaires, surveys, the raw data from these sources.

Of course, it is not just writers of scholarly articles who use research. Magazine writers, including journalists writing for a "niche" market or for the mass market, may conduct extensive research. The success of a journalistic essay often depends on the effective use of a *specific kind of primary source*: quotations from those who observe or experience something first-hand and are directly involved in the issue. Magazine writers know the impact that these individuals' stories can have on the emotions of the reader and the way that being "brought into" a story of human perseverance, exultation, or suffering can make the reader directly relate to the issue. For example, Marla Cone begins and ends her essay "Dozens of words for snow, none for pollution" (p. 475) by describing the way of life of a typical Greenland Inuit family. Showing that technology dramatically affects real people enables readers to see its negative impact with much greater immediacy than a string of statistics could ever do.

Investigative essays may even use some secondary sources. But a journalist, unlike a scholarly writer, does not usually provide a citation for the source, whether primary or secondary. Documenting sources by using citations is a feature of academic writing.

Why is it essential for academic writers to cite their sources? Purpose and audience provide the answer: academic writers seek to add to the store of knowledge in their discipline; to do so, they are assisted by the findings of previous studies. In turn, future researchers will attempt to use the conclusions of these current studies to help answer a question, test a hypothesis, or solve a problem of their own. It would be very difficult to locate important studies if the writer failed to say where they appeared. Thus, the writer provides a bibliographic "trail" that future researchers can follow to the source. Although the advent of the Internet has made tracking down an unacknowledged source less difficult than it used to be, all academic writers provide this courtesy for their readers.

An academic publication usually employs one documentation method consistently, using a set of established standards (conventions) for citing sources. The method varies from publisher to publisher, and academic journals in similar disciplines may not always use the identical documentation method. However, there are four basic formats preferred by most book and journal publishers, which are described in detail in the major manuals published by university presses and research organizations:

- *MLA Style Manual and Guide to Scholarly Publishing*, 2nd edn. Published by the Modern Language Association of America (MLA). The MLA also publishes a manual designed for student writers and researchers: *MLA Handbook for Writers of Research Papers*, 6th edn.
- *Publication Manual of the American Psychological Association*, 5th edn.
- *The Chicago Manual of Style*, 15th edn. Published by the University of Chicago Press.
- *Scientific Style and Format: The CSE Manual for Authors, Editors, and Publishers*, 7th edn. Published by the Council of Science Editors.

See pages 174–80 for a summary of specific documentation methods and formats.

Although it is not unusual for scholarly bibliographies (the alphabetical list of sources at the end of the essay) to run to four or five pages or more, articles in the history field typically include extensive notes as well, either at the foot of the page (footnotes) or at the end of the essay (endnotes), suggesting the unique engagement of the historical researcher with other scholars in the field. The following essay focuses on academic historical writing, although some of the comments about using research sources apply across the disciplines.

The Active Voice

The Historian's Critical Apparatus

The heart of most academic writing in a field such as history lies not in the text on the page but hidden away either at the bottom of the page or at the end of the book in the references. Here, the whole story is told about the writer, the audience, the subject, and the standards of the discipline. Certainly references serve to document sources: to provide the origin of a quote, to substantiate a fact that might otherwise be disputed, to guide readers to find their place in the original source material. So much more than that is being revealed, however, and that is why many historians prefer notes to the more abbreviated "in-text" reference system that is favoured in some social science and science disciplines.

A text with no notes (or what we might also call a critical apparatus) has been written with a particular audience in mind. The author has assumed a position of absolute authority on the subject being discussed and is saying to the reader that he or she is to be trusted as a source. Such writing is often deemed "popular" in academic circles. It suggests that the historical "facts" are known for certain and that there are accepted ways of understanding the flow of history that need no debate.

A few footnotes or endnotes providing direct sources of information or quotes do not indicate much about the writer's imagined audience, but they do reflect honesty on the part of the researcher in disclosing his or her debts to other scholars. For the reader, they give a few hints of a different nature: they tell you about other relevant sources for this topic of discussion, names of authoritative writers in the field, and sometimes the theoretical perspective that is implicit in the essay being read. Academics tend to work within a single intellectual trend of their discipline. The sources indicated in authors' notes give the first hint of the genealogy of their ideas and perspective. History is being revealed to be more complex; these notes suggest that writing history is not just a recounting of data but an intellectual reconstruction through a framework built upon theoretical generalizations.

It is in the essay with an elaborate note apparatus that a scholar's full range is displayed. Not only will you find a bibliography on the topic and its related aspects packed into these notes, but you will also find the traces of the debates that the discipline of history engenders and the methodological issues that produce divergent perspectives. Such documentation tells the reader—especially one who is approaching a field for the first time—a good deal about the extent to which the essay being considered has a particular perspective or even bias that needs to be taken account of in using it as a source.

The full experience of scholarly reading incorporates the aptly called footnote: it is the foundation and the support of the entire endeavour, the key to decoding the values of the writer and the value of the writing. That said, a question lingers. What is the best way for the reader to tackle an essay laden with notes, whether the latter be brief, long, or a combination of the two? As surprising as it may seem, one way is to skim the notes first. For this to be a fully meaningful exercise, it is necessary for you to know something of the subject about which you are reading first. If you do, then the notes can reveal quite quickly all the hidden secrets that are their very purpose. By reading the notes first, you can make an initial and rapid assessment of whether the essay is relevant to your research topic. If it is, then you can turn to the text and read it through, ignoring most of the notes except where a quick glance might suggest that the note has something relevant to tell. That completed, your critical reflection upon the whole essay is possible. Certainly this is a process which takes practice. It also does not work as well if you are learning a subject for the first time. In that situation, there is little alternative to the opposite strategy of reading the text without the notes first and then reviewing them subsequently for their hints for further reading and the like. With practice and some immersion in your topic of research, however, that initial quick skim of the notes will prove rewarding.

Such are the joys of historical writing. The same set of data is repeated in different essays, but the picture that emerges varies in the hands of different writers. The notes can frequently be the key to understanding the hows, whys, and wherefores of the discipline.

Andrew Rippin, Dean, Faculty of Humanities, University of Victoria

VOICE AND STYLE

The voice in academic essays is generally objective and analytical. Although the authors may express an opinion, it will be seen as arising out of the findings of the study and their possible consequences or as a result of their careful analysis of the subject of investigation. It will be closely linked to their own research, in other words, and not based on their attitude toward the subject itself. Thus, it is useful to consider academic writing as expository rather than argumentative writing, since academic writers do not usually try to persuade their audience of the rightness of a system of values or of a course of action.

However, academic writing can be considered persuasive in that it seeks to convince its reader of the accuracy and validity of the findings. And, of course, academic writers do have opinions and a stake in what they are investigating. Objectivity, then, is not synonymous with a lack of involvement but refers to the degree of detachment that acts as a kind of guarantee that the writer will not be swayed by contrary or faulty evidence or by imprecise reasoning. Such a guarantee is necessary if the author is to be seen as reliable and the findings as credible.

Writers who use the scientific or empirical method tend to sound the most detached. As observers and recorders of natural phenomena, scientists must assume a distance from the object of study to avoid influencing the results or raising the perception of bias. Thus, writers may use voice in specific ways to convey this distance:

- They may use **passive constructions** (the passive voice). In passive constructions, the subject of the sentence is being acted upon, not doing the action. Student writers are often told to avoid the passive voice in their writing—for good reason, because it often results in a weaker sentence. However, if the purpose is to de-emphasize the subject, such as the researcher, or to stress the object (receiver of the action), such as that which is being studied, then a passive construction may be preferable to an active one. Note the difference between passive and active in the following example:

  Active voice: Researchers have carried out several studies to assess psychiatric risk factors in motor vehicle accidents. "Researchers" is the active subject, but in this case, the "studies" (object of the verb) are more important than the generic subject, "researchers." By changing the construction of this sentence to the passive, the writer can replace an active but unimportant subject with a passive but more important subject, "studies." Note that in passive constructions, the active subject may not even be expressed. In the sentence below, the original, unimportant subject is indicated by the use of brackets.
  Passive voice: Several studies have been carried out [by researchers] to assess psychiatric risk factors in motor vehicle accidents.

- If the **active voice** is used, writers may displace themselves as the subject, substituting "this study shows" or "the research confirmed." When the article is multi-authored, as it often is in the sciences, the writer may employ the *exclusive* "we" point of view. By contrast, in many argumentative essays, the writer deliberately uses the *inclusive* "we" or "us" in order to appeal to values that writer and readers hold in common; these latter forms of the first-person pronoun, then, include both author and reader.

  As is the case with the passive voice, student writers are often discouraged from these practices in the interests of direct, "reader-based" prose. Journalists, too, make minimal use of them because for the reader unacquainted with the conventions of academic writing, they may make the writing appear overly formal and uninteresting—anathema in journalistic writing.

Concise summaries, or abstracts, that precede many journal articles in the natural and social sciences typically use the above strategies to convey detachment and objectivity. In the example below, the first abstract, from the journal *Child Development*, uses the passive voice and displaces the authors of the study. The second abstract, from the *Canadian Journal of Forest Research*, uses the displaced subject and the exclusive "we." The passive voice is italicized, the displaced subject is bolded, and the exclusive "we" is underlined.

> Using a genetic design of 234 six-year-old twins, **this study examined** (a) the contribution of genes and environment to social versus physical aggression, and (b) whether *the correlation between social and physical aggression can be explained by* similar genetic or environmental factors or by a directional link between the phenotypes. For social aggression, *substantial (shared and unique) environmental effects but only weak genetic effects were found.* For physical aggression, *significant effects of genes and unique environment were found.* . . .
>
> **This paper considers** the question of whether sustainable forest management (SFM) should continue to incorporate sustained yield (SY) requirements. . . . <u>We</u> evaluate the extent to which SY and SFM are consistent with notions of weak and (or) strong sustainability. . . .

Many readers can identify scholarly writing simply by considering the language itself. Two important aspects of this language include the predominance of specialized diction, or **jargon**, and the difficulty level of academic prose. Compared to literary writing, however, academic writing is characterized by a lack of ornamentation. Writing in the sciences, in particular, is marked by direct, straightforward prose with minimal use of modifiers (adjectives and adverbs). (See "The Active Voice: How to Write a Scientific Paper," p. 107.) Academic writers are also much less likely to use figurative language, such as metaphors, similes, personification, and the like, than literary writers. They may, however, use analogies to help explain a point. An **analogy** is a systematic comparison between one item and another one that is otherwise unlike the first one. Analogies can be used to make the first item more understandable.

In spite of this lack of ornamentation, academic writing may strike ordinary readers as hard to understand. Although jargon and language level can be major obstacles to understanding, other elements of style, such as complex sentence and paragraph structure and intrusive documentation, can hinder comprehension. Many of these obstacles can be overcome, however, by frequent exposure to this kind of writing, partly through learning the writing and other conventions of the various disciplines.

Undeniably, however, inexperienced readers must read more closely, more slowly, and more consciously than they have to do when presented with simpler material. Part of the problem is that it is generally not until college or university that students encounter scholarly writing, although it quickly becomes a focal point in their academic lives. In terms of complexity, literary works probably come closest to the academic model, but, as mentioned, there are many differences between literary and academic works. Furthermore, the popularity of non-written media, such as television, film, and video and computer games, contributes little to the incremental development of reading skills. As well, the increasing prominence of the Internet, with its emphasis on writing and reading as entertainment and diversion, has enhanced personal, informal communication at the expense of knowledge-based communication and learning.

In spite of this, however, new reading habits can be cultivated by adopting specific strategies, such as learning to differentiate more important ideas from less important ones and to use context to identify crucial words and concepts. Fortunately, clarity is a major aim of all successful academic writers, as it should be for writers in general, and academic writers usually employ deliberate techniques to make this goal attainable. Inexperienced readers, with patience and diligence, can overcome the legitimate difficulties they encounter. Many of these difficulties are discussed in Chapter 2, "Keys for Reading Challenging Essays."

PREVIEWING CONTENT

True to their purpose as "knowledge-based" rather than "interest-based" writing, academic texts usually provide a "preview" of the article's content through an informative, often lengthy title and an abstract. By contrast, interest-based writing may attempt to "tease" the reader by asking a provocative question, setting a scene, using personal experience, or addressing the reader directly, such as by using the inclusive "we."

Titles

The title of a scholarly article is designed to give the reader important information about content at a glance. This not only serves the interests of regular readers but also is helpful for student researchers because it enables them to gauge an article's potential usefulness by a quick scan of the table of contents. Typically, key terms in the article appear in the title; thus, searching by "keyword" in an electronic database often yields many useful entries. Although it is difficult to generalize when it comes to titles, many titles include two parts separated by a colon. In this example from the *Journal of Clinical Child and Adolescent Psychology*, the first part summarizes the study's finding while the second part reveals the method: "School connectedness is an underemphasized parameter in adolescent mental health: Results of a community prediction study." In this example from *Essays on Canadian Writing*, an attention-grabbing phrase precedes the colon while the second phrase focuses more on content: "Venus envy: The depiction of the feminine sublime in Gayla Reid's *All the seas of the world*." If you turn to Part Three, "The Active Reader," in this book's table of contents, you will often be able to predict whether the title refers to an academic or a journalistic essay by looking at the amount of detail included in the title and at its format.

Abstracts

An abstract is a kind of summary or condensed version of an article. Abstracts precede most journal articles in the sciences and social sciences and give a preview of content by focusing on the study's purpose, method, results, and conclusion. They may also briefly explain background (for example, the need for the study) or consider the findings' significance. Abstracts today often include keywords, which enable a researcher to find the article electronically when searching for words and phrases related to the topic. The function of the abstract is not so much to introduce the essay as to provide a concise overview so that readers can determine whether they should read the entire article. Abstracts are usually written by the study's author(s) and range in length from 100 to 250 words but can be considerably longer.

Section markers

Writers may choose to announce upcoming content explicitly throughout their essay by using section markers or headings. In empirical studies, these markers serve a formal function by dividing the essay into conventional categories, each serving a particular purpose: for example, "introduction," "methods," "results," "discussion," and "conclusion." In longer essays, writers may include subsection markers as well. In other kinds of academic writing, the markers serve a descriptive function, enabling readers to preview content.

Descriptive section markers are one way that writers can make essay structure clearer to their readers. You can consider them as equivalents to the informal or scratch outline that can be used to help you organize your main points before you begin writing an essay. Descriptive headings are especially useful in orienting the reader of long academic essays or those that deal with complex material. Because the essays students write for class are usually much shorter, such markers are seldom necessary. However, if you are writing a scientific, engineering, or business report, you may be required to use formal markers to designate the standardized sections of your report (see "The Active Voice: Report Writing," p. 104).

Structural markers are not restricted to section headings. Because of the complex organizational scheme of many academic essays, writers may use markers throughout the essay, including in the introductory section where they can be used to preview the essay's organizational scheme (see **essay plan** in the next section). Markers can be used to announce where the writer is going, but they can also be used to review where he or she has been; thus, summaries can serve as markers and are often strategically placed after a particularly detailed or complex section. Used that way, they recapitulate content before the writer moves on to a new area.

FEATURES OF INTRODUCTIONS IN ACADEMIC WRITING

Most of the discussion so far has focused on general characteristics of academic writing and on the kind of information you can get when you preview an essay. This section reviews some of the common characteristics of the introductions of academic essays. They include the **essay plan**, the **justification**, and the **literature review**.

Activity

A good way to prepare for reading academic essays is to look at specific academic articles and see how they make use of the general academic conventions discussed so far. Browse current issues of periodicals on your library's shelves or use a periodical index or electronic database (your library's home page can likely guide you to listings of both), and evaluate a sample issue of a humanities, social sciences, and natural sciences journal, noting some of the differences among them. You can answer the following questions by scanning the table of contents and a representative number of essays—say, three or four.

What kinds of articles did the journal contain? How long were they? What were some typical titles? Were most articles written by a single author or by multiple authors? Did the articles include abstracts? How many articles per issue? Were book reviews included? Were there editorials? How were the essays laid out (for example, the use of formal/standardized or content/descriptive headings or other markers)? Typically, how many sources were used per article (you can determine this by looking at the last pages of the article where references are listed alphabetically)? Was specialized language used? Was the level of language difficult?

Like virtually all essays, academic essays, including book chapters, begin with an introductory section. It may be titled "introduction" or "background" or have no heading, but its purpose is to set the scene for the body of the essay by introducing important concepts or summarizing previous studies in the subject. If the purpose is primarily to summarize scholarship, a review of relevant literature might be included; if a review of the literature is not included in the introduction, it may closely follow under a separate heading. (The term "literature" in this context does not refer to literary works but to the broader meaning of something written—it comes from the Latin *littera*, letter— so "literature review" refers to a focused survey of the related scholarship in the field of study.) Literature reviews are a general characteristic of academic writing.

Student writers are familiar with the common practice of including a thesis statement in their introductions. Academic writers refer to their thesis near the end of their introductions, but the form that the thesis takes can vary. For students, the thesis statement consists of a claim that is supported in the body of the essay and reiterated in the conclusion. It must go beyond a simple statement of what they will be writing about: it must include a comment *about* the topic or focus on the specific approach to be taken *toward* the topic.

In academic articles with an empirical methodology, the thesis may consist of a **hypothesis** that will be tested or a **question** that will be answered through a formal experiment. It could also consist of a simple statement of intention. One common academic form for a thesis to take is an **essay plan**, a generalization of intent. An essay plan outlines the areas to be explored in the order they will appear. Authors may refer to the plan throughout the essay; in this way, it is used to orient the reader as he or she is conducted through the different stages of the essay's development.

An essay plan sounds like, and in effect *is*, an announcement, signalling where the writer intends to go. Since it announces *where* as much as *what*, it is rather like a map with directional arrows. Students may ask why essay plans can be essential parts of academic essays but may not be considered acceptable in their own essays. The answer is simple: academic essays are longer and more complex than most undergraduate student essays; they have more parts. Announcing a plan in the introduction of an essay that will be only 1,000 to 1,500 words long is usually unnecessary.

Academic essays, unlike student essays, usually include a **justification**; in other words, the author will explicitly or implicitly state the reason for his or her study. While students generally write essays to become more proficient planners, researchers, and writers (as well as to satisfy a course requirement and receive a grade, of course), academic authors need to convince their peers that their essay is worth reading. And although student writers should be clear about their purpose in writing before composing, academic writers usually need to go one step further and *announce* this purpose to justify it in light of how their work will contribute to the field of study. As mentioned earlier, academic essays are always written with a view toward what *has been* written; if an academic writer naively jumped right in and ignored previous studies, he or she would be dismissed as uninformed. In justifying the study, the writer is announcing why the investigation is necessary or beneficial. He or she also establishes credibility in appearing informed about what other scholars have written. The literature review, in turn, provides support for the justification.

By reviewing related studies on the topic, the author demonstrates where his or her contribution fits in and how it furthers knowledge about the subject. In the **literature review**, the writer briefly considers the findings of different scholars, often but not always in chronological order, and ends either with the most recent studies or those most closely related to the author's approach. Surveying what has been written underscores the interdependence of the current study and previous scholarly studies in the field, an interdependence at the heart of virtually all academic writing.

All in all, academic writers must be concerned with presenting their credentials for the work they undertake; the justification and the literature review serve as a kind of badge of membership in the academic community.

Two essay plans from articles in "The Active Reader" are reproduced below. In the first one, note that the justification for the study lies in the absence of such studies in Canada; therefore, no review of the literature is included. Academic writers often make it clear as part of their justification that the reason for undertaking the study is the neglect of scholars or their failure to investigate an area thoroughly.

> The epidemiological knowledge regarding heavy drinking in the US is longstanding, but the history of such studies in Canada is recent, sparse, and regionalized, and no study has been conducted

nationally. This paper will describe the prevalence and frequency of heavy drinking among a nationally representative sample of Canadian undergraduates and assess the character of subgroup differences related to key demographic and campus lifestyle factors. (Gliksman et al. "Heavy drinking on Canadian campuses," p. 436)

We argue that the recent alarm over girl violence is the product of a moral panic that has had a significant impact on social, educational, and legal policy-making. Drawing on the moral panic and risk society literature, as well as the work of Michel Foucault, this paper examines how the recent concern with girl violence emerged; what effects that concern has had on policy-making in particular and on society in general; and why the panic over young females is occurring today. (Barron and Lacombe. "Moral panic and the Nasty Girl," p. 366)

In the excerpt below, from the introduction of an article dealing with conduct codes in secondary schools, the author includes a thorough literature review. Because she uses a parenthetical citation style, novice readers may find the passage difficult to read. However, this difficulty can be overcome by making a conscious effort to read "between the parentheses," following the meaning of the text by essentially ignoring the names and numbers mentioned in the sources. It takes some practice to learn to read this way because, in the literature review section, the information is often very compressed to make it as comprehensive as possible.

Current literature on school rules focuses primarily on two areas: zero tolerance policies and uniforms. Zero tolerance policies delineate specific, inevitable consequences ranging from suspension to expulsion for a series of behaviours, including bringing a weapon to school. Uniforms and zero tolerance policies are often introduced in the interest of violence prevention in the school (Casella, 2003; Sughrue, 2003; Day et al., 1995). For example, Shannon and McCall's (2003) overview of school codes of conduct and zero tolerance policies in Canada was created to assist schools in developing discipline policies to address violence. Zero tolerance policies have been introduced in Ontario and in a number of American schools with the argument that they increase school safety. Recent researchers and popular commentators have responded critically, however (Sughrue, 2003; Casella, 2003; Insley, 2001; Gabor, 1995), with particular emphasis on inappropriate and unfair applications to learning disabled and non-white students (Boyle, 2003; Keleher, 2000). (Rebecca Raby. "Polite, well-dressed and on time: Secondary school conduct codes and the production of docile citizens")

The final example, below, is from an author's preface to a book-length study, a chapter of which is reproduced in "The Active Reader." In the third paragraph of the preface, the author states his purpose in the form of important questions that are addressed in the individual chapters. In the final paragraph of the preface, he briefly explains the scope of his book and justifies his study of human survival:

> For each environment, the book asks these central questions: How does the human body respond to the change in environment, and what happens when adaptive mechanisms fail? When does biology reach its limits, and when must technology take over? How do scientists evaluate the biological responses to extreme states that involve life-support problems under such conditions? These intriguing questions and their implications offer a fresh look at the human condition. . . .
>
> The debate over human evolution is beyond the scope of this book, which deals with the individual, for whom the outcome of environmental stress can be reduced to tolerance and adaptation or death. These outcomes, however, have important ramifications for the long-term survival of humans both on this planet and elsewhere in the solar system. Thus, understanding how individuals adapt to the environment is a step on the road to discovering how the physical world shapes human biology.

TWO COMMON KINDS OF ACADEMIC ESSAYS

Although the forms of academic writing share many characteristics, most academic essays can be divided into two categories with divergent formats. You can think of them as Type A (for "arts") and Type B (for "biology," one of the largest disciplines within the natural sciences).

Type A is common in the arts/humanities disciplines and in other disciplines in which an author's methodology is not one of direct experimentation. In Type B essays, the writer's research design involves an experiment or some other empirical process through which primary sources, such as raw data, are generated. If the researcher analyzes data that already exists in order to put it to use in a new way to address a problem or answer a question, the writer might also use a Type B format. Research of this kind is sometimes called **original research** to distinguish it from the kind of research that depends heavily on what other people have said. Many scientific journals publish only original research, just as many arts and humanities journals publish only research that interprets primary or secondary source material. Still other journals publish both. For example, the *Canadian Journal of Psychiatry* publishes various kinds of articles but includes the heading "original research" and other headings to inform its readers about the nature of the research that follows.

The main differences between these two categories are that Type A essays use qualitative research methods while Type B essays use quantitative ones and that Type A essays do not use standardized divisions (indicated by formal headings) while Type B essays do. These divisions, in effect, replicate the chronological stages of the experiment, beginning with "introduction," followed by "methods" (or "materials"), "results" (or "findings"), and "discussion" and/or "conclusion." The basic categories may then be subdivided. For example, "methods"/"materials" may be divided into "subjects," "participants," "measures," "procedures," "statistical analyses used," and so on. Other sections, too, may be divided into formal or descriptive categories with corresponding subheadings.

The following essays in "The Active Reader" are examples of Type B essays: "Conditions for success? Gender in technology-intensive courses in British Columbia secondary schools," "Intended and unintended effects of an eating disorder educational program: Impact of presenter identity," "Safer injection facility use and syringe sharing in injection drug users," and "Heavy drinking on Canadian campuses." "Climate change, health, and vulnerability in Canadian northern Aboriginal communities" would also be considered a Type B essay, although it does not include original research (see chart, Type B, below). The other academic essays in "The Active Reader" are examples of Type A essays.

Although not all academic essays conform precisely to the characteristics outlined in the chart below, the vast majority do conform in most respects to either Type A or Type B. Book chapters generally follow the formats of Type A. The chart is set up to highlight differences rather than similarities, but as mentioned above, Type A and Type B essays share many characteristics.

Some other kinds of writing models follow the basic divisions outlined above. Much journalistic writing, for example, is closer to Type A than to Type B in its methodology and structure. On the other hand, case studies, proposals, and business and other kinds of formal reports commonly use the methodology and structure of Type B essays. In your career as a student, you will be asked to write essays and reports that conform to one model or the other. Inevitably, you will write formal essays in several of your classes; the essay format, as it has been taught for many years in college and university, resembles the Type A academic essay format. You will likely also be asked to write a lab report as a result of a specific experiment you performed in order to satisfy a course learning objective in a science or social science discipline. Such empirically based reports resemble the Type B academic essay. For information on how to write reports, see "The Active Voice: Report Writing," p. 104; for information on how to write a scientific paper, see "The Active Voice: How to Write a Scientific Paper," p. 107.

Feature	Type A	Type B
Methodology	qualitative (concerns ideas, values, qualities); may have theoretical base	usually quantitative; centred on data that is generated, observed, and recorded
Author	often single author	often two or more authors
Abstract?	not usually	yes
Purpose	variable: may inform, generate new knowledge, or seek to interpret knowledge in a new way	to generate new knowledge
Structure	variable: may use content headings as structural markers	formal, standardized headings and sections
Introduction	• includes thesis and/or plan • justifies need for study; often includes literature review • claim is interpretive[1]	• includes hypothesis to be tested or question to be answered • justifies need for study; includes literature review • claim is fact-based[1]
Primary sources	interprets/analyzes them; often uses direct quotation	generates raw (numerical) data in order to test hypothesis, arrive at conclusions
Secondary sources	interprets/analyzes them; uses both direct quotation and summary	refers to them in literature review; uses summary
Source treatment	uses analysis and synthesis throughout essay	uses analysis in "results" and/or "discussion" section; uses synthesis in literature review and may use it in "discussion" or "conclusion"
Voice	variable: may be relatively detached (humanities) or involved (some social science research involving group observation, for example); active voice preferred	objective, detached; passive voice often used
Style	variable: may be discursive and complex; longer sentences and paragraphs; sentence variety; moderate/difficult language level	straightforward, direct; simple sentence structure
Terminology	specialized diction but may borrow terms from other disciplines and define their specific usage in essay; may use terms applicable to a particular theory	specialized diction; assumes reader familiarity with terms as well as experimental and statistical processes
Ancillary material	not usually included; illustrations may be used in book chapters	charts, graphs, tables, figures, photos, appendices are common
Conclusion	may reiterate (circular conclusion) or focus on implications of the study's findings (spiral conclusion)	spiral conclusion: indicates whether hypothesis proved/disproved or how question has been answered; often suggests practical applications/further research directions

[1]In an interpretive claim, the author weighs and interprets the evidence of the primary or secondary sources, using close analysis and sound reasoning. In a fact-based claim, the author presents his or her hypothesis and proceeds to test it under controlled conditions. An interpretive claim could use factual material as evidence; similarly, the evidence in a fact-based claim could be interpreted various ways.

A community within communities

While some students may interact with the academic community throughout their careers, most eventually leave school and the academy behind forever. What have the "isolated" interests of the scholarly community to do with those outside this community, whose everyday lives may be focused on the struggle to get or keep a job?

In fact, the academy and the world outside it benefit from one another in unmistakable ways. The rigour of academia provides training for those who take the skills they acquired in college or university out into the world. They are better equipped to confront the problems they encounter, both in their personal lives and in dealing with the larger problems of our society and world because of their exposure to the specialized skills, along with the general reading, writing, and critical thinking skills, that the academy seeks to instil.

In less obvious ways, the influence of academic research is far-reaching and consequential. For one thing, the results of major academic studies often help shape our future by influencing the policies of governments. Government agencies and independent think tanks may consult scholars or commission scholarly research before making recommendations about a particular course of action; they may even provide the funds for research in areas of interest or concern.

Since 1990, governments and scientists, including many with connections to universities, have joined forces to produce four assessment reports and many special reports on climate change through the agency of the Intergovernmental Panel on Climate Change (IPCC). The creation of these non-binding but highly influential reports on "the current state of knowledge on climate change" suggests that, notwithstanding the many tensions that can exist between governments and researchers, the relationship between them is necessarily symbiotic. Furthermore, the role of the media in disseminating the content of these reports underscores its vital relationship with the academic community.

SCHOLARLY WRITING AND THE MEDIA

People may think that the relationship between academic writing and popular writing is not a close one, since the former is dominated by highly educated individuals conversing in a specialized language to other "insiders," whereas popular writers speak the language of the rest of us. However, the relationship is really one of interdependence. Research creates new knowledge or opens up new areas for speculation; this knowledge, in turn, is disseminated to the general public, mostly through the media. We often do not consider this basic relationship, or we may take it for granted.

Although the most traditional media—newspapers, magazines, and television—provide their readers and viewers with information about the news of the day, they also act as conduits for the dissemination of new knowledge generated through research. Much of this new knowledge is transmitted through print, in special sections or feature articles in newspapers or magazines, or through news features or specialized

TV channels. However, an increasing number of people get their daily news from the Internet. Internet search engines usually include in their general interest categories stories derived from scholarly research. For example, on a typical day, Google featured the following and other research-generated stories on its news home page:

- a study showing that people who spoke on cellphones while driving were as likely to cause accidents as those who drove while intoxicated;
- a study that found an inverse relationship between high income and perceived happiness;
- findings from medical research on preventing blindness and the relationship between diabetes and heart attacks;
- the conclusions of a report, commissioned by the Canadian federal government, that examined wait lists for medical treatment. Its author was the director of a research centre and a university professor.

Translating the complex findings of research into the language of everyday readers is often the work of media agencies—"wire services" like the Canadian Press—which search out current research of significance and rewrite it for use by daily newspapers. Academic writers direct their studies to those with similar expertise and interest— their peers—while the popular press disseminates this knowledge, making it known to the very people whom it will most directly affect—for example, people who use cellphones and who may at some time in their lives reap the benefits of new medical discoveries. In this way, the connection between scholarly research and the reporting of this research to the public is seamlessly affirmed every day.

The following excerpt from a Canadian newspaper illustrates the way that research can be disseminated through the mass media. The article, which recently appeared in *The Daily News* (Halifax), was also published in other dailies across the country, usually in a similar format, suggesting that it was rewritten only minimally after the newspapers received it from the Canadian Press. (See "Conventions of the journalistic essay," p. 29, for more information about journalistic prose.)

> The simple opening, designed to attract interest by relating a common observation, marks it as journalistic.

> The short paragraphs that follow the first one focus on condensed summary and, in the third paragraph, on the researchers' methodology.

Kids can be cruel. Everyone knows that.

But a Canadian study published in the journal *Child Development* suggests that social aggression—acts like a kid purposely ignoring another for seemingly no reason—is learned behaviour and can be prevented.

Researchers from the University of Montreal, University of Quebec at Montreal, and Laval University studied 234 sets of six-year-old twins.

Based on ratings from the children's teachers and peers, researchers found environmental factors, such as parents and peer influence, accounted for about 80 per cent of a child's social aggression.

By contrast, genes make up more than half of individual differences in physical aggression.

"It's about 60 per cent of genetics that determine whether you are aggressive or not, period," says Mara Brendgen, lead researcher in the study.

The writer quotes the first author in the multi-authored study.

"But this aggressiveness is initially expressed as physical aggressiveness, but the environment determines whether you make the shift from physical to social aggressiveness."

Brendgen says as physically aggressive kids grow older, they can learn to adapt their behaviour into a social form of dominance, like spreading rumours and excluding a certain child from social groups.

"These strategies are extremely successful in hurting the victim, but they carry much less risk of detection and punishment."

Brendgen says the research suggests that if aggressive children can learn to replace their physical impulses with social aggressiveness, they can also learn to curb their social bullying.

In referring to Brendgen, the writer uses a combination of direct quotation and summary. Another expert, Wolfe, contributes to the newspaper story, someone uninvolved in the study but interested in its outcome.

David Wolfe, a child psychologist at the Centre for Addiction and Mental Health in London, Ont., agrees that early prevention is key.

"Parents for younger kids play a very important role to set the boundaries and say that's wrong, let's work it out, let's talk," Wolfe says, noting the huge push in schools to teach that bullying is not just physical intimidation.

The study is of interest to parents, teachers, and caregivers because, Brendgen says, victims can feel the effects of social aggression for months and years after the bullying has stopped. . . .

Toward the end of the article, the author focuses on those who might be interested in and affected by the results. Compare with the original study in which the authors speak to a different audience in their conclusion, below.

It is safe to assume, without having to read the research article, that the language of the original is very different from that of the newspaper. Furthermore, aside from the brief mention of the subjects of the study and the ratings measure used, the section on methods, always an important one in a Type B academic essay, is hardly represented in the newspaper article. It is clear that this article was written for a very different audience from that of the research paper.

In their "conclusion," the authors of the original 17-page study address their intended audience, not so much "parents, teachers, and caregivers" as future researchers in the field of social aggression. Note, however, that, in spite of the different audience addressed, the conclusions of both articles focus on the practical implications of the findings in reducing the prevalence of social bullying:

The present results have important implications for preventative interventions as they suggest that reducing physically aggressive behaviour at an early age might also help prevent the development of social aggression. In this context, it will be important to identify in future studies the putative moderating factors that might qualify the pathway from physical to social aggression. Identification of such moderating conditions will help improve the existing preventative intervention programs aimed at reducing aggressive behaviour in all its forms. (Brendgen et al. "Examining genetic and environmental effects on social aggression: A study of six-year-old twins." *Child Development*)

Large social and cultural changes permeate our world so gradually that we are scarcely aware of them or where they came from; however, many of these changes have their origin in scholarly debates that have been ongoing for years. To take one of many examples of the way that academic debate has produced wholesale changes in our way of thinking, consider the once-novel perception of the relationship between language and the construction of our identities, a perception that has had radical implications across societies, cultures, and races. What began as speculative thought, much of it in linguistics and anthropology, now permeates virtually all disciplines from art to women's studies—and well beyond into the non-academic world.

A SELF-REGULATING COMMUNITY

There is another important fact about the academic community that helps to make it a true community: academic writing, by its very nature, is self-regulating. Researchers are always questioning, testing, retesting, and, in some cases, criticizing one another's work. Even a well-established journal is not immune from criticism, as one incident dramatically shows: in 2005 the editors of the journal *Cell* decided to retract without explanation an article published in its own pages the previous year. The decision unleashed a furor. What the critics objected to was not the retraction per se but the failure to give a reason for it. In the world of academic writing, accountability is crucial, and, in the opinion of some, the journal editors were not acting responsibly.

Academic writers often anticipate criticism or, at least, challenges to their methodology or findings. To assure readers that they are aware of the study's possible weaknesses, the authors often include a section at the beginning or end of the article that directly addresses possible limitations, such as a small sample size. A small sample might mean that the findings cannot be generalized. This does not mean that the study is flawed but rather extends an invitation to future researchers to replicate the original experiment or conduct similar studies using a larger sample size in order to make the results more reliable, more applicable to larger or more diverse groups.

The academic writer as a specialist in his or her subject area is familiar with what has been written and able to assess the strengths as well as the limitations of others' work. He or she can discriminate between a study that satisfies its objectives and one that does not, between one whose methods are consistent with its aims and one whose methods are not. In other words, self-criticism is built into the model of research-oriented scholarship.

Conventions of the journalistic essay

Clichés about journalists abound from the days when reporting was a legendary male preserve and the newsroom a smoky conclave of cigar-chomping editors, tough veterans of the beat, and raw recruits eager to make their name by "cracking a top story." With the marriage of news and image in the TV newscast, print media had to adapt to the new reality that television could report the news quicker and with greater impact. One of these adaptations was through specialization: the diversity of narrow-market "niche" periodicals and special sections in high-circulation dailies is one indication of this specialization.

CATEGORIES OF PERIODICALS

Narrow-market publications include trade magazines and "house organs" that speak directly to a niche audience by industry, business, vocation, or membership in an organization; the wide variety of cultural and ethnic magazines; regional and local magazines whose readers may share civic or environmental concerns; hobbyist magazines catering to those with a passion for anything from dance to interior design, from aviation to opera; and advocacy magazines whose shared concerns might focus on women's issues, health issues, or the environment.

Other publishers target demographics like age group or income, with examples of the latter ranging from glossy magazines with costly advertising to "street newspapers" promoting the interests of the homeless. Many niche magazines in Canada are short-lived, constrained by tight budgets and staff turnover and by competition from better-funded US publications. The advent of web-based publishing, from non-academic on-line journals to personal web logs (blogs) and Internet spaces, has introduced an economically viable way for individuals with no previous forum to communicate to do so, anonymously if preferred, with people of similar interests, tastes, obsessions, or fantasies.

The line between the various kinds of periodicals is often unclear, but there are major distinctions between them and academic journals. Although many different kinds of periodicals are represented in the journalistic essays in "The Active Reader," most could be considered "ideas" magazines in which professional writers, including many with academic affiliations, address compelling issues in the broad field of culture and the arts. The mandate of such magazines could be summed up by that of *Inroads*, a 15-year-old Canadian periodical that aims to publish "content [that] is well-researched but not academic." Depending on the magazine, topic, and other factors (such as the requirements of the assignment), these magazines may be considered valid sources for some of your essays.

In general, journalistic essays differ markedly from academic essays in their use of specialized language (although language level may vary considerably), in their use and acknowledgement of secondary sources (written sources in particular), and in their formats and organization.

In addition, they are fundamentally interest- rather than knowledge-centred, much less concerned with generating new knowledge than with disseminating and synthesizing knowledge produced by the academic and research communities. Investigative essays typically bring to the public eye knowledge that has been suppressed or overlooked. Some essays, unlike the vast majority of academic essays, take an argumentative stance toward their topic; if not explicit, argument is often implied.

Activity

To get an idea of the variety of Canadian periodicals and their content, visit an on-line website of Canadian magazine publishers, such as the Canadian Magazine Publishers Association, or obtain a copy of the most recent directory from your library. Prepare a short oral or written report that canvasses some of the categories mentioned above, referring to the relative number of magazines in each; include a summary of at least one specific magazine for two of the categories mentioned, including its purpose and audience. Consider what the magazines, taken collectively, might say about Canadians and their interests in today's world. If you are preparing a written report, you may set it up informally or formally (if the latter, see "The Active Voice: Report Writing," p. 104 and "The struggle for superior sources," a sample student report, p. 184).

LANGUAGE

The language level of journalistic essays varies depending on whether the essay has been written for a narrow-market or a mass-market audience in which the education level of readers might differ considerably. Although journalistic essays seldom use highly specialized language, they may target an educated audience. This is particularly the case with articles and commentaries in arts and culture ("ideas") magazines. Such narrow-market magazines are much more likely to expect their readers to be highly literate than mass-market magazines and newspapers would. In addition, many special interest magazines use words and terms that would be familiar to their niche readers but not necessarily to general readers.

The level of formality in the language varies, but journalistic writing is almost always more informal than academic writing. In most mass-market publications, writers use the language of everyday speech. Contractions and colloquial expressions are acceptable—in fact, preferable to their more formal alternatives. Sentences are usually short and of simple construction; to maintain interest and create "white space," paragraphs may also be short. The stress is on ease of reading so that readers can skim an article if they are in a rush or return to it easily if they are interrupted. On the other hand, sentence and paragraph construction in essays appearing in arts and culture publications may be similar in their variety and complexity to some Type A academic essays.

Whether the essay appears in a narrow- or mass-market publication, journalistic writing is active writing, and the active voice is preferred to the passive voice (in the active voice, the subject is acting, not being acted on; see p. 14).

USING SOURCES

Journalistic essays rely greatly on experts or on the informed opinion of the author. Experts are essential if the main purpose of the essay is to inform or to disseminate new knowledge, such as the results of a research study. Journalistic writers use a combination of direct quotations, especially those that will make the greatest impact on the reader, and summary, which is used when complex material needs explanation. Technical information will almost always be simplified, or omitted if unimportant, unless the magazine is designed for those with technical expertise in the subject, such as readers of computer or auto magazines.

How journalists use their sources depends greatly on the specific purpose for writing. Most often, journalists are simply informing their readers about a current item of interest, ranging from the coverage of a fast-breaking news story to a recent development in a general field like technology, culture, or psychology. However, journalists often venture into less familiar areas, using the specialized conventions that apply, depending on the purpose for writing. The following three subsections discuss two specialized journalistic forms—literary journalism and investigative journalism—and the way that the journalistic essay treats sources.

Focus on human interest

In contrast to most academic essays, human interest is usually a focus, to varying degrees, in journalistic essays. Writers will interview those most directly affected by an event, as well as observers, often shaping the story around the emotions of those directly or indirectly involved.

Writers seek ways to find a human connection, even if the focus of the essay is not primarily on people. In fact, the inclusion of the obligatory "human interest" factor is sometimes criticized as formulaic (what journalism instructor Don Gibb has referred to as the "warm-body syndrome"), so journalists must ensure that they choose relevant and representative sources. For example, Clive Thompson chose to begin his essay "Game theories" (p. 332) by introducing a "gamer," an economics professor who discovered a connection between economic theory and "capital" accrued by on-line gamers. Thompson's essay illustrates another, less common relationship between journalistic and academic writing: although he draws on a few well-known academic sources in his essay, Thompson reports on an area relatively untouched by research: Internet addiction. A journalist attuned to the fine vibrations of contemporary life can sometimes anticipate an area of future research, as Thompson did in 2004; there are now an increasing number of scholarly studies on this topic.

A common practice of journalists today is to write themselves into their essays, using the first-person voice to take on the role of an "expert." This practice goes back to writers like American journalist Tom Wolfe, who coined the term "new journalism" in 1972 to refer to a kind of subjective writing through which the writer could break free from the strictures of impersonal journalism. Like the warm-body syndrome, this technique is sometimes criticized. At its best, however, the writer becomes a stand-in for the reader, experiencing the immediacy of a situation as he or she interacts with it, asking the kinds of questions the reader might ask, recording subjective experience, and, sometimes, reflecting on that experience and the way it affects the writer.

In the hands of a skilled journalist, this kind of writing, which is sometimes called **literary journalism**, is as close to literary fiction as it is to traditional journalism. The writer may use fictional techniques, such as irony, imagery, dialogue, and figurative language, and may make considerable use of narration and description, which are avoided by journalists reporting "just the bare facts." Wolfe even used "stream of consciousness" writing, which records, unedited, sensual stimuli, thoughts, and emotions as the writer experiences them. Creative non-fiction, like literary journalism, is a general term in which the authors may blur the line between "fact" and "fiction," acknowledging that such absolute distinctions are misleading if not downright false. (See "The Active Voice: A Brief History of Creative Non-fiction," p. 40). However, some creative non-fiction forms, such as the **personal essay** and the memoir, derive much of their emotional power from the artful blending of candid and honest recollection with literary techniques (see Susan Olding's "Push-me-pull-you" as an example of a personal essay, p. 388).

Other journalistic forms, such as opinion pieces or lifestyle features like travel writing, may also employ the first person. Where literary journalism differs from opinion pieces and other forms of first-person journalism is in the degree of interaction with the human situation: literary journalists immerse themselves in the moment, creating a full, satisfying sensual and intellectual experience for the reader. In doing this, the literary journalist moves beyond the local scene or moment to ponder large human questions of endurance and suffering, life and death. Two examples of literary journalism in "The Active Reader" are "Sulfur Island," by P.J. O'Rourke, and "The poison stream," by Mathew Power. (The latter also has many of the characteristics of an investigative essay—see below.) Still other essays, such as "A box full of history," by Robert Fulford, "Fear and loathing in Toontown," by Richard Poplak, and "9/11: The day the world changed," by Robin V. Sears, use literary techniques selectively, combining them with high-quality writing, yet the result is less a literary essay than a **commentary**, a category of journalistic writing that depends more on ideas and the analysis of cultural, social, or political issues. (See "Classification by rhetorical mode/pattern or style," p. xviii, and "Classification by genre—Literary/investigative journalism and personal essay," p. xv.)

Focus on truth

Investigative journalism often seeks to uncover an under-reported or misrepresented side to an issue. The writer may call on unused or unofficial sources to look for a new perspective that will bring a fresh light to bear—a new truth—on a matter of public interest. While the literary journalist seeks to create a new awareness by evoking a human situation and the emotions associated with it, the investigative journalist seeks to create a new awareness by unearthing a new truth, one that appeals to a reader's sense of ethics or justice.

However, the term "investigative journalism" is sometimes reserved for a hard-nosed style of reporting that relentlessly works to expose corporate crime, political corruption, or some similar large-scale deception. In these cases, the writer's sources typically include "insiders," former employees, archival records, or recently declassified documents that the reporter has been able to obtain. *Washington Post* reporters Bob Woodward and Carl Bernstein received a Pulitzer Prize in 1973 for their series of articles about the Watergate scandal in what is probably the most famous example of investigative reporting in the last century. One of the most infamous also involved a *Washington Post* reporter, who wrote in "Jimmy's world" about an eight-year-old "heroin addict" who in fact never existed. The writer falsified the character to make the story seem more dramatic, and her 1980 Pulitzer Prize was withdrawn when the deception was revealed.

The stakes that writers and newspapers invest in such stories are high, and there is a real danger that the writer may cross the line of objective reporting. On the other hand, writers may deliberately cross the line, revealing their self-interest in the story—or, as in the case of contemporary filmmaker Michael Moore in *Bowling for Columbine* and *Fahrenheit 9/11*, the documentary—to present their version of the truth to the uninformed.

While many reporters and their editors dream of the fame that could come from blowing the whistle on power-hungry politicians or high-ranking executives, most investigative work by journalists today is modest in scope, the efforts of dedicated reporters from major newspapers or news organizations posted to bureaus throughout the world, particularly in the politically sensitive areas of Asia and Africa. They may move around the country or from country to country, reporting on important but under-represented global issues. Journalists in Africa, for example, uncover problems that might otherwise escape the notice of readers in developed nations—political turmoil, drought and starvation, the ravages of the AIDS epidemic. In "The poison stream" (p. 446), Matthew Power reports on how aerial spraying of a dangerous pesticide may have affected local communities in the state of Kerala, India, interviewing ordinary people and "experts." Many others work to uncover sensitive political and social issues closer to home, such as the retreat of Canadian politicians on the issue of Canada's sovereignty in the Far North (Gordon Laird. "On thin ice," p. 468).

Depending on what they are investigating, these journalists may use written sources more than the literary journalist does. This is because the information they require to support their claim about government or corporations may lie buried in forgotten or secret documents. However, like virtually all journalists, they do not provide documentation for the sources within their essays, in stark contrast to the standard practice of academic writers. They may not even name their sources, referring to "a source close to the government" or using a similar phrase. The confidential relationship between the journalist and his or her source has always been controversial. Journalists have been jailed for their refusal to name a source, and it was 31 years after the Watergate scandal that the real name of the major informant, "Deep Throat," finally came to light.

Treating sources

In an academic essay, information from primary and secondary sources may be analyzed (broken down) or synthesized (put together); usually, both processes are involved. However, in journalistic essays, as in many student research essays, synthesis can be considered the more important. The reason differs in each case: a primary goal in assigning research essays is to enable students to learn how to use secondary sources in their own essays, to integrate important information from these sources with the student's own ideas—synthesis. (Of course, analysis can also play an important role in research essays; analysis is involved in critical thinking, for example.) On the other hand, the main purpose of journalistic essays is to inform the reader. This information comes from what others have discovered or said. Journalistic writers, then, use other people's words and ideas, synthesizing them in an interesting and entertaining way for their audience.

However, some kinds of journalistic essays—the **review**, the **editorial**, and the **commentary**—stress analysis over synthesis. In these forms, independence of opinion counts for more than evaluating and integrating what others have said, although editorials and commentaries often refer to others' opinions. (See "Classification by rhetorical mode/pattern or style," p. xviii, and "Classification by genre—Commentary/editorial," p. xiv.)

FORMATS

The formats of journalistic essays are just as variable as the many kinds of journalistic writing that can be found in today's newspapers and magazines. Many formats, however, are readily identifiable to readers because they have become formulaic through their frequent use over the years. Common examples include the hard-news story with its traditional inverted pyramid structure in which the writer tries to answer the "five W's" (*Who, What, Where, When, Why*) and the one "H" (how) in the first paragraphs. Cooking and gardening features may be set up to present the chronological stages in an activity; this rhetorical pattern is known as **process analysis.** Equally formulaic are travel features, with their journal-style structure, use of the present tense, reliance on the **descriptive** and **narrative** rhetorical patterns, and on many photos, including the obligatory sunrise or sunset.

Other journalistic essays depend much less on formula and more on conscious strategies and techniques, which make these essays worthy of study. Formulaic writing well serves the needs of writer and audience: it can be efficiently produced and quickly consumed. However, other journalistic essays go much further to explore or expose an issue of vital concern to readers. Such essays do not rely on formulas but on conventions, sets of implicit instructions that facilitate communication between writer and reader. Many of the conventions of the kinds of journalistic writing represented in "The Active Reader" essays are discussed below.

Introductions

Like the kinds of introductions you may be asked to write (see "Writing introductions," p. 90), introductions in journalistic writing are designed to attract the attention of readers and draw them into the essay. There are many ways to interest readers:

- Sketching a familiar scenario to which the reader can relate or one that will be striking because it is so *un*familiar. In a variant on this method, the writer makes a common observation or draws a familiar scene, only to use the reversal strategy to counter it.
- Recounting a personal experience that introduces the topic.
- Posing a provocative question.
- Beginning with a rich descriptive or narrative passage or a short, challenging statement.

> It is the medium we most love to hate. The glowing black cube, the cathode-ray cyclops lodged in our living rooms. We regard it with fascinated horror, feel powerless before it, sucked into its evil vortex.... Television: bane of our existence, the hardest of hard drugs.
>   Except it isn't.
>
> (Mark Kingwell. "The goods on the tube")
> *reversal strategy*

> Is science on the verge of explaining the mystery of existence once and for all?
>
> (John Horgan. "Can science solve the riddle of existence?")
> *question strategy*

> To each generation comes at least one day that changes their world: Sarajevo, Black Friday, Pearl Harbor, Hiroshima. For mine it was a cold fall day in November 1963.
>
> (Robin Sears. "9/11: The day the world changed")
> *personal experience/observation*

On a sheet of ice where the Arctic Ocean meets the North Atlantic in the territorial waters of Greenland, Mamarut Kristiansen kneels beside the carcass of a narwhal, the elusive animal sometimes known as "the unicorn of the sea" for its spiralled ivory tusk.

(Marla Cone. "Dozens of words for snow, none for pollution")

narration

Nuclear power is a child of war.

(Elaine Dewar. "Nuclear resurrection")

challenging statement

In the introduction, the writer quickly reveals the essay's subject, but thesis statements are less common in journalistic essays than in the kinds of essay that students are usually asked to write. The reason? Thesis statements are not designed as much to attract the interest of a reader as to inform the reader of the essay's content, its main point(s). In most interest-centred writing, this kind of formal announcement can work against the writer, deflecting the reader's interest when it is most needed—at the end of the introduction before the body of the essay begins. In your own essays, a thesis statement serves to inform the reader; in early drafts, it also ensures that you, the writer, are clear on your purpose and main point.

Instead of a clear thesis statement, the journalistic writer may continue to draw out the reader's interest throughout the introduction, indirectly conveying detail about the topic while doing so. Many successful journalistic essays contain no clearly articulated thesis or delay the thesis until somewhere in the body of the essay. Fewer still include an essay plan, a characteristic feature of academic essays. Instead, the journalistic writer relies on tools of the trade to lead the reader on, using linguistic resources, evoking a distinct tone or mood, or seizing on a human interest angle.

Organization

Journalistic writing is organized logically, and the transitions from one point to another will be clear through the use of organizational patterns common to all writing. For example, a writer could organize points chronologically (time order), beginning with the oldest and ending with the most recent. As mentioned earlier, journalistic writers often use description and narration to organize information, and all writing benefits from the use of examples to develop and amplify abstract concepts.

If journalistic writers do not typically use theses or essay plans to unify complex material, what do they use in their place? In many cases, especially those that utilize literary techniques, it would be more precise to speak of a theme rather than a thesis. Students are familiar with themes from literary analysis. A **theme** can be defined as the overarching meaning or the universal qualities manifested in a work through elements like plot, setting, character, and point of view. Rather than *announce a thesis*, a journalistic writer can *convey a theme by evoking one or more universal qualities in the essay*. While thesis statements are supported by various kinds of evidence, they are particularized through the essay's main points. A theme, on the other hand, is sounded through the use of **motifs**, a literary term borrowed from the fine arts and referring to recurrent patterns that help in developing or expanding the theme. Motifs are often images; for example, the repeated image of the witches in William Shakespeare's *Macbeth* evokes the supernatural or fatality theme in the play.

In some journalistic writing, the writer may rely less on logical organizational patterns, such as chronology, and more on descriptive ones: **vignettes** are brief scenes or descriptive passages that refocus a theme visually and with immediacy. In the opening of the essay "Dozens of words for snow, none for pollution," Marla Cone uses a vignette, and she continues to use vignettes throughout to help organize her essay.

In academic writing and in student writing, coherence can be achieved by the use of transitional words and phrases. Such transitions are widely used in journalistic writing, but writers do not always want to lead the reader smoothly from one point to the next. Rather, using a filmic technique of rapid "cuts," writers may abruptly shift from one point or scene to another. In the **montage** method, a writer combines different narrative or thematic elements, organizing these elements by the principle of **juxtaposition** (the word means "place beside") rather than that of logical relationships. Sometimes, the "cuts" mark a change in location or time period, as they often do in "On thin ice," by Gordon Laird (p. 468) and "The poison stream," by Matthew Power (p. 446); at other times, they may reflect the writer's style, one in which an essay's pacing or internal rhythm takes precedence over the use of watertight reasoning. Literary essays and many personal essays make extensive use of the montage organizational method; argumentative essays, which depend on logical links in a solid chain of reason, seldom do.

DICTION AND TONE

Academic essays seldom use the kinds of indirect techniques that are features of literary writing. Their language may be difficult owing to specialization or sophistication, but diction serves a utilitarian function: to communicate complex information as precisely and directly as possible. Literary writers often use words that have more than one connotation (implication); they may aim for richness, even ambiguity, through their language, rather than precision. The same cannot be said of academic writers: although the language of academia may frustrate inexperienced readers, this frustration should not be due to ambiguity. An ambiguous academic writer would frustrate experienced and inexperienced readers alike.

Unlike academic writers, journalistic writers, especially those who know their audience well, sometimes use indirect techniques and expect their readers to be aware of them. Such authors can safely make statements that a different audience might take issue with. For example, when P.J. O'Rourke says of the young marines in "Sulfur Island" that "[s]ome of them will be sent to deal with the antique absurdities of

Afghanistan and Iraq," he can be confident that most readers of the *Atlantic* magazine, where the essay first appeared, would be on the same side of the issue concerning the US presence in these countries; on the other hand, readers of *The American Conservative* or the *National Review* might not be.

Writers can convey their attitude to their subject by their **tone**. One of the ways that you can infer a writer's tone—what he or she is *really* saying—is by employing critical thinking skills, by asking questions like: Does the writer always say what she means? Does she sometimes deliberately manipulate the reader's response? When and why does she do this? What effect is she trying to create? Tone can be defined as the *use of language to convey the writer's attitude toward the subject.* A writer could use a tone that is serious or solemn, light or comic, mocking or earnest, intimate, thoughtful, or ironic. Journalistic writers may use an **ironic** tone if they are directing their readers to look under the surface, transparent meaning of the words or a situation. They may use irony occasionally, as P.J. O'Rourke does, or pervasively, as Zebedee Nungak does in "Qallunology" and Richard Poplak does in "Fear and loathing in Toontown." If a writer uses irony throughout the essay, he or she must make this fact clear to the reader. If the reader misses the ironic tone, the purpose in using irony will be lost.

Pervasive irony is often used in **satire**, a genre that *mocks or criticizes institutions or commonly held attitudes.* One way that satirists "tip off" their readers is through exaggeration. For example, in the thesis of the famous satire "A modest proposal" (1729), Jonathan Swift proposes the sale of infants to Ireland's rich to be served up for dinner! The false thesis is so extreme that readers are able to see beneath the literal meaning and realize that Swift is actually attacking the callous attitude of the rich toward the poor. In his argument, he is really making an indirect plea to Ireland's wealthy classes to help combat poverty, which is his "true" thesis.

STYLISTIC TECHNIQUES

Journalistic writers may use other techniques and devices common to literary writing. For example, they may use sound devices, such as **alliteration** (the repetition of sounds at the beginning of successive words). Such devices can cause the reader to slow down and pay more careful attention to these passages; they also enhance the reading experience.

Writers frequently vary the length and rhythm of their sentences. A succession of short sentences can create a dramatic effect, while longer, more flowing sentences can be used to draw forth a speculative idea. In **periodic** sentences, the writer builds towards the main idea, which is expressed at the end of the sentence. In **cumulative** sentences, the writer begins with the main idea and follows with words, phrases, or clauses that extend this idea. In the examples below, note the different rhetorical effects created by these two sentence types, especially in the third, strongly cumulative sentence (the third sentence also contains an example of alliteration, the repetition of the "c" sound in "*c*ashew," "*c*urling," "*c*ool," "*c*ave," and "*c*loser"):

Moderately periodic: Perched at the top of the Arctic food chain, eating a diet similar to a polar bear's, the Inuit also play unwilling host to some 200 toxic pesticides and industrial compounds. (Cone. "Dozens of words for snow, none for pollution")

Moderately cumulative: I keep returning to the poignant question posed by the essayist Wendell Berry: "How will you practice virtue without skill?" I thought that I was responding to this question during weary nights in uncomfortable call rooms, acquiring the skills that would allow me to make my contribution to society, to turn noble ideals into action. (Wohlgemut. "AIDS, Africa and indifference")

Strongly cumulative: I can feel the weight of all the earth above me, the cashew roots curling like warped fingers through the soil, and the cool cave walls seem to gather closer, the moss to reach out tendrils, the ferns at the distant cave-mouth to stiffen like a dog's hackles. (Power. "The poison stream")

The sentences above also demonstrate the use of parallel structures for rhetorical effect (the phrases beginning "perched" and "eating" are parallel, as are those beginning "the moss" and "the ferns"). Parallel structures contribute to the coherence of a paragraph, making it easier to follow (see "Writing strong paragraphs," p. 95).

Other kinds of parallelism are used less for rhetorical effect than to convey information efficiently. For example, an **appositive** is a word or phrase that names, specifies, or explains the previous word or phrase; it is grammatically parallel to the preceding word or phrase. Although appositives are common in all writing, they are used routinely in articles designed for mass-market consumption because they enable the writer to express information economically. The first sentence below contains the same information as the second, but in the second, the writer uses an appositive, which specifies or explains the previous phrase, "The Alliance for Childhood," in the interests of concise writing (note the commas in the second sentence, separating the appositive from the main idea in the sentence):

1. The Alliance for Childhood has called for a moratorium on new computers for preschool and elementary classrooms. The Alliance for Childhood is a group of 60 health, child-development, education, and technology experts.

2. The Alliance for Childhood, a group of 60 health, child-development, education, and technology experts, has called for a moratorium on new computers for preschool and elementary classrooms. (Ferguson. "How computers make our kids stupid")

LEARNING FROM JOURNALISTIC PROSE

Student writers and readers can learn a great deal by studying both the conventions of prose designed for specialized niche markets and the more formulaic kind of prose that appears in newspapers and mass-market magazines. From the former, you can learn about different strategies designed to engage your reader intellectually or emotionally. You can study the way that tone and voice can direct readers to subtle nuances of thought, features that are especially important when you are reading a work for its "true" or intended meaning. From the latter, you can learn the importance of concision, of producing clear prose that can be read quickly. Professional writers, of course, do not always think in black-and-white terms: the successful writer for a niche market also knows the value of readable, concise prose, just as the writer for the mass market knows the importance of stimulating his or her reader.

It is important to remember, however, that most mass-market writing is designed for casual readers who lack the time for complex arguments or detailed analysis. Some of the techniques writers use to make their prose more economical and immediate are not suitable for the kind of writing you will be asked to do as a student. Your instructor, for example, may not allow you to use contractions or sentence fragments, which save on space but are a sign of informal writing. On the other hand, you may be permitted to use contractions in *some* writing, such as personal responses, or to use fragments for dramatic effect in personal essays or selectively in other kinds of semi-formal writing assignments.

The Active Voice
A Brief History of Creative Non-Fiction

In the beginning was the news story, and the news story was in a prescribed form known as the inverted pyramid: all pertinent information (*Who, What, Where, When,* and *Why*) was crammed into the first couple of sentences, while less significant details, like flabby thighs, were allowed to range free—spreading and meandering into the lower reaches of the column.

According to legend, editors once plied their trade with a knife. If a story ran too long, a quick "endectomy" was performed. Afterwards, the story could lead a normal life. In contrast, the news feature story could not be dealt with as stolidly. Its structure, more like a pyramid proper way up, digressed conversationally, with its meat packaged someplace in its middle.

With the advent of professional ethical standards for journalism, a major consideration for both of these story types was "objectivity." It was believed, and is still believed by some, that whether the story was inverted or upright, a reporter could write it with a completely dispassionate eye—seeing an event in a totally objective way. This school of thought adopts the premise that one's personal history, gender, race, economic situation, can be neatly put aside and "the truth" (or at any rate "the factual truth") of a situation can be reported untarnished by bias.

It was in the early 1960s that the writer Tom Wolfe had a journalistic crisis, or maybe it was just a case of writer's block, or perhaps it never really happened but has just gone down in the annals as what went wrong or right with journalism (depending on which side of the fence you're standing). The story goes that Wolfe wrote to his editor and said, "I'm having a heck of a time writing this piece on hot rods . . . !!!" (Tom Wolfe was notorious for over-punctuating), and his editor said, "I'll tell you what, why don't you just send me what you'd like to say, and I'll help you?" So Wolfe dashed off a few pages that were wild and personal, and sent them to his editor in the form of a letter. While these notes defied any kind of journalistic model, they were informative and fascinating. The editor ran the notes as: "There goes (varoom! varoom!) that kandy-kolored (thphhhhhh!) tangerine-flake stream-line baby (rahghhh!) around the bend (brummmmmmmmmmmmmmmm) . . ."

Some argue that this was the beginning of what Wolfe would later call "the new journalism": realistic writing about real events, but employing certain techniques and devices of fiction that are able to render "story." And while the term "new journalism" faded into the landscape of its era, its seed propagated and multiplied like the versatile tomato, which is a fruit to science and vegetable to the culinary arts. Under the genre title "literary journalism" (in the discipline of journalism) and "creative non-fiction" (in the discipline of creative writing), the formerly named new journalism flourished, becoming if not the most popular genre of writing today, then certainly the most purchased.

Whereas journalists of old strove to remain emotionally detached from their subject matter and presented the facts in the most neutral language possible, today's creative non-fiction writers and literary journalists see things differently. They understand, for example, that even if they try to detach themselves from a subject and report "only the facts, ma'am," it's actually going to be their subjective perception that determines which facts they deem newsworthy and noteworthy. Instead of seeing subjectivity in writing as a besetting sin, many writers consider it inevitable and strive to convert their presence and perceptions into strengths.

But the creative non-fiction/literary journalism story does not stop here. As in current issues in genetic engineering, we move into questions about the ethics and extent to which fact and fiction can be intermingled. In 2006, creative non-fiction became a household phrase when James Frey's memoir *A million little pieces* was selected as an Oprah Book Club choice and then was found to have economized on the truth. Frey had embellished and even invented certain material he presented in his book as fact. Was this a cheat? Was it unethical? Defenders of Frey maintain that the genre he worked in allowed him to take certain liberties with the facts in order to present an even more emotionally authentic work—a work truer than truth. Others, who cannot defend him, see great dangers looming in the boundary transmigration and the blurring of fact and fiction. Frey himself admits "lying" but claims that much of the lying had to do with his self-image and perception, which were not introspective enough for him to discern between events as they actually were and as he'd come to see them. While Frey has expressed contrition and claims that he has learned from his mistakes and will try never to lie again in print, the controversy over his work cannot be resolved in such black-and-white terms for the genre of creative non-fiction: the way writers experience events, their emotional states, their neurosis and delusions, their pride and their prejudices will all inevitably shape their perceptions of "the truth." Facts that seem important and intrinsic to the stories they are telling will be included, while others that don't will be discarded. Is the writer who leaves something important out of a memoir as culpable as the one who adds something important to it? And ultimately, what is a fact? Aren't all facts, as they exist in a story, pieced together by the subjective glue of their author?

Madeline Sonik, M.F.A., Ph.D. (Education), University of British Columbia

Chapter 2

Keys for Reading Challenging Essays

Although the focus of this section is on academic writing, the reading strategies discussed apply to all the essays in "The Active Reader" and to many of the other readings you will undertake as part of your education. As the previous sections stress, there is no mystique surrounding scholarly writing: conventions exist to ensure effective communication and ease in understanding, not to privilege this kind of discourse from other genres or to segregate the writing in one discipline from the writing in another. Consistently applying the thinking and reading strategies discussed below will make you a more conscious and active reader and, in the end, make reading less a matter of overcoming challenges and more a matter of personal satisfaction.

Critical thinking

Academic essays call on the reader's use of critical thinking skills. Other kinds of writing, such as literary works, do this as well, but exercising the range of critical thinking skills is of paramount importance when you read academic prose because academic arguments are frequently based on tight logic or a series of unfolding claims that increase in complexity or significance. Various assumptions and premises underlie the claims of academic writers. Questioning and testing these assumptions are at the heart of critical thinking; a spirit of enquiry guides the critical thinker throughout the reading process.

Writing at the post-secondary level also requires readers to make inferences, to draw valid conclusions based on evidence. What is common to all forms of interactive reading is its reliance on critical thinking. Analyzing, questioning, hypothesizing, evaluating, discriminating, reconsidering, judging, synthesizing, concluding—all are part of critical thinking. And one more characteristic should be added: remaining open to new interpretations as you read and reread a text.

If you look up the words "critical," "critic," or "criticism" in a dictionary, you will see that each word has several meanings. One meaning of "critical" is to make a negative judgment, to criticize. However, the root of "critical" comes from a Greek word that means to *judge* or *discern*, to weigh and evaluate evidence. It is this meaning that is implied in the term *critical thinking*.

WHEN DO YOU USE CRITICAL THINKING?

Many of your assignments will require you to form conclusions about what you have read. Thus, you might employ critical thinking to decide whether to use a secondary source in your research essay. As well as deciding whether the topic and the writer's approach to the topic are close to your own, you will need to form a judgment about the reliability of the source and the validity of the findings—which means you will use critical thinking.

It might seem that you do not have to employ critical thinking if you are asked to summarize a text as an end in itself, as you do in a précis. However, such "stand alone" summaries require you to carefully discriminate more important from less important ideas, so critical thinking *is* involved. More generally, critical thinking skills are triggered whenever you read a work in order to comment on it; this could be in the form of a classroom discussion or debate or a written assignment, such as a review, a critical response, or a critical analysis. In research assignments, you will have to assess the validity of your sources and, quite likely, compare the claims and conclusions of these sources.

However, critical skills do not apply just to reading: they are used in many everyday situations, like those described below ("Inferences and critical thinking"), and in fieldwork projects, like those discussed in "The Active Voice: Silent Witnesses to the Past" (p. 52) in which the fieldworker observes phenomena in their natural or original surroundings and draws conclusions as a result of these observations.

For a writer, critical thinking is stimulated whenever analysis is involved, as it is in most kinds of problem-solving. A writer asks a question about a relevant topic in his or her discipline and uses the methods and processes of the discipline in an attempt to answer it. For example, criminologists Christie Barron and Dany Lacombe question the so-called phenomenon of the "nasty girl," account for its general acceptance, and draw on related literature and social policy to propose their own theory for its popularity ("Moral panic and the Nasty Girl," p. 366). Using a combination of journalistic and scientific methods, Kevin Krajick attempts to find the reason for the disappearance of the ivory gull from Canada's Arctic ("In search of the ivory gull," p. 483).

Although critical thinking involves typical activities, they vary somewhat from discipline to discipline. Empirical studies in the natural and social sciences often identify problems, generate hypotheses, predict occurrences, create raw data, analyze using cause and effect, and attempt to generalize on the basis of their findings. Studies in the arts/humanities often identify problems, ask questions, propose a thesis (which is supported by a theoretical framework), interpret primary and secondary sources in light of the thesis, and analyze using definition, examples, compare/contrast, and other patterns.

INFERENCES AND CRITICAL THINKING

Context clues can be utilized to infer the meaning of an unfamiliar word (see "Word meanings," p. 71). More broadly, **inferences** apply to ideas and the way we use them to form conclusions. Writers do not always explicitly state all they mean but leave it to the reader to infer these meanings. When you **infer**, *you arrive at a probable* *conclusion about the meaning of a word or about what the evidence shows or points to, its meaning or significance.*

Many research methods rely on inferences: astronomers, for example, study the phenomenon of black holes by observing the behaviour of matter that surrounds the black hole. They know that before gas is swallowed up by a black hole, it is heated to extreme temperatures and accelerates. In the process, X-rays are created, which escape the black hole and reveal its presence. Scientists cannot actually *see* black holes, but they can *infer* their existence through the emission of X-rays.

We practise critical thinking in our daily lives, inferring probable causes or consequences on the basis of what we observe—the evidence—and our interpretation of this evidence. For example, say you are jogging and wearing a headset. Another jogger catches your eye and points to her wrist. What is the probable reason (cause)? You might infer that she is asking whether you know the time. Other inferences are possible too, but the most valid inference is the one with the greatest probability of being correct. If you shouted out the time and she looked puzzled, you might infer that your original inference was incorrect; on the other hand, she may not have heard you, another valid inference.

If you are impatiently waiting for a bus and someone at the bus stop tells you that the buses are running 15 minutes late, you might be more interested in inferring the consequence than the cause: you will be late for class. However, if the bus immediately arrives, you might revise your original conclusion, which was based on the testimony of the person at the bus stop. You might also infer that this person is not a reliable source.

You use critical thinking as you read whenever you evaluate and draw conclusions about claims (assertions) and their evidence or the source of these claims, the writer. Although critical thinking can involve all the activities mentioned above—analyzing, questioning, hypothesizing, evaluating, discriminating, reconsidering, judging, synthesizing, and concluding—there are three general activities that will promote critical thinking skills as you read a text: reading closely and objectively, asking questions, and drawing logical conclusions. However, although most texts are linear (that is, we read them from beginning to end), our engagement with them is not always linear. It is important to remember that critical thinking is a *process of rigorous but flexible engagement* with a text (or a non-textual situation) that may change as you read (or learn more about the non-textual situation).

CRITICAL THINKING AND SCEPTICISM

Focused reading is a systematic method that can be used in reading for content (see "Focused reading," p. 64). But the aim in a focused reading embraces not just *what* is being read but also *how* the reader responds to a text. Only by reading a text very closely, by attending objectively to its claims, to the details that support these claims, and to the writer's language and tone will you be in a position to go beyond simple comprehension and apply critical thinking skills.

Activity

The passages below contain specific statements from which readers may be able to make inferences either about the information in the passage or about the writer's attitude toward the subject. Choose the most valid (most probable) conclusion:

1. Surveys of public opinion conducted before and after the [end-of-the-world disaster] film [*The Day after Tomorrow*] was released found that it made people think climate change is less likely. (Note: This statement was part of an introduction to a book review; if the reader does not make the correct inference, he or she may not be receptive to what the writer goes on to say in the review itself.)

    a.   Viewers seldom interpret movies correctly.
    b.   Viewers may sometimes confuse fact and fiction.
    c.   It is a simple matter to predict viewer response to disaster films.
    d.   No inference is possible about the responses of movie viewers.

2. [The students at the school] work in isolated workstations; their desks face the walls. Social interaction is structured and supervised. Time-out rooms are small, windowless areas without furniture or carpeted floors; the doors have keyed locks. The cells are painted bright colors: pink, yellow, and blue; the light switch for each cubicle is on the outside.

    a.   The students at the school are thoroughly dedicated to their studies.
    b.   School designers have provided the optimal conditions for study.
    c.   The school has been designed for students with behavioural problems.
    d.   No inference is possible about the students or their school.

3. All was not eager anticipation for Meghan. She chose to attend the largest university in the state, and she found herself frequently feeling lost, both geographically and socially. She had to take a campus bus to get to some of her classes on time. Most of her classes were large with well over 100 students; one class had 250 students. She was used to smaller class sizes in high school with support from her resource teacher. Although she arranged for support through the university's Office of Disability Services, Meghan realized that she would have to approach the professors to describe her learning problems and request accommodations. . . . Meghan also felt disorganized. Although her roommates had purchased their texts, yearly organizational calendars, and other materials, Meghan had no idea where to begin; her fear of failure was increasing by the moment.

    a.   Meghan will likely face many challenges at the university.
    b.   Meghan will likely give up and go home.
    c.   Meghan's fears are likely unfounded, since the many resources available at the university will help her adjust to her new life.
    d.   No inference is possible about Meghan's future at the university.

Activity – *continued*

4. Binkley paid for all the travel and expenses, and what was only 12 months ago a very new and controversial transaction has today left Binkley a healthy man—and the first of 16 people who have successfully received organs through MatchingDonors.com.

   a.   The author believes that this method of soliciting donors is wrong.

   b.   The author believes that this method of soliciting donors is, at the very least, ethically questionable.

   c.   The author sees nothing wrong with this method of soliciting donors.

   d.   No inference is possible about the author's beliefs.

5. Two recent studies have found that those arrested for property or financial crimes (such as embezzlement) were disproportionately likely to have used marijuana. However, when the researchers looked at crime rates rather than arrest rates, the connection disappeared entirely. (These correlations are determined by comparing a community's rate of pot use with its overall crime and arrest rates.)

   a.   Marijuana users are more likely to break the law but are less likely to get caught.

   b.   Marijuana users are less likely to break the law and less likely to get caught.

   c.   Marijuana users are more likely to break the law and more likely to get caught.

   d.   Marijuana users are less likely to break the law but are more likely to get caught.

Reading closely, then, means becoming more conscious of how you interact with a text, approaching it in a state of preparedness—that is, being open to challenges to your own ways of thinking but not being swayed by other views unless they stand up to the tests of logic and consistency. One attitude often used to describe this state of readiness is *scepticism*. Adopting an attitude of healthy scepticism does not mean you are obliged to mistrust everything you read (remember that openness is an important characteristic of critical thinking). A sceptic is very different from a cynic, as explained in the philosophical statement of the Skeptics Society, a group of scholars who publish the quarterly magazine *Skeptic*:

> Some people believe that skepticism is the rejection of new ideas, or worse, they confuse "skeptic" with "cynic" and think that skeptics are a bunch of grumpy curmudgeons unwilling to accept any claim that challenges the status quo. This is wrong. *Skepticism is a provisional approach to claims.* It is the application of reason to any and all ideas—no sacred cows allowed. In other words, skepticism is a method, not a position. Ideally, skeptics do not go into

an investigation closed to the possibility that a phenomenon might be real or that a claim might be true. When we say we are "skeptical," we mean that we must see compelling evidence before we believe.

In critical thinking, you constantly test and assess the evidence presented, considering how it is being used and where the writer is going with it. Key activities in a close reading of a text are questioning, evaluating, and discriminating.

THE SPIRIT OF ENQUIRY

The popular tabloid the *National Enquirer* promotes itself as a magazine "for enquiring minds." In fact, it is nothing of the sort: a more typical tabloid reader is one who believes anything he or she is told or at least finds humour in having his or her credulity stretched to the breaking point.

A truly enquiring mind analyzes what it reads and does not take everything at face value. The critical thinker operates in the interrogative mode, questioning assumptions, testing the evidence, and accepting (or rejecting) conclusions on the basis of careful analysis. When questions arise, the critical thinker first seeks for answers within the text itself but may also consider relevant knowledge gleaned from outside sources or from personal experience. How might such sources address or answer the question? Are these answers consistent with or different from those found in the text being read?

In analyzing arguments, the critical thinker should be aware of the potential force of counter-arguments, especially those unacknowledged by the writer. Is the writer avoiding or minimizing certain issues by not mentioning them? By considering all sides and angles and by questioning all easy or glib answers, the critical thinker sets firm and logical boundaries within which the text can be understood.

CRITICAL SITUATIONS FOR CRITICAL THINKING

For some texts, reading is a relatively fluid and stable activity. As we silently assent to what we read, we may scarcely be aware that we are thinking critically. However, at times, critical thinking is brought to the fore. A writer might make a claim that directly contradicts what our knowledge or common sense tells us—for example, that cats are more intelligent than humans. Another example might be a writer making a claim about a topic that experts have been debating for years—for example, that cats are smarter than dogs. In the first case, if you believed that the writer was completely serious in her claim, you might dismiss her as flaky or worse. But the second claim would probably cause you to respond differently, using critical thinking to evaluate the following:

• *The writer's credibility:* Is the writer considered an expert? What is the nature of his or her expertise? A researcher into animal behaviour? A veterinarian?

An animal trainer? Someone who has owned dogs and cats? Someone who has owned dogs only? Could the writer have a bias? Are there any logical fallacies in the argument? Has fact been carefully distinguished from opinion?

- *Nature of the claim (assertion):* Specific claims are stronger than general ones, and they are often easier to prove (bear this in mind if you are ever tempted to use a very general claim for a thesis statement). Since variability has been found among dog breeds, it would be difficult to generalize about the intelligence of all dogs.

- *Basis of the claim:* Some claims are more straightforward than others. A claim may depend on an underlying assumption, such as a particular definition (in argument, this is referred to as the *warrant*; see "Connecting claim to evidence," p. 119). There are different ways to define and measure intelligence: physiologically (e.g., the weight of the brain in proportion to the weight of the body) and behaviourally (e.g., trainability, adaptability, independence). Advocates of a dog's superior intelligence may point to trainability as the intelligence factor, while advocates of cat intelligence may point to adaptability or independence. Both could be valid criteria, but by themselves they do not offer proof.

- *Methodology:* How does the writer attempt to prove the claim? Is the methodology compatible with the claim? Intelligence can be measured (but see previous point). Therefore, a methodology that sought to measure intelligence scientifically would be more credible than one that relied on personal observation especially since many pet-lovers are quite opinionated about their pets' intelligence and may not always distinguish between fact and opinion.

- *Support:* A credible writer needs to provide more than opinion or personal observation to back up a claim. In critical thinking, you must evaluate the nature of the evidence and the way the writer uses it. Typical questions might include the following: What kind of evidence did the writer use? Has the writer relied too much on one kind of evidence or one source? How many sources were used? Were they current sources (recent studies may be more credible than older ones)? Did the writer ignore or minimize some sources (e.g., those that found dogs more intelligent than cats)?

- *Conclusion:* See below, "Drawing conclusions."

There is another scenario in which critical thinking is inevitably involved: comparing the arguments of two writers who arrive at different or even contradictory conclusions, even though both appear to reason logically and bolster their points with the use of solid evidence. The kinds of analysis employed in these cases will be primarily those of relating, comparing, connecting, and discriminating.

Expository writing as well as argumentative writing can produce disagreement and contradictory findings. For example, researchers conducting experiments to determine the effectiveness of a new drug or to investigate the connection between television viewing and violence may arrive at very different conclusions although their methods appear credible. A researcher's attempts to replicate an experiment may fail in spite of the scrupulous care taken to follow the precise methods of the original experiment. What can account for the differing results? Attempting to answer this question, to account for variation, involves critical thinking. Critical thinking is a necessary part of all problem-solving.

DRAWING CONCLUSIONS

Remember that an inference can be defined as a conclusion drawn from the evidence. However, drawing a conclusion about a work you have read involves more than making an inference; it results from the *incremental process of reading critically*. In arriving at a conclusion, you weigh the various factors involved in your analysis of the text. But while analysis and its associated activities were paramount when you were reading the work, as you complete your reading, you are synthesizing this information in order to say something definitive about it, about its presentation, and/or about the writer.

To form conclusions, you might assess the way that the parts relate to the whole, assigning relative values to these different parts. Obviously, some points are more important than others, and some evidence is more effective than other evidence. *Your goal is to determine whether the accumulated weight of evidence supports the writer's claim*, or, as members of the Skeptics Society would ask: Is the weight of evidence "compelling?" You might consider how weaker or less substantiated points affect the validity of the findings. Were there any gaps or inconsistencies in the chain of reasoning? Was the writer's conclusion logically prepared for?

Ultimately, you are determining whether the writer's findings/conclusion reflect what he or she set out to investigate. Was the original hypothesis proved/disproved? Was the original question answered? And if you have been using your critical thinking skills to write a critical analysis of the work, you will need to make explicit the critical thinking that led to your conclusion. In a critical analysis, you use critical thinking not just as a means to an end, a way of extracting as much as you can from a work; it is also the most beneficial way to engage with the work of other writers and with others who have read the same work or who are interested in the same topic.

Student readers and researchers may think that what they find in academic journals should not be questioned. After all, one would expect that these authors are trained experts with unimpeachable critical thinking skills. An obvious inference that arises from the following letter shows, however, that the assumptions and conclusions of all writers *should* be subjected to the rigours of critical thinking. In this case, a group of students criticized the prediction of the authors of a study that appeared in a highly respected journal, *Nature*.

Biology students find holes in gap study

Sir—

We are students aged 16–18 in a Texas high school. Our biology teacher Vidya Rajan asked us to comment on the paper by A.J. Tatem and colleagues (*Nature* 431, 525, 2004); we believe the projection on which it is based is riddled with flaws.

The idea of women running faster than men—although not novel (see B.J. Whipp and S.A. Ward *Nature* 355, 25, 1992; and Correspondence *Nature* 356, 21, 1992)—is interesting, but one cannot draw these conclusions based on generalization by extrapolation. Tatem et al. used a domain of 104 years to extrapolate to a domain of 252 years. It is not logical to say that the first 104 years will have data with exactly the same regression as the next 148 years. Using similar reasoning in 1992, Whipp and Ward suggested that women would run the marathon faster than men by 1998. This has still not happened.

In Tatem and colleagues' study, men were measured for 32 more years than women. This ignores the possibility that women might be reaching a plateau: had women's times been unexpectedly high before 1934, one could trace a decreasing rate of change for post-1934 Olympians.

Improvements due to the increase in numbers of women running are likely to level off as the rate of increase in participation slows down (see www.olympics.org.uk/olympicmovement/olympicissueswoman.asp).

Finally, both men and women may reach a physiological limit beyond which they cannot progress. With these factors taken into consideration, the predictions made from the extrapolation seem less than sound.

A&M Consolidated High School, College Station, Texas 77840, US

Activity

Respond to the following questions:

1. How do these students establish their credibility to critique a study in an academic journal?
2. Of what use do the students make of the study by Whipp and Ward?
3. What year did Tatem et al. begin studying women's times? How can you infer this?
4. How many points do the students use to support their claim? Which do you consider the strongest? Why?

Activity – *continued*

5. The letter above appeared in *Nature* in 2004 (volume 432, issue 7014, page 147), along with other letters that criticized the findings of Tatem et al. Following the letters, the authors of the study responded to these criticisms. What tone did they use in their letter? After reading the letters and the authors' response, consider whether the authors effectively answered the charges. Note: It is not necessary to be familiar with the models mentioned by the authors.

extrapolation: an inference in which a sequence or series of known facts in the past are used to make a prediction.
regression: a statistical operation that shows the relationship between two variables.

The two essays below, from the disciplines of classical studies and women's studies, demonstrate how critical thinking can be used to make or challenge constructions of reality, enabling us to revise inaccurate perceptions or limited "truths." Clearly, the effects of critical thinking, whether applied to small practical problems or to fundamental social issues, have the power to let us better understand our past and radically transform our future.

The Active Voice
Silent Witnesses to the Past

No academic subject can claim a greater longevity in the Western educational system than the study of Greek and Latin. From the Renaissance on, it was thought that the mastery of these two difficult languages would provide a mental training without equal. The consequences of this belief were still apparent until quite recently. During the Second World War, for instance, classicists came second only to mathematicians in the recruitment of code-breakers, having intellectual capabilities, it was believed, perfectly honed to tackle complex problems. That said, despite their formidable reputation, classical languages have of late suffered an astonishingly rapid decline. Dominant for some 500 years, the study of Latin all but disappeared from schools in a single generation, while Greek is in an even more perilous state.

University departments of classics (now usually called something along the lines of "Greek and Roman Studies") have generally shown themselves to be highly adept at adjusting to the changing circumstances. Their new mission is to introduce students to classical civilization through non-linguistic media. None has proved more successful than archaeology.

Classical archaeology is, of course, much more than an inferior substitute for the ancient languages. It is a highly effective way for students to gain a direct and tangible connection with antiquity, in many ways far more direct than they ever could from the written text. I might illustrate this from my own experience with a training excavation conducted on behalf of the University of British Columbia. The practicum, conducted for academic credit at the Lunt Roman Fort, near Coventry, England, from 1985 to 2002, was in each of those years attended by 35 or so students from UBC and elsewhere in North America.

The Lunt Fort was first built in the early sixties AD (during the reign of Nero) and remained under occupation for about 30 years. Our work concentrated on its defensive system, in the form of a turf rampart fronted by a series of ditches. In the course of excavation, the students brought to light objects that had remained untouched since they were discarded nearly 2,000 years ago by the fort's original occupants. The term "discarded" is deliberate, since most of the material was there because its owners had thrown it away: pieces of pot, old nails, a belt buckle, a broken brooch, and the like. For students sensitive to the spirit of history, the thrill of gaining this direct physical contact with the ancient Romans proved to be a life-transforming experience.

Archaeology is not, of course, a mere treasure hunt. The students, usually from faculties of arts, were obliged to acquire a whole new set of skills. They were given thorough training in the techniques required of the modern archaeologist. They learned to plan, to survey, to enter items into a systematic database. They were taught to date fragments of pottery, to identify different types of corroded metal, to distinguish between natural strata in sandy soil and deposited material compacted over hundreds of years. This last is not an easy task but a crucial one on a site like ours, where no stone construction was used and the residual material is often detectable only through variations in the colour of the soil.

More importantly, however, beyond these essentially technical skills, the students developed crucial expertise in applying logical thought processes to the investigation of complex evidence. Archaeological remains are silent witnesses to the past. Like other witnesses, they surrender their testimony only under skilful cross-examination. Let me illustrate this with a concrete example. The most useful features on any Roman fort are the "V"-shaped defensive ditches. When forts were demolished to give way to civilian settlements, the ditches were filled, and the material deposited in them came primarily from the fort's upper structures. In the ensuing centuries, the surface area would almost invariably be subject to human activity, usually ploughing. The evidence at ground level would thus often be destroyed or damaged. But the fill of the ditches would survive intact, and much of the history of the site can be recovered from it. Students noticed when they drew a plan of a section of a ditch that there was, at the bottom, at the point of the "V," a roughly square-shaped slot. What had caused this? They soon learned to dismiss such fanciful ideas such as "ankle-breakers" by observing what happened in the newly excavated ditches when it rained: they filled with silt.

The slots were clearly made by Roman soldiers dragging buckets along the ditch-bottom to remove the silt. Students were then told to observe whether the excavated slot was silt-free or full of silt. What could that observation tell us? We made the students try to think in Roman terms. In the case of a silted-up ditch, why would the Romans have stopped removing silt from the bottom of the ditch? Almost certainly, it means that the occupants anticipated that they would be abandoning the fort at some point in the near future and saw no need to keep the ditch clean. In other words, it suggests an orderly redeployment. Conversely, a meticulously cleaned ditch suggests that the fort was abandoned and the ditches filled in as the immediate result of an order to move, perhaps because of some military crisis.

Archaeology thus involves not only the collection of material from which evidence is derived but, most importantly, the interpretation of that evidence by a series of logical mental sequences. It is a never-ending process. Examination of surviving material will reveal the size and nature of wall foundations. Foundations of a certain size token walls of a certain size. Why do walls have to be so high, so thick? Would that size have been needed for storage? If not, it presumably means that the walls were needed for defence. But, let us suppose, the period was peaceful and the region settled, at least according to Tacitus and the like. Does the evidence on the ground suggest that we have to question the literary evidence (written, after all, in Rome, usually by historians who never set foot in a military camp and almost certainly had never been to Britain)? There are numerous permutations of this kind of questioning.

Interestingly, the very mental discipline that the detailed knowledge of the ancient languages reputedly bestowed on previous generations is now well matched by what archaeology offers the students of today. The vast majority will not become professional archaeologists. But after their training, they see their world differently and will have developed considerable proficiency as problems-solvers, acquiring broad skills that stand them in excellent stead in their chosen future careers.

Anthony Barrett, Professor, Department of Classical, Near Eastern and Religious Studies,
University of British Columbia

The Active Voice

Feminist Thinking in Composition and Literature Classes

Feminist thinking has revolutionized the way we write, as well as the way we read, in university English classes. A feminist approach to these activities encourages us to investigate the (sometimes unconscious) assumptions about gender that inform both our own writing and the array of cultural "texts" we encounter every day: the television and movies we watch, the advertising we take in, the music we listen to, the books we read, the world around us. The human body itself constitutes another example of a text; intentionally or not, whenever we dress, speak, move, or adorn our bodies (or not), we present ourselves to others for interpretation. All such texts, we have come to realize, are charged with meaning, and a feminist approach encourages us to become active, rather than passive, interpreters of them.

In other words, feminism encourages us to practise critical thinking in the study of both composition and literature. Indeed, feminism itself constitutes a primary example of how critical thinking can produce wholesale change, both inside and outside the university. Particularly since its grassroots upsurge in the women's liberation movement of the 1970s, feminist thinking has questioned the authority of conventional gender hierarchies, calling attention to the inequity (and the impossibility) of forcing individuals to comply with stereotypical notions of masculinity and femininity.

Feminism has come a long way since then, becoming first of all academically legitimate—in the establishment of women's studies departments at all major universities—and then more theoretically sophisticated, evolving into the study of gender more generally. The popular stereotype of feminists as man-haters, albeit persistent, has generally given way to an understanding of gender as a cultural construct and of feminism as a means of critiquing this construct. Masculinity, as well as femininity, has become the object of intellectual scrutiny, and the possibility and/or desirability of maintaining a binary gender system has been called into question.

Closely related to questions about gender are questions about sexuality, another concept that has been rigorously examined by feminist thinking. Is there any necessary connection between gender and sexuality? Is an individual's sexuality always unambiguous, and does it remain constant over time? The gay/straight binary, like the masculine/feminine binary, has come under scrutiny, giving rise to the branch of gender studies known as "queer theory." Such a questioning of identity binaries constitutes a post-modern theoretical move that has become indispensable to the study of all cultural texts, including literary texts and our own writing. The automatic classification of individuals or concepts into binary oppositions, we have come to realize—oppositions such as self/other, black/white, culture/nature, as well as man/woman and hetero/homosexual—misses many of the groups and nuances that do not fall neatly into one category or the other.

This critical approach has given rise to exciting new interpretations of traditional texts, as well as an expansion in the category of texts available for literary study. Asking why texts written by women were traditionally excluded or ignored in the study of literature, feminist scholarship has transformed the canon—the body of literary texts considered worthy of study—to include a much more equitable proportion of women's writing. Following this, texts by women (and men) of colour, by women (and men) of all socio-economic groups, and by gays, lesbians, and bisexuals have become legitimate objects of literary study along with the "great literature" of the past—which has itself been subjected to rigorous feminist critique.

Discussions of texts in twenty-first-century literature and composition classrooms, accordingly, encourage readers to ask searching questions about gender and sexuality. How are male and female characters represented in any given text—including those we write? Is gender represented as a fixed or fluid category of identity? Is the sexuality of the characters represented as definite or ambiguous? What is the attitude of the narrator, speaker, or implied author to such issues? Most importantly, what are the ideological implications of the answers to these questions?

At the very least, an awareness of gender issues requires us to regard our own writing as a culturally significant activity, one that produces results that readers will interpret in light of cultural norms. Gender-neutral terminology such as inclusive pronouns ("he/she" or "they" instead of "he") and designations ("humanity" instead of "mankind"; "firefighter" instead of "fireman") sends a message, as do the images we create, the figurative language we use, and the humour we draw on. Texts, we have come to realize, are not interpreted "neutrally" but in the context of the culture in which they are produced or consumed.

Along with an awareness of issues of class and race, our awareness of gender issues has profoundly influenced the way we write, the way we read literature, and our understanding of literature itself. In our post-modern world, we have become aware that the texts a culture produces and consumes command enormous power, the power to affect the beliefs and behaviours of individuals in that culture. Feminist thinking in university English classrooms can help us to develop the critical skills we need in order to create and interpret the texts that shape our world.

Judith Mitchell, Associate Professor, Department of English, University of Victoria

Interacting with texts[1]

As suggested above, reading is not a passive process in which you simply register the meanings of words and, aided by your knowledge of English syntax and other rules, combine words, phrases, and clauses to construct meaning. Although reading does rely on such competencies, it is more of an active process or, more accurately, an *interactive* process in which you assume a relationship *between* you and the text you are reading ("inter" is a prefix meaning "between"). Because of the interactive nature of this relationship, it often changes as you read and apply critical thinking skills. That is why when you read a text for the second time, you uncover new meanings, make new inferences, and become aware of things you were not aware of before.

If reading were actually not interactive, when you read an essay and are asked to write a critical response, yours would look much like anyone else's. Most likely, there would be many differences between yours and those of other readers because you would have approached the essay with the ideas, beliefs, and specific knowledge about the topic that reflect who you are and your unique experiences. You would therefore have interacted differently with the text from the ways others have (see "The critical response: A meeting place," p. 136).

The interaction between you and the text you are reading is not just a function of who you are and your prior knowledge and beliefs. The nature of the text itself, the purpose of the author in writing, the audience it was intended to reach, and the reason for reading it—all play a role in the way you interact. So do the ideas, beliefs, and background of the author, along with the ways that all these factors are expressed: the specific choices—for example, in diction, style, and tone—that he or she makes in writing.

Consider, for example, what you might find yourself thinking about as you begin to read an essay by David Suzuki about wind power (wind farms) as an alternate source of energy (it appeared in *New Scientist* in 2005):

> *Questions about the subject itself:* What do I know about wind farms? Where did my knowledge come from (the media, teachers or textbooks, conversations with friends, my own observation)? Have I any personal experience that might have a bearing on my reading? Do I have opinions about the topic? Are they open to change? What could cause them to change?

---

[1] The word "text" has a variety of meanings. It can refer to a textbook, like the kind you are reading. But in contemporary usage, a *text* can refer to any written material that serves a purpose. One can say that graffiti is a text, along with a private journal entry. Most texts, however, are designed to be read or seen by others. Texts vary in their purpose and scope; for example, an informal essay varies in both respects from a scholarly book, yet both are texts.

Questions about the writer: Is the author's name familiar? What do I associate with him and his writing? Where did these associations come from (previous work by the author or by another author, something mentioned in class or in general conversation)? Do I consider him an authority? Why or why not? How would the average Canadian respond to an essay written by this writer? How do I know this?

While many readers have different knowledge and opinions about wind farms, most know something about the author, a noted Canadian scientist and environmentalist. The following comments on his essay illustrate the different ways that reader and writer can interact based on prior knowledge and experience. What they reveal is that each writer's point of view is coloured, at least somewhat, by his or her experience with the subject of wind farms and, in one case, with the author. Each writer, therefore, has likely approached the essay in a different way. Canvassing your knowledge of the subject and author(s) is a practical pre-reading activity because it will make you more conscious of the background, opinions, and possible biases that could come into play as you read.

Suzuki's introduction

Off the coast of British Columbia in Canada is an island called Quadra, where I have a cabin that is as close to my heart as you can imagine. From my porch on a good day you can see clear across the waters of Georgia Strait to the snowy peaks of the rugged Coast Mountains. It is one of the most beautiful views I have seen. And I would gladly share it with a wind farm.

But sometimes it seems like I'm in the minority. All across Europe and North America, environmentalists are locking horns with the wind industry over the location of wind farms.

Student comments

Katherine W.: I wasn't very knowledgeable about the "windmill issue" before I read this article, but by the end, I was pretty much convinced that it is an important issue. Of course, my viewpoint might have been a little biased because I've always been a fan of windmills (no practical reason) and have a lot of respect for David Suzuki. I guess that's the main reason I was convinced.

Tristan H.: Since I grew up in southern Alberta, I am no stranger to windmills, but I never imagined they were an issue with certain groups. Whenever we talked about windmills, it wasn't to say how ugly or unpleasant they were. They were more of an accent to the background. Without reading this essay, I would never have thought they were an environmental issue at all.

Andrew M.: In the first paragraph, David Suzuki speaks of his cabin on Quadra Island and the fact he would "gladly share it with a wind farm." I have flown over and around Quadra Island numerous times as well as across the Georgia Strait to the Coastal Mountains referred to in his article. The island is covered by forest, as are the mountains across the strait. I have seen wind farms in various parts of Alberta, all of them in non-forested areas. I don't see his point as credible, as it is impractical to set up wind farms in forested areas.

As you continue to read an essay, of course, many other factors arise. Your initial impressions or preconceptions may intensify or weaken through the accumulating evidence the writer presents. A simple issue may begin to appear more complex, or the level of detail may make it increasingly difficult to follow the writer's points; on the other hand, of course, points could become clearer. Whatever the case, some general reading strategies can make the reading process more manageable, ensuring that you remain in control of the reading situation.

STRATEGIES FOR READING ACADEMIC AND OTHER ESSAYS

One simple way of responding to an essay is just to reflect on what the author has written. If your purpose for reading is to prepare for a general discussion of a topic for the next class, this might be adequate preparation. On the other hand, if the discussion is two days away or if you are to write a critical response to the essay, simply thinking about it is probably not sufficient. You will need to jot your ideas down, to **annotate** the essay—annotate = *ad* (to) + *nota* (note).

Making annotations about the text you are reading is an important (perhaps the *most* important) reading strategy, not just because it enables you to return to the essay later and have your questions and other responses fresh in your mind but also because your written response, your annotation, will almost certainly be more complete than a mere thought would have been. When you annotate an essay, you are *beginning your actual work on the assignment*: you are translating abstract ideas and impressions into concrete language, solidifying those ideas.

Purpose in reading

As mentioned, the reading process is interactive; therefore, it is vital that you take steps to interact with the text you are reading. Since the author is not there to explain, clarify, or otherwise engage with you, this interaction will be somewhat limited, but you can annotate the text as if he or she *were* there—that is, by posing the kinds of questions that come up, by writing "?" in the margin for a statement that is not clear or "!" for a statement you agree with or that strongly makes a point, or by adding your own comments as they occur to you. The difference is that in the absence of an obliging author, you need to exercise your own reading and critical thinking skills to answer these questions and to expand on your comments in order to make practical use of the text you are reading.

It is important to know why you are reading the text; the reason affects the way you respond to it. This advice might seem obvious. Yet there are many different reasons for reading—beyond the obvious one of satisfying a course requirement. Are you reading it to determine whether the essay is related to your topic? To extract the main ideas? To use the text as a secondary source in your essay? To write a critical response to the text? To write a critical analysis? Each of these questions affects the way you respond to the essay and necessitates a conscious reading strategy:

- *Reading to determine whether the essay is related to your topic (to explore):* When you search for potential sources for a research essay, you are looking for essays that seem promising, perhaps on the basis of their title or the fact that they are listed in bibliographies of general works such as textbooks or in encyclopedias, indexes, or subject directories. If you are using an on-line resource, you might want to search for articles or books by keywords related to your topic. Since you are reading for exploratory purposes, you do not want to waste time by closely reading each text, so a different strategy is essential.

  Once you find a potentially useful essay, you can read the abstract, if available, the introduction, and all section markers (headings). If you are encouraged by what you read, turn your attention to the main parts of the essay, scanning for topic sentences and other content clues (See "Reading paragraphs: Identifying main ideas," p. 66). Finally, read the concluding section. Scanning prevents wasting time on what might not be useful, giving you more time to apply these reading techniques to other potential sources. Underlining and annotation can be minimal at this stage since you are assessing the essay to determine whether it will be useful.

  It is vital, however, that you carefully write down all relevant bibliographic information for every potential source—title, author, journal or book title (and include names of editors if the source is an edited book), journal volume and issue numbers, and page range. This information will enable you to access the source quickly when you are ready. It often happens that you end up using some information you recall from a source you were not planning to use. Having the bibliographic information at hand can be a life-saver for late-stage additions to your essay.

- *Reading to extract main ideas (to summarize):* You might read an essay in order to write a formal summary, or précis, of it (see p. 148). In this case, your annotations will be minimal because you are focusing on content. Instead, you identify the important points, possibly by underlining them. However, do not underline until you have read the text through once. Since most formal summaries include *only* the main points, you do not want to confuse yourself by excessive underlining; you may not know which are the main and which the sub-points until you have completed your reading. (This practice applies to other reading purposes too: save the underlining for later readings—after you have become familiar with the entire contents of the essay, its purpose, its tone, and so on.)

There are many other reasons that you might read a work to summarize its main ideas: you may want to synthesize these ideas with your own ideas in a research essay or to provide some background for a critical response to the essay.

• *Reading to use the text as a secondary source in your essay (to synthesize):* After you have explored to find out what research is available on your topic, you need to flesh out the general areas of each article that you identified as potentially useful. Thus, you must read closely now, take careful notes, and think in terms of how each point relates to your thesis. If your source is borrowed from the library, you should make a photocopy of the article or relevant chapters of a book; in the case of a journal or magazine article, you can check your library databases to see whether a full-text version exists. If so, you can download the pages and print them.

How much you annotate depends on the importance of the source to the essay you are writing, so your initial task is to attempt to answer this question. It may be that after scanning the entire essay (if you have not done this earlier), you decide that only one section directly pertains to your topic. You may then wish to summarize this section for use in your essay. If a phrase or sentence is particularly significant or expressed in a memorable way, you can record its wording exactly for future use. (See "Integrating your sources," p. 170.) Make sure that you record the page numbers of every potential source whether you are quoting directly, summarizing, or making a passing reference.

• *Reading to respond and analyze:* Reading to respond critically to a text is very different from reading to summarize content or to synthesize information. The goal is to look for possible connections between the text and your own thoughts and opinions. To do this successfully, you must engage with the text in a way that is very different from the way you would if you were summarizing content. Annotation is therefore important. Writing speculative comments in the margin can help with this engagement. Asking basic questions like "what have I heard about this topic before?" or "how does this relate to me or others I know?" can provide starting points. It is also important in critical responses that you frequently refer to the text. By keeping the text front and centre, by citing it specifically, your essay becomes truly a response to the *text* and not just to the *topic*.

A critical analysis is not the same as a critical response, so the way you read a text to write an analysis is not the same as if you were reading it to respond. While, typically, you will use your own experience and the first-person voice, at least partly, in a response, in an analysis you are concerned with breaking down (analyzing) the text to determine the author's premises, to test the validity of the claims and conclusion, and to examine the specific methods and strategies used. Thus, your interaction with the text will involve such activities as identifying and scrutinizing; it will involve critical thinking and objective analysis. (See "The critical response: A meeting place," p. 136, "The critical analysis: Explaining and how and why," p. 139, and "Critical thinking," p. 43).

Of course, there are other reasons for reading: to write a review of a book or film, to prepare an informational or evaluative report, to compare/contrast two essays, to study for an exam, to see whether an essay topic interests you, for pure pleasure, and many more. Asking "how am I going to use the text?" before you begin can orient you appropriately and help you select the most useful approaches and strategies from among those discussed below.

THE LARGE PICTURE: READING STRATEGIES

People often assess their own strengths by saying, "I like to look at the large picture" or "I'm a detail person." Many of us do seem to have a natural aptitude—or at least a preference—for one or the other. It is nonetheless true that in order to complete many tasks, both skills are required. In much scientific research, a professor or senior researcher will oversee an experiment; the success of the experiment, however, depends just as much on the painstaking work of graduate students or junior researchers, all of whom may be mentioned among the study's authors. Of the many real-world examples of what can happen when a detail is overlooked, one of the strangest is the architect who forgot to include washrooms in his design for a theatre!

Successful essay writing, too, requires attention to the large and the small: while large-scale concerns relating to essay organization and paragraph structure (sometimes referred to as *macro-composing*) tend to occupy the writer in the early and middle stages of the process, by the final-draft stage, the focus will have changed to detail-oriented tasks (*micro-composing*), such as sentence construction, word choice, grammar, and source integration. These details increasingly become the focus throughout the revision process. This general pattern applies to reading as well, with some significant differences.

One difference is that you may not have to go beyond the large scale to consider the small scale; scanning an essay might give you all the information you need. Scanning is a form of **selective reading**, which is planned, conscious reading. Selective reading is different from the kind of reading you may be used to. In selective reading, your reading strategy is governed by your pre-reading choices, which can depend on what you are reading (for example, an introduction, a book chapter, an academic essay, or a book review) and your purpose for reading, as discussed above. It is therefore very different from simply sitting down with a book or essay and closely reading every word from beginning to end. This, too, could be considered a strategy of sorts but not a very efficient one; it wastes resources—your time, in particular. Selective reading can be contrasted with reading for pleasure or entertainment in which you have no particular plan in mind—you just read.

Scanning

In a **general scan**, you read to get the gist of a text. You read rapidly, keeping an eye out for content markers, such as headings and places in which the author summarizes material (in academic Type B essays, this summary could include tables, graphs, and other visual representations used to condense textual explanation). You try to identify main ideas in the essay by locating topic sentences within major paragraphs (topic sentences are often, but not always, the first sentence of the paragraph). Thesis statements, plans, or hypotheses are found in academic essays at the end of the introductory section. You proceed to skim, skipping detail such as examples or explanatory matter. General scanning is a good way to start reading a text since it will give you an overview of content. From a general scan, you could then practise another selective reading method.

In a specific scan, or **targeted scan**, you look for specific content. You might use this method if you are trying to determine whether a text will be useful. Say, for example, that the text is mentioned in a source that you definitely plan on using. You then look up the title of the potentially useful text and read its abstract, but neither the title nor the abstract confirms its usefulness. To investigate further, you *target scan* the entire text for specific content: you look for words and phrases related to your topic.

If you are looking for information in a book, you are likely able to locate it by referring to the **subject** or **author index**, a standard feature of most full-length reference and scholarly texts. These indexes, found at the back of books after any appendices or bibliographies, may give you many page references, so you may have to scan a number of pages in order to access the information you seek.

If your source is a journal article involving original research, the conventional structure of these kinds of studies may make it unnecessary for you to target scan the whole article—only the appropriate sections. But if your potential source is a journal article that is not divided into formal sections, you may have to scan the entire text. If you are accessing a text on-line, however, you can use your word processing program's "Find" function under "Edit" to locate occurrences of significant words or phrases in the text.

A general scan is helpful if you know you will be using the whole text since it can give you an overview of content—for example, if you are going to summarize a work or refer to it often in your essay. A targeted scan is helpful if you want to assess the usefulness of a text; if you decide that it does contain relevant content, you can then apply another method of selective reading, such as focused reading.

Focused reading

Because focused reading is time-consuming, you will probably have scanned the essay beforehand to find the most relevant portions of the text, which you then read in detail. College and university-level reading across the disciplines often involves both scanning and focused reading.

As the term **focused reading** implies, you read the text closely line by line and word by word. You may want to analyze the text for rhetorical strategies, tone, or stylistic elements. You may want to subject it to a critical analysis by testing the

Activity

Below are 10 reading situations with two variables for each—reading purpose and kind of text. Consider how the variables would help you decide on the most appropriate reading strategy(ies) to use in each situation.

Reading Purpose	Kind of Text	Reading Strategy(ies)?
To provide an overview or general summary	journalistic essay	
To see whether the topic interests you sufficiently to write an essay on it	informative essay	
To summarize results	journal study that describes original research (an experiment)	
To prepare for an exam question with a topic assigned in advance	short story you have never read before	
To study for a final exam	your class notes	
To write a critical response to an essay about a recent controversial topic (e.g., face transplants)	journalistic essay accessed on-line	
Compare/contrast two essays with differing points of view (e.g., two tax systems)	edited collection of essays published by an academic press	
To write a critical analysis	argumentative essay	
To pass the time before your dentist appointment	popular magazine	
To check the accuracy of a direct quotation you used in your essay	academic essay	

author's premises or questioning the conclusions he or she draws from the evidence. Or you may simply want to extract the text's main ideas. Many of the strategies for focused reading are discussed below under "Dividing the whole"; "The detail work" is also applicable.

In a focused reading, you often concentrate on one or more short or medium-length passages and relate them to a main idea or to other sections of the text. For example, if you are writing an essay for a literature or history class, you might concentrate on specific passages from a primary text, such as a novel or historical document, in order to connect key ideas in the passage to a work's theme, a main character, or some such literary (or historical) element. The purpose of analyzing the specific passage(s) is to support your thesis about the theme or main character.

Dividing the whole

Information is more easily grasped if it is presented in orderly chunks. Therefore, if your goal is to study an entire text, you can facilitate this goal by breaking the text into logical divisions, if the writer has not done so. Empirical studies (Type B academic essays) are divided into formal categories, each labelled according to convention; formal reports also use standardized headings. Such conventional categories are useful in telling you where specific kinds of information can be found; for example, in the "methods" section, the writer describes how the study was set up, the number of participants, how they were chosen, what measurements were applied, and similar details. If you are interested in whether the author proved a hypothesis or answered a question, you would read the abstract or the introduction and then read the "discussion" and/or "conclusion."

However, not all academic or journalistic essays clearly indicate how they are broken down. In long Type A academic essays, descriptive headings may be used, but you might want to subdivide the essay further to create more manageable content subcategories. Some writers of longer essays do not use descriptive headings but may nevertheless separate sections by leaving additional spaces between the end of one section and the beginning of the next. If descriptive headings are used in journalistic essays, their primary function may be less structural than interest-centred; thus, the heading may not well represent the content that follows it.

One way to begin figuring out an academic essay's structure is to return to the introduction and reread the essay plan, usually located near the beginning of many Type A essays, where the author announces the essay's organization. Fortunately, most academic and professional writers are aware of the importance of structure and organize content in the body of their essays according to a logical rationale. In the absence of an essay plan, headings, additional spacing, or similar aids, your job is to determine that rationale and use it to create manageable subdivisions. Although the primary purpose for doing this might be to make the essay easier to read, when you do it you are also familiarizing yourself with the parts of the essay that are going to be the most useful to you.

Information can often be organized by specific **rhetorical patterns**. Identifying these patterns makes the text easier to follow. For example, in the chronological method, the writer traces a development over time, usually from old to new. In the spatial method, the writer describes an object or scene in a systematic way, from top to bottom, for example, or from one side to another. In enumeration, points are listed in a numbered sequence (see "Rhetorical patterns and paragraph development," p. 98).

In addition, the relationship between ideas is often shown through **transitional words and phrases**. These transitions can indicate whether an idea is going to be expanded or more fully explained or whether there will be a shift from one idea to another one. Paying attention to organizational patterns and transitions can help you break down an essay into smaller and more manageable units. In the passage below, the writers use enumeration to indicate the development of one point and the transitional phrase "in addition" to indicate what could be either a new point or a major expansion of the earlier point. (Ellipses show that sentences in between have been omitted.)

> So, what can be done to reduce the start-up costs for young Canadians? *First*, political parties have a role to play. . . .
>
> *Second*, the problems with the permanent voters list need to be resolved. . . .
>
> *In addition* to these short-term solutions, various long-term solutions should be considered. (Gidengil et al. "Enhancing democratic citizenship")

Reading paragraphs: Identifying main ideas

Scanning paragraphs for important information is not just a mechanical process. The paragraphs in much academic writing may be very long and replete with detail; sentences may also be long and of complex construction. Furthermore, although student writers are often encouraged to announce their main idea in the first sentence of the paragraph, in academic and journalistic prose, topic sentences can occur at the beginning or the end of a paragraph—even in the middle. And not all paragraphs contain topic sentences. Some studies have shown that only half of paragraphs contain identifiable topic sentences. The style of professional writers varies considerably, a variability that may be reflected in paragraph construction.

A topic sentence states the central idea of the paragraph. It is usually the most general statement (although it should not be vague or overly broad), which can be developed by examples or analysis throughout the rest of the paragraph. In paragraphs constructed this way, the writer builds *from* the topic sentence, the first sentence. However, a writer may build *toward* the central idea, in which case the topic sentence may be the last one in the paragraph. The function of topic sentences is primarily structural—providing a foundation for the paragraph; however, this anchoring can occur in different places in the paragraph.

The following paragraphs illustrate two methods of paragraph construction in which topic sentences are, respectively, the first and last sentences in the paragraph (they are italicized):

Whether someone lives through extreme exposure can be boiled down to a few physical and biological factors. In its minimal form, survival analysis requires an accounting of four factors, which can be defined as critical variables. The first two variables are beyond human control, while the latter two are amenable to intervention. These critical variables are as follows: (1) the physics of the environment, (2) the limits of human physiology, (3) the length of the exposure, and (4) behavioural adaptation, including what the victim understands about survival requirements and the plans made to prepare for a failure. (Piantadosi. "The human environment," p. 403)

Lately I've discovered a British series called "Playing Shakespeare" in which John Barton of the Royal Shakespeare Company works through a few scenes with half a dozen actors. Together they unlock a text, discovering what words and phrases to stress, where to breathe, what meaning Shakespeare encoded in the words, how the actors should react to each other. Barton comes across as a master teacher and a bit of a TV star (like Buddy Rich, he forgets the camera). What makes this historic is that the lessons take place in 1982 and the actors he works with—Ben Kingsley, Judi Dench, Ian McKellan—are among the best of their generation, all caught relatively early in their distinguished careers. *It offers a privileged glimpse of a long-ago reality.* (Fulford. "A box full of history: TV and our sense of the past," p. 315)

Does the variability of paragraph construction mean that every paragraph needs to be closely read in order to determine its main idea? The reason that it is useful to scan by focusing on the first sentences of paragraphs is not just because they may contain the main idea: they often suggest the way the paragraph will be developed. Also, typically, important words and phrases recur throughout related paragraphs in an essay, and since topic sentences anchor the thought in the paragraph, they often contain these recurring words. The first place to look is the first sentence of the paragraph.

Clues can be picked up from the first sentences in the paragraphs above. In the first paragraph, the opening sentence makes a general statement; a quick glance at the numbers below it reveals the paragraph's development through division, a kind of analysis. The paragraph can be said to have been developed **deductively**: the topic sentence makes a general statement after which more specific statements are used for support ("evidence"). In contrast, the second paragraph begins with a specific personal observation, which is explored until its significance is revealed in the final (topic) sentence. The paragraph can be said to have been developed **inductively**: the topic sentence is a general statement arrived at after specific "evidence" has been considered.

Thus, many first sentences in well-constructed paragraphs provide clues to where the main idea will be found. In the following paragraph excerpt, the first sentence provides a transition from the previous paragraph as well as a **prompt** for the topic sentence, which follows immediately:

> The new rationality and concern over bullying is not only targeting the aggressive girl. *It also actively seeks the participation of school authorities in the informal control of girls.* (Barron and Lacombe. "Moral panic and the Nasty Girl")

In the following excerpts from the same essay, the authors provide clues through transitional and repeated words and phrases to guide the reader to the main ideas in the paragraphs. Note that in the first paragraph, the reader would need to read beyond the generalization to find the topic sentence, which follows the semicolon in the second sentence; the first sentence and the first clause in the second, then, act as a prompt. In the interests of efficiency, several of the middle sentences in the paragraphs are omitted. If you were scanning these paragraphs, you might not read these middle sentences at all since they do not contain main ideas but are expansions on the topic sentences. (Main ideas are italicized, and transitional and repeated words are bolded.)

> Girl violence is not a new phenomenon. A glimpse at newspaper articles in 1977 reveals that acts of girl violence are not new; *rather, the attention paid to them is novel.* **For example**, one article reports a violent confrontation between a group of teenage girls who had been feuding for a week. . . .
>
> **Despite** a rich description of violent details, *the tone of the article is non-threatening.* The title, "Teenager girl in knife feud says: 'We're friends again,'" certainly prepares the reader for an account of violence, but it also emphasizes the fact that the dispute has been resolved amicably. . . . The article ends with the assurance that this violent incident is not typical of girl behaviour, a conclusion justified by the knowledge that the weapon used in the girl feud did, after all, belong to a boy. In the **wake of fear** created by Virk's murder, the relationship between girls and violence is presented differently.

> **Also** *central to the creation of a* **climate of fear** *is statistical manipulation of crime data to establish the amplitude of girl violence....*
>
> **However**, *most articles failed to recognize that the increase was in reference to minor assaults,* such as pushing or slapping, which did not cause serious injury....

Note that the transitional words/phrases "for example," "despite," "also," and "however" suggest specific relationships between what has preceded and what follows (respectively, relationships of illustration, contrast, addition, and qualification). By attending carefully to prompts, along with transitional and repeated words in these paragraphs, a reader could quickly find the most important ideas and focus on them.

Thinking of transitions, repeated words, prompts, and other strategies for reading reiterates the importance of using them to create coherence in your own writing. In fact, they are usually discussed as *writing* rather than as reading strategies, ways to ensure that your ideas are communicated clearly to your readers. Looking at them as reading strategies highlights the essential relationship between writing and reading: writing consciously by using strategies for coherence facilitates conscious readers in their decoding of a difficult text. Less conscious writers who do not focus on strategies to make their writing coherent put their readers at a distinct disadvantage, possibly frustrating them. See "Writing middle paragraphs" (p. 94), which discusses strategies for producing coherent writing.

It is important to realize that the hints above can serve only as rough guides to where the main ideas in any text can be found. The best way to become familiar with the reading process is to read frequently and to be conscious both of the author's attempts to create coherence through specific strategies and your own attempts to find coherence by being aware of these strategies and responding to each writer and text as a unique learning experience.

THE DETAIL WORK

As useful as it is to think in terms of the large picture and to be able to identify important information in essays and paragraphs, sooner or later you will find yourself grappling with the elements of the sentence—words, phrases, and clauses. When you look more closely at a text, you may be confronted by problems in any of the three areas listed below, but the last two typically present most of the challenges for student readers:

1. The relationships among words and the other syntactical units in a sentence, phrases and clauses (grammar and sentence structure).
2. The variety of linguistic resources used by the author (you can think of this as the *way* that the author uses words or the range of linguistic options at a writer's disposal).
3. Word meanings (vocabulary).

Grammar and sentence structure

Knowing the meaning of words is not going to help with comprehension unless you are familiar with the conventions that govern the arrangement of these words in a sentence. Fortunately, native English speakers entering college or university have been practising these conventions for years, albeit unconsciously, in their daily speech and writing. It is the conventions that determine the order of words and other relationships among the syntactical units in a sentence (syntax refers to the order of words, phrases, and clauses in a sentence).

English sentence structure and rules of grammar are governed largely by these syntactical relationships. Non-native English speakers must learn these rules in order to speak, read, and write in English. Native speakers need to learn these rules too in order to speak and write in Standard English; however, it is possible to read most English texts without being familiar with fine points of English grammar. Indeed, most native English speakers do not need to think much about the conventions of grammar in order to grasp the meaning of a passage. The reason that some writing professionals—especially teachers and editors, those who analyze prose—return to study the rules of grammar closely is that they need to know the basis for the rules in order to explain them to others. And when you *write* in English it *is* necessary to know these rules well, whether you are a native or non-native speaker. Poor grammar or sentence structure undermines your credibility as a writer.

Linguistic resources

All readers need to know *how* a writer is using words before they can make assumptions about the meaning of a text. Individual words carry **connotations**, or implications, beyond those of their dictionary meanings, or **denotations**. Paying careful attention to context—the surrounding words—can help you determine a word's connotation and orient you to the intended meaning. Sometimes dictionaries suggest a word's connotations, although often, when you look up a word in a dictionary, you find one or more of its common definitions and have to look at the passage itself to discern precisely how it is being used (its connotation). Dictionaries are often not the "final word" on meaning but necessary starting places.

A word can acquire different connotations through its use over time or within a specific group. In some cases, positive or negative values have become associated with the word. Many common words have several connotations. Consider, for example, the implications of the words *slender, slim, lean, thin, skinny, scrawny,* and *emaciated,* which suggest a progression from positive (graceful, athletic . . .) to negative (. . . weak, sick). Sometimes only context will make a word's connotation clear.

Writers often indirectly signal their true or deeper intentions to their readers, and if these readers fail to pick up the signals, they will fail to "read" the work as intended; they will not be properly oriented to the work. Finding the appropriate orientation toward a passage or an entire essay might involve more than figuring out contextual clues: it might involve asking how the author's purpose in writing should be reflected in your reading of the text. It might involve asking questions like *What response is the author looking for from me? Does the author want me to read literally, or does the surface level of words hide another meaning?* Although these kinds of questions relate to the author's purpose, their answers are inevitably embedded in the language of the text. Therefore, the author's use of language is the place to find answers.

Such questions are more pertinent to essays written to persuade or entertain than to those written to explain. Thus, writers might adopt an ironic tone to make the reader question a commonly accepted or simplistic perspective. In **irony**, you look beyond the literal meaning of words to their deeper or "true" meaning. The object might be to make you aware of another perspective, to poke fun at a perspective, or to advocate change.

Authors whose primary purpose is to entertain may do so by using **humour**. Although some humour engages us directly, much does not but rather relies on subtle linguistic techniques revealed through implication or through devices like word play or allusion; many essays, of course, use humour not just to entertain but to criticize people or institutions, employing irony as well. Literary works present yet another way in which writers seek to encode multiple meanings and resonances beyond those of literal representation. You would not read a novel or short story in the same way you would read an essay; your orientation toward these two kinds of texts varies with the author's purpose in writing.

Word meanings

Dictionaries are an indispensable part of the writing life whether you are a professional writer or a student writer, whether you do your writing mostly by hand or use a sophisticated word processing program from start to finish. They are also an essential part of the reading life, and every student needs at least one good dictionary—two are preferable: one mid-sized dictionary for the longer, more complex writing you do at home and a portable one for the classroom or school computing station (you may also be able to access reliable on-line dictionaries through your library). But while a good dictionary is part of the key to understanding challenging texts, it is not the only one—often it is not even the best one.

This is because the texts you read at the post-secondary level may be a good deal more challenging than you are used to. To look up every word when the meaning is unclear would require too much time; as well, if you interrupt your reading too often, it will be hard to maintain continuity, reducing your understanding and retention of the material. Thankfully, you do not need to know the precise meaning of every word you read; you need to know the exact meanings of the most important words but only approximate meanings for many of the others.

We all have three vocabularies: a speaking vocabulary, a writing vocabulary, and a reading, or *recognition*, vocabulary. The speaking vocabulary is the smallest, and 2,000 words can be considered sufficient for most of our conversational needs. Our recognition vocabulary is the largest, but it includes words we would not use in our writing. That is why, if you are asked the meaning of a word from your recognition vocabulary, you might struggle to define it, even though you might *think* you know what it means; however, you know it only within the contexts in which you have read it.

Since relying *only* on a dictionary is both inefficient and unreliable, you should cultivate reading practices that minimize—not maximize—the use of a dictionary. Use a dictionary when you have to or to confirm a word's meaning; otherwise, try to determine meanings by utilizing contextual clues. In the following passage, the omission of first words in the lines has very little effect on comprehension:

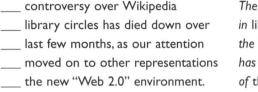

___ controversy over Wikipedia	*The* controversy over Wikipedia
___ library circles has died down over	*in* library circles has died down over
___ last few months, as our attention	*the* last few months, as our attention
___ moved on to other representations	*has* moved on to other representations
___ the new "Web 2.0" environment.	*of* the new "Web 2.0" environment.

In this passage, the missing words are small words—prepositions, articles, and an auxiliary verb. However, important nouns, verbs, adjectives, and adverbs are also often revealed through context—the words around them. Writers may define difficult words or may use synonyms or rephrasing to make their meanings easy to grasp; such strategies are used if the author thinks the typical reader may not know them. On the other hand, authors may, without conscious effort, use an unfamiliar word in such a way that the meanings of the surrounding words clarify the meaning and connotation of the unfamiliar word.

Context clues: Specialized words, such as words borrowed from another language or culture, are defined for general audiences:

> The birds were nesting on *nunataks*—sheer-cliffed islands of rock surrounded by vast glacial icefields. (Krajick. "In search of the ivory gull")

Particularly important concepts may be given an expanded definition:

> [T]he Buddhist concept of *duhkha*, often translated as "suffering," is not simply an unpleasant feeling. Rather, it refers most deeply to a basic vulnerability to suffering and pain due to misapprehending the nature of reality. (Ekman et al. "Buddhist and psychological perspectives")

Even in highly specialized writing, the writer may define terms the reader might not know:

> Young female larvae of bees, wasps, and ants are usually *totipotent*, that is, they have the potential to develop into either a queen or a worker. (F.L.W. Ratnieks and T. Wenseleers. "Policing insect societies")

Rather than being stated directly in a clause or phrase that follows, a definition can be implied in a preceding sentence:

> Ruttenbur and the soldier have a joint house and property in the game, even though the soldier is married in real life. Such in-game *polygamy* is common. (Thompson. "Game theories")

When a writer does not define a word, you may be able to infer its meaning through context—by looking at the words around it and the idea the writer is trying to express. In the following example, both the preceding word, a verb, and the following word, a noun, help reveal the word's meaning:

> Only after women had overcome *formidable* barriers . . . were they able to analyze the predominant patterns of knowledge. (Ruth Hayhoe. "Universities, women, and the dialogue among civilizations")

In the example below, the author's use of the correlative conjunctions *either . . . or* shows us the contrastive relationship between two words in close proximity. Since you probably know that "virtuous" means "morally good," you can deduce that "insidious" must mean something bad—deceptive or treacherous:

> We are blinded by cuteness, and the very traits that make a character either virtuous or *insidious* are lost on us. (Poplak. "Fear and loathing in Toontown")

By carefully reading the following sentence, you can see that "perturbations" is a near synonym of the word "change"; in this case, it is necessary to look at more than the immediate context and consider the idea being expressed:

> Being alive requires being attuned to natural *change*, and many organisms are exquisitely sensitive to even tiny *perturbations* in environmental conditions. (Piantadosi. "The human environment")

What follows a word may suggest its meaning, not by defining or rephrasing but by expansion or illustration through examples. In the first passage, examples of *changes across* the spectrum of light are given (it also helps to look at the etymology of the word; see "Word puzzles," below: *trans* = across + *mutare* = change):

> [N]atural philosophers assumed that coloured rays of light were *transmutable*. To change blue into red, white into yellow, or orange into violet, they reckoned that one simply had to find a way to quicken or retard the speed at which the pulses moved through the aether. (John Waller. "Sir Isaac Newton and the meaning of light")

> In the Nevada desert, an entire city, Las Vegas, has been turned into spectacle, a neon-lit 24-hour wonderland of *ersatz* experience, complete with fake Eiffel Tower, fake Venetian canals. (Posner. "Image world")

In the sentence above, the use of the word "fake" implies that "ersatz" means something fake or artificial. If the author had not expanded on the phrase "wonderland of ersatz experience," it might have seemed that "ersatz" meant "spectacle."

Reading carefully to determine both the immediate context and the encompassing idea of the sentence or passage can help you determine a word's meaning. Remember that the object is not necessarily to make the word part of your writing vocabulary but to enable you to know how the author is using it—to recognize its particular connotation. Of course, if you are still in doubt, you should look up the word. By examining a word's denotations (dictionary definitions) and at least one of its connotations (the way it is used by the author in a particular context), you are well on the way to making it part of your writing vocabulary.

Family resemblances: If context does not help you to determine a word's meaning, you can look for resemblances, recalling words that look similar and whose meanings you know. Many words in English come from Greek or Latin (most English words of more than one syllable are derived from Latin). A "family" of words may arise from the same Latin or Greek root or word element. While it is helpful to know some of these roots (see below), you may be able to infer the meaning of a new word by recalling a known word with the same word element. For example, you can easily see a family resemblance between the word "meritocracy" and the familiar word "merit." You can take this a step further by looking at the second element and recalling that "meritocracy" and "democracy" contain a common element. In a *democracy*, the *people* determine who will govern them. In a *meritocracy*, then, *merit* determines who governs.

Word puzzles: In the following sentences, it is difficult to determine meaning either by context or by family resemblance:

> [T]he number of biographies of public figures has shrunk over the last few decades to virtual non-existence. And those that are written are rarely *hagiographies*. (Saul. "Anti-Heroism")

> When there was wind, it was an *eructation*. (O'Rourke. "Sulfur Island")

Using a dictionary in such instances is certainly a good recourse, but another way of determining a word's meaning without resorting to a dictionary is to break it down to discover its **root** (its base) and, if applicable, its **affixes** (its prefix and/or suffix). A **prefix** precedes a root, changing or qualifying the word's meaning; a **suffix** follows the root, changing or qualifying the word's meaning and indicating its grammatical function. Not all words have prefixes and suffixes, of course, and some contain more than one root. Assembling the "pieces" of an unfamiliar word is much like putting together a puzzle; it can enable you to make an educated guess about the word's meaning, which is often sufficient for reading purposes.

The study of the origin of roots can be a mystifying process that is bound up in the complex development of the English language. Often, the basic root of a word does not much resemble the form it takes in an English word. For example, in the word "tactile," the basic root is "tang," while "tact" is a secondary root formed from "tang," the past participle of a Latin verb. Thus, the charts below give the secondary root or roots when applicable because that makes it easier to see the connection between the root's meaning and the meaning of the English word that contains the root. Some of the roots, prefixes, and suffixes can be used to help define the key and difficult words that follow each of the essays in "The Active Reader."

Examples

antecedent: *ante* (before) + *cede* (goes) + *ent* (noun). An antecedent of an event occurs before the event (and is usually a cause); it is also the grammatical term for the noun that a pronoun replaces (so it "goes before" the pronoun).

autocratic: *auto* (self) + *crat* (power) + *ic* (adjective). An autocratic ruler does not share power with others but rules absolutely (and usually harshly). The word is formed from two roots plus a suffix indicating its function as an adjective.

Specialized language: The strategies discussed above for understanding unfamiliar words apply to all kinds of writing. However, the academic disciplines have their own specialized vocabularies that scholars use to communicate with each other. This language is known as **jargon**, and even the jargon of two subdisciplines, such as plant sciences and zoology, can vary considerably. When you take undergraduate courses in one discipline or the other, you begin to acquire this specialized vocabulary, which has developed over the years as the discipline itself has developed. To acquire knowledge about a subject is to simultaneously acquire its language, along with the other conventions of the discipline.

Where does this leave the novice reader? In the case of long essays dealing with highly technical subject matter, it might leave him or her feeling in the dark. But such readings are not usually assigned until students are well acquainted with the language, methods, and practices of the particular discipline. In addition to the strategies discussed above, both novice and more seasoned readers can make use of the variety of discipline-specific dictionaries, encyclopedias, and research guides that can be accessed through many libraries. For example, Oxford University Press has published a series of subject dictionaries in art and architecture, the biological sciences, classical studies, computing, earth and environmental sciences, and many other disciplines.

Prefix	Meaning	Root	Meaning	Suffix	Meaning/Use[1]
a; an before vowel/*h*	*not, absence of*	alter	*other (of two)*	-able/ible	*capable of* (adj.)
ab; a before *v*; **abs** before *c, t*	*away, from*	amphi/ampho	*both, on both sides*	-acy/ocracy	*government* (n.)
ad; may add first letter of root *(allude/affix)*; usually assimilates with first letter of root	*to(ward)*	ann	*year*	-ade	*result of action* (n.)
ante	*before (in temporal sense)*	anthrop	*human being*	-age	*result, act* (n.)
anti; elides before vowel	*against*	arch	*beginning, old, ruler*	-al/ial	*relating to* (adj.)
bi; bin before vowel	*double*	aud	*hear, listen*	-an/ian	*pertaining to* (adj.)
circum	*around*	auto	*self*	-ance	*state of, action* (n.)
con; co before vowel/*h*; assimilates with *l* and *m*	*together, with*	bi	*life*	-ant	*agent, cause* (n.)
contra	*against*	capit	*head, chief, leader*	-arium	*place, housing* (n.)
de	*away, from, down*	cathar	*purge, purify*	-ary	*relating to, place where* (n.)
di	*two, double, separate*	ced	*go, yield, surrender*	-ate	*associated with* (n.) (adj.) (v.)
dia	*through, across*	chron	*time*	-cule	*small* (n.) (adj.)
dis	*take away, not, deprive of*	cid	*kill*	-dom	*quality, state* (n.)
e (Latin); **ex** before vowel, *h, c, p, q, s*; **ef** before *f*; **ec** (Greek); **ex** before vowel, *h*	*out, from*	clud	*shut*	-eer	*one who* (n.)
en; em before *b, m, p*	*into*	cis	*cut*	-ed/en	*past participle* (adj.)
hyper	*over, above, excessive*	cord	*heart*	-en	*consisting of* (adj.)

[1](n.) = noun; (adj.) = adjective; (v.) = verb

Prefix	Meaning	Root	Meaning	Suffix	Meaning/Use
in; im before b, m, p	not, into	crat	power	-ent	quality of (n.) (adj.)
inter	between, among	cosm	world	-ence/ency	state of, action (n.)
macr	large	cred	believe	-er/or	doer (n.)
mal	bad, evil	dem	people	-ese	native/language of (n.) (adj.)
ob	facing	dic	speak	-ful(l)	full of (n.) (adj.)
pan	all	dogm	belief, opinion	-ic	like, nature of (adj.)
per	through	epistem	knowledge	-ion/sion/tion	act, result, state of (n.)
post	after, behind	fac	make	-ism	system, condition (n.)
pre	before	fort	strong	-ize/ise	make (v.)
pro	forward, forth, before	grad/gress	step, degree, walk	-ness	state of (n.)
re	again, back	greg	crowd, group	-ory	place (n.)
sub	under	hagi	sacred	-ous	full of (adj.)
syn; sym before b, m, p	with, together	icon	image	-ster	one who is, belongs to (n.)
trans	across	log	word, study	-ure	state of, act, process (n.)

Thirty Additional Roots

luc/lum/lun	light	man	by hand	met	measure
mis	hate	mitt	send	mut	(ex)change
nasc/nat	born	omni	all	palp	touch
path	feel, suffer, disease	phil	love	phren	mind, brain
pon/pos	place	port	carry	punct	point
put	think	rect	straight, right	rid/ris	laughter
ruct	belch	tax	order	tel	end
sci	know	scrib	write	simil/simul	like, resembling
stru	build	tact/tang	touch	taut	identical
trib	pay, bestow	vad	go	vert	turn

Activity

Using contextual, word resemblance, or word puzzle strategies whenever necessary, determine the meanings of the italicized words in the following passage:

Some physicists are so troubled by the *arbitrariness* of the cosmos that they *espouse* a quasi-theological concept known as the *anthropic* principle. According to the anthropic principle, the universe must have the structure we observe, because otherwise we wouldn't be here to observe it.

The anthropic principle actually comes in two forms, weak and strong. The weak anthropic principle, or WAP, holds merely that any cosmic observer will observe conditions, at least locally, that make the observer's existence possible. The strong anthropic principle, SAP, insists that the universe must be constructed in such a way as to make observers possible. WAP is *tautological* and SAP *teleological*. . . .

Many scientists have argued that life must be a *ubiquitous* phenomenon that *pervades* the universe, but they can offer precious little *empirical* evidence to support this assertion. After decades of searching, scientists have found no signs of life elsewhere in the universe; a 1996 report of fossilized microbes in a meteorite from Mars turned out to be *erroneous*. Researchers still cannot make matter *animate* in the laboratory, even with all the tools of modern biotechnology. (Horgan. "Can science solve the riddle of existence?")

PART TWO

Academic Writing

Academic discourse can be thought of as *a set of oral and written procedures used to generate and disseminate ideas within the academic community*. Most of the classes you take in college or university focus on *written* discourse: by writing down your thoughts, you are recording them to be analyzed by others (and, yes, usually graded). Familiarity with the conventions of written discourse will be valuable to you throughout your college or university career and beyond because it is primarily through writing that knowledge is transmitted. By contrast, oral discourse lacks staying power, though modern technology has altered this distinction somewhat.

By the time that students approach college or university, most are familiar with the rudiments of reading and writing. They probably know the ground rules for writing essays, though they may find the requirements of reading and writing at the post-secondary level somewhat alien. Thus, you may find that some of the essays you are asked to read and respond to seem more challenging than you are used to. The same applies to the writing skills in which you are required to demonstrate competence. One thing you will find is a greater variety of challenges. You will probably be writing essays and reports in most of your courses. They may share certain similarities with one another but will also contain marked differences. To write a lab report for a chemistry class, for example, you use different standards and procedures, or conventions, from those you use in a literary analysis for an English class, which, in turn, are different from those you use to write a marketing plan for a business class or a feasibility study for an engineering class.

Despite these differences, there are two relatively distinct forms that academic writing can take: the **essay** and the **report**. You will be required to write essays in many of your undergraduate courses. Writing reports may be limited to your science courses, some of your social sciences courses, along with any business, engineering, or health sciences courses you take. Chapter 3 reviews the fundamentals of writing academic essays, followed by an overview of report writing ("The Active Voice: Report Writing," p. 104) and a step-by-step guide to writing science papers ("The Active Voice: How to Write a Scientific Paper," p. 107).

Chapter 4 introduces specific kinds of essays. In the section on the argumentative essay, you will learn about applying general academic writing skills to the mode of argument: in argumentative essays, you assert and defend a claim, usually one of value or policy. When you try to convince someone that something is good or bad or to adopt a particular course of action, you may not have to use outside sources to help support your claim. However, when you write a critical response or a critical analysis, you use your critical thinking skills to analyze one or more specific texts. Learning summarization skills enables you to represent the ideas and words of other writers in your own essays. When you summarize, then, you focus more on *re-presenting* than on analyzing. Research essays display the fullest range of skills for student readers and writers because they combine various skills, including representation, analysis, synthesis, and critical thinking. Although they may also use argument occasionally, they *always* call on what is for many students one of the most challenging of skills at the post-secondary level: research—locating, evaluating, and effectively utilizing library resources in your essays.

Chapter 3

An Overview of the Essay

There are two major models of essay writing: the sequential (or chronological) model and the structural model. Each approaches the essay in a distinct way, although you will no doubt use both at different times.

The sequential model

The sequential model quite logically implies that essays, like most extended projects, are written in chronological stages. Although academic writing may place more emphasis on the later stages than you are used to, such as the revising and editing of the rough draft, or on research, students approach academic writing with the knowledge that it is a chronological process that usually begins with a broad topic.

FORMULATING A THESIS

Using inventing and pre-writing techniques, you explore the topic, asking what you know about it and what you want to find out about it. The objective is to narrow the topic to express the specific focus or approach to the topic, which you formulate as a **thesis statement**. Some students find this the most difficult stage: intimidated by a blank page or screen, they may associate this with a blank mind and feel hopeless or frustrated. Fortunately, there are several pre-writing techniques that help to ease the transition from blank to written page.

Students who are assigned a topic of their choice may find the task more daunting than those who are given specific topics on which to write. Although they may be relieved when the instructor offers as preliminary guidance "write on what you're interested in," they may nonetheless feel that many of their interests do not seem to lend themselves to the kind of writing they are being asked to produce at the college or university level; for example, how does an interest in cats, comic books, or Christian rock translate into a topic for a research essay?

Let us say that you are interested in dance, having taken classes for several years in jazz and hip hop. To refine this broad area, try the "subject test": dance is considered a subject or subdiscipline within fine arts, often associated with the faculty of arts or humanities, yet this subject could be explored from a number of different angles within other disciplines:

- dance as self-expression (humanities—fine arts);
- dance as entertainment (humanities—fine arts);

- the history of dance (humanities—history);
- the function of dance in other cultures (humanities—cultural studies; social sciences—anthropology);
- dance as the expression of a collective identity (social sciences—sociology);
- dance as therapy (social sciences—psychology);
- dance as physical movement (science—physiology/kinesiology);
- dance as an area of skill acquisition and study (education).

Each of these approaches suggests a way of narrowing the broad subject of dance in order to write on it for different classes or as an assignment for your English class. In fact, the approaches could already be considered topics, but they are, as yet, undeveloped. *What would you like to know about it?* Let us say that you are planning to major in psychology. Therefore, the topic of dance as therapy is something you would like to know more about. One option is to begin your research now by finding out what has been written about this topic. Accordingly, you could check out your library's databases, such as *Humanities index* or *Periodical contents index*, which cover journals focusing on the performing arts. However, there are other techniques you can use to narrow your topic further before you commit yourself to research, if research is a requirement for your essay. These techniques can also be used when you have only a broad subject (such as dance) and want to make it more specific.

Pre-writing techniques

Freewriting utilizes your associations with something. To freewrite, begin with a blank piece of paper or a blank screen and start recording these associations. Do not stop to reflect on your next thought or polish your writing: simply write continuously for a predetermined time—such as five or 10 minutes. A good starting point is a sentence that includes the subject you want to find out more about, such as a tentative definition: Dance as therapy is. . . .

After you are done, look back at what you have written. You may find much of it repetitive or that you have started thinking about one thing and suddenly switched to something else. That is to be expected. But it is also possible that what you have written reveals consistencies or subtleties you had not considered before or were not aware of when you were writing. Underline potentially useful points. You can take the best one and use it as a starting point for another freewriting session, or you could summarize one significant section in a sentence and use that sentence as a starting point. The sample below is the result of one freewriting session. The writer might have continued by summarizing the last three lines in a sentence and attempted to refine her topic further by a second session.

> Dance as therapy is i don't really know what it is as i've never thought about dance that way but i know that my dancing can be therapeutic in that i lose myself self self as i spin or split leap and

once the teacher had everyone look at me as i was doing a fou-
ette and i was not even aware only of concentrating on one spot
as you're supposed to and i was blocking out everything else and
not thinking about what i'm going to wear the next day or my
problems at work getting more hours so i can pay for these
classes so therapy is healing and there must be a method to follow to heal yourself just as there is a method or technique for
learning different kinds of dance i would like to learn about integrating healing into my dancing but i think i do anyway so maybe
i am learning about therapy as i dance.

Madison Mauberly

In the **questioning** technique, you ask questions pertinent to the topic. Initially, these questions could be the basic *who, what, where, when, why, how.*

- What is dance therapy? What are its basic elements/divisions/stages? What are its goals?
- Who would use dance as therapy? Who would benefit from it?
- Where can you go to study dance therapy? Where is it practised?
- When did dance therapy begin? Why?
- How does it work? How is it similar to/different from other kinds of creative healing techniques?

Each question suggests a different approach to the topic and a different rhetorical pattern. For example, the first question might lead you to the definition pattern; the second question might lead you to divide dance therapy into different types or other subcategories (division/classification). The last question could lead you to focus on comparison and contrast (e.g., dance therapy versus music therapy) or to analyze the costs and benefits of different creative healing techniques (see "Rhetorical patterns and paragraph development," p. 98).

Brainstorming and **clustering** (mapping) work by generating associations. In brainstorming, which can be done either collaboratively or individually, you list your associations with a topic, writing down words and phrases, until you feel you have covered the topic thoroughly. Although you do not intentionally look for connections when you generate your list, you can then look back to explore possible connections between items on your list.

While brainstorming works linearly, clustering is a spatial technique that generates associations and seeks connections among them. You begin by writing a word or phrase in the middle of a blank page and circling it. As associations occur to you, you write them down and circle them, connecting them by a line to the word/phrase that gave rise to the association. As you continue this process beyond the first words/ phrases circling the original word/phrase, you will develop larger clusters in some places than in others. The well-developed clusters may suggest the most promising ways to develop your topic. The spatial organization of the individual clusters themselves may suggest connections, but you may also be able to draw lines to connect one item in a cluster to another item in a separate cluster. These clusters and interconnecting lines can suggest ways to extend your topic (what is circled in the centre of the page) and develop your essay's structure in the process.

The thesis statement you come up with should always reflect your purpose in writing. For example, if you were writing a personal essay on dance as part of your application to a performing arts program it would be very different from one you would write for a research essay.

Exercise

Three sample thesis statements on dance follow. Determine which one would be applicable to (1) a personal essay; (2) an argumentative essay that attempts to persuade the reader to take a particular course of action; (3) a research essay concerned with the historical development of dance therapy:

With its roots in modern dance and its stress on self-expression over performance, dance therapy has evolved into a vibrant profession that today serves such diverse groups as disabled people and employees of large corporations.

One of my earliest memories is of pulling myself up close to the TV so I could follow the intricate moving shapes before my eyes, trying to make sense of the patterns they formed. Now, at 18, I want to personally explore what it is like to be a part of the visual pattern called dance.

Cuts to the operating budgets of performing arts programs at this university must be curtailed so these students can feel the security they need to succeed in their studies and the university community can experience the benefits of the performing arts on campus.

FINDING SUPPORT

In the next stage, you attempt to back up your thesis. Thesis statements are claims of some kind. A claim must have **support**; otherwise, it is an empty claim that will be disregarded. For example, although you could claim that the dog ate your homework, your instructor is not likely to take such a claim seriously. But if you produced your vet bill, the claim would at least have some support and may demand your instructor's consideration. If you were writing a critical analysis of a poem, the support would need to come from the poem itself. If you were writing a research paper, you would need to find out what other people have said or written about the topic as it related to your thesis. However, if you were writing a personal essay or response, you might have to do no more than think about how you were affected by the topic, and so your support might consist of memories, experiences, or perceptions.

Your general claim (thesis statement) must be supported by more specific claims (main points), which, in turn, require support in the form of references to primary sources (English or history essay), factual information such as statistics or secondary sources (research essay), or personal experience (personal essay). If during this stage it becomes clear that you are unable to adequately support your thesis, you can consider adapting the thesis to be in line with the support you have found; occasionally, you may have to abandon the thesis and begin again. (See "Kinds of evidence," p. 101; see also "Kinds of evidence in argumentative essays," p. 120, and "Selecting resources" in "The Active Voice: A Beginner's Guide to Researching in the Digital Age," p. 158.)

RELATING PARTS AND DISCOVERING STRUCTURE

When you have found enough support, it is time to begin thinking about how you will use it in your essay—how, in other words, you will connect the general claim (thesis statement) to the specific claims (main ideas related to the thesis). With this in mind, you begin organizing claims and support in a logical and consistent way, one that clearly expresses the relationship between each claim and its support. One way to clarify these relationships is to construct an **outline**, a diagrammatic representation of the essay and a plan you can use in the composing stage so that you do not get off-track. An outline can be a brief listing of your main points, a **scratch** or **sketch outline**, often used for in-class or exam essays for which you do not have the time for much more than a rudimentary sketch of your essay. With longer essays, an outline can be extensively developed to include levels of sub-points (developments of main points) along with details and examples. The **formal outline** uses a number/letter scheme to represent the essay's complete structure. The conventional scheme goes like this:

I. First main point (topic sentence of paragraph)
    A. First sub-point (development of main point)
        1. first sub-sub-point (development of sub-point: detail or example)
        2. second sub-sub-point
    B. Second sub-point
        1. first sub-sub-point
        2. second sub-sub-point

This example represents a paragraph with a three-level outline—that is, one main point and two sub-points—presumably, a very important paragraph in the essay. Not all paragraphs are developed this extensively; in fact, such a paragraph might be too long to hold a reader's attention, and it might be advisable to divide it into two paragraphs.

When you are considering your outline, especially if it is a formal outline, remember that it serves as the blueprint for the essay itself. Therefore, to construct a useful outline, you should ask questions like the following:

- How do the main points in my outline relate to my thesis statement?
- How do the sub-points relate to my main points?
- Do I have enough main points to support my thesis?
- Do I have enough sub-points (at least two) for each main point?
- Are there any points that seem either irrelevant or out of place? (If the latter, where do they belong?)
- What is the most effective order for my points? (In argumentative essays, you should order points according to their persuasiveness—for example, least to most persuasive, the climax order. In expository essays, you often order them according to a consistent organizational method—for example, compare/contrast, cause/effect, chronology.)
- Are my points logically related to each other (i.e., each one should naturally follow from the previous point)? Will these relationships result in a coherent essay (one that is easy to follow)?
- Can points be expanded? Have I covered everything my reader would expect me to cover?

COMPOSING

Making the commitment to the first draft is difficult for many people—students and non-students alike. It is important to realize that a first draft is inevitably "drafty"— incomplete, uneven, and much in need of revising. These possible deficiencies should not hold you back from putting forth a determined effort to record your thoughts on paper—imperfectly expressed as they may be. See "The structural model" (below), which considers the drafting of introductions, middle paragraphs, and conclusions.

REVISING

Most essays require more than one draft before you begin to think about the final stage in which you train a critical, objective eye on what you have written. In composing the first, "rough" drafts, your focus is on getting ideas down, explaining, clarifying, integrating, and ordering. During the revision stage, however, you should not expect to be simply dotting i's and crossing t's. The word "revise" means to "see again." First, you should take a hard, objective look at your essay's purpose and audience, structure, solidity of ideas and connection to your thesis, and clarity of expression. Review these areas as if you are seeing them for the first time. Waiting at least several hours after you have completed a rough draft before revising is sensible advice. Ask the kinds of questions you originally asked (for example, when you were creating an outline), and see if you are completely satisfied with the results.

Next, you must check conscientiously for grammatical correctness and stylistic efficiency. *Then*, it will be time to dot the i's and cross the t's—checking for spelling errors and typos and ensuring that the essay conforms to the format your instructor has asked for.

The importance of these end-stage activities cannot be underestimated, although it is understandable that they sometimes are. After all, when you have finished the rough draft, the paper looks physically complete. It has a beginning, middle, and end; it makes a claim in the thesis statement that is supported through various kinds of evidence. Besides, there are other classes now demanding your attention, and nothing is ever perfect, is it? Perhaps not, but you should remember that your instructor may look at things differently. A quick glance might convince him or her that it is not as good as it could be—a point may seem incomplete or a paragraph may lack coherence. But what often strikes a marker first are the very things you may have glossed over as your deadline approached: grammatical errors, wordiness and other stylistic glitches, typos, and mechanical errors that could easily have been fixed.

Though nothing will replace careful attention to every detail, here is a checklist that will help you "re-see" your essay:

Content and structure

✓ Is the essay's purpose clear? Is it conveyed in the introduction, consistent throughout the middle paragraphs, and reinforced in the conclusion?

✓ Is it written for a specific audience? What would show a reader this (for example, level of language, voice or tone, kinds of evidence used, citation format)?

✓ Is the thesis statement aligned with the focus of the essay and its main points? If not, consider adjusting the thesis—sometimes a word or phrase will clarify this alignment.

✓ Are all paragraphs adequately developed and focused on one main idea?

✓ Are any paragraphs noticeably shorter or longer than others? If so, can you combine short paragraphs, ensuring a logical transition between them, or break up longer paragraphs, ensuring each can, in fact, stand on its own?

✓ Have different kinds of evidence been used for support? Does any part of the essay seem less supported than other parts?

✓ Would an example, illustration, or analogy make an abstract point more concrete or a general point more specific?

✓ Is there a possibility a reader could misunderstand any part of the essay? If so, would this be due to the complexity of a point or the way it is expressed? If your draft has been commented on/edited by a peer, pay particular attention to any passages noted as unclear. If one reader has difficulties in comprehension, no doubt others will too.

Grammar and style

✓ Are there any sentence fragments (i.e., "sentences" missing a subject or predicate), run-on sentences (two "sentences," or independent clauses, with no punctuation between them), or comma splices (two "sentences" separated only by a comma)?

✓ Is punctuation used correctly? For example, are commas used (1) to separate independent clauses with a coordinating conjunction (*and, or, but, for, nor, yet, so*) and to separate an introductory word, phrase, or clause from a following independent clause; (2) to separate items in a list or series; (3) to separate parenthetical or non-essential words and phrases from more important (essential) information? Are semicolons and colons used correctly? Dashes and parentheses used correctly and sparingly (dashes for emphasis, parentheses for asides)?

✓ Are apostrophes used correctly to indicate possession and similar relationships in nouns and indefinite pronouns (e.g., the book's author—one book; the books' authors—more than one book; anyone's opinion—indefinite pronoun)?

✓ Do verbs agree in number with their subjects and pronouns with their antecedents (the noun they replace)?

✓ Is the relationship between a noun and its antecedent clear (i.e., every pronoun should refer back to a specific noun)?

✓ Has the principle of pronoun consistency been maintained (i.e., pronouns should not arbitrarily change from third person [he/she, they/them] to first or second person [I/me, we/us, you])?

✓ Is parallelism present in sentences with elements that must be parallel (lists, compounds, correlative conjunctions, and comparisons)?

✓ Are there any misplaced or dangling modifiers?

✓ Are you satisfied that every word you have used is the best word and expresses precisely what you want to say? Is the level of language appropriate and have you avoided contractions and slang in formal essays?

✓ Have you avoided repetition? Have you managed to eliminate unnecessary words and phrases? Doing so will greatly help you achieve clarity and precision.

Mechanics

✓ Have all outside references been cited correctly? Have you used the documentation style favoured by your instructor or by your discipline?

✓ Have you met word length, essay/page format, and other specific requirements?

✓ Have you proofread the essay at least twice (once for content and flow, once for minor errors such as typos—breaking each word into syllables and reading syllabically throughout is the best way to catch minor errors)?

ALTERNATE METHODS

Most essays are not written mechanically using the sequential model: you may often find yourself going back and forth—from composing to outline, for example, if you find you need to rethink your original structure, or from composing to the research stage if you need to check on a source or bolster the support of a point. In fact, it is a sign of your maturity as a writer if you *do* go back and at least reconsider changes as the writing process is ongoing.

However, some instructors encourage a writing approach that stresses *exploration* over goal-centredness. In addition, many writers, including professionals, do not follow a traditional-linear process at all but instead write more discursively; that is, they begin composing without any firm plan in place, trusting to their instincts and realizing that it is sometimes only by writing something down and taking the risk of going off-topic occasionally that they can discover what they really want to say. In both the exploratory models discussed below, your intentions and goals are revealed through the act of writing itself; in both models, outlines are less important than in the linear, highly planned approach. Below, Frans de Waal, primatologist and author of *Our Inner Ape*, describes his personal process. Few instructors would recommend it, but it does illustrate the important notion that writers need to find the approach that works best for them:

> I write my books without much of an outline except for the chapter titles. My main strategy is to just start writing and see what happens. From one topic follows another, and before you know it I have a dozen pages filled with stories and thoughts. . . . I have a very visual memory, and remember events in great detail. When I write, my desk fills up with ever higher piles of papers and books used for reference, until it is a big mess, which is something I cannot stand. I am very neat. So, at some point I put all that stuff away, print out the text I've written, and sit down comfortably with a red pen. By that time I have already gone over the text multiple times. With pen in hand, I do a very rigorous rereading and again change things around.

Exploratory models

Exploratory models are gaining credibility through recent research in composition studies. In the aptly named **discovery draft**, you keep your topic in mind as you write, but allow yourself to go off on "tangents" if your mind urges you that way. In reality, you are not really going off-topic but exploring the topic's ramifications and subtleties. The aim of the discovery draft, sometimes called "directed freewriting," is to discover your purpose in writing. Along with a lack of concern for formal structure (structure comes later, perhaps in the second draft or later still), writers who use this method are unconcerned with the writing niceties, grammar, style, or spelling but instead focus on recording the progress of their thoughts on a topic. When the discovery draft is completed (i.e., when the discovery has been made), you look back on what you have written, identifying the most useful points. Exchanging your discovery draft with a peer enables someone to look over your draft with an objective eye. After striking out passages that are unimportant or irrelevant to your discovered purpose, you may begin a second draft that explores and expands specific points by adding relevant detail.

While discovery drafts are written with minimal self-consciousness and no self-censure, the **process-reflective draft** involves a self-conscious approach to what you are writing. When de Waal reveals, above, that he has "gone over the text multiple times" before he stops to consider large-scale changes, he is revealing his preference for a writing process in which he pauses to reflect, re-examine, and change, if necessary, before continuing—a kind of revision on the fly. As with the traditional-linear and the discovery drafts, however, you should not be concerned with mechanical correctness as you write.

Typical activities in process-reflective drafts are rephrasing, clarifying, evaluating, amplifying, and connecting: you concern yourself with making logical transitions from one thought to the next and checking to see that your developing points are consistent with your general plan. You may begin with a few rough points and "reminders," such as important authors or quotations you want to use, but as in discovery drafts, you do not have a definitive plan. The main difference is that in process-reflective drafts, the plan evolves as you write rather than being revealed to you after you have finished writing. Process-reflective writing can be used for in-class and exam essays in which there is seldom time to outline your points in detail or to write two or three exploratory drafts.

The structural model

Like the sequential model, the structural model is somewhat familiar to most students because it is often stressed in high school. The essay is divided into an introduction, middle or body paragraphs, and a conclusion. Each part contributes in a different way to the overall essay.

WRITING INTRODUCTIONS

Introductions are more than just starting places. Their primary function is to inform: generally, they inform the reader about the essay's purpose and topic; more specifically, they tell the reader what the writer's approach to the topic will be (this is usually conveyed through the thesis statement) and, in some cases, also mention the essay's main points. As well, introductions may indicate the primary organizational pattern for the essay. In all these ways, the introduction previews what is forthcoming.

All good introductions are inherently persuasive: they must sufficiently interest the reader, encouraging him or her to read on, perhaps by conveying the importance of the topic. As science writer Bradley Anholt puts it, "You need to convince your readers to care enough about the subject to invest their time in reading your paper."

Introductions not only introduce the essay but also introduce its writer; therefore, you must come across as credible and reliable. Nobody, except a college or university instructor, is going to continue reading an essay if the writer has not come across as credible. (See "Issues of credibility," p. 102.)

Not all essays contain introductions that work in these ways. For example, many journalistic essay introductions contain no conventional thesis statement. Instead, the writer may be concerned with building the essay, through a variety of interest-centred strategies, to the most important point, which may occur near the end of the essay. Academic writers may put less stress on creating interest since it can be assumed that most readers of a journal article or scholarly book are interested in the subject. Furthermore, academic essays often include an essay plan rather than a traditional thesis statement, and empirical studies may substitute a hypothesis or central question in place of a thesis statement. The essay plan and the hypothesis are specialized forms that the thesis can take, and they serve the different purposes of the academic writer. For the function of introductions in academic and journalistic essays, see pages 18–22 and 35–6.

Student writers are often advised to write their introductions last because they will not know precisely how the topic will develop until the body of the essay is written. On the other hand, many writers like to have a concrete starting point. If the latter describes you best, you should return to the introduction after you have completed drafting your middle paragraphs to ensure that it fits well with them.

Thesis statements

The Greek word *thesis* refers to the act of placing or setting down. *A thesis statement, then, is a formal assertion, a generalization that is applicable to the entire essay.* However, this generalization can take different forms depending on purpose and audience. Student writers usually place the thesis statement in their introductions. It announces the topic and includes a comment about the topic (*simple thesis statement*); thesis statements may also incorporate the major points to be discussed (*expanded thesis statement*). The thesis statement usually embodies a **claim**, the nature of which depends on the essay's purpose. Typical argumentative claims are ones of **value** or **policy**. **Fact-based** claims are common in expository essays in the sciences and social sciences, while **interpretive** claims are used in many humanities essays in which the writer sets out to analyze one or more primary sources by using a specific frame of reference, such as a critical theory of some kind, or a set of discipline-related standards that are announced in the claim. For example, a poem could be analyzed through the lens of feminist theory or by looking at literary motifs occurring in it.

The introduction of an essay that focuses on the results of original research may include a question to be answered or a **hypothesis** to be tested. Essays that are set up to answer a hypothesis (an unproved assumption) usually take the form of a report, such as those assigned in biology, geography, or psychology classes or in any other discipline in which you are required to investigate a phenomenon or problem and report on what you have discovered (see p. 184 for an example of such a report). An introduction that includes a hypothesis clearly announces the essay's purpose: to test the validity of the hypothesis under controlled conditions.

In academic essays that do not include original research, the thesis may take the form of a generalization of intent (**essay plan**): the author will state the areas he or she intends to discuss—in the order in which they will appear in the essay. Essay plans may systematically outline the structure and, in this way, prepare the reader for what is to follow. Because student essays seldom exhibit the depth and complexity of long academic essays, essay plans are usually unnecessary.

For comparative purposes, the following statements illustrate the different forms that theses can take:

> Conventional thesis statement from an expository student essay (fact-based claim): Xenotransplantation, the transplantation of organs across a species barrier, is emerging as a possible alternative to transplants from human donors.

> Conventional thesis statement from an argumentative student essay (policy claim): Despite the variety of equipment, aerobic classes, and availability of personal trainers, joining a fitness club will not meet a person's complete needs today. Canadians need to step out into their backyards to find the many wonders the outdoors and sports have to offer.

> Thesis in the form of a question: In Europe, stirrups changed the warfare of the time, but could they have also had an impact on society beyond the battlefield?

> Thesis in the form of a hypothesis: It was hypothesized that obsessive passion, but not harmonious passion, would be related to greater gambling involvement and greater problem gambling severity. (Steven A. Skitch and David C. Hodgins. "A passion for the game: Problem gambling and passion among university students." *Canadian Journal of Behavioural Science*)

Creating reader interest

Although giving some thought to techniques that will generate reader interest is especially important when you are writing for a general audience, all readers need to be convinced at the outset that your essay is worth reading. The most traditional way to generate interest and persuade your reader of the topic's importance is to use a **logical opening**: to begin with a universal statement that becomes more specific and ends with the most specific claim, the thesis itself; this method is referred to as the inverted triangle method. One risk in this approach is that in making the first sentence too broad or familiar, it fails to interest the reader. Therefore, student writers are often encouraged to use a **dramatic opening**. Examples of dramatic openings include those that use personal experience, description, or narration or that ask a pertinent question that intrigues the reader. An opening could also make an emotional appeal; however, use these appeals cautiously because you cannot always assume that a typical reader will respond in the way you wish. The following paragraphs illustrate two different ways of attracting reader interest:

> **Logical:** The writer begins with a statement about the beginning of World War I and proceeds to discuss Canada's contribution to the war effort. He then briefly refers to Canadians of British descent before focusing on the contribution of Aboriginal peoples.

> Canada was only 47 years old when it entered World War I on the same day as Britain in August 1914. Canada saw the war as an opportunity to define itself as a great nation and contributed by supplying, among other things, materials and soldiers. By the time peace was declared, over 400,000 Canadians had fought in World War I, of whom approximately 60,000 lost their lives (Gaffen 15). Canadians of direct British descent were not the only people willing to help their country; Aboriginals also enlisted, eager to prove their right to be called British subjects. Early on, there was some question as to whether or not Aboriginals should be allowed to participate in the war. Their lack of British lineage, together with the false stereotypes of violence created by books like *The last of the Mohicans*, initially made the Canadian government reluctant to officially accept them into the army. Eager to disprove any previous stereotypes, and with a desire to be accepted as British subjects, Aboriginals fought hard and contributed immensely during World War I. (student writer Mike Mason)

> **Dramatic (questions):** The writer begins with two questions, referring to the popular connotation of perfectionism. Using the reversal strategy, she then cites the definition of experts. Her final sentence makes it clear that her essay will focus on the problems of the "maladaptive perfectionist."

> What does it mean to say that one is a perfectionist? Does it mean that one does everything perfectly? In common language, the term "perfectionist" carries the connotation that the perfectionistic individual does everything perfectly, but according to perfectionism experts in social psychology, perfectionism is a

term referring to a mentality, or set of cognitions, that are characteristic of certain people. According to Hollender (as cited in Slade & Owens, 1998), perfectionism refers to "the practice of demanding of oneself or others a higher quality of performance than is required by the situation" (p. 384). Although the name suggests to the layperson that perfectionism would be a desirable trait, this quality is in fact often unrecognized for its detrimental effects on the lives of people who are maladaptively perfectionistic. Perfectionism is associated with mental illness and can contribute to problems in areas of life such as academic success and intimate relationships. (student writer Erin Walker)

WRITING MIDDLE PARAGRAPHS

The structure of middle paragraphs is often said to mirror that of the essay itself: the paragraph begins with a generalization that is supported by the sentences that follow. In terms of structure and function, the essay's thesis statement is equivalent to the **topic sentence** of a paragraph, which announces the main idea (topic) of that paragraph. This is a useful, if somewhat restrictive, analogy—useful because it stresses the importance of a predictable order for both essays and paragraphs but also somewhat limiting because, in reality, paragraphs are not always constructed this way.

When a writer uses a topic sentence to announce the central idea, the rest of the paragraph provides support, such as examples, reasons, statistical data, or other kinds of evidence. In some way, it illustrates, expands on, or reinforces the topic sentence. In the following paragraph, student writer Leslie Nelson expands on the main idea, first by explaining the function of talking therapies and then by dividing them into three different subcategories and explaining the function of each (the topic sentence is italicized):

Talking therapies—especially when combined with medication—are common to treatment of adolescent depression. There are several kinds of talking therapies, including cognitive and humanistic approaches, and family and group sessions. Each of these therapy types confronts depression in a different way, and each is useful to adolescent treatment. Cognitive therapies confront illogical thought patterns that accompany depression; humanistic therapies provide support to the patient, stressing unconditional acceptance. Group therapies, on the other hand, encourage depressed patients to talk about their feelings in a setting with other people who are undergoing treatment for similar problems. This therapy can inspire different coping strategies, and it allows people to realize that they are not alone in their problems.

However, in the following paragraph, the writer uses his first sentence to set up a common opinion with which he disagrees. His own position is not fully explained until the final sentence, the paragraph's topic sentence, italicized below:

> Some suggest that we should actively limit our reliance on technological props and aids, not just to protect our privacy but to control our own destinies and preserve our essential humanity. Here, the title of the book gives me away. Human-machine symbiosis, I believe, is simply what comes naturally. It lies on a direct continuum with clothes, cooking, bricklaying, and writing. *The capacity to creatively distribute labour between biology and the designed environment is the very signature of our species, and it implies no real loss of control on our part, for who we are is in large part a function of the webs of surrounding structure in which the conscious mind exercises at best a kind of gentle, indirect control.* (Clark. "Bad borgs?")

Students can experiment by trying different placements for their topic sentences. The common placement as the first sentence tends to make for a coherent paragraph, while a succession of such paragraphs contributes to a readable, coherent essay, but students should choose the order that best reflects the paragraph's purpose. For example, in the first paragraph above, the writer is dividing a general category into subcategories, while in the second paragraph, the writer is raising a point in order to counter it with his own point. These purposes require contrastive approaches to paragraph construction.

Writing strong paragraphs

Effective paragraphs are unified, coherent, and well-developed. A **unified** paragraph focuses on only one main idea; when you move to another main idea, you begin a new paragraph. If, however, a paragraph is excessively long, you should consider dividing it into two paragraphs even if each contains the same idea. Look for the most logical place to make the division; for example, you could divide the paragraph where you begin an important sub-point.

A **coherent** paragraph is simple to follow, which is not the same as saying that the thought behind it is simplistic. Coherent paragraphs are both clear and carefully arranged to place the emphasis where you want it to be. Compositional theorists use the term **reader-based prose** to suggest a focus on the concerns of the reader. In reader-based prose, the writer takes pains in designing the paragraph, directing it to a specific audience using understandable and well-organized prose, stressing what is most important and omitting what is irrelevant, and clarifying the relationships among the points and sub-points. Coherence can be achieved by considering the following points:

1. *Logical sentence order:* In logical sentence order, one sentence follows naturally from the preceding one, and there are no sentences out of order or off-topic (an off-topic sentence would also not result in a unified paragraph); there are no gaps in thought that the reader has to try to fill.

2. *Organizational patterns:* You can order the paragraph according to specific patterns (see "Rhetorical patterns and paragraph development," below).

3. *Appropriate adverbial transitions:* Transitional words and phrases enable you to convey precise relationships between one idea and the next.

4. *Selective rephrasing and reiteration:* Knowing the knowledge level of your audience will determine whether and when you should rephrase in order to clarify difficult concepts.

5. *Repetition of key words/phrases or the use of synonyms:* Repetition can be used to emphasize important ideas. Of course, *needless* repetition should always be avoided.

6. *Parallel/balanced structures:* Employing parallel/balanced structures creates coherence, in part, through the use of familiar syntactic patterns. William Shakespeare and Charles Dickens are two acknowledged literary masters of balanced structures, which makes their words memorable and easy to recall:

> Now is the winter of our discontent
> Made glorious summer by this sun of York;
> And all the clouds that lour'd upon our house
> In the deep bosom of the ocean buried.
> Now are our brows bound with victorious wreaths;
> Our bruised arms hung up for monuments;
> Our stern alarums chang'd to merry meetings,
> Our dreadful marches to delightful measures.

> Shakespeare. *Richard III.*

Being aware of organizational and syntactical patterns as you write will make you a more conscious writer, focused on the needs of your readers. The first two points above concern the paragraph as a whole, while the last four focus on forging connections between individual sentences or parts of sentences by using transitional words/phrases or some form of repetition.

After defining the term "nanotechnology," student writer Jeff Proctor makes effective use of transitions (noted by italics) to help explain a difficult concept to general readers. He uses a balanced structure in sentence 4 to make a comparison understandable and repeats the key word "precision" at strategic points in the paragraph (the beginning, middle, and end); other words, too, can be considered near-synonyms for "precision" (synonyms and repetition are underlined):

Nanotechnology will allow the construction of compounds at nanometre <u>precision</u>. *Essentially*, this capability would allow scientists to form a substance one atom at a time and to put each atom <u>exactly</u> where it needs to be. *Consequently*, any chemical structure that is stable under normal conditions could theoretically be produced. In comparison to semiconductor lithography, which <u>could be imagined as</u> the formation of electrical circuits by joining large heaps of molecules, the techniques of nanotechnology <u>could be imagined as</u> the <u>careful</u> arrangement of molecules with a pair of tweezers. With this incredible degree of <u>precision</u>, electrical circuits could be designed to be smaller than ever before. *Currently*, each component in a computer is the size of thousands of atoms; *however*, if nanotechnological processes were used to produce it, one component could be on the scale of several atoms. This fact alone emphasizes the potential efficiency of next-generation computer circuits, for smaller components are closer together and, *thus*, able to communicate with each other in less time. *Furthermore*, it could be guaranteed that products are reproducible and reliable as a result of the absolute <u>precision</u> of these formation processes.

Transitions in the paragraph above convey various relationships: *essentially* (transition of summary), *consequently, thus* (cause/effect), *currently* (time), *however* (contrast), *furthermore* (addition). Other relationships include concession or limit (e.g., *admittedly, although, though, it is true that, of course*), illustration (e.g., *for example, for instance, such as*), sequence (e.g., *first, second . . .; then, next*), and emphasis (e.g., *certainly, especially, in fact, indeed, undoubtedly*).

It is important to realize that striving for coherence throughout the writing process should not just enable a reader to follow you but also assist you in clarifying your train of thought as you write. Successful writing is never simply the result of a mad dash to the finish line but of a complex process that utilizes varied cognitive activities at different times. To clarify your own thoughts, it is useful to consciously rephrase ideas and specific passages as you write. Without crossing out what you wrote, follow it with transitions like *in other words, in short, in summary, to reiterate, that is* and a paraphrase or expansion of the original. If your "second attempt" is clearer—and it often is—you can then consider crossing out the original to avoid needless repetition.

For more information on paragraphs, see "Dividing the whole," p. 65, and "Reading paragraphs: Identifying main ideas," p. 66.

RHETORICAL PATTERNS AND PARAGRAPH DEVELOPMENT

Rhetorical patterns are systematic ways by which to present and organize information in your essay; they apply to both the essay itself and to paragraphs within the essay. All the claims you make in your essay—your general claim, or thesis, and your specific claims, which are usually made in your topic sentences—must be well-supported or they will not be convincing. You can support a general claim through one **primary rhetorical pattern**; the pattern you choose will depend on the purpose of your essay. For example, the first of the thesis statements above, p. 92, on xenotransplantation, will likely be developed through the problem/solution pattern (this transplantation method offers a possible solution to a problem); the second will likely use cost/benefit, with the writer arguing for the benefits of exercising outdoors, although perhaps acknowledging that exercising in gyms is also beneficial; the third and fourth examples will use the cause/effect pattern.

Writers also use these and other patterns to help develop individual paragraphs, supporting the specific claims in the topic sentences. An important ingredient in the success of an essay is choosing the most appropriate rhetorical pattern to develop a claim. Several different methods are described below; two important methods are then given a more detailed treatment.

Most topics can be developed by using one or more of the methods above or the two below. For example, if you were looking for ways to develop the topic "fighting in hockey," you could use description or narration to convey the excitement of a hockey brawl; conversely, you could use either method to convey it as an unseemly spectacle. You could use the process analysis pattern to depict the step-by-step procedures officials use to break up a fight, the chronological pattern to trace the history of rules governing fighting, or the pattern by example to call attention to notorious fighting incidents in recent years.

Definition

The importance of using definition as a rhetorical pattern is pronounced in expository essays written for a general audience who would be unfamiliar with specialized terms. Thus, definitions often precede large sections that focus on explaining or analyzing, as in this introduction to an essay on the effects of trans fat on human health:

> In the early 1900s, William Normann invented the hydrogenation process in which trans fat, short for trans-fatty acid, is the by-product. A tiny amount of trans fat is found naturally, usually in animal fat; however, the majority of trans fats are made when hydrogen is added to vegetable oil in a process called hydrogenation. Hydrogenation is the modification of vegetable oil to allow it to be a solid at room temperature. The way the atoms of the fatty acids are bonded shows whether the fat is saturated or unsaturated: saturated fats have only single bonds while unsaturated fats

Purpose	Rhetorical Pattern	Description/Explanation
To create an image or picture of something	Description	Uses images related to sight or the other senses to create immediacy and involve the reader; uses modifiers (adjectives and adverbs) to add detail; may systematically focus on a scene, using a logical method such as from left to right, top to bottom, etc.
To tell a story	Narration	Relates an occurrence, usually in chronological order; stresses action through the use of strong verbs; anecdotes are brief narratives that introduce or illustrate a point.
To show how something works or is done	Process analysis	Breaks down a (usually) complex process into a sequence of successive steps, making it more understandable; provides instructions or directions.
To show the way something changed/ developed	Chronology	Uses time order to trace something, often from its beginning to the present day; can be applied to people, objects (like inventions), or situations.
To particularize the general or concretize the abstract	Example	Gives particular instances of a larger category, enabling readers to better understand the larger category; gives immediacy and concreteness to what can seem otherwise broad or abstract.
To analyze why something happened or a result/outcome	Cause/effect	Uses inductive methods to draw conclusions; works from causes to effects or from effects to causes; for example, to determine whether smoking leads to (causes) heart disease or to determine whether heart disease results from (is an effect of) smoking.
To account for or justify something	Reasons	Uses deductive methods that draw on one's knowledge or experience (which may ultimately be derived from inductive findings); for example, you should not smoke because it often leads to heart disease (reason derived via empirical evidence).
To analyze by dividing into subcategories	Classification/division	Classification: groups according to shared characteristics (e.g., types of bottled water: purified, mineral, sparkling). Division: separates large category into constituent parts (e.g., the essay into introduction, middle paragraphs, conclusion).
To look at two sides/ views of something	Cost/benefit analysis	Weighs the pros and cons of an issue, question, or action, usually to decide which is stronger; in argument, cost/benefit analysis is used to support a value or policy claim and/or refute an opposing claim.
To identify a problem or solve/resolve it	Problem/solution	Analyzes or explains a problem or proposes a solution; may incorporate other methods, such as reasons, cause/effect, or cost/benefit analysis.
To better understand something	Analogy	Points to a surprising way in which one subject is similar to another to reveal or clarify the nature or a feature of the first subject.

have double bonds. A trans fat is a fat that was once an unsatu-
rated fat but has had its double bonds weakened through the
process of hydrogenation. (student writer Kim Snyder)

Using definition can also be an effective strategy in argument. Value claims, in particular, often rely on definition: after explaining what you mean by something, you can
support the claim by demonstrating the validity of the definition through various
kinds of evidence. For example, if you were arguing that gymnastics should or should
not be considered a sport, you would need to state what you meant by a "sport."
Ensuring that this was a definition with which most readers would agree, you could
then use the definition as a springboard into your claim and main points by showing
how gymnastics fit or did not fit this definition.

Comparison and contrast

Comparison and contrast can be used to develop one or more paragraphs or to organize an entire essay. When you compare, you look at how two items are similar; when
you contrast, you consider their differences. However, the term *compare* is generally
used to refer to both similarities and differences. You can compare ideas, issues, people, places, objects, or events—as long as bases of comparison exist to make such comparisons valid. For example, you can compare two jobs by looking at their salaries,
workweeks, levels of responsibility, and so on. However, if you were comparing two
things in order to evaluate them, you would have to ensure that the same evaluation
standards could be fairly applied to each. For example, you could not evaluate two
universities that were vastly different in size. That is why the compilers of *Maclean's
guide to Canadian universities* categorize universities by their size before applying their
performance measures, such as student body, classroom size, and calibre of faculty,
which serve as the bases of comparison.

Organizing a comparison and contrast essay can be more complicated than organizing essays that use another primary rhetorical pattern. Consider using the three-step
approach when organizing these kinds of essays. First, determine whether the two
items you want to compare *can* logically be compared. The health care system in the
US cannot be compared to the education system in Canada. Although the health care
systems in the two countries are comparable, such a large undertaking might prove
unmanageable. More reasonable would be a comparison between two provincial
health care or education systems.

Next, carefully select the bases of comparison, or criteria for comparing (choosing
at least three should help make the comparison valid); each basis can serve as a main
point in your essay. Finally, choose one of two possible methods for organizing your
main points: the **subject-by-subject** (**block**) method or the **point-by-point** method.
In the first, you begin with the first subject of comparison and apply your bases of
comparison to it; you then do the same for the second subject, keeping your points
(criteria) in the identical order. In the more commonly used point-by-point method,

you begin with a basis of comparison and apply it to the first, then the second subject. You continue to do this until you have represented all your bases of comparison.

Which is the better method? The block method stresses the subjects themselves, while the point-by-point method stresses the criteria for comparison. If there seems no compelling reason to prefer one over the other, consider that the point-by-point method can be more efficient and easier to follow because in the block method, the reader needs to keep in mind each basis of comparison as it has been applied to the first subject while it is being raised for the second subject. For this reason, essays that use the block method can be more challenging to write and to read.

The following paragraph uses one basis of comparison, communication skills, as part of an essay that explores biological and environmental factors for differences between men and women:

> Some studies have shown that women perform better than men in specific areas of verbal and language skills, but the difference is small and emerges only when data from thousands of individuals is considered (Pool 55–6). In her book *You Just Don't Understand*, Deborah Tannen explores the differences in the way that men and women communicate, but Carol Tavris argues that these patterns of speaking are simply products of the division of power in our society: men, in the superior position, need not fear giving offence and so speak directly and bluntly, while women, in a subordinate position, must be more finely attuned to the sensitivities of men. Tavris points to studies showing that when the positions are reversed, women speak more directly and men demonstrate greater empathy (65–6). (student writer Guy White)

For examples of essays in "The Active Reader" that employ different rhetorical patterns, including definition and comparison and contrast, see "Classification by rhetorical mode/pattern or style," p. xviii.

KINDS OF EVIDENCE

Although it is good to use various kinds of evidence in your essay, it is likely that some are going to be more important than others. The choices you make depend on your purpose, audience, topic and claim, and the type of essay you are writing. For example, if you are writing an evaluative report on the credibility of two sources, your essay will focus on those primary sources; if you are writing a research essay, your focus will likely be on secondary sources. For kinds of evidence typically used in argumentative essays, see p. 120.

Kinds of evidence favoured also tend to vary from discipline to discipline: humanities writing often uses extensive direct quotation from primary sources; social sciences writing tends to focus on statistics, interviews, questionnaires, case studies, and interpersonal observation, while the sciences rely on direct methods that involve experimentation.

Some kinds of evidence are more authoritative than others, depending on the discipline and other factors like purpose and audience. In fact-based writing, "hard" evidence—facts, statistics, and the findings of empirical research—provides the strongest grounds for much of the support. Various kinds of "soft" evidence, such as expert opinion, examples, illustrations, and analogies, may also be important to help explain a concept but will likely be less important than "hard" evidence. This is not the case with personal essays in which the writer strives to make a personal experience meaningful to the reader; similarly, argumentative essays may make considerable use of personal experience, analogies, precedents, and expert opinion.

One kind of example that is often pertinent to fact-based social sciences writing, as well as writing in business and education, is the **case study**, a detailed exploration of one particular case, such as a real-life situation, in order to gain a depth of understanding of the issue being investigated. Case studies use empirical methods of observing and recording, although typically, the data produced and then analyzed is qualitative rather than quantitative, based, for example, on interviews, questionnaires, and personal observation. Because of their systematic methodology and the wealth of detail that is analyzed, the findings from case studies can often be generalized, while ordinary examples cannot.

ISSUES OF CREDIBILITY

When you analyze a source to write a critical analysis or to use it for support in your own essay, you must consider the credibility of the writer. This credibility must be established in the introduction and be maintained throughout. By the same token, you must establish your own credibility with the audience to whom you address your essay.

Credibility factors include **knowledge**, **reliability**, and **fairness**. You exhibit your knowledge by appearing well-informed about your topic and supporting each claim with solid and substantial evidence. You convey reliability in many ways:

- using the accepted conventions of the discipline in which you are writing; this includes using the appropriate citation style, being aware of the specialized language of the discipline, and adhering to format requirements, such as the use of an abstract and formal sections (report writing);
- writing effectively, ensuring that you follow the rules of grammar, punctuation, syntax, sentence structure, and spelling; that your prose is efficient; and that you use words that express exactly what you want them to;
- using credible and authoritative sources (research essays);
- reasoning logically and avoiding logical fallacies (argumentative essays).

Although fairness applies particularly to argumentative essays, it can also be important in research essays, since synthesis could involve acknowledging and accommodating sources whose findings contradict your claim or hypothesis; this entails accounting for contrary evidence. The following criteria, however, apply mostly to argument. You convey fairness in several ways:

- using an objective voice and not showing bias;
- acknowledging and accurately representing the opposing view;
- looking for common ground;
- avoiding slanted language and emotional fallacies.

WRITING CONCLUSIONS

Like introductions, conclusions can vary considerably depending on the kind of essay and other factors. While conclusions are always a vital part of essays, their functions differ. In student essays, the conclusion refers back to the thesis statement, reasserting its importance and usually rephrasing it. The conclusion may also look ahead by considering a way that the thesis can be applied or the ways that it could be further explored.

In report writing and Type B essays, the conclusion is a separate section titled "conclusion" or "discussion." Its specialized function is to interpret the results of the subject investigated or to answer whether the hypothesis has been proved. Conclusions also consider the results within a broader context than just the present study, either by discussing its significance to the field of study or by suggesting follow-up research, or both.

Although essay conclusions may both look back to the thesis statement and look ahead to the thesis's implications, the stress often falls on one or the other. **Circular conclusions** are primarily concerned with reminding the reader of the writer's thesis and with reinforcing it. Even so, if you want to emphasize these functions, you should not repeat the thesis word for word, nor should you simply summarize what you have already said in your introduction. You should draw attention to the significance of the paragraphs that follow your introduction and precede your conclusion—after all, they are probably the most substantial part of the essay. One way you can do this is to summarize the most important point.

Spiral conclusions refer to the thesis but are more concerned with looking beyond it by considering its larger importance. In argumentative essays, you may want to use the occasion not just to reinforce your claim but also to make an emotional appeal or, especially if your purpose is to reach a compromise, to suggest common ground between your view and the opposing one. Other strategies in spiral conclusions include ending with a relevant anecdote or personal experience (informal essays) or a question or hypothesis that extends from your findings or that of the research you have used (formal essays or reports). If your focus has been on a problem, this may be the time to suggest ways to solve it, or if your topic was applicable to a relatively small number of people, you can suggest how it could be generalized to a larger group, ideally one that would include the reader.

The paragraph below uses the circular pattern. Although it repeats some information from the introduction, it uses different words and introduces a new term, "adaptive perfectionism," from the middle paragraphs of the essay. In the final sentence, the writer advocates further research in the field to benefit people who are maladaptive perfectionists. You can compare the conclusion to the introduction, reproduced on page 93.

As an infiltrating personality characteristic, perfectionism is often deleterious and psychologically harmful. Although adaptive perfectionism has been associated with positive elements such as a proclivity for excellence, it has also been associated with increased levels of depression as compared to non-perfectionists. Maladaptive perfectionism is that much more detrimental to an individual's life in that it is associated with more elements of mental illness and with difficulty in academics and intimate relationships. Since, as Costa and McCrae (1986) point out, personality is relatively stable, research on perfectionism is a warranted endeavour to better understand, and to better help people suffering from, this quality. (student writer Erin Walker)

The following "Active Voice" essays, "Report Writing" and "How to Write a Scientific Paper," give guidelines relevant to students writing reports and papers in the sciences, social sciences, engineering, and other disciplines in which an adaptation of the Type B essay is required. Note the emphasis in both essays on clear, direct, and active writing.

The Active Voice
Report Writing

AIMS AND GOALS

Of all types of writing, report writing is the most categorically active. It's built on *doing something*, then writing about what was discovered as a result of doing it—a lab experiment, for instance, or a survey, or a site visit. "Planned," "designed," "measured," "saw," "researched," "interviewed," "calculated," "analyzed," "evaluated," "solved": verbs—dynamic action or "doing" words—lie at the heart of all report writing. That's because reports record the results of a study undertaken to *find out something specific*: answer a question, clarify an issue, solve a problem, analyze a policy, establish a cause or consequence, decide on a course of action, evaluate possible outcomes, make a recommendation, or give an update on a project. In all these cases, reports "write up" the results of a study conducted to yield specific, concrete information that's otherwise missing, unknown, or incomplete.

Original findings based on original research. That's what reports typically deal with. In fact, "Report of original research" is a common name for this type of writing in the science and social science disciplines, where the principal goal is to expand the field of knowledge—

to fill gaps in the current state of research. The audience for such reports is typically other scientists or scholars. The report writer's job is to convince experts in the field that the findings are valid, making an original contribution to knowledge.

In other situations, however, report writing may answer more practical goals. Investigative reports, recommendation reports, feasibility reports, and progress reports are what engineers may end up writing. The information compiled in these types of reports is usually intended to promote a specific course of action—for example, to implement (or scrap) a policy, develop a community program, approve an expansion of medical facilities, upgrade a highway, purchase new educational software, build a new gas line, or restore polluted waterways. As a result, they tend to be written for a mixed audience—other engineers as well as managers, policy-makers, public administrators, budgeting personnel, or company clients. Consequently, while they're generally technical in scope, they're often written so as to make sense to non-experts as well, with the goal of persuading them to act on the findings.

ORGANIZING REPORTS

We've said that the goal of report writing is to provide specialized, concrete information, based on empirical research, in response to a question, problem, or project. At the same time, to ensure the report is sufficiently persuasive—allowing important decisions to be made on the information presented—reports also record *how* the information was compiled. They provide a **methodology**. This is a key way in which science and much social science writing differs from humanities writing. It explains not only the facts but how the facts were derived. This is important because knowing *how* the data was compiled means readers can gauge its trustworthiness for themselves.

Report writers therefore **organize** reports with an eye to showing *how* the information was found so they can demonstrate its reliability. Luckily, organizational *templates* make this a relatively easy task. Formal reports have a rigidly defined **structure** that report writers are expected to follow to meet disciplinary demands for clarity and accountability. The **American Psychological Association** (APA), the disciplinary body that regulates report writing in the social sciences and some of the sciences, requires an **IMRAD** style of organization: **introduction**, **methods**, **results**, and **discussion**, with each section clearly signalled by headings.

Introduction

Introductions provide context and needed background, explaining **topic** and **purpose**, describing what the study was intended to find out and why. In the academic disciplines, this usually involves giving an opening **literature review**, an overview of current research in the field. A **research question** that the study is designed to answer may also be stipulated.

The introduction often ends with a **hypothesis**, a "prediction" about expected results that the study is designed to test.

Methodology

This section explains *how* the study was conducted. It outlines steps taken to compile the data, giving details about *where*, *when*, and *how*. In many cases, this section may also explain *why* the study was designed the way it was. The methodology section, in short, stipulates the techniques used to gather information:

- lab experiment;
- fieldwork;
- "on-site" observations;
- tests, surveys, or questionnaires;
- primary and secondary sources (print and electronic);
- interviews;
- technical descriptions or specifications;
- mathematical formulas or calculations;
- computer modeling.

Results

This section **objectively describes** the findings yielded by the study. The focus is on presenting the "raw data": no discussion of its significance takes place yet. What the data *means* (interpretation and evaluation) is reserved for the next section.

Discussion

The *APA Publication Manual* (1998) is very specific about **key functions** of a conclusion (usually called "discussion") of an APA report. Primarily, this is where the study's findings are evaluated or interpreted. Their significance is explained. This section answers the questions: What do the results mean? What conclusions can we derive from them? If a hypothesis has been presented, the discussion should likewise state whether it's been confirmed or not, always bearing in mind that a negative result can be as valuable as a positive one. In either case, something new has been discovered.

Finally, a discussion worth its salt ends with a closing **peroration**, a final "heightened appeal" for the significance or worth of the study. The goal here is to avoid a "so what?" response. The *APA Manual* suggests that report writers should aim to answer the following questions:

- What have I contributed here?
- What has my study helped resolve?
- What broader theoretical implications can I draw from my study?
- Can meaningful generalizations be drawn?
- Does further research need to be done to clarify any remaining uncertainties?

Monika Rydygier Smith
Instructor, Technical Writing, Department of English, University of Victoria

For an example of a student report, see p. 184.

The Active Voice
How to Write a Scientific Paper

The scientific enterprise requires that ideas and results be subject to scrutiny by others. Errors are thus recognized, and genuine advances can be incorporated into current thinking. No matter how brilliant your theory or experiments might be, if you don't write them up and publish them in accessible form, you might as well not have done the work. Editors and reviewers for scientific journals are busy people. If they can't understand your paper, they will reject it. In biology, most journals now accept 25 per cent or less of submissions. Most submitted work has merit, but poor writing will make it hard for the reader to appreciate your research and easy to consign your research to the reject pile.

RULE 1: APPLY BUM TO CHAIR

Writing is simply hard work. No amount of inspiration is going to generate beautiful, pleasing, elegant prose. Waiting for the muses to inspire you is a guaranteed way of never submitting a paper for review (or for your instructor). The goal of the scientific paper is to accurately transfer information to the reader. If it is done elegantly and gracefully, so much the better, but this isn't the object of the exercise. Start by writing the paper accurately; let inspiration come along the way.

RULE 2: REMEMBER YOUR AUDIENCE

Your first audience is the editors and reviewers of the journal you intend to submit to. Journals have stylistic conventions so read the "instructions to authors." Then read a collection of papers in that journal to see how successful authors have presented their work. Native English speakers are lucky because the language of scientific communication is English. The other side of this coin is that you have to remember that your worldwide audience comes to English as a second (or third or fourth) language. This means you should avoid obscure words and complex sentence constructions. You won't become famous by writing obscure papers no one can understand. It is your responsibility to write as clearly as possible to communicate your results. Don't make reading painful for your audience.

RULE 3: BEGIN WITH AN OUTLINE

This may seem obvious, but for some reason people don't. The scientific paper has four main sections: introduction (what is the question?), methods (what did I do?), results (what did I find?), and discussion (what does it mean?). Sections are sometimes combined, called something else, or placed in a different order, but these four elements are found in every paper.

If you create a point-form outline of what should be in each section, you will have the topic sentence of almost every paragraph in the paper. Obviously, the outline will change as you fill in the outline. You will reorder the outline, add topics and drop others, expand in some places and simplify in others—this is called editing. Spend more time editing your paper than writing the first draft.

RULE 4: TELL A STORY, BUT DON'T WRITE A MYSTERY

Tell the reader what you have learned in the order that is easiest to follow. This might not be the order in which you learned them. Tell the reader early what is in the paper. Often, this will entail telling the reader what you have concluded in the last paragraph of the introduction. The perfect paper would only need to be read once. A bad, confusing paper needs to be read several times in a search for the clues that support the conclusions. State your rationale clearly and don't build up to a surprise ending.

RULE 5: WRITE THE "METHODS" FIRST

This isn't a hard and fast rule but is usually the easiest. The "methods" outline what you did: the experimental or sampling design, study subjects, protocols, any chemical analyses that had to be done, the data analysis, and so on. Use the active voice whenever feasible. This varies markedly among disciplines and journals. Some journals prefer the passive voice: "the samples were collected," as opposed to the active voice: "I collected the samples." The active voice is almost always simpler and more direct than the passive. It also places responsibility on the person who performed the action. For example, the sentence "I broke the lamp" places responsibility in a way that "The lamp was broken" never could.

RULE 6: WRITE ABOUT YOUR "RESULTS," NOT THE FIGURES AND TABLES

Write the "results" after the "methods." Remember that you are telling a story; the figures and tables are illustrations. You don't need to include all of the tables and figures you generated, just enough to adequately illustrate the story. Tell your readers what you found and then refer to the figure. "Females were 10 per cent heavier than males (figure 1)" is shorter and clearer than "The data plotted in figure 1 show that females were 10 per cent heavier than males." Data should only be presented once in one table or in one figure but not both. Too many tables and figures are confusing. Remember, the results are a description; leave interpretation for the discussion.

RULE 7: EXPLAIN HOW TO UNDERSTAND A FIGURE OR TABLE IN ITS CAPTION

Your readers should be able to get the gist of a paper by reading the introduction and looking at the figures and tables. Briefly summarize the results presented in the figure, even if this seems redundant to the text.

RULE 8: TELL THE READER IN THE "DISCUSSION" WHAT YOU LEARNED

Begin by restating your most important results and put them into the context of what has been reported before. This means being able to draw conclusions based on what you did. Your readers want to know what you learned: Is it the same or different from what has been reported before? What are the limitations of the study? And what needs to be done next? Avoid over-interpretation and wild speculation.

RULE 9: INTRODUCTIONS ARE DIFFICULT

So write them last. A good introduction sets the general context for a paper. You need to convince your readers to care enough about the subject to invest their time in reading your paper. You do this by explaining the general context of your study and by summarizing current understanding of the problem. Explain how your study will address a general theory or problem and what is novel about your hypothesis or approach. At the end of the introduction, outline your main results. Readers will evaluate your conclusions as they read the methods and results. They won't have to go back and reread your entire paper to determine whether they agree with you. They will have been thinking about it while they are reading. Explain why your paper is interesting and give your readers a road map to your paper.

RULE 10: FOCUS ON IDEAS, NOT AUTHORITIES

"Anholt and Werner (1995) found that food level affected predation mortality" takes the emphasis away from the result and puts it on the citation. This is sometimes good when you want to emphasize that this is an old problem, but usually you want to emphasize the result. In contrast, "food level can affect predation mortality (Anholt & Werner, 1995)" is shorter, and the citation doesn't get in the way of the presentation.

RULE 11: USE PARALLEL CONSTRUCTION

Set up the "results" to follow the same order as the "methods." Discuss subjects in the "discussion" in the same order they are presented in the introduction. If there are four explanations for a result, explain them in the same order you first mentioned them. If you refer to two things in a sentence or paragraph, don't change the order later in the paper. In the same vein, don't use two different words to describe or refer to the same thing. Using the same wording allows your readers to make connections throughout the paper. If you use different wording, your readers will wonder whether you are referring to a different observation. You can enhance the parallel construction among sections by using subheadings to guide the reader. When your reader is going through topic X of the results, they can easily find topic X in the methods, rather than being forced to reread the entire section. Be consistent in your presentation.

RULE 12: REVISE, REVISE, REVISE . . . AND REVISE AGAIN

When I submit a paper for publication, it typically has had 10 to 15 drafts. Even so, it will come back from the journal with requests for revision because there are questions about the work. Most of those questions can be resolved by more careful writing, because the reviewers did not understand exactly what I meant. The secret of great writing is editing and revision. After you finish a draft, give it a few days rest before going back. You will be appalled at the horrors you have committed in the rush to get everything written down. It is difficult to edit your own work, especially at the beginning. Get someone else to read it. If they ask a question about anything, then the writing is not clear enough. Don't be offended, but rather benefit from their comments and questions.

RULE 13: MAKE COPIES OF YOUR WORK

Writing papers is hard work. Make back-up copies. I emphasize copies. Put them someplace other than where you keep your computer (a bank vault is not too extreme). There is nothing more miserable than losing days or weeks of work to a dog, electrical storm, demonic possession, virus, or theft. Don't be careless.

These rules are subject to bending and interpretation. Different disciplines have their own conventions, as do different journals. No matter the discipline, the goal is the same: to write a comprehensible account of your research so that anyone in your discipline, with even an imperfect grasp of English, can understand and repeat it. With practice, your writing will also become more compelling and graceful.

Bradley R. Anholt
Professor, Department of Biology, University of Victoria

Chapter 4

Kinds of Specialized Essays

Writing argumentative essays

Classical argument has its origins among the ancient Greeks. To prove that a wrong or injustice was done to them, Greek citizens had to appear before a tribunal of fellow citizens and argue their case. This was a formal process in which the accuser and the accused tried to establish their credibility, exchanged claims and counterclaims, and ended with a rhetorical flourish. In the absence of compelling evidence, the more persuasive speaker often won the day.

Another kind of oral discourse using argument, the formal debate, was considered a training ground for males seeking public professions during the nineteenth century, and debating societies are still alive on the campuses of many North American universities (with female debaters more than welcome, of course). Successful debaters are thought to exhibit life skills such as mental dexterity (quick thinking), verbal acuity (repartee), and poise (calm under pressure). In the classical Western tradition, however, argument often went hand in hand with an "us versus them," "winner take all" divisiveness.

Today, argument can serve several purposes:

- to settle an issue (i.e., win an argument);
- to critique a viewpoint, position, text, etc.;
- to expose a problem or raise awareness of a problem;
- to consolidate an opinion;
- to reach a compromise.

Arguing to reach a compromise, in fact, often constitutes a more realistic purpose than arguing to claim a victory. Thus, in her essay on a section of the Criminal Code that permits corporal punishment "if the force does not exceed what is reasonable under the circumstances," student writer Danielle Gudgeon steers a middle ground between those who want the law upheld and those who want it abolished. Her middle position makes it likely that an audience on both sides will consider her points, making her argumentative goal more attainable:

> Section 43 of the Criminal Code has a social utility for both teachers and parents, but it is an old law that must be amended to reflect society's progression. The addition of clear guidelines to the law regarding the severity of discipline and the use of

objects as weapons will create a distinction between abuse and discipline. This will prevent subjectivity within the courts and discourage future abuse, while affording parents the option of disciplining their children.

The kinds of evidence and the argumentative strategies you use depend on your purpose in arguing, your audience, and the topic itself. It is useful to look at three diverse forms that written argument can take in the media in order to see how these various elements interact: the letter to the editor, the review, and the editorial. Each has a different purpose, which is reflected in its structure, voice, language, kinds of evidence, and typical reader/viewer. The letter to the editor is the most subjective, in which writers can "have their say"; most published reviews reflect the informed opinions of experts; the voice of the editorial writer is usually the most objective of the three, but editorials are sometimes perceived as dull. Within these categories there can be much variation; for example, editorials do not always represent a collective viewpoint: "op-eds" (opinion-editorials) are usually written by one person, a "guest" editor or representative of an involved group. And certainly not all letters to the editor contain inflamed rhetoric.

An equivalent to the letter to the editor today is the web log (blog); "bloggers" range from opinionated novices to informed experts. Unlike letters to the editor, blogs often take the form of journal entries and are not restricted by length requirements. Another obvious difference is that bloggers can incorporate interactive elements in the design of their site, including direct feedback.

Which of the above is most like the kind of argumentative essay you are likely to be assigned? In terms of its structure, the argumentative essay resembles the review. In your language and use of voice, you should aspire to the objectivity of an editorial; however, letters to the editor are sometimes more interesting than editorials, and you should look for ways to interest your readers—especially neutral readers, those who have no strong position one way or the other.

Argumentative essays can be challenging to write because the methods and strategies that go into planning them vary depending not only on your writing purpose but also on the topic itself and the audience you are writing for. Furthermore, several common misconceptions surround argument today, so before beginning to plan, you need a clear picture of what argument is and what it is not.

Misconception 1: "I never argue"

People who say this may have in mind the pugilistic conception of argument. However, consider the following scenario: you have moved into a residence at your university only to find the rules and regulations there particularly unfair (a 10 p.m. curfew for social functions, for example). You might well discuss your disagreement with other residents and write a petition that argued for more reasonable rules. The impulse to argue can easily arise if we perceive our values or beliefs challenged; similarly, we may

Letter to the Editor	Book/Film Review	Editorial
Purpose: to sound off, settle an issue; other purposes are possible as well.	*Purpose:* to critique a text; the subjective nature of reviewing is assumed; thus, if you were reading reviews to decide whether to see a film, you would likely read several reviews.	*Purpose:* to critique a position, expose a problem, or reach a compromise. Editorials in niche publications (e.g., a union newsletter) may attempt to consolidate an opinion.
Writer: anyone may write a letter to the editor, which may be published if it is not libellous and the writer provides name and contact information.	*Writer:* is named; is knowledgeable in the field; may have a degree or other credentials; may make a living as a reviewer.	*Writer:* member of an editorial board; writer's name not given; represents views of the newspaper.
Audience: no particular audience in mind but often appeals to those with similar values and views.	*Audience:* written for book readers, film-goers, readers with interest in movies, etc.	*Audience:* educated readers, often the politically informed.
Structure: usually short; might be edited for length and for style; might not be highly structured or well-organized.	*Structure:* varies in length; usually follows conventional structure of argument: generalization with value claim followed by supporting evidence from the film/book.	*Structure:* usually short; tight structure: focused on one issue.
Claim: may be of value or policy; argument may present only one side.	*Claim:* of value; will consider the pros and cons but will come down on one side or the other—"thumbs up" or down.	*Claim:* often of policy; will carefully weigh both sides; may argue for one side, but argument characterized by careful, scrupulous reasoning.
Voice: subjective—"I."	*Voice:* sometimes uses first person—"I."	*Voice:* objective—the "editorial we."
Language/tone: variable; may be colourful, emotional, or volatile: "I'm appalled by our political leaders"; conversational, informal.	*Language/tone:* may use some specialized words and terms; may be ironic or sarcastic, direct or evocative.	*Language/tone:* elevated, sophisticated; formal, detached.
Evidence: personal opinion may predominate.	*Evidence:* mostly expert opinion on primary source (text); may refer to other books/films; evaluates according to agreed-on standards of excellence.	*Evidence:* facts and figures; precedents—reason-based evidence.

argue to defend our self-interest or those of a group with which we identify, such as our family, school, or community.

Whenever you send a resumé to a prospective employer, you are implicitly arguing that you are the best person for the job and supporting your claim by facts about your knowledge and experience. If you are asked during the interview why you believe you should be hired, you will have to marshal your strongest persuasive skills in response. Argument in its myriad forms is engrained not only in our society—in our legal and legislative systems, for example—but also in our daily lives.

Misconception 2: "My opinion is as good as anyone's"

Once declared, opinions reveal a great deal about the speaker or writer. For example, a racist opinion reveals the speaker as intolerant or as misinformed at best. Certainly, an uninformed opinion *is* as good (bad) as anyone's. It is difficult to argue against someone who holds racist views, because they are not grounded in either logic or reasoned experience. However, an informed opinion, especially one based on various kinds of evidence—for example, statistics, personal experience, and research findings—is much more likely to be credible. On the other hand, a person may hold the opposite opinion, which may be equally informed. An **opinion**, then, is not the same as a **fact**, which can be verified by observation or research; opinions are challengeable.

The *basis of a fact*, however, can change, and if the basis changes, what was once considered a "fact" may no longer be so. The basis for the "fact" that the planetary bodies revolved around the Earth was the Ptolemaic system, which was influential until the seventeenth century when the Copernican system changed the nature of this "fact." From Pluto's discovery in 1930 until August 2006, it had been a "fact" that our solar system had nine planets. However, the basis of this fact changed when astronomers declared that Pluto did not fit the newly revised definition of a planet.

The *interpretation of facts*, too, can be challenged. Interpreting facts in light of the claim that the arguer makes is an important strategy in argument. For example, the fact that just over 50 per cent of lung transplant recipients have a five-year survival rate could be used to support a claim that more resources should be allocated to boost this rate. The same statistic could be used to support a claim that fewer resources should be allocated to this procedure since the result is less promising than for other kinds of transplants in Canada (see "Connecting claim to evidence," below).

Misconception 3: "Arguments are boring"

Some kinds of argument are, indeed, boring for many people. However, the tedium of a subject is often synonymous with a lack of personal investment in it. For example, political speeches may be boring for a neutral observer but exciting for a member of the same political party as the speaker. Undoubtedly, one reason that media analysts focus attention on externals such as a politician's posture and expression, as well as on gaffes or hesitant responses to questions, is their effort—some would say a misguided one—to make up for the typical viewer's lack of interest in content by stressing human interest.

Many people find TV commercials boring. Over the years, some advertisers have attempted to rectify this perception by infusing greater novelty into their commercials, making each one more outlandish than the previous. Although commercials that appeal to our sense of surprise this way may amuse us, even exotic commercials become boring if we see them too often. Numbing repetition is anathema in advertising, as it is in other forms of argument. The aim of commercials is simple: to persuade members of the audience to buy a product. Not all arguments are designed to persuade their audience to act directly this way, of course, but the challenges of both the media analyst and the advertiser are similar in some ways to the challenges of the writer of argumentative essays: to interest and involve the reader in order to make him or her more receptive to the argumentative claim (see "Giving life to logic," below).

Claims in argument

The term **claim** is particularly appropriate to argumentation: when you set up your position in the introduction of your argumentative essay, you are doing more than *stating* a thesis: you are *actively asserting* one. When you claim something, you assert your right to it. The claim is the assertion that you will actively attempt to prove through logic and various kinds of evidence in the body of the essay. However, simply claiming something does not entitle you to it: you must convince people that the claim is merited, which is what you do when you argue effectively. Recall that a thesis statement/claim is a generalization about the essay's content: it includes your topic and sums up your main point(s), approach to your topic, or, in the case of argument, thrust of your argument.

An argumentative claim is usually one of value or policy. In a **value claim**, you would argue that something is good or bad, right or wrong, fair or unfair, and so on. A **policy claim** advocates an action. In this sense, a policy claim goes further than a value claim on which it often rests. However, value claims may be appropriate if you wish to make your audience consider something in a more positive light. For example, if you argued in favour of euthanasia to a general or unreceptive audience, you might not want to argue a policy claim, one that might focus on changing laws. A value claim instead would focus on changing attitudes, getting the reader to see, as a first step perhaps, that euthanasia relieves the suffering of a terminally ill patient. Value claims are especially relevant if you are critiquing a viewpoint or text (as reviews do) or trying to reach a compromise (i.e., to arrive at a middle ground); less frequently, they are used to settle an issue.

Argumentative claims must be *arguable*, *substantial*, *specific*, *realistic*, and *manageable*.

ARGUABLE CLAIMS

Most factual claims are not arguable because, as mentioned, a fact is different from an opinion. Facts can be questioned, and their interpretation is sometimes open to debate, but facts themselves cannot serve as the basis of an argumentative claim—for example, you could not argue against the fact that the closest star to Earth is 4.2 light years away or that more than 80 per cent of single-parent families in Canada are headed by women (as Statistics Canada has found). However, you could use the latter fact as evidence to support a policy claim, say, for allocating more financial resources to women who head households, especially if you found their per capita incomes were lower than those of men.

In addition, a belief is not arguable—for example, that God exists—although you could argue the merits or interpretation of something within the belief system, such as the meaning of a passage from the Koran or another religious text. Similarly, you could not logically argue that one religion is better than another since there are no clear and objective standards that reasonable members of your audience could agree on (and on which to base your claim, see "Connecting claim to evidence," below). Of course, comparisons between aspects of two belief systems could well be discussed as a fact-based claim. However, arguable claims must be capable of being supported through objective evidence, *not just opinion*.

More subtle are essays that set out to extol the benefits of something: for example, exercise, a clean environment, or a good diet. However, if a general consensus exists about an item's value, you would find yourself arguing in a vacuum. You do not have a meaningful claim if your audience accepts it as a truism (i.e., it is self-evident and does not need proving). *If you cannot think of a strong opposing view to the one you want to argue, consider revising the topic so that it is arguable, or choose another topic.*

On the other hand, if you set out to argue that one method or system is better than another—for example, that the flat tax system is better than the progressive tax system—you may find yourself considering the pros and cons of each in a point-by-point rebuttal, although your purpose at the outset of would be to argue in favour of one side. You could also write a comparison and contrast *expository* essay on this topic, but in that case, you would set the essay up as a question to be answered (e.g., which system most benefits taxpayers in the middle-income bracket?) and use factual evidence to answer the question. There can be a fine line between cost/benefit argumentative and cost/benefit expository essays; therefore, it is necessary to clearly announce your overall purpose—argumentative/persuasive or investigating/explaining—in your claim.

SUBSTANTIAL CLAIMS

A reader has a right to expect you to argue about something of importance and may dismiss a claim perceived as trivial. Readers should see how the claim could affect them, their community, or their society. A relevant claim for one group may not be relevant for another. If you want to use the claim, you must make the reader see its relevance (see "Appeal to reader interests," below).

Some claims are trivial by their very nature—for example, that one brand of deodorant is better than another. Of course, many commercials "argue" precisely this way, often using irrelevant or misleading "evidence." Needless to say, in such claims, specific detail is lacking or is couched in such general terms as to be meaningless: "Now 97% improved!!!"

Be careful not to use an exaggerated or weak claim as the basis for your argument—for example, that all cellphones should be banned in public places because they are distracting when they go off. A stronger argument would be for banning hand-held phones in automobiles—it is stronger because it is more important and has a much better chance of being implemented, as it has been in some US states.

SPECIFIC CLAIMS

A claim should not promise more than it is able to deliver. This applies particularly to claims that are too broad: "we need to change our attitude toward the environment"; "we need to do something about terrorism." On the other hand, if your claim relates to a problem that most people are not aware of, your argumentative purpose would be different—to draw attention to a problem—and it might be possible to argue a broad claim.

One way to narrow a general claim, or amend it so it is more specific, is to think about how it might apply to a subject you are knowledgeable about. If you have come up with a broad topic, you can ask how it might affect people you know. For example, if you wanted to argue that the media promotes unhealthy weight loss in teenagers, a very big topic, and you were an athlete, you could consider what rules or procedures can lead to unhealthy weight loss in your sport. Many sports, such as rowing, have weight categories. In some provinces, the junior female lightweight category is 135 pounds and under. As a rower, you may be aware of unhealthy eating or purging habits that can develop in rowers seeking to remain in a lower weight category in order to be competitive. Your thesis statement might take this specific form: *To help prevent unhealthy and dangerous activities in young rowers, junior lightweight categories should be eliminated from provincial regattas.*

A broad claim can also be made more specific (and manageable) if you can apply it to a particular group. It might be unwieldy to apply an anti-smoking claim to Canada or even to an entire province, since municipalities may have their own smoking bylaws; you might therefore restrict the focus to your city or even your campus.

REALISTIC CLAIMS

Unrealistic claims are usually policy claims that have little chance of being implemented. One could argue for almost anything that would make life easier or that would fulfill a need, but if it cannot be instituted, the argument becomes moot. You may be able to muster some points in favour of a return to Prohibition or the legalization of all currently illegal drugs, but since such arguments would not take account of social conditions today, the claim would not be realistic. Unenforceable policy claims are also unrealistic.

MANAGEABLE CLAIMS

Like a broad claim, an overly complex claim may not appear doable within an essay of a reasonable length. You should take a realistic approach to your topic, ensuring that it can be convincingly argued within the assigned word length. As is the case with overly broad claims, you can make a complex topic more manageable by limiting its scope in some way.

Exercise

In discussion groups, evaluate the 10 claims below, determining whether they would make good thesis statements for an argumentative essay. Are the claims arguable, substantial, specific, realistic, and manageable? If they are not, consider what changes would need to be made to make them arguable. Revise them accordingly.

1. Cloning should be prohibited because it will mean the end of natural selection.
2. In order to represent the interests of voters more accurately, give voters a wider selection of candidates, and provide a stronger voice for minority issues, British Columbia should adopt the single transferable vote (STV) electoral model.
3. *South Park* is a much better show than *Family Guy*.
4. E-mail is a very useful form of communication today because it is accessible, fast, and far-reaching.
5. The Wii is a more popular gaming system than the Xbox 360 or PlayStation 3.
6. No-fault insurance is very beneficial because it has made it easier for insurance companies to stay in business.
7. Internet dating services are an innovative, convenient, and affordable alternative to the singles scene.
8. The culture of consumerism is responsible for many of the problems that our world faces today.
9. There need to be legal guidelines for genetic testing because it may threaten our privacy, lead to harmful gene therapy, and have dangerous social costs.
10. Because of the dangerousness of the sport utility vehicle, people should have to prove that they really need an SUV before being permitted to purchase one.

Connecting claim to evidence

Strong arguments do not simply consist of an arguable claim and supporting evidence: there needs to be a link between claim and evidence, showing why the evidence is relevant to or supports the claim. Philosopher Stephen Toulmin called this the **warrant**. If a man with a bleeding cut on his face ran up to you and asked you to call the police, you would probably infer that the person had been attacked. The link between the claim (request to call the police) and the evidence (the bleeding cut) would be the common sense notion that the police will arrest the perpetrator (the warrant). The man would not need to explain the warrant (how the claim relates to the evidence) since it would be self-evident, as it is in many arguments. Warrants can arise from common sense/intuition, physical laws, human laws, standards, assumptions, aesthetic values, ethical principles, and so on. Readers may not accept your claim or the evidence you present unless they first accept the warrant.

The underlying assumption of Douglas Morris in "Enemies of biodiversity" (p. 410) is also unstated. Morris claims that humans are "in a deadly race" to save endangered species. As evidence, he cites data from the website of the Committee on the Status of Endangered Wildlife in Canada. The warrant arises from an ethical principle: it is vital that we conserve biodiversity.

Consider the warrants in the following example (referred to under "Misconception 2," above) in which the same evidence is used to support different claims. It is the underlying assumption, the warrant, that links evidence to the claim in each case.

Claim #1: More resources should be allocated to boost the survival rate of lung transplant recipients.

Warrant: **The survival rate could be improved if we allocate more resources** (an assumption; it could be based on the economic principle that allocating more resources is likely to improve a result).

Evidence: Just over 50 per cent of lung transplant recipients have a five-year survival rate.

Claim #2: Fewer resources should be allocated to this procedure since the result is less promising than for other kinds of transplants in Canada.

Warrants: **The survival rate does not justify the allocation of the present level of resources for this procedure** (an ethical principle); **the resources could be better allocated to help more people** (an economic principle).

Evidence: Just over 50 per cent of lung transplant recipients have a five-year survival rate.

Exercise

What warrant(s) could be used to connect the following claim to the evidence?

Claim #3: The allocation of resources for lung transplant recipients should be maintained at its present level.

Warrant(s):

Evidence: Just over 50 per cent of lung transplant recipients have a five-year survival rate.

Kinds of evidence in argumentative essays

Argumentative essays often make ideal in-class and exam assignments because they do not require research and you are not usually called on to demonstrate specialized knowledge about the topic. However, although an effective argument can be built around reasonable points with logical connections between them, specific kinds of evidence can bolster a claim. Some are more common to argument than to exposition, but most can be used in both:

- *Experts and authorities:* **Experts** are directly involved in the issue you are arguing. You will usually use expert testimony to support your claim; however, the occasional use of experts with whom you disagree can make your argument more balanced. Sue Ferguson ("How computers make our kids stupid," p. 195) uses a variety of experts in her essay, which argues against the overuse of information technology in Canadian schools. Most of her experts are teachers and researchers who support her claim, but she also makes sparing use of those who favour technology in the classroom. An effective way to stress experts who agree with you is to cite them directly (direct quotation), while putting the words of opposing experts in your own words (summarization or paraphrase), ensuring that you do so accurately and fairly.

  Authorities can also lend credibility by virtue of who they are and what they say. Although authorities may not have direct experience in the issue you are arguing, they may make the reader pay more attention to it. Pico Iyer ("Canada: Global citizen," p. 273) begins his essay by citing three internationally respected authorities. None is Canadian, but all are used to support Iyer's point about the way Canadians are perceived internationally.

- *Examples and illustrations:* Using **examples**—specific instances or cases—can make a general claim more concrete and understandable, enabling the reader to relate to it. An **illustration** could take the form of an anecdote (a brief informal story) or other expanded example. Student writer Tyler Nichol sets up his thesis about the value of fine arts programs in schools with an illustration: the case of a school that cut such programs in order to focus exclusively on academic achievement. Using the reversal strategy, he then questions the costs to students of eliminating fine arts programs from the curriculum (see "Analysis of a sample student argumentative essay," below).

- *Precedents:* In law, a **precedent** is an important kind of example: it is a ruling that can apply to subsequent cases that involve similar facts or issues. To *set a precedent* means to establish a formal procedure for dealing with future cases. In argument, appealing to precedents—the way something was done in the past—can be particularly effective in policy claims. To use a precedent, you must show: (1) that the current situation (what you are arguing) is similar to that of the precedent and (2) that following the precedent will be beneficial. (Of course, you can use a precedent as a negative example as well, showing that it has not produced beneficial results.) Precedents can be used to legitimize controversial issues, such as banning smoking in public places, decriminalizing marijuana or prostitution, or providing universal access to post-secondary education. Matt James ("Being stigmatized and being sorry: Past injustices and contemporary citizenship," p. 293) uses the Japanese-Canadian successful redress experience as a precedent to argue that redress is urgently necessary for other ethnic groups, which, like many Japanese Canadians during World War II, were robbed of their civil rights in the past.

- *Personal experience:* The selective use of personal experience in argumentative essays can be a highly effective way to involve your reader. In some cases, it can also increase your credibility; for example, if you have worked with street people, you may be seen as better qualified to argue a claim about homelessness. Personal experience could take the form of direct experience, of observing something first-hand, or of reporting on something that happened to a friend.

  Some kinds of personal experience are less successful. Simply announcing that you experienced something and benefited by it does not necessarily make your argument stronger; for example, saying that you enjoyed physical education classes in high school is not going to convince many people that it should be a required subject in the schools. What is important is the way you use personal experience: you should stress the ways that an occurrence or situation has been a learning experience for you and that, by mentioning it, the reader can learn something too. The following introduction serves as a compelling set-up for the carefully phrased value claim (italicized):

  > On a Friday night in February 2005, many friends of mine, including Tommy Stanwood, decided to party in Esquimalt's Cairn Park. When the crowd decided to move to Gorge Kinsmen Park to merge with another party, five of my peers got in the car with a 17-year-old who had also been drinking. Tommy, among three other male high school seniors and two ninth-grade girls, was nearly killed when the intoxicated driver flipped his Buick by slamming it into a concrete divider at high speed. Miraculously, no one was killed. Both girls suffered broken limbs, the driver was badly injured, and Tommy broke his pelvis and had his left ear severed in the crash. Tommy's life was spared, but he now walks with a limp, has many scars and only one ear. More tragically, he seems like an entirely different person. *Although it is not possible to legislate perfect judgment into the young people of British Columbia, the current laws regarding youth driving and alcohol take the wrong approaches to try to prevent these tragedies, which often result in death.* (student writer Alex Smith)

- *Facts, statistics, scientific studies:* Policy claims can often benefit from factual support. Ensure, however, that all factual data is accurate and clearly represented. You are no doubt familiar with the truism that "statistics lie"—that is, they can often be manipulated to suit the purpose of the arguer. Use the most current statistics available from the most reliable sources. Be especially wary of sources that do not reveal where the facts they cite come from or the methods used to obtain the statistical data. All secondary sources need to be acknowledged in your essay; your citations will reveal both the currency and the reliability of the source.

Referring to a fact, statistic, or study that is outdated or otherwise lacking authority can damage your credibility (see "Issues of credibility," p. 102).

Two kinds of reasoning

Two methods of reasoning are **inductive** and **deductive reasoning**. In inductive reasoning, you arrive at a probable truth by observing and recording specific occurrences. Flaws in inductive reasoning can occur if not enough observations have been made—that is, the evidence is insufficient to make a generalization—or if the method for gathering the evidence is faulty. Thus, researchers try to include as large a sample as possible within the population they draw from; this makes their findings more reliable (see Appendix, "The Active Voice: What Students Need to Know About Statistics"). Similarly, researchers reveal the details of their experiment's methodology. They need to show that their evidence-gathering methods are thorough and free of bias.

While inductive reasoning works from detail to generalization, deductive reasoning begins with a major premise, which can be summed up by a general statement assumed to be true. A second premise, which is a subset or instance of the major premise, is then applied to the major premise. If both statements are, in fact, true and logically related, the conclusion follows as true. The deductive reasoning method can be set up in the form of a **syllogism**, a three-part structure that nicely illustrates how deductive reasoning works in forming conclusions. Syllogisms have very complex applications in logic and mathematics. However, in its simple form, the syllogism can be useful in sorting out the validity of a conclusion. The conclusion of the following is true because both premises are true and are logically related:

Major premise: All students who wish to apply for admission to the university must submit their grade transcripts.
Minor premise: Deanna wishes to apply for admission to the university.
Conclusion: Deanna must submit her grade transcripts.

USING REASON IN ARGUMENTS

Most arguments rely on both inductive and deductive reasoning, although we may not be aware of it when we hear or read an argument. Instead, we may silently assent to a plausible premise or one that seems borne out by our own experience. Whatever the purpose in arguing—whether to settle an issue, expose a problem, or reach a compromise—getting the listener/reader to agree with your premises is vital. It is also vital to make a neutral or hostile reader receptive to what you have to say; thus, it can be important to use specific strategies like concessions and appeals to common ground. Emotional appeals are often part of argumentative strategies as well. But most successful arguments begin and end with your effective use of reason.

However, reason can also be misused in arguments. Consider the following statements, the first of which illustrates the misuse of inductive reasoning because there is inadequate evidence to justify the conclusion; the second illustrates the misuse of deductive reasoning in which a false premise results in a faulty conclusion. Avoiding logical fallacies (failures in reasoning) in your own essays and pointing them out in the arguments of others will make your arguments stronger and more credible.

> **The premier broke a promise he made during his election campaign. He is a liar, and his word can no longer be trusted.** It is not reasonable to distrust a politician because he broke one promise. Politicians do not always deliver on their pre-election promises (this could almost be considered a generalization peculiar to campaigning politicians!). If the premier broke several promises, there would be much stronger grounds for the conclusion. Thus, in most people's minds, there is not enough inductive evidence to prove the claim.

> **Eduardo is the only one in our family who has a Ph.D. He's obviously the one who inherited all the brains.** Underlying this statement is the assumption that having a Ph.D. indicates your intelligence. Possessing an advanced degree could be partly a measure of intelligence; it could also indicate persistence, a fascination with a particular subject, a love of learning, inspiring teachers, an ambitious nature, strong financial and/or familial support, and so on.

FAILURES IN REASONING

Errors in reasoning fall into several categories, termed the **logical fallacies**. To argue effectively and to recognize weak arguments when you read them, it is not necessary to be able to categorize every failure in logic. Most errors are the result of sloppy or simplistic thinking—the failure to do justice to the complexity of an issue (sometimes deliberate in the case of conscious distortions but often unconscious). Developing your critical thinking skills will make you alert to errors of logic. A few examples of fallacious reasoning follow:

- *Oversimplification:* An arguer may consider only two possibilities, one of which may be clearly unacceptable (*either/or fallacy*):

  > **If you don't get a college degree, you might as well resign yourself to low-paying jobs.**

- *Cause/effect fallacy:* Among the many cause/effect fallacies is the one that argues a claim on the basis of a coincidental (non-causal) relationship between two occurrences:

Re-elect your prime minister; the economy grew by 4 per cent while she was in office. The question is whether the government's policies were primarily responsible for that growth.

If homosexual marriages are legalized, the next thing people will want to do is marry their pets! In the **slippery slope fallacy**, the arguer claims that a challenge to the status quo will lead to a break-down in order or of human values; recently, it has been used as an argument against such practices as euthanasia, legalizing marijuana, and the screening of embryos. Of course, arguments can be made against these claims, but using "slippery slope" logic does not make for a sound argument.

- *Deductive fallacy:* The arguer constructs a faulty generalization and uses it to prove a claim. The following could be set up as a syllogism:

  Major premise: It is human nature to take the easy way.
  Minor premise: Downloading music is the easy way.
  Conclusion: It is only human nature to download music from the Internet, so why fight human nature?

- *Circular reasoning:* An arguer may assume something is true simply by citing the premise as if it validated the claim:

  I'm an "A" student. How can the teacher give me a B- on the assignment? The student has appealed to a premise that needs to be proven before being accepted as truthful.

- *Irrelevance:*

  He can't be trusted for public office. After all, he admitted to an extramarital affair. This fallacy of irrelevance is a **non sequitur**—literally, "it does not follow"—as the "evidence" (supposed questionable personal conduct) has no logical connection with the claim (trustworthiness as a public official); it does not *follow from* the claim.

Another fallacy of irrelevance is **name-dropping**, citing a famous person as if his/her views are evidence in something's favour; in the **guilt by association fallacy**, the arguer uses the fact that some allegedly disreputable person or group supports a view as an argument against it (or opposes it as an argument in its favour).

- *False analogy:* In a false analogy, you make a comparison between two things that are not comparable because they are, in fact, not alike or they differ greatly in one respect. In the heat of the moment (see emotional fallacies), people sometimes compare a perpetrator of a minor tyranny to Adolf Hitler or another bona fide tyrant.

- *Slanted language:* An arguer may use highly charged language to dismiss an opponent's claims. Simply characterizing an opponent as "ignorant" or "greedy" serves no constructive purpose. Of course, you may be able to show through unbiased evidence that the opponent has demonstrated these characteristics.

- *Emotional fallacies:* These statements appeal to the emotions of a reader in a manipulative or unfair way, such as a partisan appeal, guilt by association, name-calling, or dogmatism (simply asserting something without offering proof—often, over and over). They are very different from legitimate appeals to emotions:

  > Don't believe the claims of those neo-liberals. They just want to take your hard-earned money away from you. (partisan appeal)

- A common emotional fallacy is the **bandwagon**, which asserts that because something is popular, it has value:

  > All my friends' parents give them unrestricted curfews on Friday nights.

In the two quotations below, the speakers appeal to the emotions of New Orleans's voters in the post-Katrina election shortly after the hurricane devastated the city. Lost in the emotional appeal (a variant of the bandwagon fallacy) is manipulation of the truth: neither man had won when he spoke, but in the election they received, respectively, the highest and the second-highest number of votes, resulting in a run-off to decide on the mayor:

> "There have been too many people who said we were dead, too many people who said we were way too divisive. There were too many people who said this city should go in a different direction. But the people have said they like the direction." (incumbent mayor Ray Nagin. In fact, fewer than 50 per cent of the people "said" this.)

> "Today in this great American city, African-American and white, Hispanic and Vietnamese, almost in equal measure, came forward to propel this campaign forward and loudly proclaim that we in New Orleans will be one people. We will speak with one voice

and we will have one future." (mayoral candidate Mitch Landrieu. In fact, people did not speak with one voice but, as usual in a democracy, with many voices. If people had spoken with one voice, there would have been no need for a run-off: one of the candidates would have been elected unanimously.)

Giving life to logic

As noted, argument at the post-secondary level depends heavily on your use of reasonable claims supported by convincing evidence, but logic alone will not necessarily convince readers to change their minds or adopt your point of view. The following strategies can be used, depending on your topic, purpose, and audience, to shape a logical and appealing argument, one that will make your readers more responsive to your claim.

- *Dramatic introductions:* Dramatic introductions are used more often in argument than in exposition because they may enable the reader to relate to a human situation. The introductory paragraphs on pages 122 and 134 illustrate dramatic introductions to essays on impaired driving in youth and fine arts programs. (See also "Creating reader interest," p. 92.)

- *Establishing common ground:* Getting your readers to see that you share many of their values enables you to come across as open and approachable, making them potentially more receptive to your argument. Although familiarity with your audience is important in knowing where and how your values and those of your audience intersect, you can assume that most readers will respond favourably to universal qualities like generosity, decency, security, and a healthy and peaceful environment.

- *Making concessions:* In granting concessions, you acknowledge the validity of an opposing point, demonstrating your fairness and willingness to accept other views, at least in part. After conceding a point, you follow with a strong point of your own. In effect, you are giving some ground in an effort to get the reader to do the same. The concession can be made in a dependent clause and your own point in the independent clause that follows: "Although it is valid to say . . . [concession is made], the fact is . . . [your point]." Concessions can be vital in cases in which there is a strong opposition or in which you wish to reach a compromise.

- *Appeal to reader interests:* When you appeal to the interests of your readers, you show how they might be affected by your claim. For example, in a policy claim, it could consist of showing how they might benefit by the implementation of a particular policy—how it will be good for them—or what costs could be incurred if it is not implemented—how it will be bad for them. Arguing in favour of a costly social program may be a hard sell to those whose approval and support are vital, such as business leaders. Therefore, you could explain how the program could benefit these leaders—for example, by helping to prevent a bigger problem, such as increased health care costs or taxes. If you know the values and motivations of your readers, you may be able to use this knowledge to make your points directly relevant to them.

- *Emotional appeals:* While dramatic openings can be successful in many argumentative essays, the success of an opening that includes an appeal to emotion depends greatly on your audience. Beginning an essay on animal testing by describing a scene of caged animals at a slaughterhouse may alienate neutral readers. If you do use such an opening, you need to ensure that a typical reader will respond in the way you wish. Emotional appeals, however, are commonly used in the conclusion of an essay. They provide an effective coda, a final way that the audience can reflect on the topic. In the following conclusion, student writer Mary McQueen appeals to landlords in order to subtly reinforce her claim advocating a more open policy toward pets in apartments:

> The human/animal bond is special and worth preserving and promoting. Landlords who allow pets make an important, generous contribution towards the solution of the pet-friendly housing problem and have the opportunity to make the partnerships of landlords, tenants, and companion animals so successful that they become role models to inspire others around the community, the province, and the country.

Refutation strategies

Since the existence of an opposing viewpoint is needed for an argumentative claim, it is advisable to refer to this viewpoint in your essay—otherwise, it may appear that you are avoiding the obvious. Although you may use concessions as part of your argument, for the most part you will be concerned with refuting the competing claims on the other side. In your **refutation**, or **rebuttal**, you show the weaknesses or limitations of these claims. Here are three general strategies to consider. Which one you use depends on the three factors that you need to take into account when planning your argumentative essay: your topic, purpose, and audience. There may be additional factors involved too, such as essay length.

ACKNOWLEDGEMENT

You may need to do no more than simply acknowledge the opposing view. Such a strategy may be appropriate if the argument on the other side is straightforward or obvious. In the case of arguing for more open policies toward pets (above), the position of landlords is simple: allowing pets increases the potential for property damage. Similarly, this strategy would be a natural choice if the claim argued against the use of pesticides in lawn maintenance. Again, the opposing view is obvious: lawn owners use pesticides to make their lawns look attractive. After acknowledging the competing claim, the writer would go on to raise strong points that refute this claim without necessarily referring to it again.

If your argumentative purpose is to raise awareness of a problem, a simple acknowledgement may not be enough. In his essay on the seeming indifference of the developed nations to AIDS in Africa, Joel Pauls Wohlgemut (p. 190) argues for the need to act. However, actions are contingent on awareness and on the belief that action is possible. Accordingly, Wohlgemut's purpose is partly to get his audience to acknowledge the problem and confront some of its complexities. In his case, topic, purpose, and audience (fellow physicians) all played a role in his argumentative strategies.

LIMITED REBUTTAL

In a limited rebuttal, you raise and respond to the major point(s) on the other side, then follow with your own points without mentioning any minor competing claims. One obvious reason for using a limited rebuttal is that in a short essay, you will not have space to respond to all the competing claims. This strategy may also be appropriate if the strength of the opposing view is anchored by one or perhaps two very significant claims. You would not want to give strength to the other side by raising and refuting less important issues, especially if your purpose is to settle an issue. When you are analyzing the main argument on the other side, however, it is important to represent that position fairly; concessions are often helpful in this regard.

Whether you adopt the limited rebuttal strategy can depend on your audience and purpose for arguing. For example, if your audience is only generally knowledgeable about an issue, mentioning less important points on the other side might be counterproductive since they might not have been aware of them. If you are arguing to critique a position, you might be fundamentally concerned with one important claim relating to a topic. Raising other claims could confuse or obscure the important claim to which you are responding. In his essay "Kyoto: Mother of intervention," (p. 462), Peter Foster makes it clear that he is not arguing against the need to combat global warming but against what he considers the "nonsensical" argument that the Kyoto Protocol will stimulate the economy through the development of new technologies.

FULL REBUTTAL

There are two ways to organize a full rebuttal. You may systematically raise competing claims and respond to them one at a time (**point-by-point rebuttal**). Although concessions could be involved, especially if your purpose is to arrive at a compromise, usually you point out the flaws in each before responding with your own counter-claim. Alternatively, you could summarize the competing claims before you present the support for your claim, right after your introduction or after you have presented that support, just before your conclusion (**block rebuttal**). In some essays, you will not have the space or the need for a full rebuttal, let alone the more systematic form, the point-by-point rebuttal—for example, when you are limited by word length or when you are asked simply to give your opinion on an argumentative topic.

Point-by-point rebuttals can be very effective if the competing claims of an argument are well-known or if there is strong opposition to your claim. In his essay on contemporary redress movements in Canada, Matt James responds in detail to his opponents using the point-by-point strategy (see p. 293). Such a thorough response is necessary, he believes, because of the increasing opposition to redress movements, opposition that he sees as "extremely dangerous." However, if your argumentative purpose is to reach a compromise, you might also choose to use the point-by-point strategy. Here, however, you would be attempting to reach out to the other side (or both sides), showing that you understand the points that define their position. This strategy would demonstrate your knowledge and fairness.

The paragraph below illustrates the effective use of the point-by-point strategy in an essay on mandatory physical education classes in high school. Notice how student writer Meghan Cannon skilfully uses a concession (sentence two) to help turn a competing claim into a point in her favour:

> Some individuals argue against mandatory physical education because they believe that many teenagers feel self-conscious about their bodies and, therefore, self-conscious about physical activity. While the initiation of physical activity may be difficult for one suffering from body image issues, the long-term effect is invariably one of satisfaction. Students learn to appreciate what they can do with their bodies instead of being completely concerned with how it looks. Physical activity promotes self-awareness and acceptance. Self-confidence soars from participation in sport and the social interaction induced by sport.

Final considerations

Before you begin an outline or an audience plan (see below), you should decide on the order of your points. For most argumentative essays, this will mean choosing between two orders: the **climax order** or a **mixed order**. In the first, you begin with the weakest point and build toward the strongest; in the second, you could begin with a strong point—but not the strongest—follow with weaker points, and conclude with the strongest. It may be advisable not to begin with the weakest point if your audience opposes your claim, since an initial weak point may make your readers believe your entire argument is weak without reading on. Other orders are also possible. For example, if you are arguing to reach a compromise, you might need to focus the first part of your essay on one side of the debate, the second part on the opposite side, and the third on your compromise solution.

There is nothing inherently wrong in ending with your weakest point either (**inverted climax order**), although some advise against it. If you have presented a strong argument, a weaker concluding point is not necessarily going to undo your work. The last point could contain something humorous, anecdotal, or personal, for example, and serve as a fitting transition to a strong conclusion. Whatever order you use, it should be identical to the order of points in your thesis statement, assuming you use an expanded thesis statement.

Whichever refutation strategy you use, you should consider outlining the points on the other side before writing the essay—constructing a theoretical argument, as it were. In particular, consider how someone who disagreed with your claim might respond to your main points. This could reveal the strengths on the other side and any weaknesses in your own argument. More important, perhaps, it should serve to keep the opposing view in focus as you write, causing you to reflect carefully on what you are saying and how you say it.

Collaborative exercise: The audience plan

Taking the audience factor into account is very important as you prepare to write an argumentative essay. Constructing an audience plan will enable you to consider your approach to the essay, including the kinds of strategies to use. Team up with two other students and interview the other members of your group to determine their knowledge level, their interest level, and their orientation (agree, disagree, neutral) toward your topic; they will serve as your "audience." Based on this information, construct an audience plan. Include an audience profile and a summary of the strategies you would use to persuade this audience. Include your topic and your writing purpose in the plan. A sample plan on the topic of raising the minimum wage follows:

Topic: Should the minimum wage in British Columbia be raised?

Argumentative purpose: To convince readers that the minimum wage should be raised.

Audience profile:
To determine a plan for my argumentative essay, I questioned two student-peers on their knowledge, interest, and orientation in regard to my topic.

Knowledge: I would characterize both of them as moderately knowledgeable about the subject of minimum wage in British Columbia. Both have either earned minimum wage working or know someone who is or was earning minimum wage.

Interest: The topic was of interest to both students. They asked many questions about the issue and were interested in learning more. Also, as university students soon to graduate, both were concerned about employment and the level of wages once they graduated. One of the students was also concerned about how low income affected the community as a whole.

Orientation: Both agreed that the minimum wage in BC is too low and should be raised, although one student voiced a stronger opinion on the subject and suggested a much higher increase than the other. This student had had a job where she was making minimum wage. The second student, who approached the idea of an increase much more cautiously, was concerned about the pressures that a "drastic" increase would put on small-business owners.

Audience plan:

It is important for the audience to know a few more specific background points before I can effectively argue my claim. It may be of interest to them to know what the poverty index in Canada is and how many people earning minimum wage live below this index. Other information could also be useful, for example, cross-provincial comparisons. Many other provinces have had or are proposing minimum wage increases: Manitoba and New Brunswick will be increasing their minimum wage in 2007, and Alberta had an increase in 2005. By contrast, BC's last increase was in 2001.

Of considerable interest to my audience was how minimum wage affects the overall welfare of the community. I will make this the main point of my essay by looking at the relationship between minimum wage and homelessness as well as exploring other links between minimum wage and quality of life. A key assumption on which I base my claim about homelessness is that if people are not able to earn enough for housing working full-time on minimum wage, one of the solutions would be to increase the minimum wage so they can live above the poverty index. I will also look for studies that found relationships between wage level and self-esteem and/or psychological states, such as depression. Also of interest is the potential for students with an undergraduate degree to earn minimum wage, especially while they are looking for work related to their education and, perhaps, paying back loans.

In order to address concerns brought up by the second student I interviewed, I will use a limited rebuttal strategy to look at the possible opposition to raising the minimum wage, especially addressing the concerns of small-business owners. Here I will attempt to establish common ground and appeal to reader interests, perhaps by stressing the link between an adequate wage and the purchasing power that comes with it.

Student writer Meleisa Ono-George

Analysis of a sample student argumentative essay

When student writer Tyler Nichol wrote on the importance of fine arts programs in the school curriculum, he did not use studies or statistics to bolster his claim, though doing so might have assisted him. However, in order to write within the assigned word length, he focused on three main points that were developed through sound reasoning. Initially, however, Nichol had to decide his purpose in arguing, the kind of audience he wanted to address, and the claim (value or policy) that would be the most effective given the topic, purpose, and audience. From there, he had to decide which refutation strategy to use. In addition, he considered the role that concessions, establishing common ground, appeals to reader interests, and emotional appeals would play in strengthening his argument. After weighing these options, he decided to use a point-by-point rebuttal, trying to establish common ground with his readers, and make subtle use of concessions. He did not use emotional appeals in his essay.

Other choices he faced are those common to most essay writing: deciding on what kind of introduction to use, what evidence to present, what order of points to use, and so on.

Purpose: Nichol is primarily concerned with settling an issue, with a secondary purpose of exposing a problem—the difficulties that can result if fine arts programs are cut from the curriculum.

Audience: In his introduction and conclusion, Nichol refers to school administrators, yet his argument seems directed toward a more general audience, perhaps of parents and teachers. In this case, why does he mention the administrators? He likely does this because they are the ones who make the decisions about curriculum. With pressure from parents and the community, he believes that administrators might have to act to reinstate fine arts programs.

Refutation strategy: Limited rebuttal. Nichol responds to two competing claims, those he believes are the strongest: the claim that discounts the practical value of fine arts classes and a related claim that argues the value of traditional academic classes over fine arts classes. This was an effective strategy because most of his readers would be familiar with these arguments. Nichol mentions these familiar points before replying with his strong rebuttal. If he simply acknowledged the other side without specifically referring to its main arguments, his readers might think he was avoiding them.

Fine Arts Are a Crucial Element of a Child's Learning

by Tyler Nichol

Newport High School, a fairly large school in the fairly large city of Bellevue, Washington, was selected as a Blue Ribbon National School of Excellence in 2003 by the US Department of Education. Earning this prestigious award was the result of years of steady increase in SAT scores, ITED scores, and the number of AP (advanced placement) tests taken by its students. Newport also offers the widest range of AP classes available to students in the Bellevue School District. How were they able to do this? It is simple: administrators worked hard to cut most of the fine arts programs to make room for a large number of academic classes. This is a serious problem facing many schools in North America today as school administrators push aside creative learning classes to make room for honours and advanced placement classes, convinced that it will boost their school's reputation and prestige. This may be so, as was the case for Newport High School, but what is the cost to the students attending these schools? Fine arts are crucial to the development of the child's self-image, intellectual capacity, and mental health. Time must be allotted for such classes in high school.

High school spans an important period in a child's life. It is a time when many young adults struggle with self-awareness, self-confidence, and self-esteem issues. With so much pressure put on the students by the schools to take a rigorous academic schedule, there is little time left for a student to let the mind wander and explore the depths of his or her own inner being. One of the best ways to help a child through this awkward phase is through fine arts classes. Classes that encourage students to be creative and use their imagination help them gain confidence and develop a strong sense of "self." In a time marked by self-discovery, it is important that students have an artistic outlet through which they can explore their innermost being.

Fine arts, such as ceramics, music, and photography, are also important to the development of the brain. The vast majority of academic classes challenge students to think logically and make rational connections between topics. This sort of activity is usually carried out by the left hemisphere of the brain. Creatively oriented activity calls on the right hemisphere; however, learning and thinking are improved when both sides of the brain are able

---

Nichol uses a dramatic introduction, referring to the example of a US high school. He initially paints this school as an exemplary one, but then uses the reversal strategy to point out the problem in making academic preparation the sole criterion for learning.

Claim: a broad policy claim but grounded in value. He uses an expanded thesis that lists his main points. *Fine arts are crucial to the development of the child's self-image, intellectual capacity, and mental health. Time must be allotted for such classes in high school.*

Common ground: Most people would assent to this generalization, including those with the opposing viewpoint. If you can get a reader to respond favourably to a reasonable claim like this one, it is easier to get your own view across; you are more likely to be listened to.

to function adequately and in a well-balanced manner. Many would argue that fine arts are a waste of time and that students do not learn anything practical from such classes. In a sense this is true: most students who take a ceramics class in high school will never again mould clay; however, the class helps exercise that right hemisphere, providing a foundation that allows the child to begin to think creatively in everything he or she does. This is very important for, among other things, making relationships and communicating with others. In addition, most people will not need to remember how to apply Snell's law of refraction to find the critical incidence angle of a light beam leaving a glass medium unless they pursue a degree in the sciences. When high school is considered in that light, a physics class is just as unimportant as a fine arts class to a student destined to become a stockbroker. It is because high school lays the foundation for future learning, rather than career preparation, that fine arts classes are just as important as academic classes.

> Concession: Nichol raises a common argumentative point on the opposing side, agrees with it ("in a sense, this is true...") but then points out its limitations.

> Although Nichol builds a strong argument by making careful choices, consider his inclusion of the final sentence in paragraph 3. Could it alienate some readers? Do you think he should have rephrased the sentence?

With the ever-increasing rigour of high school schedules these days, students are finding less and less time for creative classes as they need more academic classes to graduate. The general sentiment is that the more students are educated in the basics—history, math, English, science—the better prepared they will be upon entering university. However, a schedule devoid of artistic classes not only is detrimental to the development of the brain but also has a negative effect on a student's mental health. The pressure to excel in so many different and difficult subjects can be overwhelming for many students, causing them to be frantic and worried. That pressure can be relieved with classes that provide a creative outlet. Having just a couple of classes a day where students can relax and focus their attention and energy on something they enjoy doing can rid their minds of all the worries and frustrations and enable them to be happier individuals; furthermore, it will allow them to perform better in their academic classes, as they will be more relaxed and able to concentrate. Fine arts classes help students maintain a healthier state of mind, which is crucial to success in school as well as in life.

> Nichol uses the climax order, with his strongest point reserved for the paragraph before his conclusion. To strengthen this point, he connects the need for creative classes to academic success, directly addressing his audience and attempting to appeal to their interests (strong academic performances).

Although a school in which students spend all day performing complex calculations and examining the reasons for the fall of the Ottoman Empire may sound appealing to many administrators, it is important for them to take into consideration the needs and interests of the students. Fine arts classes, when taught in conjunction with academic classes, provide the framework for students to excel in any discipline they enter. For this reason, school administrators need to recognize the importance of fine arts classes and make a wide variety of these courses available to their students.

For examples of essays in "The Active Reader" that use argument, see "Classification by rhetorical mode/pattern or style," p. xviii.

The critical response: A meeting place

In a critical response, you reflect on your response to a work, using your critical thinking skills and supplementing them with your own perspective on and/or experience about an issue. You can write a critical response to a written text, but it can also be used to record your thoughts about a film, speech, performance, or public event.

Because they provide a forum for opinion, critical responses can be considered somewhat argumentative, although their main purpose is not to persuade a reader, unlike a book or film review, for example. Critical responses have an expressive component. Like personal essays, they can serve as a medium for self-exploration: they can clarify your thoughts about an issue or reveal your feelings about it. That does not mean, however, that you should force your opinions on the text or that your thoughts and feelings should predominate in your response. The main function of critical responses is to engage with the text and through this engagement to share your views with others.

Critical responses provide the opportunity for you to explore an area of personal interest, using the text, in part, as a springboard into this exploration, but it is important that you remain "grounded" by the text: it should serve not only as the point of departure but also as the focus of your main points. Interweaving textual references with your own observations and opinions results in a different kind of synthesis from that of a research essay in which you integrate research sources to help support a thesis, answer a question, or prove a hypothesis. Critical responses may be loosely structured and seldom require a thesis statement or even a separate introductory section. Their flexible structure reflects their exploratory function.

One additional function of a critical response to a reading is to call attention to what you do naturally as a reader, at least to a degree: process a text—whether it is argumentative, literary, or expository—through the filter of your own experience. Of course, the way you respond in *writing* to texts in these three genres will usually necessitate your standing back and making objective assessments, creating the distance to apply the standards of critical thinking.

Because of the different way you interact with texts in critical responses, you could consider responses as meeting places between you and the author or between you and others who have read or might read the work. Thus, the critical response resembles some classroom discussions in which you join other class members in exploring a topic by offering your unique perspective and sharing it with others. Of course, in a written response, you have more time to reflect on this perspective and on the text itself and, as with all written discourse, your response should adhere to the conventions of the form. Below are some of the objectives and conventions of response writing:

- Although critical responses do not include thesis statements, the general approach to the work you are analyzing should be evident early on; your first sentences could include an overview of or a generalization about the text or the central issue(s) it raises.
- If your reader is unfamiliar with the text, you will need to briefly summarize its main ideas (or plot, if the text is a literary work or a film).
- It can be a good idea to refer to your background or the place you "are coming from" in addressing the issue or topic before you offer concrete observations. Doing so will help pave the way for your more specific comments and may also enhance your credibility. For example, you could mention your ethnic heritage, if you consider it relevant, before addressing the specifics of an essay on Canada's multiculturalism policy or mention your experience as a gamer before analyzing an essay on computer games.
- Do not lose sight of the fact that you are primarily reacting to a *text* and that the text should remain front and centre in your analysis. Personal experience should not *replace* analysis.
- You do not need to research the topic unless your instructor requires it.
- Critical responses are written more informally than many other kinds of writing. Since personal experience is often important, using the first-person voice—"I," "me," "we," "us"—is natural.
- The length of critical responses can vary considerably from a couple of substantial paragraphs to several pages, depending on the nature of the assignment and length of the work you are responding to. Sometimes, instructors choose to initiate a response by posing specific questions about the text.
- In some critical responses, you may be required to respond to more than just the text—for example, to another student's response to the text. In that case, you will need to filter your perspective through that of another reader, considering the validity of his or her views and the degree to which you agree or disagree with them. In the sample critical response below, the writer criticizes the way that some of her peers have responded to the text being analyzed.
- If you have trouble generating a response, consider utilizing one or more traditional pre-writing techniques, such as freewriting, brainstorming, or thinking of specific questions pertaining to the topic. Remember that in a response you do not have to consider the entire essay but can narrow your response to one or more main points or even consider what is *not* in the essay as opposed to what is. What has the writer left unsaid?

- Critical *responses* are typically less focused on the techniques and strategies of the author than are critical *analyses*; however, if the essay is argumentative, pointing out its strengths and/or weaknesses, its limitations, and any fallacies, for example, might well form a substantial part of your response. In general, the critical response considers *your response to the text*, while a critical analysis is focused on *the text itself* and very little, if at all, on your personal response.

Can you write a successful critical response if you have no particular opinion on the topic or interest in it? In most cases, the answer is "yes." A "response" or a "reaction" is not the same thing as an opinion. You may have no opinion, but it is difficult *not* to react to topics of common concern or to the beliefs and viewpoints of others. It is certainly just as valid to respond to a topic by reflecting on how it can affect others or how it affects society as it is to reflect on how it has affected you. In the following critical response, the student writer uses the text extensively, along with her own experience, in questioning some of the author's ideas as well as the responses of other students. The response was part of an on-line discussion of the essay "Fear and loathing in Toontown," reproduced in "The Active Reader" on p. 321.

Critical response to "Fear and loathing in Toontown," by Richard Poplak

by Kara McBee

Poplak's writing style in "Fear and loathing in Toontown" is surprisingly ingenious. He utilizes irony to ridicule the people out there who believe cartoons are detrimental to children. Presumably, he was aware that the vast majority of his audience would agree that cartoons are not dangerous. By taking on the opposing argument's side, Poplak is able to stir emotion in his audience.

Reading through my classmates' responses, however, I see some have interpreted Poplak's argument differently. Without appreciating his irony, some denounce him as paranoid and without credibility. If they had read closely, they would have seen that Poplak is indeed ridiculing Dobson and that Saturday morning cartoons are not under attack. Poplak refers to "Dobson and others like him, who so courageously wrestle the animated industry monolith" (para. 3) without actually including himself. He also questions their logic: "since when does wearing no pants necessarily denote homosexuality?" (para. 4).

He undermines his own argument continually by making ridiculous statements—for example, that the video *We are family* could only make people "tolerant, open-minded, and/or homosexual" (para. 1). This is obviously a huge leap: if watching a half-hour film can alter one's sexual orientation, I might as well be Peter Rabbit! Such cleverly biased statements are found throughout the article. Key phrases for me were "indiscriminate inclusiveness" and "excessive tolerance" (para. 11), both of which put limitations on fundamentally all-encompassing ideas, shrewdly emphasizing the illogical nature of the argument. I also enjoyed the ironic statement "healthy and well-exercised paranoia" (para. 7) in alluding to the relationship between Goofy and Pluto; in what context can paranoia be considered healthy?

While I am quite impressed with the effectiveness of Poplak's argument and respect his writing style, I do not agree with all he says. He ridicules extensively those who think cartoons are harmful, but I for one do see some validity in parts of Dobson's argument. I watched *Duck Dodgers* today to gain a little insight. Within five minutes, the duck had made various sexual references as well as used his newfound super-powers to secretly watch a "babe" from her balcony. Harmful? Probably not. A bit strange? Definitely. Any child watching cartoons is probably too young to pick up on sexual innuendo, but that doesn't mean it should be present, and in many cases prevalent, in cartoons.

The critical analysis:
Explaining the how and why

Both critical responses and critical analyses comment on other texts and are in this way different from traditional student essays, which often use other texts (primary and secondary sources) to support the essay writer's claims. But while the response is *mainly* focused on the text, the focus of the critical analysis is *exclusively* on the text or texts being analyzed. When you critically analyze a work, you break it down in order to scrutinize its constituent parts, using your critical thinking skills.

The critical analysis assumes a different relationship with the text from that of the critical response, one of a knowledgeable reader familiar with how such texts are written and capable of evaluating the author's success in achieving his or her objectives. And while the main purpose of the critical response is exploratory, the main purposes of critical analyses are (1) to explain and (2) to evaluate/critique the text. As can be inferred from the above, the response has a subjective element to it, but the critical analysis should be rigorously objective both in content and voice.

Analyses can be more challenging to write than responses, so they need to be planned carefully; for example, it is often a good idea to outline your points before beginning your draft. The reader of your analysis should not get the impression that spontaneity has been your organizing principle. By contrast, in critical responses, you may be guided by where the text or your interest in one particular part of the text takes you.

Writing a critical analysis makes you more conscious of the way that texts written by academics and other professionals are put together, as well as the kinds of strategies that can be used to make content clear and accessible. In this sense, you critically analyze a text in order to see what works and what does not—and why. Honing your analytical abilities in this way helps you use the essays you analyze as models for your own writing. Of course, the text under consideration could also serve as a negative model in some respects.

EXPLAINING AND EVALUATING

The purposes of critical analyses help determine the way you approach and organize them. As is the case with traditional student essays, most critical analyses begin with an introduction that includes a generalization about the essay and the author's approach. They should also include a summary of the author's thesis or what question he or she tried to answer. If a reader of your analysis is likely to be unfamiliar with the source text, you should briefly summarize the complete essay or at least enough to enable the reader to understand its essence. Summarization can be an important part of a critical analysis, but critical analyses are more than simple summaries.

In the body paragraphs, your analysis should "break down" the most relevant features of the essay, attempting to explain how these features, such as the author's methods and rhetorical strategies, reflect his or her purpose, objectives, and audience. The aim is to explain and evaluate the how and the why of the source text: How does the author explore the subject, prove the claim/hypothesis, and support the main points? Why are those particular methods and strategies used and not other ones? What are the essay's strengths and weaknesses? How could the text be improved?

Critical analyses can be weighted in different ways, depending on the nature of the source text. In many analyses, you may do little more than explain how the elements of the text relate to one another and function to make up a whole. If the source text presents the findings of original research, your analysis might mainly involve evaluating the essay according to the formal conventions of this kind of writing. Further, when original research appears in academic journals today, it often includes a section that discusses the study's limitations. In such cases, your analysis should mention these limitations, but the analysis itself might consist mostly of explanation and include minimal evaluation.

Because authors of Type A academic essays usually make interpretive rather than fact-based claims, this kind of essay is often more amenable to evaluation and critique. Nevertheless, student readers may find themselves reluctant to find fault with academic writers, believing that they lack the expertise to address the writers on their own terms. It is helpful to remember, however, that critical analyses do not necessarily involve a direct negative critique of the author or his or her methods. And, importantly, not all academic essays require a highly specialized level of knowledge in their readers: a non-specialist reader may be perfectly able to evaluate the effectiveness of an essay's organization or its clarity without being an expert in the subject. Although in some cases you may not be able to tell whether the writer has accurately represented a problem, proved a hypothesis, or answered a question, it may be evident that he or she has not addressed all sides of the issue or all implications of the question. In such cases, in your evaluation/critique you could point to undeveloped areas, suggesting why it would have been beneficial to expand on a point and what it could have contributed to the essay. For example, Gidengil et al. in "Enhancing democratic citizenship" (p. 282) canvas the literature in order to suggest ways of raising the level of participation in Canada's democratic process. You could ask yourself whether they have failed to consider other methods than those mentioned. Pointing out what a writer has not said is as much a critique as pointing out flaws in an essay's presentation or in the author's reasoning.

In a critical analysis of an argumentative essay, you might question the validity of an author's assumptions or premises (premises underlie many kinds of thinking, especially deductive reasoning in which conclusions can be drawn from specific premises). One conclusion that might be drawn (inferred) from the previous statement is that essays employing argument are often more easily critiqued than those that do not because in most arguments, an author's assumptions are clearly expressed in the form of an argumentative claim; argumentative claims are debatable. Remember, though, that a critical analysis of an argumentative essay should focus on the hows and whys of the author's methods and strategies. Unlike critical responses, they should not be used as a forum for expressing your personal agreement or disagreement with the author's opinions but for evaluating the logic and effectiveness of the argument itself.

In any analysis, being specific is vital. Support all claims you make about a text by referring specifically to examples from the text that illustrate your point. The best critical analyses proceed from a close and detailed reading of the source text (see "Focused reading," p. 64).

One common form of a critical analysis applies to literary works. The literary analysis "breaks down" the elements of the literary text—in the case of fiction, such elements would include plot, character, setting, point of view, and language—showing how they relate to one another. Of course, such texts contain no thesis or hypothesis but rather themes, which can be inferred from the interconnections among these elements. Like other kinds of texts, literary texts can be analyzed according to their conventions, which vary by genre (poetry, drama, fiction, creative non-fiction) and by subgenre (lyric, dramatic, and narrative poetry, for example).

The questions below, organized according to purpose, can be used as a basis for a critical analysis. Note that many of the questions and activities that follow individual essays in "The Active Reader" are the kinds of questions you can ask of a text as you read it in order to analyze it; on the other hand, other questions and activities in "The Active Reader" are more applicable to critical responses. The nature of the text itself will help determine which questions of those below are the most relevant to your analysis; for example, the author(s) of a study appearing in an academic journal article do not need to consider special strategies in order to create reader interest.

Explaining

- When was the essay written relative to similar studies in the field?
- Why was it written? Is it intended to inform, explain, persuade, entertain?
- What kind of audience is it written for? How do you know this?
- Is there an identifiable introduction? What is the writer's thesis, hypothesis, or central question? What is the justification for the study? In what way(s) does the author propose to add to his/her field of knowledge? Is there a literature review?
- Is there an essay plan? How does the author convey essay structure?
- What are its main points (Type A or journalistic essay)?
- What format does the essay follow? How does the text reflect the conventions of the discipline for which it was written? Does it follow these conventions exactly, or does it depart from them in any way?
- What kinds of evidence does the author use? Which are used most extensively?
- What is the essay's methodology?
- Is there a stress on either analysis or synthesis in the essay? On both equally?
- What inferences are readers called on to make?
- How is the essay organized? Is there a primary rhetorical pattern? What other kinds of patterns are used?
- What do you know about the author(s)? Does he/she appear to be an expert in his/her field or otherwise qualified to write on the topic? How is this apparent (if it is)?
- What level of language is used? Does the author include any particular stylistic features (e.g., analogies, metaphors, imagery, unusual/unconventional sentence structure)?
- Are tables, charts, or other kinds of graphic representation used (Type B)?
- Is there an identifiable conclusion? What is its primary purpose?

Evaluating/critiquing

- Does the author successfully prepare the reader for what is to follow in the essay? Generally speaking, authors prepare their readers by revealing the essay's thesis (Type A) or the results of the study (Type B) in an introduction and/or abstract. In some journalistic and argumentative essays, however, the author may choose to delay the thesis.
- Does the author manage to create interest in the topic? How is this done? Would other strategies have worked better? (These questions are relevant to interest-based essays.)
- Main points: Are they identifiable (in topic sentences, for example)? Are they well supported? Is supporting detail specific and relevant?
- If secondary sources are used, are there an adequate number? Are most of them current references? You can determine this by looking at the year in parenthesis in the text of the essay or in the alphabetical listing of sources at the end of the essay.

- What kinds of sources were used? Books? Magazines? Journal articles? Have the author(s) published related works in the field of study? Although this is no assurance of their credibility, many academic authors, especially in the natural and social sciences, publish more than one work in the area being investigated—sometimes in the same year.
- Are some sources more important than others—for example, are they used more often? Is there an overreliance on a particular source or a kind of source? For example, could the essay benefit from a greater use of primary source material?
- Does the author adequately respond to findings that are at odds with his/her own? How does he/she do this?
- Are the kinds of evidence used relevant to the topic, audience, and discipline? Are examples and illustrations used to make points more concrete?
- What kinds of strategies and techniques does the author use to facilitate understanding? Are they effective? Are there other ways that organization or content could have been made clearer?
- Is the voice or tone appropriate, given the kind of essay and the audience? Does the author make it clear that he/she is using a distinctive voice/tone for a specific purpose?
- If graphic material is used, is it used effectively to supplement the study's findings? Is it obvious what findings the material illustrates? Does it clarify rather than confuse?
- Does the conclusion answer the question/prove the hypothesis that the author sets out to investigate? Does it explain the relevance of the study, what it contributes to the field? In most essays written by academics and other professionals, a circular conclusion—one that does no more than paraphrase the thesis—is inadequate. In various ways, the writer should use the conclusion to look beyond the immediate context and consider where the study fits into the whole. One way to do this is to propose directions for future research.

The following questions are particularly relevant to argument:

- Is it clear in the introduction that the essay will focus on argument rather than on exposition? Is the claim one of value or policy?
- Does the author appear reasonable? Has he/she used reason effectively, establishing a chain of logic throughout? Are there failures in logic (logical fallacies)?
- Does the author succeed in making the issue relevant to the reader? Does he/she appeal to the reader's concerns and values?
- Does the essay appear to focus on exposing a problem, critiquing a problem, or settling an issue? Is this focus the best one, given the nature of the topic and the audience?
- Is the order of points appropriate? From weakest to strongest (climax order) or strongest to weakest (reverse climax)?

- Does the essay appear free of bias? Is the voice as objective as possible, given the argumentative stance? Has slanted language been avoided? An accusatory tone? Authors sometimes openly declare their opinions. If this is the case, do you think it was a good strategy?
- Has the author acknowledged the other side? How has he/she responded to the opposing viewpoint? Limited rebuttal? Full rebuttal? Has the author tried to establish a common ground with the reader?
- Does the author make emotional appeals? Are they extreme or manipulative? Are there any emotional fallacies?
- Is the conclusion strong and effective? What makes it so (or does not)?

There is not always a firm line between critical responses and critical analyses, and your instructor may clarify the degree to which you may express your personal views in your analysis. In addition, he or she may require a particular format—for example, one of a specific length. A critical analysis like the one below on "Universities, governments and industry," by Simon N. Young (see p. 216), highlights some of the main features of the source text, using summary, explanation, and evaluation.

A critical analysis of "Universities, governments and industry: Can the essential nature of universities survive the drive to commercialize?" by Simon N. Young

by Emily Kay

Simon N. Young organizes his concerns about today's universities by first making note of significant historical events in the development of higher education, by presenting current trends among universities, and finally by speculating on the anticipated negative effects of these changes. It is reasonable that this essayist expects an audience of university students and faculty to take interest in his claims regarding the changes in today's universities, and Young immediately highlights his credibility by drawing on his 40 years spent in universities. According to Young, these years have provided him with ample opportunity to gain insight into the "idiosyncrasies, foibles and problems" (para. 1) faced by and encountered at the modern university. More specifically, he focuses on his growing concern about the commercialization of universities and the negative effects of this trend. Despite this, Young neglects to propose any feasible resolution. Instead of attempting to settle the issue, Young concludes with a hopeless tone, noting that he "[does] not see any solution" (para.14).

In his introduction, Young plainly announces his purpose "to discuss the current state of university research" as well as "explain why . . . some aspects of the current situation" disturb him (para. 1). The introductory paragraph also clearly presents Young's belief that commercialization "threatens to subvert the very nature of universities." Young then provides an admittedly preferential definition of a university as a "whole body of teachers and scholars engaged in the higher branches of learning" (para. 2). He strategically cites this definition in the beginning of his essay and utilizes it to augment later points.

What follows in the body of his essay is a collection of brief points regarding the historical stages of the evolution of universities and the commercialization that has ensued more recently. Although Young avoids bias, it is clear that social values are at the forefront of his opinions. Young's use of words such as "threat," "danger," and "distortion" in association with commercialization (paras. 8–10) convey his concern for the preservation of universities as a means of broadening knowledge for everyone's benefit—as exemplified in his initial definition of a university. Young frequently refers to today's university researchers as "entrepreneurs" and, in paragraph 8, boldly claims that "there was no threat to the fundamental nature of universities until the drive for commercialization began." Throughout his essay, Young suggests that an either/or situation has occurred at universities, where increasing pressure for economic gain has resulted in the abandonment of concern for widespread societal enrichment. In the latter part of the essay, his focus shifts to the future: he argues that universities are producing a new generation of researchers whose "breadth of vision . . . characteristic of . . . creative researchers" has not been cultivated (para. 12). Young refers again to the definition of a university and leaves readers with the ironic suggestion that modification of this definition may be necessary as the chief priority of universities shifts to "turning ideas into profit" (para. 13).

In general, Young's essay is not discouraging but rather exposes readers to the increasing commercialization among universities. However, his conclusion is not particularly satisfactory as he dwells on the hopelessness of the issue. Instead of making proposals for resolution, Young notes that he remains faithful only because universities have historically adapted to change. In his final comment, Young admits that universities surely can resist commercialization, but he is "just not sure how." This conclusion is ineffective as it leaves the reader feeling helpless. After all, Young has established his credibility with 40 years in the university community; if he cannot suggest alternatives to the current disturbing trends, who can?

Writing summaries

Student researchers are often told that when they use secondary sources in their research essays, they must do more than simply summarize them. Similarly, when students analyze literature, they may be advised to "avoid plot summary." It might be possible to conclude from these examples that summarization plays a relatively minor role in academic discourse and should be discouraged except in special situations. Nothing could be further from the truth: although there are specific times and places for summaries, they are a major part of research-related writing.

Just how important summaries are depends on writing purpose and audience. For example, in book or film reviews written for a general audience, some summary is essential; on the other hand, if you are writing a critical analysis of a book or film for your professor, you might not include summary at all. In the former case, readers need to know the gist of the work being reviewed, perhaps the basic plot and a description of the main characters, since you cannot assume that your readers will have read or seen the work. In the latter case, you can assume that your instructor was sufficiently familiar with the work to assign it, so plot summary would waste precious space. Of course, your instructor *could* assign something that he or she was unfamiliar with, in which case you would probably use some summary.

However, research never occurs in a vacuum; it is part of a collaborative effort. Even the most novel theories and innovative research must be placed within the context of what has been thought and written before. And that is often where summarization comes in.

TIMES AND PLACES FOR SUMMARIES

Summarization is a broadly inclusive term for an activity concerned with *representing the ideas of a writer in a condensed form, using mostly your own words*. The key words in this definition are "represent"—*re*-present—and "condensed"—concentrated. A summary does no more than re-present; it does not interpret or analyze, for example. What a summary re-presents is the essence of the original. Summaries are more concentrated than the work being summarized because they contain only the main ideas, and sometimes only *the* main idea, of the original.

There are many occasions when you will be called on to represent the main ideas of a source. As mentioned, if you are reviewing a work, you will typically summarize its plot or characters before you begin your analysis. If you are critiquing a specific text in order to argue against the author's position, you might begin by summarizing the author's arguments before replying with your own points.

In Type B academic essays, very concentrated summaries called **abstracts** precede the essay, giving an overview of what follows. Unlike most other summaries, however, writers may lift entire phrases directly from the essay itself. Another form of summary occurs in the **literature review** section in which the author, often in a phrase or sentence for each, summarizes the relevant studies in the field, connecting them to his or her own thesis or hypothesis.

However, not all summaries come at the beginning of an essay. Sometimes they occur at the end. Students are familiar with summaries that conclude the traditional "five-paragraph essay." In the conclusion, according to the conventions of this essay type, you reiterate your thesis, using different words but in essence summarizing what you have already told your reader. Academic writers may occasionally use this kind of circular conclusion as well. If the student or academic writer does choose to summarize in the conclusion, the stress will be on reminding the reader about the thesis rather than on applying the thesis or suggesting future research in the subject area.

A special kind of summary is the **annotated bibliography**, found at the end of some academic texts. It is an expanded bibliography that includes not only the bibliographic information of standard bibliographies but also highly condensed summaries of related works. These include studies referred to in the text, but they may also include those not cited there but nonetheless deemed significant. Typically, each entry in the bibliography includes the main point, or thesis, and a comment on what it contributes to the field as a whole—where it fits in. Annotated bibliographies may form appendices to book-length studies.

Some authorities in a subject compile such bibliographies as independent projects. For example, *The world Shakespeare bibliography online* is a massive compilation of annotated entries for "all important books, articles, book reviews, dissertations, theatrical productions, reviews of productions, audiovisual materials, electronic media, and other scholarly and popular materials related to Shakespeare" created in the last 40 years. It includes 40,000 articles, 18,000 books, and more than 500 films in various languages. Students may be assigned a more modest annotated bibliography to be handed in as part of a research project or as an independent project. In either case, the purpose will be to demonstrate students' ability to research and summarize relevant works on a topic.

Summarization can also be used in the middle of an essay. In fact, most of the summarizing you will do in your research essays will be of your sources. Summary is an important feature of scholarly discourse, whether practised by students or academics, because it enables writers to situate their own points relative to those of others. By presenting the main idea(s) of your sources and synthesizing them with your own ideas, you are developing and supporting your thesis. Writers of academic essays, especially Type A essays, rely on this form of development: academic writers summarize the ideas of other writers to support their own point, set up a contrastive point, or otherwise respond to what other experts have said. Student writers may be reluctant to summarize a source, particularly a scholarly one, in order to disagree with him or her, but academic writers often summarize a point, which they proceed to critique, as a way of setting up their own point.

As mentioned previously, students should not shy away from summarizing a source to reveal its shortcomings or limitations. After all, critical thinking, an indispensable reading skill, involves questioning and evaluating, and a full engagement with the text you are using for your research goes well beyond the passive acceptance of its methods and its results.

The amount of space you devote to a summary depends on how you want to use it and on its importance to your thesis. In the case of a review, you want to provide enough plot to enable your reader to grasp what the work was about. If you are summarizing an author's position with which you disagree, you do not want to do more than briefly sketch the main arguments on the other side, unless your purpose in arguing is to reach a compromise rather than to win the argument. If one source is particularly important to your research essay, your summary should be longer than those of less important sources. Summaries, then, can range greatly in length.

THE STAND-ALONE SUMMARY: THE PRÉCIS

Summaries can also serve as ends in themselves. A stand-alone summary, sometimes called a **précis** (meaning something precise), represents all the main points in a complete work or section(s) of a work. In effect, it is a miniature version of the original, following the same order of points as the original but omitting less important sub-points and all detail. The specific guidelines that apply to stand-alone summaries do not apply to all types of summaries, but learning these guidelines and practising them is the best way to learn the exacting art of summary writing. The important skills required in précis writing include the following:

Comprehension skills: Because précis summaries, like most summaries, require you to change the wording of the original, you focus more closely on comprehension than if you quoted the words of the source directly: you have to be clear on content in order to write a successful summary. If you are unsure of a writer's meaning, you need to work at deciphering it before you can re-present it in summary form. Of course, this could mean using contextual clues to determine a word's meaning or looking it up in a dictionary. It could also mean understanding relevant concepts. You can hardly express another's ideas with clarity if you are not clear on their meaning yourself.

Prioritizing skills (establishing a hierarchy of importance): Distinguishing the main ideas from the less important ideas is a fundamental part of the reading process. In précis writing, you often have to go further than this: if you are assigned to write a summary that is 20 to 25 per cent the length of the original (the average range for a précis), you may have to include one or more important sub-points or a key example in addition to the main points in order to achieve the word quota; on the other hand, if your summary is too long, you may have to omit a main point or an important sub-point. In effect, you need to think about the overall importance of a point relative to other points, the importance of a sub-point relative to other sub-points, and so on.

Concision skills: A crucial principle applies to précis writing: the more economical your writing, the more content you can include and the more informed a reader of your summary will be. Therefore, you should strive for concision in your own writing. Wherever possible, too, you should try to tighten up the writing of the original without sacrificing clarity. Focusing on conciseness will serve you well in any writing you do, making you a more conscious and disciplined writer.

Nine pointers for précis writing

When writing précis-style summaries, you should keep the following guidelines in mind:

1. **Follow the exact order of the original**. Points out of order will not result in a summary that mirrors the source. Begin the summary with the thesis or first main point.

2. **Include only the most important points** (the thesis and its major developments). You may include the most important sub-points as well, depending on space. Most sub-points develop or expand a main point in some way.

3. **Avoid all detail**. Detail can be important for support, but in a summary you want only the essence; if a reader wants more information, he or she can read the original. Do not include examples unless they are very important; if an example is important, the writer will probably mention it more than once.

4. **Avoid repetition and reiteration**. Writers often rephrase points to make them clearer. For your summary, choose either the point as first expressed or the rephrasing, not both. However, writers also reiterate to emphasize a point. Ideas stressed in the original should be stressed in your summary too but without creating redundancy.

5. **Do not repeat the author's name or the work's title** any more than necessary.

6. **Do not add your own opinions**. Do not analyze or interpret—simply re-present. Summaries require you to be objective, not to judge the writer or his/her views.

7. **Use your own words**, keeping direct quotations to a minimum. If a significant part of the source is not paraphrasable, you may quote it directly, but ensure that you use quotation marks to show the reader that those exact words occurred in the source. You can also use direct quotation if a word/phrase is significant or memorably expressed. Common everyday words from the original do not have to be placed in quotation marks unless they occur in a phrase of four words or more (the number of words necessitating quotation marks can vary; check with your instructor).

8. **Write economically**. Rephrase the original concisely and check to ensure that you use no more words than you must; use basic words—nouns and verbs, adjectives and adverbs if they are important and can be expressed concisely, and transitions (though sparingly) to create a logical flow between one idea and the next.

9. **Ensure that the verbs you use reflect the author's rhetorical purpose**. For example, if the writer is arguing rather than explaining a point, use a verb that reflects this: The author *argues . . . claims . . . believes . . .* (argument); the author

states . . . explains . . . discusses . . . (exposition). Avoid using strongly argumentative verbs like "condemns" or "denounces"; "criticizes" would be acceptable if the writer is in fact criticizing.

A how-to of précis writing

Reading strategies: Reading to summarize means you should use the forms of selective reading appropriate for this activity. Begin by scanning the text to get its gist—its thesis—and to determine its structure—that is, how the author has divided the text. Determining structure is vital if you use method 2 below, but it is also important in method 1, as can be seen in the sample précis that follows. You can use one of these methods to construct your summary:

1. *Outline method:* Identify main ideas (you can underline them). In paragraphs, these ideas may be found in topic sentences, often but certainly not always the first sentence of the paragraph. Individual sentences may be made up of an independent clause (containing the main idea) and one or more dependent clauses (containing less important ideas). You should also identify important sub-points (developments). For more information, see "Reading paragraphs: Identifying main ideas," p. 66. Prepare an outline that contains all main points and important sub-points. If you wish, you can indent sub-points as in a formal outline. Then write your summary from the outline, using your own words as much as possible and adding transitions to create coherent prose. If the summary exceeds the allowable length, omit the least important sub-point(s). *This method is particularly useful for shorter summaries.*

2. *Section summary method:* Prepare a section-by-section breakdown. Sections can be determined by headings or additional spacing between paragraphs. If there are none, try to determine where the writer has shifted focus or introduced a new concept. Summarize each section in your own words. Aim for one sentence for short sections, two sentences for mid-length sections, and two or three sentences for longer sections. As in the outline method, look for main ideas by trying to identify topic sentences. However, since you are dividing the text differently from the way you would in the outline method, pay strict attention to the opening paragraphs of each section, where the main idea(s) in the section may be introduced. Then combine your section sentences to write your summary, adding transitions to create coherent prose. If the summary exceeds the allowable length, omit the least important sentences. *This method is particularly useful for longer summaries.*

SOME SUMMARY WRITING STRATEGIES

In addition to the guidelines discussed above, you might find the following summarization strategies helpful:

✓ If you find it difficult to identify what is important in a passage, ask whether or how it connects with or contributes to the thesis. Main points usually provide support for the thesis or expand it in some way. If you are summarizing part of a complete work and not all of it, you may not find a thesis; still, every section should contain a controlling idea.

✓ You might find it easier to identify main ideas after you have first put parentheses around what you know are unimportant details and examples. Eliminating the non-essential can make it easier to identify the essential.

✓ For longer works, pay particular attention to the writer's own summaries, which may occur in the introduction, in the conclusion, or toward the end of particularly long or complex sections.

✓ Remember that there is not necessarily a mechanical relationship between ideas and paragraphs. Not all paragraphs are equally important, and not all contain topic sentences. In addition, the introductory paragraph(s) will not necessarily contain important information. In much journalistic writing, for example, opening paragraphs may serve to attract the reader's interest; they may contain little of substance and should in that case be omitted.

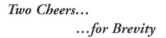 *Two Cheers...*
            ...for Brevity

The following is a section from a book chapter. In the chapter (entitled "Bad borgs?"; see p. 415), the author, Andy Clark, categorizes what he calls "spectres," possible threats to our autonomy posed by today's technology. Read the passage and consider strategies for summarization. The passage is 488 words; a 97-word summary would represent 20 per cent of the original, a typical length for a précis summary.

Overload

One of the most fearsome spectres . . . is that of plain simple overload—the danger of slowly drowning in a sea of contact. As I write, I am painfully aware of the unread messages that will have arrived since I last logged in yesterday evening. By midday there will be around 60 new items, about 10 of which will require action. Ten more may be pure junk mail, easy to spot or filter, but it is the rest that are the real problem. These I read, only to discover they require no immediate thought or action. I call this e-stodge. It is filling without being necessary or nourishing, and there seems to be more of it every day.

The root cause of e-stodge, Neil Gershenfeld has suggested, is a deep but unnoticed shift in the relative costs, in terms of time and effort, of *generating* messages and of *reading* them. Once upon a time, it cost much more—again in terms of time and effort—to create and send a message than to read one. Now, the situation is reversed. It is terribly easy to forward a whole screed to someone else, or to copy a message to all and sundry, just in case they happen to have an opinion or feel they should have been consulted. The length of the message grows as more and more responses get cheaply incorporated. Other forms of overload abound. The incoming messages aren't all e-mail; there are phone calls (on mobile and land lines) and text messages, even the occasional physical letter. There is the constant availability, via the Google-enhanced web, of more information about just about everything at the click of a mouse.

One cure for overload is, of course, simply to unplug. Several prominent academics have simply decided that "e-nough is e-nough" and have turned off their e-mail for good or else redirected it to assistants who sift, screen, and filter. Donald Knuth, a computer scientist who took this very step, quotes the novelist Umberto Eco, "I have reached an age where my main purpose is not to receive messages." Knuth himself asserts that "I have been a happy man since January 1, 1990, when I no longer had an e-mail address."

We won't all be able to unplug or to avail ourselves of intelligent secretarial filters. A better solution, the one championed by Neil Gershenfeld, is to combine intelligent filtering software (to weed out junk mail) with a new kind of business etiquette. What we need is an etiquette that reflects the new cost/benefit ratio according to which the receiver is usually paying the heaviest price in the exchange. That means sparse messages, sent only when action is likely to be required and sent only to those who really need to know—a 007 principle for communication in a densely interconnected world. E-mail only what is absolutely necessary, keep it short, and send it to as few people as possible.

Preparing to summarize: The gist of the above passage should not be hard to determine. If you read the essay carefully, you will see that it is divided into two parts: the first two paragraphs describe a problem, while the last two present possible solutions. The summary, too, should be equally weighted. Unfamiliar words in this section might include "stodge" and "screed," examples of informal diction, meaning, respectively, "something dull or stupid" and "a long piece of writing." Since the passage to be summarized is relatively short, it is best to use the outline method to focus on the main ideas and important developments. These might include the following:

> Para. 1: *Main point* (topic sentence): "One of the most fearsome spectres . . . is that of plain simple overload—the danger of slowly drowning in a sea of contact." This is the controlling idea in this section.

Very important development: E-mail that creates the "real problem" is that which "require[s] no immediate thought or action. I call this e-stodge. It is filling without being necessary or nourishing, and there seems to be more of it every day."

Para. 2: *Main point* (topic sentence): "The root cause of e-stodge, Neil Gershenfeld has suggested, is a deep but unnoticed shift in the relative costs, in terms of time and effort, of *generating* messages and of *reading* them."

Sub-point 1: It is easy today to "forward a whole screed to someone else, or to copy a message to all and sundry."

Sub-point 2: In addition to e-mail, "Other forms of overload abound."

Para. 3: *Main point* (topic sentence): "One cure for overload is, of course, simply to unplug."

Sub-point: "Several prominent academics have simply decided that 'e-nough is e-nough' and have turned off their e-mail for good or else redirected it to assistants who sift, screen, and filter."

Para. 4: *Main point* (topic sentence): "A better solution, the one championed by Neil Gershenfeld, is to combine intelligent filtering software (to weed out junk mail) with a new kind of business etiquette." Note that the first sentence in paragraph 4 connects the main idea in paragraph 3 to paragraph 4, serving as a prompt for the topic sentence in paragraph 4, the second sentence.

Very important development: "E-mail only what is absolutely necessary, keep it short, and send it to as few people as possible." Note that the last three sentences become progressively more specific. The best choice, then, is the final sentence—the most specific.

An important consideration is Clark's reliance on Neil Gershenfeld. The references to Gershenfeld occur in two important points. In constructing the summary, then, it would be advisable to specifically mention Gershenfeld.

What follows is a summary based on the outline above but using different words. Note that the summary does not include sub-point 2 in paragraph 2, because this development is not specifically about the problem of *e-mail*. The sub-point in paragraph 3 is an example that supports the main point in this paragraph but which was deemed relatively unimportant. Of course, there is more than one way to summarize this section. To check its effectiveness, you can refer to the summarization goals on pages 142–4. Does it satisfy these goals?

Summary of "Overload," by Andy Clark

Users of today's technology are in danger of being overwhelmed by unimportant e-mail, which Clark calls "e-stodge." While creating messages used to take longer than reading them, today's problem results from the ease with which one can forward or copy an e-mail to numberless contacts. Although it is possible to sever connection with e-mail entirely or let subordinates handle the problem, Clark favours Neil Gershenfeld's solution, one that uses sophisticated spam filtering with "a new kind of business etiquette." Such a protocol requires that all e-mails be essential, concise, and carefully directed to a select few. (96 words)

Writing research essays

Research essays call on various kinds of reading and writing skills, many of which have been discussed in this text. The usual formats for academic research writing are the essay and the report, discussed in Chapter 3, "An Overview of the Essay." Since research requires you to read your sources closely, it is wise to adopt specific strategies to facilitate this process; such strategies were discussed in Chapter 2, "Keys for Reading Challenging Essays." Further, comprehension of the material depends on your ability to utilize critical thinking skills, which was discussed in the Chapter 2 section "Critical thinking." Responding to texts in writing involves such processes as evaluating, assessing, and comparing sources. These kinds of activities were discussed in "The critical analysis: Explaining the how and why" earlier in this chapter. In addition, identifying which ideas from a source are the most relevant to your topic and integrating them into your own essay are key research skills essential in summarization, which was discussed in "Writing summaries," the previous section of this chapter.

However, the fundamentals of research extend beyond these skills. In this section, we focus on: (1) locating sources in the modern library; (2) assessing the reliability of sources, particularly those accessed electronically; and (3) integrating ideas and words smoothly and efficiently—summarization is only one means of doing so—and giving appropriate credit to your sources. But first, let us begin with some brief comments on the nature of the research process.

PREPARING FOR RESEARCH

A logical question for a student contemplating research is: When is the best time to begin preliminary research? One approach is to begin as soon as you have decided on a topic, although if you wanted to write on something like "energy sources in today's world," you would need to narrow the topic considerably before beginning even the most basic research: the topic is much too large and the information available is overwhelming. However, you can use any of the pre-writing strategies discussed on p. 82 to make the topic more manageable.

One way to narrow the topic of energy sources is to focus on alternatives to fossil fuels, a major contributor to global warming; nuclear power, with its safety and environmental concerns; and thermo-mechanical energy, which is often considered a less viable long-term energy source. You could begin your research into alternative sources by consulting general reference works, such as textbooks, encyclopedias, or dictionaries, along with indexes and guides in the fields of applied science, engineering, and technology. Most of this research must be done either in the library or on-line using your library's electronic resources, since most reference material cannot be taken out of the library.

Your reading will narrow the topic further. It could lead you to three specific energy sources: bio-diesel, solar energy, and hydrogen. However, writing on all three sources in one essay would probably prevent you from going into detail about any of them. Although one option might be simply to randomly select one of the three alternative sources, a better option would be to ask what you or your potential readers might want to know about these energy sources: *Why are these sources important? Who would be interested in knowing about them, and what more do you need to find out about them in order to inform others? Whom could they benefit? What are the potential benefits? What are the potential costs?* Posing these kinds of questions can provide valuable direction and help focus your research. In this case, all these energy sources offer a potential global solution to the energy crisis. *Which of the three offers the best potential?* With this last question in mind, you can recall what you have read about each or continue to browse general works for more background information—in particular, information concerning the costs and benefits of these three energy sources. In the end, you might decide that the most promising is hydrogen. Your thesis statement might take this form:

> Current research into the development of alternative fuels provides hope for an oil and nuclear-free future, but of the different types of alternative fuels, hydrogen is the most promising because it satisfies the requirements for a long-term energy plan.

Now, with a tentative thesis and organizational pattern (cost/benefit analysis), you can conduct further research by turning to specific journals, especially peer-reviewed journals in which academics, scientists, and researchers publish their findings. This is where library search skills enter the picture. Knowing how the modern library works will save you a lot of time and help you find high-quality sources. By following the guidelines in "The Active Voice: A Beginner's Guide to Researching in the Digital Age," below, you will be able to locate specific sources directly relevant to a topic like energy sources in today's world in peer-reviewed journals such as *Renewable and Sustainable Energy Reviews*, *Applied Energy*, and *International Journal of Hydrogen Energy* and non-peer-reviewed but reliable journals such as *New Scientist* and *Scientific American*.

As with most projects involving a combination of skills that develop through *doing them*, doubts, false starts, and occasional frustrations are inevitable. The information that follows on research methods and sources is designed to make this process a more comprehensible and satisfying learning experience, with long-term benefits for your research endeavours.

RESEARCH PROPOSALS

Before you undertake your major research, it is useful to write a **research proposal**, although it can also be written after your research but before you begin composing, in which case it may include an essay outline. The main purpose of a proposal, whether a research proposal for your instructor or the kind of fully developed proposal used in various professions, is to convince a reader that the project you propose is worth doing and that you are the right person to do it. If a professional writer is able to persuade the reader to whom the proposal is directed, such as someone in government, it will be approved, and the writer will receive the funding to proceed. For you, the student researcher, a successful proposal will persuade your instructor that you have done adequate preparation and are on the right track to a successful research essay.

At a bare minimum, research proposals need two parts: (1) a description of what you are undertaking and (2) your methodology. In the first part, you include your thesis and, if known, your main points. You could also include your reason for wanting to research the topic; thus, you could mention your interest in the area or summarize the importance of research in this field to others. You will not be held to the specific terms of your proposal if you discover on further research that you need to amend your thesis or your main points. The proposal represents a *probable* plan: your thesis and main points are tentative at this stage and can be revised if necessary.

In the second part of the proposal, you should include the sources you have found useful so far and the kinds of sources that you will be looking at as you continue your research. Be as specific as possible here as well. Give names of books, journals, websites, and so on, along with article titles. If you are planning other kinds of research, such as interviews or questionnaires, mention them too. The more detail you provide, the more your reader will be convinced. Being specific makes your proposal credible.

A final function of the research proposal is that it gives you a preliminary plan to follow; it solidifies your topic and your approach to the topic in your own mind.

A proposal may even include projected dates, such as the date you plan to begin your major research and the date you plan to complete it.

RECORDING IMPORTANT INFORMATION

Keeping methodical and accurate records during the research phase of the essay-writing process allows you to read material efficiently as well as save time (and your sanity) when you write your paper. You should record notes as you research, ensuring that they include the following information:

- a direct quotation, a summary, or a paraphrase of the writer's idea (if it is a direct quotation, make sure you put quotation marks around it);
- the complete name(s) of the author(s), ensuring correct spelling;
- the complete name(s) of any editors or translators;
- the complete name of the book, journal, magazine, newspaper, or website;
- the title of the specific article, chapter, section, or webpage;
- full publication details, including date, edition, and translation (if appropriate);
- the name of the publisher and the company's location (including province or state) for books;
- in the case of Internet sites, the day you viewed the page, as well as the date of the site or its most recent update;
- the call number of a library book or bound journal (to help you find it again if necessary);
- the page numbers you consulted, both those from which specific ideas came and the full page range of the work (or some other marker, such as paragraphs, for unnumbered Internet documents).

Ensure that you keep your research notes, such as summaries and direct quotations, separate from your personal annotations. Use a method that clearly distinguishes between the two; otherwise, you could end up plagiarizing by failing to attribute the idea or words of a source, thinking they were your own.

Organizing research notes

There are many ways to organize information from your research in order to consult and use it later. The manual method is probably the most familiar to students: cardboard recipe cards, for example, are portable and practical. You can also record notes in a notebook or journal and use tabs to divide the book, using distinct subject headings. In addition, there are a number of software programs available designed to help with planning and organization. For example, *RefWorks* (https://www.refworks.com/) is an Internet-based "citation manager" that allows you to import references from popular databases like *Academic search elite*, *MLA bibliography*, and *EconLit*. Others are databases, such as *EndNote* (http://www.endnote.com/), *Bibliographix* (http://www.bibliographix.com/), and *Nota bene* (http://www.notabene.com/). Students can usually take a tutorial for these programs on their websites or even through their own institution if it has purchased licences allowing students to use them. These programs offer many benefits, such as automatic formatting for a great variety of citation and bibliographic systems.

The Active Voice

A Beginner's Guide to Researching in the Digital Age

The twenty-first-century academic library can seem like an overwhelming conglomeration of print and electronic resources, especially to the undergraduate researcher. In addition to the "traditional" materials found in the library's on-line catalogue (OPAC), there are numerous on-line resources available, including databases, e-journals, e-books, and other digital formats.

The sheer volume of information resources in today's academic library need not be intimidating. On the contrary, an effective research strategy will enable you to take full advantage of the wealth of print and electronic information resources available to you. An effective strategy should include three important considerations:

- your topic or research question;
- the resources that are most likely to contain information about your topic;
- the search strategy you will use to obtain information from those resources.

When you understand how to choose a well-defined research topic, where to look for information on that topic, and how to construct an effective search in a catalogue or database, you will have the basic tools required for most research projects at the first-year level. As you become a more confident researcher, you can expand on these basic strategies by exploring more specialized resources and experimenting with advanced search strategies.

THE RESEARCH TOPIC

The starting point for your research will invariably be your topic. If you are choosing your own topic, you will want to select one that is not too broad or too focused. If your topic is too broad, you will have difficulty focusing your research and writing. If your topic is too narrow or obscure, you may not be able to find enough relevant information to support your thesis. For instance, you may want to write about *homelessness* or *the homeless*.

It would be difficult to write a focused paper on such a broad topic. To narrow your focus, you might want to research homelessness in a particular age group, such as teenagers. However, this would probably still be too broad. You could narrow your focus further by looking at particular health problems of homeless teens or risk factors associated with homelessness in teens, like poverty, addiction, abuse, and so on.

SELECTING RESOURCES
Subject or research guides

Once you have decided on a topic, you must then decide which resources to search for relevant information on your topic. Most academic libraries provide subject or research guides on the library website. These guides are prepared by librarians who are specialists in their particular subject areas. Many research guides provide valuable information on reference resources like dictionaries, encyclopedias, biographies and bibliographies, call number ranges for the subject, key databases, and scholarly websites.

The library catalogue (OPAC)

The OPAC is an important resource for finding print sources like books, encyclopedias, dictionaries, and journals available in your library. Most catalogues also provide hyperlinks to any on-line versions that might be available. Encyclopedias and dictionaries are useful for finding background information on your topic. Books tend to provide a broader overview of your topic as well as the kinds of detail that may not be found in journal articles. Books also feature tables of contents that can help you to identify important aspects of the subject that you may want to examine and bibliographies to help you locate other resources.

On-line databases

A good multidisciplinary database like *Academic search elite* should provide relevant information on most topics. This can be a good place to start your search for journal articles. However, you will also want to take advantage of the many subject and specialized databases available. Most subject areas feature a "core" database that indexes the key journals for that discipline, such as ERIC for education literature or MEDLINE for medical literature. It is important to get to know the core databases in your subject area. If your library has subject guides, these will usually include core databases for each subject. Most libraries will also allow you to select databases by subject in addition to providing an A–Z list. This is especially helpful if the databases include information or abstract pages. These pages provide useful information on the kinds of resources indexed in the database, whether it includes full text, coverage dates available, whether it can be accessed remotely, and anything else that may be pertinent to that particular database.

You will also need to think about the kind of information you require. There is no point searching for complex data or statistical information in an article database. It is unlikely you will be able to find the information you need unless you search a statistical database. Again, the database abstract or information page can help you in determining the types of information the database contains.

Bibliographic versus full-text databases

Bibliographic databases contain a bibliographic record for each item included in the database. The record usually includes the title, author, and other publication information. The database may also provide a brief summary of the article, called an abstract. Full-text databases include the full text of the article or journal in HTML or PDF format in addition to the bibliographic record. Many bibliographic databases also provide linking to on-line journals available through your library's catalogue or document delivery and interlibrary loan (ILL) system. So you should not eliminate a database from your research just because it is not a full-text database. By doing so, you might also eliminate relevant books or articles that might be available in print in the library or that could easily be obtained via document delivery or ILL.

SEARCH STRATEGIES
Determining keywords

The first step of your search strategy is to identify the key concepts from your topic. You will use these concepts as keywords or search terms in the OPAC or databases. For instance, if you want to search for information on risk factors associated with homelessness in youth, you will want to identify keywords that embody the concepts *risk factors* associated with *homelessness* and *youth*. Some risk factors might be *poverty*, *addiction*, *abuse*, etc. *Risk* or *factors* used as search terms would be far too broad and would not provide good search results. *Risk factors* combined as a single term would not find results unless the books or articles used this exact term as well.

Boolean operators

The actual search process, to be effective, should employ some form of Boolean strategy. The most common Boolean operators, AND, OR, and NOT, are used to combine, expand, or eliminate keywords in your search. For instance, AND combines the two different terms homelessness AND youth. A search conducted using AND will also narrow your results compared to searching for each of the keywords separately because sources retrieved must include both terms. The OR operator is used to expand your search results by including other concepts. These may be synonymous concepts or different aspects of a broader concept. In this example, you might want to search for results that include the keywords youth OR teens OR adolescents, which are synonymous concepts. Or you may want to search for poverty OR abuse OR addiction as different aspects of the risk factors concept. The NOT operator eliminates concepts you don't want to be included, such as children, if you don't want results that discuss young children. The NOT operator should be used cautiously, however, because you may eliminate an article that discusses both children and teens and which, therefore, may be relevant to your topic.

Truncation and wildcards

Another useful search strategy is truncation. Truncation symbols enable you to include all variants of a search term. Using the asterisk as the truncation symbol in teen* will ensure that your search results include all the terms: teen, teens, and teenager. Truncation symbols can also be used as wildcards within a word—for instance, in colo*r or wom*n. Used in this way, the wildcard searches for colour and color, woman and women. Most databases and OPACs use the asterisk (*) or a question mark (?) as the truncation or wildcard symbol. However, if you are not sure what symbol to use, check the "help" menu. The help menu will also provide information on other advanced search strategies that can be used in that particular catalogue or database.

Search options

On-line catalogues and databases usually feature simple or basic search and advanced search options. The basic search field can be used to enter single terms or more complex search statements using Boolean operators. To construct a search statement using Boolean in the basic search field, you must use parentheses to separate the OR terms from the AND terms as indicated below:

(Homeless* OR runaway*) AND (teen* OR adolescen* OR youth) AND (poverty OR abuse OR addiction*)

Also, if you want to use a combined term such as "risk factors," you must use quotation marks unless the field provides the option to search two or more words as a phrase. The advanced search option is set up to allow you to insert your terms and then select AND, OR, or NOT from a drop-down menu. The advanced search option also allows you to search for terms in various fields, such as *keyword* (usually the default), *abstract*, *title*, *descriptor* or *subject heading*. By selecting a specific field, you limit the search for your term to that field alone. It is often best to try a search in the keyword field initially and then try other advanced strategies to refine your results if necessary.

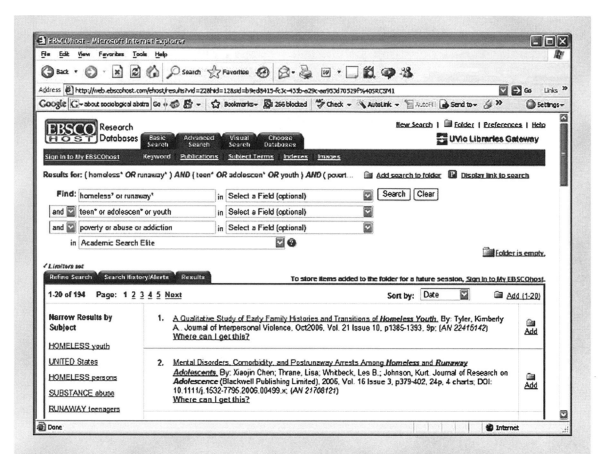

Subject headings or descriptors: Subject headings or descriptors are very useful for refining your search strategy. One or more Library of Congress subject headings are applied to most of the resources found in your library's OPAC. Subject headings are included in the bibliographic record to indicate what a book, journal, or other resource is about. Most on-line library catalogues provide subject headings that are hyperlinked to other resources with the same heading. This is a good way to find other titles that have been assigned the same subject heading. Additionally, there may be a hyperlink for the call number that will direct you to other items in the immediate call number range.

Subject headings or descriptors in databases constitute the thesaurus or "controlled language" of the database. The headings have been applied to each entry to describe what it is about. It is not merely a keyword found in the article or abstract, although it may be that as well. Take note of the subject headings for your most relevant hits in your initial keyword searches. Using these terms in a repeat search will often produce more relevant results.

Limiters: Another search strategy is limiting or using the limiters available to you in a particular database. This strategy is generally used to limit your results if there are too many

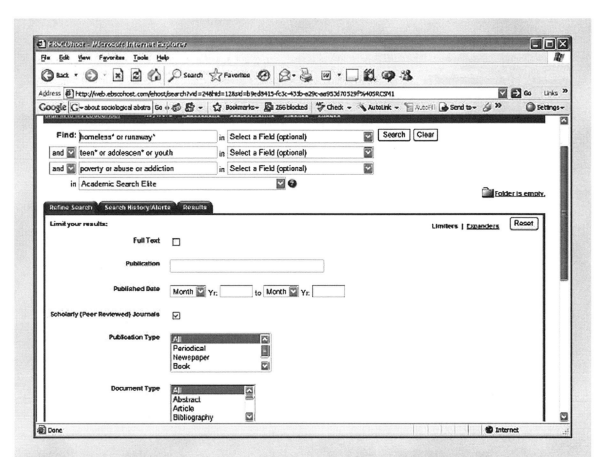

or to limit them to a particular date range, article type, format, publication, etc. One very useful limiter found in many databases is the scholarly or peer-reviewed limiter, if you want your results to include only scholarly articles. Some databases will do this for you automatically. Others require you to check off a box or select "peer-reviewed" from a drop-down menu.

Saving your results: Most databases and OPACs provide a marking and saving feature. You can select your most relevant results, mark them by ticking a check box or adding them to a folder, and then choose from several options—usually print, e-mail, or save. Saving often enables you to download or export to the bibliographic management software of your choice. Some databases also save your search history so that you can go back and make revisions or combine one or more searches you have previously attempted.

Refining your strategy

One final consideration for effective library research is refining your strategy throughout the process. It may be necessary to re-evaluate your topic or your choice of databases. You may also want to try different search terms and Boolean combinations. This is not an indication that your strategy is not a good one or has failed. Rather, it is a natural part of the research process to try different approaches and strategies in order to find the most relevant information. It is important, therefore, to start your library research early. This will allow you the necessary time to find and evaluate your information and obtain any materials unavailable on-line or in your library by interlibrary loan.

Danielle Russell, information services librarian
English and rare books, University of Victoria

Using credible sources
CREDIBILITY ISSUES

Critical thinking applies to more than just the writer's ideas, the validity of claims, and the adequacy of their support. If the premise behind a claim seems invalid or any piece of evidence suspect, the credibility of the writer will be in doubt. The explosion of information via the Internet has made it more difficult to assess the validity and authority of written information. Because the boundaries are sometimes blurred between knowledge and speculation, fact and opinion, those who surf the net, reading indiscriminately, may not be able to distinguish readily between what is valid information from a credible source and what is not. (See "The Active Voice: Google and the Invisible Web: Using Library Resources for Deeper and Broader Research," p. 167.)

Assessing credibility applies to non-electronic sources too, of course, but the Internet has increasingly become a forum for personal opinion, some of it informed, some of it uninformed. Today's student researcher must be able to distinguish between reliable and potentially unreliable sources by reading carefully and asking questions about the source's sponsor(s) and/or author(s), along with the accuracy, currency, objectivity, and scope of the information.

The criteria above apply particularly to open-access resources, from Google Scholar to the enormously vast array of commercial, governmental, and personal websites that anyone sitting in front of a computer screen can view. In contrast to these are the more predictably authoritative resources accessed through your institution's library home page. The way you use these open-access resources, or *if* you use them in your research (your instructor may specify whether he or she considers them legitimate sources for your essay), depends on what kind of information you are looking for. You should first consider your purpose for seeking out a source. Is it for reliable information from an objective source with evidence-gathering methods beyond reproach (Statistics Canada, for example), or is it to learn about a particular viewpoint? In the latter case, it might be acceptable to use a website that advocates a position or supports a cause. If you were writing an essay on animal rights, you might want to access People for the Ethical Treatment of Animals (PETA) or Animal Rights Canada, since their advocacy of animal rights is clear and above board—which is not to say that their information is always factual or accurate.

Not all websites, however, are forthcoming in acknowledging their true stake in an issue, nor do all websites use quality control to ensure the accuracy of their content. Even seemingly reliable and objective websites, such as those affiliated with governments, may be a source of misleading or outdated information. The criteria below are therefore relevant to most sources you access via the Internet.

Sponsors and authors

- What group or individual has erected the site or assumes responsibility for its content? If the organization/individual is unfamiliar, try to find (a) its parent organization, (b) affiliated organizations, or (c) a mission statement or similar claim concerning the organization's and/or website's purpose. If this information is not on the home page, it could be accessible from the home page. You should be suspicious of websites lacking these forms of self-identification.
- Who are the authors of the material on the website? Are names and affiliations given? Biographies? If the names of specific writers are not provided, what about names of the group's officers or officials? Is contact information provided? Mailing address, telephone number, e-mail address? Note the domain of the website or e-mail address: the most common ones in North America are ".edu" (US) and ".ca" (Canada), preceded by an abbreviated form of the institution's name (these indicate degree-granting colleges or universities); ".gov" (a government source); ".org" (a non-profit organization); and ".com" (a commercial site).

Accuracy and currency

- What is the source of the content? Are informational sources identified—by author, title, date? How has statistical information been calculated (e.g., through censuses, surveys, questionnaires by reliable organizations)? How are statistical information and other factual data being used? Does the use seem consistent with the website's purpose?
- Are all claims and other statements reasonable and well-supported?
- What is the original date of the site? Has it been updated recently? Does factual information appear verifiable? Can it be verified by checking a reliable and unaffiliated website? Does the website have a maintainer and a way to contact this person?

Objectivity

- Does the content seem presented without bias? Could it be considered politicized in any way? Does it seem to address a specific reader (e.g., is the voice familiar and informal?) or directed more toward a general reader? Do statements seem provocative? Is the tone neutral? Can you identify any slanted language or bias?
- If opinion is evident, is it clearly differentiated from fact? Are other points of view besides those of the author/organization represented? How are they treated?
- Is there any advertising on the site?

Scope and comprehensiveness

- Does the site appear to include different views of and approaches to issues?
- Is there a menu or site map that provides an overview of content? (You could get an indication of scope from that.)
- Are there links to other sites? Do these sites appear reliable?
- Does content primarily consist of text, or are there photos or other graphics? What is the approximate proportion of text to graphics (it is no hard and fast rule, but unless the purpose of the site is to display visual material, text should outweigh graphics)? Are there accompanying charts, graphs, or other illustrative material? If so, do they seem designed to explain and summarize (as opposed to having a merely decorative purpose)?

Other issues

- Is the information on the website easy to access? Does it appear well-organized? What specific resources are designed to enhance accessibility or ease of site navigation? A site that is designed to facilitate access to information has at least thought about its potential readers.
- Is the site appealing and attractive rather than just glitzy?

See p. 184 for an example of a student report that critically evaluates a website and a peer-reviewed article for credibility and other related factors.

In the following essay, the writer uses the techniques referred to in "The Active Voice: A Beginner's Guide to Researching in the Digital Age," p. 158, to compare the effectiveness of the search engine Google with that of the resources of the "deep" web, such as bibliographic databases that can be accessed through your institution's library.

The Active Voice

Google and the Invisible Web: Using Library Resources for Deeper and Broader Research

The world wide web (WWW) is a window on many worlds. A few words in Google can lead to more than enough information on almost any topic. But is it the "best" information? Can this information be retrieved comprehensively? Much of the "best," more scholarly information is not accessible, either hidden in private sources or available only for a fee. These commercial and private sources represent much of the "deep" or "invisible" web,[1] the huge part of the world wide web not reached by the spiders of the search engines.[2] This essay argues that Google and similar tools open up windows to only some of the worlds accessible via the WWW. It draws attention to the commercial bibliographic databases indexing the literature of specific subjects and providing retrieval tools more appropriate for the subject than Google. Libraries are licensing these databases for their clientele, opening up the "deep" web and the information inaccessible on the surface of the web through search engines.

The web is indiscriminate, with no restrictions on what may be put up by whom. Web search engines rate sites using various criteria. Google uses word frequency counts and gives priority to sites that are linked on many others. In the scholarly literature, books and articles more highly cited are considered better, but this basic principle does not always apply to Google: because the web is so inclusive with commercial, popular, and self-published as well as scholarly sites rated by popularity, much of the best material—especially on popular topics—is not given priority because it is less popular than the material on non-scholarly sites.

Even though the WWW is undergoing rapid change and more information is easily accessible, two unvarying features of the use for information mean that a Google search may never be enough. First is the need in searching for an adaptable view that brings together similar items, even if they don't use the same words for the same concepts. For example, computers do not recognize terms from their context; they cannot tell if a hedge is a row of plants or a type of fund. Humans recognize that information on Shakespeare and Chekhov would be relevant to a search on playwrights, but all terms, general and specific, must be input into Google to ensure a comprehensive search. Second is the need for critical appraisal, bringing out features other than word frequency or popularity. The availability of tools for extracting the best items (peer-reviewed, in more important journals) and selection of what is indexed based on quality address this need. While Google pulls *more information*, these features lead to a focus on the *best* information.

Bibliographic databases licensed by libraries for their users bring together and index items, print and electronic, of the literature on particular topics. They give structure to this literature by using standard vocabulary and, often, concepts. Examples are *PsycInfo* for psychology and the *MLA (Modern Language Association) bibliography* for literary criticism. As a health librarian, I use *MEDLINE* daily. It indexes some 13 million citations and gives structure to the literature of the health sciences from research to clinical practice.

Comparing search results on Google to bibliographic databases makes the differences apparent. For example, a search[3] on "seasonal affective disorder" on *PsycInfo* led to 671 articles focusing on that topic, including a chapter from a 2006 book. The particular interface I used, Ovid, allows limits to be applied, including restricting the search results to review articles only, leading to 32 articles; for many of these, my university offered direct connections to the full text. Google provided some useful information but mostly targeted patients. Google Scholar did not work well for this topic, linking to many older scholarly articles. Interestingly, my library's catalogue provided some good, recent printed books on this topic that neither source retrieved. In summary, Google and *PsycInfo* both led to quality articles on seasonal affective disorder; however, Google provided information at a more basic level understandable to patients while *PsycInfo* accessed more scholarly material.

I also tried a search on music in eighteenth-century literature using Google and the *MLA bibliography*. This search proved treacherous, particularly for Google, with retrieval including sites and articles discussing music <u>and</u> literature, not music <u>in</u> literature, in the eighteenth century. I tried the "advanced search" with "music in literature" in Google. A few of the hits looked useful, leading me to use Google Scholar for the same topic. It performed even better (no CVs of faculty studying music in literature), although some citations on Shakespeare and Thomas Mann showed the indiscriminate nature of a Google search. A basic search in *MLA bibliography* pulled some good hits but also much dross. Using "advanced search" allows searches to be entered using "period"—I used "1700–1799"—and "literary theme"—I used "music OR musical." All hits were relevant, although a number were in foreign languages. More specific topics—music in the writing of Goethe and Rousseau—suggested themselves. In this example, once more I found Google and Google Scholar generated more links that were irrelevant, while *MLA bibliography* enabled me to gain access to information specific to the topic.

Four similar examples were examined more carefully in a recent article.[4] The authors found that "Google is superior for coverage and accessibility. Library systems are superior for quality of results. . . . Improving the skills of the searcher is likely to give better results from the library systems, but not from Google."

There are hundreds of bibliographic databases, large and small, general and specific, reflecting the structure and communication patterns of the literatures of many subjects.

Some of these databases are accessed via web search engines such as Google Scholar, but access is generally restricted to users verified as members of a library's clientele. While there are sometimes a number of interfaces to a database, and some interfaces are better than others, the various databases can generally be searched using techniques and vocabulary that suit the particular discipline indexed. Precise searches can be executed on specific topics. Databases collecting together and organizing the information of a discipline and made accessible with effective retrieval tools represent powerful adjuncts to the wide-ranging, indiscriminant search engines of the WWW.

So, Google away. But are Google and friends good enough? As a librarian, I say "No!" Using Google, you will find much useful information, much of high quality, some the "best" available. For complete and more precise searches, you will need to augment Google with the databases of the deep web that index the literature on the topic you are exploring. How scholars communicate, even who are "scholars," is being changed by the web and the free flow of information. Google will turn up items made available outside the controlled world of scholarly communication and that increasingly reach into that world. Databases indexing the published literature point to items beyond standard search engines using more varied concepts and interfaces adapted to the topic of the literature. As a librarian, I am pleased that a variety of tools is making information more accessible. I am thrilled that the value placed on using information, applying what is known, has increased. With the surface of the web readily accessible via Google and friends and with increasing understanding of the value of databases provided by libraries, more of the best information is going to reach and address the needs of more people.

---

[1] For a bibliography, see Egger-Sider F, Devine J. "Beyond Google: the invisible web." May 2003, revised August 2005. http://www.lagcc.cuny.edu/Library/invisibleweb/webography.htm (accessed 9 October 2006). It includes the key paper, Berg MK. "White paper: the deep web: surfacing hidden value." *Journal of electronic publishing.* 7(1) 2001. http://www.press.umich.ued/jep/07-01/bergman.html (accessed 9 October 2006).

[2] At least, these robots did not reach them until recently. With Google Scholar, a small number of commercial sources were opened, although the sources themselves still require payment before they can be viewed.

[3] All searches done October 2006.

[4] Brophy J, Bawden D. "Is Google enough? Comparison of an internet search engine with academic library resources. *Aslib proceedings: new information perspectives.* 57(6) 2005: 498–512.

Jim Henderson, life sciences librarian, McGill University

Integrating and documenting sources

When you integrate your research sources into your essay, you can use one or more of several methods to combine the source material with your own words. When you document these sources, you use a standardized format to show your readers where you obtained this material. Typically, you integrate, or synthesize, your sources as part of the composing process. Documenting your sources is often the final stage in the composing process—either of the rough draft or of a later draft. The value in documenting as early as possible in the process, however, is that it will give you ample time to check and double-check the accuracy of your sources.

INTEGRATING YOUR SOURCES
Summary versus paraphrase

When you **summarize** a source, you extract an idea (ideas) from the source that is directly relevant to your essay, expressing it in your own words. If you wanted to summarize a large portion of the original, you would follow the guidelines for précis summaries (see p. 148). What distinguishes a summary from a **paraphrase** is that summaries are selective: they focus on main ideas. When you paraphrase, you include *all the original, putting it in your own words.* You could paraphrase anything from a part of a sentence to one or two paragraphs. Paraphrasing is reserved for very important information. Whereas a summary condenses and is thus an efficient method for synthesizing material, a paraphrased passage is not usually shorter than the original—in fact, it may be longer. Because you include so much in a paraphrase, you must be careful to use completely different wording or you may unknowingly be plagiarizing. Changing the order of the original will also help you avoid plagiarism (see "Plagiarism," below).

Direct quotation and mixed format

Like a paraphrase, a direct quotation applies to specific content. When you represent a source by **direct quotation**, you use exactly the same words as the original, enclosing them within quotation marks. Reports and Type B essays make sparing use of direct quotations, but they are often used with other essay formats. Humanities essays that analyze primary sources, such as literary or historical texts, may depend on direct quotations for support. Researchers in the social sciences who use interviews or observe group interactions as part of their methodology may also rely on direct quotations.

With the exception of such discipline-related situations and the specific contexts outlined below, prefer summary or paraphrase to direct quotation. When you summarize or paraphrase, you concretely demonstrate your comprehension of a source by "translating" it into your own words. Quoting directly may demonstrate no more than your understanding of the relevance and importance of the source to your topic. Therefore, if there is no compelling reason to use direct quotation, use summary, paraphrase, or a mixed format (see below) instead.

> Direct quotation unnecessary or inappropriate: "Pilot error accounted for 34 per cent of major airline crashes between 1990 and 1996, compared with 43 per cent from 1983 to 1989." Statistical detail does not need to be quoted directly.

Paraphrase: In the six-year period between 1990 and 1996, 34 per cent of major airline crashes were due to pilot error, a decrease of 9 per cent over the previous six-year period.

"Students often find ways to compensate for their symptoms of ADD in their earlier years so that the disorder reveals itself only with the increased intellectual and organizational demands of college." If factual material can be easily put in your own words, prefer summary or paraphrase to direct quotation.

Summary: Because of the greater demands of college compared to those in the earlier grades, students with ADD may not have to confront their disorder until college.

In a **mixed format**, you combine summary or paraphrase with direct quotation. Effective use of mixed format demonstrates both your understanding and polished writing skills since it requires you to seamlessly integrate the language of the source with your own language. You can use this format when you want to cite part of an important passage in which key words or phrases occur, carefully choosing the significant words and excluding the less important parts.

Specific contexts for using direct and mixed quotations: You can use direct or mixed quotations if you want to define something or if the exact wording is important for another reason—for example, to lend authority to your point or if the wording of the source is particularly significant or memorable:

The Yerkes-Dodson law "predicts an inverted U relationship between arousal and performance and that the optimal level of arousal for a beginner is considerably less than that for an expert performing the same task" (Oxford dictionary of sports science and medicine). The definition of a specialized term makes direct quotation a good choice.

"The genius of a free and democratic people is manifested in its capacity and willingness to devise institutions and laws that secure fairness and equitable opportunities for citizens to influence democratic governance" (Royal Commission on Electoral Reform and Party Financing). Using direct quotation is appropriate because the writer wants to stress the authority of the source.

According to Sir Clifford Sifton, Prime Minister Wilfrid Laurier's interior minister, Canada was to be "a nation of good farmers," meaning Asian immigration was discouraged (Royal Commission

24). The writer uses a mixed format, quoting a significant phrase to reveal discrimination against Asians in the first decade of the twentieth century in Canada.

Integrating quotations: When you incorporate direct quotations into your essay, you must do so grammatically and smoothly; you must also provide enough context for the reader to grasp their significance. The following shows a poorly integrated quotation and its well-integrated alternative:

> An unloving parent-child relationship can be characterized as "unaccepted, unacknowledged, or unloved" (Haworth-Hoeppner 216).
>
> Well-integrated: An unloving parent-child relationship exists when the child feels "unaccepted, unacknowledged, or unloved" (Haworth-Hoeppner 216).

Omitting, adding, or changing material

You may choose to delete quoted material in the interests of efficiency or add material in the interests of completeness or clarity. You may also have to make minor changes to a source for grammatical or stylistic reasons. Whenever you alter a direct quotation, you must indicate these changes to the reader.

Omitting: You may want to omit part of a sentence if it is irrelevant or unimportant for your purposes. To indicate an omission of one or more words in the middle of a sentence, use an **ellipsis** (the word means "omission"), which consists of three spaced dots. If you leave out all the words to the end of the sentence (and even if you leave out the following sentence), add a fourth dot, which represents the period at the end of the sentence:

> Original: Hockey—indeed almost any professional sport today—may be taken as an example of what the late French philosopher Guy Debord called the "triumph of visual spectacle": reality constantly filtered through the distorting prism of contrived images. And it's a pernicious development. (Posner. "Image world")
>
> Words omitted in the middle of the first sentence: "Hockey . . . may be taken as an example of what the late French philosopher Guy Debord called the 'triumph of visual spectacle': reality constantly filtered through the distorting prism of contrived images."
>
> The rest of the sentence omitted: "Hockey—indeed almost any professional sport today—may be taken as an example of what the

late French philosopher Guy Debord called the 'triumph of visual spectacle.'. . . And it's a pernicious development."

Note that the single quotation marks around "triumph of visual spectacle" shows that the phrase was in quotation marks in the original.

Adding and changing: If you add or change material, you need to indicate this by using **brackets** (brackets are square; parentheses are rounded). Changes can be made for grammatical, stylistic, or clarification purposes. The following examples from "Being stigmatized and being sorry: Past injustices and contemporary citizenship," by Matt James, illustrate some of the different reasons for using brackets to add or change the words of a source. James also uses ellipses to indicate omitted words:

Grammatical (plural required): Cairns suggests that the increased constitutional emphasis on equality, which followed the 1982 entrenchment of the Charter of Rights, has encouraged redress movements to seek "compensatory treatment . . . for past injustice[s]. . ." (Reconfigurations 25).

Stylistic (upper case "T" to begin a sentence): As former residential-school student Gilbert Oskaboose wrote in 1996: "when we returned to our communities we had become strangers. . . . [T]he politics of assimilation . . . brought pain, suffering, lost lives, vicious in-fighting, divisions, waste and sorrow" (4).

Clarification (to replace "they"): As survivor John Amagoalik has recounted, "we just went into a panic because [the RCMP] had promised that they would not separate us" (qtd. in Marcus 21).

DOCUMENTING YOUR SOURCES

Documenting sources serves several practical purposes: it enables a reader to distinguish between your ideas and someone else's, and it makes it possible for any reader to access the source itself, either to ensure its accuracy or to focus on its content. Documentation formats (called **styles**) provide a coherent and consistent way for scholars to communicate with other scholars (and also with student researchers, who must learn the fundamentals of documentation formats in order to use them in their essays).

Plagiarism

Plagiarism is an extremely serious academic offence. A surprisingly large number of students approaching post-secondary study believe that plagiarism is limited to cases in which they use direct quotations and fail to cite their sources. In fact, plagiarism encompasses much more than this: you plagiarize if you use any material that is not your own—whether you quote directly, summarize, paraphrase, or refer to it in passing in your essay—without acknowledging it. But it is not only lack of acknowledgement that constitutes plagiarism: you also plagiarize if you use the exact words of the source and do not put them in quotation marks; in the former case, you would be passing off someone else's *ideas* as your own, while in the latter, you are, in effect, passing their *words* off as your own. Finally, you are plagiarizing if you follow the structure of the original too closely.

Specifically, what kind of information must be acknowledged and what does not need to be? Two principles can guide you as you consider the question—to document or not to document. You do not need to cite anything that falls under the category of **general knowledge**. If a typical reader is likely to know something, a citation may be unnecessary. Further, if a fact or idea is **easily obtainable**, a citation may also be unnecessary. (However, you may be asked to mention a specific number of sources to satisfy the "easily obtainable" factor—often three.) Both these categories depend on your audience; for example, if you were writing for an audience that was knowledgeable about the topic, your essay would probably contain fewer citations than if you were writing for a general audience that was less knowledgeable and would probably find it difficult to trace the information. If in doubt, err on the side of caution and make the citation.

MAJOR DOCUMENTATION STYLES

There are four major documentation styles but many variants on these styles. The *Modern Language Association* (MLA) style is widely used in the humanities, including English. The *American Psychological Association* (APA) style is used in many social science disciplines and some science disciplines, as well as in education and business. Both are parenthetical styles, meaning that a brief citation including the author's name and page number (MLA) or name and publication year (APA) follows the reference in the text of an essay.

Both the *Chicago Manual of Style* (CMS), used in history, and the *Council of Science Editors* (CSE) style, used in mathematics, biology, health sciences, and some other science disciplines, follow a number/note method. Superscript (raised) numbers are placed after the in-text references; they correspond to the numbers at the end of the document where full bibliographical information is given (in the Chicago style, these notes can also be placed at the foot of the page). MLA, APA, and CMS styles also require a final-page listing of sources alphabetically by last name. CSE style requires a listing of sources that follows the order they were used in the text. Note: CSE also gives guidelines for an author/year system similar to that of the American Psychological Association; however, as the number/note method is more common, it is outlined below.

Students and teachers alike are sometimes frustrated by the many small differences among the styles, especially between the parenthetical styles, MLA and APA. This frustration may be compounded by the existence of variant style guides in disciplines like chemistry, engineering, law, and others. Many book publishers use a distinct "house" style, and different departments at your institution may publish their own set of guidelines applicable to students in that discipline. The major manuals are also constantly changing as new editions are brought out. Fortunately, there are an increasing number of on-line resources for those confused by the array of documentation styles; college or university library sources are the most reliable. Each of the organizations that produce the manuals also maintains websites where updates are posted. Further, when you decide on an area of study, you will become familiar with the style prominent in your discipline.

Many of the distinguishing features of the styles are given below. Examples of the most common bibliographic formats are then provided. Note: A **signal phrase** names the author before the reference is given; thus, in MLA and APA styles, the parenthetical citation will not include the author's name if a signal phrase precedes it.

Electronic formats in all styles should include as much information as is available. If an author's name is not given, use the name of the organization or sponsoring group in its place. If there is no sponsor, use the work's title alphabetized by the first major word. MLA, APA, and CSE styles require you to include date of access for Internet citations; CMS style does not. Paragraph number or section heading can be used to identify location, if necessary, in the absence of standard page numbering.

MLA (Modern Language Association) style

- MLA uses an "author/number" referencing format. Basic parenthetical format includes author's last name and page number with no punctuation in between.
  e.g., (Slotkin 75); (Rusel and Wilson 122)
- If a signal phrase is used, only the page number will be in parentheses.
  e.g., "Slotkin states . . . (75)"
- Block quotations should be used for important passages at least four typed lines long. They are indented 10 spaces from the left margin, double-spaced, and do not include quotation marks. The end period precedes the parenthetical citation.
- The final page, titled "Works Cited," alphabetically lists by author's last name all works used in the essay. Entries are double-spaced with the first line flush left and successive lines indented one-half inch. All major words in titles begin with a capital letter. Names of books and journals may be italicized or underlined (MLA prefers underlining for student research essays).

APA (American Psychological Association) style

- APA uses an "author/year" referencing format. One basic format includes author's last name and year of publication (general references and summaries); the other basic format also includes page number (for direct quotations and paraphrases).
- Commas separate author's name from year and year from page number (if required); "p." or "pp." (for more than one page) precedes page number(s).
  e.g., (Huyer, 1997, p. 43); (Bryson & de Castell, 1998, pp. 542–544)
- If a signal phrase is used, the year will follow the author's name in parentheses.
  e.g., "Huyer (1997) explains . . ."; if a page number is required, it will be placed in parentheses after the reference: e.g., " . . . (p. 43)"

- Works by the same author(s) from the same year are assigned different letters—e.g., 2004a, 2004b. They are listed this way in "References" alphabetically by title.
- Block quotations should be used for important passages more than 40 words long. They are indented five spaces from the left margin, double-spaced, and do not include quotation marks. The end period precedes the parenthetical citation.
- The final page, titled "References," alphabetically lists by author's last name all works used in the essay; authors' initials are used, not given names. Entries are double-spaced with the first line flush left and successive lines indented five spaces. In article and book titles, only the first letter of first words, first words following colons, and proper nouns, along with all letters in acronyms, are capitalized.

CMS (Chicago Manual of Style) style

- CMS uses the "note" referencing format with numbered footnotes (at the bottom of the page) or endnotes (at the end of the text) corresponding to superscript numbers in the text of the essay. Each entry is single-spaced with the first line indented five spaces and successive lines flush left.
- Full bibliographic details are given for first references, beginning with author's first name(s), followed by surname, work's title, and (in parentheses) place of publication, publisher, and date, and ending with page number(s).

  e.g., "As is well known, the sociobiologist E.O. Wilson has entitled one of his books *Consilience*."[15] The note would look like this:

  15. Edward O. Wilson, *Consilience: The Unity of Knowledge* (New York: Alfred A. Knopf, 1998).

  Successive references are condensed forms of the first citation:

  18. Wilson, *Consilience*, 55.

  Consecutive references to the same work:

  19. Ibid. (the page number would follow if different from preceding note)
- Block quotations should be used for important passages at least four typed lines long. They are indented five spaces from the left margin, double-spaced, and do not include quotation marks. The end period precedes the parenthetical citation.
- On the final page, titled "Bibliography," entries are listed alphabetically by author's last name. Entries are single-spaced with double-spacing between them; the first line is flush left, and successive lines are indented five spaces.

CSE (Council of Science Editors) style

- CSE uses the "citation/sequence" referencing format with superscript or bracketed numbers corresponding to numbered sources at the end of the text in a separate section.
- To cite more than one source for a specific reference, each source number is included, followed by a comma with no space between; a dash is used to indicate consecutive sources (e.g., 2–5).

e.g., "There is increasing evidence for the efficacy of exercise [10,11] and fish oils [12,13] in the treatment and prevention of depression."

- For references to a source for a second time or more, the number first assigned to the source continues to be used.
- On the final page, titled "References" or "Cited References," authors are listed beginning with author's last name followed by initial(s) with no spaces or periods between initials. The order of entries is based on their sequence in the text (i.e., the first cited source is assigned the number 1, the second one the number 2, etc.). Entries are single-spaced with double-spacing between them.

COMMON FORMATS: SAMPLE CITATIONS
Book (one author)

MLA: Berger, Arthur Asa. Video Games: A Popular Culture Phenomenon. New Brunswick, NJ: Transaction, 2002.

APA: Heyd, D. (1992). *Genetics: Moral issues in the creation of people.* Berkeley: University of California Press.

CMS: *Note:*
1. Keith D. McFarland, *The Korean War: An Annotated Bibliography* (New York: Garland, 1986), 91.
Bibliography:
McFarland, Keith D. *The Korean War: An Annotated Bibliography.* New York: Garland, 1986.

CSE: 1. Fleiss JL. The design and analysis of clinical experiments. New York (NY): John Wiley and Sons; 1986.

Book/journal (multiple authors)

MLA: Bolaria, B. Singh, and Peter S. Li. Racial Oppression in Canada. 2nd edn. Toronto: Garamond Press, 1988. (second author's name is not reversed)
More than three authors: Name of first author given, followed by a comma and "et al."

APA: Sahalein, R., & Tuttle, D. (1997). *Creatine: Nature's muscle builder.* Garden City Park, New York: Avery Publishing Group. (second author's name is reversed.)
Three to six authors: give all names; *more than six:* list first six followed by "et al."

CMS: *Note:*

2. Bob Beal and Rod Macleod, *Prairie Fire: The 1885 North-West Rebellion* (Edmonton: Hurtig Publishers, 1984), 104–7.

More than three authors: name of first author given, followed by "and others."

Bibliography:

Beal, Bob, and Rod Macleod. *Prairie Fire: The 1885 North-West Rebellion.* Edmonton: Hurtig Publishers, 1984.

More than three authors: all authors are named (second author's name is not reversed).

CSE: 2. Thursby, JG, Thursby, MC. Intellectual property: university licensing and the Bayh-Dole Act. Science 2003;301:1052.

More than 10 authors: names of 10 listed, followed by "and others."

Selection in edited work

All entries give page range; in-text citations in MLA, APA, and CMS give specific page(s) referred to.

MLA: Wright, Austin M. "On Defining the Short Story: The Genre Question." <u>Short Story Theory at a Crossroads</u>. Ed. Susan Lohafer and Jo Ellyn Clarey. Baton Rouge: Louisiana State UP, 1989. 46–63. (UP is the abbreviation for *University Press*)

APA: Chesney-Lind, M. & Brown, M. (1999). Girls and violence: An overview. In D. Flannery & C. R. Huff (Eds.), *Youth violence: Prevention, intervention and social policy* (pp. 171–199). Washington, D.C.: American Psychiatric Press.

CMS: *Note:*

3. Marcia K. Lieberman, "'Some Day My Prince Will Come': Female Acculturation through the Fairy Tale," in *Don't Bet on the Prince*, ed. Jack Zipes and Ingrid Svendsen (New York: Routledge, 1987), 185–200.

Bibliography:

Lieberman, Marcia K. "'Some Day My Prince Will Come': Female Acculturation through the Fairy Tale." In *Don't Bet on the Prince*, edited by Jack Zipes and Ingrid Svendsen, 185–200. New York: Routledge, 1987.

CSE: 3. Saper CB, Iversen S, Frackowiak R. Integration of sensory and motor function: the association areas of the cerebral cortex and the cognitive capabilities of the brain. In: Kandel ER, Schwartz JH, Jessell TM, editors. Principles of neural science. 4th ed. New York (NY): McGraw-Hill; 2000. p. 349–380.

Journal article

MLA: Fetterley, Judith. "*Little Women:* Alcott's Civil War." Feminist Studies 5 (1979): 369–83.

Journals with continuous pagination use volume number only (as above); journals paginated by issue (i.e., page numbering begins with each issue) include issue number in addition to volume number—e.g., Feminist Studies 5.2 (1979).

APA: Clegg, S., Mayfield, W., & Trayhurn, D. (1999). Disciplinary discourses: A case study of gender in information technology and design courses. *Gender and Education, 11*(1), 43–55.

Volume number is italicized; issue number (where required) is not italicized.

CMS: *Note:*

4. Robert Garner, "Political Ideologies and the Moral Status of Animals," *Journal of Political Ideologies* 8 (2003): 235.

Issue number (where required): 8, no. 1 (2003).

Bibliography:

Smith, John Maynard. "The Origin of Altruism." *Nature* 393 (1998): 639–40.

CSE: 4. Bayer R, Fairchild AL. The genesis of public health ethics. Bioethics. 2004;18(6):473–492.

CSE uses abbreviations for most journal titles; for example, Can J Psychiatry is the abbreviation for *Canadian Journal of Psychiatry.*

Internet source

MLA: American Educational Research Association. Sources of Health Insurance and Characteristics of the Uninsured (Issue Brief No. 123). 2001. 24 Jan. 2001 <http://www.ilt.columbia.edu//publications/papers/newwine.html.>

The first date is that of the site; access date follows. Angle brackets enclose website address.

APA: Statistics Canada (2006, March 26). Gasoline and fuel oil, price by urban centre. Retrieved November 20, 2006, from http://www40.Statcan.ca/101/cst01/econ154a.htm.

CMS: *Note:*

5. The Internet Encyclopedia of Philosophy, "Deductive and Inductive Arguments," http://www.iep.utm.edu/d/ded-ind.htm.

Bibliography entry would be listed alphabetically by first major word; if access date is required, it can be placed in parentheses—e.g., (accessed March 21, 2007).

CSE: 5. Health Canada. A report on mental illnesses in Canada [Internet]. Ottawa (ON): Health Canada; 2002. [modified 2002 Oct 15; cited 2006 Nov 28], Available from: http://www.phac-aspe.gc.ea/publicat/miic-mmae/.

Sample student research essay and report

The essay below uses MLA citation style; the evaluative report that follows uses APA citation style.

Gambling addictions:
An increasing hazard among youths

by Selina Gonzalez

Addictions, particularly among adolescents, are usually associated with drugs, alcohol, smoking, and even sex. Rarely is gambling considered a hazardous addiction. Of those who do realize that gambling can be potentially harmful, most do not believe it is a prevalent issue in today's society, especially among youths. Furthermore, gambling addictions are often considered less damaging and therefore less important than other types of addictions (e.g., drug or alcohol). These are misconceptions. Unfortunately, gambling addictions among adolescents are escalating in number, and their effects are becoming increasingly adverse; however, steps can be taken to control these issues and reverse these trends.

Gambling addictions are neither rare nor are they exclusive to adults. Youths' gambling addictions are increasing in number and severity internationally. Studies by Youth Gambling International (YGI) show that currently about 80 per cent of high school students participate in some sort of gambling; 4 to 8 per cent of teenagers have severe gambling problems, and 10 to 14 per cent of teenagers are at high risk of developing serious gambling problems. Furthermore, studies have shown that adult pathological gamblers usually began gambling at approximately 10 years of age (Problem Gambling par. 1–2). Engagement in gambling typically begins at a much younger age than engagement in other potentially addictive behaviours such as drinking, smoking, and using drugs. Also, gambling is the most popular high-risk activity among youths (<u>Prevention</u> par. 1). Since 1977, problem gambling among adults has more than doubled; still, adolescent problem gamblers outnumber adult problem gamblers five to one (Cromie par. 3–5). In addition, adolescents are approximately five times as likely as adults to become addicted to gambling (Pridmore par. 10). These statistics show that gambling addictions among youths are a growing hazard and that their severity should not be underestimated. Nevertheless, the majority of parents and their children continue to see gambling as a harmless pastime (YGI, <u>Problem Gambling</u> par. 1).

Gambling's apparent harmlessness is one reason why youths engage in it. Parents and guardians are not likely to restrict their children from an activity they find innocuous; therefore, these children are left feeling that gambling is safe. Many children and adolescents are introduced to gambling by their parents: 78 per cent of youths gamble at home, and 80 to 90 per cent of parents report they are aware of and yet unconcerned about their children gambling. Children are also drawn to gambling because of the way it is advertised—it is "glamoriz[ed]," and even though it is prohibited to minors, these laws are not firmly enforced in several areas. Also, various types of gambling are now available on-line, which makes them that much more accessible, illegally, to underage persons (Derevensky et al. 242, 250–51). Doors are constantly opening up to facilitate access for youths to the world of gambling. Additionally, many youths begin gambling due to peer pressure because it is a pastime that is considered "socially acceptable and entertaining" (Derevensky et al. 242–43). Just because a teenager begins gambling, however, it does not mean he or she will necessarily become an addict.

The reasons underlying a person's gambling addiction are more difficult to pinpoint than those explaining why that person began gambling in the first place. There are several personality, physiological, and psychological factors, however, that are common to most youth gamblers and may suggest reasons why these youths become addicts. Young gambling addicts are found to be more impulsive, excitable, extroverted, anxious, self-blaming, and emotionally unstable than young non-gamblers. They are also greater risk-takers, have an "increased physiological resting state," and are less self-disciplined than the average teenager (Derevensky et al. 244). These traits make adolescent gamblers more likely to develop addictive behaviours and may be the fundamental causes of their disordered behaviour in some cases. Many adolescents with gambling problems also have "unresolved underlying issues" (Pridmore par. 4); these youths may use gambling as a way of escaping from their inner trauma and forgetting about their deeper issues. Gambling addictions may also be considered an "expression of depression" (Cromie par. 14). Perhaps these emotional disturbances are not the gambling addiction's results but rather its initiators and sustainers. Because adolescence is such an emotionally difficult time in the average person's life, teenagers are especially likely to develop gambling addictions.

Unfortunately, contrary to the perceptions or wishes of youth addicts, gambling fails to resolve a person's issues. It leads only to further, more serious problems. Gambling addictions may lead to other dangerous, co-morbid addictions and self-destructive behaviours, including delinquency, criminality, substance abuse (Derevensky et al. 240–45) and, in extreme cases, suicide (Canada Safety Council par. 3–7). Gambling can also twist and falsify a person's logical perception of reality. Many gambling addicts develop "cognitive distortions": they begin to erroneously believe that they have power over chance and over the outcome of randomly occurring events (Pridmore par. 18). Furthermore, gambling addictions often lead to academic difficulties and destruction of familial and peer relations (YGI, Problem Gambling par. 3). Gambling addictions harm not only the addict but also his or her friends, family, and peers as they must endure the addict's negative changes in character, personality, and lifestyle.

Treatment for youth and adolescent gamblers is more difficult and must be approached more delicately than for adult problem gamblers. One main reason youths and adults refuse treatment is because they are in denial of their problems. For a variety of reasons, however, adolescents are more likely than adults to avoid treatment options. Youths often see themselves as invincible, invulnerable, and immortal; they feel adults cannot understand them; they would rather try to solve their own problems than ask for help; they may see treatment as a symbol of personal failure, and they may be afraid that treatment could stigmatize them (Chevalier and Griffiths 3–5). Consequently, they generally choose to avoid treatment. Treating youths is often more difficult than treating adults because "pharmacological interventions" have recently become available for adult gambling addicts, but these treatments are not often recommended for youths because their efficacy among youths has not yet been adequately researched (Grant 93–94).

Since treatment of young gambling addicts is so difficult and cannot always guarantee satisfactory results, a more effective method of minimizing problem gambling among younger populations is prevention. If youths can be diverted from gambling, the number of gambling addictions among them can be significantly decreased. School-based programs for youths should be implemented at various age levels, starting in elementary school and proceeding through high school. Schools should communicate to teachers, parents, and adults in general the potential harmfulness and prevalence of this issue among today's youths. The older population, which directly influences the younger population, must realize that this issue is not to be taken lightly. Additionally, qualified psychologists (not just counsellors) should be available to work with school children of all ages to provide professional assistance for those in need and to teach them to adopt healthy, non-destructive methods of approaching emotional, social, and psychological distress. If youths' underlying issues "are treated [competently], gambling problems should disappear" (Chevalier and Griffiths 3–4).

Preventive action must extend further than just in-school programs, though, if it is to be effective and successful. In addition to prevention measures taken by schools, legal forces controlling gambling and its promotion must be strengthened. Laws governing the prohibition of underage gambling must be more strictly enforced to ensure that gaming environments are unavailable to youths. Gambling via the Internet should also be closely regulated to make it inaccessible to minors. Furthermore, laws should be imposed on the advertisement of gambling. The glamorization of gambling should be stopped, and gambling commercials should be aired only during programs available to adults (Canada Safety Council par. 14). Ideally, gambling advertisements should be prohibited.

Today's society is largely ignorant of gambling addictions among youths. The health and welfare of youths are being increasingly jeopardized because society lacks education about the costs, risks, and dangers of gambling. The growing number of gambling addictions among adolescents signifies not only that gambling is becoming too easily accessible and acceptable for minors but also that adolescents need help in dealing with their personal problems. Society must realize that its attitudes and perceptions about gambling are flawed and then establish prevention programs that deal carefully with the fragile nature of the youth psyche because, ultimately, it is only with the help and support of society that gambling problems among youths can be reduced.

WORKS CITED

Canada Safety Council. Canadian Roulette. 2004. November 8, 2005. <http://www.safety-council.org/info/community/gambling.html>.

Chevalier, Serge, and Mark Griffiths. "Why Don't Adolescents Turn up for Gambling Treatment." Electronic Journal of Gambling Issues. 11 (2001).

November 20, 2005. <http://www.camh.net/egambling/archive/pdf/JGI-issue11/JGI-Issue11-chevalier.pdf>.

Cromie, William J. "Gambling Addictions on Increase." The Harvard University Gazette. 12.11 (1997). November 19, 2002. <http://www.news.harvard.edu/gazette/1997/12.11/GamblingAddicti.html>.

Derevensky, Jeffrey L., et al. "Youth Gambling: Some Social Policy Issues." Gambling: Who Wins? Who Loses? Ed. Gerda Reith. Amherst, New York: Prometheus Books. 2003. 239–57.

Grant, Jon E., et al. "Adolescent Problem Gambling: Neurodevelopment and Pharmacological Treatment." Gambling Problems in Youth: Theoretical and Applied Perspectives. Ed. Jeffrey L. Derevensky and Rina Gupta. New York, NY: Kluwer Academic/Plenum Publishers. 2004. 81–98.

Pridmore, Lisa. Family Service Canada. The High Stakes of Gambling Addiction: Gambling Hurts the Whole Family, Not Just the Wallet. 2003. November 10, 2005. <http://www.familyservicecanada.org/resources/index2_e.html>.

Youth Gambling International. Prevention. 2005. November 20, 2005. <http://www.education.mcgill.ca/gambling/en/prevention.htm>.

Youth Problem Gambling. 2005. November 20, 2005. <http://www.education.mcgill.ca/gambling/en/problemgambling.htm>.

The struggle for superior sources: Critical evaluation of a website and a peer-reviewed journal article

by Danica Poje

Abstract: All information sources are not equally credible or valuable, but careful evaluation of a source helps to ensure reliability. NIDCD's (2006) website, "Apraxia of speech," and a peer-reviewed journal article by Ogar et al. (2005), "Apraxia: An overview," were compared to determine the efficacy and value of each in introducing apraxia of speech, a speech disorder. The articles were evaluated based on their content, credibility, and organization. It was found that the journal article contained more detail and depth and included more references than the website. While both sources were determined to be equal in content and organization, details and references provided additional credibility to the journal article.

The articles were determined to be equally valuable and effective for their intended audiences.

Critical analysis of any literary source is crucial to ensure that information is up-to-date, accurate, and understandable. Although the Internet has an abundance of health-related information, there is considerable risk of misinformation as there is no supervisory committee to regulate this information. There are numerous Internet sites and peer-reviewed journal articles regarding apraxia of speech (AOS), a disorder that hinders the person's ability to say what he or she wants, but many of these have conflicting opinions and suggestions. A website and a peer-reviewed journal article, both addressing the question of "what is AOS?," were selected and objectively analyzed to determine which presented a more valuable introduction to AOS.

The electronic posting "Apraxia of speech," by the National Institute on Deafness and Other Communication Disorders (NIDCD) (2006) was intended to inform the general public about acquired AOS and developmental AOS and the symptoms, method of diagnosis, treatment, and ongoing research of each.

"Apraxia: An overview" was written by Ogar, Slama, Dronkers, Amici, and Gorno-Tempini (2005) and published in *Neurocase*. The purpose was to inform and "review clinical hallmarks of AOS, the evolution of terminology associated with the disorder and the ongoing controversy regarding lesion sites associated with AOS" (p. 427). Confusion with other communication disorders, such as aphasia, are described, and the authors explain how inconsistencies make AOS difficult to diagnose and treat.

It is expected that the peer-reviewed article will be more complex and will also contain a greater depth of information than the Internet article. Thus, for general information, the website would be more valuable.

RESULTS

The content of an article is a critical measure of its usefulness. NIDCD's (2006) article provides information that is adequate and practical for someone unfamiliar with the subject. The article begins with a general definition of AOS and outlines different varieties, then works through the causes, symptoms, diagnosis, and treatment options of each type. It concludes with a brief review of ongoing research on the subject. Comparison and contrast between the types of AOS is useful in understanding who would be affected and how the disease effects the lives of those who are. Numerous examples are provided to illustrate the information presented;

for example, magnetic resonance imaging, speech tasks, reading and writing tests, and observation are all techniques that can be utilized during diagnosis. Specialized terms, such as "prosody" (the rhythms, stresses, and inflections that help give express meaning in speech), are defined. There are several suggestions for further reading, including the American Speech-Language-Hearing Association (ASHA) and *PubMed*, a journal database, but no references or citations are provided. In contrast, Ogar et al.'s (2005) peer-reviewed journal article cited over 60 primary and secondary sources to support the authors' research. This article begins with a brief introduction and definition of AOS and an outline of the topics covered. An in-depth look at the history, clinical presentation, and anatomy are informative as the authors describe, using examples, how AOS is confused and mistaken for other communication disorders. Definitions are provided for a few words, but most, including "prosody," assume a reader's prior knowledge. Ogar et al. (2005) use a substantial amount of jargon, including anatomical terms and linguistic references, which also assume reader familiarity. In summary, the content, including definitions, examples, and citations, must be examined to ascertain the value of a particular source.

Credibility is another defining factor of a source's validity. The author of the web-based article was the NIDCD, an organization focused on conducting biomedical and behavioural research into the process of hearing and other senses (NIDCD, 2006). The NIDCD is a subset of the US Department of Health and Human Services, whose goal is to "acquire new knowledge to help prevent, detect, diagnose, and treat disease and disability" (About Us, para. 1). The information in the article is current and updated regularly, most recently on March 23, 2006. The peer-reviewed article was written by five individuals from the University of California in San Francisco and Veterans Affairs in Northern California in December 2005. All the authors have previous experience in the area, and each has participated in multiple research projects concerning AOS and other communication diseases. Ogar et al.'s (2005) article was published in the peer-reviewed journal *Neurocase*, which features case studies and review-type papers such as this one. The study was funded by, among others, the California Institute of Health and the National Institute for Neurological Diseases and Stroke. Consideration of the authors' credentials and the currency of the articles supports the credibility of both sources.

Finally, the organization of an article is fundamental to the ease with which information can be located and understood. NIDCD's (2006) website is organized using clear headings phrased as questions, such as "What are the types and causes of apraxia?" (Types and Causes, para. 1). An outline is presented with hyperlinks directly to the definition, causes, symptoms, diagnosis, treatment, and ongoing research of AOS. Using a question and answer pattern of development makes the information clear and easy to follow. There are no graphics or distracting pop-ups on the site. Some words have definition hyperlinks that open a glossary in a new window, and additional resources, also with hyperlinks, are included. Ogar et al.'s (2005) paper does not conform to the typical APA format because it is an overview rather than a presentation of original research. The abstract and conclusion of the introduction outline the five headings: history and definition, clinical presentation (symptoms) and diagnosis, neuroanatomy (cause), models of understanding, and treatment. Two tables, presenting the historical terms and articulation characteristics of AOS, are included as visual aids in the first two sections, respectively. The authors demonstrate confusion within the subject area by comparing the similarities between AOS and aphasia, for example, but then using contrast explain how to differentiate between the two disorders. The organization of the website and the journal article is clear and understandable, which facilitates navigation and comprehension.

DISCUSSION

In conclusion, the credibility and organization of the two articles are comparable. The content within Ogar et al.'s (2005) peer-reviewed *Neurocase* article, however, is much more in-depth and provides numerous citations for those familiar with AOS or neurology. The NIDCD website would be most useful for the general population: the brevity, simple language, and ease of navigation facilitate learning for someone lacking previous knowledge of the subject. Those interested in learning about AOS could find specific details overwhelming and would rarely require the specifics provided by the journal article. Furthermore, most readers would accept the governmental organization as an authoritative resource that would present accurate, up-to-date, non-biased information. Although citations would increase the credibility, they are most useful for those doing in-depth research who would generally utilize journal articles before websites. The question and answer format facilitates understanding and ease of navigation through the site, and a link to *PubMed* encourages further research.

Thus, the hypothesis has been confirmed: although Ogar et al.'s (2005) article provided the detail and citations required by those in the field of biomedical research, simplified information and clear presentation make

NIDCD's (2006) website more valuable to someone unfamiliar with the subject. This study illustrates the usefulness of websites as a general information source, but with the exponential increase in articles available on-line, an objective and critical evaluation of sources based on content, credibility, and organization is crucial to ensuring value and reliability.

REFERENCES

Ogar, J., Slama, H., Dronkers, N., Amici, S., & Gorno-Tempini, M.L. (2005). Apraxia of speech: An overview. *Neurocase, 11*, 427–432. Retrieved March 9, 2006, from http://www.metapress.com/media/e3dnrguqqncn7 qxqmxfr/contributions/w/5/1/1/w5111171672u2540.pdf.

National Institute on Deafness and Other Communication Disorders. (2006). *Apraxia of speech*. Retrieved March 24, 2006, from http://www. nidcd.nih.gov/health/voice/apraxia.htm.

PART THREE

The Active Reader

The Knowledge Society

AIDS, Africa and indifference: A confession

Joel Pauls Wohlgemut

(2,000 words)

Not everybody wants to be a saint.
Jonathan Hullah, M.D.,
in Robertson Davies, *The Cunning Man*[1]

The activities of the World Trade Organization (WTO) do not normally attract much attention from the medical community. However, the defence by manufacturers and governments of patent protection for antiretroviral drugs—despite the catastrophic HIV/AIDS crisis in Africa—ensured that the November 2001 meeting of the WTO in Doha, Qatar, would be different. At issue was the Agreement on Trade-Related Aspects of Intellectual Property Rights (TRIPS), common rules for protecting proprietary interests in ideas, processes and products (including pharmaceuticals) and for circumventing those rights in the case of a "national emergency." In the days after the conference, all sides seemed to be, for the time being, satisfied. An African delegation believed its proposal that "nothing in the TRIPS Agreement shall prevent Members from taking measures to protect public health" had carried the day: it had won wording to this effect, including a specific reference to HIV/AIDS as a disease that could constitute a "national emergency."[2] On the other hand, the final document took pains to point out that this position was only a clarification of the WTO's existing agreement on intellectual property rights, obliquely suggesting that all this furor was a matter of misunderstanding rather than disagreement.

Before the conference, other conflicts had flared over the role that drug manufacturers might play in stemming the tide of HIV/AIDS in sub-Saharan Africa. The 17 October 2001, issue of *JAMA* offered Amir Attaran and Lee Gillespie-White's answer to the question, "Do patents for anti-retroviral drugs constrain access to AIDS treatment in Africa?": a clear No.[3] Their analysis of existing antiretroviral patents in African countries suggested that few such patents were actually in place and that "geographic patent coverage [did] not appear to correlate with antiretroviral treatment access."[3] Instead, they fingered insufficient international aid to fund therapy as the biggest culprit in maintaining the status quo. Nongovernmental organizations (NGOs) such as Médecins Sans Frontières and Oxfam wasted no time firing back.[4] Patents do matter, they contended: the most practical and sought-after formulations have been strategically patented, while drugs left unprotected typically are impractical in resource-poor communities (e.g., owing to increased need for monitoring).[4] Arguing that the drug companies were using the research published in *JAMA* as justification for further inaction (and querying a $25,000 grant from Merck to Gillespie-White's institution), Médecins Sans

Frontières unflaggingly pressed on with its Access to Essential Medicines campaign in the lead-up to Doha.

What are we to make of these clashes between NGOs and academics, between impoverished nations and an institution of global commerce? Everyone agreed in 2001 that the infection of 28 million Africans with HIV is a public health disaster of epic proportions. Clearly, a Herculean effort will be required to combat the disease, involving international health organizations, drug manufacturers, governments and local health care workers. I am absent from this list.

I have never been to Africa. I am not black. I do not have HIV. I am a middle-class man (married, 2 kids) living a middle-class life (family medicine resident) in a middle-class neighbourhood (London, Ont.). By virtue of my work, I have cared for people—transiently—who have HIV/AIDS. But, as politically incorrect as it may sound, I am not connected to the tragedy that is AIDS in Africa. And, as crass as it may sound, I do not have to be. Perhaps, as part of my effort to be reasonably well-informed about the world, I cannot avoid hearing about it. Perhaps, as a physician who spends much of his time considering how best to help people who are sick, I cannot avoid thinking about it. But I can avoid doing anything about it, and no one will call me to account for my inaction.

This is the downside of globalization: self-interest is still paramount. Cheaper televisions, cheaper bananas, cheaper running shoes. At best, we can make arrangements that are mutually beneficial. But tragedy is not an easily exported commodity, and we prefer that it be handled behind national borders. In wealthier nations, we look after our own: Americans pledged $1.2 billion to New Yorkers in the two months following the terrorist attacks of 11 September 2001 that left thousands dead.[5] The US Agency

for International Development budgeted $320 million to target HIV/AIDS in Africa in 2001, a disease that had killed an estimated 2.3 million people on that continent over the preceding year.[6,7]

Where can we turn for help in sorting out our responsibilities in the face of human disaster? "Ethics" was a word I heard frequently during my medical education. I approached it warily, with the jaundiced eye of a former graduate student in the humanities, all too conscious of the ways by which words can become ends in themselves. "There are no right answers!" was a common invocation intended to break down our reticence. I appreciate the pedagogical point, but the notion that there are no right answers is a dangerous partial truth. The mistake is to conclude that we cannot have a rational discussion about better answers, nobler answers, more virtuous answers.

The Code of Ethics of the medical profession in Canada,[8] like many other such codes, focuses on the relationship between physicians and individual patients. There is a passing exhortation to "accept a share of the profession's responsibility to society in matters relating to public health," but this clearly seems directed at domestic matters. Defining ethics within a framework of duties and rights (as many are inclined to do) works in a clearly delimited community where people are required to interact with one another and must find mutually agreeable ways of doing so. However, disasters seen at a distance require something different—something capable of generating compassion from across an ocean.

There are forms of discourse that permit us to think in these terms. Some of us turn to the philosophical tradition, from Aristotle to Alasdair MacIntyre, for reflection on virtue. Others seek direction in religious scriptures, such as the New Testament story of the good Samaritan (Luke 10: 25–37), who breaks free of the constraints of culture and race in the face of human need. This is not to say that virtuous action necessarily relies on such traditions; however, they highlight the inability of modern medical discourse—the languages of pathophysiology, epidemiology and genetic determinism—to word-find when confronted with human tragedy.

Of course, as Robertson Davies so wryly observed, "Not everybody wants to be a saint." More truthfully, few aspire to such a state, whether their vocation is religious or medical. There is a small cadre of physicians who commit themselves to working on the international front lines, and I envy their self-sacrifice, the "rightness" of their lives. But my envy, or guilt, or shame will not make the world a better place or make one shred of difference to someone dying of AIDS in Uganda.

I keep returning to the poignant question posed by the essayist Wendell Berry: "How will you practice virtue without skill?"[9] I thought that I was responding to this question during weary nights in uncomfortable call rooms, acquiring the skills that would allow me to make my contribution to society, to turn noble ideals into action. But AIDS in Africa, a crisis that is so classically medical, slides nonetheless through the therapeutic templates I learned so painstakingly. Perhaps if I restricted myself to talk about reverse transcriptase and protease inhibitors I might be on more familiar ground, although our tendency to place AIDS care in the hands of a knowledgeable few leaves me adrift just the same. Move on to other factors such as national health budgets of $8 per capita, patriarchal power structures that leave women with few choices, and civil violence that cripples countries' abilities to act, and I am out of my league. I suspect that if I were airdropped into a Soweto township I would be next to useless.

Hand-wringing is not a particularly constructive enterprise. As I reflect critically on my own response, a few starting points emerge: skeletons of thought, pointing a shaky finger, requiring substantial "fleshing out." I offer them briefly, inviting comment:

1. As medicine in Western democracies becomes increasingly reliant on biomedical engineering (both pharmaceutical and technical), physicians become increasingly incapable of practising effectively without those costly supports. It is unclear why we tolerate such obvious discrepancies in medical infrastructure around the globe and why we seem bent on widening that gap.

2. As we reflect on the staggering health needs of developing countries, it becomes apparent that the North American medical research machine is in desperate need of retooling. The questionable value of spending millions to prove the marginal benefit of ever-more expensive therapies (which, once they are proven, become medico-legally obligatory) is a case in point. Naturally, we cannot expect leadership from the pharmaceutical industry, whose livelihood is at stake. There may not even be much public support for this (not from the "diseased" public, at any rate). However, investment in projects that find their principal application outside our own borders could be one measure of our compassion.

3. Obviously, there is a deep need for international money to fund programs to combat HIV/AIDS in developing countries.[10] Governments should be exhorted to do their part: Canada's last federal budget committed $500 million over 3 years to a trust fund for sustainable development in Africa,[11] and politicians should be encouraged to amplify this trend. On the other hand, physicians should look carefully at their own ability to make independent contributions as wealthy individuals in a wealthy society.

4. We must remind ourselves that a strictly medical approach to HIV/AIDS will be inadequate. The feasibility of large-scale antiretroviral therapy (which has been instituted on a very small scale in a number of developing countries[12]) is not at all clear. It may be that the most critical interventions will be nonmedical in nature (e.g., culturally relevant public health education aimed at curbing the transmission of HIV), a fact that should both humble us and motivate our cooperation with others.

It is hypocritical for me to write, from the comfort of my suburban backsplit, about the horror of Africans dying by the millions of AIDS. Perhaps I am not qualified to write at all. Perhaps only they can write who have seen the grim realities first-hand, who have suffered the heat and the heartbreak in an effort to bring healing to the dying. Yet perhaps I am someone who must write, representing as I do the many thousands of physicians in this country who live in the tension of believing that things ought to be otherwise and chastising themselves for doing so little.

Even our best efforts, coming as they do from a position of power and privilege, may not afford us the distinction of saintliness. But sainthood is not the goal. Instead, we need to shake off the inertia of the overwhelmed and take our first, feeble steps on the road to responsibility.

Canadian Medical Association Journal. 2002. 3 September: 167 (5).

REFERENCES

1. Davies R. *The cunning man.* Toronto: McClelland & Stewart; 1994.
2. *Declaration on the TRIPS agreement and public health* [Doc no WT/MIN(01)/DEC/2]. World Trade Organization; 2001 Nov 20; Doho, Qatar. Available: www.wto.org/english/thewto_e/minist_e/min01_e/mindecl_trips_e.htm (accessed 2002 Aug 6).
3. Attaran A, Gillespie-White L. Do patents for antiretroviral drugs constrain access to AIDS treatment in Africa? [special communication] *JAMA* 2001; 286:1886–92.
4. *Patents do matter in Africa according to NGOs* [joint statement]. Oxfam, Treatment Action Campaign, Consumer Project on Technology, Médecins Sans Frontières, Health GAP; 2001 Oct 17. Available: www.accessmed-msf.org/prod/publications.asp?scntid=171020011428553&contenttype=PARA& (accessed 2002 Aug 7).
5. *American Red Cross offers to refund donations* [online news article]. Ottawa: Canadian Broadcasting Corporation; 2001 Nov 8. Available: cbc.ca/cgi-bin/templates/view.cgi?category=World&story=/news/2001/11/07/red_cross011107 (accessed 2002 Aug 7).
6. *USAID combatting HIV/AIDS: a record of accomplishment* [press release]. Washington: US Agency for International Development; 2001 June 22. Available: www.usaid.gov/press/releases/2001/fs010420.html (accessed 2002 Aug 7).
7. *Estimated adult and child deaths from HIV/AIDS during 2001* [graphic]. Geneva: Joint United Nations Programme on HIV/AIDS; 2001 Dec 1. Available: www.unaids.org/worldaidsday/2001/EPIgraphics2001/EPIgraphic6_en.gif (accessed 2002 Aug 7).
8. *Code of ethics of the Canadian Medical Association.* Ottawa: Canadian Medical Association; 1996. Available: www.cma.ca/cma/common/displayPage.do?pageId=/staticContent/HTML/N0/12/where_we_stand/1996/10-15.htm (accessed 2002 Aug 7).
9. Berry W. *The gift of good land.* San Francisco: North Point Press; 1981.

10. Canada's commitment to AIDS relief in Africa [editorial]. *CMAJ* 2001; 164(13):1825.

11. *Budget 2001.* Ottawa: Department of Finance Canada; 2001. Available: www.fin. gc.ca/budget01/toce/2001/budlist01_e.htm (accessed 2002 Aug 7).

12. *Time to start treatment: AIDS treatment is working in developing countries* [press release]. Geneva: Médecins Sans Frontières; 2001 Dec 1. Available: www.msf.org/content/page. cfm?articleid=A622E063-E539-4540-BB231F1440B04D90 (accessed 2002 Aug 7).

KEY AND DIFFICULT WORDS

Define the following, using context or other clues if possible: **antiretroviral, proprietary, transient, exhortation, pathophysiology, epidemiology, determinism.**

QUESTIONS

1. What is a confession? Does this essay fit your definition of a confession?

2. If you hadn't read the essay's title or epigraph, what would you expect the essay to be about? Do you think the author made a good choice to begin the way he does? Would it be a stronger or a weaker essay if he had started with paragraph 3 or 4?

3. (a) What does the author say is the problem with applying ethics, as he has dealt with the concept as a doctor, to the real problems of developing nations? (b) What other ways does he mention through which the problem of ethics can be addressed? (See paragraphs 6–8.)

4. What is the importance of Robertson Davies's quotation to the essay? Of Wendell Berry's?

5. Identify the point in the essay when Wohlgemut seems to lose hope. As a reader, how did you respond to this? Do you think it was a wise strategy on his part to express these feelings?

6. Who are his "skeletons of thought" directed to (paragraph 11)?

7. What kinds of sources does the author use, and how effective are they? Are there an adequate number? A sufficient variety? Where are the sources taken from? Are they reliable?

COLLABORATIVE ACTIVITIES

1. Wohlgemut's essay on the AIDS epidemic in Africa is one global problem with a scope that seems beyond human comprehension. What other global examples of mass suffering have taken place in the past? Consider how they have developed and been resolved (if they have) and how they might be compared to the AIDS situation in Africa.

2. What role does the awareness of individuals in developed nations have to play in situations like that described in the essay? Can the knowledge of single individuals help bring about large-scale change, and if so, how? Discuss or debate this issue.

ACTIVITY

Choose one of the four starting points Wohlgemut mentions (the numbered points). (a) In one sentence, summarize the point; (b) in two to three paragraphs, respond to the point. You could consider the validity of the point and/or whether the suggestion(s) are practical and viable.

How computers make our kids stupid

Sue Ferguson

(3,800 words)

The first thing you notice opening the door to Les Black's classroom is the smell. It's a dank, earthy aroma from a dozen planters perched on shelves or suspended from the ceiling. Sunlight filters through a row of wood-framed windows onto the 27 fourth-graders. A boy standing at the front relates the story of his grandfather's life, impressing upon his audience that the old man did not always act within the letter of the law. His classmates squirm in their seats. Some fiddle with pencils. One boy thoughtfully caresses a papier mâché snake resting on his desk. Behind the presenter is a chalkboard and, above it, the age-old series of placards displaying the alphabet, exquisitely drawn in cursive form.

This scene in a private school in the Toronto suburb of Thornhill is not unlike thousands of others across Canada. But wait a minute—something is strangely amiss. Where are the keyboards? Where are the darkened screens framed by dull grey plastic? The tangle of cables cascading over the backs of the tables? How strange: a classroom without a gigabyte in sight, not even on the teacher's desk. How will these children ever get a job? How will their teachers ever instil in them a love of learning?

It's never been easier for kids to get their fingertips on a keyboard or to cruise cyberspace. Statistics Canada reports three out of four households with school-aged children regularly access the Internet, and a growing number of users are turning to high-speed connections. Our schools now have about a million computers, 93 per cent of which are on-line. Although we already boast a 5:1 ratio of students to computers (compared to an average of 8:1 in the developed world as a whole), the push is on in many districts to equip each middle- and high-school student with a wireless laptop. With homes and classrooms crawling with mouses and modems, anyone resisting the digital impulse seems either hopelessly naive or in a state of downright denial.

Yet, in bucking the trend, the Toronto Waldorf School—home to Les Black's class—is arguably doing its students a favour. While computers clearly have a place in education (Waldorf introduces them in Grade 9), the evidence is mounting that our obsessive use of information technology is dumbing us down, adults as well as kids. While they can be engaging and resourceful tools for learning—if used in moderation—computers and the Internet can also distract kids from homework, encourage superficial and uncritical thinking, replace face-to-face interaction between students and teachers, and lead to compulsive behaviour.

At least some teens recognize the problem. Fifteen-year-old Colin Johnson of Toronto sits down at his computer at 4 most afternoons. He whizzes through his homework in half an hour, and then starts surfing, gaming, and chatting with friends on MSN until 1 a.m., when he goes to bed. The tenth-grader is failing science, but otherwise getting by. "I procrastinate a lot more than before," he says, acknowledging that "everybody's marks suffer to some degree" if they spend as much time as he does on-line.

Perhaps the most persuasive evidence for taking a more critical view is a broad-reaching and rigorous study published last November. University of Munich economists Thomas Fuchs and Ludger Woessmann analyzed the results of the OECD's PISA international standardized tests. Not only did they tap into a massive subject pool—174,000 15-year-olds in reading, 97,000 each in math and science from 31 countries (including Canada)—but they were also able,

because participants filled out extensively detailed surveys, to control for other possible outside influences, something remarkably few studies do. Their results, which are only now starting to make waves among pedagogy experts, confirm what many parents have long intuited: the sheer ubiquity of information technology is getting in the way of learning. Once household income and the wealth of a school's resources are taken out of the equation, teens with the greatest access to computers and the Internet at home and school earn the lowest test scores.

At school, the economists found, some exposure to computers seems beneficial. For instance, students who never or rarely use the Internet and computers in the classroom don't do as well as those who make moderate use of them. But the difference in achievement levels is significant in math and science only, not in reading. And those same computer-less students outperform peers who frequently access the technology. The optimal level for computer and Internet use at school, Fuchs and Woessmann suggest, is pretty low, somewhere between "a few times a year" and "several times a month." Seventeen-year-old Tilo McAlister has some idea why that may be so. By Grade 7, the Waldorf student was aware that friends in other schools were more computer-savvy than he. (McAlister had limited use of his father's home-office computer at the time.) Upsetting as that was to him then, four years later, he has caught up. And "looking back," he says, "I'm glad I didn't have them in school. Anything I would have learned from a computer, I'm sure I learned better from a teacher."

Irene Freeman is Brooke Elementary School's resident technology guru. The 63-year-old teacher first introduced computers to her Delta, BC, classroom in the early 1980s. She's since facilitated the installation of the school's computer lab, designed the school's website, led countless workshops for teachers, and spent two years as an e-learning consultant for her district. Now in the last of 39 years of teaching, Freeman takes every opportunity to put her first-graders on the road to becoming seasoned technophiles. Along with twice-a-week trips to the lab, her 23 six- and seven-year-olds spend a chunk of each day in front of the five hand-me-down computers in her classroom, where they navigate a selection of commercial educational software and Internet sites.

Freeman estimates she delivers about a quarter of the curriculum in this way. "In September, we talk about the parts of the computer," she says. "Where to put your left hand, your right hand—and they play games with the alphabet." By the end of the school year, the children (who have already used computers in kindergarten, though not as extensively) can, among other things, write stories, draw pictures and insert them into documents, build geometric patterns, organize their thoughts (with the help of a graphics program called Inspiration that prompts them to "web," or connect, their ideas), and even create slides for a PowerPoint presentation. Freeman's convinced that computers help students master the alphabet, reading and writing more quickly than they would in a tech-free environment. "Pretty well all the kids really like it," she notes, "so they're motivated to learn."

The computer is frequently cited by educators as the great motivator. "It's not that you couldn't teach without it," says Brooke principal Barbara Hague, "but we need everything in our power to keep kids engaged." More significantly, however, PCs are part of their world. If schools failed to integrate them into the curriculum, she insists, "we'd be missing a huge part of their life—it would be like not including physical education" in the school day.

Yet the accoutrements and relentless upgrading they demand are expensive. At Brooke, which is located in a solidly middle-class neighbour-

hood, parents are helping foot the $10,000 cost of an upgrade to the lab this spring, which added 14 computers for a total of 32. And although some have questioned the school's priorities (especially as spending on "all aspects of school life," says Hague, has been cut back in recent years), the students' current level and sophistication of use means they need to be working at their own screens. "They're way beyond sharing."

The push for more—more modules, more speed, more software—can take on a life of its own. In fact, labs and classroom PCs like those at Brooke school are considered dinosaurs—"not that different from someone wanting to install an eight-track tape player in a 2005 sports car," according to Ron Rubadeau, superintendent of schools for BC's Central Okanagan district. Students don't get enough time in labs, he stresses in a report released earlier this year, "Technology unplugged," and classroom modules are located "in spaces that may already be too cramped to fully accommodate student learning." The wave of the future is wireless laptops which, although "costly," will lead "to an improved focus on teaching and learning," he predicts. That's the same reasoning behind the province's $2.1-million program to equip each child in select Grade 5 to 12 classrooms next fall with their own laptop computers.

Rubadeau's confidence is born of a seemingly impressive stack of research. When 1,150 Grade 6 and 7 students in BC's Peace River North school district were given their own Apple iBooks, for instance, writing skills improved (especially among students whose teachers were more experienced with the technology), and the achievement gap between girls and boys, and between non-Aboriginal and Aboriginal students, narrowed. Studies from Quebec, Maine, and Maryland, where iBooks have been used for a few years, back up those results. Wireless laptops distributed on a one-to-one basis, concludes

Rubadeau—whose middle- and high-school students are part of the province's initiative—are "revolutionizing instruction."

Now surely that should silence the critics—the parents, educators, and others who have, over the years, objected to the massive outlay of cash on what they argue is an unproven medium. (No one has kept tabs in Canada, but in the US, one estimate puts the federal expenditure on digitizing schools at nearly $6 billion a year.) Yet, rather than clamming up in the face of such persuasive evidence, the opposition, like a dog with a bone, has grown bolder—and has its own growing body of contrarian evidence, including the Munich economists' study. "The jury is in," says Alison Armstrong, Toronto co-author of 1999's *The Child and the Machine: Why Computers May Put Our Children's Education at Risk*. "There's no compelling evidence that computers help develop intellectual or emotional intelligence in any way."

South of the border, the Alliance for Childhood, a group of 60 health, child-development, education, and technology experts, has called for a moratorium on new computers for preschool and elementary classrooms. In its report "Fool's gold: A critical look at computers in childhood," the Alliance argues, "We do not know what the consequences of such a machine-driven education in adulthood will be. But we suspect that they will include a narrower and more shallow range of intellectual insights, a stunting of both social and technical imagination, and a drag on the productivity that stems from imaginative leaps. In short, a high-tech agenda for children seems likely to erode our most precious long-term intellectual reserves—our children's minds."

Meanwhile, the Munich economists found that on the home front, kids without a PC do better than those with one or more. This changes only when specific computer uses are taken into account. Educational software, e-mail and web page access—and this will come as no surprise—are associated with higher achievement than gaming or chat rooms, precisely the activities on which teens spend the most time. Or, as a new British Department for Education and Skills document advocating e-learning puts it, booting up at home can be beneficial, "but not many pupils have yet integrated such uses with their school experiences."

So, it's quite simple, really. There's no harm in buying your teen his own computer and dedicated Internet access, so long as you're confident that the *Encyclopaedia Britannica*, and not an on-line game of Doom, will keep him glued to the screen. And while American author Steven Johnson argues in his new book, *Everything Bad Is Good for You*, that video games and certain popular TV shows are making the next generation smarter (because their multi-layered, unresolved soap-opera plots stimulate underused neural pathways), this sort of virtual multi-tasking clearly has its drawbacks. Not only, as Fuchs and Woessmann propose, can recreational uses be a distraction, crowding out time spent on homework, but our brains—at least, once we go to work—appear to suffer in other ways. According to a University of London study commissioned by Hewlett-Packard, the constant interruption of employees' concentration by e-mails and telephone calls lowers a person's IQ by 10 points—more than double the four-point drop that results from smoking a joint.

One reason students don't "integrate" their school work with their home computer use, the British government report goes on to suggest, is that "teachers do not have direct control over what pupils do outside school hours." In many ways, this goes to the heart of the issue. Computers don't, on their own, dumb us down. But so long as schools treat computers as if they are indispensable, and teachers continue to assign homework that either requires or assumes research will be carried out on the web, kids will inevitably be pulled into gaming, chat rooms, and other distractions. This, as Woessmann and Fuchs have shown, bodes poorly for their achievement levels. It also arguably interferes with their capacity for deep and sustained reading, thinking, and understanding—a point *Everything Bad Is Good for You* author Johnson eventually comes around to acknowledging. "Now for the bad news," he writes at the end of his book. "Complicated, sequential works of persuasion, where each premise builds on the previous one, and where an idea can take an entire chapter to develop, are not well-suited to life on the computer screen."

And it's not just the students who are losing out. Heather Menzies, author of the recently published *No Time: Stress and the Crisis of Modern Life*, and York University sociologist Janice Newson surveyed 100 faculty members from six of the country's universities. About a third of them reported short-term memory problems and difficulties concentrating, which they link to the digital revolution. Seventy per cent said that rather than read deeply, reflectively, and broadly, they scan for usable bits of information. What's more, the overwhelming use of e-mail is affecting their interactions with students and colleagues, making communication more "superficial" and less personal.

As for why kids with a surfeit of school computers don't perform as well as others, Fuchs and Woessmann suggest what Waldorf student McAlister suspects about his own experience: time spent at the screen may crowd out personal interaction with teachers and creativity. They're referring to the 15-year-olds in their study, but in an interview, Fuchs speculates that younger children whose lessons depend excessively on computers suffer even more. "I would suggest that for the reading literacy of nine-year-olds, very frequent computer use at school could have a more

severe effect, since the learning of reading requires a lot of interaction between teachers and students." The general message of the German study is this: at home and at school, computers may well have a time and a place, but not just any place and any time. As Canadian schools eagerly embrace the next wave of e-learning—and PCs, laptops, and the Internet become as common as pencils and erasers in ever-earlier grades—it's not clear that message is getting through.

All this makes it harder to accuse the staff at the Toronto Waldorf School of being either naive or living in denial. "We're not Luddites or anti-computer," says the Toronto school's faculty chair, Todd Royer. "But we are for introducing important technologies at the right time in the development of children." The right time for computers, he says, arrives in Grade 9, when students move from a purely sensual, experiential curriculum to a more abstract, conceptual level of learning. According to the Waldorf approach—first espoused by Austrian philosopher and scientist Rudolf Steiner in 1919—the elementary years are for engaging children with natural phenomena, like gardens, animals, and light. The child is expected to store such encounters in her memory and, from an accumulation of experiences, create and test her own concepts. In experiencing (as opposed to intellectualizing) the world, says Royer, students come to develop their capacities for wonder, interest, reverence, and love—a key step in "holding their intellect in check so that they can deal with it responsibly."

Computers are of no use in this process. "They don't present us with phenomena," he explains. "They present us with something that is pre-digested—a concept of something" created by someone else. For the same reason, textbooks are also scarce in Waldorf classrooms. The children write and illustrate their own records of what they've learned using good, old-fashioned pens, pencils, crayons, and paper. That process, says Royer, goes a long way toward building a child's self-esteem—a task the Waldorf elementary curriculum puts front and centre in the belief that intellectual life should develop from emotional and moral maturity.

Letting a child loose on the Internet (where three million new web pages are created every day) before they've developed a strong sense of self, he says, "can extend them beyond their capacity to understand." They lack the maturity to deal with it responsibly. Obsessive use of the Internet is a prime example. Not only can gaming and chat rooms distract a kid from homework, but more than 10 per cent of students show signs of compulsive Internet use, experts say. In such cases, cautions University of Calgary computer scientist Tom Keenan, computers themselves are not to blame. "There's always something to take kids away from studying. Thirty years ago, at universities, it was bridge." But whereas card games require some effort to coordinate, the Internet is "ubiquitous and cheap," he adds. And in the absence of parental supervision, "it's always ready for you, always friendly, always happy. It's the crack-cocaine of time-wasters"—a point some kids are well aware of. "MMORPGs" (massive multi-player on-line role-playing games) "are highly addictive," notes Toronto teen Colin Johnson. "A lot of people have screwed up their lives playing them." In fact, one Sony product, EverQuest, in which gamers create characters using "a powerful customization system for unprecedented player individuality," according to the company's website, is widely known as EverCrack.

Even more troubling, notes Royer, is that the things kids read and see on-line invade their imagination. The recent incident at Royal St. George's College—in which two boys (one Jewish) at the Toronto private school spewed anti-Semitic insults at a chat-room participant, Rod (a moniker for four Jewish girls from another pri-

vate school)—is a case in point. Not only did one of the students pick up some of the racist vocabulary from surfing the web in the first place, but it's not clear he fully understood the impact of posting his diatribe on the Internet. In a cyberworld glutted with undifferentiated information, students desperately need to be able to distinguish valid information from hate propaganda and other irresponsible messages. In light of such incidents, it doesn't seem entirely grandiose when Royer suggests, "The force of thinking is like the power of the gods that we hold in our hands. We have the power to do incredible things, both for good and evil. It's a force that needs to be protected within humanity."

The Waldorf school's 100 high school students share a modest 17-unit lab for a limited menu of courses—math, programming, and business. In waiting until a child's character is more fully formed, Royer hopes his students will understand computers for what they are, a tool, and use them responsibly. Student McAlister does much of his homework on the PC he recently bought for himself and acknowledges that the allure of surfing, downloading music, and e-mail was initially a distraction. But he started to feel guilty, his marks were dropping, and, he says, "that got me to get on top of it"—without parental nagging. Classmate Kaz Iguchi transferred from the public system to the Waldorf school in Grade 9. "I close all other programs so I don't get distracted when I do my homework," he says. A one-time video-game aficionado, he sold all his games in January. Iguchi, 17, credits his school environment with that decision. "In Waldorf, not many kids play games," he says. "If I still went to a public school, I'm pretty sure I'd still be playing."

As for the standard rationales for digitizing the classroom, Royer trots out a variety of curt responses. To the claim that the world is full of computers and schools need to be relevant to children's lives: "The world's full of all kinds of things—automobiles, sexuality, and we have appropriate times and places for all these aspects of our lives." But surely engagement is an issue. Don't kids get revved up about lessons presented on a computer? "Sure," he responds. "It's an addictive medium." Okay, what about helping students gain the skills they need to get a job? "Our grads go everywhere and anywhere."

This last rebuttal is less impressive when you consider that Waldorf is a private school with tuition fees between $11,000 and $12,200. Most of its students, in other words, are going to be ahead of the curve by virtue of their advantaged background. But it's also the case that a 2005 survey asking Canadian corporate leaders what they look for in new hires consistently emphasized self-discipline, an inquiring mind, and loyalty over technical know-how, which can be picked up on the job. Add to this evidence cited by Fuchs and Woessmann that computer skills have no substantial impact on an employee's wages, while math and writing abilities do, and Royer's glib response gains credibility.

Delta teacher Irene Freeman is also a big believer in hands-on, experiential learning. The first week of May, her class spent a morning making strawberry jam for Mother's Day, arranging baby food jars of preserves in baskets fashioned out of berry containers woven with strips of coloured paper, topped off with a homemade card—no mousing or keyboarding required (except for Freeman, who found the design for the cards on the web). But even experiential learning can be digitized. For one previous project, her students picked fallen leaves, which Freeman then laminated. After writing about where they found each leaf and what kind of tree it dropped from (using Microsoft's Talking First Word software), the students mailed their work to dozens of other North American schools participating in the same project. In return, says Freeman, "we got some unusual looking leaves—from trees like the sugargum in Florida." The experience "didn't replace books," she stresses. "We started by reading *The giving tree* by Shel Silverstein," and ended by looking up the leaves they were sent in reference books.

It's hard to see much harm in such judicious use of technology. But for every positive example, there are other troubling ones. Of course we hope our kids will discover that mouses, websites, and e-mail are useful educational tools. But as we allow curricula and computers to cozy up ever closer, we risk letting technology run the show.

Maclean's. 2005. 6 June.

KEY AND DIFFICULT WORDS
Define the following, using context or other clues if possible: **pedagogy, OECD PISA, ubiquity, accoutrements, Luddites, allure.**

QUESTIONS
1. How does Ferguson's introduction evoke the older, traditional classroom? What is her reason for doing this?
2. Do you think the essay's title accurately represents the essay's content or its tone? Why or why not? (Titles and headlines in magazines and newspapers are often chosen by an editor, not the writer.)

3. What is the most important study of computer use in the school, according to Ferguson? Why does she consider it such an authoritative study?

4. Identify the thesis statement. What kind of claim does Ferguson make? According to the thesis statement, what are her main points? How does she qualify her claim?

5. The author uses various kinds of evidence to support her claim, particularly authorities. Identify two such authorities. Could the 15-year-old student, cited along with other teenage students in the essay, be considered an "authority?" Why or why not?

6. Why might it be advantageous for Ferguson to cite the opposing side near the beginning of her essay (paragraph 8), and why does she return to teacher Irene Freeman in her concluding paragraphs? Find another example in which she refers to an opposing claim before refuting it.

7. Ferguson spends parts of two paragraphs critiquing the views of Steven Johnson as expressed in his book *Everything bad is good for you*. Summarize her critique of Johnson.

8. Would you say that Ferguson's main purpose is (a) to expose a problem, (b) to settle an issue, or (c) to critique a position?

COLLABORATIVE ACTIVITY

There are really two issues addressed in Ferguson's essay: computer use in the classroom (her main topic) and the effect of computers on various groups of people, including students and adults in the workplace. Focusing on one issue or the other in groups, attempt to come to a consensus about computer use.

ACTIVITY

Most students today are at least somewhat familiar with computers, although not everyone is comfortable with them. Using at least partly your own experience with computers, write a 500- to 700-word essay on their value to the individual or to society today.

Related reading: Clive Thompson. "Game theories"; Mary Bryson et al. "Conditions for success?"

Wikipedia grows up

Peter Binkley

(1,500 words)

The most common title for an encyclopedia in the Middle Ages (when the genre was formalized, at least in the Western tradition) was Speculum, or "Mirror." Such a work was intended to reflect the entirety of nature, history, and doctrine. The pre-eminent example, Vincent of Beauvais's monumental *Speculum maius*, ran to nearly 1,400 large double-column pages in a seventeenth-century edition of its history volume alone. Don't believe me? Look it up in Wikipedia: I just inserted that (true) figure in the article on Vincent.

The controversy over Wikipedia in library circles has died down over the last few months, as our attention has moved on to other representations of the new "Web 2.0" environment: social bookmarking services, blogs, etc. Nothing, of course, illuminates a complex question like a good buzzword—such as "Library 2.0"—but we should not let the new emphasis prevent us from following the development of one of the forerunners of Web 2.0. Wikipedia is entering its adolescence, at least in web terms: it passed its fifth birthday in January.

To review: Wikipedia aims to be a "multilingual free encyclopedia of the highest possible quality." Its English edition is closing in on one million articles. Anyone can create an account for himself or herself and create or edit articles; even without an account anyone can edit. Every article has a discussion page, where contentious changes can be discussed before they are implemented in the main article. Every article also has a history page where all past changes can be reviewed and reversed. It takes four clicks to restore any earlier version.

Changes are ascribed to the user who made them; users have their own wiki pages with the Wikipedia site where they can list their interests, store work in progress, and receive and respond to comments from readers and other users.

PROBLEMS

Can such a process produce an authoritative encyclopedia? Common sense says no. Even when a knowledgeable author writes something worthwhile, any ignoramus can replace it with whatever nonsense he or she cares to paste into the edit form. Those of us who work in the information professions may well ask why we should involve ourselves in a forum where amateurism rules. Why should you go to the trouble to write a good and correct entry, only to see it defaced?

The openness of the Wikipedia model irritates its critics beyond endurance. The Parents for the Online Safety of Children have found the answer to the question of who edits it: "there is an underground cabal of pedophiles who edit Wikipedia" [*sic*].[1] Their evidence is in the discussion page for the article on pedophilia, where advocates for "childlove" argue for a more lenient attitude toward those who are sexually attracted to children. Perhaps you were unaware of this movement (I certainly was). It is difficult to imagine a more sensitive topic. But the article itself, in its present form, reports the existence and aims of the "childlove" movement without undermining its coverage of the medical and legal aspects of pedophilia. The "cabal" has certainly failed in its attempt to use Wikipedia to infect the world's youth.

Recently a series of minor scandals have drawn public attention to the dangers of Wikipedia's open editing model. A practical joke let a preposterous statement about a Tennessee journalist's involvement in the assassination of John F. Kennedy stand on the record for months. Congressional staff tidied up their senators' entries, in one case consigning an inconvenient campaign promise to the memory hole. Other celebrities were found to have taken a less than neutral approach to their own entries. Even IP addresses traceable to Canada's House of Commons have been found on Wikipedia history pages.

If you are outraged at the way that Wikipedia considers itself above the law, and you feel you have been personally maligned, you might care to join the budding class action suit and claim your share of the "substantial monetary damages" the organizers hope to recover. Wikipedia's problems, the anonymous proponents of the suit claim, "are intentional in design and purposeful in their intent; to cause harm, to permit and encourage a system of anonymous libel."[2] Even if you haven't been libelled yourself, you can still support their cause by clicking on one of the Google ads on their site.

WIKIPEDIA vs. BRITANNICA

There are a thousand reasons why Wikipedia should have been stillborn. And yet it moves, as Galileo said. A recent study published in the journal *Nature* found that Wikipedia compared well to the Encyclopaedia Britannica in a side-by-side blind comparison of 42 articles conducted by experts.[3] The two encyclopedias were tied in major errors at four apiece; Wikipedia led in minor errors 162 to 123.

The sample articles were from the hard sciences. Where Wikipedia really excels is in the areas that you might expect to attract a demographic willing to sit in front of a browser and show off his or her knowledge: popular culture and current technology. If your question concerns a current indie band, an anime character, a class of monster in a particular role-playing game, wireless routers, or even OpenURLs, Wikipedia will often be an excellent source. Jon Udell made this point well last year with his screen-cast "documentary" on the Wikipedia article "Heavy metal umlaut."[4] This article traces the history of the extravagant use of umlauts by bands such as Mötley Crüe—a field of inquiry that Britannica, so far as I know, has yet to address.

Even in the realm of politics, Wikipedia has much to offer. Dip into the article on the Swift Boat Veterans for Truth, who were so prominent in the US election in 2004. You'll find a detailed chronology of the ads and descriptions of their contents and a reasonably balanced account of the issues at stake. The "neutral point of view" (NPOV) so prized at Wikipedia was not achieved in this case without controversy bordering on bloodshed: just look into the discussion page. This, I submit, is one of the most remarkable documents to emerge from the 2004 campaign. If you need a guide to the issues and the passions they provoked, reading this discussion among fierce partisans for both sides is as good as scanning a thousand political blogs. And what is most remarkable is that the two sides actually engaged each other and negotiated a version of the article that both can more or less live with. This is a rare sight indeed in today's polarized political atmosphere, where most on-line forums are echo chambers for one side or the other.

Such negotiations are never easy, and in fact Wikipedia has more institutional structure than at first appears. Some 800 experienced users are designated as administrators, with special powers of binding and loosing: they can protect and unprotect, delete and undelete and revert articles, and block and unblock users. They are expected to use their powers in a neutral way, forming and implementing the consensus of the community. The effect of their intervention shows in the discussion pages of most contentious articles. Wikipedia has survived this long because it is easier to reverse vandalism than it is to commit it; but it still requires an enormous amount of volunteer monitoring to keep the ship afloat.

IDEAL PATRONS

To get a sense of the scale of activity in the Wikipedia community, dip a toe. Click the "Random page" link in the navigation menu a few times, until you find a typo to fix (it won't take long). Fix it, and save the perfected version. Admire your work, and click the "History" page to see your IP address immortalized in the annals of Wikipedia. Now click the "Recent changes" link in the navigation menu. You'll typically find that in the seconds since you saved your change, dozens of other pages have been modified. If you moved too slowly, your change may have scrolled off the list.

What is most striking about this community from the perspective of libraries is that it is made up of ideal library patrons. These are people who are passionate about acquiring and sharing information. Many of them are graduates enjoying an opportunity to maintain contact with their academic discipline and to make use of their scholarly skills. If you enter their community, you may be exposed to ideas that are unsavoury or worse. You will certainly encounter claims that are palpably inaccurate. But I believe it is incumbent on libraries to engage with them.

If an encyclopedia is a mirror, what does Wikipedia reflect? Its community of passionate amateurs—and beyond them the web, in all its variety, like a city described by Whitman. Wikipedia is a glorious experiment and a challenge to us to live up to our ideals. How can we devote ourselves to making information accessible to all and then scorn these devoted amateurs who delight in building with the bricks we give them?

Canadian Library Association. *Feliciter*. 2006. 52 (2).

NOTES

1. http://news.baou.com/main.php?action=recent&rid=20679.
2. http://wikipediaclassaction.org.
3. www.nature.com/news/2005/051212/full/438900a.html.
4. http://weblog.infoworld.com/udell/gems/umlaut.html.

KEY AND DIFFICULT WORDS:
Define the following, using context or other clues if possible: **pre-eminent, contentious, ascribe, cabal, proponent, palpable, incumbent (adj.).**

QUESTIONS
1. How does the author attempt to generate interest in his introduction? Is he successful?
2. What is the author's purpose in writing the essay? Where and how does he indicate this? Who is his audience? Where and how does he indicate this?

3. How could you describe the author's tone in the sentence: "The 'cabal' has certainly failed in its attempt to use *Wikipedia* to infect the world's youth" (paragraph 5). Cite another place where he uses the same tone.

4. What does the author find "remarkable" about *Wikipedia*'s article on the Swift Boat Veterans for Truth? Summarize the paragraph in which this reference occurs.

5. Who are the "ideal patrons" that Binkley refers to in the final section of his essay? Why does he call them this?

6. (a) On the basis of reading this article, list two strengths and two weaknesses of *Wikipedia*. (b) Do you think Binkley would recommend that students use this encyclopedia for their research essays? Why or why not?

COLLABORATIVE ACTIVITY

Do you think that the "consensus" method for determining the content of an encyclopedia entry is as valid as the method of assigning experts/authorities in their field to write entries? Debate this issue.

ACTIVITIES

1. Using at least two current and reliable sources published since December 2005, summarize in 300 to 400 words the controversy that arose when the academic journal *Nature* compared articles in *Wikipedia* with articles in the *Encyclopaedia Britannica*.

2. Write an informational *or* evaluative report based on one entry from two different encyclopedias, one of which is *Wikipedia*. Ensure that the subject is one that you are familiar with so that you are qualified to compare and contrast the sources in their treatment of the subject.

Conditions for success?
Gender in technology-intensive courses in British Columbia secondary schools

Mary Bryson, Stephen Petrina, Marcia Braundy, and Suzanne de Castell

(2,500 words)

One thing is clear: claiming that current policies and practices aim to achieve 'equal opportunity' is not yet borne out in reality. The committee recommends that a program be developed to deal with these [gender] inequities.
British Columbia Ministry of Education, 1999. p. xiv.

Abstract: Gender inequities in technology are systemic in Canadian schools and workplaces (Status of Women Canada, 1997). Several recent analyses of British Columbia (BC) students' participation in technology-intensive areas of the public school curriculum have documented a range of these inequities (Braundy, O'Riley, Petrina, Dalley, & Paxton, 2000; Bryson & de Castell, 1998; Schaefer, 2000). In the BC Ministry of Education's (BC MOE) most recent technology policy report, *Conditions for success* (1999), gender inequities are treated as symptoms of poor access, rather than as a systemic part of the school conditions themselves. Because the report's authors misapprehended the extent of inequities, BC MOE's Technology Advisory Committee recommended a distribution and integration of technologies to provide the new conditions for success in technology throughout BC's public schools. We argue that the inequities in the BC schools are systemic and cannot be understood without an adequate assessment of participation and performance data. We analyze provincial trends in gender-differentiated participation and performance of students in the technology-intensive courses of BC public secondary education, at a time in Canadian history when competence and confidence with a range of technologies are essential for full cultural participation.

More financial resources are being directed to technology than to any other area in public school budgets. For the period 1998 to 2004, the BC government committed $123 million to establish a Provincial Learning Network to network BC's 1,700 public schools and improve access. Other provinces made similar commitments to information technology. Alberta, for example, invested $85 million for the same time period. Inasmuch as girls continue to be under-represented in technology courses, they have not benefited from the comparatively large financial investments in technology. Policy-makers in Canadian public education require access to sex-disaggregated data in order to create and implement equity-oriented strategies in technology. The research described here represents a step towards the development of an information-rich database for monitoring technology course enrolments in Canadian schools and has both policy and scholarly implications.

BACKGROUND

The knowledge and technology sectors represent the fastest growing areas in the Canadian economy, in Canadian cultural production, and in Canadian educational curriculum development. In 1998, the high-tech sector's contribution to

BC's GDP was 6.2 per cent, 20 times the 0.3 per cent expansion rate of the BC economy. High-tech sector job growth doubled during the 1990s, while overall job growth was 15 per cent. But the high-tech sector is male-dominated. Only 20 per cent of the high-tech positions in BC, Canada, and the United States are filled by women (American Association of University Women, 2000; Menzies, 1998; Ministry of Women's Equality, 2000: Schaefer, 2000; Status of Women Canada, 1997; Withers, 2000). Why, then, is it still the case, at the dawn of the twenty-first century, that a large number of girls and women (a) remain limited to domestic, clerical, medical, and service *uses of* technology and (b) occupy subordinate roles in many scientific and technical fields? While women are more likely than men to work in an occupation requiring significant amounts of computer use, girls in secondary school are only one-fourth as likely to complete a computer education course as boys. In the educational context, specifically, empirical evidence suggests that female staff and students (in comparison with males) (a) are disenfranchised with respect to access and variety of use, (b) are less likely to acquire technological competence and confidence, and (c) are more likely to be actively discouraged from playing a leadership role in technology (Braundy et al., 2000; Bryson & de Castell, 1998; Schaefer, 2000; Shashaani, 1994; Sutton, 1991; Withers, 2000).

In response to the persistent under-representation of girls and women in technology courses, national (e.g., Status of Women Canada, 1998) and international (Huyer, 1997) organizations have emphasized the importance of developing and maintaining comprehensive national and regional sex-differentiated analyses of trends in students' participation and performance in technology. In the United States, analyses of key access and performance indicators have shown that girls make up only a small percentage of students in computer science courses. Girls are significantly more likely than boys to enrol in clerical and data-entry courses, the 1990s version of typing. Boys are more likely to enrol in advanced computer science and computer graphics courses (American Association of University Women, 1998, 2000). The proportion of female students taking the Computer Science College Board examinations did not increase between 1987 (17 per cent) and 1997 (16 per cent) (College Board, 1997; National Science Foundation, 1997a, 1997b).

Our analysis of BC's student enrolments in all technology-intensive courses documents inequities for girls across all but the information management (business education) and clothing and textiles (home economics) courses (tables 1 to 3). Inasmuch as girls continue to be under-represented in most technology-intensive courses, they have not benefited from investments in these courses. And so there exists a double inequity: information and industrial technology courses continue to be over-funded in comparison to courses where female students predominate; only a small percentage of girls receive the benefits accrued through completion of these courses. In Canada, England, and the United States, analyses of sex-disaggregated data have indicated similar findings regarding engineering, design, and the trades. For example, the percentage of women completing baccalaureate degrees in engineering increased in the United States through the 1960s and 1970s but has remained between 15–20 per cent of the total since the late 1980s (National Science Foundation, 1997b). Women account for about 15 per cent of the total product and industrial design graduates in Canada and England and about 90 per cent of the graduates in textile design (Clegg, Mayfield & Trayhurn, 1999). In Canada, women account for between 0.51 per cent (sheet metal fabricators) and 3.5 per cent (machinists, painters/decorators) of all apprenticeships, when chefs and hairdressers are removed from the calculations (Ministry of Women's Equality, 2000;

Skof, 1994). The point of these indicators is not to belabour the under-representation of women but rather to stress the importance of sex-disaggregated data for accountability and policy-making.

METHOD AND OBJECTIVES

We analyzed BC MOE records of secondary course enrolment (participation) and performance (marks) in technology-intensive courses for all years for which sex-disaggregated data were available. We also analyzed practices in schools where either a single program or multiple programs were in place to increase participation by female students. All middle and secondary schools were contacted by the research team, via both mail and e-mail *(N = 375)*. An exceedingly small sub-set of schools (n = 13) was *self-identified* by administrators as having either a single program or multiple programs in place to increase participation of female students. This sample was unrepresentative and so small as to render any generalizations entirely suspect. However, teachers and administrators in these schools were contacted and interviewed about initiatives to increase the participation of female students in technology-intensive courses. Reports from these schools about gender-specific interventions were sketchy at best. We also contacted all of the provincial ministries of education in Canada to gain access to enrolments in technology-intensive courses, but only Ontario, in addition to BC, responded with useable data.

We have created a website (http://www.she can.com) both to disseminate the results of this project and to engage members of all stakeholder groups in public discussions of our findings, as well as to publish research findings. Our findings and recommendations represent an interdisciplinary approach to investigating gender inequities that are national in scope and of great international interest. We believe that policy makers in Canada will benefit directly from the results of this research.

FINDINGS

Key findings are as follows:

- With the notable exception of information management (i.e., business education) and clothing and textiles courses, boys dominate in most technology-intensive courses. This finding has remained essentially unaltered throughout the duration of an explicit BC MOE *gender equity* policy. In other words, the situation for girls remains one of under-representation and disciplinary ghettoization. The status of girls in BC public school technology courses has not improved over the last 15 years. While our focus was on secondary schools, we stress that gender inequities in technology are systemic in the educational system, from K-to-12 curriculum to instruction to teacher preparation and employment (tables 1 to 3).
- Female students, relative to their absolute numbers as participants in technology-intensive courses, are *over-represented* in the upper categories of the performance scale (A and B) and *under-represented* in the lower categories of the performance scale (C to F). Statistically, the comparability of performance across the sexes is suspect, because the samples are not comparable to the extent that the female sample represents a very small minority of the total number of available participants. It may be that only the most able female students choose to participate in these courses. One cannot conclude from this finding that girls 'do better' than boys in technology-intensive courses (tables 2 and 3).
- Interprovincial data for comparative purposes is generally unavailable. Record-keeping is either sporadic across the provinces or ministries are unwilling to make their enrolment data public. Enrolments in BC's

technology-intensive courses are similar to enrolments in Ontario's courses, except in Communications Technology, where female enrolments are nearly twice those of BC's enrolments in the parallel Drafting and CAD courses. Enrolment in Ontario's Technological Design course is also noticeably higher than in BC's General Technology course. More research is necessary to determine why there are differences (table 4).

Table 1: BC technology enrolments by course and sex, 1988, 1998

Course	% Female 1987–1988	% Male 1987–1988	% Female 1997–1998	% Male 1997–1998
Info Tech 12	23	77	21	79
Construction 12	4.2	95.8	6	94
Drafting & CAD 12	11	89	14	86
Technology 12	8	92	10	90

Table 2: BC technology-intensive courses and performances by enrolments, marks, and sex, 1997–1998

Course and sex	#	%	% A–B	% C	% F
Construction 11 female	322	10	65	33	2
Construction 11 male	2,779	90	55	40	5
Construction 12 female	149	6	71	26	3
Construction 12 male	2,295	94	59	37	4
Drafting & CAD 11 female	837	19	79	20	1
Drafting & CAD 11 male	3,453	81	62	32	6
Drafting & CAD 12 female	274	14	82	18	0
Drafting & CAD 12 male	1,720	86	56	42	2
Electronics 11 female	33	3	83	17	0
Electronics 11 male	965	97	57	36.2	6.8
Electronics 12 female	22	3	86	14	0
Electronics 12 male	714	97	70	34.6	3.5
Metal fab/welding 11 female	192	9	60	37	3
Metal fab/welding 11 male	2,026	91	50	45	5
Metal fab/welding 12 female	75	6	61	39	0
Metal fab/welding 12 male	1,260	94	56	39	5
Power tech/auto 11 female	461	10	40	55	5
Power tech/auto 11 male	4,266	90	44	46	10
Power tech/auto 12 female	153	4	51	45	4
Power tech/auto 12 male	3,706	96	51	44	5
Technology 11 female	128	12	67	33	0
Technology 11 male	962	88	46	49	5
Technology 12 female	52	10	75	23	2
Technology 12 male	483	90	61	36	3

Source: BC Ministry of Education, Data Management and Student Services Branch, Report TRAK2952B.

Table 3: BC technology-intensive courses and performance by enrolments, marks, and sex, 1997–1998

Course and sex	#	%	% A–B	% C	% F
Information tech 11 female	2,692	34	67	30	3
Information tech 11 male	5,264	66	58	36	6
Information tech 12 female	733	21	76	22	2
Information tech 12 male	2,734	79	66	29	5
Info management 11 female	760	69	68	31	1
Info management 11 male	335	31	55	39	6
Info management 12 female	339	74	71	28	1
Info management 12 male	119	26	57	38	5
Clothing & textiles 11 female	1,643	96	72	24	4
Clothing & textiles 11 male	77	4	48	44	8
Clothing & textiles 12 female	735	98	76	21	3
Clothing & textiles 12 male	13	2	38	62	0

Source: BC Ministry of Education, Data Management and Student Services Branch, Report TRAK2952B.

Table 4: Ontario technology enrolments by secondary course, grade, and sex, 1996–1999

Course	Female 1997–98	Male 1997–98	Total 1997–98	Female 1998–99	Male 1998–99	Total 1998–99
Communications	21,173	47,822	68,995	24,221	50,590	74,811
	30.6%	69.4%	100%	67.7%	32.3%	100%
Transportation	5,394	50,609	56,003	5,400	50,913	56,313
	9.6%	90.4%	100%	9.5%	91.5%	100%
Construction Tech	6,067	35,283	41,350	6,702	37,453	44,155
	18.4%	81.6%	100%	15.1%	74.9%	100%
Tech Design	6,694	26,235	32,929	15,739	40,064	55,803
	20.3%	79.7%	100%	28.2%	71.8%	100%
Manufacturing	2,422	24,923	27,345	3,647	27,731	31,428
	8.8%	91.2%	100%	11.6%	88.4%	100%
Electronics	108	1,121	1,229	71	756	827
	8.7%	91.3%	100%	8.5%	91.5%	100%
Computer Tech	150	1,011	1,061	439	1,251	1,690
	14.1%	85.9%	100%	25.9%	74.1%	100%
Hospitality Services	8,164	9,077	17,241	9,397	10,294	19,691
	47.3%	52.7%	100%	47.7%	52.3%	100%
Cosmetology	11,962	1,536	13,498	12,769	1,720	14,489
	88.6%	11.4%	100%	88.1%	11.9%	100%

Source: Ontario School Report Course Enrolment, Ontario Ministry of Education.

- Of the 375 secondary schools in BC that were contacted by the research team by both e-mail and regular mail, only 13 (3.4 per cent) responded to our request for information concerning *any* local, school-based initiatives designed to increase participation by female students in technology-intensive courses. Clearly, there is good reason to be concerned that administrators at BC secondary schools are not addressing the problem of the significant and persistent under-representation of female students in technology-intensive secondary schools.

- One out of every 30 technology teachers and one out of every eight information technology teachers are female. Neither the BC Ministry of Education nor the university administrators in BC have demonstrated leadership in redressing these inequities, which correlate directly with enrolments in technology-intensive courses. While the research on gender and role modeling is contentious, there is no excuse for wholesale inattention to gender inequities in the technology education teaching force.

- In 1998 the BC Ministry of Education ceased to collect sex-disaggregated data on most courses in the secondary school curriculum, citing in explanation the cost of collecting these data, as well as their perceived use value to educational decision-making. However, policy-makers for Canadian education require access to sex-disaggregated data in order to create and implement equity-oriented interventions in technology.

DISCUSSION

Girls and boys are required to take one or more of the applied skills courses in Grade 8 (business education, home economics, information technology, technology education), and most administrators have chosen to make *all* of these a requirement. Hence, the percentage of girls enrolling in Grade 8 technology courses in BC increased from 32 per cent in 1986 to 42.3 per cent in 1996. We are tempted to celebrate this as a milestone in gender equity in BC education history, but practices in some districts have remained unchanged. In Grades 9 and 10, where boys and girls elect the applied skills courses, girls' participation rates are one-third to one-half lower than in Grade 8. When given options, both girls and boys choose stereotypically gendered courses. Requiring girls to take technology (or boys, home economics or business courses) is a solution to only part of the problem (Braundy et al., 2000).

In BC's senior secondary courses, the current percentage of girls enrolled in technology-intensive courses remains extremely low, while performance data indicate that those female students who participate in these courses do better, on average, than male students in these courses. In Information Technology courses, the participation of female students is 34 per cent of total students enrolled in Grade 11, declining precipitously to 21 per cent in Grade 12, yet female students in Information Technology continue to earn A and B more often than their male peers. Girls represent 74 per cent of the enrolments in information management courses and 98 per cent of the enrolments in clothing and textiles courses (tables 1 to 3). One could make an argument for enrolling more boys in these technology-intensive courses.

Total enrolments in the most popular technology courses dropped by 20 per cent between 1987 and 1998, but the percentage of girls increased by 2.4 per cent. The percentage of girls enrolled in Grades 11 and 12 technology courses increased from 7.9 per cent in 1987 to 10.3 per cent in 1998. In Grade 11 and 12 Construction, the enrolment of girls was 10 per cent and 6 per cent respectively in 1998. The enrolment of girls in Grade 11 Electronics was 3.6 per cent; for Grade 12 the percentage of the total dropped to 3.0 per cent. Despite the relevance of electronics to high-technology careers, this course has never been able to overcome the average 3 to 4 per cent enrolment of girls. Girls' enrolment in Grade 11 Power Technology was 10 per cent and in Grade 12, 4 per cent; in Grade 11 Metal Fabrication, 9 per cent and in Grade 12, 6 per cent. Drafting and CAD courses had significantly higher enrolment rates than the other technology courses (19 per cent in Grade 11 and 14 per cent in Grade 12). Enrolments of girls in the senior, general technology courses increased by 3 per cent between 1987 and 1998, while total enrolment increased by 26 per cent in the same decade. Enrolments of girls declined in the Construction, Electronics, Metal Fabrication, and Power Technology courses. There is work to be done if we are to be accountable for equity as a policy initiative.

Girls in secondary school courses in BC have proved that they have high levels of knowledge and skill, so it is not an issue of technophobia. In Grade 11 Construction during 1997–1998, the percentage of girls awarded A was 29.7 per cent, while the percentage of boys awarded A was 21 per cent. In Grade 12 Construction during that year, 45.7 per cent of the girls were awarded A-level final marks and 27 per cent of the boys were awarded A-level marks. If girls have proven themselves willing and able to succeed in technology, then what is the problem, or more specifically, what is the solution?

RECOMMENDATIONS

Public knowledge of trends in the gender-differentiated participation and performance of girls and boys in technology-intensive courses in Canadian schools can underwrite accountability and support intelligent and informed interventions. This knowledge can facilitate policy initia-

tives aimed at redressing current inequities. Ought an equitable representation of females and males in technological careers and practices to remain a pipe dream? The BC MOE's *Conditions for success* (1999) report articulates a vision for the integration of information technology in the public school curriculum at all levels, and this is one place where the report's authors are uninformed. "Technology should be integrated into curriculum rather than having technology as a separate course," the Technology Advisory Committee mistakenly recommended to BC MOE (p. vii). Here is the naive assumption that technology is merely a tool; students do not need to study technology (Petrina, 2002). It was not until Grade 11, the Technology Advisory Committee suggested, that a course in information technology should be available for students to choose. While there is nothing patently wrong with the integration of technology into all subjects, integration is irrelevant to equity. We argue that only through structural interventions (such as courses) and systematic instruction will systemic inequities be adequately addressed. Current gender inequities are, in part, the result of the mere integration of technology and the resultant unstructured, unsystematic way in which technology is addressed in the schools. Research has repeatedly demonstrated that boys dominate technology use in contexts of integration and regular classroom use and that teachers have proven reluctant and unable to integrate computers into the K-to-12 curriculum (Ungerleider, 1997, p. 13). So our recommendation is the antithesis of that of the Technology Advisory Committee. We recommend that more courses be made available and be required for girls rather than fewer, but the caveat is this: access and outcomes must be redefined by equity. Access to technologies must follow access to equities; equities must precede outcomes. Equity is amorphous as a value, but it is also structural as a policy. Equity can have accountability. To redress inequities, we recommend accountable, gender-specific, intensive experiences in technology for all boys and girls rather than chance integration. When the BC MOE removed the acclaimed *Information Technology K-7* and *Technology Education K-7* curricula from the schools in 1998, another potential gender intervention was abandoned. The curriculum was pulled from the shelves of the schools (including the ministry's website), structure was destroyed, and the result was maintenance of the *status quo*. The decision to stop the collection of enrolment data in 1998 made evidence for accountability inaccessible. These are hardly conditions for success in any subject!

ACKNOWLEDGEMENT

This research was funded by a grant from the British Columbia Ministry of Education.

Canadian Journal of Science, Mathematics and Technology Education.
2003. 3 April: (2).

REFERENCES

American Association of University Women. (2000). *Gender gaps: Where schools fail our women.* Washington, DC: Author.

American Association of University Women. (2000). *Tech-savvy: Educating girls in the new computer age.* Washington, DC: Author.

Braundy. M., O'Riley, P., Petrina, S., Dalley, S., & Paxton, A. (2000). Missing XX chromosomes or gender in/equity in design and technology education? The case of British Columbia. *Journal of Industrial Teacher Education, 37*(3), 54–92.

British Columbia Ministry of Education. (1994). *The kindergarten to grade 12 education plan.* Victoria, BC: Author.

British Columbia Ministry of Education. (1999). *Conditions for success* (Report of the Teaching, Learning and Education Technology Advisory Committee to the British Columbia Ministry of Education). Victoria, BC: Author. Available: http://www.bced.gov.bc.ca/technology/advisoryreport/toc.htm.

Bryson, M., & de Castell, S. (1998). New technologies and the cultural ecology of schooling: Imagining teachers as Luddites in/deed. *Educational Policy, 12*(5), 542–567.

Clegg, S., Mayfield, W., & Trayhurn, D. (1999). Disciplinary discourses: A case study of gender in information technology and design courses. *Gender and Education, II*(1), 43–55.

College Board. (1997). *Ten year increases in percentages of men and women taking AP examinations.* Available: http://www.collegeboard.com/press/senior97/table14.html.

Huyer, S. (1997). *Supporting women's use of technologies for sustainable development.* Toronto: Women in Global Science and Technology.

Menzies, H. (1998). *Women and the knowledge based economy and society.* Ottawa: Status of Women Canada.

Ministry of Women's Equality. (2000). *Women count 2000: A statistical profile of women in British Columbia.* Victoria, BC: Author.

National Science Foundation. (1997a). *Science and engineering Bachelor's degrees awarded to women increase overall, but decline in several fields.* Washington, DC: Author.

National Science Foundation. (1997b). *Women and minorities in science and engineering: An update.* Washington, DC: Author.

Petrina, S. (2002). Getting a purchase on the school of tomorrow and its constituent technologies: Histories and historiographies of technologies. *History of Education Quarterly, 42*(3), 75–111.

Schaefer, A. (2000). *G.I. Joe meets Barbie, software engineer meets caregiver: Males and females in BC's public schools and beyond.* British Columbia Teachers' Federation.

Shashaani, L. (1994). Gender differences in computer experience and its influence on computer attitudes. *Journal of Educational Computing Research, 11*(4), 347–367.

Skof, K. (1994). Women in registered apprenticeship training programs. *Education Quarterly Review, 1*(4), 26–33.

Status of Women Canada. (1997). *Economic gender equality indicators.* Ottawa: Author.

Status of Women Canada. (1998). *Gender based analysis: A guide for policy-making.* Ottawa: Author.

Sutton, R. (1991). Equity and computers in the schools: A decade of research. *Review of Educational Research, 61,* 475–503.

Ungerleider, C. (1997). *West Vancouver teachers' association teacher computer technology use survey.* Unpublished manuscript, University of British Columbia.

Withers, P. (2000). Mismatched? Why so few women seem to be taking advantage of this high-tech business bonanza. *BC Business, 28*(10), 102–111.

KEY AND DIFFICULT WORDS

Define the following, using context or other clues if possible: **systemic, inequity, disaggregated, disenfranchised, ghettoization, contentious, caveat, amorphous.**

QUESTIONS

1. What is the function of the epigraph and abstract? How is this abstract unlike the more typical ones that precede scientific experiments?

2. What does the essay's title refer to? How does the title reflect the purpose and findings of the study?

3. Does this essay include a review of relevant literature? If it does, where is it and what is its specific function?

4. What limitations are mentioned in the "Method and objectives" section? What was done in an attempt to remedy these limitations?

5. What data is presented in table 1? Why do you think the authors chose to present similar data in two different tables (table 2 and table 3)?

6. In what section do the authors refer extensively to the data from tables 1–3? Are any conclusions drawn in this section?

7. Explain how the heading of the final section, "Recommendations," is consistent with the purpose of the authors in writing this study. Summarize this section in approximately 100 words (25 per cent of the total); *OR*, identify two specific criticisms of the government's Ministry of Education that the authors make in "Recommendations." Addressing one of these criticisms, explain why you think it is valid (or why you think it is not).

COLLABORATIVE ACTIVITIES

1. "Conditions for success?" deals more with problems and solutions than with causes and effects. However, many of the problems addressed in the essay raise questions about possible causes. What or who do you think is primarily responsible for the lack of progress in reducing gender inequities in technology courses in Canadian schools? Discuss.

2. "There is little that can be done about gender inequities in the school or the workplace until society changes its stereotypical views of men and women." Debate this statement.

ACTIVITY

Write a critical response to the essay in which you consider your own experience with technology as a student, and address at least one of the recommendations of the study.

Related reading: Sue Ferguson. "How computers make our kids stupid."

Universities, governments and industry: Can the essential nature of universities survive the drive to commercialize?

Simon N. Young

(3,000 words)

Having spent 40 years in universities, I have had sufficient time to consider some of the idiosyncrasies, foibles, and problems of these academic institutions. The purpose of this editorial is to discuss the current state of university research and explain why I find some aspects of the current situation disturbing. Changes that started during the second half of the twentieth century and that have continued into the twenty-first threaten to bring about fundamental changes in the nature of universities. Some of the changes are commendable, for example, the large expansion in the proportion of the population attending universities, at least in the richer nations. Other trends are disturbing, especially the increasing tendency of governments and industry to view universities as engines for short-term economic gain. While universities certainly cannot ignore the context in which they function and the needs of society, responding purely to short-term economic considerations threatens to subvert the very nature of universities and some of the benefits they provide to society.

So what exactly is a university, and what is its purpose? I much prefer the *Oxford English dictionary* definition of the word "university" to some of the more utilitarian definitions in other dictionaries. The Oxford definition reads, in part, "whole body of teachers and scholars engaged in the higher branches of learning." Thus, it is the community of faculty and students that is the essence of a university. The higher branches of learning in which teachers and scholars engage have two important products: the educated minds that are essential for the well-being of society and new knowledge and ideas. Some of that new knowledge will enrich society by producing economic growth, directly or indirectly, but the benefits of new knowledge go far beyond economic gain.

Universities have always been subjected to outside influences. The oldest European university, the University of Bologna, has existed at least since the 1080s. Some time before 1222, about 1,000 students left Bologna and founded a new university in Padua because of "the grievous offence that was brought to bear on their academic liberties and the failure to acknowledge the privileges solemnly granted to teachers and students."[1] The outside interference came from the Roman Catholic Church, and for several centuries, Padua was home to the only university in Europe where non-Catholics could get a university education. Both Bologna and Padua were student-controlled universities with students electing the professors and fixing their salaries. However, in spite of marked differences, there are similarities between what happened then and what is happening today, with important outside influences—then the dogma of religion, now the dogma of business— threatening to change the activities of the community of teachers and scholars.

The seeds of what is happening now were sown in the years following World War II. Before the war, the most important influence on a faculty member was probably the departmental chair, who in those days had power to influence in an important way what went on in the department. Nonetheless, a faculty member would have had access to departmental resources and would not necessarily have required outside research funding (although such funding was sometimes available from private foundations). The mechanism of funding research, and the amount of money available for research, changed greatly in the postwar years. In 1945, Vannevar Bush's landmark report to President Harry Truman, *Science the endless frontier*,[2] had an important influence on university research. In this report, Bush stated, "The publicly and privately supported colleges, universities, and research institutes are the centers of basic research. They are the wellsprings of knowledge and understanding. As long as they are vigorous and healthy and their scientists are free to pursue the truth wherever it may lead, there will be a flow of new scientific knowledge to those who can apply it to practical problems in Government, in industry, or elsewhere." Bush supported the idea that the US government should provide strong financial support for university research but also supported the idea that the individual investigator should be the main determinant of the topics for investigation, with statements such as "Scientific progress on a broad front results from the free play of free intellects, working on subjects of their own choice, in the manner dictated by their curiosity for exploration of the unknown."[2]

In the latter half of the last century, many countries adopted the model of granting councils, which used a system based on peer review to distribute money for investigator-initiated research. This model has been a great success, but it has also contributed to important changes in universities. Much more money has been available to support medical research, basic science research, and engineering research than has been available for the social sciences or arts. Thus, decisions about support for different disciplines devolved from the universities to governments, who decided on the budgets of their various grant-giving bodies. Also, individual researchers who were successful in obtaining grants no longer depended as much on departmental facilities. In my opinion, this not only weakened the power of departmental chairs but also decreased collegiality within departments.

With increased enrolments, as a university education became accessible to a greater proportion of the population, and an increased need for infrastructure for the larger student population and for complex research equipment, administrators became more concerned about sources of funding and consequently more detached from the faculty. There is always a tendency for senior academic administrators to speak and behave as though they *were* the university (when of course they are there to serve the community of teachers and scholars). This is of course a normal human trait, no different from the tendency of politicians to forget that they are elected to serve the people. However, this increasing detachment of senior university administrators from the faculty has facilitated the erosion of collegiality within departments and universities. The individual personalities of university faculty probably also facilitated this change. I learned recently, when looking at the literature on personality, that an inverse correlation between intelligence and conscientiousness has been demonstrated in a number of studies (see, for example, Moutafi et al[3]). Thus, it might be more than just my paranoia leading me to believe that the small proportion of university faculty who lack conscientiousness and collegiality is larger than in

some other walks of life. The erosion of collegiality is not a matter of great significance, except that it probably played a role in making researchers more open to the efforts of governments to transform them into entrepreneurs.

The most recent and possibly the most important change in university research resulted from the push by governments to commercialize the results of such research. In the United States, the Bayh-Dole Act of 1980 encouraged universities to license to private industry discoveries made with federal funds.[4] The push by governments for commercialization of new knowledge grew during the 1980s and 1990s and continues to have an important influence on universities. Recently, Lord Sainsbury, the science and innovation minister in the United Kingdom, boasted that there had been a cultural change in universities there, which has resulted in a substantial increase in university spin-offs.[5] In 2002 the Association of Universities and Colleges of Canada entered an agreement with the government to double the amount of research performed by these institutions and to triple their commercialization performance by 2010.[6] Although this agreement was reached in the absence of any broad consultation with the faculty who are supposed to commercialize their work, the universities seem to be well on track to achieve this objective, with a 126 per cent increase in revenues from licence royalties between 1999 and 2001.[7] Most major universities now have a technology transfer office, and at many universities success in commercialization is taken into account when faculty are considered for tenure. Will there come a time when success in commercialization carries the same weight as (or more weight than) teaching and research in the awarding of tenure?

The end result of all the changes discussed above is that individual faculty members have become much more like entrepreneurs whose main allegiance is to the maintenance or growth of their own research programs and not infrequently to the commercialization of their research. The researcher exploring Vannevar Bush's "endless frontier" could be considered the modern equivalent of the homesteader taming the seemingly endless frontier of the nineteenth-century American West.[8] This is not necessarily detrimental if a new generation of university research entrepreneurs provides the new knowledge that will benefit patients and society. However, the change in culture that made university faculty more like entrepreneurs also made them more open to the desire of governments to make them entrepreneurs in the economic sense. Although the nature of universities has been changing, there was no threat to the fundamental nature of universities until the drive for commercialization began.

A recent report of the Canadian Association of University Teachers[9] states that university administrators have been "building increasingly hierarchical management structures" that "place the future of academic medicine in danger." The report's main concern is that "incentives to create commercializable products push economic concerns, rather than scientific and ethical considerations, to the forefront." [9] In the fields of biologic psychiatry and behavioural neuroscience, the emphasis on commercial applications has already, to some extent, moved research priorities away from an emphasis on mental well-being to an emphasis on commercial products. There are many examples of this shift. For example, more research is being carried out on antidepressant drugs than on psychotherapy, even though in mild to moderate depression (the majority of cases) drugs and psychotherapy are approximately equal in efficacy. There is increasing evidence for the efficacy of exercise[10,11] and fish oils[12,13] in the treatment and prevention of depression. However, these strategies receive

much less attention than antidepressant drugs. Even an established antidepressant treatment such as S-adenosylmethionine (SAMe)[14] receives little attention. Searching the abstracts of the 2004 meeting of the Society for Neuroscience, I found 179 with the keyword "antidepressant" and only four with the keyword "S-adenosylmethionine," and none of those four was concerned with the antidepressant action of SAMe. SAMe is a major methyl donor and seems to work in a fundamentally different way from any product being investigated by drug companies. Surely we could expect that an antidepressant acting through a different mechanism would be a popular topic of investigation. However, SAMe is a natural product and not of commercial interest. Similarly, insights into what exercise or fish oils do to the brain may provide important insights into the pathophysiology of depression and its treatment, but these subjects receive little attention.

Many basic science researchers investigating the mechanisms of antidepressants produced by drug companies do not receive funding from those companies. However, enough are lured by drug company research funds into working on topics of interest to the companies to significantly influence what are fashionable topics of research. Laboratories with funding from industry can often afford more trainees, who may then adopt a more industry-centred approach in their own research. While the availability of funds from industry has certainly influenced research, the pressure on university faculty to commercialize the results of their research will undoubtedly cause even greater distortion in the areas of research that are most popular.

Granting agencies have increasingly tried to foster research in neglected areas by allocating funds to specific areas of research and requesting applications in those areas. Although this approach is certainly necessary, it has not done much to alter the effects of drug company money on research output. Also, in some ways it moves research even further away from the ideal in Vannevar Bush's report that "Scientific progress on a broad front results from the free play of free intellects, working on subjects of their own choice, in the manner dictated by their curiosity for exploration of the unknown."[2] This model was notably successful in the last half of the twentieth century, but it may not survive the pressure to commercialize. While there is still much scope for curiosity-driven research, the curiosity of researchers is likely to be aligned increasingly with the interests of drug companies. As mentioned above, a cultural change has accompanied the increasing commercialization of university research. The pressure to commercialize has been critiqued in some quarters, but many university faculty have nonetheless embraced commercialization or at least remained unconcerned about it. Are we far from a time when a researcher without a patent that is being commercialized will be regarded in the same way as those who do not publish regularly in the top journals? And how long will it be before governments make commercialization a mandate of granting councils and a requirement for the majority of grants?

A fascination with the workings of the brain and how it can malfunction in mental illness is the usual motivator for researchers in neuroscience and psychiatry research. As a result, curiosity-driven research will always tend to serve the best interests of patients. Although research driven by commercial interests will certainly benefit psychiatric patients in some ways, it cannot serve their overall needs, as it is much too narrowly focused. The designation of funds by granting agencies for specific neglected topics will help but is unlikely to produce any large changes in the direction of research. Thus, the biggest losers from the pressure to commercialize will be psychiatric patients. In addition, I am

concerned whether students who are trained to focus on the short-term commercial implications of their research will be able to maintain the breadth of vision that is a characteristic of the majority of creative researchers.

Changes due to pressure from governments to commercialize are not limited to researchers. The increased emphasis on commercialization in universities has in some ways distorted the perceptions of senior university administrators about the purpose of the institutions. For example, there seems to be a lack of concern about some of the sources of funds that universities receive. Universities now hold patents on many life-saving drugs. These patents sometimes limit access to the drugs, particularly in low-income countries.[15] In Canada, one-quarter of the faculties of medicine receive funding from the tobacco industry.[16] Perhaps a suitable future definition of a university will be a "whole body of teachers and scholars engaged in turning ideas into profit."

In thirteenth-century Italy, the response to interference by the Roman Catholic Church in the work of scholars was a move to another location to escape the interference. In the twenty-first century, that option is not available even to the minority who are concerned about the drive to commercialize. However, the picture is not entirely bleak. Charitable foundations will remain immune to commercial interests. In addition, even though charitable foundations will probably remain relatively small players in the funding of research, there are promising signs. For example, the Bill and Melinda Gates Foundation, created in 2000, has an endowment of about US$27 billion and is striving to use its money for the benefit of humankind in areas neglected by governments. This foundation is not involved in psychiatric research, but its focus on preventive approaches may help to direct interest to that important area. Research on prevention in psychiatry is still in its infancy and will certainly remain that way if short-term commercial considerations stay paramount. However, charitable foundations cannot be expected to have any large effect on the change in university culture brought about by the drive to commercialize. Although I would like to be able to end this editorial on a more hopeful note, I am concerned about these cultural changes, and I do not see any solution. Still, one lesson from history is that the communities of teachers and scholars making up universities have adapted to many changes over the centuries without changing the fundamental nature of universities, and they will surely continue to do so. I am just not sure how.

Journal of Psychiatry & Neuroscience.
2005. 30 (3).

REFERENCES

1. *History*. Padua (Italy): Università Degli Studi di Padova. Available: www.unipd.it/en/university/history.htm (accessed 2004 Dec 13).

2. Bush V. *Science the endless frontier. A report to the President by Vannevar Bush, Director of the Office of Scientific Research and Development, July 1945*. Washington: US Government Printing Office; 1945. Available: www.nsf.gov/od/lpa/nsf50/vbush1945.htm (accessed 2004 Dec 13).

3. Moutafi J, Furnham A, Paltiel L. Why is conscientiousness negatively correlated with intelligence? *Pers Individ Differ* 2004;37:1013–22.

4. Thursby JG, Thursby MC. Intellectual property. University licensing and the Bayh-Dole Act. *Science* 2003;301:1052.

5. Sainsbury L. A cultural change in UK universities [editorial]. *Science* 2002;296:1929.

6. Allan Rock welcomes framework on federally funded university research [press release]. Toronto: Industry Canada; 2002 Nov 19 [modified 2003 Jun 16]. Available: www.ic.gc.ca/cmb/welcomeic.nsf/558d636590992942852564880052155b/85256a220056c2a485256c76004c7d44 (accessed 2004 Dec 13).

7. Berkowitz P. Spinning off research: AUCC sets new tool to measure universities' commercialization performance. *Univ Aff* [serial on-line] 2004;June/July. Available: www.universityaffairs.ca/issues/2004/junejuly/print/spinningoff.html (accessed 2004 Dec 13).

8. Kennedy D. Enclosing the research commons [editorial]. *Science* 2001;294:2249.

9. Welch P, Cass CE, Guyatt G, Jackson AC, Smith D. *Defending medicine: clinical faculty and academic freedom*. Report of the Canadian Association of University Teachers (CAUT) Task Force on Academic Freedom for Faculty at University-Affiliated Health Care Institutions. Ottawa: Canadian Association of University Teachers; 2004 Nov. Available: www.caut.ca/en/issues/academicfreedom/DefendingMedicine.pdf (accessed 2004 Dec 21).

10. Salmon P. Effects of physical exercise on anxiety, depression, and sensitivity to stress: a unifying theory. *Clin Psychol Rev* 2001; 21:33–61.

11. *Depression: management of depression in primary and secondary care*. Clinical guideline 23. London (UK): National Institute for Clinical Excellence; 2004 Dec. Available: http://www.nice.org.uk/pdf/CG023NICEguideline.pdf (accessed 2005 Mar 8).

12. Nemets B, Stahl Z, Belmaker RH. Addition of omega-3 fatty acid to maintenance medication treatment for recurrent unipolar depressive disorder. *Am J Psychiatry* 2002; 159:477–9.

13. Su KP, Huang SY, Chiu CC, Shen WW. Omega-3 fatty acids in major depressive disorder. A preliminary double-blind, placebo-

controlled trial. *Eur Neuropsychopharmacol* 2003;13:267–71.

14. Papakostas GI, Alpert JE, Fava M. *S*-Adenosyl-methionine in depression: a comprehensive review of the literature. *Curr Psychiatry Rep* 2003;5:460–6.

15. Kapczynski A, Crone ET, Merson M. Global health and university patents [editorial]. *Science* 2003;301:1629.

16. Kaufman PE, Cohen JE, Ashley MJ, Ferrence R, Halyak AI, Turcotte F, et al. Tobacco industry links to faculties of medicine in Canada. *Can J Public Health* 2004; 95:205–8.

KEY AND DIFFICULT WORDS

Define the following, using context or other clues if possible: **dogma, collegiality, infrastructure.**

QUESTIONS

1. Paraphrase the author's statement of purpose and thesis statement in the first paragraph.

2. Explain why it is important for Young to define the common word "university" in the second paragraph.

3. Do you believe that the comparison in the third paragraph between what happened at Italian universities before 1222 and what is occurring at today's universities is valid? Why or why not?

4. Name two negative consequences that resulted from adoption of the "model of granting councils" in the second half of the twentieth century.

5. Analyze the paragraph beginning "A recent report of the Canadian Association of University Teachers. . ." Among the factors you could consider are the method(s) of development (rhetorical patterns), the kinds of support, and the writer's credibility.

6. Who does Young believe will ultimately be most affected if research in neuroscience and psychiatry research continues to be "driven by commercial interests?"

7. Could Young have ended his editorial more positively or assertively than he did? Does the concluding paragraph add or detract from the strength of the essay?

8. Would you say that Young's main purpose is (a) to expose a problem, (b) to settle an issue, (c) to critique a position, or (d) to reach a compromise? How might his audience affect his purpose?

COLLABORATIVE ACTIVITY

As students who may be going on to intensive undergraduate work or perhaps graduate school, are you concerned about the increasing ties of university research to commercial interests? How do you think it could affect you or students like you in the next few years?

ACTIVITIES

1. It is well known that substantially more money is given today to research in science, engineering, and medicine than to research in the arts. Do you think this allocation is inevitable? Do you think it is fair? Do you believe that students, administrators, or society should be concerned about the possible consequences to arts programs throughout the country? (Hal Niedzviecki's "The future's books from nowhere" discusses a related issue.)

2. Reflect on the idea of a "student-controlled university" (see paragraph 3). Write up a one- to two-page proposal in which you urge your government to finance such a university. In your proposal, you should outline the need for the project, along with goals and objectives, and provide a few specific features of such a university.

Buddhist and psychological perspectives on emotions and well-being

Paul Ekman, Richard J. Davidson, Matthieu Ricard, and B. Alan Wallace

(3,000 words)

Abstract: Stimulated by a recent meeting between Western psychologists and the Dalai Lama on the topic of destructive emotions, we report on two issues: the achievement of enduring happiness, what Tibetan Buddhists call *sukha*, and the nature of afflictive and nonafflictive emotional states and traits. A Buddhist perspective on these issues is presented, along with discussion of the challenges the Buddhist view raises for empirical research and theory.

Buddhist thought, which arose more than 2,000 years ago in Asian cultures, holds assumptions that differ in important ways from modern psychology. The particular branch of Buddhist thinking we consider here is Indo-Tibetan, a tradition having roots in Indian thought and further developed by Tibetan theorists. It is a line of thinking that is more than 1,000 years old. Although different aspects of Buddhist thought have already influenced a number of psychologists, its challenges for research on emotion are not widely known. Some suggestive convergences between Buddhist thinking and, for example, findings in neurobiology, suggest the fruitfulness of integrating a Buddhist view into emotion research.

The traditional languages of Buddhism, such as Pali, Sanskrit, and Tibetan, have no word for "emotion" as such. Although discrepant from the modern psychological research tradition that has isolated emotion as a distinct mental process that can be studied apart from other processes, the fact that there is no term in Buddhism for emotion is quite consistent with what scientists have come to learn about the anatomy of the brain. Every region in the brain that has been identified with some aspect of emotion has also been identified with aspects of cognition (e.g., Davidson & Irwin, 1999). The circuitry that supports affect and the circuitry that supports cognition are completely intertwined—an anatomical arrangement consistent with the Buddhist view that these processes cannot be separated.

We have chosen two issues, the achievement of enduring happiness and the nature of afflictive emotions, to illustrate the usefulness of considering the Buddhist perspective in work on emotion. Given the space allowed, we present illustrative examples of possible areas for research, rather than a more complete discussion.

This report is a collaborative effort of Buddhists (Matthieu Ricard and B. Alan Wallace) and psychologists (Paul Ekman and Richard J. Davidson). Our report grew out of an extraordinary meeting with His Holiness the Dalai Lama, in Dharamsala, India, in March 2000, that focused on destructive emotions.[1] The Buddhist authors wrote the sections titled "The Buddhist View," and the psychologist authors wrote the sections on research directions and theory.

Achieving enduring happiness

THE BUDDHIST VIEW

Buddhists and psychologists alike believe that emotions strongly influence people's thoughts, words, and actions and that, at times, they help people in their pursuit of transient pleasures and satisfaction. From a Buddhist perspective, however, some emotions are conducive to genuine and enduring happiness, and others are not. A Buddhist term for such happiness is *sukha*, which may be defined in this context as a state of flourishing that arises from mental balance and insight into the nature of reality. Rather than a fleeting emotion or mood aroused by sensory and conceptual stimuli, *sukha* is an enduring trait that arises from a mind in a state of equilibrium and entails a conceptually unstructured and unfiltered awareness of the true nature of reality. Many Buddhist contemplatives claim to have experienced *sukha*, which increases as a result of sustained training.

Similarly, the Buddhist concept of *duhkha*, often translated as "suffering," is not simply an unpleasant feeling. Rather, it refers most deeply to a basic vulnerability to suffering and pain due to misapprehending the nature of reality. (The terms *sukha* and *duhkha* are from Sanskrit, one of the primary languages of Buddhist literature.)

---

[1] The participants at this meeting, besides the Dalai Lama, were Richard J. Davidson, Paul Ekman, Owen Flannagen, Daniel Coleman, Mark Greenberg, Thapten Jinpa, Matthieu Ricard, Jeanne Tsai, Francisco Varela, and B. Alan Wallace. We thank the Mind and Life Institute of Boulder, Colorado, for organizing the meeting in India and a subsequent meeting during which we wrote this article.

How is *sukha* to be realized? Buddhists believe that the radical transformation of consciousness necessary to realize *sukha* can occur by sustained training in attention, emotional balance, and mindfulness so that one can learn to distinguish between the way things are as they appear to the senses and the conceptual superimpositions one projects upon them. As a result of such training, one perceives what is presented to the senses, including one's own mental states, in a way that is closer to their true nature, undistorted by the projections people habitually mistake for reality.

Such training not only results in shifts in fleeting emotions but also leads to changes in one's moods and eventually even changes in one's temperament. For more than two millennia, Buddhist practitioners have developed and tested ways of gradually cultivating those emotions that are conductive to the pursuit of *sukha* and of freeing themselves from emotions that are detrimental to this pursuit. The ideal here is not simply to achieve one's own individual happiness in isolation from others but to incorporate the recognition of one's deep kinship with all beings, who share the same yearning to be free of suffering and to find a lasting state of well-being.

TWO RESEARCH DIRECTIONS

We have begun to examine highly experienced Buddhist practitioners, who presumably have achieved *sukha*, to determine whether that trait manifests itself in their biological activity during emotional episodes (Lutz, Greischar, Rawlings, Ricard, & Davidson, in press) or increases their sensitivity to the emotions of other people and to see how their interactive style may transform the nature of conflictual interactions. Such study of Buddhism's most expert practitioners may change psychology's conception of what at least some human beings are capable of achieving.

Another possible area of research concerns the reliability of self-report about mental states.

Although much of the research on emotion has presumed that research subjects and our patients during psychotherapy can readily report on their subjective experience through questionnaires and interviews, findings to date show that most people report only the most recent or most intense of their emotional experiences (e.g., Kahneman, Fredrickson, Schreiber, & Redelmeier, 1993; Rosenberg & Ekman, 1994) and are subject to bias. Research could determine whether those schooled in Buddhist practices could offer a more refined and complete account of their immediately past emotional experience, exhibiting fewer judgmental biases. In a related vein, other research has demonstrated that most people are poor predictors of what will make them happy (e.g., Wilson & Gilbert, in press). It would be interesting to determine whether those who have engaged in Buddhist contemplative practices sufficiently to achieve *sukha* are more accurate in affective forecasting.

Afflictive mental states
THE BUDDHIST VIEW

Buddhism does not distinguish between emotions and other mental processes. Instead, it is concerned with understanding which types of mental activity are truly conducive to one's own and others' well-being and which ones are harmful, especially in the long run.

In Buddhism, a clear distinction is made between affective states that are directly aroused by the experience of pleasurable stimuli (sensory, as well as aesthetic and intellectual) and *sukha*, which arises from the attentional, emotional, and cognitive balance of the mind. (For a similar distinction, see Sheldon, Ryan, Deci, & Kasser, 2004.) The experience of pleasure is contingent upon specific times, places, and circumstances and can easily change into a neutral or unpleasant feeling. When one disengages from the pleasant stimulus, the resultant pleasure vanishes, whether or not it is connected to any afflictive state.

The initial challenge of Buddhist meditative practice is not merely to suppress, let alone repress, destructive mental states but instead to identify how they arise, how they are experienced, and how they influence oneself and others over the long run. In addition, one learns to transform and finally free oneself from all afflictive states. This requires cultivating and refining one's ability to introspectively monitor one's own mental activities, enabling one to distinguish disruptive from non-disruptive thoughts and emotions. In Buddhism, rigorous, sustained training in mindfulness and introspection is conjoined with the cultivation of attentional stability and vividness.

In contrast to Aristotelian ethics, Buddhism rejects the notion that all emotions are healthy as long as they are not excessive or inappropriate to the time and place. Rather, Buddhism maintains that some mental states are afflictive regardless of their degree or the context in which they arise. Here we focus on three mental processes that are considered to be fundamental toxins of the mind.

The first of these is craving. This mental process is based on an unrealistic, reified distinction between self and others—or between subject and object more generally—as being absolutely separate and unrelated. Craving is concerned with acquiring or maintaining some desirable object or situation for "me" and "mine," which may be threatened by "the other." One assumes that desirable qualities are inherent in the object desired and then exaggerates these qualities, while ignoring or deemphasizing that object's undesirable aspects. Craving is therefore an unrealistic way of engaging with the world, and it is harmful whenever one identifies with this afflictive mental process, regardless of how strong it is or the circumstances under which it arises. Craving is said to be afflictive, for it disrupts the balance of the mind, easily giving rise to anxiety, misery, fear, and anger; and it is unrealistic in the sense that it falsely displaces the source of one's well-being from one's own mind to objects.

Hatred is the second of the fundamental afflictions of the mind and is a reverse reflection of craving. That is, hatred, or malevolence, is driven by the wish to harm or destroy anything that obstructs the selfish pursuit of desirable objects and situations for me and mine. Hatred exaggerates the undesirable qualities of objects and deemphasizes their positive qualities. When the mind is obsessed with resentment, it is trapped in the deluded impression that the source of its dissatisfaction belongs entirely to the external object (just as, in the case of craving, the mind locates the source of satisfaction in desirable objects). But even though the trigger of one's resentment may be the external object, the actual source of this and all other kinds of mental distress is in the mind alone.

The third, most fundamental affliction of the mind is the delusion of grasping onto one's own and others' reified personal identities as real and concrete. According to Buddhism, the self is constantly in a state of dynamic flux, arises in different ways, and is profoundly interdependent with other people and the environment. However, people habitually obscure the actual nature of the self by superimposing on reality the concepts of permanence, singularity, and autonomy. As a result of misapprehending the self as independent, there arises a strong sense of the absolute separation of self and other. Then, craving naturally arises for the "I" and for what is mine, and repulsion arises toward the other. The erroneous belief in the absolute distinction of self and other thus acts as the basis for the derivative mental afflictions of craving, hatred, jealousy, and arrogance. Such toxins of the mind are regarded, in Buddhism, as the sources of all mental suffering.

THEORETICAL ISSUES AND RESEARCH DIRECTIONS

Psychologists do not distinguish between beneficial and harmful emotions. Those who take an evolutionary view of emotion (e.g., Cosmides & Tooby, 2000; Ekman, 1992) have proposed that emotions were adaptive over the history of the species and remain adaptive today. Even those who categorize emotions as simply positive or negative (e.g., Watson, Clark, & Tellegen, 1988) do not propose that all of the negative emotions are harmful to oneself or to others. The goal in any psychologically informed attempt to improve one's emotional life is not to rid oneself of or transcend an emotion—not even hatred—but to regulate experience and action once an emotion is felt (Davidson, Jackson, & Kalin, 2000). (Note, however, that not all theorists consider hatred an emotion.)

One point of convergence between the Buddhist and psychological perspectives is that hostility, which is viewed in the West as a character or personality trait, is considered to be destructive to one's health. Impulsive chronic violence is also considered to be dysfunctional and is classified as pathological (Davidson, Putnam, & Larson, 2000). But neither of these is considered in psychology to be an emotion per se.

Rather than focusing on increasing consciousness of one's inner state, the emphasis in much of psychology is on learning how to reappraise situations (Lazarus, 1991) or how to control (regulate) emotional behaviour and expressions (Gross, 1999; but see Ekman, 2003, for a psychological approach to enhancing awareness of emotions as they occur).

The growing literature based on self-report measures of well-being indicates that punctate

events, even significant ones such as winning the lottery, phasically alter an individual's state of pleasure but do not change an individual's trait level of happiness. Buddhists agree that events such as winning the lottery would not alter an individual's dispositional level of happiness, but they do assert that happiness as a dispositional trait (*sukha*) can be cultivated through specific practices. Although the term trait positive affect as it has been used in the mood and temperament literature has some elements in common with *sukha*, it does not capture the essence of the Buddhist construct, which also includes a deep sense of well-being, a propensity toward compassion, reduced vulnerability to outer circumstances, and recognition of the interconnectedness with people and other living beings in one's environment. Moreover, *sukha* is a trait and not a state. It is a dispositional quality that permeates and pervades all experience and behaviour.

Another important difference between Buddhism and psychological approaches is that the Buddhists provide a method for modifying affective traits and for cultivating *sukha* (Wallace, 2005), whereas in psychology the only methods for changing enduring affective traits are those that have been developed specifically to treat psychopathology. With a few notable exceptions (e.g., Seligman, 1998), no effort has been invested in cultivating positive attributes of mind in individuals who do not have mental disorders. Western approaches to changing enduring emotional states or traits do not involve the long-term persistent effort that is involved in all complex skill learning—for example, in becoming a chess master or learning to play a musical instrument. Typically, not even psychoanalysis or the most intensive forms of cognitive-behaviour therapy involve the decades of training Buddhists consider necessary for the cultivation of *sukha*.

Buddhists, as we said, consider craving to be one of the primary toxins of the mind. Unlike psychologists, who restrict the idea of craving to states produced by substances of abuse or by strongly appetitive opportunities that offer the potential for abuse (e.g., gambling, sex), Buddhists use the term more generically to encompass the desire to acquire objects and situations for oneself. A growing body of neuroscientific literature has shown that activity of the neurotransmitter dopamine in a part of the brain called the nucleus accumbens is common to states of craving, including both pharmacologically induced addictions and activities such as gambling. Although activation of this system is highly reinforcing (i.e., it leads to the recurrence of behaviours associated with the system's activation), it is not associated with pleasure in the long run. Of course, what is not included in this neuroscientific framework is anything akin to the notion of *sukha*.

Buddhist contemplative practices are explicitly designed to counteract craving. It would thus be of great interest empirically to evaluate how effective these methods may be as interventions for addictive disorders, which are disorders of craving, and to determine if the brain systems associated with craving are altered by such training.

The Buddhist, but not Western, view considers hatred to be intrinsically harmful to people who experience it. This perspective suggests that it would be valuable to examine the different ways in which those who have been exposed to a major trauma react emotionally to the cause of their trauma—for example, how people whose children have been murdered react to the perpetrators once they are apprehended. In a study of such individuals, various biological, health, and social measures would provide information about the consequences of maintaining hatred or forgiveness toward the perpetrator.

Joint conclusion

Buddhist conceptions and practices that deal with emotional life make three very distinct contributions to psychology. Conceptually, they raise issues that have been ignored by many psychologists, calling on the field to make more finely nuanced distinctions in thinking about emotional experience. Methodologically, they offer practices that could help individuals report on their own internal experiences, and such practices might thereby provide crucial data that is much more detailed and comprehensive than that gathered by the techniques psychologists now use to study subjective emotional experience. Finally, Buddhist practices themselves offer a therapy, not just for the disturbed but for all who seek to improve the quality of their lives. We hope what we have reported will serve to spark the interest of psychologists to learn more about this tradition.

Current Directions in Psychological Science.
2005. 14 (2).

REFERENCES

Cosmides, L., & Tooby, J. (2000). Evolutionary psychology and the emotions. In M.L. Lewis & J. Haviland-Jones (Eds.), *Handbook of emotions* (2nd ed., pp. 3–134). New York: Guilford Press.

Davidson, R.J., & Irwin, W. The functional neuroanatomy of emotion and affective style. *Trends in Cognitive Science, 3,* 11–21.

Davidson, R.J., Jackson, D.C., & Kalin, N.H. (2000). Emotion, plasticity, context and regulation: Perspectives from affective neuroscience. *Psychological Bulletin, 126,* 890–906.

Davidson, R.J., Putnam, K.M., & Larson, C.L. (2000). Dysfunction in the neural circuitry of emotion regulation—a possible prelude to violence. *Science, 289,* 591–594.

Ekman, P. (1992). An argument for basic emotions. *Cognition and Emotion, 6,* 169–200.

Ekman, P. (2003). *Emotions revealed: Recognizing faces and feelings to improve communication and emotional life.* New York: Times Books.

Gross, J.J. (1999). The emerging field of emotion regulation: An integrative review. *Review of General Psychology, 2,* 271–299.

Kahneman, D., Fredrickson, B.L., Schreiber, C.A., & Redelmeier, D.A. (1993). When more pain is preferred to less: Adding a better end. *Psychological Science, 4,* 401–405.

Lazarus, R. (1991). *Emotion and adaptation.* New York: Oxford University Press.

Lutz, A., Greischar, L.L., Rawlings, N.B., Ricard, M., & Davidson, R.J. (in press). Long-term meditators self-induce high-amplitude gamma synchrony during mental practice. *Proceedings of the National Academy of Sciences, USA.*

Rosenberg, E.L., & Ekman, P. (1994). Coherence between expressive and experiential systems in emotion. *Cognition and Emotion, 8,* 201–229.

Seligman, M.E.P. (1998). *Learned optimism.* New York: Pocket Books.

Sheldon, K.M., Ryan, R.M., Deci, E.L., & Kasser, T. (2004). The independent effects of goal contents and motives on well-being: It's both what you pursue and why you pursue it. *Personality and Social Psychology Bulletin, 30,* 475–486.

Wallace, B.A. (2005). *Genuine happiness: Meditation as the path to fulfillment.* Hoboken, NJ: John Wiley and Sons.

Watson, D., Clark, L.A., & Tellegen, A. (1988). Development and validation of brief measures of positive and negative affect: The PANAS scales. *Journal of Personality and Social Psychology, 54,* 1063–1070.

Wilson, T., & Gilbert, D. (in press). Affective forecasting: Knowing what to want. *Current Directions in Psychological Science.*

KEY AND DIFFICULT WORDS

Define the following, using context or other clues if possible: **convergence, discrepant, affect (noun), transient, conducive, afflictive, reify, punctate, dispositional, generic, nuance.**

QUESTIONS

1. What is the justification for the study? What paragraph contains the essay plan? How does the plan clarify or make more specific the title of the essay?

2. What is the first Buddhist concept that finds confirmation in psychological research to be mentioned in the essay?

3. Which of the two comparison methods (see p. 100) do the authors employ? Comparisons can focus on similarities, differences, or both. Do you think that this essay calls more attention to similarities or to differences? Support your contention.

4. According to Buddhist thought, why do most people not see the "true nature of reality?" How can one be brought to see it?

5. Summarize one of the three paragraphs that identify the three "toxins of the mind" (paragraphs 15–17).

6. Why is it necessary to distinguish between a *state* and a *trait*? (See paragraph 21.) What is the fundamental difference?

7. What is the function of the "Joint conclusion?"

8. In your view, does this study suggest any flaws or limitations in the traditional Western approach to the study of emotion? Does the study suggest any flaws or limitations in the Buddhist approach? Refer specifically to the essay in your response.

COLLABORATIVE ACTIVITY

Do you believe it would be worthwhile for modern psychological research to try to "[cultivate] positive attributes of mind" (paragraph 22) in those without mental disorders or, as suggested in the conclusion, to seek "a therapy, not just for the disturbed but for all who seek to improve the quality of their lives?" Is such an approach possible? Could it change our society in any way? Discuss the implications of these questions.

ACTIVITIES

1. What do you know about Buddhism? Freewrite in order to answer this question. Note: This could be used as a pre-reading or post-reading activity.

2. Is there anything you learned from this essay that has changed your views or made you think differently about the traditional Western approach to "emotions and well-being?" Write a personal response in which you consider the answer to this question.

Situating disability:
Mapping the outer limits

Tanya Titchkosky

(5,500 words)

For the past five years, I have lived in a small university town, Antigonish, Nova Scotia. During the summer, most students leave to look for work, and many tourists come to visit the town. Both new students and tourists receive verbal and pictorial maps of the town. Despite the town's small size, I have seen at least a dozen professionally produced maps of it and many more hand-drawn ones. Some maps are so sparse in their detail that they could be used only to arrive at the event they are intended to advertise—the Highland Games at Columbus Field or the Ceilidh at Pipers' Pub. Other maps, especially the ones oriented to students as consumers, contain so many details that the path of travel is obscured by the indication of stores and sights along the way. Maps come in many different shapes and sizes and communicate many different intentions. Even maps of the same locale can appear radically different from each other and have different interests and aims. Maps do not simply correspond to the geography of a place. Instead, different maps draw out different meanings that a place holds. All maps try to impart a sense of the significance of place as this relates to the map producers' interpretive relation towards the readers of the maps.

Culture, too, gives us many different maps of various things, including disability (Gleeson, 1999). One such map represents buildings and events that are accessible to disabled people; Braille maps with embossed configurations are constructed for use by blind persons. But there are other types of maps that are not so conventional, maps that point out disability itself. Sometimes disability is regarded as a place requiring some delineation of its appearance and its significance. The criteria necessary to qualify for a disability pension, for example, are one such map; government officials use this map to locate disability and to manage disabled people. There are others, such as demographic counts that map out disability rates in a population. They aim to show what part of a population is made up of disabled persons, as well as what part of a person is made up by disability by locating it in the body—"mobility impairment," "vision impairment." These maps point out the severity of the disability landscape by using such terms as "mild," "moderate," and "severe." These maps are also used as a way to predict one's chances of arriving in the place of disability. According to Zola (1982: 242–3), such statistical mapping shows that disability is the norm and that "anyone reading the words on this page is at best momentarily able-bodied." Still, most cultural maps refer to disabled people as a "them" and not as an "us." This separation performs the functions, says Bauman (1990: 40, 42), of dividing people into categories and calling for different attitudes and different behaviours; this, in turn, lends cohesiveness, inner solidarity, and emotional security to any "us" who has something to say about "those" disabled people.

All maps of disability reflect a conception of its place and space within culture (Pile and Thrift, 1995). The mapping of disability is an imparting of some version of what disability is and thus, contains implicit directions as to how to move around, through, or with it. Disability is mapped differently by various societal institutions and cultural practices, and these representations influence one's relation to disability.

In this chapter, I begin to show some of the ways in which disability is mapped, and I show how each topography supports a different conception of disability. I do not follow, however, any single path provided by these maps. Instead, I interrogate the representations of disability found within them. I argue that this critical relation to maps and their use serves as an alternative topography that points out the socio-political character of body anomaly and identity. This alternative depicts disability as a social space (Grosz, 1995: 83–101), constituted from the inter-subjective relations to the disabled body, disability identity, and interpretive relations that are developed to both. As a way to develop a full sense of the social topography of disability, I make extensive use of my own experience as a dyslexic woman living with a blind person, as well as the post-modern principle that reality is a discursive accomplishment (Corker, 1999, 1998; Corker and Shakespeare, 2002). My social mapping of the inter-subjectively constituted place of disability supports the idea that disability is not merely an individual matter but a socio-political one (Oliver, 1996, 1990; Shakespeare, 1998). My aim is to demonstrate that disability is social and political, not only in regards to what culture "makes" out of impaired bodies but also because the body in all of its vicissitudes already comes to us through cultural maps and is, thus, *always-already constituted from social and political discursive action.*

MAPPING DISABILITY: OPPOSITION AND AMBIGUITY

Recall that more than 10 years ago I began sharing my life with fellow sociologist Rod Michalko, who is blind. Sharing life with Rod has meant experiencing a life of blindness in varied and often dramatic ways. Rod has spent most of his life on the outermost edge of the legal blindness continuum —"10 per cent of normal acuity." Measuring a person's percentage of visual acuity is a medical way to map blindness. This map says little about blindness itself but says much about how far a person is from "normal" sight.

When I first met Rod, I did not experience "10 per cent of a normal acuity." I met Rod as a blind man, but one who could see. He could see . . . but not quite; what I could understand, count on, or see as seeing was never all that clear when I was with Rod. It was a confusing state of affairs that threw into question for me what seeing and blindness were supposed to mean. Back in the beginning of our relationship, Rod pointed down and said, "Your shoelace is undone." I thanked him, and picked up my pencil . . . and wondered. Perhaps Rod had regained his sight. Yet, if he had, why did he see my pencil as a shoelace? Still, if he is blind, how did he see my pencil? Rod certainly could see, but I could not understand what or how.

This confusion flowed from my conception of blindness and sightedness as radically opposite. Either Rod was sighted or he was blind. "Fixed oppositions," according to Joan Scott (1998: 33), "conceal the extent to which things presented as oppositional are, in fact, interdependent." Not only did my oppositional conception of blindness and sightedness conceal their interdependence in Rod, it also concealed from me the need to think about this interdependence—thus, their interdependence in me was also concealed. I was working with a "cultural map" that pointed out the land of blindness and that of sightedness with a clearly defined border between the two. What's more, my map did not indicate any border crossings;

either you were in the land of the blind or in the land of the sighted. Rod seemed to be on the border. But, instead of thinking about how sight and blindness rely on each other for their meaning, I tried only to decipher whether I was seeing a blind person, or not. As obvious as it is now, it was not so obvious then; blindness, be it 10 per cent, total, or what lies between, or notions such as going blind and being blind, are not clear-cut matters. Clearly, my cultural map was oversimplified. Between all the different ways that sight and blindness appear lies something much more meaningful and much more complex than sheer opposition.

Living with Rod meant living with the experience of uncertainty in the face of things of which I was so certain that never before did I question them—things like "being blind" and "having sight." Notice that our language frames the concepts of "blind" and "sight" in different ways: a person can *be* blind or a person can *have* sight, and it sounds as if these are two very separate things. Outside of the disability movement, people are not usually referred to as being able-bodied; nor is "non-disabled" a common way to categorize people. Instead, the common expression is that people *have* normal acuity, normal hearing, normal mobility, or normal use of their appendages. We grow up with a language that allows us to speak of our bodies while, at the same time, giving us ways of conceiving of them. We conceive of our bodily faculties, for example, as a possession, and we conceive of disabilities as neither a faculty nor a possession but, instead, as a lack of both.

The words "disability," "handicap," and "impairment" have a complicated history (Barnes, 1998: 65–78; Davis, 1995: 1–22; Gleeson, 1999: 18–19; Oliver, 1990; Shogan, 1998; Susman, 1994: 15) and diverse social and political meanings. Despite the nuanced meaning of these words and various attempts to pin

down or simplify them, all these words are regularly made use of in everyday life to refer to bodies for which something has gone wrong or is missing or to bodies that lack. This way of speaking gives people a map of disability through a series of negations—something in the body is *not* there, *not* right, *not* working, *not* able. Blindness, for example, is regularly conceived of as simply *not* seeing, and during Rod's 10 per cent days, I wondered and I was asked by others what it was that Rod *could and could not* see. I was not asked about blindness as an "in itself." By speaking about disability in the way that people typically do, disabled people are brought to life as if the entire meaning of being disabled can be grasped simply as *not being* able-bodied. So common is it to map disability through a series of negations that it might be easy to miss the strangeness of such a process. This strangeness is revealed if we try to map other types of people in a similar fashion; for example, a man is a person lacking a vagina. It would seem ridiculous today to conceive of gender in terms of negation. The feminist movement has shown us that gender is not a matter of simple negation. Woman is not woman because she is not man, and man is not man because he is not woman. The language of everyday life does not provide for such expressions as "There goes not-a-man." But it does provide for expressions such as "There goes someone who can't see" or "There is that woman without arms."

Language suggests that we regard the disabled body as a life constituted out of the negation of able-bodiedness and, thus, as nothing in and of itself. If, as Smith (1999: 133) insists, discourse *is* social organization, the everyday ways that the body is spoken about organize being disabled and having able bodies *as if* they are radically opposed phenomena. Our language tempts us to think that the "normally working body" has nothing to do with the ways in which we organize our world, go about our daily affairs, or speak about disability. Our language recommends that we conceive the non-disabled body as something that just comes along as we go about daily existence. People *just* jump into the shower, run to the store, see what others mean while keeping an eye on the kids or skipping from office to office, and, having run through the day while managing to keep their noses clean, finally hop into bed—all of this glosses the body that comes along while, at the same time, brings it along metaphorically. However, if we have a bad day, we must stumble through, limping along while blind to the ramifications of not standing up to the boss and letting the kids run all over us. Through this way of speaking, "normal bodies" escape from being understood as something that could be mapped, insofar as such a body is regarded simply as movement and metaphor.

Like other sighted people who follow the recommendations given by culture and its language (maps), I thought that blindness and sightedness were polar opposites. Such opposition was dependent upon my being secure in the illusion that Rod did not have sight and, thus, was blind, whereas others, including myself, simply have sight. Adhering to these categorical oppositions meant that I possessed sight, really good sight— I saw that my pencil was not a shoelace—and in seeing this I also saw Rod as blind.

MAPPING SIGHTEDNESS

While opposition was one way that I initially tried to map the significance of blindness, there were other ways. Rod and I would often walk together. Initially, no hand-holding, cane, or elbow guidance was part of these walks. I began to pay attention to how I watched out for bumps and obstacles and to how Rod must be doing the same. Rod, however, was not doing the same. He was watching me.

Before I met Rod, I had moved through the world with the implicit assumption that my sight would see whatever needed to be seen. Walking with Rod, I paid attention to how my sight worked, and I assumed that Rod's partial sight would work the same way, albeit with more effort and more time. "Less of the same" did not, however, capture my experience of Rod's way of seeing. What Rod did was observe me as a sighted person, and it was his stance (Harding, 1996: 146) between blindness and sight that provoked him to do so. My belief in the illusion that sight is *the* means to observe the world but is not itself observable began to disintegrate— sight too could be mapped.

Experiencing and attending to the outer edges of legal blindness can bring to consciousness the ambiguity that lies between sight and blindness and can show that some of the security that sighted people possess is indeed illusory. Wittgenstein (1980, 14e–15e: 75) puts the matter this way:

> I can observe . . . I can also say, "You see, this child is not blind. It can see. Notice how it follows the flame of the candle." But can I satisfy myself, so to speak, *that men see?*
>
> "Men see."—As Opposed to *what?*
> Maybe that they are all blind?

Of all the things that sight can see, it often does not observe the intimate relation between sight and blindness as ways of being in the world. As Wittgenstein indicates, attending to sight usually only occurs in relation to blindness and what we have to say about blindness.

Blindness made me take notice of myself as sighted and helped me understand that being sighted was more complex than ownership of yet another, albeit highly valued, possession. Sight need not be regarded as simply one more possession, since it influenced who I was, how I acted, and my engagement with the world around me. My body and my life are the terrain upon which sight can be understood as inscribing itself (Bordo, 1993: 142; Foucault, 1979). Rod became expert in deciphering these inscriptions. While walking or sitting in a pub, for example, Rod could see that I had just seen something worthy of note. Sighting a server or an unnerving glance of a stranger was observable to Rod in the position of my head, my posture, my movement. Rod's blindness began to teach me that sighted people look as though they have seen something. Living with Rod included living with disability and non-disability (sight) as an ambiguous experience. This ambiguity grows out of the assumption that blindness and sightedness are not opposites but do express an interrelatedness observable on the level of interaction.

Ten per cent of normal vision is not simply the outer limit of blindness; it is also the outer limit of sightedness, and it is both at the same time. The first five years, or so, of our life together were spent in this mix of sight and blindness. It was for me a curious mixture. I wanted to see blindness, or see what it saw, perhaps influenced by the illusion that seeing *is* understanding.

One day, in yet another of my attempts to see his blindness, Rod and I mapped out what ophthalmologists would refer to as his visual field. Rod focused on the centre of a tabletop, and I moved objects from his point of focus towards the edge of the table until Rod indicated that the object had appeared in his peripheral vision. I left the objects in the places where Rod began to see them. Soon, using fork, spoon, knife, salt and pepper shakers, the tabletop displayed a circle of sorts—his field of vision.

There it was—Rod's visual field and his blind spot, concretely represented for me to see. Rod, too, took a look. He took many looks, moving his gaze around his visual field and blind spot, both the one on the table and the one of his vision. This reminded him of some of his ophthalmological examinations: the same sort of mapping of his vision occurred when he was asked to look at eye charts or when photographs of his retinas were taken. Despite this somewhat painful reminder of past mapping, Rod worked to give me a representation of his vision, and he worked to see this representation for himself.

Mapping, measuring, or providing a kind of topography of blind spots and fields of vision is one way to conceive of blindness, as well as sight. It is, literally, a static way: Rod could not move if his vision was to be charted; and once charted, the representation itself was immobile, objectified. As static, such an image is already distanced dramatically from the lived experience of blindness and sight. No matter how precisely produced and minute in its detail, such a map could not tell me how Rod moved, used, and lived with this blind spot and this peripheral vision. Although forks and knives are not part of the ophthalmologist's tools of examination, the procedure of objectively mapping is tied to the common-sense desire to come to know disability. But such a map told me little. It could not tell me much about how I could or should travel or move with a blind person. This mapping procedure did serve to announce that Rod was different, which, of course, we already knew, for why else would we be involved in such an activity?

Measures, such as inability to see the big *E* on the eye chart, ability to see hand movements at three feet, field of vision charts, photographs of bodily damage including retinas, or surveys of activity limitations resulting from bodily differences (Gadacz, 1994: 31–4; Harrison and Crow, 1993), help to make blindness, and other disabilities, into a concrete *individual* issue, abstracted from *interpersonal* interaction and interpretation. The social practice of measurement always needs to measure some *thing*; in this case, we were making and measuring what Taussig (1980: 3) refers to as a "biological and physical thinghood." Through measurement, disability can be made into a thing, a reality in and of a person's body (Murphy et al., 1988; Scott, 1981).

These measures objectify blindness, making it concrete and easier to deal with, and "to see," than do the complex self-reflective practices of noticing and reading the work of blind persons as they interact with sighted others in situations, environments, and histories not of their own making. "The thingification of the world, persons and experience," says Taussig (1980: 3), produces a "phantom objectivity" and "denies" and "mystifies" the body's fundamental nature as a "relation between people."

The great quantity of statistical data that is produced and disseminated by governmental, medico-rehabilitative, and even political organizations is testimony to Western culture's proclivity to regard disability as thing-like. For example, the statistical rendering of disability can be found, in one form or another, repeated over and over again, in various governmental department publications, at disability-related websites, in textbooks and policy statements, in fundraising material of various helping organizations, and in disability community coalition documents. Many of these sources, which have something to say or to do for disabled people, begin with quantification and thus the objectification of disability. Even among those who recognize that the definition of disability has much to do with how disability gets measured, there is still the unquestioned assumption that disabled people are best understood as measurable objects of limit and lack.

The measurement, the counting, and the policies that follow are dependent upon the illusion that disability is objectively given (Goode, 1996: 1–5). This conceptual map of disability begins with the assumption that disability is readily observable, easily quantifiable, impervious to interpretation, set in stone. As the plethora of disability statistics indicate, being counted as disabled means being given a probable fate of unemployment and poverty. As with disability and the need to measure it, so too can unemployment, poverty, etc., now be spoken of *as if* they are dictated by, or caused by, the disabled person's body. For example, learning that only 2.3 per cent of disabled Canadians (530,000 persons) make use of the disability tax credit, and that many more disabled persons are unemployed, do not participate in the labour force, or are poor, has led to multiple nationwide governmental task forces, all of which recommend changes to the disability tax credit and to employment, training, and rehabilitative programs for disabled people (Fawcett, 1996). Report after report—*Obstacles, The will to act, In unison* (Canada, 1981; 1996; 2000)—recommends, on the basis of these statistics, that something ought to be done, and what ought to be done often includes the reproduction of these statistics. The objectification of disability reaches its highest sophistication in the current development of fetal tests oriented to eliminating disabled persons before they enter the population (Hubbard, 1997: 187–201; Langer 1997: 47–66). And such objectification processes have even supported sterilization and extermination programs (Russell, 1998: 13–55). The unquestioned map of disability as a thing leads to the unexamined presupposition that programs oriented to ameliorating disability or managing disabled people are just as objectively given as are impaired bodies themselves.

The problem with the measurement and management of disability is not simply that it begins and ends with an unexamined conception of disability as objectively given. Nor is the problem only that such measurement and control practices must take for granted the current social milieu that says that it is right and good to measure, count, track, and manage disabled persons. The problem is that this thing-like conception of disability requires, as did Rod's and my measurement of it on the tabletop, a bracketing off of the Really real work involved in being disabled. Disability as objective lack and inability understood as located within a person's body means ignoring disability in relation to the social character of our bodies. The problem, too, is that ideology and assumptions of non-disability often remain unmapped and unexamined, even though it is from a non-disability perspective that disability is most often objectified.

The body's significance *is* social in the sense that bodies are only found within locales of interaction, within interpretive milieus and ideological structures, such as health and beauty, and the specific language or genre (Bakhtin, 1986) through which all this is expressed. This sociality lies behind every conceptual map of disability, even at the level of "mere bodies" and "impairment." The work involved in being disabled is always accomplished in the midst of the social character of bodies and their political arrangements. Mapping disability as if it is an object and developing policy on the basis of such a map is a little bit like giving people a map of the city of Toronto that only indicates its hills, rivers, and valleys and telling them to find Paupers' Pub. Adhering to the belief that disability is concretely given in some people's bodies requires that we do not get close to the lived actuality of disability. Yet such mapping is often accompanied by the illusion that all sorts of things about disability can be mapped.

LIFE WITH MAPS

There is, however, a more life-filled reality to disability to which we can attend. This reality appears within the objectifying practices of measuring and managing disabled people, and it even appears within the objectification of blindness accomplished around the table that day with Rod and me. Consider, for example, what might be learned if we shift our attention away from the objective representation of Rod's vision that was laid out on the tabletop and "focus" instead on all that went on *around* the tabletop. This is a shift in attention to the making of the map and away from the map itself.

Around the tabletop, Rod produced a different image of blindness, one that was more difficult to attend to but more dynamic, filled with effort, interest, and work. Rod had to work to see. He had to take an interest in seeing forks and knives. He had to use his knowledge of a context to figure out what there was to see— what should be seen and what not. Big blind spot or not, charting its existence could not answer routine questions such as should I tell Rod that something is in his way or leave well enough alone. The image of blindness produced *around* the tabletop that day told me that whatever is in Rod's way could only be deciphered by reading his use of vision in relation to the people and the environment around him.

To gain even a slight understanding of the production of Rod's vision would require that I attend to something much more dynamic than the facticity of his blind spot, much more complex than the concrete stuff of the physical environment. In Rod's terms, seeing is a project insofar as we always see through a life (Michalko, 1999: 15–17; 1998: 39–40; on the body as project, see Shilling, 1997: 69). The project of seeing for a legally blind person on the outer edges of both blindness and sight is one filled with conscious effort, will, and desire. For sighted people, the project of vision is usually something to which no attention is paid.

But Rod paid attention. Not only did he focus on the tabletop, but he also focused on that which surrounded the tabletop and on that which brought it into view. He saw that he was in a bar and that he was surrounded by other tabletops around which people sat. Music, sounds of drinking and eating, laughter—all of these sounds Rod "saw" as his "being in a bar." The forks and salt and pepper shakers I used to map his visual field were seen by Rod not only by his peripheral vision but also through the lens of his being in a bar. Rod never saw these things when an ophthalmologist mapped out his visual field. The map we drew was drawn with the material of our life. And as objective as this map was, it was constructed from Rod's "subjective seeing" of his world. We were engaged in a project of vision, transforming Rod's "seeing" into the objective fact of vision. Ophthalmologists were engaged in the same project with Rod, but this project is not "seeable" through the ophthalmological lens.

Any project of vision is accomplished not only in relation to the things and events of the physical world but also in relation to the habits and customs of a culture—Rod expected to see forks and knives on a tabletop in a bar, and so did I. Vision is accomplished in relation to other people, with conflicting interpretations of what there is to see and with shifting meanings of blindness in different and changing circumstances. What did people see as Rod and I walked into the bar, his hand on my elbow? Did they see a blind person and sighted guide? Did they see an ordinary intimate couple? Did they see both or neither? Did they see a sighted person mapping out the visual field of a blind person on a table? Did they see two people engaged in animated conversation, perhaps about staging a play or the moves of football players?

Like the people in the bar, Rod's seeing is embedded in the particularity of his body, his interests, his attention, his energy, and his effort. Around the tabletop, Rod worked to give me a representation of his vision. Moreover, he worked to see this representation for himself. In both the making and the observation of his representation of blindness, Rod showed me that his way of being in the world meant living with a conscious awareness of vision as an accomplishment. To help or hinder, to experience or ignore, Rod in this accomplishment would be dependent upon the kind of attention that I paid to it. Blindness began to teach me that seeing is culturally organized. Blindness and sight conceived of as an accomplishment, as *work*, more clearly represents that which I actually was experiencing with Rod.

THE MAP OF INTERACTIONAL WORK

Insofar as seeing is cultural, sight is a social accomplishment, and blindness is a kind of forced consciousness of the work necessary to achieve it. This is a key lesson, which accompanies my shift away from attempts to reduce disability to a concrete reality and towards mapping disability as a complex set of social and discursive interactions. This lesson did not simplify my understandings of "being blind" and "having sight." It showed me that there is no way to concretize what will be seen and what will not. There is no rule book or chart that will tell me what being blind or sighted means. For example, doors left ajar, which are normally closed, are hazards for anyone who lives on the outer edges of sight. Using objective measures, such as Rod's ability to see hand movements at three feet but no farther, I could invoke a rule that I will now announce to Rod all such doors within a four-foot radius. The rule that Rod would also need to invoke is that such announcements will be made. Our movement through the world would now involve a series of announcements. But announcing open doors opens up the necessity for announcing a plethora of other features—

curbs, stairs, posts, pedestrians. The list never ends. The world would no longer be experienced by Rod; it would be announced. This rule would mean that the world would now come to me in an interpretation of what is announceable and to Rod as announcements. This rule would mean that I would rule what Rod experiences.

Together with the production of the hegemony of sight, such a rule is also impractical and, indeed, works against gaining any sense of the social topography within which we live. The knowledge of blindness that comes with rules and charts excludes any experience of my sight or Rod's blindness as an accomplishment. Mapping the accomplishment of vision requires that I pay attention to context; for example, what events surround the door that has become ajar? To address this question, I need to take into account Rod's bodily position in relation to the door, the people around the door, my judgment of their ability or inability to imagine the standpoint of blindness, whether or not Rod is orienting to the particular environment as familiar and routine or as uncertain and hazardous. All of these interactional factors need to be read in the process of making a decision regarding my role in Rod's way of being in the world.

The interaction between blind and sighted people, disabled and non-disabled people, and everything in between always involves such decisions. One of the most important decisions a sighted person needs to make is *not* "What should I do or not do?" Nor is it "Should I tell the blind person this or should I not?" The crucial decision is whether or not the sighted person, in the face of blindness, will be oriented to her or his decisiveness. To be oriented to such decisiveness requires that the sighted person begin to do what the blind person is almost always doing—engage in the conscious work of seeing as a social accomplishment and do so in relation to the reality of blindness. Reading the topography of the social environment permits the understanding that the significance of sight and blindness cannot simply be found in their objectified physicality and must, instead, be sought in the lived actuality of self and others. Only by attending to the ways in which disability is conceptualized (mapped) can we gain any social understanding of disability. "In fashioning some kind of theoretical approach to disability," Lennard Davis says (1995: 11), "one must consider the fact that the disabled body is not a discrete object but rather a set of social relations."

In Tanya Titchkosky. *Disability, self and society*, 46–63. Toronto: University of Toronto Press.

REFERENCES

Bakhtin, Mikhail Mikhailovich. 1986. Trans. Vern W. McGee. *Speech Genres and Other Late Essays.* Austin: University of Texas Press.

Barnes, Colin. 1998. "The Social Model of Disability: A Sociological Phenomenon Ignored by Sociologists?" Pp. 66–78 in *The Disability Reader: Social Science Perspectives.* Ed. Tom Shakespeare. London: Cassell Academic.

Bauman, Zygmunt. 1990. *Thinking Sociologically.* Oxford: Blackwell Publishing.

Bordo, Susan. 1993. *Unbearable Weight: Feminism, Western Culture, and the Body.* Berkeley: University of California Press.

Canada. Parliamentary Special Committee on the Disabled and the Handicapped. 1981. *Obstacles.* Ottawa: Minister of Supply and Services Canada.

Corker, Mairian. 1998. "Disability Discourse in a Postmodern World." Pp. 221–33 in *The Disability Reader.* Ed. Tom Shakespeare. London: Cassell Academic.

———. 1999. "New Disability Discourse, the Principle of Optimization and Social Change." Pp. 192–209 in *Disability Discourse.* Ed.

Mairian Corker and Sally French. Buckingham: Open University Press.

————, and Tom Shakespeare, eds. 2002. *Disability/Postmodernity: Embodying Disability Theory.* London: Continuum Press.

Davis, Lennard J. 1995. *Enforcing Normalcy: Disability, Deafness and the Body.* London: Verso Press.

Fawcett, Gail. 1996. *Living with Disability in Canada: An Economic Portrait.* Hull: Office for Disability Issues, Human Resources Development Canada.

Foucault, Michel. 1979. *Discipline and Punish: The Birth of the Prison.* Trans. Alan Sheridan. New York: Vintage Books.

Gadacz, René. 1994. *Re-Thinking Dis-Ability: New Structures, New Relationships.* Edmonton: University of Alberta Press.

Gleeson, Brendan. 1999. *Geographies of Disability.* London: Routledge.

Goode, Erich, ed. 1996. *Social Deviance.* Boston: Allyn and Bacon.

Grosz, Elizabeth. 1995. *Space, Time, and Perversion.* New York: Routledge.

Harding, Sandra. 1996. "Standpoint Epistemology (a Feminist Version): How Social Disadvantage Creates Epistemic Advantage." Pp. 146–60 in *Social Theory and Sociology: The Classics and beyond.* Ed. Stephen P. Turner. Cambridge, MA: Blackwell Publishers Ltd.

Harrison, Felicity, and Mary Crow. 1993. *Living and Learning with Blind Children: A Guide for Parents and Teachers of Visually Impaired Children.* Toronto: University of Toronto Press.

Hubbard, Ruth. 1997. "Abortion and Disability." Pp. 187–200 in *The Disability Studies Reader.* Ed. Lennard Davis. New York: Routledge.

Langer, Lawrence L. 1997. "The Alarmed Vision: Social Suffering and Holocaust Atrocity." Pp. 47–65 in *Social Suffering.* Ed.

Arthur Kleinman, Veena Das, and Margaret Lock. Berkeley: University of California Press.

Michalko, Rod. 1998. *The Mystery of the Eye and the Shadow of Blindness.* Toronto: University of Toronto Press.

————. 1999. *The Two in One: Walking with Smokie, Walking with Blindness.* Philadelphia: Temple University Press.

Murphy, R., J. Scheer, Y. Murphy, and R. Mack. 1988. "Physical Disability and Social Liminality: A Study in the Rituals of Adversity." *Social Science and Medicine* 26(2): 235–42.

Oliver, Michael. 1990. *The Politics of Disablement.* London: Macmillan.

————. 1996. *Understanding Disability: From Theory to Practice.* New York: St Martin's Press.

Pile, Steve, and Nigel Thrift, eds. 1996. *Mapping the Subject: Geographies of Cultural Transformation.* London: Routledge.

Russell, Marta. 1998. *Beyond Ramps: Disability at the End of the Social Contract.* Monroe, ME: Common Courage Press.

Scott, Joan. 1998. "Deconstructing Equality-Versus-Difference: Or the Uses of Postcolonial Structuralist Theory for Feminism." *Feminist Studies* 14(1): 32–50.

Shakespeare, Tom, ed. 1998. *The Disability Reader: Social Science Perspectives.* London: Cassell Academic.

Shilling, Chris. 1997. "The Body and Difference." Pp. 63–120 in *Identity and Difference.* Ed. Kathryn Woodward. London: Sage Publications.

Shogan, Debra. 1998. "The Social Construction of Disability: The Impact of Statistics and Technology." *Adapted Physical Activity Quarterly* 15: 269–77.

Smith, Dorothy E. 1999. *Writing the Social: Critique, Theory, and Investigations.* Toronto: University of Toronto Press.

Susman, Joan. 1994. "Disability, Stigma and Deviance." *Social Science and Medicine* 38(1): 15–22.

Taussig, Michael. 1980. "Reification and the Consciousness of the Patient." *Social Science and Medicine* 4(1B): 3–13.

Wittgenstein, Ludwig. 1980. *Remarks on the Philosophy of Psychology.* Volume 2. Chicago: University of Chicago Press.

Zola, Irving Kenneth. 1982. *Missing Pieces: A Chronicle of Living with a Disability.* Philadelphia: Temple University Press.

KEY AND DIFFICULT WORDS

Define the following, using context or other clues if possible: **anomaly, discursive, vicissitude, ophthalmologist, topography, disseminate, ameliorate, facticity, hegemony.**

QUESTIONS

1. From the essay's title through to the last paragraph, it is evident that maps and mapping serve as much more than key images and metaphors but as a conceptual framework for Titchkosky's essay. (a) What are some other words she uses that are connected literally or conceptually with mapping and that are important in the essay ("limits," in the title, is an example of one such word)? (b) Come up with a one-sentence definition of "mapping" as the author uses the term.

2. One of the reasons that Titchkosky begins her essay by discussing maps may be to *defamiliarize* her readers (i.e., to surprise them into a new awareness, enabling them to reflect on an unfamiliar context in which the word can be used). Why is it important that her readers are able to "see" a new meaning for maps and mapping?

3. Identify the paragraph that announces the essay's plan; identify the author's thesis.

4. "Situating disability: Mapping the outer limits" is an academic essay but uses a lot of personal experience. Pointing to at least one specific example, explain why first-person experience might be especially useful in this essay. The author also uses secondary sources extensively. Do you think she synthesizes these two kinds of evidence well (again, be specific)? Does she use one kind too much at the expense of the other kind?

5. What is the difference between the medical and cultural maps discussed in the first few paragraphs of "Mapping disability: Opposition and ambiguity" and the "map of interactional work" discussed in the final section of the essay?

6. According to the author (and many others), language can "frame" and thereby limit our perceptions and conceptions. What are the implications of the phrase "being blind" versus "having sight" (in "Mapping disability: Opposition and ambiguity")? Summarize the paragraph that follows.

7. In "Mapping sightedness," Titchkosky addresses the practice of objectifying and measuring some aspect of a disability. What is the problem with quantifying and objectifying disability and the disabled, according to the author? What can it lead to?

8. What did the experiment of arranging objects around the tabletop set out to prove (see "Mapping sightedness" and "Life with maps")? How did it help lead the author to a new awareness?

COLLABORATIVE ACTIVITY

Did your reading of the essay change your conception of blindness or of disability in general? Discuss the essay's purpose and its success in achieving that purpose. (It might be a good idea if you began by summarizing or paraphrasing the author's objective as she expresses it in her introduction.)

ACTIVITY

Did it surprise you that the author seemed so little concerned with the legal rights of the disabled and with the management of disabilities? How do you think advocacy groups for the disabled might respond to her essay? Write a 200- to 300-word response from the point of view of the president of such an advocacy group. *OR* Write a 200- to 300-word response from the point of view of a person who has a disability (it could be blindness or any other disability).

Qallunology: An introduction to the Inuit study of white people

Zebedee Nungak

(2,200 words)

Like many Inuit boys of my generation, I had a fascination with Qallunaat that bordered on awe. Growing up, the few we encountered lived in warm wooden houses, while we lived in igloos. They seemed to lack no material thing. Their food was what the word delicious was invented for. All their women were beautiful, and even their garbage was good! As a boy, I had an innocent ambition to be like them. The measure of my success would be when my garbage equalled theirs.

I lived among the Qallunaat for seven years in their land, the Qallunaarjuani fantasyland of my early childhood. In that time, my discoveries of their peculiarities sparked my interest in what could be called Qallunology.

Many of us who have been exposed to Qallunaatdom through deep immersion in their world could write some credible discourses on the subject. Their social mores and standards of etiquette could fill several volumes. Their language contains scores of weirdnesses. Their sameness and distinctness can be utterly baffling. An Irishman from Northern Ireland looks exactly the same as one from the south. A close look at Albanians and Serbs has them all looking like bona fide Qallunaat. Why such savage conflict among such same-looking civilized people? Some rate their own calling: Jaamaniit, who were so long the enemy, and the Ouigouit, whose label could have been different if the first of their arrivals had kept saying "Non-non" instead.

Several fat books' worth of subject matter is being condensed to bare introductions here. But enjoy this launch of a new branch of academia.

Qallunaat were born to be nicknamed. Each Arctic community has its own set of gems. Here are but a few to which I myself can attach a name in English or French: Qirnitagalaak (Slightly Black); Miqquituq (Furless One, attributed to baldness); Navvaataaq (Found By Chance While Lost); Aupaqtualuk (Big Red); Qungisialuk (Big-Necked One); Kigutaittuq (Toothless One); Angajuqqaakutaak (Long Tall Thin—or Slender—Boss).

Many who caught on to their Inuktitut nicknames came to appreciate them as special symbols of regard. It is a point of pride for some Qallunaat to have been "badged" with an atinnguaq (nickname). If some seemed derogatory, it was in a most inoffensive and affectionate manner, as in calling somebody Qarliingasik (Drooping Pants), if that happened to be the most telling description of an individual.

Atinnguat were mostly descriptive of a physical characteristic or habit. Guides in a fishing camp had a fisherman who weighed 360 pounds, whom they immediately called Ammalukitaaq (Round, Circle-shaped). Some outsiders who study Inuit ways are quite proud of being called Apiqquq (One Who Is Always Asking Questions).

Even for prime, well-known Qallunaat, most older Inuit could only manage Pai-Minsta Tuutu for former Prime Minister Trudeau. Then there was Pai-Minsta Ma-ROO-ny, and now Pai-Minsta Jaa-KUIT-sia.

But it was not mere inability to pronounce English or French names that gave rise to this custom. There was an attitude, an element of "during your time in my space and environment, I will call you as I see you" about it. There's nothing scientific in how one got endowed with an atinnguaq. A tourist visiting for one week was as likely to be zinged with one as a nurse, teacher, or clergyman who spent years in the Arctic. It was an equal opportunity practice.

There is no Inuit Bureau of Qallunaat Nicknames, but a compilation of all that have existed would be just wonderful. The practice of nicknaming Qallunaat is not so slowly dying out. They are now so common in such great numbers all over the Inuit homeland that they have ceased to be the novelty they once were. Besides, the Qallunaat turnover rate is such that it is literally impossible to get a "feel-it-in-the-bones" handle on a subject sufficient to rate him/her with a decent atinnguaq.

Look! Look! See Sally run! Oh Dick, Oh Jane! Why do your parents have no name? Are all dogs in Qallunaatdom Spot, all cats Puff? There was absolutely no Fun with Dick and Jane as we Inuit children crashed head-on into the English language. The cultural shocks and tremors have never completely worn off those of us from the first generation to be zapped with such literature.

Against all odds, many of us became functional, and some even fluent, in Qallunaatitut, this Queen's English. But Inuit who have mastered its nuances so as to speak and command the language as would a Qallunaaq are very, very few. I have never been one of them, trudging along in a version that I call Eskimo English. For example, I talk about precipitation in a stragedy, not participation in a strategy.

This is nothing strange. Qallunaat who are functional in Inuktitut are also many, scores of them trudging along in a Taipsomanialuk Okagunna-launngilang sort of way. Anglo-Inuktitut, it could be called. Only four Qallunaat have ever fooled me into believing I was listening to an Inuk, so flawless was their command of the language.

In Qallunology, we take a look at some names that can be considered translators' delights: Lipscomb (Qaniup Illaigutinga), Featherstone (Suluk Ujaraq), Noseworthy (Qingagatsangijai), Goodenough (Piujuq Naammatumik), Middlemiss (Qitiraqsaungittuq). Some have no obvious translation but sound like they have character: McCorkindale, Vandervoort, Ottenheimer, Hotchkiss, MacAninney. If sorting out Inuit names was a tribulation for early traders, clergy, police, and government officials, beholding Qallunaat names can be an unperverted joy.

The Qallunaat custom of abbreviating first names does not seem to follow a standard formula. Robert can be Rob, Robbie, Bob, Bobby, or Bert. Joseph is Joe, James/Jim, Sidney/Sid, Arthur/Art, and Peter/Pete. Charles is Charlie but can be Chuck. What sleight of hand makes a Henry a Hank? And how does Richard become a Dick, if not a Rich or a Rick? Do you see a B in William on its way to be a Bill? Don't ever say SEEN for Sean (sh-AWN) or JOHN for Jean, if the person is a francophone male, gh-AWNG.

Qallunaat women can have very masculine names clicked feminine by ending them with an A: Roberta, Edwina, Donalda, Phillippa, Edwarda. Shortened names are mostly chopped versions; Katherine/Kate, Deborah/Debbie, except for some ready-mades like Wendy and Kay. Liz is drawn from the mid-section of Elizabeth, unlike in Inuit use, where these names are entirely separate as Elisapi and Lisi. Many names can fit both sexes: Michael, Beverly, Pat, Jan, and Leslie.

For a real treat, watch the NHL, not for the hockey, but for the names: Zhitnik, Cunneyworth, Nieuwendyk, and some, like Vanbiesbrouck, covering the sweater from armpit to armpit. There's even a Satan, though fortunately not pronounced as the Evil One. (Imagine him playing for the New Jersey Devils!) Some are even coincidentally Inuktitut sounding: Tkachuk, Sakic, Otto. Some names sound musical in their un-Englishness: Jaromir, Teemu, Pavel, Mats.

For all of this, we Inuit have been sneaking up on Qallunaat with what I call names not to be associated with hunger or starvation: Kevin, Curtis, Travis, Willis, Brenda, Linda, Stephanie, and Lindsay. But that is a point for Eskimology, not Qallunology.

One of the most distinctive features of life among Qallunaat, the one most markedly different from Inuit life, can be summed up in this expression of theirs: Keeping up with the Joneses. Not much is communal and very little of life's essentials are shared. It is based on competition, going to great lengths to "get ahead," and amassing what you gain for yourself. People around you may be in want, but that is their problem.

There is a hierarchy of labels for different classes of Qallunaat. There are the poor (yes, there are poor Qallunaat!), the lower middle class, middle class, upper middle class, upper class, and many variations of sub-descriptions for their wealthy. One can be old-money rich or nouveau riche. There are Baby Boomers and Generation X. Whole sections of towns and cities tend to cluster people by their station in life or economic status.

We know Qallunaat, of course, by the way they eat: with a fork and a dull knife known by Inuit as nuvuittuq (without point). There is a whole etiquette to eating too cumbersome to describe in detail. But if one has the misfortune to burp, belch, or fart during the meal, one has

to be civil and say, "Excuse me!" in a sincere enough demeanour. Never forget to say "Please" in asking for the salt or potatoes to be passed. Don't ever just up and walk away from the table.

Having visitors over (having Company) is mostly attached to some ritual of activity, such as a bridge game. If alcohol is served to guests, it is amazingly incidental and not the main item of attention. Nobody gets drunk, but there is a lot of talking! Then there seems to be an obligation to talk even more at the door before leaving. Guests and hosts lingering forever at the entrance to talk volumes about nothing in particular is one of the surest trademarks of being in Qallunaatdom.

There is a ritual called dating, which is hard to describe in Inuit terms. It can't really be described as husband- or wife-hunting. Maturing and onward people of opposite sexes mutually agree to "go out" to some form of enjoyable activity. Sometimes it is to test their compatibility as a possible couple, sometimes simply to genuinely enjoy each other's company. It seems to be a permanent occupation of some, whom Inuit might call uinitsuituq or nulianitsuituq, meaning "unattachable to a husband or wife."

Some people have attempted to characterize my discourses on Qallunology as racist. Such criticism simply glides off my hide. Over the years, I have winced countless times upon reading Qallunaat observations of Inuit. The earliest Qallunaat, especially, had a tendency to grossly misunderstand what they saw of our people. In comparison, my snapshots of Qallunaat folk are focused, vivid, and delivered in good humour.

I don't proclaim to be an expert on Qallunaat and what makes them tick. But my commentaries on Qallunology are based on having eaten, slept, and breathed their life for some years, learning their language and tumbling along in their tidy-squares thought processes.

The resulting recollections are no more superficial than those of the first Qallunaat, who unwittingly illustrated their educated ignorance when they tried to describe Inuit.

Consider British explorer Sir John Ross's account of meeting Inuit in the Central Arctic's Boothia Peninsula on January 9th, 1830: "Going on shore this morning, one of the seamen informed me that strangers were seen. . . . Knowing that the word of salutation between meeting tribes was 'Tima Tima,' I hailed them in their own language. . . ."

The next day, the Qallunaat visited the Inuit encampment: "The females were certainly not beautiful; but they were at least not inferior to their husbands, and were not less well behaved. . . . Their features were mild, and their cheeks, like those of the men, ruddy; one girl of 13 was even considered to have a pretty face. . . ."

In his book, *Northward over the great ice*, American Polar explorer Robert E. Peary does a take on the Inuit of High Arctic Greenland, from the year 1891: "Without government; without religion; without money or any standard of value; without written language; without property, except clothing and weapons; their food nothing but meat, blood and blubber; their clothing the skins of birds and animals; with habits and conditions of life hardly above the animal, these people seem at first to be very near the bottom scale of civilization; yet closer acquaintance shows them to be quick, intelligent, ingenious, and thoroughly human."

In the past, Qallunaat seemed to hold a monopoly on being the only ones who knew what to do. This has changed, and their previously held appearance of invincibility has been cut down a few notches. Qaujimajualuit, those of them who "know a great deal," with strings of academic degrees attached to their names, are more often seeking guidance from the reservoir of traditional knowledge possessed by Inuit.

Eskimology has long been a serious field of study by Qallunaat. Scores of museums and universities all over the world have great departments and sections devoted solely to the subject. Eskimologists have become world-renowned. Serious Qallunologists, on the other hand, are likely to sweat and toil in unrewarding anonymity until the academic currency of their field of study attains the respectability of being labelled officially with an "-ology."

Eskimologists have carted off traditional clothing, artefacts, hunting implements, tools, ancient stories and legends, and human remains for display in museums, bartering these for very little. Qallunologists will find nothing worth carting away for display. All Qallunaat stuff is for immediate use, much of it disposable, easily replaceable, and now available in mass quantities to Inuit as well, from their cordless drill to their satellite telephone to their Viagra pill. It all costs quite a lot, and one will be prosecuted for stealing any of it.

Eskimology was triggered by others' curiosity about who we are and how we live. It has done so well that we Inuit have in some ways benefited from it by reclaiming some essences of our identity from various collections in others' possession. Qallunaat, meanwhile, are not in any danger of having to go to museums to pick up remnants of who they once were.

This Magazine. 2003. November/December.

KEY AND DIFFICULT WORD

Define the following, using context or other clues if possible: **mores.**

QUESTIONS

1. The author purports to be introducing the reader to "a new branch of academia." What is this branch, and how does he establish himself as an authority on it?
2. Who does the author indicate is being addressed his essay? Is this his real audience?
3. Give one example of a neologism (a new or coined word). Give an example of an old word that is used in a striking or unusual way.
4. What is the author's attitude towards Eskimology? How do you infer this (be specific)?
5. Does Nungak successfully defend himself against charges of racism (paragraph 24)?
6. How would you characterize the humour in this essay? Identify examples of satire (satire uses humour and irony to promote change and can range from gently mocking to harshly critical).
7. What does Nungak mean in his last paragraph? Paraphrase the paragraph and identify its tone.

COLLABORATIVE ACTIVITY

Did this essay change your thinking in any way (i.e., about the way that non-Inuits have seen Inuit peoples or about the way that Inuits have seen non-Inuits)?

ACTIVITIES

1. Write a formal report on the status of Inuktitut or another traditional language spoken by a Canadian indigenous group. You can follow the guidelines for a formal report outlined in "The Active Voice: Report Writing," p. 104, or write an informal report on the subject.
2. Consider the author's purpose for writing his essay: to introduce his readers to a new field of study, Qallunology. Write a 500- to 750-word critical response to or critical analysis of this essay in which you address the purpose of the essay as well as his success in achieving this purpose.

Defining Canadians: Identity and Citizenship

Anti-heroism

John Ralston Saul

(1,900 words)

> *Napoleon would have been a nobody here.*
> George Bowering. *A Short Sad Book.*

It is difficult to think of a country where the modern idea of the Hero is less celebrated. This is not to say that thousands of people haven't acted in an heroic manner, in wars and out of wars. The hero of the heroic action has nothing to do with modern Hero worship. And it must be said that, even when it comes to the hero of the heroic act, Canadians are willing to show respect, but little more. They are nervous that anything more might slip into that other thing.

George Woodcock examined this phenomenon in his biography of Gabriel Dumont. "The pattern is clear. Canadians distrust heroes, partly because heroism is always a kind of imposition; the hero is dominating us by his strength, by his brute courage, and we have become suspicious of such qualities." He put this down to the sense that "we see ourselves generally imposed upon," an idea that Margaret Atwood first explained and that any number of francophone writers would echo in their own way. Arthur Buies, for example: "Egotism pushes us to false glory and there is scarcely a hero of the people who is not at the same time the jailer of another."

All of this is sensible and probably true, but I wonder if our reaction to Heroes doesn't go beyond the idea of sufferance. After all, that is something we share with many other countries, and they have more often than not adopted a classic attitude towards heroism. Many throw themselves into Hero worship as the solution to sufferance. Heroic nationalism with Heroic leadership and Heroic martyrdom are rather common among those who feel put upon.

As Woodcock points out, we do actually identify easily with martyrs. But even then, this is rarely an Heroic identification. Perhaps it's because we like to think of ourselves as martyrs. Perhaps we simply find it an easier relationship to assume since the Hero, being dead, is less able to impose himself on us.

Whether they are alive or dead, our aversion to Heroes seems to come from something else. After all, how could a country built on ideas not conquest, a place of three dominant minorities and many others, a poor place that evolved, thanks to a sense of individualism as cooperation, embrace the worship of Heroes?

The very form of the country is an anti-Utopia. This is what makes it interesting. And Hero worship is dependent on a willingness to believe in Utopias: to believe in the perfect place that has never and will never exist. The utopian ideal is the original form of ideology. Most countries slide between the unreasonable belief that a utopian form is possible and a realization that the utopian quest is exclusionary and catastrophic for real societies. But various phenomena—the illusion of racial unity or of cultural unity or a dominant historic mythology—lead some people to believe that fulfillment—le salut—can only come by embracing one or more of these false unities. From time to time, the combination of utopian leaders and favourable circumstances pushes a perfect solution to the fore. The result is usually disastrous.

Canada has never embraced these illusions of unity. The effect of trying to impose one—as various leaders have tried and continue to try to do—is merely to convert complexity into division. To suggest on the other hand that Canada is not a real country because it lacks the illusion of unity is to evoke the Heroic vision. I would say that it isn't worth preserving Canada if it can be reduced to a utopian ideal.

Let me go back for a moment to our peculiar attitudes towards war. These have seemed to divide us—francophone versus anglophone, but also rural versus urban. In spite of this, we have sent unusually high per-capita levels of soldiers to fight, with not equal but reasonable representation from all language and regional groups, and they have fought as well as or better than others.

And yet, once the propaganda and excitement have died down, virtually no heroic literature is produced. A great deal is written, much of it of very high quality, and it isn't exactly an anti-war literature. Again, Canadians lack the easy romanticism of being able to pretend that something that has always existed is likely to disappear. On the other hand, this literature contains a curiously consistent internal line—it is anti-heroic. Heroic acts are admitted to but invariably put down to accident or misadventure.

The doctor based on Norman Bethune, in Hugh MacLennan's *The watch that ends the night*, admits that he won his military medal after a suicidal charge, having caught the clap in his first sexual experience. He was actually trying

to kill himself. "For committing murder because I'd caught the clap, I was called a hero."

In a scene eerily similar to that in *War and peace*, when Napoleon decorates one of the tsar's soldiers, Robertson Davies's main character in *Fifth business* finds himself staring into the eyes of George V as the king pins a Victoria Cross onto his chest. "Here am I, I reflected, being decorated as a hero, and in the eyes of everybody here I am indeed a hero; but I know that my heroic act was rather a dirty job I did when I was dreadfully frightened. I could just as easily have muddled it and been ingloriously killed. But it doesn't much matter because people seem to need heroes; so long as I don't lose sight of the truth, it might as well be me as anyone else."

The same atmosphere can be found in Colin McDougall's novel *Execution* or Timothy Findley's *The wars* or Farley Mowat's memoirs, *My father's son: Memories of war and peace*, or Kevin Major's dramatization of the massacre of the Newfoundland Regiment in *No man's land* or Oakland Ross's *Guerilla Beach*, with its contemporary Latin American war stories.

Jacques Brault's wonderful—

They say you died for our Honour   they say
and stroke their sagging belly they say that you
died for Peace   they say   and suck on their cigar
long like a barrel

might be put down to an anti-war atmosphere in Quebec, except what then do you do with a Westerner like Nellie McClung, feminist leader, friend and supporter of Mackenzie King, who wrote—

Oh! her sunny-hearted lad! So full of love and tenderness and pity, so full of ambition and high resolves and noble impulses, he is dead—dead already—and in his place stands "private 355," a man of hate, a man of blood!

And what do you do then with most of the pictures painted by Canada's official war artists during the First World War?

There were some traditional heroic canvases, but nothing more anti-war was produced by any writer than F.H. Varley's pictures *The sunken road* and *For what?* with their corpses, not like fallen heroes but like clods of mud, indistinguishable from the heaving landscape. Or there was A.Y. Jackson's dark, ironic picture of seared tree trunks, water-filled craters and mud. He called it *A copse, evening*. Varley wrote home of the effect the war was having on him. "You must see . . . the dead on the field, freakishly mutilated—headless, legless, stomachless, a perfect body and a passive face and a broken empty skull—see your own countrymen, unidentified, thrown into a cart."

The dominant Canadian war images were not those of the heroic school. The general image produced by the official war art came from that of the Group of Seven and David Milne and was profoundly anti-heroic. Emily Carr recounts Lawren Harris lecturing in the years after the war "about the churches and their smugness, and of mothers offering their sons as sacrifices, and the hideous propaganda of politics and commerce exploiting war with greed and money for their gods while we stupidly, indolently, sit blindfolded, swallowing the dop ladled out to us. . . ." The Group of Seven may have been a nationalist school. But it was not nationalism of the old school. It was not about race or Heroes.

In truth, there seems to be no heroic war literature and in general little heroic war culture, at any rate of a quality that could survive the propaganda drive of the moment. Even those who were eager to fight or to send others to fight have shown no interest in the classical representation of glory.

And yet various nationalist schools of historians and politicians have attempted to introduce a taste for great men. Abbé Groulx was full of the glories of great men, as in his own way was Donald Creighton. But it didn't catch on. For example, the number of biographies of public figures has shrunk over the last few decades to virtual non-existence. And those that are written are rarely hagiographies.

This frustrates experts in communication who would prefer to find a taste for advanced personality worship in the population. You can see this in the desperate reworking of hockey over the last years. There have always been great players, and they have had something of the heroic about them. But both they and the public have seen the game for what it is—a profoundly cooperative experience. The great teams have been just that, teams. They also have a few great individual players.

The needs of commerce in an era dominated by the Heroic Hollywood entertainment myth have endlessly twisted the game to look and sound like an undertaking of great players who, incidentally, play for good teams. Still, you can feel that Canadian audiences are only marginally interested in this Heroic approach to the game. They watch it as they know it is played at its best—a flying, rough, corps de ballet.

This is probably because every Canadian male has played hockey at some age or ends up believing he has. The game has thus become one of those basic physical mythologies which reveal and reflect the larger myths. If Canadians are anti-heroic, they will treat their basic game as anti-heroic and team-oriented. You can see the forces that now control the professional level of the game struggling with, or rather against, these attitudes. Their conforming commercial attitudes require a game of Heroes and goals. Canadian audiences persist in an interest in how the game is played.

Among the same experts in communications there is a constant moaning about our lack of heroes and leaders in public affairs. Pierre

Trudeau, the most personally successful politician in Quebec and throughout Canada since Laurier, refused to play by these new rules and instead based his popularity on a relatively abrupt and intellectually direct public manner. He broke all the formulae of Heroic communications, while men like Jean Chrétien, Preston Manning, and Lucien Bouchard are each in their own way obedient to those rules.

Even so, the citizenry seem to have withdrawn even farther into their shell, as if wary of such public figures, while leaving a surface impression of acquiescence. They have become increasingly indecipherable, perhaps loyal to the view laid out by George Frederick Cameron in the middle of the nineteenth century.

> I am not of those fierce, wild wills,
> Albeit from loins of warlike line,
> To wreck laws human and divine
> Alike, that on a million ills
> I might erect one sacred shrine. . . .

In John Ralston Saul. 1998. *Memoirs of a Siamese twin*. Toronto: Penguin Canada.

KEY AND DIFFICULT WORDS

Define the following, using context or other clues if possible: **sufferance, hagiographies.**

QUESTIONS

1. In paragraph 1, what does Saul mean by "that other thing?" Why does he use this phrase rather than name it directly?
2. Why is it important for Saul to discuss utopias and anti-utopias in his first section? Summarize the paragraphs in which he defines and discusses utopias and their opposite (paragraphs 6–7).
3. How many sections does the essay have? Provide section headings, using an appropriate descriptive phrase for each.
4. Saul chooses to use many examples from primary sources to support his claim about anti-heroism. Give three examples of primary sources. (a) Do you think that it would have been better to use more secondary sources, such as those mentioned in the first paragraph of the last section? (b) Of the following considerations, which do you think had the greatest bearing on his choice: essay topic, purpose in writing, intended audience?
5. For most of his essay, Saul is concerned with supporting his claim concerning the existence of Canadian anti-heroism. At what points, specifically, does he try to account for this phenomenon? Do you think he does so successfully?
6. Using your experience as a participant or observer, do you accept Saul's appraisal of the attitude of most Canadians toward hockey?
7. How does the popularity of Pierre Trudeau exemplify the Canadian preference for the non-heroic?

COLLABORATIVE ACTIVITY

It is sometimes said that Canadians and the Canadian identity can be defined by a negation or a lack of something, by what Canadians are not rather than what they are. Discuss the validity of this assessment.

ACTIVITIES

1. Who is John Ralston Saul? Write a one-paragraph biography of Saul, including his qualifications for writing about the Canadian identity, using your own words and naming your source(s).

2. (a) Using biographical information obtained from a reliable hard-copy or electronic source, explain why the exploits of Gabriel Dumont (see paragraph 2) could be considered heroic, defining first what you mean by a "hero." OR
(b) Find an image of a suitable Canadian painting (it could be one of those Saul refers to in the second section of his essay), and write a brief analysis of the way it portrays anti-war or anti-heroic qualities.

Related readings: Pico Iyer. "Canada: Global citizen"; and Michael A. Robidoux. "Imagining a Canadian identity through sport: A historical interpretation of lacrosse and hockey."

Imagining a Canadian identity through sport: A historical interpretation of lacrosse and hockey

Michael A. Robidoux

(7,600 words)

Sport in Canada during the late 19th century was intended to promote physical excellence, emotional restraint, fair play, and discipline; yet these ideological principles were consistently undermined by the manner in which Canadians played the game of hockey. This article explores the genesis of violence in hockey by focusing on its vernacular origins and discusses the relevance of violence as an expression of Canadian national identity in terms of First Nations and French-Canadian expressions of sport.

In *Imagined communities*, Benedict Anderson convincingly reduces the concept of nationalism to an imagining—imagined "because members of even the smallest nation will never know most of their fellow-members, meet them, or even hear of them, yet in the minds of each lives the image of their communion" (1991:6). It is this notion of communion that motivates nations to define and articulate their amorphous existence. If Anderson is correct—which I believe to be the case—the task of defining a national identity is a creative process that requires constructing a shared history and mythology(ies) that best suit the identity *imagined* by those few responsible for responding to this task. For a nation as young as Canada (confederated in 1867), this constructive process is somewhat recent and largely incomplete, which is disconcerting for Canadians who have twice witnessed the threat of national separation.[1] As a result, what it means to be Canadian is often scrutinized, lamented, and at times even celebrated (most recently through a Molson Canadian beer advertisement).[2] Yet through all of this there has been one expression of nationalism that has remained constant since Confederation, that being the game of ice hockey.[3]

Since World War II, Canadians have been internationally perceived more as peacekeepers and, perhaps, even as being unreasonably polite—both political constructions in themselves—which makes it difficult to comprehend why a game such as hockey, known for its ferocity, speed, and violence, would come to serve as Canada's primary national symbol. The mystery intensifies if we consider that the game of hockey was born out of a period of social reform in Canada, where popular pastimes that involved violence, gambling, and rowdiness were being replaced by more "civilized" leisure pursuits imported from Europe. For instance, cricket, as Richard Gruneau states, was

> especially palatable to Canada's colonial merchants and aristocrats because it combined an excellent and enjoyable forum for learning discipline, civility, and the principles of fair play with a body of traditions and rules offering a ritual dramatization of the traditional

power of the colonial metropolis and the class interests associated with it. [1983:104]

The question becomes, then, how did a game such as hockey not only take shape in Canada but become "frequently cited as evidence that a Canadian culture exists" (Laba 1992:333)? Furthermore, to what extent does the game of hockey embody a Canadian collective sensibility, or is this *imagining* of Canadian identity without justification even at a symbolic level? In order to respond to these questions, it is necessary to explore early vernacular forms of sport in this nation and consider how these sensibilities have maintained themselves in a contemporary sporting context.

THE PROCESS OF MODERNIZATION

Sport historians and sociologists have documented extensively the development of physical activity from a traditional folk (vernacular) pastime to a modern organized event.[4] Much of this discourse, however, concerns itself with the impact of modernization on traditional physical activities without taking into account the influences of traditional sporting behaviour and its role in shaping (at least from a Canadian perspective) a national sport identity. Colin Howell is critical of these prejudicial tendencies and writes:

> Modernization theory views history as a linear continuum in which any given circumstance or idea can be labeled "pre-modern" or traditional, and thus, can safely be ignored as something that the seemingly neutral process of "modernization" has rendered anachronistic. [1995:184][5]

What needs to be understood is that the process of modernization is not, in fact, a linear progression but rather a series of contested stages that maintain certain aspects of the past, while housing them in an entirely different framework. Before further discussing the relationship between traditional and modern sport, a brief explanation of these terms is necessary.

In sport theory, loosely organized, periodic, and self-governed sporting contests fit under the rubric of *traditional* sport (Metcalfe 1987:11). This form of physical activity is devoid of field or participant specifications and "was closely interwoven with established conventions of ritual . . . as well as the daily and seasonal rhythms of domestic and agrarian production, entertainment and religious festivals" (Gruneau 1988:12–13). There is a tendency to refer to traditional sport as rural, tribal, and in the past tense; in truth, however, this manner of participation continues to exist in a variety of forms. An example would be road/ball/pond hockey in which people engage in variations of the game of hockey in unspecified locales, with unspecified participants in terms of age, number, gender, and skill; these spontaneous games are performed around daily routines, whether these routines be dictated by work, school, personal, or familial responsibilities. For this reason, I have substituted the term *traditional* with *vernacular*, as it connotes similar meanings but remains viable in a contemporary context and is, in fact, clearer.

The significance of the term *modern* sport is twofold in that it relates not only to the changes that have taken place in the way people engage in play, but *modern* also implies the political motivations that dictated these changes. To begin, modern sport is not a random pursuit but rather a highly organized event played within specific boundaries and performed with uniform rules maintained by leagues and organizations. In time, equipment becomes standardized, and play becomes recorded and measured. The result is greater uniformity over time and space, reduc-

ing the "localized forms of individual and community-based expressions of pleasure, entertainment, physical prowess, and ritual display" (Gruneau 1988:13). Importantly, the consequence of this reductive process was not simply the limiting of specific expressions of sport, but behaviour itself has been reduced to satisfy a limited and highly specific social order. Pierre Bourdieu explains that "it would be a mistake to forget that the modern definition of sport is an integral part of a 'moral ideal,' that is, an ethos which is that of the dominant fractions of the dominant class" (1993:344), notions that were instilled and maintained by religious and education institutions (Wheeler 1978:192). It is through the standardization of sport that undesirable qualities of vernacular play could be eliminated—behaviours such as violence, public disorder, and mass rowdiness—thus controlling behaviour to ensure a compliant and non-volatile populace. However, it must be stressed that while levels of control were successfully manufactured through sport, and play was indeed standardized, "undesirable" vernacular elements were not, in fact, entirely reduced but actually remain critical features of specific sports such as lacrosse and hockey.

The political motivations behind the modernization of sport cannot be separated from the actual changes that occurred in expressions of physical activity. In Canada, these motivations stemmed from a British Victorian sensibility. By the turn of the eighteenth century, sport in Britain was being realized as an excellent means of social control and conditioning (Jarvie and Maguire 1994:109). The successes that church and school officials had enjoyed by providing the ever-increasing urban working class with productive non-threatening activities, such as cricket and (a "refined" version of) football, were soon being implemented in the colonies as a means of "correcting" the rougher, more vulgar vernacular pastimes. Perhaps even more importantly, there was symbolic value in having newly colonized peoples engaging in these uniquely British activities; thus, regulated sport quickly became a vehicle for cultural imperialism. Metcalfe speaks to the imperialistic role of cricket by stating that it "illustrated the powerful forces of tradition and the way in which dominant social groups perpetuated their way of life in the face of massive social change" (1987:17).

In early nineteenth-century Canada, attempts were well underway to introduce imported European games such as cricket and curling to a nation only beginning to take shape. However, in its earliest stages, organized sport was something suitable only for "gentlemen" and not worthy of the working class or ethnic minorities. Howell points out that while "middle-class reformers advocated a more disciplined and rational approach to leisure, seeking to replace irrational and often turbulent popular or working-class recreations with more genteel and improving leisure activities," these "bourgeois sportsmen" primarily "concentrated their attention on the improvement of middle-class youth" (1995:14). It was not until later in the century that schools and churches began to take a more active role in introducing structured forms of physical activity to Canadians of various class and ethnic backgrounds. The intent of making sport and physical activity more socially democratic was threefold: to acquire levels of control over increased amounts of leisure time made possible by industrialization and a shorter workweek; to reduce class conflict by enabling male participants of various backgrounds to compete on an equal playing field; and to build a physically fit yet subordinate workforce, ensuring maximum levels of industrial production. In short, advocating for institutionalized sport served as an important means of reproducing a Victorian social order in Canada, where young men learned to be honourable and genteel gentlemen. As with any hegemonic process,[6] however, control was never absolute, and almost immediately emergent and residual cultures affected the desired outcome in unexpected ways.

RESISTING AN IMPORTED CANADIAN IDENTITY

The development of "controlled" sport took an important turn by the middle of the nineteenth century with a new emergent class—led by Montreal-born dentist, George Beers—responding to impositions of British nationalism in Canada. Beers's role in Canadian sport history was that of a romantic nationalist, as his politics were comparable to Herder's romantic nationalism of eighteenth-century Germany. Like Herder, Beers understood that to construct a national identity, two things needed to occur. First, foreign influence needed to be eliminated—Herder contended with French influence; Beers contended with English imperialism. And second, a national history/mythology needed to be consciously constructed. Instead of turning to indigenous poetry and language as Herder did, Beers turned to indigenous sport as a means of portraying the soul of a nation. What better place to look, he surmised, than Canada's First Peoples whose game of *baggataway*—filled with speed, violence, and skill—appeared to best embody the harsh and gruelling existence of Canadian natives as well as the trials of early Canadian settlers in this new and untamed land.

The game *baggataway*, renamed lacrosse by French settlers,[7] was played by many First Nations (Native Canadians) across North America prior to European contact, and it proved to be a game that both fascinated and repulsed early settlers (Eisen 1994:2). Some English Europeans were least sympathetic to First Nations' leisurely activities largely because of puritanical sensibilities that tended to perceive all forms of play as wasteful and unproductive. It is not surprising that English observations of lacrosse disparaged the violence; yet negative comments were often countered with admiration for First Nations players who exuded remarkable sportsmanship and respect for their opponents. One late eighteenth-century account reads:

> The Chippewas play with so much vehemence that they frequently wound each other, and sometimes a bone is broken; but notwithstanding these accidents there never appears to be any spite or wanton exertions of strength to affect them, nor do any disputes ever happen between the parties. [Carver 1956:237]

More detailed accounts of lacrosse come from French missionaries and settlers, who, unlike the English, lived with First Nations peoples and made efforts to learn their language, customs, and social practices. One of the earliest accounts comes from Nicolas Perrot, who encountered the game while living as a *coureur de bois*[8] between 1665 and 1684:

> Il y a parmy eux un certain jeu de crosse qui a beaucoup de raport avec celuy de nostre longue paume. Leur coustume en joüant est de se mettre nation contre nation, et, s'il y en a une plus nombreuse que l'autre, ils en tirent des hommes pour rendre égale celle qui ne l'est pas. Vous les voyez tous armez d'une crosse, c'est à dire d'un baston qui a un gros bout au bas, lacé comme une raquette; la boule qui leur sert à joüer est de bois et à peu près de la figure d'un oeuf de dinde. [1973:43–44][9]

> [Among them there is a certain game of crosse that compares to our tennis. Their custom is to play nation (tribe) against nation (tribe), and if one side has more players than the other, more players are brought forth to ensure a fair game. Each has a stick, called a crosse, that has a big curve at the end that is laced like a racket; the ball that they play with is made of wood and looks a little bit like a turkey's egg.]

He continues by describing the violent nature of the sport:

> Vous entendez le bruit qu'ils font en se frapant les uns contre les autres, dans le temps qu'ils veulent parer les coups pour envoyer cette boule du costé favorable. Quand quelqu'un la garde entre les pieds sans la vouloir lascher, c'est à luy d'eviter les coups que ses adversaires luy portent sans discontinuer sur les pieds; et s'il arrive dans cette conjoncture qu'il soit blessé, c'est pour son compte. Il s'en est veü, qui ont eü les jambes cassées, d'autres les bras, et quelques uns ont estez mesme tüez. Il est fort ordinaire d'en voir d'estropiez pour le reste de leurs jours, et qui ne l'ont esté qu'à ces sortes de jeu par un effect de leur opiniâtreté. [1973:45]

> [One can hear the noise they make when they hit one another, while they attempt to avoid receiving blows in order to throw the ball to a favourable location. If one secures the ball in his feet without letting it go, he must fend off blows from his opponents who continually strike his feet; and if in this situation he is injured, it is his own concern. Some are seen with broken legs or arms, or are even killed as a result. It is common to see players maimed permanently, yet this does not change the way they play the game on account of their obstinacy.]

For many young French males, the rough nature of the sport was appealing, and as a result, these men became enamoured with not only the game of lacrosse but with its participants as well.

The radical impositions of European colonization on North American indigenous peoples has been taken to task in recent academic and popular discourse; clearly, arguments that perceive this relationship to be unidirectional are often overstated. In *The skyscrapers hide the heavens*, Miller offers some balance to this historical analysis by revisiting early Euro-Indian relations and discussing them in terms of cultural change, both "non-directed" and "directed" (2000:95). In other words, Miller understands these relations as being far more equitable than is often portrayed. Not only did First Nations peoples often *willingly* take advantage of such things as European technology to benefit their own situations, but Miller documents, as well, the gross reliance of European settlers on First Nations knowledge and technologies. In fact, he states that European survival in Canada would not have been possible without First Nations assistance and charity. Furthermore, and more importantly for our purposes, is the knowledge concerning the extensive cultural borrowings of European settlers (in this case French) from First Nations peoples.

For a certain sector of French Canadian males—later known as *les Canadiens*—the First Nations male provided an alternative model of masculinity to what they had known in France, one where physicality, stoicism, and bravado were valued and celebrated, not repressed, as was the typical Christian model of masculinity:

The young voyageurs struggled to copy the Indians' stoicism in the face of adversity and their endurance when confronted with hardship, deprivation, and pain. They also copied, to the extent that their employers and governors could not prevent, the autonomy that Indian society inculcated in its young.

French males found the liberated sexual attitudes of young Indian women before matrimony as attractive as the missionaries found them repugnant. [Miller 2000:54]

Early French settlers began emulating First Nations males and, in doing so, began sharing in their cultural practices. Occupational and survival-related pursuits such as canoeing, snowshoeing, and hunting were some of the obvious activities that were learned and performed. Native team sports such as lacrosse also proved to be of tremendous interest to *les Canadiens*, as these games gave both First Nations and French males the opportunity to prove their worth to one another as men. According to Joseph Oxendine, these white settlers did not fare very well, however, "because of the Indian's clear superiority of the game. Indians were frequently reported to have used fewer players in an effort to equalize the competition" (1988:48). First Nations proficiency at lacrosse was highly regarded by early sport enthusiasts, but these skills were also perceived by others to be violent and dangerous, a perception that began generating its own folklore among the early North American settlers.

Perhaps the most popularly known lacrosse event was a legendary contest between two First Nations tribes at Fort Michilimackinac in 1763—an ambush disguised as a sporting contest. According to Alexander Henry's account of the "contest," the tribes used lacrosse as a means of staging an attack on the British fort during the Pontiac Rebellion (Henry 1901). Francis Parkman supports this in his account, which states:

Suddenly, from the midst of the multitude, the ball soared into the air and . . . fell near the pickets of the fort. This was no chance stroke. It was part of a preconcerted stratagem to insure the surprise and destruction of the garrison. . . . The shrill cries of the ball-players were changed to the ferocious war-whoop. The warriors snatched from the squaws the hatchets, which the latter . . . had concealed beneath their blankets. Some of the Indians assailed the spectators without, while others rushed into the fort, and all was carnage and confusion. [1962:254]

It was the legendary status the sport commanded that made it the perfect vehicle for George Beers's nationalist agenda. The game ran counter to British bourgeois sensibilities that understood sport to be refined and gentlemanly, one that could ultimately serve as a breeding ground for proper British mores and values. Instead, lacrosse was a display of rugged, brutal, and aggressive behaviours that were said to embody what it meant to be a Canadian settler in this unforgiving northern territory. Thus, Beers called on Canadians to refrain from engaging in the imperial pursuit of cricket and take up lacrosse as the new national game, in effect ridding Canada of foreign influences and acquainting the new populations with the soul of the nation.

In order to make this fictious proposal possible, the native game needed to be claimed by the male settlers and then incorporated into a modern sporting climate. *Baggataway*, as First Nations peoples played it, was not merely a sport but a spiritual and religious occasion, often having healing or prophetic significance.[10] The game also had regional and tribal idiosyncrasies, which meant that there was no standard form of play, making Euro-Canadian adoption difficult. Thus, *baggataway* as a native vernacular entity needed to be transformed into lacrosse, which meant claiming the game and eliminating traits that were linked to First Nations culture. To achieve this transformation, it was necessary to standardize the rules to create a sense of uniformity. An important step was made, in fact, by George Beers, who published the first rules of lacrosse under the name "Goal-keeper" in a series of advertisements in the *Montreal Gazette* in 1860 (Cosentino 1998:15). These rules were later adopted by the Montreal Lacrosse Club and became the "official" rules of lacrosse, later republished in the *Montreal Gazette* in July of 1867 (Morrow 1989:47). Efforts to standardize the game not only eliminated regional variation but also seemed to dictate how the game of lacrosse was to be played. All that was left, then, was to attract people to the game, and, again, in this Beers was instrumental.

Through various print forms (magazines and newspapers), Beers began to promote lacrosse as Canada's national game and in the process deride cricket as foreign and irrelevant to Canadians. In an article that appeared in the *Montreal Gazette* in August of 1867, suitably entitled, "The national game," Beers writes:

> As cricket, wherever played by Britons, is a link of loyalty to bind them to their home so may lacrosse be to Canadians. We may yet find it will do as much for our young Dominion as the Olympian games did for Greece or cricket for our Motherland. [1867]

Of course, Beers makes no apologies for appropriating an Aboriginal game and promoting it as the national pastime. Instead, he sees appropriation as an accurate depiction of European presence in Canada and argues, "just as we claim as Canadian the rivers and lakes and land once owned exclusively by Indians, so we now claim their field game as the national field game of our dominion" (1867). Beer's proselytizing was enormously effective, to the extent that a National Lacrosse Association was formed—the first national sporting body in Canada—and lacrosse was being touted by many as Canada's official national game.[11]

These developments, which documented how a vernacular sporting pastime was transformed into a modern sport, were not as complete as scholars have suggested. Sports historian Don Morrow claims: "At first heralded in adoption, then transformed in nature, the Indian origins of the game were finally shunned by nineteenth-century white promoters and players" (1989:46). While ritual/sacred components and regional variations were erased from modern lacrosse competitions, there were native/vernacular elements of the game that remained, largely to the chagrin of elite sporting officials who were governing these developments. To begin, the popularization of lacrosse did not arise merely because of Beers's ideological ravings. It is incorrect to claim, as Morrow does, that the new national affinity of lacrosse was achieved through the word of George Beers. Crediting only one person simply does not allow for human agency, and while public consciousness can be influenced, it is not something that can be dictated. In other words, there needed to be some pre-existing value in lacrosse that allowed it to be so willingly adopted by Canadian sport enthusiasts. It is here, then, that we can begin examining the cultural value of lacrosse (and later hockey) and its relationship to Canadian identity.

SPORT SENSIBILITIES IN CONFLICT

One of the primary reasons lacrosse served as a viable alternative to imported British sports such as cricket was its emphasis on physical aggression, volatility, and danger. The game appealed to males who identified with a more physically aggressive notion of masculinity rather than the reserved and civil expressions of masculinity exemplified in cricket. In essence, the attraction to lacrosse was an extension of early French Canadians' infatuation with First Nations masculinity, where the emphasis was on physical superiority, bodily awareness, and perseverance. Lacrosse provided males the opportunity to display these heralded qualities and challenge themselves through formal competitions. However, in the attempt to modernize lacrosse and market it to a broader audience, the game needed to become less violent and needed to be played in a manner more suitable for "gentlemen"; otherwise the game would not enter dominant sport culture. Efforts were in place to sanitize the game, but they were not entirely successful. In fact, those who were most successful at the sport were First Nations and working-class players who played the game as it was originally designed—aggressively and intensely. Attempts to turn the game into something else merely put those who engaged in it as "gentlemen" at a clear disadvantage to those who maintained its aggressive style of play. One team renowned for its aggressive play was the Montreal Shamrocks, who "were, without question, the most successful team prior to 1885. . . . The Shamrocks were out of place both socially and athletically. Social misfits on the middle-class playing fields, the Shamrocks were Irish, Roman Catholic, and working-class" (Metcalfe 1987:196).

What is critical here is that the ideological and political value of lacrosse as advocated by those in power paled in relation to the actual meanings early participants experienced through playing it. Colin Howell, also a sports historian, correctly observes that lacrosse was "a relatively minor sport" that "was suddenly elevated to prominence because of the symbolic role that was associated with it at the time of Confederation" (Howell 1995:103). However, those elite officials who helped elevate the status of lacrosse understood the sport symbolically, not according to its literal value as a meaningful expression of Canadian consciousness. I do not wish to imply that this is a singular phenomenon, but there is evidence that lacrosse did have value for certain Canadian males as an identifiable articulation of who they were as men. In essence, lacrosse did signify class, gender, and ethnic values, but these values were generally unacknowledged by elite sporting officials who were suddenly threatened by their own ideological manoeuvrings. The official recourse was to prohibit the "people" from playing the game and to attempt to make it instead the game of an exclusive minority:

> The logical conclusion for lacrossists was that the incidence of disputes, violence, and undesirable conduct on the field of play could mean only one thing—some players were not gentlemen. The truth of this observation was given substance by the presence of Indians, who always played for money and, by race alone, could not be gentlemen, and of the working-class Shamrock team. [Metcalfe 1987:195]

This prohibition of undesirable participants eventually led to the introduction of amateurism.

Amateur athletics in Canada did not merely function as a means of ensuring that athletes engage in sport in a gentlemanly manner[12] but served as a discriminatory system that prevented "undesirable" players from playing. Prior to 1909, the year when a national amateur athletic union was formed in Canada, national sporting bodies used the concept of amateurism to best suit their sport's needs. In the case of the National Lacrosse Association, league officials decided to make it an "amateur" association restricted to those players who fit under the definition of amateur. An amateur was conveniently defined by the Amateur Athletic Union of Canada as someone who had "never competed for a money prize, or staked bet with or against any professional for any prize" or one who had "never taught, pursued, or assisted in the practice of athletic exercises as a means of obtaining a livelihood" (Metcalfe 1987:105–106). The stipulations were highly restrictive and deliberate in design.

First, the new requirements made working-class participation virtually impossible in that wage earners were no longer able to receive financial compensation for taking time off from work to play. Keeping in mind that it was illegal to play sports on Sunday and that the workweek ran from Monday to Saturday, working-class participation in sport was restricted generally to Saturday afternoons. As a result, players were not only prevented from receiving payment for time lost at work, but those players who at one time received compensation for their services were no longer eligible to play. The second aspect of the restrictions was equally effective because it denied access to individuals who at one time gambled on sport. During this period in Canadian history, gambling and sport were virtually inextricable: gambling made up part of the fabric of vernacular sporting pastimes. For First Nations cultures in particular, gambling in sport (by spectators and participants) was deeply ingrained in their traditions and at times even played a role in their overall economies (Oxendine 1988:31). Therefore, by these first two stipulations alone, most ethnic minorities and working-class players were considered ineligible and could no longer play amateur athletics. The final stipulation reinforced economic divisiveness further by making it clear that sport was not the property of the people but, rather, of men who "had the leisure, economic resources and social approval to explore intensive athletic training in a financially disinterested manner" (Burstyn 1999:224).

The restrictive measures imposed by the National Lacrosse Association did not go unchallenged, however. Teams tried to circumvent the rules by covertly using "professional" players to become more competitive and in certain cases even paid players for their services. In response, the National Lacrosse Association was compelled to enforce disciplinary measures to contend with these dissident organizations. Teams caught cheating were brought before the Canadian Amateur Athletic Union to face arbitration and potential censuring.[13] As these arbitration cases grew in number, tremendous pressures were being placed on the National Lacrosse Association to retract its strictly amateur policy and permit both professionals and amateurs into the league. Despite this, the National Lacrosse Association remained steadfast in its position to prohibit professional players and was ultimately successful in maintaining itself as an amateur association; this success, however, proved to be its inevitable downfall.

By maintaining its exclusive membership, the National Lacrosse Association forced potential lacrosse players to pursue alternative sporting options. Other team-sport leagues (i.e., baseball, football, and hockey) were not as resistive to the influences of professionalism, and thus, they provided working-class and ethnic minority players alternatives to play in these sports and be financially compensated at the same time. While baseball and football did attract many of the players, these sports did not possess the symbolic and literal value found in lacrosse. Instead, it was hockey that early Canadian sport enthusiasts embraced by the turn of century, for the same reasons they were attracted to lacrosse 20 years earlier. Unlike baseball or football, hockey was seen as uniquely Canadian in origin and character. An amalgam of modern and vernacular sporting pastimes, hockey resembled lacrosse in design and in the manner it was played. Play was aggressive and often violent, providing men the opportunity to display this emergent notion of masculinity. At a symbolic level, it was played on

a frozen landscape, perfectly embodying what life as a Canadian colonialist was supposed to be like. Thus, hockey provided all that lacrosse entailed but without the restrictions of amateurism. By the 1920s, hockey had succeeded in becoming Canada's national sport pastime.

VIOLENCE, MASCULINITY, AND CANADIAN IDENTITY

It is here, then, that we return to the politics of identity and the manner in which hockey, a game notoriously aggressive and violent, serves as a potential symbol for national expression. Along with other social scientists,[14] I have been critical of popular discourse that tends to mythologize hockey and locate it as a unifying force in this nation. Gruneau and Whitson astutely observe:

> The myth of hockey as a "natural" adaptation to ice, snow, and open space is a particularly graphic example of what Barthes is alerting us to—about how history can be confused with nature. . . . This discourse of nature creates a kind of cultural amnesia about the social *struggles* and vested interests—between men and women, social classes, regions, races, and ethnic groups—that have always been part of hockey's history. [1993:132]

While these sentiments are certainly valid, it would be incorrect to say that hockey is without cultural or historical relevance in Canada. In fact, it is my contention that hockey is more than a mythological construct; it is a legitimate expression of Canadian national history and identity. Hockey *does* speak to issues of gender, race, ethnicity, and region in this nation, albeit not in an entirely positive manner. For this reason, hockey moves beyond symbol and becomes more of a metaphoric representation of Canadian identity.

ODDS AND ENDS AT THE HOCKEY STRUGGLE

Figure 1. Odds and ends at the hockey struggle.

First, hockey was born out of post-Confederation Canada,[15] in a period of political uncertainty and unrest. Canada was a disparate nation, divided in terms of language, region, and ethnicity—lacking in identity and national unity. Thus, while hockey was used ideologically to express national sentiment, its value as a vernacular entity was equal to, if not greater than, its symbolic value. From the outset, hockey's violent and aggressive style separated itself from other bourgeois (European) pastimes, including the increasingly popular game of baseball that was entering Canada from the United States. Early games often appalled certain sport writers and sport officials who saw the violence on the ice and in the stands as unfit for gentlemen. J.W. Fitsell provides two accounts of the first recorded game of hockey, which took place in 1875. The first, from *The Daily British Whig*, states that "Shins and heads were battered, benches smashed and the lady spectators fled in confusion" (Fitsell 1987:36). The other report from *The Montreal Witness* claimed that:

> Owing to some boys skating about during play an unfortunate disagreement arose: one little boy was struck across the head, and the man who did so was afterwards called to account, a regular fight taking place in which a bench was broken and other damages caused. [Fitsell 1987:36]

These accounts of violence are undoubtedly extreme, yet what is significant is that even in its earliest stages hockey was a sport perceived as excessively aggressive and violent within a modern European context.

THEY CALL FOOTBALL BRUTAL SPORT!

Figure 2. American cartoonists took to the slash and crash of Canadian players in Pittsburgh.

It was largely because of this excessive violence that hockey became a sport Canadians could call their own, and they quickly began to showcase it in international contexts. By the mid-1890s, competitions were being staged between Canadian hockey teams and American ice-polo teams. The Canadian teams dominated these early competitions and revelled in the press they received. Newspapers did applaud their skill, but at the same time reports were critical of their rough play. *The Daily Mining Gazette* of Houghton, Michigan, described one game as "rush, slash and check continually.... Calumet were knocked off the puck by Portage Lakes 'any old way.' Many a man had to be carried to the dressing room" (Fitsell 1987:120). In a game in Sault Ste. Marie, Michigan, an incident occurred where "Stuart [an American player] was laid out by a board check from Jack Laviolette. He recovered and tangled with the same player, fans rushed on the ice and as Stuart bled from the facial cuts, police were called in" (Fitsell 1987:120). These accounts illustrate that within 20 years of organized existence, hockey was internationally known as being first, Canadian, and second, notoriously violent. Further evidence of this is found in two American cartoons depicting Canadians playing hockey in Pittsburgh in 1904.[16]

The distinction hockey received as being a rough sport also served as a means for Canadians to display their proficiency in the clearly demarcated context of a sporting event, making hockey a valuable vehicle for expressing national identity. But it was not simply proficiency on the ice, it was physical proficiency within the masculinist tradition that was earlier identified in relation to lacrosse. Hockey displayed men who were perceived to be stoic, courageous, and physically dominant: precisely the same images of masculinity valued in First Nations culture and later by early Canadian settlers. These historically pertinent attitudes attracted Canadians to hockey, as the game provided Canadian males with an identifiable image outside of a British Victorian framework. Moreover, through hockey competitions, Canadians could exude superiority over Americans, illustrating for many a "victory for the industrious Canadian beaver over the mighty U.S. eagle" (Fitsell 1987:106). In essence, hockey became a vehicle of resistance against British and American hegemony, something that Canadians continue to call on in periods of political or national uncertainty.

The political implications went beyond resistance to British and American rivalries. One such occasion was the 1972 Summit Series in which Canadian professional hockey players engaged in an eight-game series against the Soviet Union national hockey team. The event was a debacle, yet it is considered by many to be the greatest Canadian story ever told. The series was described as East meets West—communism versus capitalism. So as the players rightfully admitted, it was no longer just about hockey. Reflecting on the series, Team Canada member Phil Esposito stated: "It wasn't a game anymore; it was society against society . . . it wasn't fun.

It was not fun" (*September 1972* 1997). The series was filled with incidents of extreme violence: one Canadian player (Bobby Clarke), following instructions from a coach, broke a Soviet player's ankle with his stick. Other incidents involved a Soviet referee nearly being attacked by a Canadian player; throat-slitting gestures; kicking (with skates); fighting; and a *melee* with NHL Players Association executive director Alan Eagleson, the Soviet Guard, and the Canadian hockey team. The event, which was advertised as an expression of goodwill between nations, turned sour when the favoured Canadians were defeated in the initial games and obviously outclassed in terms of skill and sportsmanship. Canadian players were simply unaware of the tremendous abilities of the Soviets and were, hence, humiliated both on the ice by the Soviets and off the ice by an unforgiving Canadian public who lambasted them with jeers.

In response to their dire predicament, Canadian players resorted to bullying and intimidation tactics and literally fought their way back into contention. In a miraculous comeback, overcoming real and imagined barriers, the Canadian team proved victorious, winning the final game and the series. Their "heroism" became permanently etched into the memory of Canadians, despite actions that have recently been described by two American journalists as "hacking and clubbing the Soviet players like seal pups and bullying their way to a thrilling, remarkable comeback" (Klein and Reif 1998:31). While there have been critics of the series, the games in the Canadian collective consciousness remain as "an orgy of self-congratulation about the triumph of 'Canadian virtues'—individualism, flair, and most of all, character" (Gruneau and Whitson 1993:263). Historically speaking, these seemingly appalling behaviours are compatible with Canadian hockey in general and for this reason are embraced, not denounced. The players performed in a manner consistent with Canadian play, illustrating a Canadian character that has yet to be defined in more concrete fashion. Therefore, despite Canadian behaviour that was an assault on international hockey, and on international competition in general, this assault was distinctly Canadian, something that is invaluable for the construction of a national identity.

CONCLUSION

The connection I have made between hockey and Canadian nationalism is very real.

I do not make the claim that Canadians are predisposed to violence or that they condone violent behaviour. Rather, I argue that hockey enabled Canadians to display qualities that have been valued in patriarchal relations: stoicism, courage, perseverance, and proficiency. The singularity of the game and the manner in which it was played were critical for a young and disparate nation to have as its own as it faced encroaching social, political, and cultural interests from Europe and the United States. At a more pedestrian level, hockey was accessible to men of various ethnic and class backgrounds, and thus, to a greater degree than lacrosse, it became a game of the people. The fact that "people" here is specific only to males established hockey as a male preserve, making it a popular site for males to define their worth as men, drawing on notions of masculinity that date back to seventeenth-century Canada. In this sense, understanding hockey beyond its mythological rhetoric acknowledges the "social *struggles* and vested interests—between men and women, social classes, regions, races, and ethnic groups" and confirms that hockey was, as Gruneau and Whitson state, "all of these" (1993:132).

Finally, by linking hockey to Canadian nationalism I am not situating either as being positive. In fact, the Canadian penchant to understand itself through hockey repeats masculinist formulas of identification that reflect poorly the lives of Canadians. The physically dominant, heterosexist, and capitalist associations of this specific identity are certainly exclusionary, but for that matter, all nationalist expressions cannot suitably speak for the polyphony of a nation. Despite the obvious fallibility of nationalistic representation, the legitimacy of nationalistic expression remains. Canada's history is located firmly in patriarchy, heterosexism, and capitalism; thus, the use of hockey to promote national pride and unity was not random then, nor is it today. Playing hockey is a means of constructing an image of a nation in the manner in which dominant forces within it wish to be seen. With this, hockey does not merely symbolize the need to define a national identity, it offers insight into the actual imaginings of what this identity entails. Hockey provides Canada a means by which to be distinguished. As Benedict Anderson astutely observes, such distinction ought not to be characterized by the dichotomy of "falsity/genuineness, but by the style in which it is 'imagined'" (1991:6).

Journal of American Folklore. 2002. 115 (45).

NOTES

1. The province of Quebec has twice voted to separate from Canada (1980 and 1995). The most recent referendum saw only 51 per cent of Quebecers voting "no" to separation.
2. The television commercial gained national notoriety because of its pro-Canadian stance. It depicts an ordinary "Joe" pronouncing his Canadian identity in contrast to perceived stereotypes of Canadians.
3. From this point forward ice hockey will be referred to as hockey.
4. See Gruneau 1983, 1988; Gruneau and Whitson 1993; Dunning 1975; Hargreaves 1986; Burstyn 1999; Metcalfe 1987; Morrow et al. 1989; Guttmann 1994; and Guay 1981.

5. Richard Gruneau in "Modernization and hegemony" similarly recognizes the shortcomings of "overlooking, or misconstruing, the importance of social and cultural continuities in sport" (1988:19).

6. Guttmann expresses his dissatisfaction with the term *cultural imperialism* to describe sport diffusion. Instead, he prefers the term *cultural hegemony*, which better communicates the lively "contestation that has accompanied ludic diffusion" (1994:178).

7. It has been argued that the term *la crosse* was applied to the game because the sticks used by the participants resembled a bishop's crozier (Thwaites 1959:326). Maurice Jetté argues, however, that the name comes from "an old French game called 'la soule' which was played with a 'crosse' very similar to the Indian implement" that was also cross-like in shape (1975:14).

8. Literally means, "runner of the woods." More specifically, *coureurs de bois* were French male fur traders and trappers who lived as the indigenous population did during the seventeenth century. J. R. Miller writes that these young males were "neither French peasants nor Indian braves, they were a bit of both" (2000:56).

9. All translations provided by Robidoux unless otherwise stated.

10. Jean de Brébeuf, a Jesuit priest, writes in 1636: "There is a poor sick man, fevered of body and almost dying, and a miserable Sorcerer [Shaman] will order for him, as a cooling remedy, a game of crosse. Or the sick man himself, sometimes, will have dreamed that he must die unless the whole country shall play crosse for his health" (Thwaites 1959:185).

11. Despite claims made in *The story of nineteenth-century Canadian sport* (1966) and the 1894 edition of the *Dictionnaire canadien-français* that lacrosse was the national game of Canada, there are no official records that substantiate this claim (Morrow 1989:52–53).

12. Varda Burstyn writes, "For many of the founding sport associations of the late-nineteenth century, 'amateur' athletics meant 'gentlemen' athletics" (1999:49).

13. The Amateur Athletic Association of Canada changed its name in 1898 to the Canadian Amateur Athletic Union in an attempt to strengthen its position as a national sport governing body (Metcalfe 1987:110).

14. See Robidoux (2001); Gruneau and Whitson (1993); and Laba (1992).

15. Canada became a confederation in 1867, and the first recorded game of hockey took place in 1875.

16. The figures and caption are taken from J.W. Fitsell's *Hockey's captains, colonels and kings* (1987:119). The cartoons depict games that took place in Pittsburgh in 1904. No information is provided to indicate where they were originally published.

REFERENCES

Anderson, Benedict. 1991 [1983]. Imagined Communities: Reflections on the Origin and Spread of Nationalism. New York: Verso.

Beers, W.G. 1867. National Game. Montreal Gazette, August 8.

Bourdieu, Pierre. 1993. "How Can One Be a Sports Fan?" *In* The Cultural Studies Reader. Simon During, ed. Pp. 339–358. London: Routledge.

Burstyn, Varda. 1999. The Rites of Men: Manhood, Politics, and the Culture of Sport. Toronto: University of Toronto Press.

Carver, J. 1956 [1796]. Travels through the Interior Parts of North America. Minneapolis: Ross and Haines, Inc.

Cosentino, Frank. 1998. Afros, Aboriginals and Amateur Sport in Pre-World War One Canada. Ottawa: Canadian Historical Association.

Dunning, Eric. 1975. Industrialization and the Incipient Modernization of Football. Stadion 1(1):103–139.

Eisen, George. 1994. Early European Attitudes toward Native American Sports and Pastimes. *In* Ethnicity and Sport in North American History and Culture. George Eisen and David K. Wiggins, eds. Pp. 1–18. Westport, CT: Greenwood Press.

Fitsell, J. Williams. 1987. Hockey's Captains, Colonels, and Kings. Erin, Ontario: The Boston Mills Press.

Gruneau, Richard. 1983. Class, Sports, and Social Development. Amherst: University of Massachusetts Press.

———. 1988. Modernization or Hegemony: Two Views on Sport and Social Development. *In* Not Just a Game: Essays in Canadian Sport Sociology. Jean Harvey and Hart Cantelion, eds. Pp. 9–32. Ottawa: University of Ottawa Press.

———, and David Whitson. 1993. Hockey Night in Canada: Sport, Identities and Cultural Politics. Culture and Communication Series. Toronto: Garamond Press.

Guay, D. 1981. L'Histoire de l'Éducation Physique au Québec: Conceptions et Évènements (1830–1980). Chicoutimi: Gaetan Morin.

Guttman, Allen. 1994. Games and Empires: Modern Sports and Cultural Imperialism. New York: Columbia University Press.

Hargreaves, John. 1986. Sport, Power and Culture: A Social and Historical Analysis of Popular Sports in Britain. New York: St. Martin's Press.

Henry, Alexander. 1901 [1809]. Travels and Adventures in Canada and the Indian Territories between the Years 1760 and 1776. James Bain, ed. Toronto: G.N. Morang.

Howell, Colin D. 1995. Northern Sandlots: A Social History of Maritime Baseball. Toronto: University of Toronto Press.

Jarvie, Grant, and Joseph Maguire. 1994. Sport and Leisure in Social Thought. London: Routledge.

Jetté, Maurice. 1975. Primitive Indian Lacrosse: Skill or Slaughter? Anthropological Journal of Canada. 13(1):14–19.

Klein, Jeff Z., and Karl-Eric Reif. 1998. Our Tarnished Past. Saturday Night Magazine 113(10):30–33.

Laba, Martin. 1992. Myths and Markets: Hockey as Popular Culture in Canada. *In* Seeing Ourselves: Media Power and Policy in Canada. Helen Holmes and David Taras, eds. Pp. 333–444. Toronto: Harcourt Brace Jovanovich Canada.

Metcalfe, Alan. 1987. Canada Learns to Play: The Emergence of Organized Sport, 1807–1914. Toronto: McClelland and Stewart.

Miller, J.R. 2000 [1989]. Skyscrapers Hide the Heavens: A History of Indian-White Relations in Canada. 3rd edition. Toronto: University of Toronto Press.

Morrow, Don. 1989. Lacrosse as the National Game. *In* A Concise History of Sport in Canada. Don Morrow, Mary Keyes, Wayne Simpson, Frank Cosentino, R. Lappage, eds. Pp. 45–68. Toronto: Oxford University Press.

———, M. Keyes, W. Simpson, F. Cosentino, and R. Lappage, eds. 1989. A Concise History of Sport in Canada. 3rd edition. Toronto: Oxford University Press.

Oxendine, Joseph B. 1988. American Indian Sports Heritage. Champaign, IL: Human Kinetic Books.

Parkman, Francis. 1962. The Conspiracy of Pontiac. 10th edition. New York: Collier Books.

Perrot, Nicolas. 1973 [1864]. Mémoire sur les Moeurs, Coustumes, et Relligion des Sauvages de l'Amérique Septentrionale. Publié pour la première fois par J. Tailhan. Montréal: Éditions Élysée.

Robidoux, Michael A. 2001. Men at Play: A Working Understanding of Professional Hockey. Montreal: McGill-Queen's University Press.

September 1972. 1997. By Ian Davey. August Schellenberg, narrator. Robert MacAskill, dir. Ian Davey and Robert MacAskill, producers. CTV.

Thwaites, Reuben G., ed. 1959. The Jesuit Relations and Allied Documents: Travels and Explorations of the Jesuit Missionaries in New France, 1610–1791, vol. 10. New York: Pageant Book Company.

Wheeler, Robert F. 1978. Organized Sport and Organized Labour: The Workers' Sports Movement. Journal of Contemporary History 13:191–210.

KEY AND DIFFICULT WORDS

Define the following, using context or other clues if possible: **amorphous, disconcerting, connote, hegemonic, enamour, proselytize, resistive, amalgam, disparate, debacle, pedestrian (adj.), masculinist, dichotomy, polyphony.**

QUESTIONS

1. What is the purpose of Robidoux's essay? Identify the thesis statement and comment on the form it takes. The author does not include a literature review early in the body of his essay, but he does refer to the work of sports historians in note 4. Why do you think he does not include a full literature review?

2. Briefly consider why it is beneficial for the author to define the following concepts before proceeding to the body, or main part, of his essay: (a) nationalism (paragraph 1); (b) modernization (paragraph 3).

3. What is the function of the first main section, "The process of modernization," in terms of the overall essay?

4. The author uses several primary sources in his essay. Referring to one example of a primary source, briefly explain its purpose and effectiveness. Note: You can consider any *original* source in this essay as a primary source even if Robidoux cites it from a secondary source.

5. Why is it important for Robidoux's purposes that he draws attention to the "often overstated" perception that European colonization imposed only negative effects on the indigenous population (paragraph 10)?

6. Does Robidoux consider the role of George Beers an important one in the rise of the popularity of lacrosse as a national game (paragraphs 8, 12–14)? Explain his reliance (or lack of reliance) on Beers in his essay.

7. Summarize Robidoux's point concerning the regulations imposed by the National Lacrosse Association and the way they worked to exclude participation in the sport by the working-class and First Nations peoples.

8. Identify the paragraph in which the author makes the transition from discussing lacrosse to discussing hockey. Why is this an important paragraph?
9. In the final two paragraphs preceding his conclusion, Robidoux uses a relatively familiar (1972) example of hockey operating within a political/nationalistic framework. What does this detailed example contribute to the author's thesis and to the effectiveness of the essay as a whole? What is the author's tone in this passage, and how is it conveyed?
10. What do the two cartoons (figures 1 and 2) contribute to the essay?

COLLABORATIVE ACTIVITY

Do you think that Robidoux would subscribe to the common perception that sports builds character? Why or why not? *OR* Do you believe that participation in sports builds character? Discuss or debate one of these questions.

ACTIVITY

Write a critical analysis of the final two paragraphs. Support your analysis by specific references to the text. *OR* Write a critical response to the author's critique of the 1972 "Summit Series" (the final two paragraphs before the conclusion).

Related readings: Pico Iyer. "Canada: Global citizen"; and John Ralston Saul. "Anti-Heroism."

Dead cooks & clinking sandwiches: The origins of northern humour

Peter Unwin

(1,550 words)

One of the earliest known witticisms recorded in English Canada took place in 1817 in the town of Hamilton. It occurred in a prison and was uttered by a debtor confined there. The man, shackled at both feet and chained to an iron ring in the floor, offered a protest against the cold. Pointing at the stove, he warned his jailer, "Either you get that fire up, or I'm leavin'."

In 1817 this comment was thought funny enough to be preserved in memory, then finally copied on paper. Like almost all northern humour, it is based on hardship. And like almost all northern humour, it insists that only through a blind and proud stupidity can those hardships be survived.

A half-century later near Denbigh, Ontario, timber men sang a shanty song that celebrated the memory of a dead cook.

When Sandy was livin' before he was dead
He gave us good grillades to eat with our bread.

Life, the lyric writer seems fit to inform us, is that brief, inconsequential thing that happens before we die.

This brutality in either grammar or logic, and often both, is the trademark of northern humour. It is heard again in a remark uttered by the editor of the *Sault Daily Star*. In 1925 James Curran attempted to prove, once and for all, that a wolf in the wild would not attack a human being. Curran offered $1,000 to any person who could prove conclusively that he'd been set upon by a wolf. The challenge was bravely met by a CPR foreman who claimed he was operating a jigger when a wolf leapt down from a rock, landed on the speeding machine, and attempted to eat him. It seems the railway man wrestled the wolf to the ground and leapt aboard an oncoming train. The story was judged inconclusive, and the reward went unclaimed, furthering Curran's statement that "Any man who says that he's been et by a wolf is a liar."

From wolf attacks to brute labour, from cholera to forest fires, from black flies to hatchet wounds, northern humour is birthed out of everyday misery. Stripped of learning and sophistication, it is often oral humour, created not so much by the author but by the innkeeper and the jailed debtor. Examples were to be found painted on boards, such as this one hanging from an old Ontario tavern in the early 1800s: GOOD FOOD AND ACCOMMODATION FOR BOTH MAN AND HORSE. Here the formal literacy of

England has all but given up hope and is already rotting in the bush.

Three quarters of a century later, Old World cleverness had all but given up the ghost. In 1913 a sign hung in the lobby of the Stag Hotel in Golden City, Ontario, stated succinctly, WE KNOW THIS HOTEL IS ON THE BUM. WHAT ABOUT YOURSELF?

This aggressive dimwittedness is what distinguishes Canadian humour from its English parent. The epigram, the witty remark as uttered by the cultured Englishman, reveals just the opposite—the cleverness of the speaker. Two centuries ago Chief Justice Elmsley of old Toronto wrote to a friend: "There is no news here except the death of my Parrot who departed this life the day before yesterday without a will." This charming remark, though composed on North American soil, is still patently European humour, whimsical, privileged, and the product of a gentleman with too much time on his hands.

Similarly, when Oscar Wilde stood among honeymooners atop Niagara Falls and proclaimed it to be "the bride's second biggest disappointment," he was revealing himself to be a man of extreme sophistication. Not only was he slandering the performance of Englishmen in the bedroom and scandalously implying Englishwomen might *care* about this sort of thing, he was also celebrating an urbane indifference to nature. The genius does not care about water crashing over rocks. In continental humour, the mind, the wit, and the execution of one's own superior intelligence are what matter. Nature has no place here. Nature, as New York humorist Fran Leibowitz explains, is what happens between the hotel and the taxi.

In the North, however, nature *is* what matters. Nature causes the taxi to skid out of control and burns the hotel to the ground. Rather than being tedious, nature is fast and brutal and makes a mockery of sophistication, even of common sense. In the deadly cold and yawning loneliness of the North, suicide beckons but offers no real solution. As Stephen Leacock informs us, we should probably not commit suicide because "it often involves serious consequences."

The argument can be made that the shape and originality of northern wit is the result of a hard-boiled immigrant experience grafted onto the indigenous humour of the First Peoples. "The Indian," wrote Peter Spohn in 1811, "has a great sense of humour, loving jests, games, dancing, and merry-making." Unfortunately, we do not possess an extensive record of what these jests were. Possibly it was a humour expressed in physical language or song. Just as possibly it was a dry, stoical resignation to the hardships of northern life, expressed with delicious crudity.

In 1850 lecturer and author George Copway recorded the following "joke," which took place between two Ojibwa chiefs at a Washington dinner. Unaccustomed to the white man's table, one chief swallowed a bowl of mustard. Seeing the tears stream from his eyes, his companion asked, "Brother, why do you weep?" The chief answered, "I am thinking about my son who was killed in battle." The second chief swallowed his own bowl of mustard and also began to cry. The first asked, "And why do you weep?" "Because," the chief answered, "*you* were not killed in battle along with your son!"

More recently, the story is told of an Inuit elder being pestered by a visiting city journalist. The man, on assignment in Baffin Island, had grown deathly afraid of polar bears and demanded to know what he was supposed to do if attacked by one. The old Inuk gave the matter some thought, folded his arms, and answered sagely, "Use your common sense." The response reveals the chasm between two cultures, one in which "using your common sense" is a euphemism for dying an extremely gruesome death.

The humour of the North is also the humour of alcohol. There is hardly any northern or frontier humour that is not heavily soused in it.

Remove the drinking jokes from Leacock's *Sunshine sketches of a little town*, and not 50 pages would be left. The same observation can be made of the American humorist, O. Henry, who opened one of his drinking stories with the memorable line, "Baldy Woods reached for the bottle, and got it."

The line fits neatly alongside Leacock's boozy observations: "You know, I think, the peculiar walk of a man with two bottles of whiskey in the inside pockets of a linen coat." Here is heard the grammatical contortions that sound the pulse of northern humour. It is heard again when he concludes that a certain picnic cooler must be full of sandwiches because—"I think I can hear them clinking."

Often, northern humour appears in unlikely places. *The Calgary Eye Opener* once suggested that "a man driven to drink usually has to walk home." When the famous distiller Hiram Walker passed away, a newsman for the same paper who wrote Walker's obituary had the gall to conclude, "We are pleased to note that his spirit is still with us."

These sorts of liberties are a defining trademark of northern wit, regardless of whether they take place on the American or Canadian side of the border. In 1980 the town council of Eagle Harbour, Michigan, on the south side of Lake Superior, found it necessary to spend $30,000 to replace the local foghorn. A grumpy councillor complained, "Thirty thousand dollars for a new foghorn, and *we've still got fog.*"

Eventually this sort of grammatical freedom would be eclipsed by a new generation of men and women: writers, editors, critics who fawned on Europe, longed for New York, and aped the styles of London in a desperate attempt to appear sophisticated. The pages of Canadian magazines would soon fill with their yappings, and the age of indoor writing would begin.

The Golden Age of the North and of northern funny men was coming to an end. No longer would people compose and exchange such flawless couplets as:

> *My name is Johnny Hall*
> *And I'm from Montreal.*

They would not depart from each other with the benediction, "May your roof not cave in." Nor would they tell the tale of Paddy Garvey who went "up the Karcajoo" carrying an iron stove and leading a pregnant sow on a rope. Unfortunately, the sow gave birth, forcing Paddy to chase the newborn piglets around the forest while lugging a cast-iron stove on his afflicted back. Today the new and sophisticated Canadian would simply *put the stove down.*

But before that happened, this drunken wit of the Ottawa Valley was to get off one last ringing toast to northern humour. Staggering home one night in a stupor, Paddy Garvey was confronted by the village priest. "Drunk again, Paddy?" the priest demanded. To which the blithe Irishman answered, "Me too, father, me too."

The Beaver. 2004. October/November.

KEY AND DIFFICULT WORDS
Define the following, using context or other clues if possible: **epigram, urbane, euphemism, souse.**

QUESTIONS
1. What is Unwin's thesis? The author relies on many examples to support his claim. Do you think this is a good strategy for an essay of this kind and for a claim like his? Do you think that all his examples provide adequate support?
2. Although no sources are cited in this essay, it is evident that it is well researched. Give examples that illustrate different sources. What kinds of sources did Unwin primarily use?
3. Summarize the way that Unwin differentiates "Canadian humour" from "Old World humour." Come up with five adjectives that could describe Canadian humour.
4. What is Unwin's attitude to Oscar Wilde's remark about Niagara Falls (paragraph 9)? What shows you this?
5. Are the terms "northern humour" and "Canadian humour" synonymous in this essay?
6. Not surprisingly, Unwin uses humour himself in his essay on Canadian humour. Analyze his humour. What does it rely on? You could consider specific techniques, such as exaggeration or understatement, or linguistic devices, such as diction or tone. Be specific in supporting your answer.

7. Does Unwin restrict his focus to English-Canadian humour? Do you think that this focus weakens or strengthens his thesis?

8. Why do you think the author chose to conclude his essay with two stories about Paddy Garvey? How do they exemplify traits about northern humour that Unwin has discussed?

COLLABORATIVE ACTIVITY

Can Canadian humour be defined today? Why or why not? What stereotypes exist about Canadian humour today? Do you think they have a grain of truth to them? Discuss or debate these questions.

ACTIVITY

Pick one medium (such as TV) or one example from that medium (such as a TV show), and attempt to show how it embodies (or does not) Canadian humour today.

Canada: Global citizen

Pico Iyer

(3,150 words)

"Thank you, thank you, thank you," said Archbishop Desmond Tutu, his voice a whispered intimacy as it echoed around the high-vaulted spaces of Vancouver's Christ Church Cathedral one day this spring. Behind him sat the fourteenth Dalai Lama and the winner of the 2003 Nobel Peace Prize, Shirin Ebadi, the fearless lawyer from Iran. "You are Canadians," Tutu went on, "so you are too shy to applaud yourselves. But let me wave a magic wand over you for a few minutes and turn you into Africans."

He passed his hand above the assembled gathering and then urged everyone to recall how Canada's political and moral support had helped bring an end to apartheid in his native South Africa. Had Canada not followed his call for economic sanctions, he implied, his country might still be mired in institutional racism. Then the charismatic Anglican passed his hand over the crowd in the other direction and said, "Now you can be Canadians again, quiet and polite."

In fact, Canadians these days very often come from Africa—and Tibet and Iran and everywhere—and live ever farther from the pale diffidence of old stereotype. And yet the fact remains that when these three great voices of global responsibility came together to discuss how to bring peace and freedom to the planetary neighbourhood, they chose to do so not in London or Paris or New York but in Canada. Canada has become the spiritual home, you could say, of the very notion of an extended, emancipating global citizenship.

We all know that Canada has worked hard to turn the multicultural reality of the modern urban world into an opportunity. Cities like Montreal, Toronto, and Vancouver are home now to singers from Senegal and novelists from Sri Lanka, to India-Pakistan cricket matches and festivals from the Caribbean. In the 1960s, when I was growing up (I was born in England to parents from India, raised in California, and live now in Japan), barely 3 per cent of Toronto's people were "visible minorities." Now the figure comes to more than 50 per cent.

But even the many Canadians who live far from these rapidly changing cities or whose communities are largely unchanged since Queen Victoria's time have seen their lives transformed by the country's determination to stage a radical experiment, in the wake of Pierre Trudeau's inclusive immigration policies, that has given Canadians a sense of connection to both their homes and the world.

Yet what is harder to appreciate, especially if you're at home in the Yukon or small-town Manitoba or in a Newfoundland outport, is that even as more and more of the world is in Canada, Canada is in more and more of the world. Travelling across the globe for 40 years now, I've met Canadians, disproportionally numerous, at every turn: aid workers and diplomats and engineers and just plain travellers taking the spirit of hopefulness and exploration and practical know-how that seems to arise out of the country's wide expanses and seeing how they can uncover a different kind of world.

The person who showed me around Bangkok my first day in Southeast Asia was a friendly, young would-be entrepreneur from Ottawa; and

not long ago, on a plane, I found myself next to a grandmother from Saskatchewan who, when her husband died, decided that she might as well go and see the world (she was returning from three months in a small town in Mexico when I met her). I ushered in the twenty-first century in a tiny Tibetan café on Easter Island with two adventurous Torontonians who had brought themselves to a place where few Europeans or Americans were in evidence.

And two years earlier, on another New Year's Day, as I viewed the great carvings that swarm around Cambodia's central monument, Angkor Wat, I saw two Khmer Rouge leaders walking as fellow sightseers, unprotected, through a city they had orphaned. A Cambodian beside me clutched the ancient pillar nearby so tightly that his knuckles turned white. He was a Canadian now, he informed me, and had managed to escape to freedom and safety after the Khmer Rouge killed 1.7 million of his countrymen, including his mother and father. Having made it to the comfort and ease of Ottawa, though, he felt he owed it to his old compatriots, and his new ones, to come back to Cambodia and try to help it toward the peace and prosperity it so desperately needed.

Geography, of course, has long been one of the singular blessings of Canada—and with its openness of space has come an openness of spirit and an expanded sense of possibility. Fifty years ago, by some counts, 250,000 lakes in Ontario alone were unnamed. But what is newer is that Canada seems to have decided to take the gifts of its geography and history—its bilingualism, its First Nations heritage, its territory stretched across five and a half time zones—and use them to advance a wider, global sense of community and home.

Innumerable stresses arise, inevitably, from this expanded sense of boundaries: Canadian soldiers are risking their lives abroad, and the age-old hostilities of South Asia, among others, now often play themselves out on the streets of Canadian cities. The very term "global citizenship" reminds us that we're living in a global city, fractious and unwieldy, rather than in the fondly imagined global village we like to invoke.

Yet both Canada and its sense of geography have been irreversibly turned around by the mass migration that has accompanied the age of plane travel, and Canadians have to make the most of a destiny they've never faced before. As former minister of foreign affairs Lloyd Axworthy writes at the outset of his book *Navigating a new world*, Canada is no longer just a "middle power" but a "value-added nation." Its task—its blessing—is to take its particular assets and responsibilities and make them global.

"Where do you come from?" These days, the simplest question brings ever more complicated answers, when it brings answers at all. To the preacher in Halifax or the woman in Alberta who still lives in the house her great-grandfather built, it may be quite easy to answer. But to the shopkeeper in Mississauga, perhaps, or the Edmontonian sent to work on a mining project in the Congo, there may be many answers or none at all. Even the First Nations peoples, who are more deeply connected to the Canadian soil than any, may find themselves ever less sure of the ground beneath their feet as they stream into Regina and Saskatoon and Thunder Bay and find themselves approaching majority status in those cities, while feeling like exiles in their own homes.

For more and more Canadians, in short, home is a multiple or fluid concept, a work-in-progress. They may feel attachment to a piece of territory, but they may also feel a loyalty to their partner's homeland, the country where their parents were born, the very different land where they are now stationed. Home has gone portable and invisible in the modern world and may have less to do with a house or a piece of land than

with a set of beliefs or assumptions that one can share with someone in a far corner of the world or with someone one's never met. Global citizenship does not mean giving up a sense of roots so much as extending our sense of what roots involve. On the page, to take an example, Canada has one life in the deeply textured, changeless stories of Alistair MacLeod, about fishermen going about the age-old ways in Nova Scotia; but it has another life in the roaming, international stories of Yann Martel.

Within Canada itself, this sense of extended affiliation is everywhere apparent. Mexican farm workers flood into Ontario to claim the seasonal jobs they could not so easily get in the United States; a Québécoise woman is taking her knowledge of Inuktitut to the classrooms of Paris. I walked into a quaint bed and breakfast in the walled centre of Quebec not long ago—the Auberge Saint-Louis—and was greeted by a manager from New Delhi who was more than ready to explain to me in Hindi where I could find the local Lebanese and Thai restaurants. In Montreal a few days later, I saw lampposts and walls filled with flyers reminding locals of the ways they could help those in Gujarat, Palestine, Rwanda. "Does your son speak Farsi?" I asked an Iranian cab driver in Vancouver this April.

"No!" He laughed. "Punjabi, Chinese, Hindi. But Iranian language, he doesn't know."

What this means on the other side of the world, though, is that Canadians—not burdened by the complicated obligations of the United States and not weighed down by centuries of history, as older cultures are—are taking their native sense of mobility and internationalism across the planet to help draw up what could be called the outlines of a global constitution.

It's well known that a Canadian law professor helped draft the Universal Declaration of Human Rights and that a Canadian prime minister helped inaugurate the United Nations peacekeeping forces. But the tradition is brought into the present in Canadian Louise Arbour, who now heads the Office of the United Nations High Commissioner for Human Rights, and Canadian Stephen Lewis, who is leading the UN's campaign to fight AIDS in Africa. Canada's place in the global imagination has long been as a home to tolerance and non-provincialism, not so much the world's policeman, perhaps, as its magistrate, counsellor, and mediator. In the nineteenth century, slaves from the United States took the underground railroad to freedom in Canada; at Auschwitz, the personal effects stripped from prisoners were kept in a place they somehow chose to call "Canada."

To someone like me, who has spent all his life in motion, looking at the possibilities for a new kind of community peopled by "global souls," Canada seems to have worked more than anywhere I know to build up a sense of global accountability and conscience, perhaps because (unlike its neighbours to the south and east) Canada has never been in a position to imagine itself the centre of the world. The Canadian travellers I meet—hearty backpackers from Whistler, BC; Torontonians in their element in Hong Kong or Bombay; missionaries and expat bankers; and, occasionally, slippery mercenaries—are not really very different from their counterparts from Melbourne or Manchester or Wisconsin, but they travel without enmities and as emissaries from a country that most of the world has nothing against. And it still remains the case that you meet far more Canadians on the road than Americans or even Britons.

It's hardly surprising, then, that it was a Canadian, Marshall McLuhan, who came up with the notion of a global village and that the man who is credited with coining the word "cyberspace"—William Gibson—left his home in the United States to live in Vancouver. Canadians such as architect Frank Gehry are literally drafting and building the contours of our new global cities, while Canadians not ready to accept the status quo—writers like Anne Michaels and Nino Ricci, among them—are daring to dream up new notions of community in which people do not have to be defined by their past or their religion.

Again, this sense of global citizenship does not have to take away from the local; it's only human to long for attachment to something more concrete than mere abstractions and for something deeper than the "global" conveniences of CNN and the Internet. Yet Canadians, as author Michael Ignatieff has pointed out, have always had an advantage in that they live in a country held together by shared values rather than shared roots. And the very notion of a mosaic society, as opposed to a melting pot, tells new Canadians that they can think of citizenship in a less exclusionary way than they did before.

At its best, it means that a man of Indian origin, say, meeting someone of Pakistani origin in Newfoundland does not see him as an enemy—as his parents might, or as he might do himself "at home"—but, rather, as a kindred spirit who has more in common with him than apart, as another South Asian trying to shape a new destiny in North America. And the more the world is defined by war, the more people will hunger for the alternative.

To those surrounded by the complications of Canada's diverse cities, to those in rural areas largely untouched by these new developments, all this may sound very fanciful, and it may be evident, every day, how little reality conforms to our loftier hopes for it. Besides, Canada remains in many respects the Rodney Dangerfield of nations, which never gets the respect it deserves. Canadians have to look for their own country's movies, often, in the "Foreign" section of the video store (the main section being devoted to the latest offerings from Hollywood).

The second largest nation in the world is denied its own international telephone code. Its main cities are given airport codes—YYZ, YVR, YUL—that look like afterthoughts or jokes. And when Jim Carrey and Pamela Anderson and Avril Lavigne capture the world's imagination, they are gleefully taken to be American.

Yet hidden within this neglectedness lies a certain possibility. Canadians are not necessarily more upstanding or eager to do the right thing than any other people. But they enjoy a great advantage in not having a colonizing past behind them, as many European powers do, and in being closer to the world, in many respects, than the geopolitical giant on their doorstep. Canada offers the promise of prosperity without hierarchy and newness without arrogance.

"We believe that the good of all is better than the good of one," a friend in Toronto told me recently and clearly meant it, "and that each of us is better off when all of us are better off." At the same time, he added, "We have an appreciation of the space between people." I happened to fly to Ottawa from California the week of the September 11, 2001, attacks against America and was impressed that suddenly, I was hearing about the event in a larger context of geography and history and about how it related to the terrorism many other places have faced.

This means something more than just the fact that American travellers, even now, are advised to stitch a maple leaf onto their backpacks so as to ensure a warm response when they go abroad. It means that Canada, because it is seen as a home to global citizenship, attracts and encourages those who wish to think in such terms.

Philosophers from Charles Taylor to Mark Kingwell have thought seriously about a new policy of rights and about what community means when people come from everywhere; and when urban visionary Jane Jacobs came up with a new notion of a North American city, jostling and diverse, its energies not flowing out into the suburbs but consolidating at the centre, she left New York to come to Toronto to try it out. Those who have raised the most thoughtful and passionate criticisms of "globalization" have also often been from Canada, whether working through activism (like Toronto writer Naomi Klein) or through subversive media (like the Vancouver magazine *Adbusters*).

Again, this is a trend most visible to those from abroad. It was only when I started visiting other global cities, from Sydney and Cape Town to Hong Kong and Paris, that I realized Canada has the benefit of a small population in a large space, a freedom from some of the burdens of the past and yet a knowledge of history that few other places can combine. Here, you could say, is the idealism of North America tempered by the irony of Europe. In his *Dictionary of the 21st century*, French thinker Jacques Attali, a one-time adviser to former president François Mitterrand, surveyed the globe as one who travels constantly around it and singled out Canada above all as "one of the first examples of a successful multicultural, democratic country without borders, where everyone will be simultaneously a member of several communities that were formerly mutually exclusive."

Canada's first life, of course, will always be within its own borders, and it is the distinctively Canadian quality of the light, the seasons, the terrain, and the local history that will join its citizens together. The very globalism that has become so prominent has, in fact, moved many people to consolidate their attachment to the local. In his book *The new politics of confidence*, Canada's Minister of Foreign Affairs Pierre Pettigrew points out that 20 years ago, only 5 per cent of Manitobans regarded themselves as first and foremost Manitobans; recently, 20 per cent of them did.

Earlier this year, Canadian-born Oxford philosopher Jennifer Welsh described, in her Hart House Lecture at the University of Toronto, how more and more young Canadians think of themselves as "Can-globalists." Canadians, she said, "consider themselves more Canadian than ever and are proud of their national accomplishments. At the same time, there has been a noticeable increase in the number of Canadians who describe themselves as world citizens." Welsh says all this, she stresses, as the proud descendant of generations of Métis bison hunters from Saskatchewan.

Globalism is only as useful, one might say, as its connection to a real universalism. More and more people on the planet are linked, at the shallowest level, by a shared culture of MTV and McDonald's and Microsoft; but what unites us profoundly and with the greatest consequences is some deeper convergence of belief and commitment. That, in truth, is the higher form of global citizenship that drew Archbishop Tutu, the Dalai Lama, and Shirin Ebadi to Vancouver this spring. "We are, in fact, composite, communal bodies," Tutu declared, while Ebadi pointed out, "We cannot bring democracy with tanks and guns and bombs to other countries." Every one of us has a responsibility, the Dalai Lama said, and that is to make a good society.

I am always moved when I think of Roméo Dallaire, the Canadian soldier who tried in vain to rally the forces of global peacekeeping in Rwanda in 1994. Broken and close to suicide, unable to continue a normal life after seeing 800,000 people killed in 100 days and having been powerless to stop the genocide, the lieutenant general still found it in himself to write of his home country, "This nation, without any hesitation or doubt, is capable and even expected by the less fortunate of this globe to lead the developed countries beyond self-interest, strategic advantages and isolationism and raise their sights to the realm of the pre-eminence of humanism and freedom."

With dreams, the poet said, come responsibilities. But with responsibilities, as Canada knows as well as anyone, come new dreams.

Canadian Geographic. 2004.
1 November 124 (6).

KEY AND DIFFICULT WORDS
Define the following, using context or other clues if possible: **diffidence, fractious, affiliation, inaugurate, enmity, emissary, exclusionary, consolidate.**

QUESTIONS
1. Do you think that Iyer is well-qualified to write on Canada's reputation as a "global citizen?" Explain what makes him qualified (or not).
2. (a) Identify the thesis statement. (b) What kinds of evidence does Iyer use the most extensively?
3. What do you think the author means by the phrase "pale diffidence of old stereotype" (paragraph 3)?
4. Would you classify Iyer's essay as expository, argumentative, or expressive (personal)? What is his purpose in writing?

5. According to the author, what makes Canada and Canadians well-suited to the role of "global citizen?"

6. Come up with three adjectives not used in the essay that express Iyer's conception of the Canadian character.

7. Iyer has a very positive perception of Canada as a representative of global citizenship. Are all his points valid? Has he oversimplified at any time? Are there any "downsides" to his claims about global citizenship? Point to specific passages.

COLLABORATIVE ACTIVITY

Does Iyer succeed in giving you a clear sense of what it means to be a Canadian? How does he do this (or fail to do this)? Be as specific as possible in discussing these questions (they can be applicable to both Canadians and non-Canadians).

ACTIVITIES

1. Using a hard-copy or reliable Internet source, write a one- to two-paragraph biography of two people cited in the essay. In your response, include the reason(s) why Iyer uses them as authorities to lend credibility to his essay.

2. You find yourself on an airplane next to Pico Iyer. (You identify him by the fact he has forgotten to remove his nametag, which reveals that he has just attended a conference on global citizenship.) Having recently read his essay, you are eager to strike up a conversation about the role of Canada as a "global citizen." Reproduce the dialogue between the two of you.

Related reading: John Ralston Saul. "Anti-Heroism"; and Stephen Henighan. "White curtains."

White curtains

Stephen Henighan

(1,000 words)

During the power cut that paralyzed Ontario in August 2003, the residents of my townhouse condominium complex began talking to each other. It was an event that took me by surprise.

Under normal circumstances, human interaction in our development is limited to someone reporting a neighbour to the condominium authorities for putting up curtains of a colour not permitted by regulations. (This means any colour other than white.) But, facing darkened apartments, darkened television screens, darkened stoves—a darkness that even pristine white curtains could not repel—we wandered out to sit on the hard cinder-block steps overlooking the parking lot. In the fading light we traded wild-eyed rumours about the power outage. People who habitually passed each other on the way to the mailbox without stopping to speak progressed from discussions about the power cut to stories of childhoods spent in countries where electrical power was a luxury. I was at the point of succumbing to the illusion that the mood of communal bonding might outlast the blackout when, all at once, conversation stopped.

My neighbour Dragoslav walked out to the patch of grass next to his parking spot carrying a small kerosene stove, a frying pan, some cooking implements, and a steak. He sat down in the grass and coaxed a muted roaring from his stove. Crouched in the shadow of his high-fendered 1970s sedan, he began to fry the steak. The gush of kerosene and the sizzle of tenderloin carried across the parking lot. No one spoke. We did not look in Dragoslav's direction, and we did not comment on what he was doing. The Dragoslav we knew was a man who drove a second-hand car, lived with a woman who spoke less English than he did, and walked his dog when he came home from work. The Dragoslav who was cooking in the grass next to the parking lot was a foreigner: a Yugoslav who had learned survival skills in a grisly war.

Contrary to custom, no one reported Dragoslav to the condominium authorities. We sat on the steps in the dusk, mute and embarrassed. All of us had arrived in Canada as immigrants (even though some, such as I, had been here since childhood). We were happy to talk about the countries in our pasts, but we were mortified to see one of our neighbours acting as though he were living in the past. It was normal to be an immigrant; it was unacceptable to act like one. As proven members of southern Ontario multicultural society, we knew how to respond to Dragoslav's lurch into antediluvian behaviour: we tolerated him. We neither reproached Dragoslav nor approached him. We kept our distance and turned conversation to other subjects. When darkness fell, we all went back inside to sleep behind our white curtains. Two days later, when our television screens lighted up again, we stopped talking to each other.

In 1994 Neil Bissoondath published *Selling illusions: The cult of multiculturalism in Canada.* At the time I joined the chorus denouncing Bissoondath's book as a silly right-wing tract. Since moving to southern Ontario, where the idea of multiculturalism is more dominant than in eastern Ontario or Quebec (my earlier Canadian residences), I have modified my view. There is silliness in Bissoondath's book, but there is also wisdom. Bissoondath's analysis of "tolerance," the central tenet of Canadian multiculturalism, is particularly trenchant. Tolerance, Bissoondath writes, "requires not knowledge but wilful ignorance, a purposeful turning away from the accent, the skin colour, the crossed eyes, the large nose. . . . Understanding, in contrast, requires effort, a far more difficult proposition, but may lead to acceptance." To tolerate people is to fail to engage with who they are and how they differ from you. The fact that we define our multiculturalism in terms of tolerance may help to explain why it is so rare for Canadians who live in multicultural neighbourhoods to write multicultural novels.

According to an overprivileged globetrotter named Pico Iyer, Toronto is the global capital of cost-free multiculturalism. (Iyer bestows an honourable mention on Vancouver; he ignores Montreal.) Last winter, when I was invited to teach a "Topics in Canadian Literature" course for M.A. students, I assigned an article by Iyer in which he claims to find a laudatory shedding of cultural baggage in Canadian novels that disdain Canadian material. I was surprised (though, I'll admit, not disappointed) that my students, whom I had expected to embrace this hymn of praise to the city where most of them had grown up, disliked Iyer's vision of Toronto. They saw his omission of the ethnic retaining walls that channel daily interaction in urban Canada as superficial or naive. Iyer's article sparked a discussion of the students' experience of cultural barriers: of how little they knew their neighbours; of the scant communication among the various cultural cliques present in student life; of all that Iyer overlooked; of the doctrine of tolerance that makes us turn away from the accent, the skin colour, the man who cooks in the parking lot.

The writer, of course, faces the danger that dramatizing cultural differences will descend into stereotyping. But the literary writer must take risks: must challenge and extend popular understanding, not just mimic the status quo. By averting their creative gaze from the cultural dissonance that clatters around us in the shopping malls of Mississauga, the *ruelles* of Montréal-Nord, the street corners of Winnipeg, the leaky condos of New Westminster, writers actually may contribute to prolonging a polite, latent racism. You do not overcome racism by avoiding the issue and changing the subject. Racism dissolves only when you ask the awkward, embarrassing question: do all Chinese women behave that way, do all Yugoslav men cook in parking lots? Until you voice this gut reaction or, better yet, dramatize it in a scene, you cannot begin to question your own chauvinism. Such uncomfortable yet revealing moments abound in our daily lives. Our fiction could be feasting on them if fewer of our writers chose to sleep behind white curtains.

Geist. 2004. Winter 13 (55).

KEY AND DIFFICULT WORDS

Define the following, using context or other clues if possible: **pristine, antediluvian, reproach, trenchant, laudatory.**

QUESTIONS

1. What is the significance of the title "White curtains?" How is the image of white curtains thematically and/or structurally important within the essay itself?

2. Explain in your own words why Dragoslav's actions are described as a "conversation stopper."

3. Between one-third and one-half of the essay depicts the thoughts and behaviour of the author and his neighbours during an Ontario power outage. Why does Henighan devote so much time to this scene? What rhetorical pattern predominates in the first three paragraphs?

4. Who is the "we" in this essay? Who is the "other?" Identify other examples of opposites or dualities in the essay.

5. What does the title of Neil Bissoondath's book tell you about his views on multiculturalism? Paraphrase the part of paragraph 4 in which Henighan analyzes Bissoondath's book.

6. Summarize the author's attitude toward the vision of Pico Iyer. Do you believe he is able to prevent his lack of agreement with Iyer from making his essay biased?

7. In his concluding paragraph, Henighan talks about the need for writers to avoid "the status quo" in their writing. Is he addressing an audience beyond literary writers here?

COLLABORATIVE ACTIVITY

Do you agree with the students mentioned in the essay that cultural and racial "tolerance," as defined by Henighan, creates barriers to understanding and sympathy, or do you believe that tolerance is more likely to create conditions for understanding and sympathy? Discuss or debate this issue.

ACTIVITIES

1. In one to two paragraphs, summarize a review of Bissoondath's *Selling illusions: The cult of multiculturalism in Canada*.

2. The Iyer essay that Henighan refers to in "White curtains" is "The last refuge" (*Harper's*, June 2002). (a) In one or two sentences, state its thesis. (b) Based on your reading of this essay, consider whether Henighan represents Iyer's thesis fairly and accurately in "White curtains."

Related readings: John Ralston Saul. "Anti-Heroism"; Pico Iyer. "Canada: Global citizen"; and Hal Niedzviecki. "The future's books from nowhere."

Enhancing democratic citizenship

Elisabeth Gidengil, André Blais, Richard Nadeau, and Neil Nevitte

(4,700 words)

The challenges [for enhancing] democratic citizenship are clear. One is to find ways of re-engaging young citizens. A second is how to create a more informed citizenry, and a third concerns how to narrow the existing democratic divides. Identifying the challenges is easier than setting out solutions to such complex problems. But it is possible to scan the horizons to see solutions others have turned to and with what effect.

RE-ENGAGING YOUNG CANADIANS

Turnout in federal elections has declined massively among young Canadians since 1988. A recent study in the United States is suggestive;

it points to the importance of getting young citizens to vote for the first time. Once young people have paid the "start-up costs of voting," they are likely to keep on voting (Plutzer 2002). So, what can be done to reduce the start-up costs for young Canadians? First, political parties have a role to play. Political parties are representative institutions, and if they make little effort to mobilize the citizenry, then citizens are less likely to vote. Regardless of which party they heard from, people who reported being contacted by a political party or a candidate during the 2000 campaign were more likely to vote. As the data in Chapter 5 demonstrated, young Canadians were much less likely than others to report being contacted. The clear implication is that a concerted get-out-the-vote effort by the political parties could well help to reverse the downward trend in voting among the young.

Second, the problems with the permanent voters list need to be resolved (see Courtney 2004). In 2000 young Canadians were the segment of the population least likely to have received a voter information card and the most likely to have found it difficult to get their names on the permanent voters list. Part of the problem is that young people are much more mobile; they are likely to be tenants rather than homeowners. They are also less likely to file tax returns (which is one way that the list is updated). So they are either not on the list or listed under the wrong address. If these flaws in the system can be addressed, young people will find it easier to vote.

In addition to these short-term solutions, various long-term solutions should be considered. Early experiences can lay the foundation for a lifetime of democratic engagement. In this regard, research on volunteering may hold broader lessons for civic engagement. Michael Hall and his colleagues (Hall, McKeown, and Roberts 2001, 39) found that there was a clear,

albeit weakening, connection between volunteering and people's experiences early in life. Volunteering rates were higher, for example, among people who had been active in student government, who had a parent who spent time volunteering, or who belonged to a youth group. Having been helped by others in early life was also a motivating factor. If volunteering in adulthood is encouraged by experiences during people's formative years, the trend toward mandatory community service in high school could have effects that persist into later life. And as the evidence presented in Chapter 6 indicated, volunteering tends to go hand in hand with civic engagement.

In addition, a large US survey of students in Grades 9 to 12 and their parents indicates that community service enhances students' knowledge of politics. It also encourages more discussion of politics with their parents and fosters a sense of political competence (Niemi, Hepburn, and Chapman 2000). However, these benefits only seem to accrue if the amount of service is substantial. Moreover, the authors of this study sound an important cautionary note: students who were involved in few other activities, who had lower grades, and whose parents did not perform any community service were much less likely to be involved in community service themselves. In other words, unless community service is universal, it risks deepening the democratic divides. For this reason, Benjamin Barber (1992) argues forcefully that service in the community should be made mandatory rather than voluntary. But as Hepburn and her colleagues (Hepburn, Niemi, and Chapman 2000, 621) ask, "If service is required, will the students forced to participate learn from it?"

Community service seems to be most beneficial when it takes the form of "service learning." This term denotes service that is actually incorporated into high school courses in ways that encourage both awareness of the related social and political issues and reflection upon the experience (Hepburn, Niemi, and Chapman 2000; Galston 2001). The rationale for service learning is found in John Dewey's (1916; 1938) argument that schooling must be linked to real-world experience. Some educators have raised concerns, though, about the possible partisan and ideological connotations of training for citizenship.

What about civic education classes? Many see civic courses as a way of enhancing democratic engagement, and the province of Ontario actually introduced a mandatory civics course for Grade 10 students in fall 2000 (Myers 2000). But some critical questions remain unanswered:

> When should students receive civics/government instruction? . . . What classroom and extra-classroom methods are best suited to teaching about government? How much training should there be in research methods? Are the skills needed for citizenship the same as the skills needed for political analysis? What kind of instruction, if any, will make young people less cynical about (yet appropriately skeptical of) politicians? (Niemi and Smith 2001, 286)

For all the interest in revitalizing civic education, surprisingly little research systematically evaluates its benefits, especially over the long term (Niemi and Smith 2001). This is partly because conventional wisdom has long held that civics courses are ineffective. Most of the evidence about the effectiveness of civics education comes from the United States, where the experience has been mixed. The proportion of US high school students taking American government courses has risen steadily since 1980. According to a recent study (Niemi and Smith 2001), nearly 80 per cent of graduating seniors have had a government class at some stage of their high school education. And yet knowledge of politics remains low, and concern about political disengagement on the part of young adults has continued to grow. Indeed, the 1998 Civics Assessment, conducted as part of the National Assessment of Educational Progress mandated by the US Congress, found that only a quarter of high school seniors met or exceeded the standard of proficiency, while over a third tested below basic, "indicating near-total civic ignorance" (Galston 2001, 221). Evidently, civics education can fail.

Others believe that civics education can be effective, but much depends on the content (Niemi and Junn 1998; Galston 2001). Ken Osborne (1988, 228), for example, suggests that what is needed is "a genuinely political education, if the schools are to produce informed, participating citizens," and that this means bringing real-world political issues into the classroom (see also Osborne 2000). In a similar vein, Richard Niemi and Jane Junn (1998, 150) have been critical of "the Pollyannaish view of politics" that is encouraged when civics education is devoid of any serious discussion of partisan politics and interest groups. "If students can be taught to understand that political parties and interest groups form to promote and protect legitimate differences in points of view," they argue, "they would be in a much better position to understand, appreciate, and participate in the political process." It is not just a matter of *what* is taught in civics classes but *how* it is taught (Osborne 1988). Context matters, and a number of commentators have pointed to the importance of fostering a democratic classroom climate so that students are not just learning about democratic skills and dispositions but actually practising them (Levin 2000; Sears and Perry 2000). Timing also appears to be important: high school government courses seem to be most effective when they are taken in Grade 12 rather than earlier in a student's career (Niemi and Junn 1998).

The intractable problem with solutions like mandatory service learning and required civics courses is that they cannot reach those who are no longer in school. Indeed, for the long term, the key to democratic engagement may simply be to keep more young people in school. As William Galston (2001, 219) observes, "all education is civic education in the sense that individuals' level of general educational attainment significantly affects their level of political knowledge as well as the quantity and character of their political participation." Indeed, the one group of young people that has been immune to the trend toward disengagement is university graduates. It is hardly surprising that university graduates are typically the most engaged citizens, because becoming a well-informed citizen requires considerable cognitive capacity. Consider one public opinion expert's advice:

> Whenever you read or see political material, exercise skepticism. Figure out motivations and ideologies in the newspaper, magazine, or television show you are looking at; watch for its editorial thrust and for slants in the news or information it presents. What stories are made prominent? Why? What is ignored? Who is quoted, and why? What evaluative material is slipped in? Try to read between the lines, spotting what the reporter did not say, and try to dig out obscure but important bits that contradict the main story line (Page 1996, 125–6).

These tasks will be quite beyond the capabilities of people who do not even possess basic literacy skills, which are precisely what many of Canada's high school dropouts lack (Applied Research Branch 2000). Canada's dropout rates appear to be more or less in line with other OECD (Organisation for Economic Co-operation and Development) countries, but Canadian dropouts typically have much lower levels of literacy. This is because "a large proportion of those who drop out do so at an early age and at low levels of education. . . . Almost one third drop out with Grade 9 education or less and almost two thirds drop out with Grade 10 or less. . . . The earlier that students drop out, the less knowledge and fewer skills that they will have accumulated" (Applied Research Branch 2000, 13–14). And, we could add, the less likely they are to have any interest in politics or to be acquainted with the sorts of political information required for meaningful engagement in democratic politics.

CREATING A MORE INFORMED CITIZENRY

There is a lively debate about whether citizens really need to know "textbook facts" about their political world to make adequately informed decisions about how to vote. Yet one of the clearest messages to emerge from this audit of democratic citizenship is that information matters. Indeed, information is the essential prerequisite of responsive and responsible government: governments cannot be held accountable if citizens do not know what those in power have been doing. Knowing who the key political actors are may not be that consequential in itself, but "differences in knowledge of several such 'minor' facts are diagnostic of more profound differences in the amount and accuracy of contextual information voters bring to their judgments" (Converse 2000, 333; see also Neuman 1986; Delli Carpini and Keeter 1996).

Having a store of contextual information is important because it helps people to make sense of and to impart meaning to new pieces of information. This is the so-called Matthew principle: "to them that hath shall be given" or, as

Converse (2000, 335) puts it more colloquially, "them what has, gets." This principle clearly applies to campaign learning. Election campaigns actually widen the knowledge gap: those who know the most about politics in general end up learning the most, while those who know little to begin with learn the least. And information shortcuts often end up helping those who need them least, because those who need these shortcuts the most often lack the contextual information required to take advantage of them.

More important, opinion on some significant policy issues would very likely be different if Canadians were better informed about politics. This is especially true when people are misinformed about policy-relevant facts. Informed opinion on social policy questions is typically more liberal than actual opinion. The same holds for opinions about some fiscal matters and some issues concerning the role of the state versus the market. Because information can affect policy preferences and political attitudes, people who share similar background characteristics may hold very different opinions, depending on how well informed they are. This finding implies that people who are poorly informed are more likely to get it "wrong" when it comes to translating their preferences into appropriate political choices.

The extent to which citizens are informed is not a function of their own abilities and motivation alone: "Voters are not fools. . . . The electorate behaves about as rationally and responsibly as we should expect, given the clarity of the alternatives presented to it and the character of the information available to it" (Key 1966, 7). The main sources of information for citizens are the media and political actors, neither of which necessarily have a vested interest in disseminating the objective facts. Politicians and other political actors may be tempted to deploy facts in self-serving ways to build support for their preferred

positions. If politicians obfuscate and political parties fail to articulate clear alternatives, is there reason to be surprised if many citizens end up with only a vague or confused sense of what the politicians stand for?

However, even when politicians and political parties take clear stands, their messages do not necessarily reach the voters. Economic incentives encourage the media to put the emphasis on entertaining first and informing only second (Zaller 1999). Whether publicly or privately owned, broadcasters have to be concerned about audience share, just as the print media are preoccupied with circulation figures. Consequently, a party's issue positions may receive only token coverage if what the party is saying or doing is not deemed newsworthy, and newsworthiness is often determined by standings in the polls. When an issue position does receive extensive coverage, even poorly informed voters have the opportunity to learn about it.

A striking finding from recent election data is that even otherwise relatively well-informed voters had difficulty matching the parties with their promises or classifying the parties in terms of left and right. Providing more coverage of the issues and being more even-handed in the amount of coverage provided to the various political parties would help to raise the mean level of knowledge about the parties and their stands.

NARROWING THE DEMOCRATIC DIVIDES

When it comes to inclusiveness and responsiveness, diminishing the variance in political knowledge is at least as important as raising the mean. Proposals to increase the amount of information available to voters by regulating the nature and amount of coverage that broadcasters provide are going to benefit only those who are following politics to begin with. The same objection applies to another suggested solution, namely, having longer campaigns (Moore 1987). The idea is that longer election campaigns would give people more time to learn about the issues. In theory, election campaigns represent an unparalleled opportunity to engage voters (Cappella and Jamieson 1997, 241). Indeed, Popkin (1991) has likened elections to civics education, with political parties as the teachers. In practice, though, the least informed typically also learn the least during a campaign.

Eveland and Scheufele (2000, 216) actually go so far as to argue that increasing the amount of political information (and participation) "among some groups but not others . . . could be worse for democracy than no overall increase at all." This is especially true "when the group increasing in knowledge or participation is already politically advantaged and has interests at odds with the disadvantaged group." At issue is not just the low level of knowledge per se but the uneven *social* distribution of knowledge. Older Canadians know more than younger Canadians, affluent Canadians know more than poor Canadians, and men know more than women. The worry is that the needs and wants of affluent, older men are the most likely to be reflected in collective expressions of opinion. Differences would be larger on important questions of public policy if the young, the poor, and women were better informed. To the extent that this is so, public policy may well be less responsive to their needs and interests. Communications scholars put the point bluntly: "When there are disparities across social groups in political knowledge and participation, democracy is at least a little less democratic, regardless of the underlying reasons for these inequities" (Eveland and Scheufele 2000, 216).

The observation that information shortfalls are associated with democratic divides points to a deeper issue: why are some Canadians not better informed about politics? There is no shortage of potential answers to that question, and many of them take us back to the more basic question of why interest in politics is not higher. The preeminent point to acknowledge is that the costs of acquiring information are higher for some citizens than for others. The cost of subscribing to a daily newspaper, cable television, or an Internet access service may be beyond the reach of poor families. However, the effects of structural inequalities run deeper than differences in the costs of becoming informed. As Page and Shapiro (1992, 164) note, when it comes to the dissemination of political information, economic inequality tends to win out over political equality: "A large corporation has a much better chance of learning how a tax bill will affect it than do many unorganized taxpayers with small, diffuse interests."

The challenge, then, is to narrow the information gap by "lifting the bottom." Information presumes interest. If people have little or no interest in political affairs, they are unlikely to invest time and energy in seeking out political information. This is why John Zaller (1999, 2) argues that the problem is not lack of informational content in the media. On the contrary, he maintains, large numbers of citizens are being turned off by a style of politics and political communication that is "stilted, overly rationalistic, and just plain dull." Zaller takes intellectuals to task for bemoaning the rise of "infotainment" journalism when they should be seeing it as a way of re-engaging citizens' interest in politics. His point is that "infotainment" journalism offers citizens a way to fulfill "the informational obligations of citizenship . . . with less effort and more pleasure" (p. 3). Zaller supports this seemingly heretical suggestion by pointing to the disappointing experience with the free television-time experiment in the 1996 US presidential election. The provision of large blocks of free television time on the three major networks was greeted with a singular lack of enthusiasm on the part of the candidates, the networks, and the electorate alike.

Rather than "fact-packed and informationally turgid" media content, Zaller argues, what is required are more stories that truly engage people. Dan Quayle's attack on the television character Murphy Brown is one case in point. The former US vice-president took the fictional character to task for having a child outside marriage. By focusing so much coverage on this seemingly trivial incident, the media succeeded in making "the family values debate accessible to Americans in a way that traditional political rhetoric did not" (Zaller 1999, 16). The 2000 federal election provided a Canadian analogue to the Murphy Brown story in the form of the Doris Day petition. The CBC comedy program "This hour has 22 minutes" satirized the Alliance party's stand on direct democracy by inviting Canadians to add their names to a petition requesting that the party's leader, Stockwell Day, be required to change his name to Doris Day. Over one million people signed the petition through the show's website. There was a serious point: to demonstrate how easy it was to gather the requisite number of signatures required to initiate a binding referendum. And that point supports Zaller's contribution that some attention to politics is better than no attention at all, especially when viewers are being informed as well as entertained. A recent study by Matthew Baum (2002) also lends some support to this argument. He found that "due to selective political coverage by the entertainment-oriented soft news media, many otherwise politically inattentive individuals are exposed to information about high-profile political issues, most prominently foreign policy crises, as an incidental by-product of seeking entertainment" (91).

Zaller also takes a sanguine view of "horserace journalism." This is coverage that focuses on "who is ahead, who is behind, who is gaining, who is losing, what campaign strategy is being followed, and what the impact of campaign activities is on the candidate's chances of winning" (Joslyn 1984, 133). In Canada, as elsewhere, television news coverage seems preoccupied with the horserace in general and with the leaders' abilities as campaigners in particular, to the neglect of serious coverage of the issues (Mendelsohn 1993; 1996; Mendelsohn and Nadeau 1999). In Zaller's view, the unanimous condemning of the prevalence of this type of coverage is wrong. Horserace coverage, he argues, is not devoid of substantive content but can provide citizens with "a palatable mix of entertainment, information, debate, and politically useful cues," especially about the opinions of relevant groups (Zaller 1999, 19). Above all, though, this style of coverage appeals to millions of voters by making politics a spectator sport. If making politics seem like a game gets people to pay attention, Zaller maintains, then this is all to the good.

But does the prevalence of the "game frame" get viewers to tune in, or does it simply turn them off? There is evidence, for example, that some people are less active politically because they want to avoid conflict (Mansbridge 1980; Ulbig and Funk 1999; Mutz 2002). If media coverage reinforces the perception that politics is all about confrontation and competition, it may discourage such people from being politically active. We also need to ask what sort of people typically "spend many leisure hours" (Zaller 1999, 18) watching sports events on television. The audience for the sporting events that typically dominate the airwaves is still predominantly male, and politics may be just another game watched by men. After all, the players are still mostly men. We know that women are less likely than men to follow politics closely. It is not clear whether this is related to the way politics is covered, but there is certainly cause to wonder.

These are the sorts of questions, in our view, that need to be answered before Zaller's enthusiasm for horserace journalism can be readily embraced. But Zaller is surely right to encourage us to think outside the box when it comes to ways of stimulating greater political awareness.

Political interest is likely to be higher to the extent that citizens see a link between political affairs and their own lives. If politics is perceived to be remote and abstract or, worse yet, corrupt and self-serving, citizens will simply tune out. Globalization and market rhetoric encourage the view that governments are not only relatively powerless in the face of global economic forces but govern best when they govern least. That view is certainly open to challenge, but it should come as little surprise to discover that many citizens seem to have internalized the message that politics just does not matter very much.

This message has perhaps been encouraged by changes in the way that the media cover politics. Over the past two decades, media coverage in Canada (as in the United States) has taken on an increasingly negative tone; straight reporting of the facts has become subordinate to interpretation and evaluation, and the framing of stories too often highlights partisan calculation, conflict, and personal motives. The result, Richard Nadeau and Thierry Giasson (2003, 9) suggest, is a "devalued concept of politics" that discredits the electoral process "by reducing the broad debates of society to simple partisan issues." They go on to advocate a shift to "public journalism," or "civic journalism," as an antidote. This is a type of political reporting that puts citizens and their needs at the forefront of coverage: "From this angle, electoral news must principally focus on citizens' questions about issues they consider to be priorities and on party positions concerning these precise issues. The reporting in public journalism must cover campaigns by uncovering ordinary citizens' experiences" (18).

The task of the journalist is to contextualize social issues and to foster debate with citizens about the proffered solutions. While admittedly somewhat idealistic, this approach has been practised in parts of the United States for the past dozen years; it has also been associated with significant gains in citizens' political knowledge. Changing media practices is no easy task, though, given the constraints under which journalists work, be they organizational, technical, financial, or the constraints of the genre itself (see Nadeau and Giasson 2003).

The single most important step that can be taken to narrow the democratic divides is to increase the number of Canadians who complete high school and go on to post-secondary education. One of the central findings to emerge from this audit of democratic citizenship is just how well education serves democracy. The more education people have, the more interested they are in politics, the more attention they pay to news about politics, and the more they know about politics. And the more education people have, the more likely they are to vote, to belong to a political party or an interest group, to sign petitions and join in boycotts, and to be active in their communities. Education does not just provide citizens with better tools for democratic citizenship, it also provides them with the inclination for it.

A recent report by the Applied Research Branch of Human Resources Development Canada (2000, 58) outlines some of the policy options for encouraging more Canadians to complete their high school education: "awareness campaigns, raising the legal age at which youth can leave school, improving literacy, modifying programs for those who have difficulties with academic programs, developing alternative pathways to the workplace, policies directed to families, schools and the community, lowering the minimum wage, and developing non-accreditation learning options."

The HRDC report makes the point that lowering the dropout rate is good economic sense. The report estimates that the total monetary rate of return to society for completing high school as opposed to stopping at Grade 10 is 17 per cent. But a lower dropout rate is not only good for the Canadian economy; it is also good for Canadian democracy. More Canadians would be equipped with the cognitive skills and the motivation needed to be active and engaged citizens. Keeping students in school would also help to address the other root cause of democratic disengagement, namely poverty. The same study makes the relationship between socioeconomic factors and dropping out clear. Poor children are at greater risk of dropping out, and dropping out makes a lifetime of poverty more likely.

CITIZENSHIP TODAY

The picture of democratic citizenship in Canada is mixed. A core of highly engaged citizens pays close attention to politics and takes an active part in civic life. At the same time, a very significant minority of Canadians knows little about politics and cares less. Most disturbing, perhaps, is the evidence of deep pockets of political ignorance within certain groups in Canadian society. These democratic deficits diminish the inclusiveness and impair the responsiveness of Canadian democracy. And the most striking deficits are those defined by material circumstances, age, and gender. Of course there are poor young women who are highly engaged in civic life, just as there are affluent older men who are not. But the association between democratic engagement and social background is indisputable.

The systematic nature of this association should make us look to its deeper causes. The numerical under-representation of certain groups in Canada's political institutions is one factor. And patterns of media coverage and the conduct of election campaigns are implicated. But the roots of democratic disengagement also lie deep in the structural inequalities that characterize Canadian society. To the extent that they do, only by tackling those inequalities can democratic citizenship in Canada become truly inclusive.

In Gidengil et al., *Citizens*. 2004. Seattle: University of Washington Press.

REFERENCES

Applied Research Branch. 2000. *Dropping out of high school: Definitions and costs*. R-01-1E. Ottawa: Human Resources Development Canada.

Baum, Matthew A. 2002. Sex, lies, and war: How soft news brings foreign policy to the inattentive public. *American Political Science Review* 96: 91–109.

Cappella, Joseph N., and Kathleen Hall Jamieson. 1997. *Spiral of cynicism*: *The press and the public good*. Oxford: Oxford University Press.

Converse, Philip E. 2000. Assessing the capacity of mass electorates. *Annual Review of Political Science* 3: 331–53.

Courtney, John C. 2004. *Elections*. Canadian Democratic Audit. Vancouver: UBC Press.

Delli Carpini, Michael X., and Scott Keeter. 1996. *What Americans know about politics and why it matters*. New Haven, CT: Yale University Press.

Dewey, John. 1916. *Education and democracy*. New York: Macmillan.

———. 1938. *Experience and education*. London: Collier Macmillan.

Eveland, William P., Jr., and Dietram A. Scheufele. 2000. Connecting news media use with gaps in knowledge and participation. *Political Communication* 17: 215–37.

Galston, William A. 2001. Political knowledge, political engagement, and civic education. *Annual Review of Political Science* 4: 217–34.

Hall, Michael, Larry McKeown, and Karen Roberts. 2001. *Caring Canadians, involved Canadians: Highlights from the 2000 National Survey of Giving, Volunteering and Participating.* Catalogue no. 71-542-XIE. Ottawa: Statistics Canada.

Joslyn, Richard. 1984. *Mass media and elections.* New York: Random House.

Key, Vladimir O. 1966. *The responsible electorate: Rationality in presidential voting 1936–1960.* Cambridge, MA: Belknap Press of Harvard University Press.

Levin, Ben. 2000. Democracy and schools: Educating for citizenship. *Education Canada* 40: 4–7.

Mansbridge, Jane. 1980. *Beyond adversary democracy.* New York: Basic Books.

Mendelsohn, Matthew. 1993. Television's frames in the 1988 Canadian election. *Canadian Journal of Political Science* 18: 149–71.

———, and Richard Nadeau. 1999. The rise and fall of candidates in Canadian election campaigns. *Harvard International Journal of Press/Politics* 4(2): 63–76.

Moore, David W. 1987. Political campaigns and the knowledge-gap hypothesis. *Public Opinion Quarterly* 51: 186–200.

Mutz, Diana C. 2002. The consequences of cross-cutting networks for political participation. *American Journal of Political Science* 46: 838–55.

Myers, John. 2000. Ontario's new civics course: Where's it going? Paper presented at the conference Citizenship 2000: Assuming Responsibility for Our Future, McGill Institute for the Study of Canada, Montreal, 20–1 October. <www.misc-iecm.mcgill.ca/citizen/myers2.htm>. 8 February 2004.

Nadeau, Richard, and Thierry Giasson. 2003. Canada's democratic malaise: Are the media to blame? *Choices: Strengthening Canadian democracy*, vol. 9. Montreal: Institute for Research on Public Policy.

Neuman, W. Russell. 1986. *The paradox of mass politics: Knowledge and opinion in the American electorate.* Cambridge, MA: Harvard University Press.

Niemi, Richard G., Mary A. Hepburn, and Chris Chapman. 2000. Community service by high school students: A cure for civic ills? *Political Behavior* 22: 45–69.

———, and Jane Junn. 1998. *Civic education: What makes students learn.* New Haven, CT: Yale University Press.

———, and Julia Smith. 2001. Enrolments in high school government classes: Are we short-changing both citizenship and political science training? *PS: Political Science and Politics* 34(2): 281–7.

Osborne, Ken. 1988. Political education for participant citizenship: Implications for the schools. In *Political education in Canada*, ed. Jon H. Pammett and Jean-Luc Pepin, 227–34. Halifax: Institute for Research on Public Policy.

———. 2000. Public schooling and citizenship education in Canada. *Canadian Ethnic Studies* 32: 8–37.

Page, Benjamin I. 1996. *Who deliberates? Mass media in modern democracy.* Chicago: University of Chicago Press.

———, and Robert Y. Shapiro. 1992. *The rational public: Fifty years of trends in Americans' policy preferences.* Chicago: University of Chicago Press.

Plutzer, Eric. 2002. Becoming a habitual voter: Inertia, resources, and growth in young adulthood. *American Political Science Review* 96: 41–56.

Popkin, Samuel L. 1991. *The reasoning voter: Communication and persuasion in presidential campaigns.* Chicago: University of Chicago Press.

Sears, Alan, and Mark Perry. 2000. Paying attention to the contexts of citizenship education. *Education Canada* 40: 28–31.

Ulbig, Stacy G., and Carolyn L. Funk. 1999. Conflict avoidance and political participation. *Political Behavior* 21: 265–82.

Zaller, John. 1999. A theory of media politics: How the interests of politicians, journalists, and citizens shape the news. Unpublished typescript, UCLA. <www.uky.edu/AS/PoliSci/Peffley/pdf/ZallerTheoryofMediaPolitics(10-99).pdf>. 9 February 2004.

KEY AND DIFFICULT WORDS

Define the following, using context or other clues if possible: **partisan, intractable, contextual(ize), disseminate, obfuscate.**

QUESTIONS

1. In the first section of the chapter, the authors refer to many US studies in their attempt to propose solutions to the problem of "re-engaging young Canadians." Are the findings relevant to Canada, in your view?

2. What is a possible reason that civics education courses work more effectively in Grade 12 than they do in the earlier grades (see paragraph 9)?

3. How is the dropout rate in Canada related to the number of politically engaged citizens? What kinds of skills, according to Page (cited in paragraph 10), must be developed in order to produce knowledgeable citizens?

4. Summarize the ways that (a) political parties and (b) the media are often served through inaccurate or distorted reporting of the "facts."

5. Paraphrase the first sentence in "Narrowing the democratic divides."

6. The authors devote a lot of space to summarizing and evaluating the views of Zaller and other critics of "'fact-packed'" media (see "Narrowing the democratic divides"). Why? Do you think that they are basically supportive or dismissive of these views? What shows you this?

7. What do the authors believe is the single best way to bridge the disparity between citizens in terms of their political knowledge and interest? Do you agree with them?

8. Is this chapter just about the problem of low voter turnout? After reading it completely at least once, consider the nature of the concept referred to in the title, and in two to three sentences, provide a complete definition of "democratic citizenship."

COLLABORATIVE ACTIVITY

Some students may have taken civics classes at school or performed community service for school credits. Based on your direct experience or indirect knowledge of them (perhaps through friends), assess their value. Do they in fact make participants more informed about or interested in politics and citizenship?

ACTIVITIES

1. Reflect on one of the following proposals to increase democratic citizenship referred to in the essay: (a) "fostering a democratic classroom climate" (paragraph 9); OR (b) encouraging the media to adopt a practice of "'public journalism,'" (paragraph 9 in "Narrowing the democratic divides"). Adopting the role of (1) a school consultant or (2) a media consultant, begin by justifying the need for the proposal; then outline at least four to five specific and realistic recommendations that would make the proposal viable.

2. What do you believe is the major cause of voter apathy? How can it be overcome? Give yourself five to 10 minutes to freewrite, using one of the questions as your starting point.

Related reading: Matt James. "Being stigmatized and being sorry: Past injustices and contemporary citizenship."

Being stigmatized and being sorry: Past injustices and contemporary citizenship[1]

Matt James

(7,200 words)

Groups seeking redress for past injustices have made history a crucial focal point for contemporary Canadian debates about citizenship.[2] This role is fitting, because understandings about the past affect how we practise citizenship in the present.

Alan Cairns has established the significance of redress campaigns for Canadian citizenship by linking them to Canada's postwar search for a constitutional framework that is capable of attracting support from a multinational and pluralistic society. Cairns suggests that the increased constitutional emphasis on equality, which followed the 1982 entrenchment of the Charter of Rights and Freedoms, has encouraged redress

movements to seek "compensatory treatment . . . for past injustice[s] whose lingering effects are still visited on survivors" (Cairns, 1995, p. 25). As Cairns explains, these movements insist that transforming Canadian understandings of the "constitutionally significant past" is crucial to the larger project of fashioning a more acceptable future (Cairns, 1995, p. 22).

This article explores redress campaigns as bids to confront problems of civic marginalization and unequal political power. It emphasizes the importance of redress for groups whose capacity to participate in citizenship has been hampered by histories of stigmatization. In turn, I link this group interest in redress to the remarkable symbolic power of apologies. Historical episodes that violate contemporary standards of equal citizenship become potent political tools when they are made to symbolize what others must learn about and then repudiate in order to produce a more satisfactory future. For example, Ottawa's 1988 apology for the World War II Japanese-Canadian internment proclaimed that "the shame on [Japanese Canadians'] honour, their dignity, their rights as Canadians is now removed forever" (Weiner, 1988, p.2). And in January 1998, after being forced to apologize for its past policy of forcing Aboriginal children to attend residential schools, the federal government officially admitted that "the contributions made by all Aboriginal peoples to Canada's development . . . have not been properly acknowledged" (Stewart, 1998, p. A19).

As the contrast between these statements and the racist policies for which they are offered in apology may suggest, groups seeking redress strive to replace the undeserved stigma of the past with a new imagery of group honour. This imagery is usefully understood as comprising a "symbolic capital" of honour (Bourdieu, 1977): a resource of political power that traditionally marginalized groups can employ as they pursue recognition as fully accepted civic participants.

The article begins by discussing the various redress claims and the episodes from which the claims derive. It then proceeds to explain redress campaigns as responses to problems of citizenship experienced by historically stigmatized communities. This point is important to consider in the case of Aboriginals, to whom the desirability of Canadian citizenship has often seemed extremely doubtful. But neither can the differences between the residential-schools campaign and the other redress movements be ignored. Thus, I distinguish between demanding redress as an unambiguous project of citizenship inclusion and doing so in order to assess the desirability of achieving such inclusion in the future.

This article also examines the debate between redress supporters and their critics. The critics condemn what they see as the unduly divisive emphasis on historical grievances that accompanies redress politics. Although redress campaigns are often confrontational, I argue that they are potentially useful vehicles of civic integration. As the example of South Africa's Truth and Reconciliation Commission suggests, to demand apologies for past wrongdoing is also to seek more harmonious future relations with former antagonists. Thus, I conclude that the increasingly influential opposition to treating past wrongs as issues of contemporary citizenship is extremely dangerous. This opposition encourages Canadians to avoid the important work of understanding and reconciliation upon which a more inclusive and durable citizenship must rest.

REDRESS POLITICS IN CANADA

Among non-Aboriginal redress movements, the successful campaign waged on behalf of the approximately 22,000 Japanese-Canadian internees of World War II is the most well known. In September 1988, the National Association of Japanese Canadians elicited a Parliament Hill ceremony, $450 million in financial compensation, and an official apology from the federal government. Other movements have also demanded redress for historical wrongs, such as the World War I internment of roughly 5,000 Ukrainian Canadians and the racist policies (of which the notorious "head tax" is the most widely remembered) that, until 1947, severely restricted Chinese immigration to Canada.

These movements have not matched Japanese-Canadian success. The National Congress of Italian Canadians was forced in 1990, after failing to win financial redress for the World War II internment of approximately 1,000 Italian

Canadians, to settle for an informal apology from prime minister Brian Mulroney (Mulroney, 1990). The congress has continued to lobby for an official apology, the establishment of university chairs in Italian-Canadian studies, and the payment of unspecified amounts of compensation to remaining survivors (de Santis, 1997, p. A4). In 1993 the other non-Aboriginal redress movements, most notably Canadians of Chinese and Ukrainian ancestry, ended negotiations with the Mulroney administration when it became clear that financial compensation would not be forthcoming ("Hefty price tag," 1993, p. A12).

These groups were rebuffed entirely in 1994, when Liberal heritage minister Sheila Finestone announced her policy of refusing to offer monetary restitution or apologies of any sort (Canada, 1994). In protest, the Chinese Canadian National Council took its claim to the United Nations to publicize the "spectacle of elderly pioneers . . . bringing forth their individual cases of human injustice before the world community" (Wong 1995, p. A15). The Ukrainian Canadian Civil Liberties Association, like its Italian-Canadian counterpart, has persevered in pressing its case. The association seeks the erection of memorial plaques at all 24 former internment sites (it has persuaded Ottawa to establish two such memorials), an official parliamentary acknowledgement, and $563,000 to cover the costs of documenting the internment experience (Ferguson and Cunningham, 1997, p. B7).

In contrast to Italian Canadians, who received an apology but no compensation, the movement seeking redress for the hundreds of Inuit who were relocated under federal government auspices in the 1950s experienced a setback of the opposite sort. In March 1996, the Department of Indian Affairs agreed to offer $10 million in monetary compensation for the coerced relocation, which buttressed Canadian sovereignty in the High Arctic by sending the Pond Inlet and Grise Fiord Inuit thousands of kilometres north as "human flagpoles" (Aubry, 1994b, p. A6). But the department refused to apologize, and the Inuit accepted what appeared to be minister Ron Irwin's final offer (Lowi, 1996, p. B5). Ottawa also adopted the compensation-without-apology approach in response to First Nations demands for atonement and restitution for a residential-schools policy that, for many survivors, led to the near-destruction of their families and languages. In December 1997, the Department of Indian Affairs agreed to set up a $200 million fund (raised subsequently to $350 million) to help meet the health care and counselling needs of survivors but refused steadfastly to apologize or to accept responsibility for the residential-schools fiasco (Anderssen, 1997, p. A1). After difficult negotiations with the Assembly of First Nations, the Chrétien government relented: "To those of you who suffered this tragedy at residential schools," said minister Jane Stewart, "we are deeply sorry" (Stewart, 1998, p. A19).

PAST WRONGS AND CONTEMPORARY CITIZENSHIP

Many of the past policies for which redress has been sought are ones that unfairly excluded particular Canadians from some of the most basic rights of citizenship. In the case of the federal government's World War II internment operations, the denial was almost total. The vast majority of the interned "Japanese" and "Italians" were Canadian citizens who, with absolutely no proof of their disloyalty, were removed from their communities, incarcerated, forced to work without compensation, and, in many cases, stripped of their homes and possessions (Miki and Kobayashi, 1991, pp. 17–49; National Congress of Italian Canadians, 1990, pp. 7–12). Little wonder that Italian Canadians doubted "that they were dealing . . . with a democratic state" (Ramirez, 1988, p. 80) or that Japanese Canadians came to see internment as "a betrayal of democracy itself" (National Association of Japanese Canadians, 1986, p. 1).

Like internment, other past policies for which redress has been claimed also shattered communities by separating innocent individuals and their families against their will. For instance, until the early 1970s, the federal government's residential-schools policy aimed to eliminate what authorities viewed as "backward" cultures by removing thousands of Aboriginal children from their homes (Assembly of First Nations, 1994, pp. 13–19). At the church-run institutions to which these children were sent, Aboriginal cultures were condemned as inferior and barbaric, discipline was often vindictively enforced, and sexual and physical abuse were remarkably common. The 1994 Assembly of First Nations report, *Breaking the silence*, has spoken powerfully about the damage inflicted by this policy on First Nations communities. Even excepting the horrific experiences of abuse that are now the schools' most well-known legacy, prolonged periods of near-total familial separation under degrading conditions meant that children who attended residential schools "found themselves becoming alone—silent and isolated and without any hope of belonging to a sensible world" (Assembly of First Nations, 1994, p. 34). The ban on Aboriginal languages, which all the residential schools enforced, though with quite varying degrees of brutality, indicates the thoroughness of this assault on First Nations identities (Miller, 1996, p. 200).

The Inuit who were relocated from their northern Quebec homes to the High Arctic also experienced the shock of an unexpected community breakup brought about by state policy. As survivor John Amagoalik has recounted, "We just went into a panic because [the RCMP] had promised that they would not separate us" (in Marcus, 1992, p. 21).

Rather than fracturing an already existent Canadian community, Canada's "Chinese exclusion" policy (1885–1947), which made "married bachelors" (Bolaria and Li, 1988, p. 114) of two generations of Chinese men drawn to Canada by the lure of work and wages, helped to prevent viable Chinese-Canadian communities from forming. The onerous head tax and subsequent ban on Chinese immigration consigned many of these men to permanent separation from their wives and families. With a 1911 ratio of 2,790 men for every 100 women, there would be virtually no second Chinese-Canadian generation until after World War II (Bolaria and Li, 1988, p. 114).

Redress movements remember these episodes as unjust assaults launched by a hostile government and society against the very existence of their communities. As former residential-school student Gilbert Oskaboose wrote in 1996: "When we returned to our own communities we had become strangers. . . . [T]he policies of assimilation . . . brought pain, suffering, lost lives, vicious in-fighting, divisions, waste and sorrow" (Oskaboose, 1996). Unsurprisingly, redress-seekers find it difficult to discharge with enthusiasm the major obligation that accompanies citizenship: loyalty to the state within which citizenship has been assumed. In 1984, for example, an angry Roy Miki of the National Association of Japanese Canadians told the federal minister for multiculturalism that "Your government instituted a policy which was meant to destroy the community, and that policy worked" (in Miki and Kobayashi, 1991, p. 132). To seek official atonement for past injustices may thus be one way of endeavouring to reconcile citizenship's demands of loyalty with the awareness of equal citizenship denied. As one Japanese-Canadian internee remarked four years prior to the historic redress settlement of 1988: "A sense of incompleteness gnaws at me. I need to feel right about my country" (in Miki and Kobayashi, 1991, p. 15).

Redress may also be valued for reasons of a more private nature. In particular, individuals who trace severe personal difficulties back to past injustices may seek apologies and restitution in order to help further their often painful recoveries. For example, Inuit leader Martha Flaherty urged the Royal Commission on Aboriginal Peoples to understand that "the High Arctic exiles . . . deserve . . . recognition so that they can start the healing process and rebuilding their lives" (in Royal Commission on Aboriginal Peoples, 1994, p. 77). Thus, official repudiation of the relevant historical wrong is welcomed as evidence that the victims will find support from the wider society in their rehabilitation. One survivor, for instance, reacted to Ottawa's apology for the residential-schools disaster by saying: "It's a nice feeling . . . to think that the government was listening. It's certainly a better day today than it was yesterday" (in Steffenhagen, 1998, p. A3).

Although internment burdened many Japanese Canadians with psychiatric problems (Omatsu, 1992, p. 171), the focus on personal recovery has been most evident in the residential-schools campaign. With many First Nations people suffering problems of low self-esteem and family dysfunction because of the abuse they experienced in residential schools, recognition of their undeserved suffering is valued as the "beginning of respect, of feeling that [they] are capable of making a contribution to the world" (Assembly of First Nations, 1994, p. 125). This focus on the personal needs of survivors has also driven demands on behalf of former residential students for monetary compensation, which, as one advocate has argued, is necessary "to start healing, because we don't have adequate therapy, addiction treatment, child care or education" (in Fournier, 1997, p. A3). Ottawa's major response

to these demands has been the $350-million healing fund announced at the January 1998 reconciliation ceremony. However, because the monies will be disbursed only to selected community healing projects, victims of residential-schools abuse continue to bring claims for individual compensation before the courts (Barnsley, 1999, p. 10).

REDRESS AND THE SYMBOLIC CAPITAL OF HONOUR

Redress-seekers insist that Canada has a responsibility to help traumatized communities overcome the ongoing manifestations of past suffering. But their critics wonder why claimants do not seek reconciliation through the more customary routes of psychiatry or forgiving by forgetting. Indeed, opponents often leap from asking this question to portraying redress politics as a cynical attempt to raid the public purse. Thus, *Winnipeg Free Press* editor John Dafoe has complained: "The theory used to be that time healed all wounds. Now there is a growing belief that time plus about $30 million might just do the job" (1994, p. A6). Prominent columnist Jeffrey Simpson has depicted the emphasis on financial compensation similarly as a "crass multicultural politics" that aims at forcing "today's generation to pay for policies and attitudes of generations past" (Simpson, 1990, p. 78).

But redress politics is a more complex phenomenon than such comments leave room to admit. More useful is Cairns's point: redress movements employ an "adversarial, accusatory history" as they seek a "more dignified future" (Cairns, 1995, p. 24). The advocacy literature on redress abounds with references to the public humiliation that can attach to a community even after the original episode or policy that gave rise to its initial official stigmatization has passed. According to the Chinese Canadian National Council, "having been singled out by law for unequal treatment," Chinese Canadians have been labelled as "inferior and undesirable" (1988b, p. 11). The anniversary of July 1, 1923, the date the Chinese Immigration (Exclusion) Act was passed, is remembered as "Humiliation Day" (McEvoy, 1982, p. 26). For the National Congress of Italian Canadians, "Canadians of Italian origin were denigrated and discriminated against in their own country. . . . For that stigma there can never be sufficient compensation" (1990, p. 21). And Japanese Canadians, as Maryka Omatsu explains, have been "scarred by our history in this country," by a "debilitating virus that . . . filled me with a shame that I could not understand as a child" (1992, p. 39).

Undeserved stigma is an extreme form of disrespect, which can make "outsiders" or "foreigners" of persons whose citizenship histories ought to support a quite different response. For example, Chinese-Canadian redress-seekers blame the exclusion, disfranchisement, and head-tax legislation for preventing other Canadians from relating to them as civic partners. One member of the Chinese-Canadian redress movement has remarked that despite being able to trace his Canadian family history to 1906, his children were still told to "go back to Hong Kong" while attending Simon Fraser University some 80 years later (in Bolan, 1995, p. B3). As the Chinese Canadian National Council put it, "the bitter legacy of the Canadian government's 62 years of legislated racism is a Chinese Canadian community that is still seen as a new immigrant community" (in Bolan, 1995, p. B3). Similarly, the National Association of Japanese Canadians found that the public was unaware that internment "was carried out against Canadians who happened to be of Japanese ancestry, and not against Japanese nationals who happened to find themselves in Canada" (Miki and Kobayashi, 1991, p. 80).

Because they associate these problems with difficulties in becoming truly accepted and equal civic participants, redress campaigns rebel against the hesitancy and withdrawal that may follow from experiences of official stigmatization. For example, as novelist Joy Kogawa has remarked, "internment worked beyond the wildest dreams of politicians. [F]orty years later, most of the people of my generation are still hiding in the woodwork and wanting to speak" (in Miki and Kobayashi, 1988, p. 10). Omatsu, too, has written of a "passivity . . . fashioned by our history in this country, that, like some invisible undertow, pulls us down on bended knees" (1992, p. 69). A similar reaction was noticed after the World War I Ukrainian-Canadian internment. One school principal remarked that his Ukrainian-Canadian pupils, who had felt before internment that "they were really becoming Canadians[,] . . . are now hurt, bewildered, shy and drawing back into their half-discarded alien shells" (in Thompson, 1983, p. 40). Internment "conditioned the entire community to be very apprehensive about their . . . status as Canadians" ("Ukraine," 1988, p. F5). These remembrances indicate how a citizen's formal right to public participation can be compromised significantly by the (historically justified) perception that others do not regard him or her with respect.

Achieving redress is thus prized as highly public proof that the stigmatization of the redress movement's constituency was ill deserved. For example, the federal government's Statement of Reconciliation, the outcome of extensive negotiations with the Assembly of First Nations, spoke of "the assistance and spiritual values of the Aboriginal peoples who welcomed the newcomers to this continent," of "diverse, vibrant Aboriginal nations," and of "the strength and endurance of Aboriginal people": contributions that "too often have been forgotten" (Stewart, 1998, p. A19). For the National Congress of Italian Canadians, redress would "restore the positive image of Italian Canadians as significant contributors to this country of ours in this century" (1990, p. 21).

A key aspect of redress campaigns is their focus on eliciting increased civic respect by demonstrating virtue. To display public-spirited virtue can be crucial in the arena of citizenship, where people are often condemned for pursuing "special" interests. Accordingly, a prominent theme in redress politics is the movement's insistence that its aim is to prevent similar racist acts from being visited on others. The National Association of Japanese Canadians emphasized that "it is as an act of citizenship and because we refuse to see democracy betrayed that we seek an honourable resolution to the injustices of the war years" (1986, p. 1). Similarly, the Chinese Canadian National Council called for "a trust foundation . . . to ensure that similar discriminatory government actions do not happen again" (1988a, p. 21). And the Ukrainian-Canadian movement sought to "ensure that no other . . . minority in Canada will in the future experience the injustices Ukrainian Canadians did in the past" (Ukrainian Canadian Civil Liberties Association, 1988).

The successful Japanese-Canadian campaign produced lasting symbols of the community's struggle to enhance the future well-being of other Canadians. For example, because the 1988 Emergencies Act—which replaced the old War Measures Act that had enabled the various internments—was largely a federal government response to Japanese-Canadian protests, the *Nikkei Voice* newspaper could call the new Act the Japanese-Canadian community's "Gift to Canadians" (Miki and Kobayashi, 1991, p. 121). The establishment of the Canadian Human

Rights Foundation as part of the terms of the 1988 redress settlement stands similarly as proof of Japanese Canadians' concern to help protect other Canadians from potential future acts of racist oppression. By no means irrelevant to the argument that a "Japanese-Canadian human rights foundation" would "help other groups" in the future was the aim of establishing a visible reminder of Japanese-Canadian virtue (National Association of Japanese Canadians, 1986, p. 10).

However, critics ask, why do redress movements seek "conscience money . . . to appease" ("Post no bills," 1988, p. 50); why do they demand "cash to expiate the perceived sins?" (Drache, 1990, p. 84). This question is important. After all, Conservative multiculturalism minister Gerry Weiner's 1993 offer of a parliamentary ceremony and formal apologies for the various movements seeking redress was refused on the ground that redress without money was not redress at all ("Hefty price tag," 1993, p. A12). The need for better health and addictions services has given an understandably consistent monetary emphasis to the First Nations and Inuit claims. But money is not just prized by redress-seekers for what it can directly buy; it is integral to the symbolism of redress as well.

With this monetary emphasis, redress movements indicate that they are willing to forgive the wrongs of the past but only if they can elicit a persuasive indicator that those wrongs will not be repeated. One cannot, after all, be brutally robbed, accept a casual "sorry" from the thief, and feel that the exchange bodes well for the future. As the National Association of Japanese Canadians insisted, "Significant individual compensation acknowledges the severity of the injustices [and provides] an honourable and meaningful settlement" (in Miki and Kobayashi, 1988, p. 7). Indeed, Ottawa itself emphasized at the Japanese-Canadian redress ceremony that its sincerity was financially guaranteed. The $450-million compensation package, Prime Minister Mulroney declared, "is symbolic of our determination to address this issue, not only in the moral sense but also in a tangible way" (Mulroney, 1990, p. 1).

A cash settlement can also help to make the gravity of the apology more closely approximate the magnitude of the original misdeed. Groups whose past victimization caused them direct and significant financial hardship insist that an honourable apology must contain a significant financial component.[3] Thus, the Chinese Canadian National Council deplored the federal government's failure to offer "a symbolic sum to acknowledge the injustice of the [head] tax" (in "Hefty price tag," 1993, p. A12), while the Ukrainian Canadian Civil Liberties Association protested that a proposed memorial at a former internment site was utterly insufficient: "a small plaque, valued at $15,000, is not enough. The internees suffered substantial economic losses" (Luciuk, 1994, p. A7).

Perhaps most importantly, struggles for financial redress aim to show other Canadians that the redress movement has forced the government to respond to the injustices of the past with more than just vague declarations of good intent. To return to the mugging analogy, accepting apologies from absconding thieves is only likely to boost one's reputation in circles where masochism is a cherished value. Redress movements, then, view the importance of financial compensation from two major perspectives. The first perspective sees the state's willingness to pay restitution as a symbol of the integrity of its apology: it seeks to determine whether the expressed regret is appropriately sincere. The second perspective on financial restitution is concerned with what a settlement is likely to tell other Canadians about the redress movement and its constituency: it judges the settlement as potential symbolic capital.

Financial restitution as a form of symbolic capital became particularly important after the Japanese-Canadian settlement. In the wake of Japanese-Canadian success, winning financial redress has been seen as an indicator of whether the group is regarded as sufficiently worthy to deserve an "honourable and meaningful settlement" (Miki and Kobayashi, 1988, p. 7). Failure to elicit financial compensation, it is feared, will create an unflattering contrast between the apparent disregard with which the unsuccessful movement's constituency has been handled with the concrete demonstration of respect already accorded its victorious counterparts. Indicating the prevalence of this fear are remarks such as: "redress offered to . . . Japanese Canadians would be discriminatory if it ignored the experience of the Ukrainians in Canada" (Civil Liberties Commission of the Ukrainian Canadian Committee, 1987, p. 49); "compensation [was] given to the Japanese[,] the Inuit . . . deserve the same recognition" (Martha Flaherty, in Royal Commission on Aboriginal Peoples, 1994, p. 77); "how could the federal government redress . . . other past wrongs but not the . . . Chinese Head Tax?" (Wong, 1995, p. A15).

REDRESS AND CITIZENSHIP INCLUSION

Opponents of redress argue that the "search for restitution for past wrongs . . . risks piling up more division in a country already quite divided" (Simpson, 1990, p. 79) and that the "rush for compensation for past slights and indignities is likely to open old wounds" (C. Dafoe, 1994, p. 40). At the extreme, redress-seeking is depicted as a vehicle of vengeance rather than of reconciliation: "Everybody has a horror story to tell about what used to go on. The time has now come to get even" (C. Dafoe, 1994, p. 40).

But strategies that seek to secure apologies reveal with particular clarity that the aim is reconciliation rather than rupture. An apology allows the offended party to relate to the offender in a way that would not be possible if the offender failed to convincingly disavow her actions. For instance, whereas a victim may signal his desire to sever relations with a tormentor by demanding punishment, the apology-seeker demands reassurance that the attitudes that gave rise to the past offence have been repudiated. Like the victim whose condition for undertaking future relations with the mugger is receiving persuasive evidence that the former wrongdoer has renounced thievery, redress movements are motivated by the desire to engage in future interaction with other Canadians, not to reject it.

RESIDENTIAL SCHOOLS AND CITIZENSHIP AMBIVALENCE

The residential-schools campaign is a different case: it cannot be portrayed unequivocally as a push for integration within the larger Canadian society. On this point, its quite different approach to the question of honour is particularly revealing. When the movement has described itself as a vehicle for attaching honour to First Nations, the context of interaction most often cited has been that of particular status Indian communities. This focus contrasts with that of the Inuit, who spoke of their campaign as a struggle for citizenship inclusion: the relocated Inuit were described as "Canadians who suffered for Canadian sovereignty and deserve . . . recognition" (in Royal Commission on Aboriginal Peoples, 1994, p. 77).

This theme has not been as conspicuous in the residential-schools campaign, which has been more overtly concerned with using redress as a remedy for interaction problems that it sees within First Nations communities. As the Assembly of First Nations summarized the consensus among residential-schools survivors: "People realized they needed to work on themselves first, help family next, and then their com-

munities" (Assembly of First Nations, 1994, p. i). Recalled with painful regret are the tendencies of many abuse survivors to either shun interaction with their families and former neighbours (Assembly of First Nations, 1994, pp. 93–97) or return only to inflict their own suffering on others (Lazaruk, 1995, p. 3). Thus, the idea of speaking out about past abuse has been seen as a means of ending a cycle of "dishonourable behaviour" (Assembly of First Nations, 1994, p. 55) in order to create more healthy communities. Encapsulating this project has been the phrase, "the honour of one is the honour of all" (Assembly of First Nations, 1994, p. 159).

This tendency to focus primarily on the movement as a vehicle for producing respect and healing within First Nations communities, and to place less stress on the notion of Canadian citizenship, helps to point out the immense difficulty that Canada's historical legacy poses for Aboriginal peoples. Canadians cannot expect First Nations to view redress in the same way as non-Aboriginal movements, which have emphasized atonement repeatedly as a symbol of meaningful inclusion within the political community. For the First Nations campaign, redress does not necessarily lead straightforwardly to an enthusiastic push for further integration within the Canadian polity. At least equally significant has been the understanding of redress as a precedent for bolstering future court attempts to make the federal government financially accountable to individual abuse survivors (O'Neil, 1998, p. A1).

The historical legacy of Canada's "Indian policy" underscores one of the most important reasons for the distrust with which many First Nations view Canadian citizenship. As Darlene Johnston argues, past federal government policies (like the ban on traditional practices such as the potlatch and the assimilative thrust of the 1969 White Paper proposals) have conveyed the notion that equal Canadian citizenship requires repudiating—or simply becoming dispossessed of—Aboriginal lands, heritages, connections, and identities. It is only against this background, Johnston (1993) writes, that "the ambivalence and resistance that First Nations display toward Canadian citizenship [can] begin to be understood" (p. 349).

But those who worry that the First Nations stress on past wrongs augurs poorly for a common Canadian future should consider the potential implications if First Nations stopped attempting to discuss history with other Canadians. The analogy should not be pushed too far, but the near-total breach in Canada-Quebec relations following the 1990 collapse of the Meech Lake Accord has also been accompanied by a marked shift in the role played by historical grievances in Quebec nationalism. Complaints directed at English Canada about historical attitudes and policies toward Quebec were prominent in the Meech debates (Cairns, 1991, pp. 226–29). But since Meech's failure, angry remarks about Quebec's history in Canada seem much less appeals to English-Canadian consciences than bids to consolidate independence sentiment among Quebeckers. As Charles Taylor (1991) writes: "With the demise of Meech, something snapped. . . . A certain kind of compromise was for ever over" (pp. 65–66).

Of course, First Nations nationalism lacks the economic and institutional advantages that make independence a far more immediate prospect for Quebec. But there are other alternatives to joint historical discussion that First Nations may come increasingly to find as the only honourable basis from which to create future relationships with Canada. These alternatives could include, and indeed have included, engaging in campaigns of civil disobedience, launching embarrassing international complaints, or even—more subtly but also indicative of an increasing apartness that would bode ill for a common future—adopting the sullen posture of inauthentic acceptance with which inhabitants of the former Soviet empire awaited their captor's demise.

Therefore, it is important to note that the Assembly of First Nations has sought redress as part of an attempt to "forge a more conciliatory relationship with the federal government" (Anderssen and Greenspon, 1998, p. A4). The co-chair of the Nuu-chah-nulth Tribal Council, Nelson Keitlah, told the Royal Commission on Aboriginal Peoples that an apology "would go a long way toward patching up the differences between Canada's Indians and the federal government. When a person hurts another person, the first thing that comes about before a friendship can start again is that [they] say, 'I'm sorry'" ("Apologize for residential schools," 1997, p. l). *Breaking the silence* has also drawn a connection between redress and seeking greater inclusion within the Canadian polity: "Today, First Nations are reclaiming their history and affirming their place in Canada, a trend which includes speaking out about their residential school experience" (Assembly of First Nations, 1994, p. 2). Individual survivors, too, have recognized that pursuing redress is a move that involves the risk of adopting a certain openness toward non-Aboriginal Canadians. As one woman expressed this feeling: "Sometimes we have to reach out . . . I guess that's what we're doing here. Trusting the government that somehow things are going to be . . . dealt with" (in Gummerson, 1997, p. 3).

Certainly, the Métis National Council, the Native Women's Association of Canada, and the Native Council of Canada condemned the reconciliation agreement for focusing primarily on the needs of on-reserve status Indians (Anderssen and Greenspon, 1998, p. A4). Comparing minister Stewart's statement with the stronger apology given to Japanese Canadians has also occasioned bitterness (O'Neil, 1998, p. A1). As one former residential-school student put it: "If any kind of apology is going to have any meaning, it's got to come from the top. It meant nothing because one of Prime Minister Chrétien's flunkies gave it" (in Barnsley, 1998a, p. 4). Others have pointed out that Stewart apologized only to those who actually attended residential schools and thus ignored the related suffering of the former students' friends and families ("Ottawa," 1998, p. 2). The fact that Ottawa failed to admit responsibility and remorse for undertaking policies whose intent was cultural assimilation and simply expressed "regret" for the abuse associated with the schools has also invited the important criticism that the Statement of Reconciliation was intended more to assuage the guilt of non-Aboriginal Canadians rather than to repudiate colonialism (Barnsley, 1998b, p. 3). And, for many, doubtless the enormity of Canadian wrongs and Aboriginal suffering simply militated against receiving the agreement with undue enthusiasm in any case.

But it is also clear that seeking redress has been understood as a means of reaching out, of attempting to gauge the sincerity of a polity that claims to want partnership with First Nations. Many First Nations individuals reacted to the apology and healing package as an appropriate basis from which to begin reconciliation with non-Aboriginal Canadians: "I felt that we didn't have hope that this was ever going to materialize. And today it did" (in Steffenhagen, 1998, p. A3); "It's a good first step" (in Laghi, 1998, p. A4); "[it's] a historic step to break from the past" (in Steffenhagen, 1998, p. A3). As one Aboriginal editorialist summarized the mixed First Nations reaction to minister Stewart's Statement of Reconciliation: "The minister went miles ahead of where other colonial governments have gone. That much is true. But . . . if the goal was really to put paternalism to bed and call an end to cul-

tural suppression, we've still got miles and miles to go. . . . But it's a start and it's about time" ("Give us strength," 1998, p. 6).

Ottawa's previous refusal to admit that the residential-schools policy constituted an injustice for which it would accept responsibility meant that survivors seeking healing did so in an unpromising atmosphere of majority-group denial. To many First Nations, therefore, redress symbolizes a welcome shift in non-Aboriginal thinking about the residential-schools issue. In the wake of minister Stewart's apology, First Nations people reading the newspaper could find that the quotation marks once used to signify doubts about their reports of mistreatment, as in "'Atrocities' alleged in mission schools" (Aubry, 1994a, p. A1), had now been replaced with a forthright admission: "Residential schools: A sad history of abuse" ("Residential schools," 1998, p. A3). It is unwarranted to expect that such symbolism will in itself alleviate the mistrust with which many First Nations regard non-Aboriginal society and Canadian institutions. But Canada's official acceptance of responsibility and communication of belief has already begun to make a small but not insignificant difference. In British Columbia, for instance, calls to a provincial sexual-abuse helpline from First Nations persons doubled (up from 12 to 25 calls a day) immediately after minister Stewart's announcement, while the RCMP experienced a dramatic rise in abuse complaints from former residential-school students (Bell, 1998, p. A1). And approximately 2,000 lawsuits from former residential-schools students surfaced in the year after the reconciliation ceremony. Ottawa has since paid out over $20 million (a figure that is expected to reach into the hundreds of millions) in out-of-court settlements ("Abuse claims," 1999, p. 5802).

The point is not that redress is a workable substitute for settling land-claims agreements or that it can solve the political impasse between demands for self-government and opposition to "special status." Rather, it is that a willingness to address past wrongs can help First Nations people to connect with Canadian institutions, such as provincial health and counselling services, the RCMP, and the civil and criminal courts, on a footing of respect. By acknowledging its role in facilitating and perpetuating abuse, the federal government has encouraged former residential-schools students to contact institutions and authorities that history has given them good reason for distrusting. Canada has therefore earned an important opportunity to show Aboriginal peoples that a common citizenship can provide a basis from which to address pressing problems in concert with other Canadians.

CONCLUSION

Redress movements have made respect a politicized issue of contemporary Canadian citizenship. The movements have reacted against legacies of civic stigmatization by struggling to achieve the elusive status of civic honour. This status is prized for its utility as symbolic capital, which, by helping to elicit the esteem of others, makes the promise of equal participation in citizenship more attainable. As sociologist William J. Goode puts it, without the "respect or esteem of others [we] cannot as easily elicit the help of others" (1978, p. vi).

As this essay has shown, redress politics attracts criticism. Critics hold that the project of repairing historical injustices has no natural limits; they contend that redress politics is unduly divisive; and, like former prime minister Pierre Trudeau, they argue that the past is the past and that we can only "be just in our own time" (in Weaver, 1981, p. 179). These criticisms warn that attempting to amend historical wrongs will unleash a torrent of aggrieved claimants, with an ensuing politics of victimization pitting group against group. Critics insist further that this prospect is particularly real because there is no end to the list of past practices, such as discrimination against people with disabilities, gays and lesbians, communists, and others, that violate contemporary moral standards. In short, the critics say that redress politics is no way to go about building a healthy citizenship.

Only the foolish would dismiss these criticisms outright. However, it is important to warn against the notion that ignoring injustice is the best way to achieve harmony and that once the door is open to historical grievances it cannot ever be closed. These objections can easily become an argument against democracy itself. Indeed, their basic similarity to the nineteenth-century objections against giving working-class and poor people the vote is striking.[4] Enfranchisement, argued the conservative critics of the workers' movement, would pit class against class and therefore be unduly divisive. Politics, the conservatives insisted, must be conducted in the general interest rather than be held hostage by "special interests." And this general interest, the propertied critics of mass democracy believed, was best determined not by succumbing to the particular demands of the aggrieved but by ensuring that politics was approached from a rational distance capable of ascertaining the best interests of the whole. Thus, the similarity of the criticisms of redress to an older political position, which no serious observer would attempt to maintain today, suggests that both sides of the argument about redress can easily be extended to the point of absurdity. It is far better, then, to at least remain open to the possibility that some historical injustices may be appropriate candidates for reconsideration, and perhaps even restitution.

Contemporary problems of racism and colonialism might seem to suggest the existence of clear-cut criteria according to which the frivolous redress movement may be separated from the worthy. One might, for instance, distinguish claims animated by lingering, and perhaps unwarranted, perceptions of disrespect from those that aim to confront actual contemporary experiences of racism. From this perspective, the Italian-and Ukrainian-Canadian redress claims might be viewed as unjustified to the extent that group members do not face forms of disrespect that include direct instances of public discrimination or racist threats. But it is important to understand that citizens may also find their equality hampered by a comparatively benign form of subordinate status. In the words of Thomas Hobbes (1991), "to neglect is to Dishonour" (p. 64).

Because Canadian citizenship so often revolves around questions of French-English dualism, other ethnic groups may find their collective civic identities collapsed into a near-faceless membership in a larger "English Canada." As former Liberal MP Sergio Marchi has objected, "not all the people of this country have been dealt the same constitutional card, nor have they been equally credited with being a dignified and contributing part of this country" (in Cairns, 1995, p. 124). This problem of civic recognition is key to redress politics. By demonstrating the role of past experiences of racism in producing movements that are dedicated to building a healthier future, these campaigns aim to establish their traditionally overlooked constituencies as the "founding peoples" of a better Canada.

The tendency of historical patterns of inequality to furnish some groups of citizens with more promising bases of civic respect than others poses a problem that the government and citizens of Canada, if they take the notion of equal participation seriously, have a responsibility to consider. However, many Canadians seem increasingly inclined to deny the relevance of his-

torical injustices to the practice of contemporary citizenship. An angry right-wing populism, whose slogan is "equal rights for all, special rights for none," rails against what it sees as a divisive preoccupation with the past. Wondering whether "anyone [has] told France that England is sorry it burned Joan of Arc?" ("Good guys," 1991, p. 100), the neoconservatives mutter darkly about a wrong-headed fixation on "long-forgotten administrations" (Drache, 1990, p. 85) and "claims that go back to the Dark Ages" (Philip, 1990, p. 94). Some opponents of the Nisga'a land-claim deal reveal a similar zeal to forget the history of a country that is barely 130 years old. They pose as defenders of "the integrity of Canadian democracy" (Lautens, 1998, p. A23) by contrasting the "Pandora's box . . . of attempting to resolve historical 'wrongs'" with the justice of living "as equals without special status for anyone" (Lipsey, 1998, p. A10).

When offered in relation to First Nations issues, the suggestion that the past has no moral bearing on our present belies a self-serving indifference toward the contemporary outcome of a legacy of conquest. More generally, the insistence that past wrongs are unreasonable items of political discussion involves a refusal to confront historically derived civic problems of undue neglect, misrecognition, and stigmatization. To the degree that it is through participation in democracy that we shape our futures, these problems carry an importance that goes far beyond psychological issues of self-esteem.

Enjoying the benefits of equal citizenship depends, in an important and often unacknowledged sense, on being able to command the positive regard of others. Without this crucial prerequisite of successful interaction, the civic arena is a remarkably intimidating and in extreme cases even an unthinkable forum to enter. Demands from redress movements that Canada must revisit unflattering episodes and practices from its past thus afford an opportunity. This opportunity is to seek to realize in a more thorough and inclusive manner the potential of citizenship, which is the most basic instrument of solidarity that Canadians have.

In David Taras and Beverly Rasporich (Eds). 2001. *Passion for identity: Canadian studies for the 21st century*, 4th Canadian edition, 40–7. Toronto: Thomson Nelson.

NOTES

1. This article is a revised, edited, and updated version of "Redress Politics and Canadian Citizenship," which appeared in *Canada, The State of the Federation 1998/99: How Canadians Connect*, eds. Harvey Lazar and Tom McIntosh (Montreal and Kingston: McGill-Queen's University Press, 1999), pp. 247–82.

2. The following analysis is indebted to Cairns ("Whose Side Is the Past On?" in *Reconfigurations*, 1995) and to Strong-Boag (1994).

3. For example, the Price-Waterhouse accounting firm has estimated that the federal government confiscated $450 million in current dollars from interned Japanese Canadians (Miki and Kobayashi, 1991, p. 93).

4. On these latter objections, see Hobsbawm, 1988, pp. 297–99.

REFERENCES

"Abuse claims swamp Ottawa." (1999, January 1). *Canadian News Facts*, p. 5802.

Anderssen, Erin. "Natives to get $200-million fund." (1997, December 16). *The Globe and Mail*, p. A1.

———, and Edward Greenspon. "Federal apology fails to mollify native leaders." (1998, January 8). *The Globe and Mail*, p. A4.

"Apologize for residential schools says Indian leader." (1997, March). *The First Perspective*, p. 1.

Assembly of First Nations. *Breaking the silence: An interpretive study of residential school impact and healing as illustrated by the stories of First Nations individuals*. (1994). Ottawa: First Nations Health Commission.

Aubry, Jack. "'Atrocities' alleged in mission schools." (1994a, August 8). *Vancouver Sun*, p. A1.

———. "Compensation urged for 'coercive' move of Inuit to High Arctic." (1994b, July 14). *Vancouver Sun*, p. A6.

Barnsley, Paul. "Healing foundation making decisions." (1999, June). *Windspeaker*, p. 10.

———. "Apology, a compromise." (1998a, February). *Windspeaker*, p. 4.

———. "Gathering strength not strong enough." (1998b, February). *Windspeaker*, p.3.

Bell, Stewart. "Abuse claims soar in wake of apology." (1998, January 27). *Vancouver Sun*, p. A1.

Bolan, Kim. "Chinese group asks UN to act on redress." (1995, March 22). *Vancouver Sun*, p. B3.

———. "Liberal's refusal to redress head tax 'betrays' Chinese-Canadians' trust." (1994, December 15). *Vancouver Sun*, p. A3.

Bolaria, B. Singh, and Peter S. Li. *Racial oppression in Canada*. 2nd ed. (1988). Toronto: Garamond Press.

Bourdieu, Pierre. *Outline of a theory of practice*. (1977). Trans. Richard Nice. Cambridge: Cambridge University Press.

Cairns, Alan C. *Reconfigurations: Canadian citizenship and constitutional change*. (1995). Ed. Douglas E. Williams. Toronto: McClelland and Stewart.

———. *Disruptions: Constitutional struggles, from the Charter to Meech Lake*. (1991). Ed. Douglas E. Williams. Toronto: McClelland and Stewart.

———. (1989). Political science, ethnicity, and the Canadian Constitution. In David

Shugarman and Reg Whitaker (eds.), *Federalism and political community: Essays in honour of Donald Smiley* (pp. 113–40). Peterborough, Ont.: Broadview Press.

Canada. Ministry of Canadian Heritage. Ministry of Canadian Heritage News Release. (1994, December 14). "Sheila Finestone tables and sends letter on redress to ethnocultural organizations."

Chinese Canadian National Council. *It is only fair! Redress for the Head Tax and Chinese Exclusion Act.* (1988a). Toronto: Chinese Canadian National Council.

———. *Then, now and tomorrow.* (1988b). N.p.

Civil Liberties Commission of the Ukrainian Canadian Committee. Presentation to the House of Commons Standing Committee on Multiculturalism. (1987, August 12). *Minutes of proceedings and evidence.* No. 11. Ottawa: Queen's Printer.

Dafoe, Christopher. Lining up for compensation. (1994). In Lubomyr Luciuk (ed.), *Righting an injustice: The debate over redress for Canada's first national internment operations* (pp. 40–41). Toronto: The Justinian Press.

Dafoe, John. "The cash that heals wounds." (1994, August 19). *Winnipeg Free Press*, p. A6.

de Santis, Agata. "Canada's unknown PoWs." (1997, April 14). *Montreal Gazette*, p. A4.

Drache, Arthur. "Little basis for redress of long past injustices." (1990, September 6). *Financial Post* (Toronto). Rpt. in Luciuk (ed.), *Righting an injustice*, (pp. 84–85).

Ferguson, Eva, and Jim Cunningham. "Ukrainians to get federal hearing." (1997, February 1). *Calgary Herald*, p. B7.

Fournier, Suzanne. "Abused Natives seek $1 billion." (1997, December 4). *Province* (Vancouver), p. A3.

"Give us strength." (1998, February). *Windspeaker*, p. 6.

Goode, William J. *The celebration of heroes: Prestige as a social control system.* (1978). Berkeley: University of California Press.

"Good guys." (1991, May 23). *Ottawa Sun*. Rpt. in Luciuk (ed.), *Righting an injustice* (p. 100).

Gummerson, Penny. "Residential school inquiry releases report." (1997, July). *Raven's Eye*, p. 3.

"Hefty price tag delays settlements." (1993, June 1). *Calgary Herald*, p. A12.

Hobbes, Thomas. *Leviathan.* (1991). Ed. Richard Tuck. Cambridge: Cambridge University Press.

Hobsbawm, E.J. *The Age of Revolution: 1789–1848.* (1988). London: Cardinal.

Johnston, Darlene. First Nations and Canadian Citizenship. In William Kaplan (ed.), *Belonging: The meaning and future of Canadian citizenship* (pp. 349–367). Montreal: McGill-Queen's University Press.

Laghi, Brian. "Residential school left lasting scars." (1998, January 8). *The Globe and Mail* (Toronto), p. A4.

Lautens, Trevor. "Let's preserve the integrity of Canadian democracy." (1998, August 1). *Vancouver Sun*, p. A23.

Lazaruk, Susan. "77-year-old pedophile sentenced to 11 years." (1995, June). *Windspeaker*, p. 3.

Lipsey, Adrian. [Letter]. (1998, July 28). *Vancouver Sun*, p. A10.

Lowi, Emanuel. "A shameful episode." (1996, April 6). *Montreal Gazette*, p. B5.

Luciuk, Lubomyr. "Time to correct injustice." (1994, October 17). *Winnipeg Free Press*, p. A7.

Marcus, Alan R. *Out in the cold: The legacy of Canada's Inuit relocation experiment in the High Arctic.* (1992). Copenhagen: International Work Group for Indigenous Affairs.

McEvoy, F.J. "'A symbol of racial discrimination': The Chinese Immigration Act and Canada's relations with China, 1942–1947." (1982). *Canadian Ethnic Studies* 3:14, pp. 24–42.

Miki, Roy, and Cassandra Kobayashi, eds. *Justice in our time: The Japanese Canadian redress settlement.* (1991). Vancouver: Talon Books.

———. *Justice in our time: Redress for Japanese Canadians.* (1988). Vancouver: National Association of Japanese Canadians.

Miller, J.R. *Shingwauk's vision: A history of Native residential schools.* (1996). Toronto: University of Toronto Press.

Mulroney, Brian. (1990). "Notes for an address by Prime Minister Brian Mulroney to the National Congress of Italian Canadians and the Canadian Italian Business Professional Association."

———. (1988). "Notes for an address by the Right Honourable Brian Mulroney, P.C., M.P., Prime Minister of Canada, on Japanese-Canadian Redress."

National Association of Japanese Canadians. Presentation to the House of Commons Standing Committee on Multiculturalism. (1986, May 27). *Minutes of proceedings and evidence.* No. 9. Ottawa: Queen's Printer.

———. *Democracy betrayed: The case for redress.* (1984). Vancouver: National Association of Japanese Canadians.

National Congress of Italian Canadians. *A national shame: The internment of Italian Canadians.* (1990). N.p.

O'Neil, Peter. "Natives say Ottawa's apology may sway judges in civil suits." (1998, January 8). *Vancouver Sun*, p. A1.

Omatsu, Maryka. *Bittersweet passage: Redress and the Japanese Canadian experience.* (1992). Toronto: Between the Lines.

Oskaboose, Gilbert. "To the Government of Canada." (1996, December). *The First Perspective*, p. 4.

"Ottawa acknowledges mistakes." (1998, February). *Windspeaker*, p. 2.

Philip, Tom. "Haunted by history: Ukrainians, Italians and Chinese seek redress for histori-

cal ill-treatment by Ottawa." (1990, December 17). *Alberta Report.* Rpt. in Luciuk (ed.), *Righting an injustice* (pp. 93–96).

"Post no bills." (1988, November 10). *Ottawa Sun.* Rpt. in Luciuk (ed.), *Righting an injustice* (p. 50).

Ramirez, Bruno. Ethnicity on trial: The Italians of Montreal and the Second World War. (1988). In *On guard for thee: War, ethnicity, and the Canadian state, 1939–1945.* Eds. Norman Hillmer et al. (pp. 71–84). Ottawa: Minister of Supply and Services.

"Residential schools: A sad history of abuse." (1998, January 8). *Vancouver Sun*, p. A3.

Royal Commission on Aboriginal Peoples. *The High Arctic relocation: Summary of supporting information.* (1994). Vol. 1. Ottawa: Minister of Supply and Services.

Simpson, Jeffrey. "The trouble with trying to compensate groups for historical wrongs." (1990, June 14). *The Globe and Mail* (Toronto). Rpt. in Luciuk (ed.), *Righting an injustice* (pp. 78–79).

Steffenhagen, Janet. "Apology to abused Natives elicits powerful emotions." (1998, January 8). *Vancouver Sun*, p. A3.

Stewart, Jane. "Statement of reconciliation: Learning from the past." (1998, January 8). Rpt. in *The Globe and Mail* (Toronto), p. A19.

Strong-Boag, Veronica. "Contested space: The politics of Canadian memory." (1994). *Journal of the Canadian Historical Association* 5: 3–17.

Taylor, Charles. Shared and divergent values. (1991). In Ronald L. Watts and Douglas M. Brown (eds.), *Options for a new Canada.* (pp. 53–76). Toronto: University of Toronto Press.

Thompson, John Herd. The enemy alien and the Canadian general election of 1917. (1983). In Frances Swyripa and John Herd Thompson (eds.), *Loyalties in conflict: Ukrainians in Canada during the Great War* (pp. 25–46). Edmonton: Canadian Institute of Ukrainian Studies.

"Ukraine: In the shadow of Lenin: 'enemy aliens' remember." (1988, October 8). *Edmonton Journal*, p. F5.

Ukrainian Canadian Civil Liberties Association. *A time for atonement*. (1988). N.p.

Weaver, Sally M. *Making Canadian Indian policy: The hidden agenda, 1968–70*. (1981). Toronto: University of Toronto Press.

Weiner, Gerry. (1988). "Speaking notes for the Honourable Gerry Weiner, Minister of State for Multiculturalism and Citizenship, at the Japanese Canadian Redress Agreement press conference."

Wong, Victor Yukmun. "An old wrong stays wrong." (1995, January 13). *Vancouver Sun*, p. A15.

KEY AND DIFFICULT WORDS

Define the following, using context or other clues if possible: **stigmatization, internment, rebuff, buttress, onerous, atonement, enfranchisement.**

QUESTIONS

1. Explain how the author uses his introduction to lay out a framework, or structure, for the essay that follows. Do you think it was necessary to do this? Can you identify a thesis or essay plan?

2. Drawing on at least two passages in the introductory section, address the main purpose of the essay (i.e., is it argumentative or expository?). Would you say that James's claim is one of fact, value, or policy?

3. What is "'symbolic capital' of honour" (first mentioned in paragraph 4)? Define this term, using your own words.

4. James's focus is not exclusively, or perhaps even primarily, on the Japanese-Canadian redress experience. Why do you think, then, that he uses it as his first example (paragraph 3) and refers to it so often?

5. How does James respond to the claim of critics that redress campaigns "'open old wounds'" (paragraph 1 of "Redress and citizenship inclusion"). Summarize his one-paragraph response in one or two sentences.

6. Of the kinds of evidence that James uses, which do you consider the most important: (a) the words of the survivors and victims of a stigmatized group; (b) studies in books and journal articles; (c) government and/or redress group sources; or (d) contemporary newspaper sources? Pick one of the categories above, and being as specific as possible through the use of examples, explain how it is important to his overall argument; in addition, identify it as either a primary or a secondary source.

7. (a) Why do you think that James decided to organize information by topic (as indicated by the essay's descriptive headings) rather than by redress group (for

example, Japanese Canadians, Chinese Canadians)? (b) Why does the author choose to depart from his main organizational method to devote a long separate section to the residential-schools campaign before his conclusion?

8. Identify the analogy used in paragraphs 26, 28, and 31. Do you think it is a suitable and effective analogy?

9. Focusing on the last three paragraphs, critically evaluate the ending of James's essay. Do you consider his ending strong and successful? Why or why not?

COLLABORATIVE ACTIVITY

Do you agree with James that monetary restitution is a key part of redress settlements, not only for practical reasons but also for symbolic ones (see paragraphs 25–6)? How central should the issue of financial settlement be in future negotiations? Debate or discuss answers to these questions.

ACTIVITIES

1. Compose a timeline that includes the major events in the racist treatment of Aboriginal people in Canada by the imposition of the residential-schools policy; consider the significant responses of both the government and Aboriginal communities, and ensure that you include any updates since James published his essay (2001). *OR* Compose a timeline that includes the major events in the racist treatment of Chinese Canadians by the imposition of the head tax in the early 1900s up to the present day, including any updates since James published his essay.

2. Using as your writing model either the editorial or the letter to the editor, respond to one or more of the issues that James raises in his essay (remember that an editorial will employ reason and objectivity to reach a consensus; a letter to the editor may be more subjective—still, you should avoid the perception of bias).

3. Interview an individual who is a member of one of the racial or cultural groups referred to in the essay (or of any minority group)—this could be a friend or a member of your family. Address questions relating to James's points about contemporary citizenship. (Of course, the interviewee need not have had any direct experience with the issues James discusses.) What conclusions can be drawn from the interview? Did the person's responses change your own views or perspective in any way?

Related reading: Gidengil et al. "Enhancing democratic citizenship."

Media and Image

The future's books from nowhere

Hal Niedzviecki

(1,350 words)

Humber College's 2005 inaugural summer course in book publishing ended with an assignment: Develop a publishing business. Students were given a budget and asked to come up with a theoretical yet viable publishing model, including a sample catalogue of titles, the covers of those titles, how the titles will be marketed and publicized, and a detailed budget showing expenditures and predicted income. Finally, the student groups were told to prepare a presentation to a panel of judges posing as potential investors. The judges, Scott Griffin of House of Anansi Press, Kim McArthur of McArthur & Co. Publishing, and myself, were told to respond to each proposed publishing venture and, finally, pick which house we'd most likely invest in.

As students will always do when they are given a creative exercise rooted in real-world potentialities, they responded with surprisingly professional catalogues, book-jacket designs, and marketing plans. Though the judges had to pick a single winner, all the groups demonstrated sound understanding of the Canadian publishing scene and the fundamentals of book publishing.

In fact, the ideas were so eerily in step with global and domestic publishing trends, these students did more than excel at the exercise. Collectively, they also explored and exposed the future of Canadian books.

So what did these aspiring publishers, mostly in their 20s with a few senior faces among them, tell us about publishing?

Well, the first inescapable fact was that not a single one of those five proposed publishing houses planned to publish fiction. No novels, short stories, and definitely, as Scott Griffin, founder of the world's most lucrative poetry prize pointed out, no poetry.

The utter absence of made-up stories (with the exception of kids' books) reveals several important things about the future of publishing. First, it seems clear that if you want to start a new publishing house in Canada and at least come close to breaking even, starting out publishing fiction is the equivalent of trying to learn how to swim with an anchor chained to your neck. In the real world, publishers big and small have been losing money on fiction for decades. A publishing house announcing it is cutting back on its fiction titles is a regular occurrence. Despite having the lucrative rights to the Harry Potter series in Canada, this summer Vancouver distributor and publisher Raincoast announced it was dramatically reining in its publishing program and letting several editors go. If one of Canada's biggest publishing businesses can't make a go of it as a fiction publisher, then how could we expect new ventures in desperate need of capital to risk their shirts on a product as flaky as the novel?

But this isn't simply a finances argument that ends with the usual pleas for governments to subsidize economically unviable but culturally crucial books of short stories. The deeper truth is more disturbing. Increasingly attuned to the fickle winds of global cultural trends, there is reason to believe that new generations are not excited about a type of writing that resists easy packaging and relies heavily on the dynamics of communities rooted in specific times and places. As the proposed publishing houses dramatically demonstrate, even Cancon is going placeless and faceless.

The five proposed publishing businesses all had, at their core, a rootless universalist ideology—books that could be published and read anywhere. So: a children's press (with an emphasis on "edgy" non-fiction), a travel-books outfit (core product: a series of extreme-sports travel guides), and a publishing house whose business model was to do custom book publishing for corporations and institutions (a money-maker was a glossy picture book celebrating the Canadian anniversary of the domestic division of a global automaker).

Only the two remaining houses took the risk of delving into the murky world of books without pictures, books not utterly rooted in the mores of genre publishing. But these houses, too, focused on universal inchoate trends: One innovative press proposed to focus solely on the search for home; the books would circle around ideas of identity and exile. The lead title was a business book on the philosophy and can-do spirit of an entrepreneur who escaped the Holocaust of the Second World War and rose to international corporate prominence from a new locale in Canada. Other titles included the memoir of a refugee and an anthology of Arctic writing. All good ideas, particularly if you want your books to be as saleable, accessible, and as readable in Poland as they are in Peoria.

The final publishing house proposed to concentrate on serious but edgy non-fiction that would appeal to a trendy, intellectually aware audience mostly in their 20s and 30s. Interestingly enough, many of the proposed books could, with a little tweaking, just as easily have fit into the mandate of the "home" publisher. The lead title was a book about the "new man," shaped by and shaping the world of the metrosexual, to be penned by a well-known newspaper columnist. In addition, this house planned to devote considerable resources to gorgeous coffee-table books, such as one chronicling the worst architectural follies of all time.

All the presentations were sound, their economics theoretically viable, the cover designs and PowerPoint displays excellent. But when it came time to choose a winner, I couldn't help feeling defeated by the—not exactly the emptiness of the books to be published, but the rootlessness, the sense that the best and brightest soon to be attaining employment in Canadian publishing have their faces turned to a distant sun whose warm, golden glow promises more than the coming frost of yet another scarce winter in the hyper-boreal.

The last thing I would do is blame these students. They are clearly bright and bold and capable of getting the most out of a well-designed crash course in book publishing. So who to blame for a generation that doesn't want to publish fiction because they realize that the most saleable stories will be those with an international cosmopolitan interior coated with a quick veneer of Cancon?

For some time now, it's been argued that Canadian fiction publishers need to step up to the challenge of engaging new generations of readers who live in an urban, multi-ethnic, pop-culture-attuned Canada. The authors are out there, and if you look you'll find them, but so far publishers haven't found a way to connect younger readers to that talent. This country's equivalents to Jonathan Safran Foer, Zadie Smith, Michel Houellebecq, and Haruki Murakami are serving coffee at Starbucks as CanLit relentlessly rewards mediocrity in the form of poetic lyricism obscuring soap-opera plots and parochial perceptions. Though attempts have been made, Canadian fiction continues to lose ground, and culturally aware twentysomethings are increasingly attuned to international imports.

We see the result—and the future—in this student exercise. Canadian publishing will fall easily into step with the rest of the multinational corporate publishers who see books as a peripherally profitable sub-genre of entertainment. Books will capitalize on trends—not create them. Clever ideas and excellent packages will dominate, but only occasionally will real depth and substance—what books give us that no other medium offers—emerge. As the giants of CanLit retire, they'll be replaced by their non-fiction facsimiles.

In the end, we chose the metrosexual/bad architecture house as the winner. We all agreed that if we were real investors looking to make money, this would be the worst house to invest in. But we were won over not so much by the slick video presentation and crafty, diverting ideas (both were apparent) but by the passion and enthusiasm this student team brought to their venture. If there's any hope that a different future for Canadian publishing may yet emerge, it's that these students will learn to be passionate not just about the globally transparent but about the stubbornly, opaquely local as well. As my fellow judges have amply demonstrated over the years, for the best publishers, passion is always more important than profit. It's fervour bordering on obsession that ultimately transcends trend and keeps the hope of a vibrant, important Canadian literature alive.

The Globe and Mail. 2005. 13 October.

KEY AND DIFFICULT WORDS
Define the following, using context or other clues if possible: **Cancon, mores, parochial.**

QUESTIONS
1. Using a reliable Canadian resource, write a one-paragraph biography of the author in your own words and naming your source(s).
2. What is the nature of Niedzviecki's involvement in the class project he writes about and in the Canadian literary scene? Does he appear to exhibit any bias in the essay?
3. Why might it be effective for the author to use students and their final project in a publishing course to set up his claim about the future of fiction in Canada rather than directly stating his concerns?
4. Paraphrase the important passage that begins, "The deeper truth is more disturbing" (paragraph 7).

5. Who does Niedzviecki ultimately blame for the student focus on quick-sell marketability? What is Niedzviecki's prediction for the future of Canadian publishing?
6. Do you believe that the author successfully avoids turning his essay into a polemic (a harsh criticism) against the publishing industry and Canadian readers? Point to specific passages in your answer.
7. What was the reasoning of the judges in choosing the competition winner?

COLLABORATIVE ACTIVITIES

1. Do you believe that the publication of genres outside of non-fiction is doomed in Canada? Should steps be taken to prevent this? What steps are possible? Discuss.
2. It is necessary more than ever that Canadian governments establish firm guidelines for Canadian content to ensure the viability of Canadian art. Debate the validity of this statement as it applies generally to various forms of Canadian media or to one specific genre, such as music, film, or books.

ACTIVITIES

1. Do an Internet search on one of the writers mentioned in the third-last paragraph to determine why Niedzviecki used him or her as an example of the kind of writer Canadian publishers could use to engage "new generations of readers."
2. Find the website of a Canadian book publisher whose list includes at least some fiction or poetry. The object is to determine both its general publishing program (i.e., what kinds of books—for example, what genres—are published) and the promotional strategy (i.e., what kinds of books are the most prominent in the catalogue). The general publishing program can often be determined by examining the publisher's on-line catalogue, reading the home page, or following a link like "About us." Books promoted are often listed on the publisher's home page or can be found by following a link like "Current titles" or "New and noteworthy." Write a formal or a briefer informal report in which you discuss the results of your findings. How well are fictional/poetic works promoted? You could also analyze the accessibility, comprehensiveness, and visual appeal of the website itself. Examples of larger Canadian publishers include McClelland and Stewart, Penguin Canada, and Raincoast Books. Note: Scholarly presses, such as Oxford University Press, seldom publish fiction.

Related reading: Stephen Henighan. "White curtains."

A box full of history:
TV and our sense of the past

Robert Fulford

(2,800 words)

On television one recent evening, Buddy Rich (1917–87) was playing a solo as the other musicians in his band sat in patient silence, watching the master work. A drum solo can be mind-numbing, a senseless demonstration of ego and physical strength that quickly exhausts the patience of the audience. Or it can be, in the hands of a virtuoso like Rich, four or five minutes of ecstatic concentration, a sweet abandonment of self, a noisy cousin of Zen meditation.

The good drum solo stands outside the normal boundaries of music in a place all its own, beyond tonality, a separate realm of rhythm and sound dynamics. It abandons notes, chords, and melodies in favour of a structure that the drummer designs spontaneously, inventing his own logic and creating his own momentum as he goes. The great drummers ignore the audience when working, losing themselves in the ingenious deployment of their muscles as they rush down the baroque corridors of their own architecture. But even as the drummer forgets us, we realize that this event contains powerful elements of the visual. Who can watch it without enjoying the look of the equipment that the musician coaxes to life? Who can ignore the light that dances off the Zildjian cymbals or the exuberant chromium on the rims of the drums? The Cubist complexities of the drum set, with its primitive lever-and-gear technology, slowly reveal themselves under the scrutiny of the camera, making a drum solo perfect television.

Intensity rises and falls as the performer drives us through climaxes and anticlimaxes, great thunderous bursts alternated with feathery passages so delicate that they walk up to the very edge of silence before coming back to us. The drum solo, when it works, amounts to a one-player drama that subsumes all the performer's talents in a single wordless narrative, emerging as exquisite theatre.

All of this Buddy Rich, dead now for 18 years, delivered to my bedroom, unannounced as usual. Pushing the buttons on my remote-control wand, I stumbled on the solo just as it began. Where was this tape made? When? As so often happens, television did not tell me. The musician's clothes suggested it was around 1980, when Rich was in his sixties, still working, a marvel of energy and survival in a profession that killed many before their time.

Television didn't pause to celebrate this miracle and didn't seem interested in the fact that it was showing us a piece of cultural history. In truth, it seems possible that the people who run television are a little ashamed of the old tapes and films they replay, as if anything less than new carried a stigma. They haven't yet developed a sub-profession of broadcasting scholars to explain the date, provenance, and context of whatever appears on the screen. The television people are unaware that a great museum of history has fallen into their hands. It will be some time before they understand the opportunities and duties this inheritance brings with it.

A sense of the past has become one of the great gifts of television and one for which I grow steadily more grateful. Only 20 years ago it was commonplace to argue that television was creating a present-tense society in which memory lost meaning. No one could say that now. A multitude of channels, rerunning the triumphs and disasters of the past, provides viewers of the early twenty-first century with a visual history that was available to no previous generation.

History is always with us on television: soldiers storming the beaches of Normandy, the caisson carrying John Kennedy's body to Arlington, the student defying the tank in Tiananmen Square, the Berliners turning their hated wall into fragments for sale to tourists, O.J. Simpson getting away with murder before our eyes. Television displays, perhaps with even more effectiveness, another kind of history, the texture of life as lived 50 or 60 years ago. It plucks out of the past all the details no one thought important at the time, details we now view with the fascination of amateur anthropologists.

Once upon a time, public events possessed a grave formality: congressional hearings, plays, and office work all required that men show up in jackets and ties; a law, apparently, decreed that men on the street must wear fedoras at all times. Houses in situation comedies were all designed in the same style, more or less up-to-date and certainly with huge windows. In that distant era, many of the most beautiful women were heavy by twenty-first century standards, their faces heavily made up.

Television delivers a third kind of history with even more effectiveness, the history of itself. As it grows older and the channels grow more numerous, television turns increasingly to its vaults. This means that I can turn on television at an odd moment, perhaps while getting dressed in the morning, and find myself transfixed by a black and white production of *The cocktail party*, by T.S. Eliot, a now-forgotten play

that was once taken seriously as a Christian exploration of contemporary sensibility. As the work of a mid-century intellectual, it naturally deals with both psychiatry and martyrdom.

This production is from 1960, which means there was no videotape yet. We watch a kinescope, an always murky kind of early recording. We find the CBC drama department at its most self-conscious and serious, when it believed its duty was to display the "important" plays of the era before a mass audience. It might have been tedious when it first appeared; now it has the patina and charm of age. It speaks more of anglophile Canada 45 years ago than of Christianity or even Eliot; there are seven principal actors, each of them bearing a name from the British Isles. The late Jane Mallett is in the cast, her mannered performance rendered historic rather than annoying. The youngish-looking man is William Hutt, 40 years old. He's not yet Canada's favourite Lear or Tartuffe. He's sharp and sardonic in his self-absorbed way.

Moments like this give entertainment a stimulating dimension of time. We can now see television in layers, noting differences in performance, content, and above all pacing (everything was much slower then, from the commercials to the movement of cameras and the editing). The situation of television has slowly come to resemble the context in which we understand printed material; we can begin to compare one era's ideas with another, laugh at or respect our ancestors as we reinterpret what they believed according to our own knowledge and sensibility. Our understanding of the people we watch naturally colours our responses. When Judy Garland sang "The battle hymn of the republic" on her program the week after John F. Kennedy's murder, she looked grave and resolute. Today, watching the same performance, knowing that she died just six years later, we may see little but her fragility, her wan attempt to hide desperation behind the courage that the moment required.

For those who want it, this kind of experience grows more available with every season, on channels like Bravo, History, BookTelevision, the Documentary Channel, CoolTV, the Independent Film Channel, and the multitude of channels devoted to old films. Elsewhere ancient TV series reappear, from "I love Lucy" to "The Rockford files," displaying tastes and habits that the old have mostly forgotten and the young never knew.

Lately I've discovered a British series called "Playing Shakespeare" in which John Barton of the Royal Shakespeare Company works through a few scenes with half a dozen actors. Together they unlock a text, discovering what words and phrases to stress, where to breathe, what meaning Shakespeare encoded in the words, how the actors should react to each other. Barton comes across as a master teacher and a bit of a TV star (like Buddy Rich, he forgets the camera). What makes this historic is that the lessons take place in 1982 and the actors he works with—Ben Kingsley, Judi Dench, Ian McKellan—are among the best of their generation, all caught relatively early in their distinguished careers. It offers a privileged glimpse of a long-ago reality.

Ancient public affairs programs have a similar effect. In the 1950s and 1960s, Nathan Cohen chaired "Fighting words," a kind of intellectual argument that appeared on the CBC late on Sunday afternoon, bringing with it an astonishing parade of artists and heavy thinkers, from Morley Callaghan to Hannah Arendt to Isaiah Berlin. These programs, showing up now on BookTelevision, provide delightful (sometimes) glimpses of what Canadians thought was important two generations ago. Occasionally I have even come upon my young self pontificating for

the "Fighting words" audience on some now antique topic. To my horror, I once saw myself pause self-importantly, in mid-oration, to light a cigarette. Well, I was young. So was television.

In 1950 the radio critic of the London *Daily Mail* (a newspaper never considered a world-beater) wrote that "Television is the biggest time-waster ever invented. . . . People will sit watching for hours—even when they don't care much for the programmes they're viewing. . . . It's so easy to sink into an armchair and switch on entertainment until bedtime." He wanted a royal commission set up to investigate the "hypnotic effect." Poor man, he had no idea of the horrors to come. At that moment there was only one channel in England, operated by the BBC.

In the spring of 1961, Newton Minow, a previously little-known lawyer, became a celebrity by denouncing American television. As Kennedy's newly appointed chairman of the Federal Communications Commission, he was addressing a convention of the National Association of Broadcasters. He told them that when television is good it's powerful and eloquent, "But when television is bad, nothing is worse. I invite you to sit down in front of your television set when your station goes on the air and . . . keep your eyes glued to that set until the station signs off." The fact that no one uses television this way didn't discourage him. He believed he had articulated an important point. He told the broadcasters they would see a procession of game shows, violence, audience participation shows, formula comedies about totally unbelievable families, more violence, etc.

"I can assure you that you will observe a vast wasteland."

That phrase went into the dictionaries of quotations and in later years achieved even more eminence by becoming the basis of questions on

"Jeopardy!," "Trivial pursuit," and "Who wants to be a millionaire?" For years no one spoke of TV without using the word "wasteland." Minow set the tone for respectable attitudes to television. He made it acceptable for just about anyone to look down on it. The intellectually stunted, the emotionally dead, the culturally blind: they can all take a superior position when giving their views on television.

To this day, newspaper columnists who may not have had a fresh thought in decades nevertheless feel licensed to tell us that TV is worthless. They know we would be astonished if they told us anything else. Those who write regularly about television are unique among critics, being the only reviewers assigned to analyze what they find inherently despicable. They believe themselves severely put upon, and they make their readers (not to mention the broadcasters) suffer for the pain and indignity they must endure while watching programs beneath their contempt.

In order to maintain this stance, one must ignore much of television and concentrate only on current programs, if possible the worst of those—the "reality" shows are a mine of inspiration for those seeking the pleasures of chronic disapproval. Meanwhile, many of us are looking elsewhere, happily exploring the history that television so generously provides.

The most interesting moments retrieved from the past are often the result of happy accidents, the work of unsung heroes in archives departments who had the sense to keep the kinescopes or videotapes in a safe place until someone recognized their value. This is not, of course, the history that television celebrates. Pious television executives and bureaucrats like to lecture us on history as something we are compelled, out of duty, to absorb in its quasi-official form. What they admire, and vigorously sell, are programs that in structure parallel the books they studied in school—programs that select some

choice theme for examination and then deliver it coherently to the audience, if possible with an actual book published as a tie-in.

In their lectures on the significance of whatever self-conscious history programs they have just made, TV people like to quote George Santayana's "Those who cannot remember the past are condemned to repeat it," possibly the most fatuous of all contemporary mantras. Teachers, journalists, and textbook publishers use Santayana to intimidate those who are not yet impressed by the Federalist Papers or the BNA Act. But anyone who thinks about it for a moment will see the flaw in Santayana's claim. Some of the great figures of recent times, such as Winston Churchill and Harry Truman, were devoted students of history, yet they were condemned to repeat the disasters of war, though of course with variations. Surely there was never a generation more learned in history than the young men who graduated from Oxford and Cambridge in the early years of the twentieth century; and they went off to die needlessly and (some would say) thoughtlessly in the trenches of the First World War.

Yet we persist in arguing for history on instrumental grounds, as if it will help us avoid future peril. Governments and public broadcasters have other demands to make on it; they expect history to buttress national spirit, justify our system of government, fill us with something like civic pride. This impulse leads to a demagogic assertion that Canada's history is, as many popular historians argue, "just as exciting and interesting as anyone else's," which would be an invitation to ribald laughter if Canadians had not silently agreed to hear all such nonsense with solemn faces. That argument is usually made by someone trying to sell a book, justify a TV budget, or set up a new curriculum. In no other circumstances would it be possible to suggest that a history that lacks a Napoleon or a Lincoln or a Churchill is just as interesting as a history that possesses such figures.

The national and educational arguments for history as a source of social improvement are made during the promotion of programs such as "The Civil War," the 1990 series Ken Burns made for Public Television in the US, or "Canada: A people's history," which Mark Starowicz produced five years ago for the CBC. These can be good programs, but they have the disadvantage of embodying a past that's been processed by professors and broadcasters. "Canada: A people's history," for all its virtues, teaches us that from the beginning Canada has been a land of conned and defeated populations, a sea-to-sea convention of losers: natives victimized by whites, French victimized by British, Scots victimized by English (who drove them out of Scotland), and of course everyone victimized by the Americans. As the list of the oppressed grows, from program to program, a viewer may wonder how it happened that these wretched and demoralized people ended up owning a country rich enough to pay for "Canada: A people's history."

That approach to our history no doubt deserves airing, but the CBC distributes it without any indication of its flaws, as the only ambitious account of our past delivered by our broadcasters in this generation. I would not like to have missed it; but as I watched it I realized that almost every incident it portrays could have been shown from an entirely different perspective, or perhaps several different perspectives. This is the problem that never fails to arise with big-budget network history in the manner of Burns or Starowicz.

Another kind of history, unmediated and unpromoted, freed from committees and consultants, reaches us in the spaces between significant programming. It comes to us routinely and offhandedly, in romances that are at least half true to their period, in TV serials that try to create period tone (like "Little house on the prairie" or "Anne of Green Gables"), in war stories that at least suggest the nature of military life.

Santayana had it wrong when he suggested history could help us frame our future. Knowing it probably won't help us avoid the calamities to come and may not even make us any wiser. Nevertheless, it remains essential. History thickens daily existence and gives life meaning by linking us with chains of ancestors. History, if understood even a little, becomes the background against which we enact our lives. Without some personal sense of history, we work on an empty stage. Television, these days, helps fill that stage with a magnificent array of props.

Queen's Quarterly. 2005. Spring 112 (1).

KEY AND DIFFICULT WORDS

Define the following, using context or other clues if possible: **exuberant, subsume, stigma, patina, anglophile, sardonic, pontificate, oration, fatuous, demagogic, ribald.**

QUESTIONS

1. The words "history" and "TV" both appear in the essay's title. Do you think this essay is more about history or about television?
2. What kind (genre) of essay has Robert Fulford written? How does it exemplify the characteristics of this essay type?

3. Why does the author include the small detail about himself when discussing the public affairs show "Fighting words?"

4. Fulford begins the final main section of his essay by evoking some of TV's critics. How does he undermine their negative comments? Why do you think he does this?

5. The author dismisses "'reality'" shows with little comment. Do you think that if he reread his essay in 20 years, he would feel the same about them? Why might his views change?

6. Summarize the way that history is presented by professors, broadcasters, and TV executives, according to Fulford. What is wrong with this presentation?

7. Why does the author focus on "Canada: A people's history" as an example near the end of his essay?

8. For about how many years has the author been watching TV? How do you know this? Are his approach and his perceptions relevant to younger generations of TV viewers? Why or why not?

COLLABORATIVE ACTIVITIES

1. Are "reality" shows being unfairly picked on by media commentators? You could consider Fulford's statement that they "are a mine of inspiration for those seeking the pleasures of chronic disapproval." Discuss their value.

2. Fulford talks about one particular use for TV that he has found rewarding. In your opinion, do the positive aspects of TV outweigh the negative ones? Debate this question, first discussing what some of these positive and negative characteristics are.

ACTIVITIES

1. Fulford addresses several of what he might call myths about TV and about history. Pick one of these and explain how he critiques or "deconstructs" the myth. Do you agree with his assessment?

2. Select one rerun that you have watched at least a couple of times. Consider what it can show you about the past, and write an analysis of 500 to 600 words on what you can learn from it.

Related reading: Richard Poplak. "Fear and loathing in Toontown."

Fear and loathing in Toontown

Richard Poplak

(1,700 words)

When I was a youngster, I spent the bulk of my Saturday mornings in front of the television, entertained by the hand-drawn shenanigans of a host of animated cartoon characters. I remember so many of them fondly, like family members or good friends: Bugs Bunny, Tweety Bird, Scrooge McDuck, Ronald Reagan. It's only now, armed with the wisdom and hindsight that comes with age, that I realize how dangerous an indulgence this may have been. For this, I have the good Dr James Dobson, founder of Focus on the Family, to thank. He noticed the effete tendencies of a pant-wearing sponge on a video entitled *We are family: A musical message for all*. (The video bears the name of the infamous disco song that hinted at the indiscriminate inclusiveness of vice-ridden dens such as Studio 54.) *We are family* is a video that was distributed to school groups all over the United States, and by all accounts (no, I have not seen it), it can make people either tolerant, open-minded, and/or homosexual. In other words, it's like a chocolate-fudge mousse cake at a Jenny Craig convention—and by that I mean highly dangerous. Dobson, with characteristic sharpness of mind and tongue, has opened up a Pandora's box, and the torrent subsequently unleashed will change the face of popular entertainment. Forever.

Or, at the very least, for several weeks. One thing is certain—the days when the animated community could walk roughshod over our values are fast coming to an end.

Who among us can forget Robert Zemeckis's prescient *Who framed Roger Rabbit?* With great insight, this film portrayed the dark underbelly of a place called Toontown, a Hollywood ghetto where cartoon characters live out a seedy, iniquitous existence. The hero, 'toon-hating Eddie Valiant (Bob Hoskins), must put his principles and very survival at risk by navigating this wacky cesspit to get to the bottom of an atrocious crime. So it is with Dobson and others like him, who so courageously wrestle the animated industry monolith, taking it to task for its indiscretions. Their purpose, as I see it, is simple: to pore over the history and current state of animated entertainment—specifically the widely accessible televised variety—and to call out those who seek to coat the genre with a patina of social and sexual deviance. This is a more difficult undertaking than one might expect, because animators have a powerful weapon in their possession. This formidable apparatus works in a similar manner to Wonder Woman's airplane or Harry Potter's invisibility cloak. It renders certain, let's call them "traits," indiscernible.

This weapon is cuteness.

Put buckteeth, short pants, and a coat of yellow paint on a nuclear bomb, and is it not still a nuclear bomb? The obvious answer is, "Yessir!" But that wouldn't stop us from smiling and waving like idiots as it rocketed downward, about to blow us to Kingdom Come. So it is with cartoon characters. We are blinded by cuteness, and the very traits that make a character either virtuous or insidious are lost on us. We're suckers for fur, a squeaky voice, and big, blinking eyes. Take Robin Williams's recent speech at the Oscar ceremonies, when he suggested that Donald Duck lives what is nowadays dubbed an "alternative lifestyle." Mr Duck is perhaps one of animation's more masculine characters (gruff voice, no-nonsense attitude, Daisy), but Williams's trite punch line—"little sailor's cap, no pants"—brings the issue into sharp focus. One of the foremost problems with our society is that certain subcultures consider it within their rights to appropriate the dress code of certain vocations and pervert them to their own nefarious purposes. (Doubt me? Dare I mention a certain "People" who dwell in a "Village?") Mr Duck dons sailors' apparel, and his very sexuality is open to question by hirsute ex-junkie comedians? Well, excuse Donald for having a job! I happen to have met several individuals who work in seafaring-related capacities—one a midshipman on a pleasure cruiser, the other a ship-in-a-bottle builder. Despite the occasional use of choice verbiage and the odd bout of rowdy behaviour, these gentlemen are straighter than the mizzenmast on Lord Nelson's HMS *Victory*. And since when does wearing no pants necessarily denote homosexuality?

SpongeBob, I should point out, does wear pants. And he's flaming. Clearly we require a system for discerning what constitutes a deviant cartoon character and what doesn't—a frame of reference that allows us the tools to strip away cuteness and interpret the true nature that lies behind it. The dissembling of special-interest groups, animal-rights activists, Hollywood studio honchos, and home-cleaning product manufacturers must not lead us astray. We need to look at the hard facts, and for this we must peer through the dimness of time and arrive at the dawn of the animated age, an era when a duck was a duck and a mouse was a mouse.

The art form did not begin auspiciously. The first de facto animated film is attributed to James Stuart Blackton, an Englishman who made a picture misleadingly entitled *Humorous phases of funny faces*. But it is a Frenchman named Emile Cohl who consensus has dubbed the first of the great animators. In his hoary youth, Monsieur Cohl was a card-carrying member of the Incoherents, a group whose central ethos stated that all is chaos, nightmare, and insanity. How very French. The question, of course, is whether our children should be watching an art form that has such concepts as source material. Yet Cohl is the man we have to thank for quiet Saturday mornings spent reading the paper while our progeny absorbs filth, one painstaking frame at a time.

Things looked up for a while, when a gentleman from Chicago named Walter Elias Disney made his entrance on the scene. For a brief time, Mickey Mouse wrested control of the animated film industry from the freaks and perverts. Sure, when Mickey's voice was first heard on *Steamboat Willie* in 1929, alarmists may have suggested that he sure didn't sound too manly. To them I ask, "Ever heard a basso mouse?" Of course not. They are by nature a falsetto species, God bless their precious little hearts. It is in Mickey's tender, solid relationship with Minnie Mouse that parents can take comfort. This ideal union, based on love, mutual respect, and identically shaped ears, should be an inspiration to us all. Indeed, the entire Disney universe is a panoply of hand-drawn wholesomeness. Whose breast has not swelled with emotion when Snow White is kissed by her Prince Charming, when the Little Mermaid acquires the ability for land-based ambulation, or when Bambi's mother is taken down by an excellently placed high-calibre round to the torso? Although I have always been somewhat uncomfortable with the Pluto/Goofy dichotomy—this I chalk up to a very healthy and well-exercised paranoia—Disney has no flies on its back catalogue. Other studios cannot lay claim to such a spotless record.

Take Warner Brothers, for example. How it has dodged the bullet of mass derision and contempt escapes me. Looney Toons? Try Porney Tunes. The litany of subversive, deviant behaviour extant in the burrows, nests, cages, and treeknots of the Looney Toons universe is astonishing. Bugs Bunny's serial cross-dressing! Co-habiting male chipmunks! Elmer Fudd! And French—there they are again—French skunks! If one employs a discerning Dobsonian eye, the antics of the Looney Toons stable are nothing less than shameful. Despite Chip 'n' Dale—and the issues regarding those two *sciuridae tamias* requires no further discussion—Looney Toons characters don't even restrict their dalliances to the same species! The immense success enjoyed by these cartoons has provided subsequent animators a licence for licentiousness. And they have used it with abandon.

Animation's rap sheet is so lengthy that time and space do not allow for full elucidation. Some examples do, however, strengthen the case: Scooby Doo was nothing more than a drug addict's in-joke. The Teenage Mutant Ninja Turtles? Lord knows you don't keep four teenage boy-turtles cooped up together all the time without adult supervision. *Shrek 2*, as Dobson helpfully points out, is as brash an example of "pro-homosexual activism" as can be found at your neighbourhood Blockbuster. As for Winnie the Pooh—that pantless bear's relationship with Christopher Robin deserves some time under a harsh klieg light. And this brings us to that pantfull sponge, Mr SquarePants himself.

SpongeBob must go, and so too must the host of characters associated with concepts out of step with mainstream beliefs. My suggestion—one I hope to table at an upcoming Focus on Family convention—is to suggest long-time cereal pitch men, such as Toucan Sam, Snap, Crackle and Pop, and Count Chocula, star in their own shows. The reasoning behind this is simple: Instead of promoting gay sex, these hard-working characters have encouraged nothing more than the benefits of a vitamin-enriched, hearty breakfast. This initiative has the added benefit of showing children that we do indeed live in a meritocracy—hard work and consistency (I believe Toucan's been at it for more than five decades) does indeed pave the road to success.

Regardless of what pans out in the future, we must understand that cuteness is often a method of obfuscation. Parents need to remember that just because a character lives in a pineapple, sings songs, and is best friends with a starfish, he should not be free and clear of scrutiny. Dr James Dobson and his fearless congregation have pointed out that Saturday mornings can be the most dangerous time of the week, and as guardians of decency, we must be on the alert for even the slightest signs of excessive tolerance appearing in children's entertainment. Tolerance is fine and dandy to talk about in a classroom setting, but by portraying tolerant attitudes in entertainment, we run the risk of children actually adopting such a mindset. And that won't do. Unless we want the next generation of North American sons doffing sailor's caps (pants optional) without venturing anywhere near the sea, we must cast a constant, unwavering eye on the animated film and television community. SpongeBob has been caught with his pants down. He'd best pull them up quickly and the animated community's socks along with them.

This Magazine. 2005. May/June.

KEY AND DIFFICULT WORDS

Define the following, using context or other clues if possible: **effete, prescient, iniquitous, indiscretion, patina, insidious, nefarious, dissemble, auspicious, progeny, falsetto, panoply, ambulation, derision, litany, dalliance, licentious, meritocracy, obfuscation.**

QUESTIONS

1. How might knowing that *This Magazine* (where "Fear and loathing in Toontown" was first published) bills itself as "the leading alternative Canadian magazine of politics, pop culture, and the arts" affect the way you approach your reading of Poplak's essay?
2. What is Poplak's main purpose in writing: to inform, persuade, or entertain?
3. Irony can be defined as a literary device in which two levels of meaning exist simultaneously, a literal (or surface) meaning and a non-literal (or deeper) meaning. What is the first indication in this essay that Poplak may not be stating exactly what he believes, that there are two levels of meaning in the text? What other "tip-offs" are used in the first few paragraphs? Identify at least two other specific passages in the essay that illustrate irony, identifying both the literal and the non-literal meanings.
4. Comment on Poplak's language and diction. You could consider the level of language: he chooses to include many challenging words, especially words that connote criticism or negativity (e.g., iniquitous, indiscretion, insidious, nefarious, dissemble). You could also consider the significance of specific phrases (e.g., "a midshipman on a pleasure cruiser" in paragraph 4; "an era when a duck was a duck and a mouse was a mouse" in paragraph 5; and "an excellently placed high-calibre round to the torso" in paragraph 7).
5. Why does the author use the chronology method of development in paragraphs 6 and 7? Summarize paragraphs 7 and 8 in which he contrasts two major animation studios.
6. Satire can be defined as a literary genre that employs irony and humour to poke fun at or criticize an individual, group, or society. Satire usually has one or more targets to whom the ridicule or criticism is directed. Whom or what do you consider the target of Poplak's satire?
7. Can you identify a thesis statement in this essay? Hint: Since the author is using an unconventional method to disclose his true thoughts, you could look for a thesis statement in a non-traditional place. What kind of claim does Poplak make? What kind of claim does he purport (pretend) to make?

COLLABORATIVE ACTIVITY

Do you think that television executives have a responsibility to portray positive or mainstream values to their viewers? If not, should any constraints or limits be placed on what appears on prime time TV? Discuss or debate this issue.

ACTIVITIES

1. In one sense, Poplak's essay puts a new spin on an old argument about animated TV shows and movies, which have sometimes been criticized for their extreme violence and possible effect on young children. Comment.
2. Write a letter to the editor or to a television network executive in which you argue that a program or type of program should be taken off the air (of course, you do not have to argue, as Poplak appears to do, that the show is immoral). *OR* Write a critical response to a television show or one particular episode of a show.

Related reading: Robert Fulford. "A box full of history: TV and our sense of the past."

Image world

Michael Posner

(3,300 words)

A picture, according to the old cliché, is worth a thousand words. That is because the message it communicates is unmistakable and instantaneous. We relate to images in more direct ways than we do to words. Words require more work, and we increasingly feel that we are already busy enough simply trying to absorb everything our multimedia world is throwing at us. But unless we take care, we will soon be unable even to imagine that there is anything wrong with this picture.

Not long ago, a friend invited me to accompany him to a Toronto Maple Leafs hockey game at the Air Canada Centre. We had front-row seats behind the goalie, the best in the house. Yet, perversely, I found myself repeatedly glancing up at the vast in-house screen positioned over centre ice. Somehow, the big pixel board seemed to frame the action on the ice in a more optically manageable way. And I wasn't alone; all around me, I noticed, other eyes were doing the same. The gritty, hard-contact reality was right before us, yet we were essentially watching the game on television, exactly as we've been conditioned to do.

Hockey—indeed almost any professional sport today—may be taken as an example of what the late French philosopher Guy Debord called the "triumph of visual spectacle": reality constantly filtered through the distorting prism of contrived images. And it's a pernicious development. It warps our core sensibility, making us confuse the image with the real thing. It forces us to encounter and comprehend our environment indirectly. And—most significantly, perhaps even ominously—it makes all of us easy prey to manipulation—to what Debord termed "hypnotic behaviour."

Consider, for a moment, pornography. Last year, in the US alone, there were more than 700 million rentals of porn videos, roughly two million a day. That figure, incidentally, does not include web-based porn sites (the biggest, most profitable business on the Internet) or pay-per-view movies. At a conservatively estimated $10 billion a year and growing, the American porn industry is now a more lucrative enterprise than professional football, basketball, and baseball—combined. For millions of people, what passes for sexual gratification can only be achieved through the act of watching paid performers do it for them.

"The world of media fantasies is more real than everyday life," writes French philosopher Jean Baudrillard.

> Video or computer games are more compelling than school or work. Porno videos or web sites simulate sex in abstraction from the problems of real relations with others, while simulated environments like Las Vegas, Disney World or shopping malls are cleaner and prettier than the actual world.

According to Baudrillard, "This is the artificial universe of the hyper-real, and the hyper-real is thus the death of the real."

It is no exercise in profundity to say that we now live in what Canadian uber-designer Bruce Mau has termed a "global image economy," a world dominated by the mesmerizing power of the visual. Its principal product and expression, of course, is film—diced, spliced, and rendered in myriad forms: television, movies, video, photography. But Mau's phrase also embraces the iconic phenomenon of branding—goods and services that we instantly identify by virtue of logos, typefaces, and graphic design. Think of Nike's "swoosh," a trademark so universally recognizable that the company's ads no longer need even to use the word "Nike." Think of McDonald's golden arches, or Starbuck's mermaid, or Coca-Cola's flowing red and white script.

Logos, billboards, banks of televisions, video monitors, camcorders, games downloadable to cellphones—one might be forgiven for thinking that the modern world has become afflicted by the tyranny of the visual. The importance of this hegemony ought not to be underestimated or explained away as simply the dominant modality of Western popular culture. Indeed, it *is* the dominant modality of Western popular culture, but its implications transcend the purely cultural.

To keep us interested, and hypnotically responsive, the ante of visual culture is always being raised. Everything, it seems, has been turned into pageant, a distended, mind-numbing, synthetic, high-octane visual glorification. On Broadway, in London's West End, and in other major urban centres, the nightly curtains rise on the theatre of spectacle—enduring megamusicals such as *The Lion King*, *Mamma mia!*, *Aida*. In Cannes, the annual orgiastic prayer rituals in worship of the Armani-suited gods of cinema have recently concluded—although somewhere on the planet, at any given moment, another film festival is opening, closing, or being announced. On any given weekend, before television audiences in the many millions, the sweat-soaked deities of hockey and baseball, tennis and golf perform. This is what professional sport has become—spectacle. In Paris and Milan, New York and London, the paparazzi assemble, jostling to capture stick-thin women draped in the latest absurdities of fashion designers, while their previous creations are being advertised by celebrities at some gala televised awards show, an almost weekly spectacle of self-congratulation.

Even for ordinary Joes and Janes, the modern world more and more resembles a movie set. We take our children to theme parks, a fraudulent, antiseptic universe of enforced gaiety. The highest rated show on TSN is professional wrestling —a two-hour extravaganza of garish costume, dry ice, pounding heavy metal, soap opera, and bad grammar (the scripts right out of some low-budget B-movie) . . . and, of course, 12 minutes of fake fighting. Our political campaigns and conventions, once occasions for legitimate policy debate, have been utterly transformed and devalued, now resembling a cacophonous swirl of balloons, placards, marching bands, and stump speeches, every candidate's appearance carefully programmed for sound bites and the six o'clock news.

More examples? Rock concerts (another venue where more people watch the screen facsimile than the real performer)—elaborate sound and light shows that have less to do with music (ear-shattering regardless) than with the Event. The Olympics, now staggered so that every two years we have a winter or summer fever of nationalism that grips athletes and global television audiences: stirring anthems, flag-raising ceremonies, torch-lit parades. Video games, now a bigger business than the movies, and tutoring an entire generation in the dubious principles of virtual reality. Buses turned mobile billboards. The Rainforest Cafe and comparably themed restaurants. The sham universe of shop-ping malls. It's a Disneyfied World, indeed—one marathon photo opportunity.

In the Nevada desert, an entire city, Las Vegas, has been turned into spectacle, a neon-lit 24-hour wonderland of ersatz experience, complete with fake Eiffel Tower, fake Venetian canals. Annual tourist traffic: roughly 35 million. One of its best draws is a made-in-Canada tenant—Cirque du Soleil, the circus rendered as sumptuous visual feast.

But Las Vegas's virtual city is simply the logical extension of New York City's Times Square, Miami's South Beach, Paris's Champs Élysées, Tokyo's Roppongi, Berlin's Kurfuerstendamm, and the dazzling streetscapes of Hong Kong. According to Princeton professor M. Christine Boyer,

> . . . these carefully manipulated visual and social environments make the real city and its chaos, class distinctions . . . disappear from view. Our optic nerves blinded by glitter, we fail to see highways in disrepair, charred and abandoned tenements, the scourge of drugs, the wandering homeless, subway breakdowns and deteriorating buses.

Even those who rail against this trend are increasingly ensnared by it: as writer Naomi Klein has observed, the now routine brick-throwing demonstrations against the evils of free trade and corporate branding (Seattle, Quebec City, Genoa) have made social protest itself a commodified spectacle. To get attention, demonstrators must invoke theatre: not long ago, some 7,500 women in London walked 26 miles stripped to their ornament-decorated bras to raise funds for breast cancer. The power of theatre: it's a safe bet they raised more money half-naked than they would have fully clothed. More recently, the entire world became spectators to the first war in history to be fought—

live—in our living rooms: the American-led attack on Saddam Hussein's Iraq, a genuine reality show about survival.

In the modern conditions of production, said Guy Debord presciently, all of life announces itself as an immense accumulation of spectacles. Or as Seth Feldman of York University puts it: "Every day is Halloween."

It wasn't that long ago that literature—novels, poetry, essays, drama—stood at the very acme of artistic expression. It wasn't that long ago that literary critic F.R. Leavis called the notion of filming D.H. Lawrence's *Women in love* "an obscene undertaking," as if the simple act of transforming a classic novel into mere celluloid was by definition a desecration. Today, Leavis's sentiment seems almost laughably outdated. Today, as social critic Camille Paglia has put it, " . . . the rhythms of our thinking in the pop culture world, the domination by image, the whole way the images are put together . . . are way beyond the novel at this point."

In a recent book, *Lifestyle*, Bruce Mau argues that film (and its progeny) now colonize all social space, a process he calls "cinematic migration." By this he means that in order to be understood, or even recognized, artists from diverse disciplines feel compelled to express themselves through the language of film. Certainly, over the past several decades, its influence has seeped ever more steadily into other genres. The impact that film language and technique have had on literary novelists is probably deserving of a Ph.D. thesis, but there is no doubt that more commercial writers increasingly write—and publishers increasingly publish—with a view to the sale of film rights. So much of commercial fiction reads like movies rendered into prose that half the fun of reading the book is mentally casting the film.

Older literary modes, richer in memory, psychology, and interior monologue, are now deemed too slow and complicated for film. In a preface to a recent anthology of 15 short stories, editors Matt Thorne and Nicholas Blincoe argue that the problem with contemporary literature is that it isn't more like the movies. "Today," they maintain, "fiction should be focusing on visual culture, and attempting to prove itself the equal of these mediums." It's a jejune viewpoint, obviously, but arresting in its brazen dismissal of textual narrative.

But it's not only writers who find themselves drawn into the cinematic force field. The same holds true in the visual arts. Post-modern painters like Julian Schnabel (*Before night falls*, *Basquiat*), Matthew Barney (the Cremaster series), David Salle (*Search and destroy*), Robert Longo (*Johnny Mnemonic*), and Cindy Sherman (*Office killer*) increasingly use film and video to express their ideas. Sherman's photographic oeuvre is virtually inseparable from film; it's her essential vocabulary. Her most famous collection, *Untitled film stills*, consists of small black-and-white photographs of Sherman impersonating various female character types from old B-movies.

A few years ago, in a catalogue essay for a retrospective of Robert Longo's work, Los Angeles curator Howard Fox cited the artist's fascination with fascism. "Fascism isn't just dictatorial regimes," Fox wrote. "It's a way of thinking. And it doesn't just come in on leather jackets and motorcycles; it comes in on bumper stickers and television. Fascism is our visual culture."

Everyone from sculptors to advertising designers is struggling to find cinematic correlatives for their work. "What links film to contemporary visual art practice . . . is its twin ability to reach large audiences and to evoke that ephemeral quality I call glamour," says Mark

Betz, professor of film and media studies at the University of Alberta. As Betz notes, the art world has experimented with film before. Avant-garde painters such as Fernand Léger, Salvador Dali, Hans Richter, and Marcel Duchamp did it in 1920s Europe. Four decades later, the Situationists and Lettrists in France and Pop movements in Britain and the USA did it again. "Andy Warhol is the key figure here," Betz contends, "as he was able to address both the mechanically reproducible features of film . . . and the glamour of film that visual artists were clamouring for." Today's cutting-edge artists, he argues, "recognize that Warhol was right: [visual] art now is, simply put, popular culture."

Not surprisingly, the visual imperative is particularly pronounced in youth culture—in the silos of pop music and video games. Few songs today become major hits without a simultaneous big-budget video release—in effect, a three-minute movie, however nonsensical its content. The emphasis on visuals means that the manufactured stars, more and more, must resemble Britney Spears or Ricky Martin, musical Barbies and Kens, air-brushed, acne-free, and dripping sexuality.

Ugliness is allowed—even mandated—in rap or heavy metal music; it's the tattoo of admission. But even here, the performers are usually draped with chorus lines of under-attired women. In all of this, the actual music becomes secondary. Does anyone really know what such performers as Janet Jackson or Madonna sound like? The truth is that how well pop stars sing is almost irrelevant—the music is largely massaged in the engineering studio. What counts is visual: cleavage, buns, smiles, how well they move. Unable to separate the sound from its glossy video wrapping, the younger generation is losing the ability to appreciate the art of listening to music.

But even more serious musical exponents have been affected by film's gravitational pull. Not long ago, electric guitarists Tom Verlaine (founder of the now-defunct rock band Television) and Jimmy Ripp improvised soundtracks to several films screened live in a Boston auditorium. Minimalist composer Philip Glass has done the same with written scores, playing live to screenings of films like Cocteau's *La Belle et la Bête* and writing scores for old silent films like *Dracula*. "This has really become the main thing that I do," Glass said in an interview, "combining images and music." And the work of other composers—such as soundscape artist Brian Eno, godspeed you black emperor, and Glenn Branca—play like soundtracks for non-existent films.

And then there are the vast, omnipresent, Cyclopian eyes: television and the Internet. According to A.C. Neilsen, the average American spends almost four hours a day (more than 52 days a year) watching TV. It is our chief source of news, information, and, especially, what passes for entertainment. By age 65, most of us have spent nearly nine years thus passively engaged, roughly 15 per cent of our lives. Internet use is climbing steadily. As of last March, almost 50 per cent of the English-speaking world had Internet access, and in Canada 64 per cent of adults aged 19–54 surf the web at least an hour a day.

Thus, like Prairie Wheeler, a character in Thomas Pynchon's *Vineland*, most of us now reside in a world mediated by layer upon layer of film and television. We don't confront reality so much as we encounter it through screens, large and small. "Film rolls up the mat of the world," observes media critic Nelson Thall. "You reel up the real world and reconfigure it for presentation. TV is a new meme for reality." Thall quotes Marshall McLuhan: " . . . the new media are not ways of relating us to the old real world; they are the real world and they reshape what remains of the old world at will."

A picture, according to the old cliché, is worth a thousand words. That's because the message it communicates is unmistakable and instantaneous. We relate to images in more direct ways than we do to words. Text requires another level of mediation, a mental or intellectual filter of some kind that distances us from what we are reading. Images are immediate. They require less judgment, less interpretation. They appeal not to our reason but to our intuition, not to thought but to feeling. Inevitably, therefore, the ascendancy of the image economy, and the concomitant decline of print culture, means that ever larger percentages of the population are being conditioned to respond emotionally and viscerally to the daily blizzard of images that bombard them. Both literally and figuratively, these images are carefully manipulated to achieve desired effects—whether it's a tearful, sympathetic reaction to a *cinéma vérité* film about child prostitution or the illusion of freedom that the average television commercial for cars tries to create; the exhilaration of the open road or the promise of easy sex embedded in so many contemporary rock and rap music videos.

This trend, long underway but gathering momentum, is weighted with serious social and indeed political implications. That it marches hand-in-hand with two other worrisome developments—the relentless dumbing down of the population through the deliberate erosion of standards in learning and culture and, under the pretext of greater security, the increasing subjection of people to video surveillance in public spaces—constitutes additional grounds for concern.

These, it need hardly be said, are the formative, incipient grammars of fascism. A liberal or neo-fascism, to be sure, where the expected smorgasbord of consumer choice—in politics, automobiles, or what to watch on television—remains more or less intact. But fascism nonetheless, in its essential anti-humanistic form, where society is increasingly susceptible to top-down governance, often in the seemingly innocuous name of public safety or health or in whatever name the moment requires. The concern, baldly stated, is that we are moving at pace toward a much higher degree of social control and engineering, responsive to omnipresent, officially mandated iconography and to which, more and more, we will lack the wherewithal, the intellectual capital, needed to resist. Witness the 150,000 video cameras that monitor the world of central London, keeping watchful eyes over the citizenry, and with negligible protest.

Media gurus Arthur and Marilouise Kroker have called this the post-alphabetic reality. Mere writing can't keep up to the speed of electronic society, they have said. The result is the end of the Gutenberg Galaxy and the beginning of the Image Millennium.

> Images moving at the speed of light. Images moving faster than the time it takes to record their passing. Iconic images. Special-effect images. Images of life past, present and future as culture is fast-forwarded into the electronic nervous system. Images that circulate so quickly and shine with such intensity that they begin to alter the ratio of the human sensorium.

Visual culture, Bruce Mau maintains, is more primitive, more tribal, than its print-based antecedent in that it works directly on the ancient nervous system. In other words, it is pre-rational, harkening back to an epoch in which meaning was communicated by pictographic symbols. "Unless we recognize the techniques being used to manipulate us," Mau warns, "we are doomed to a life of decorating and redecorating."

Debord went further. He rightly considered the spectacle a tool of pacification and depoliticization—a permanent opium war designed to stupefy and distract us. Even now, long after his death, in an age of mindless interactivity, we remain consumers, increasingly disconnected from reality and our own lives—and mesmerized by images.

Queen's Quarterly. 2003. Summer 110 (2).

KEY AND DIFFICULT WORDS

Define the following, using context or other clues if possible: **pernicious, iconic, hegemony, cacophonous, ersatz, commodify, desecration, progeny, jejune, brazen, oeuvre, ephemeral, omnipresent, meme, mediation, innocuous.**

QUESTIONS

1. Why do you think the author chose the brief title "Image world?" Does it tell you much about the essay? Evaluate its effectiveness.

2. How is the first paragraph of the essay different from the rest of the essay? Does it function as a successful introduction? Why or why not?

3. What kinds of sources does the author use? What do these sources tell you about the kind of audience he is writing for?

4. Consider Posner's diction. In particular, consider word choice in paragraph 7. How can you characterize words and phrases like "high-octane visual glorification," "mega-musicals," "Armani-suited gods," and "paparazzi?" What do they contribute to the essay?

5. How would you define "fascism" (if you are not familiar with the word, look it up in a reliable dictionary or encyclopedia)? What connection does the author attempt to draw between fascism and Western culture (see paragraphs 18 and 27)?

6. Some of Posner's points could be debated. Pick one of his more contentious statements, and explain why you agree or disagree with the statement, drawing on your knowledge and/or personal experience. You could consider one of the following: "So much of commercial fiction reads like movies rendered into prose that half the fun of reading the book is mentally casting the film" (paragraph 15); or "Unable to separate the sound from its glossy video wrapping, the younger generation is losing the ability to appreciate the art of listening to music" (paragraph 21).

7. Summarize paragraph 25. Then explain how it provides a transition between the body of the essay and the conclusion.

8. What is the real subject of Posner's essay? What or whom is he critiquing?

COLLABORATIVE ACTIVITY

(a) In the second-last paragraph, Posner quotes Bruce Mau (also cited earlier in the essay), who believes that visual culture is "primitive" and "pre-rational." Do you agree with this assessment? Discuss this issue. *OR* (b) Referring to the beliefs of Guy Debord in the final paragraph (also cited earlier in the essay), discuss his depiction of visual culture as "a permanent opium war designed to stupefy and distract us."

ACTIVITY

Posner appears pessimistic about the ability of Western culture to escape from its reliance on the image. Should or can this dependence be reduced? What can we do as individuals to reduce it? What can we do as a culture? Write a 500- to 700-word personal essay in which you address at least one of these questions.

Game theories

Clive Thompson

(6,200 words)

Edward Castronova had hit bottom. Three years ago, the 38-year-old economist was, by his own account, an academic failure. He had chosen an unpopular field—welfare research—and published only a handful of papers that, as far as he could tell, "had never influenced anybody." He'd scraped together a professorship at the Fullerton campus of California State University, a school that did not even grant Ph.D.s. He lived in a lunar, vacant suburb. He'd once dreamed of being a major economics thinker but now faced the grim sense that he might already have hit his plateau. "I'm a schmo at a state school," he thought. And since his wife worked in another city, he was, on top of it all, lonely.

To fill his evenings, Castronova did what he'd always done: he played video games. In April 2001, he paid a $10 monthly fee to a multi-player on-line game called EverQuest. More than 450,000 players worldwide log into EverQuest's "virtual world." They each pick a medieval character to play, such as a warrior or a blacksmith or a "healer," then band together in errant quests to slay magical beasts; their avatars appear as tiny, inch-tall characters striding across a Tolkienesque land. Soon, Castronova was playing EverQuest several hours a night.

Then he noticed something curious: EverQuest had its own economy, a bustling trade in virtual goods. Players generate goods as they play, often by killing creatures for their treasure and trading it. The longer they play, the more powerful they get—but everyone starts the game at Level 1, barely strong enough to kill rats or bunnies and harvest their fur. Castronova would sell his fur to other characters who'd pay him with "platinum pieces," the artificial currency inside the game. It was a tough slog, so he was always stunned by the opulence of the richest players. EverQuest had been launched in 1999, and some veteran players now owned entire castles filled with treasures from their quests.

Things got even more interesting when Castronova learned about the "player auctions." EverQuest players would sometimes tire of the game and decide to sell off their characters or virtual possessions at an on-line auction site such as eBay. When Castronova checked the auction sites, he saw that a Belt of the Great Turtle or a Robe of Primordial Waters might fetch $40; powerful characters would go for several hundred or more. And sometimes people would sell off 500,000-fold bags of platinum pieces for as much as $1,000.

As Castronova stared at the auction listings, he recognized with a shock what he was looking at. It was a form of currency trading. Each item had a value in virtual "platinum pieces"; when it was sold on eBay, someone was paying cold hard American cash for it. That meant the platinum piece was worth something in real currency. EverQuest's economy actually had real-world value.

He began calculating frantically. He gathered data on 616 auctions, observing how much each item sold for in US dollars. When he averaged the results, he was stunned to discover that the EverQuest platinum piece was worth about one cent US—higher than the Japanese yen or the Italian lira. With that information, he could figure out how fast the EverQuest economy was growing. Since players were killing monsters or skinning bunnies every day, they were, in effect, creating wealth. Crunching more numbers, Castronova found that the average player was generating 319 platinum pieces each hour he or she was in the game—the equivalent of $3.42

(US) per hour. "That's higher than the minimum wage in most countries," he marvelled.

Then he performed one final analysis: the Gross National Product of EverQuest, measured by how much wealth all the players together created in a single year inside the game. It turned out to be $2,266 US per capita. By World Bank rankings, that made EverQuest richer than India, Bulgaria, or China, and nearly as wealthy as Russia.

It was the 77th richest country in the world. And it didn't even exist.

Castronova sat back in his chair in his cramped home office, and the weird enormity of his findings dawned on him. Many economists define their careers by studying a country. He had discovered one.

I first met Castronova at a piano lounge last summer at the Caesar's Palace casino in Las Vegas, where he was attending a high-tech conference. We talked over a few drinks, though our conversation was soon drowned out by the bar's syrupy Frank Sinatra impersonator, belting out a version of "New York, New York." Castronova winced. "Where better in the world to talk about virtual worlds than Las Vegas?" he said. "This place invented the idea of virtual life."

Castronova is a natural role-player. He's a short, nebbishy guy with a neat goatee and horn-rimmed glasses. When he lectures, he radiates charisma; he is the cool professor you wish you'd had when you were trying to grasp the dry mechanics of price theory. Until recently, he acted in a Shakespearean troupe, and in his spare time he explores the world of "multiple-user domains"—Internet chat environments where people assume different personae as they hang out together.

Castronova suspects his eclectic background is why he never made the powerful connections necessary to secure a good academic job. "I've always been an outsider. I've just been floating around outside communities, sort of flitting from topic to topic," he said.

With virtual worlds, he had finally hit upon a subject that was exploding into the mainstream. Experimental on-line worlds had been kicking around for years, but they took a leap forward in 1997 when Ultima Online—a medieval fantasy world similar to EverQuest—launched and quickly amassed a hundred thousand users. The idea of having a second life on-line suddenly didn't seem so geeky, or, at the very least, it seemed a profitable niche; companies like Sony and Microsoft swarmed on-line. Today there are more than 50 active games worldwide and anywhere from two to three million people playing regularly in the US. The games range from Star Wars Galaxies (where you can wander around as a Wookie and fight the Dark Side) to There.com (where you can wander around Disneyfied islands as an attractive Gap-style model and admire your hot new body). In Korea, a single game called Lineage claims more than four million players.

To figure out precisely who was playing EverQuest, Castronova persuaded 3,500 users to fill out a survey. As one might expect, the average age turned out to be 24, and the players were overwhelmingly male. The amount of time spent "in game" was staggering: over 20 hours a week, with the most devoted players logging six hours daily. Twenty per cent of players agreed with the cheeky (if alarming) statement "I live in Norrath but I travel outside of it regularly"; on average, each of these "residents" possessed virtual goods worth about $3,000 US. "When you consider that the average real-life income in America is only, like, $37,000," Castronova tells me, "you realize these people have a non-trivial amount of wealth locked up inside the games."

When he finished his research, Castronova assembled it in a paper called "Virtual worlds: A first-hand account of market and society on the cyberian frontier." He submitted it to an academic website, the Social Science Research Network, that distributes working papers, free for anyone to read. The site has 43,982 papers, by more than 37,000 authors. He didn't expect too much. "I thought maybe 75 people would read it," he recalls, "and that'd be great."

He was wrong. The paper sent a shock wave through the on-line world. EverQuest players pounced on it and wrote up excited descriptions on game-discussion boards. That led to a flurry of posts on popular blog sites. Soon, academics and pundits in Washington were rushing to read it. Barely a few months later, Castronova's paper became the most downloaded paper in the entire database—beating out works by dozens of Nobel laureates. Today, it's still in the top three.

Why the rush of interest? What can a game filled with elves and warrior dwarves tell us about the real world?

Quite a lot, if you believe the economist Edward Chamberlin. In 1948 Chamberlin admitted that all economists face a critical problem: they have no clean "laboratory" in which to study behaviour. "The social scientist . . . cannot observe the actual operation of a real model under controlled circumstances," he wrote. "Economics is limited by the fact that resort cannot be had to the laboratory techniques of the natural sciences." Instead, classical economics tries to predict economic behaviour by theorizing about a completely fair marketplace in which people are rational actors and all things are equal.

The problem with this—as plenty of left-wing critics have pointed out—is that all things aren't equal. Some people are born into rich families and blessed with great opportunities. Others are born into dirt-poor neighbourhoods, where even the most brilliant mind coupled with hard work may not forge success. As a result, economists have warred for centuries over two diverging visions. Adam Smith argued that people inherently prefer a free market and the ability to rise above others; Karl Marx countered that capital was inherently unfair and those with power would abuse it. But no pristine world exists in which to test these theories—there is no country with a truly level playing field.

Except, possibly, for EverQuest, the world's first truly egalitarian polity. Everyone begins the same way: with nothing. You enter with pathetic skills, no money, and only the clothes on your back. Wealth comes from working hard, honing your skills, and clever trading. It is a genuine meritocracy, which is precisely why players love the game, Castronova argues. "It undoes all the inequities in society. They're wiped away. Sir Thomas More would have dreamt about that possibility, that kind of utopia," he says.

Virtual worlds have produced some surreal rags-to-riches stories. When the on-line world Second Life launched, the players were impressed to see a female avatar industriously building a sprawling monster home. An in-game neighbour stopped by to say hello, only to discover she was a homeless person in British Columbia, logging on using her single remaining possession, a laptop. Penniless in the real world, she belonged to a social elite in the fake one.

Not all social inequities are absent, of course. For instance, Castronova discovered that women in the game are worth less than men, in a very measurable way: when he compared the sale of male and female avatars, he found that female characters sold for 10 per cent less than male ones at precisely the same power level. Players with female avatars also say it's harder to advance in the game, at least initially—even though the female characters are often being played, in real life, by men. (A study by the game academic Nick Yee found that male players "cross-dress" as female characters at least one-third of the time.)

Men play as women characters partly for the kinky thrill but also because female characters are given random presents of free stuff by other players, a chivalric custom known as "gifting." "Personally, you receive a lot more stuff when you start out as a female," as one male cross-dresser wrote to Yee.

Ultimately, Castronova says, EverQuest supports one of Adam Smith's main points, which is that people actually prefer unequal outcomes. In fact, EverQuest eerily mirrors the state of modern free-market societies: only a small minority of players attain Level 65 power and own castles; most remain quite poor. When game companies offer socialist alternatives, players reject them. "They've tried to make games where you can't amass more property than someone else," says Castronova, "but everybody hated it. It seems that we definitely do not want everybody to have the same stuff all the time; people find it boring." It is a result that would warm the heart of a conservative.

Yet progressives, too, have been drawn to Castronova's research. Robert Shapiro, formerly an undersecretary of commerce for Bill Clinton, views the economist's findings as nothing less than a liberal call-to-arms. EverQuest players tolerate the massive split between the virtual rich and the poor, Shapiro tells me, only because they know that this is a level playing field. If you work hard enough, you'll eventually grow wealthy. In Shapiro's view, Castronova's research proves that the only way to create a truly free market is to support programs that give everyone a fair chance at success, such as good education and health care. "This may provide the most important lesson of all from the EverQuest experiment," he wrote in an essay. "Real equality can obviate much of a democratic government's intervention in a modern economy. . . . If EverQuest is any guide, the liberal dream of genuine equality would usher in the conservative vision of truly limited government." In other words, maybe the best way to save the real world is to make it more like EverQuest.

A few months ago, a powerful warrior showed up on EverQuest. He was at Level 50, an indication that he was an experienced player. But when he tried to join a group of other similarly powerful players on a quest to kill a dragon, they quickly realized he had no idea what the hell he was doing. He didn't understand teamwork or even the basic language of the game. Then they discovered his secret: he was a 13-year-old kid whose parents had gone to PlayerAuctions.com and bought him the character for $500.

"He kept getting killed over and over and over again. People were like, Who is this idiot?" says Sean Stalzer, a 33-year-old who is a five-year veteran of EverQuest. Stalzer runs The Syndicate, one of the game's most respected "guilds." Guilds are groups of powerful characters who co-operate to defeat the deadliest monsters (which provide the richest loot). The most elite guilds generally have a no-buying ethic. They accept only players who have "levelled up" their characters the old-fashioned way. "They put hours and hours into it," Stalzer says. "So when someone comes along to make a profit or buy a character, it makes a mockery of what they do. Why should you be better than me because you have more money?" His disdain is like that of a hardscrabble kid from the projects who works for years to get into Yale—only to watch George W. Bush sail in because his daddy is a rich donor.

This culture war underscores the big irony of EverQuest politics. Sure, most players love a level playing field—but they love a leg up even more. Adam Smith might smile at EverQuest's booming marketplace, but beneath the surface, Marx's bleaker vision of capital might be winning the day.

Of course, many people buy "pre-levelled" characters not to cheat at the game but to save time. They're usually busy professionals who can't waste six numbing hours a day killing bunnies to make their warrior elf more powerful. Game companies frown on the selling of characters because they feel it destroys the meritocratic feel of their worlds. But because so many millions of players clearly want to buy their way to power, the companies have mostly turned a blind eye to the on-line auctions. Last year, Ultima Online caved in and began to sell "pre-levelled" characters to new players; demand was so high on the first day that their phone banks crashed.

Even the most stoic guild members are tempted by the booming market. Stalzer's guild was once offered $50,000 for all of its characters and loot. The members declined. But sometimes, when individual guild members run into financial difficulties in the real world, they quietly pawn off virtual goods on the side. "One guy had an 'Enchanter,' and he sold it for $2,000," Stalzer tells me. "That happens a lot. You get a guy who says, 'Dude, I just graduated, and I can't find a job, so I gotta sell this thing.' But I don't mind it when it's real financial need."

Guild members hesitate to sell their goods in part because they do not feel they are the sole owners. When a guild vanquishes a monster, it divides the loot among the members. Each player's booty winds up feeling more like a piece of communal property. At the Las Vegas computer conference, Castronova and I ran into a blue-haired 19-year-old who plays EverQuest as a Level 55 "cleric" in a powerful guild. "I've got dozens of reagents, these magical potions," she said. "And some of them are probably worth, like, a hundred bucks apiece. I could totally sell them. But I always think, damn, I only have this stuff because of how other people helped me get it. So they sort of own it too. It's not my right to sell it." In EverQuest, even socialism finds a home.

Within months of Ultima Online's launch, in 1997, the game spiralled into a currency crisis. The developers woke up one morning to discover that the value of their gold currency was plummeting. Why? A handful of sneaky players had discovered a bug in the code that allowed them to artificially duplicate gold pieces (called "duping"). The economy had been hit by a counterfeiting ring. Inflation soared, and for weeks, players would log in each day to find their assets worth less and less.

Ultima programmers soon fixed the bug. But then they had a new problem: How do you drain all the excess gold out of the economy and bring prices back to normal? They hit upon the idea of creating a rare type of red hair dye and offering it for sale in small quantities. It had no real use, but because it was rare, it became instantly popular and commanded an enormous price—which leached so much gold out of the system that inflation subsided. But the programmers had to meditate for hours on what possible side effects their "fix" might have.

Game designers are, in a sense, the government of their worlds, continually tweaking the system to try and keep it from ruining the lives of their "citizens." In essence, they face the political question that bedevils real-life politicians everywhere: How much should a government meddle in the marketplace?

In Ultima Online, players pick jobs and produce goods: blacksmiths make iron tools; tailors make shirts. In the early days, the players were forced to find other players to buy the stuff. They had to act like entrepreneurs, and as it turned out, few people really wanted to do that; they just wanted to do their jobs and get paid. So the game designers created "shopkeepers," robot characters that would automatically buy whatever goods the players made. This forced the designers to behave like Soviet central planners, micromanaging every aspect of the marketplace

with arcane algorithms of supply and demand. How much would a chair be worth compared to a rabbit skin? If horseshoes were suddenly in low supply, how would that affect the price of magical healing potions? How much inflation is too little, or too much?

Citizens, too, began to complain that the economic system was bafflingly arbitrary. One irate player pointed out that a spool of thread could be bought for two gold pieces, then instantly transformed by a tailor into a shirt worth 20 gold pieces—a profit margin that massively overshot any other activity, for no apparent reason. Eventually, the game designers mostly gave up and built a system in which players could trade more easily among themselves. The Berlin Wall fell, and capitalism rushed in.

The free market made things more fluid but also more unfair. Soon, rich players drove the price of basic goods so high that poor players became much poorer. Once again, the designers had to step in. They would "drop" objects in places where new players could easily scavenge them, giving them a chance to amass a bit of wealth. The designers also set up programs to buy the otherwise useless items generated by poor players (such as animal skins) to give them a chance to make money. In essence, they created handouts for the disadvantaged. Ultima Online had morphed into a modern welfare state, where a free market coexists uneasily with an activist government. "As a developer, I would love to leave it all as a free market," says Anthony Castoro, one of Ultima Online's first designers. "But people who are new to the game would have nothing, and the big players would have everything."

A year after Castronova began his writings on the field, on-line games were sufficiently mainstream that he was a media celebrity, with CNN, National Public Radio, and endless newspapers calling him for comment. But economists at universities still weren't impressed. Castronova submitted his original EverQuest paper to a few economics journals. They rejected it instantly. One reviewer wrote a snippy note saying he preferred "to stick with things that are real rather than virtual."

One can appreciate the economists' confusion. Even the most highly valued virtual goods do not seem, in some essential way, real. An Axe of the Heavens may be great for killing virtual orcs, but it cannot be enjoyed in the physical world. You can't eat virtual food to stay alive. But that distinction shouldn't matter—at least not in economics, which is, as Castronova never tires of pointing out, the study of the entirely arbitrary values that people ascribe to things. "Most of a diamond's value is virtual, too," he adds.

The ultimate proof of this idea is in the game world's emerging merchant class—people who make their real-world income purely by "flipping" virtual goods. Much of their everyday jobs is conducted within the game.

One of these merchants is Robert Kiblinger, a 33-year-old West Virginian. A commercial chemist by training, he worked for Febreze, the company that invented the popular cleaning agent, for which he still holds a couple of patents. ("I was basically selling perfumed water," he jokes.) But then he started playing Ultima Online, where he ran into a player who was tired of the game and wanted to sell his entire account. The player owned two houses and towers and oodles of rare items and only wanted $500, which Kiblinger figured was a steal. He drove to Cincinnati to close the deal. "I met him in a Taco Bell parking lot, and I gave him a cheque," he recalls. The next day, they met inside the game, and the seller handed over the virtual goods. Kiblinger turned around and resold the whole shebang a few days later to another player on eBay for $8,000, producing a tidy profit.

He was hooked. He began buying up items from anyone who was willing to sell and set up a website—UOTreasures—to advertise his inventory. Today the site gets 35,000 visitors a week. Kiblinger employs 500 people inside the game, paying them a small stipend (in Ultima Gold and cash) to act as virtual couriers, scurrying around inside the game to deliver the goods to the players who've paid for them. A few elite customers have bought more than $20,000 of stuff from him. A couple of years ago, business was so good that Kiblinger quit his job as a research associate at Procter & Gamble to work full-time as a virtual vendor, though he won't tell me his exact income. "It's in the six figures," he says. "It's a decent living."

Kiblinger introduced me to one of his clients, Becky Ruttenbur, a 37-year-old woman in Montana. Outside the game she's a single mother; inside she is "married" to another virtual character, played by a soldier who is currently stationed in Iraq. Ruttenbur and the soldier have a joint house and property in the game, even though the soldier is married in real life. Such in-game polygamy is common; Ruttenbur has even met her cyberhusband's real-life wife and says, "She thinks we're nuttier than you could imagine." After playing Ultima Online for five years, Ruttenbur has a huge estate of in-game property, including a set of potted plants that goes for an average of $75 in real US dollars on an auction board. Her stash of on-line goods would fetch $15,000 if she sold it.

Now there's a company rich enough to buy the entire lot. Three years ago, a company called IGE, whose sole function is to buy and sell virtual goods, launched. I met one of the company's founders, Brock Pierce, at a gaming conference in New York. A fresh-faced, blond 23-year-old who is based in Boca Raton, Florida, he said IGE has "thousands of suppliers" who scout the games all day long to find cut-rate goods. He has a hundred full-time staff members at an office in Hong Kong to handle customer service. On any given day, he says, they handle "several million dollars'" worth of virtual inventory.

Several *million*? "We're 10 times the size of anyone else," Pierce bragged. Many players call IGE the Wal-Mart of virtual games. But it is more like a Morgan Stanley or a Long Term Capital Management, a company whose holdings are significant enough to singlehandedly affect the cash flow of the markets.

Of course, every booming economy has not only its white-shoe financiers but also its lowly offshore workers. A few years ago, a company called Black Snow Interactive opened up a "levelling" service for the game Dark Age of Camelot. It had a digital sweatshop in Mexico; there, ultra-low-wage workers would click away at computers, playing the characters 24 hours a day to level them up. Mythic, the company that runs Dark Age of Camelot, got wind of the scheme and closed down Black Snow's accounts and auctions. The operators vanished and have not been heard of since.

An even more intriguing financial institution opened for business a few months ago: the Gaming Open Market. Based in Toronto, it is an on-line service that exists solely for trading the currencies of virtual games—Gold/Silver from Horizons, Linden Dollars from Second Life, Therebucks from There.com. If you're a player who wants some quick virtual currency for your favourite game, you can buy it there using real-world US cash. Sometimes people who play several different virtual games use the market to transfer money from one world to another, like travellers at an airport exchanging currencies.

As on Wall Street, the value of each game currency fluctuates wildly depending on how badly it's needed. "It's just supply and demand. If somebody really wants a currency, it can drive the price sky-high," says Jamie Hale, the 30-year-old founder of the Gaming Open Market. The day I spoke to him, a single player had bought every Linden Dollar on the market, about $500 (US) worth. It cleaned out the Market's entire stock and produced a sudden spike in the Linden Dollar's value. Sometimes Hale himself will jump in to do some quick currency trading if he spots a profitable spread. He admits he has no official training in finance; in fact, he's a programmer by trade, and his co-founder—who helped write the Market's software—is an astrophysicist. "We keep a bunch of economics texts on my shelf to appear smart," he jokes.

Hale's operation is still small, with only 900 users. But as it grows, it could conceivably produce a virtual George Soros—someone who amasses so many billions of units of a currency that he could provoke a crisis in that game's economy for the purposes of profiting off it, much as Soros destroyed the British pound in September 1992. "The value of the currency would drop through the floor," Hale notes. "But that's the game company's problem."

As virtual worlds increasingly mirror the real one, game companies are already dealing with another problem: crime. Indeed, there's even organized crime in The Sims Online, the cyberspace version of the top-selling computer hit. In the game, players assume control of tiny suburbanites, build houses, and work at jobs to earn "Simoleans," the in-game currency. The Sim Mafia was founded by Jeremy Chase, a 26-year-old in Sacramento. Players who want to destroy another character's reputation turn to the mob. The game has a system of black marks for punishing bad behaviour. If Chase is paid to "tag" someone, he gets his crime family—a loose collection of a hundred players—to place dozens and dozens of red tags on the victim. When they're done, other players will assume the character must have done something awful and refuse to speak or trade with him.

Peter Ludlow, a professor of philosophy at the University of Michigan, became fascinated by The Sims Online last year and founded a blog—"The Alphaville Herald"—that reports on interesting social situations inside the world. Last November, he discovered something truly strange: The game had a chain of cyber-brothels, run by a family of avatars, all played by a character named "Evangeline." Evangeline had organized a handful of Sim women to perform hot-sex chat inside the game for customers, who paid in Simoleans. "Girls set their own prices," she told Ludlow. "Bj's" were 20,000 Simoleans, the equivalent of roughly $4.50 (US); Evangeline reserved the richest customers for herself, making up to $40 or $50 (US) a trick. Ludlow later discovered that some of Evangeline's "girls" were underage girls in real life and that Evangeline herself was a 17-year-old boy living in Florida. When he blogged about his findings, reporters nationwide snapped to attention, and soon The Sims Online was on the front page of *The New York Times*.

Maxis—the company that runs the game—struck back. They cancelled Ludlow's account, claiming he had broken the game's rules by advertising his blog inside the world. (Maxis prohibits anyone from advertising real-world services or goods inside the game.) Ludlow insists he never made a dime off "The Alphaville Herald" and that he was booted out solely because his research had embarrassed the game company.

Either way, Ludlow lost most of his goods. When game owners cancel your account, it's like having your house instantly destroyed in a fire: your property winks out of existence. Ludlow figures he had about $200-worth of virtual goods deleted, including a pet cheetah ("which is like a 15-dollar animal") that he'd bought from a vendor on-line. Yet Maxis could not entirely delete his virtual wealth. A week before his account

was deleted, Ludlow had deposited 800,000 Simoleans into an account at the Gaming Open Market. And Maxis has no power over the Market; it cannot forcibly demand that Hale, the owner of the exchange, delete that money. In effect, Ludlow had parked his money in the virtual-world equivalent of an overseas bank, where no game government could touch it.

Ludlow's case points to the ultimate question, with enormous legal implications for the real world: What, precisely, is the legal status of virtual property? Does anyone actually "own" it?

Last November, I accompanied Castronova to a legal conference in New York devoted to this subject. There, game-company executives argued that when a player joins a world such as Ultima Online, he or she agrees to a user licence that explicitly says the game company owns everything that happens on the servers. "It's a game, and what we're doing is inviting you in to play with the toys. But you don't own the toys. We do," said Richard Bartle, who pioneered the first virtual world back in the 1980s.

The problem is that people who play the games act as if their virtual castles were their own private property. And when it comes to property issues, courts in the US, at least, have traditionally tended to take the view that if it quacks like a duck, it is a duck. If enough people treat their Robe of Primordial Waters as though it's genuine personal property, the law might respect that—no matter what the game companies say.

This debate may appear rather abstract right now. But sooner or later, one of these game companies will start losing money and decide it can't afford to keep its virtual world. (Many observers expect at least one major world to go bankrupt this year.) If a game shut down, it would instantly destroy hundreds of thousands—perhaps even millions—of dollars. The homeless woman with the virtual mansion, for instance, could probably sell her goods for several hundred dollars; she would lose her single most valuable possession.

For now, there is no clear precedent on how to deal with virtual property. Owning a virtual castle is not like owning other virtual things, such as stock in a company, because the value is not in an external, tangible object, such as a corporation, but in the work and money invested in acquiring it.

With stakes like that, said Jack Balkin, a Yale law professor and a host of the legal conference, players will probably fight back with lawsuits or by going right to politicians, demanding legislation to prevent worlds from closing down. Julian Dibbell, a journalist who began trading virtual goods himself last summer—he aims to report "revenue from the sale of virtual goods" as the single biggest line-item on his 2004 tax return—later suggested an even stranger scenario. He said that players could well band together and try to buy back the world at the company's bankruptcy hearing—and then run it themselves as a breakaway republic. "Some renegade players have done things like that before, actually," he noted. "They've gotten access to the code of the game and then illicitly created their own duplicate world."

In a few years, these questions will creep into the mainstream, because on-line environments such as EverQuest are likely to become a significant way that people interact with the Internet. Only a small chunk of the population will ever go into a brooding medieval-fantasy such as EverQuest, but virtual worlds have emerged that are much friendlier and do not use dungeons-and-dragons themes at all. Indeed, they're not even games: they have no goals, no "levels" to achieve, no points to score.

There.com, for example, is a 3-D world devoted to nothing but chatting and socializing, using avatars that look like seductive, attractive models. You'd probably prefer it to real life,

because everything is just so much prettier in There. As in the real world, one of the main activities in There is shopping. The company created a currency, Therebucks, and tied it directly to the value of the American dollar to prevent inflation. Players spend a lot of time customizing their appearance (often for the purposes of flirting), so Nike and Levis have virtual clothes that they sell solely inside the game. Individual players, too, have become designers, creating outfits they sell to other There citizens. "One of the leading clothes designers is making $3,000 to $4,000 a month, which is a full-time job," says There's founder, Will Harvey.

A place like There is not so much a game as a platform for life. A large chunk of our everyday experiences—meetings, conversation, music, shopping—could port nicely to a 3-D space. There Inc. is already talking to companies about licensing "land" inside the game so that far-flung employees can conduct meetings there instead of on the old-fashioned Internet. It's not as far-fetched as it sounds. The US military has already licensed a private chunk of There and created a simulation of the planet on it. The army is currently using the virtual Baghdad in There as a training space for American soldiers.

The prospect of life moving into an area such as There both amazes and terrifies Balkin. "So what happens when people start doing therapy inside a virtual world?" he asked. "Or teaching? It's a convenient place to meet, but literally everything can be recorded. So what do you do when doctors are meeting to talk with patients in a virtual world?"

Castronova sighs. Though he has made his career out of studying these economies, he is dismayed by how the real world has bled into the virtual one. "I liked it better when they were just, you know, games," he says wistfully. He preferred the meritocratic feel of EverQuest, before all the duping and the auctions and the bidding wars for powerful avatars. He liked the idea of on-line worlds as a place you migrated to when, like an immigrant, you wanted a new lease on life—just as three years ago, when, depressed and lonely, he first stumbled into EverQuest.

His own voyage had a good ending. A few months ago, the communications department at Indiana University in Bloomington called. They had read his work and wanted to talk. Weeks later, they offered him a fully tenured position in a new department. Castronova had still never published a single one of his EverQuest papers in print; all his analyses had been distributed on-line. "It's all PDFs and websites," he joked. Like an avatar in the game, he had levelled up.

The Walrus. 2004. June.

KEY AND DIFFICULT WORDS

Define the following, using context or other clues if possible: **eclectic, egalitarian, chivalric, obviate, meritocratic, arcane, algorithm, morph, precedent, illicitly.**

QUESTIONS

1. How much of the essay would you consider the introduction? Why does Thompson spend so much time introducing Edward Castronova, giving his background and reporting his observations about him?

2. How does the author use quotation marks for different purposes in paragraphs 14 and 15 (find at least three different uses).

3. What main question does the author attempt to answer in his essay? How does he attempt to answer it? Do you believe that he provides a clear answer in the body of his essay?

4. A paradox is a term for a statement or situation that seems contradictory or untrue on the surface but is revealed as truthful in some sense when examined closely. What use does Thompson make of these "truths" in his essay?

5. Summarize paragraph 24. Are Shapiro's comments undermined or supported in the following three paragraphs?

6. Pointing to specific passages, briefly analyze Thompson's writing style. For example, you could consider use of first-person and third-person voice, diction (word choice), paragraph and sentence structure, and tone.

7. What kinds of sources does Thompson rely on in his essay? Using two specific sources, assess their reliability and overall effectiveness.

8. Why in his concluding paragraphs does the author change his focus from fantasy worlds like that of EverQuest to the world of There.com? Do you think it strengthens or weakens his conclusion?

COLLABORATIVE ACTIVITIES

1. Castronova makes many connections and draws several surprising comparisons between the real and virtual worlds. Are they all legitimate? Do some seem far-fetched? In groups, discuss the validity of some of the connections and comparisons.

2. "[M]aybe the best way to save the real world is to make it more like EverQuest." Debate this statement.

ACTIVITIES

1. Do you think that players of Ultima Online, EverQuest, or Second Life would like or dislike Thompson's essay? Why or why not?

2. Is Thompson successful in conjuring up the virtual game world? Using your own experience if you are familiar with computer worlds like EverQuest or relying on this essay and/or what you have heard second-hand about these worlds, write a critical response in which you look at specific strategies through which the author tries to evoke the "in game" reality.

Related reading: Andy Clark. "Bad borgs?"

Intended and unintended effects of an eating disorder educational program: Impact of presenter identity

Marlene B. Schwartz, Ph.D., Jennifer J. Thomas, M.S., Kristin M. Bohan, Ph.D., Lenny R. Vartanian, Ph.D.

(3,700 words)

ABSTRACT

Objective: This study examines the impact of presenter identity on the intended and unintended effects of an eating disorder educational program.

Method: High school students viewed one of two identical videotaped discussions about eating disorders. In one condition, the presenter was identified as an "eating disorder specialist"; in the other condition, she was identified as a "recovered patient." Before and after watching the video, participants reported on their awareness of various eating disorder symptoms, their beliefs about individuals with eating disorders, and their opinion of the presenter.

Results: At Time 2, both groups reported increased knowledge about eating disorders. There was also evidence of increased endorsement of a number of implicit messages, particularly among those in the "recovered patient" group (e.g., "Girls with eating disorders are very pretty"; "It would be nice to look like" the presenter).

Conclusion: The unintended effects of eating disorder educational programs should be investigated before implementation because of their potential to undermine program efficacy.

Keywords: eating disorder educational programs; implicit messages; intended effects; unintended effects

INTRODUCTION

The US House of Representatives has deliberated the Eating Disorders Awareness, Education, and Prevention Act[1] in several successive congressional sessions from 2000 to the present. If passed, this legislation would promulgate the use of federal education funds to increase the awareness of eating disorders among parents and students, as well as to train educators in eating disorder prevention techniques. The prospect of implementing a nationwide prevention curriculum underscores the importance of identifying empirically supported strategies. A recent meta-analysis of research on eating disorder prevention programs indicated that 53 per cent of interventions resulted in the reduction of at least one eating-disorder risk factor (e.g., body dissatisfaction) and 25 per cent led to the reduction of eating pathology (e.g., reduced frequency of binge eating and purging).[2] Importantly, a number of moderators of intervention effects were identified. For example, larger effect sizes were observed among programs that targeted high-risk populations (compared with those presented to a more general audience), and interactive programs were more effective than didactic programs.

One factor that has been relatively neglected in the empirical literature on eating disorder intervention and prevention programs is the impact of the characteristics of the presenter herself or himself. Clinicians and other specialists who work in the area of eating disorders are often recruited by various community groups (e.g., schools) to give educational talks about eating disorders. Their expertise is desirable as a means of effectively communicating information about eating disorders to audience members. Another common approach is to have presentations delivered by individuals who have themselves recovered from an eating disorder. The notion that listening to the personal story of a recovered individual would be preventative or therapeutic for vulnerable audiences is intuitively appealing. Twelve-step self-help programs, which are widely implemented in treating drug and alcohol addiction, feature personal recovery stories within a group format.[3] In the context of educational programs for eating disorders, not only can recovered individuals provide information about the etiology, symptoms, and treatment of eating disorders in general, but they are also uniquely disposed to provide descriptions of their own personal experiences with the illness, which the audience members might find particularly moving. These types of activities appear to be commonplace at colleges and universities; in one study, 13 of 18 randomly selected campuses with eating disorder prevention programs reported using recovered students as presenters.[4]

Despite the intuitive appeal of having individuals who have experienced and recovered from an eating disorder deliver educational materials, the effectiveness of these prevention efforts has been debated in the literature.[4,5] Several theorists have suggested that such interventions might be problematic in that they risk unintended iatrogenic outcomes by providing suggestive information about unhealthy weight control techniques or even normalizing and glamorizing eating disorder symptoms,[6] particularly among at-risk individuals. In particular, Garner[7] proposed that personal stories, especially those of celebrities, may inspire vicarious learning and emulation of disordered behaviours. The finding that some individuals have reported attempting self-induced vomiting after learning of the behaviour via magazine articles about eating disorders[8,9] lends credibility to these concerns. More recently, investigators have expressed growing apprehension over pro-eating disorder websites, which promote anorexia nervosa and bulimia nervosa as lifestyle choices rather than psychiatric conditions by featuring weight loss and purging tips, chat rooms, and "thinspiration" photos of ultra-slim models. In a study of eating disorder patients, Wilson et al.[10] found that 61 per cent of those who had visited pro-eating disorder websites reported learning and implementing new weight loss or purging techniques as a result.

To our knowledge, only two studies[4,11] have investigated the impact of recovered patients on prevention program participants' eating attitudes and behaviours.[*] First, Mann et al.[4] conducted a controlled study of small group panel discussions with two "poised, self-assured, attractive and personable" (p. 217) campus leaders who had recovered from anorexia and bulimia nervosa. The presenters provided educational information on etiology and treatment as well as personal accounts of their struggles. Eating disorder symptoms were assessed before the intervention, as well as four and 12 weeks after the intervention. When the researchers conducted a within-subjects analysis that included participants who completed the survey at all three time points, they found no effect of the intervention on eating disorder symptoms. In contrast, using a "more exploratory assessment" (p. 220) that included between-subjects comparisons of all participants who completed the survey at any time point, the researchers reported that at the four-week follow-up, the intervention group had significantly higher eating disorder symptoms than were found in the control group. This latter finding was interpreted as indicating an iatrogenic effect of the intervention. However, the appropriateness of the exploratory analyses and subsequent conclusions have been challenged.[2]

In another study, Heinze et al.[11] presented 7th-graders and 10th-graders with an educational video in which the presenter, an actress who had previously recovered from anorexia nervosa, differentially identified herself as a recovered anorexic, a peer, an expert, or did not provide a specific identity. After viewing these videos, participants expressed decreased drive for thinness and intentions to diet regardless of alleged presenter identity. In their study, the recovered-anorexic presenter did not provide any personal details related to her ill state or recovery, and this might have been a critical difference between the Heinze et al.[11] study and the Mann et al.[4] study.

The issue of presenter identity and disclosure of personal experiences in primary prevention for eating disorders remains a contentious one. The purpose of the present study was to explore one potential mechanism through which presenter identity could impact audience members. In particular, we focused on the explicit messages (intended effects) and on some possible implicit messages (unintended effects) of educational

---

[*]A third study[12] also used a recovered patient as a part of a prevention program, but the authors did not directly assess the impact of that particular component on the various outcomes.

programs. We predicted that an eating disorder specialist and a recovered patient would be equally effective in communicating key information about the symptoms of eating disorders and the seriousness of those conditions. We also predicted, however, that the specialist and recovered patient would diverge with respect to the unintended or implicit messages that they conveyed. Based on previous theorizing regarding the normalization and glamorization of eating disorders, we hypothesized that an educational program delivered by a recovered patient would result in more positive views of women with eating disorders in general and of the recovered-patient presenter in particular.

METHOD
Participants

Participants were 376 students who were present at their all-female, predominantly Caucasian, parochial high school on the day the data were collected. Participants ranged in age from 12 to 18 years ($M = 15.50$, $SD = 1.16$); 25.3 per cent ($n = 95$) were in 9th grade, 23.7 per cent ($n = 89$) were in 10th grade, 26.3 per cent ($n = 99$) were in 11th grade, 20.7 per cent ($n = 78$) were in 12th grade, and 4.0 per cent ($n = 15$) did not report their grade level. The protocol for this study was approved by the Yale School of Medicine Human Investigation Committee.

Materials
Educational videotape. We produced two professional quality 12-minute videotapes depicting a clinical psychologist interviewing the third author (KMB) about eating disorders. The two videotapes were identical except that the 29-year-old female presenter was introduced by the interviewer as "Dr. Kristin Siebrecht, eating disorders specialist" in the first tape and as "Kristin, a recovered eating disorder patient" in the second. This information also appeared on the screen

periodically throughout the video. The presenter was of normal weight, was well groomed and conservatively dressed, and wore light makeup. The first minute and a half of the interview described the personal story of a woman with an eating disorder who began dieting, binge-eating, and purging after being teased by her peers. In the specialist condition, the story was described as that of a typical patient, whereas in the recovered-patient condition, it was represented as the presenter's own experience. Each of the videotaped interviews then presented identical information regarding the symptoms, prevalence, etiology, health consequences, and treatment of anorexia nervosa and bulimia nervosa.

Eating disorders awareness questionnaire. The Eating Disorders Awareness Questionnaire (EDAQ) was constructed for the present study to assess the educational impact (intended effects) of the video. The scale contained 14 items addressing material that was explicitly discussed in the video presentation, including basic knowledge about eating disorders and the perceived seriousness of eating disorders. To simplify wording, most items were phrased referring to "girls" because the participants were enrolled in an all-female high school and most of those who develop eating disorders are female. Sample items include: "Girls who have anorexia nervosa are very afraid of becoming fat," "Girls who lose a lot of weight can stop getting their periods," and "People can die from eating disorders." Participants rated their agreement with these statements on a five-point scale ranging from 1 (*strongly disagree*) to 5 (*strongly agree*). After some items were reversed scored, responses were summed and averaged, with higher scores indicating greater knowledge (Cronbach's $\chi = .70$).

Implicit message items. Interspersed throughout the EDAQ were an additional eight items regarding the personal characteristics of individuals with eating disorders, how difficult it is to recover from an eating disorder, and whether recovered individuals can lead normal lives. These items were designed to measure the implicit messages (unintended effects) that might be communicated by the video and were based on previous theorizing regarding the normalization and glamorization of eating disorders. The eight implicit message (IM) items were as follows: "Having an eating disorder would not be that bad if it meant you could look like a model," "Girls with eating disorders are usually very smart," "Girls with eating disorders are usually very pretty," "Girls with eating disorders are very strong (their personalities)," "Girls with eating disorders are especially in control of their lives," "It's not that hard to recover from an eating disorder if you get one," "People who recover from eating disorders can go on to lead normal lives," and "Having an eating disorder is a good way to lose weight." Participants rated their agreement with IM items on the same five-point EDAQ scale ranging from 1 (*strongly disagree*) to 5 (*strongly agree*). The internal consistency for these items was low (Cronbach's χ = .38); therefore, each item was treated separately in the analyses described below. Two additional IM items regarding the presenter herself were assessed only after participants viewed the video: "Kristin [Dr. Siebrecht], the woman being interviewed in the video, is a good role model for girls my age" and "It would be nice to look like Kristin [Dr. Siebrecht], the woman being interviewed in the video."

Procedure

Participants were divided into two conditions by the first letter of their last names (A–L and M–Z) and led to separate rooms where they would complete the study; both groups participated simultaneously. Participants first completed the EDAQ, including the eight IM items.

Participants then watched one of the two 12-minute videotaped interviews. After watching their assigned video, participants again completed the EDAQ, the IM items, and the two additional items about the presenter being "a good role model" and "nice to look like." Participants were then debriefed as to the study purpose and were informed that the presenter in both videos was actually an eating disorder specialist. The presenters then led a media literacy discussion of the idealized body shapes depicted in television and magazine images.

RESULTS

Of the 376 initial participants, 17 had missing data, leaving 359 participants with complete data available for the following analyses. Of these 359, 127 were assigned to the specialist condition, and 232 were assigned to the recovered-patient condition.

EDAQ

A time x condition analysis of variance (ANOVA) on EDAQ scores revealed a significant main effect of time, $F(1,357) = 252.80$, $p < .001$, $\eta_P^2 = .42$, indicating that participants' overall understanding of basic facts about eating disorders and the relative seriousness of those disorders increased after watching the educational video (see **Table 1**). As predicted, there was no significant time x condition interaction.

Implicit messages

The unintended effects of the education programs were examined using a 2 x 2 (time x condition) multivariate analysis of variance (MANOVA) on the IM items, which revealed a significant main effect for time, $F(8,347) = 5.13$, $p < .001$, $\eta_P^2 = .11$, as well as a significant time x condition interaction, $F(8,347) = 2.70$, $p = .01$, $\eta_P^2 = .06$. Each IM item was then examined in separate univariate analyses (see **Table 1**).

Table 1. Means (SD) for the Eating Disorders Awareness Questionnaire (EDAQ) and implicit message (IM) items

	Specialist		Recovered Patient	
	Time 1	Time 2	Time 1	Time 2
EDAQ	47.57^a (5.58)	51.28^b (5.75)	47.00^c (5.39)	51.54^d (4.48)
IM items				
Model	1.50^a (0.97)	1.39^b (0.98)	1.53^c (0.98)	1.39^d (0.90)
Strong	2.18^a (1.09)	2.28^b (1.07)	1.94^c (0.99)	2.19^d (1.05)
Not hard to recover	1.39^a (0.80)	1.69^b (1.00)	1.68^c (1.14)	1.92^d (1.15)
Smart	3.02^a (0.77)	3.07^a (0.78)	2.79^c (0.89)	2.92^d (0.87)
Normal lives	3.65^a (1.24)	3.58^a (1.14)	3.62^c (1.16)	4.00^d (0.99)
Pretty	2.54^a (0.93)	2.60^a (0.92)	2.39^c (0.96)	2.61^d (0.91)
In control	1.82^a (1.00)	1.67^a (0.94)	1.59^c (0.95)	1.76^d (1.17)
Lose weight	1.39^a (0.82)	1.26^a (0.74)	1.40^c (0.84)	1.37^c (0.87)
IM post-test only				
Role model	—	3.59^e (1.03)	—	3.90^f (1.06)
Nice to look like	—	2.45^e (1.16)	—	3.04^f (1.21)

Note: Superscripts a, b, c, d, e, and f denote group differences at $p < .05$.

There was a main effect of time for the item "Having an eating disorder would not be that bad if it meant you could look like a model," with ratings decreasing after the interventions ($p = .01$, $\eta_P^2 = .02$). There was also a main effect of time for the items "Girls with eating disorders are very strong (their personalities)" ($p = .01$, $\eta_P^2 = .02$) and "It's not that hard to recover from an eating disorder if you get one" ($p < .001$, $\eta_P^2 = .04$), indicating that ratings increased after watching the video. A trend was found for a main effect of time for the item "Girls with eating disorders are usually very smart" ($p = .06$, $\eta_P^2 = .01$).

For the item "People who recover from eating disorders can go on to lead normal lives," there was a main effect of time, $F(1,354) = 6.55$, $p = .01$, $\eta_P^2 = .02$, qualified by a significant time x condition interaction, $F(1,354) = 12.70$, $p < .001$, $\eta_P^2 = .04$. Simple-effects analysis revealed that participants in the recovered-patient group significantly increased their ratings ($p < .001$), whereas participants in the specialist condition did not ($p = .53$). For the item "Girls with eating disorders are usually very pretty," there was a main effect of time, $F(1,354) = 8.61$, $p = .004$, $\eta_P^2 = .02$, qualified by a marginally significant time x condition interaction, $F(1,354) = 3.00$, $p = .08$, $\eta_P^2 = .01$. Simple-effects analysis revealed that participants in the recovered-patient condition significantly increased their ratings ($p < .001$), whereas those in the specialist condition did not ($p = .45$). For the item "Girls with eating disorders are especially in control of their lives," there was only a significant time x condition interaction, $F(1,354) = 5.35$, $p = .02$, $\eta_P^2 = .02$. Simple-effects analysis again revealed that ratings increased in the recovered-patient condition ($p = .04$) but not in the specialist condition ($p = .19$). Finally, there was no main effect or interaction for the item "Having an eating disorder is a good way to lose weight."

A one-way MANOVA on the two post-test items ("good role model" and "nice to look like")

yielded a significant effect of condition, $F(2,350) = 10.98$, $p < .001$, $\eta_p^2 = .06$. In both cases, ratings were higher in the recovered-patient condition than in the specialist condition (good role model: $p = .01$, $\eta_p^2 = .02$; nice to look like: $p < .001$, $\eta_p^2 = .05$).

CONCLUSION

The aim of the present study was to determine whether an educational program designed to increase awareness about eating disorders would have a differential impact, particularly in terms of some possible implicit messages, when delivered by an eating disorder specialist, as compared with someone who herself had purportedly recovered from an eating disorder. As hypothesized, the educational video successfully increased knowledge about the specific symptoms of eating disorders and the seriousness of those conditions (the intended effects). Also as hypothesized, the presenter's purported identity did not differentially impact knowledge acquisition. The observed increase in knowledge about eating disorders is consistent with the findings of Stice and Shaw's[2] meta-analysis that most prevention programs were successful in increasing such knowledge. The finding is also consistent with previous research in showing that presenter identity does not differentially influence knowledge acquisition.[11,13] Perhaps it is the case that both types of presenters were viewed as being "experts" on eating disorders, one because of professional training and the other because of personal experience.

In addition to the intended effects of the educational videos on knowledge about eating disorders, we also found preliminary evidence of some unintended effects, or implicit messages, associated with the educational videos. Several of these unintended effects emerged irrespective of presenter identity. After watching the video, participants in both the specialist and recovered-patient conditions were less likely to indicate

that having an eating disorder would be "not that bad if it meant you could look like a model," were less likely to indicate that it is difficult to recover from an eating disorder, and were more likely to agree that girls with eating disorders have strong personalities. Other IM items, however, were differentially affected by the presenter's identity. Participants who saw the recovered-patient video (but not the specialist video) were more likely to indicate that girls with eating disorders were pretty, were in control of their lives, and could go on to lead normal lives when they recover. In addition, those who saw the recovered-patient video were more likely to perceive the presenter as a "good role model" and as "nice to look like" than were participants who saw the specialist video.

It should be noted that, in general, the ratings for each of the IM items were fairly low and mostly below the midpoint of the scale. This might (1) reflect a general reluctance to strongly agree with what might be considered socially undesirable statements (e.g., "Having an eating disorder is a good way to lose weight") or (2) suggest that our measures were not sensitive enough to fully capture the implicit messages that were conveyed through the videos. Nonetheless, the observed effects were statistically reliable and in the small-to-moderate range. The fact that even these modest changes emerged after watching a single 12-minute video is remarkable.

Although we have attributed the unintended effects observed in the present study to implicit messages contained in the educational video, it is also possible that having participants complete the same questionnaire pre- and post-video may have created demand characteristics for participants to change their item ratings when completing the questionnaire the second time. The fact that impact of the videos varied across items and across conditions, however, suggests that such demand characteristics cannot fully account for the data. Future studies including a control group viewing a video on a topic unrelated to eating disorders would be useful to further rule out demand characteristics as an alternative explanation for the results of the present study.

Taken as a whole, our findings suggest that educational programs designed to increase awareness about eating disorders communicate not only the intended educational information but also implicit messages about the characteristics of individuals with eating disorders and the prospects of recovery. This might be particularly true when the program is delivered by someone who is believed to have herself recovered from an eating disorder. Theoretically, the implicit messages observed in the current study could be viewed as being positive or negative. On the one hand, eating disorders are to some extent socially stigmatized.[14,15] This stigmatization was in part reflected in the present study in that baseline ratings of some of the personal characteristics of individuals with eating disorders, such as smart and pretty, were fairly low. One possible effect of these implicit messages, therefore, is that they could serve to partially reduce the stigma of eating disorders and could in turn promote self-disclosure of symptoms, which is associated with a higher likelihood of subsequent treatment seeking.[16] Similarly, promoting the belief that recovery is attainable and that individuals can go on to lead normal lives after recovery may also be beneficial; one study found that messages emphasizing the efficacy of current treatments as well as the medical seriousness of eating disorder symptoms were the most effective in prompting individuals with bulimia nervosa to seek professional help.[17]

In contrast, it is also possible that some of these implicit messages could contribute to the glamorization of eating disorders, which might in turn have negative consequences. Several theorists have expressed concern over the potential effects of the glamorization of eating disorders on people's eating attitudes and behaviours,[6,7,18] and these concerns are particularly salient in the context of media presentations of eating disorders. A recent cross-sectional study found that individuals with higher levels of eating disorder symptoms exhibited greater implicit associations between anorexia and glamour than did low-symptom participants.[19] In the present study, we found preliminary evidence that participants perceived people with eating disorders more positively after watching the educational program, particularly when it was delivered by a recovered patient. It is possible that some implicit messages might have iatrogenic effects on at-risk individuals' eating attitudes and behaviours. A worthwhile endeavour for future research would be to determine whether, and to what extent, existing eating disorder prevention programs convey implicit messages that glamorize eating disorders.

Some limitations to the present study are worth noting. First, the sample was drawn from a single all-female high school. It is possible that students at all-female schools might differ from students at co-educational schools on certain characteristics (e.g., socioeconomic status, achievement orientation) that could potentially influence the study results and limit their generalizability. A second limitation is that, although the measures that we created for the present study showed adequate internal consistency, other indices of reliability and validity remain unknown.

A final limitation of the present study is that we did not assess the impact of the implicit messages on recipients' eating attitudes and behaviours, so the broader implications of our findings remain unknown. We suggested earlier that one explanation for the difference between the findings of Mann et al.[4] and Heinze et al.[11] was that in the former study, the presenter provided a personal account of her struggles, whereas in the later study, the presenter did not. Insofar as implicit messages might emerge from personal accounts of eating disorders in particular, it is possible that the differential effects observed in those two studies are related in part to the implicit messages that were conveyed. An important consideration for future research, therefore, would be to examine the extent to which these implicit messages impact people's eating attitudes and behaviour in the longer term. Developing a better understanding of the implicit messages communicated in prevention programs, as well as the impact of these implicit messages on attitudes and behaviour, could ultimately lead to the development of more efficacious programs.

International Journal of Eating Disorders.
2007. 40 (2).

REFERENCES

1. Eating Disorders Awareness, Prevention, and Education Act of 2005.
2. Stice E, Shaw H. Eating disorder prevention programs: a meta-analytic review. Psychol Bull 2004;130:206–227.
3. Kelly JF. Self-help for substance-use disorders: history, effectiveness, knowledge gaps, and research opportunities. Clin Psychol Rev 2003;23:639–663.
4. Mann T, Nolen-Hoeksema S, Huang K, Burgard D, Wright A, Hanson K. Are two interventions worse than none? Joint primary and secondary prevention of eating disorders in college females. Health Psychol 1997;16: 215–225.
5. Cohn L, Maine M. More harm than good. Eat Disord 1998;6:93–95.
6. O'Dea JA. School-based interventions to prevent eating disorders: first, do no harm. Eat Disord 2000;8:123–130.
7. Garner D. Iatrogenesis in anorexia nervosa and bulimia nervosa. Int J Eat Disord 1985; 4:701–726.
8. Murray S, Touyz S, Beumont P. Knowledge about eating disorders in the community. Int J Eat Disord 1990;9:87–93.
9. Thomsen SR, McCoy JK, Williams M. Internalizing the impossible: anorexic outpatients' experiences with women's beauty and fashion magazines. Eat Disord 2001; 9:49–64.
10. Wilson JL, Peeble R, Hardy KK, Mulivhill LC, Kretzschmar AY, Litt I. Pro-eating disorder website usage and health outcomes in an eating disordered population. Presented at the Pediatric Academic Society, Washington, DC, May 14–17, 2005.
11. Heinze V, Werthein EH, Kashima Y. An evaluation of the importance of message source and age of recipient in a primary prevention program for eating disorders. Eat Disord 2000;8:131–145.
12. Phelps L, Sapia J, Nathanson D, Nelson L. An empirically supported eating disorder prevention program. Psychol Schools 2000; 37:443–452.
13. Moreno AB, Thelen MH. A preliminary prevention program for eating disorders in a junior high school population. J Youth Adolesc 1993;22:109–124.
14. Crisp AH, Gelder MG, Rix S, Meltzer HI, Rowlands OJ. Stigmatisation of people with mental illnesses. Br J Psychiatry 2000;177:4–7.
15. Fleming J, Szmukler GI. Attitudes of medical professionals towards patients with eating disorders. Aust NZ J Psychiatry 1992; 26:436–443.
16. Becker AE, Thomas JJ, Franko DL, Herzog DB. Disclosure patterns of eating and weight concerns to clinicians, educational professionals, family, and peers. Int J Eat Disord 2005;38:18–23.

17. Smalec JL, Klingle RS. Bulimia interventions via interpersonal influence: the role of threat and efficacy in persuading bulimics to seek help. J Behav Med 2000;23:37–57.

18. Schulze E, Gray J. The effects of popular and textbook presentations of bulimia nervosa on attitudes toward bulimia nervosa and individuals with bulimia nervosa. Br Rev Bulimia Anorexia Nervosa 1990;4:83–91.

19. Thomas JJ, Judge AM, Brownell KD, Vartanian LR. Evaluating the effects of eating disorder memoirs on readers' eating attitudes and behaviors. Int J Eat Disord 2006; 39:418–425.

KEY AND DIFFICULT WORDS

Define the following, using contextual or other clues if possible: **implicit, didactic, etiology, iatrogenic, vicarious, contentious, prevalence, differential, efficacious.**

QUESTIONS

1. Using your own words, explain the justification for the study, its specific purpose, and the hypotheses.

2. Why do the authors choose to include such an extensive review of the literature in their introduction? (You could compare its length with those of "Conditions for success?" p. 207, and "Heavy drinking on Canadian campuses," p. 436.)

3. Why do the authors question the findings of the two studies discussed in paragraphs 4 and 5? In a brief paragraph, summarize the importance of these studies to their own work.

4. What is the reason for adding two IM items to the EDAQ after the participants viewed the video?

5. Returning to the introduction, determine (a) whether the first hypothesis was proved and (b) whether the second one was proved. In (b), you will have to be specific in your answer.

6. What are "demand characteristics" (paragraph 21), and what role could they have played in the results?

7. Explain the use of synthesis in the conclusion section of the study (see especially paragraphs 21 and 22).

8. A common practice in the conclusion/discussion section of Type B academic essays is for the researcher(s) to suggest directions for future research—particularly studies that might validate, broaden, or make more relevant the study's findings. Referring to two such suggestions for future research, (a) briefly explain how each study would validate, extend, or make the present study more relevant, and (b) come up with a prediction ("hypothesis") for each.

COLLABORATIVE ACTIVITIES

1. "Theoretically, the implicit messages observed in the current study could be viewed as being positive or negative" (paragraph 22). In discussion groups of three or four, consider the interpretations offered in this paragraph. How valid do you believe they are?

2. In their introduction, the authors refer to research into the effects that "pro-eating disorder websites" (see paragraph 3) could have on site visitors. Do you believe that such websites could fulfill a useful purpose? Do you believe that governments should be able to take lawful action against them, such as shutting them down? Discuss these or related questions.

3. This study investigates the possible effects of one form of media used as part of an educational program. To what extent are the media to blame for the prevalence of eating disorders today?

ACTIVITY

This study appeared in the *International Journal of Eating Disorders* (2007. 40 [2]). Consulting three other articles from the same issue, write an informal report or short essay (600–750 words) that summarizes content. For each, write briefly on the study's objective, methodology (for example, questionnaires, interviews, psychological assessment), participants, and findings. The purpose of the report is to demonstrate the variety of approaches of researchers to eating disorders. Note: Most of this information can be obtained from the individual abstracts. If your library does not allow you access to this journal, find three other recent articles on eating disorders in other journals.

War and Aggression

Sulfur Island

P.J. O'Rourke
(3,000 words)

As a memorial to the astonishing war slaughter of the modern age, I propose the island of Iwo Jima—for its ugliness, its uselessness, and its remoteness from all things of concern to the post-modern era.

Iwo Jima can be visited only with military permission and, usually, only by military transport. A comfortless C-130 Hercules propeller craft flies from Okinawa over more than 700 miles of blank Pacific, moving as slowly as the planes of Iwo's battle days. The island is five miles long, running northeast from a neck of sand at the base of the Mount Suribachi volcanic cone and spreading to a width of two and a half miles in the shape of a paint spill, with Mount Suribachi (really a 550-foot hill) as the can of paint. The colors are gray, gray-green, brown, and black—the hues of camouflage. From the air, Iwo Jima looks as small as it is, a reminder of the insignificance of the great tactical objectives of war. The landscape at Ypres is banal. The beaches at Normandy are not as nice as those in East Hampton. From the top of Cemetery Ridge, at Gettysburg, the prospect is less awe-inspiring than the view from many interstate rest stops. And Iwo Jima protrudes unimpressively from an oceanic reminder of the insignificance of everything.

I went to Iwo Jima with a director and a cameraman. We were working on a one-hour cable-television documentary about the battle. From 19 February to 26 March of 1945, 6,821 Americans and about 20,000 Japanese were killed in the fight for the island. How could a one-hour anything—prayer, symphony, let alone cable-television documentary—do justice to that? The director, the cameraman, and I had worried about it the night before in an Okinawa bar. We decided that 26,821 men would have told us to knock off the chickenshit worrying and drink.

The three of us were guests on a trip that is offered periodically to young enlisted marines in recognition of exemplary performance and attitude. The journey is spoken of as a "morale booster." It was July. Iwo Jima is almost on the Tropic of Cancer, parboiled by the north equatorial current. In the sun its rocks become charcoal-coloured briquettes in a hibachi. The temperature was 100° in the daytime and 100° at night. The humidity was 100 per cent. When there was wind, it was an eructation. The volcanic vents on Iwo Jima are still active. The name means "Sulfur Island" in Japanese. The visiting marines were not allowed to smoke or swim or explore on their own. They slept on the ground. Reveille was at 5 a.m. They were led on hikes all day, covering the island's eight square miles. I was never in the military, but if this is what boosts morale, I want nothing to do with what causes morale to deteriorate.

However, young men and women do not join the marines to get comfortable. And going to Iwo Jima is a way for new marines to imbue themselves with the spirit of the corps. The battle for the island was fought by what was at that time the largest force of marines ever assembled. The casualties were shocking. More than a third of the approximately 72,000 marines who landed on Iwo Jima were killed or wounded. The bravery, too, was shocking. Of the 353 Congressional Medals of Honor awarded during World War II, 27 were given for heroism on Iwo Jima, 13 of them posthumously.

Iwo became a byword for fighting while it was still being fought. The US military had hoped the island could be taken in two weeks. The battle lasted 36 days. Japanese resistance was expected to be stubborn. It was ferocious. Only 1,083 of the approximately 21,000 Japanese defenders surrendered or were taken prisoner. The landing on Iwo Jima occurred as the war in Europe was ending. The Allies were on the Rhine. Warsaw had fallen. Attention turned to the Pacific theatre. The secretary of the navy himself, James V. Forrestal, was on the beach at Iwo Jima on D-Day (as the day of the landing was called) plus four. When secretary Forrestal saw the flag-raising on Mount Suribachi, he said, "This means a Marine Corps for the next 500 years."

And there is that flag-raising. The Associated Press photographer Joe Rosenthal's shot is the best-known image of combat in World War II—perhaps the best-known image of combat in history. The word "icon," dull with use, can be applied precisely to the picture of the flag-raising on Mount Suribachi. Rendered in bronze at the Marine Corps War Memorial, with men 32 feet tall, the flag-raising is more impressive than the mountain where it happened.

To the young—very young—marines who were looking at that mountain when I was there,

the flag-raising must seem to have happened a full-secretary-Forrestal-500 years ago. For someone born in 1984, the war between Japan and the United States feels almost as distant in time as the war between Japan and Tsarist Russia does for me. During that long meander of chronology, Iwo Jima acquired a slight, untoward comic tinge. There were numerous parodic representations of the monument, the photo, the pose. There were Johnny Carson's "Mount Suribachi" tag lines. There was a period of years when every drunk of a certain age who'd ever been a marine claimed to have fought at Iwo, my uncle Mike included. (Uncle Mike's World War II Marine Corps stint was spent in a stateside hospital with an infected toe.) John Wayne didn't fight there either, but he gave a clumsy imitation of doing so in Sands of Iwo Jima. When televisions became common, that movie appeared on them constantly. The photograph itself showed not the first American flag atop Suribachi but, rather, its larger replacement. It is an image of combat in which no combat is involved. One or two too many men are trying to shove an iron pipe into a pile of rocks. And the flag-raising was not a signal of victory. It happened on the fifth day of the invasion, when most of the fighting and dying were yet to come.

The young visiting marines woke up on their first morning on Iwo Jima and hiked about four miles from their campground to the top of Suribachi. They did it so quickly that they were there for sunrise, at 5:45. They hung their dog tags at Suribachi's peak, on a bas-relief of the flag-raising mounted on a granite plinth. The monument is decorated with hundreds of dog tags, many bearing dates of birth more recent than my last dentist appointment. But if there was anything that struck the young marines as antique or absurd about this battlefield, they didn't show it. Some of them will be sent to deal with the antique absurdities of Afghanistan and Iraq.

The director, the cameraman, and I—antiques in our 40s and 50s—proceeded on our own absurd errand. Bearing camera, tripod, battery packs, tapes, and so forth, we trudged through a satire of tropical paradise. The beaches were black, not white. The sea looked like agitated dishwater. The sky was cloudless but dull with heat haze. Palm trees did not sway, nor did bougainvillaea flower in the botanically anonymous uninterrupted scrub. The weather didn't warm the blood, it broiled the bald spot and baked the feet. In place of grass shacks and tiki huts were the ruins of Japanese pillboxes and gun emplacements.

The three of us carried our stuff across the island and up Suribachi and down. We didn't faint in the heat or get too dizzy and sick. Iwo Jima is not a place, we complained to one another, where you feel you're allowed to complain. We went out into the deep, steep-pitched, sucking sand of the D-Day landing beaches. Thirty thousand men were put ashore that morning in a space hardly adequate for a UCLA pan-Hellenic luau. Tanks, amphibious vehicles, and marines themselves sank to immobility. On D-Day, 2,420 Americans were killed or wounded.

Combat now is a less crowded affair and more dependent on sophisticated electronic equipment. We were lugging some. It didn't compare in heft to what a marine carried on an amphibious landing. In 1945 one man's weapons, ammunition, and gear might have weighed as much as 122 pounds. Killing is not as physical as it once was. It's time for young, hopeful people to be relieved of fighting duties. War should be fought by the middle-aged men who are the ones who decide that war should be fought anyway. We don't have our whole lives in front of us. We're already staring down the bar-

rel of heart disease and SEC investigations. Being wrenched from home, family, and job would not be that wrenching for many of us. We wouldn't need these morale-boosting trips.

The idea that we should be doing the fighting and they should be having the fun didn't seem to occur to the young marines. They had brought pocketfuls of small zip-lock bags and were filling these with the sands of Iwo Jima.

Perhaps that movie deserves an unironic look. *Sands of Iwo Jima*, released in 1949, doesn't have much to do with the battle, although the final scenes are set on Iwo and incorporate harrowing footage shot by marine combat cameramen. The movie's real subject is a change in America—a nationwide, 150-million-person shift in values. John Wayne, a marine sergeant, is tough as nails. John Agar, a private in Wayne's platoon, is sensitive and has been to college. They clash. "I won't insist that [my son] be tough; instead I'll try to make him intelligent," Agar tells Wayne, who is shown to be pretty damn sensitive himself and more intelligent than you'd think. Then Wayne gets shot, and Agar realizes that sometimes the sensitive, intelligent thing to do is to be tough as nails. *Sands of Iwo Jima* thus traces US foreign policy from Teddy Roosevelt's Big Stick through Woodrow Wilson's Fourteen Points to George W. Bush's Whatever It Turns Out to Be.

It's tempting to believe that the Japanese defenders of Iwo Jima weren't as sensitive as the Americans of today. The Japanese fought for the island mostly from underground, hiding in as many as 16 miles of tunnels and caves. They died in there from flamethrower attacks, satchel-charge explosions, and suffocation. Many Japanese dead remain in these catacombs. Small, scary orifices of the tunnel system open all over the island. Visiting relatives have placed small altars by the holes. Offerings of cigarettes and sake sit beside incense burners. Broken and rusted weapons are arranged gracefully. It's just not possible for a sensitive American peering into the grim apertures to think that every person inside was as miserable and frightened as Bill Moyers would have been.

In fact, the Japanese military men on Iwo Jima—the officers, at least—were arguably more sensitive and intelligent than their American counterparts. The island's commander, Lieutenant General Tadamichi Kuribayashi, was an accomplished artist. He was fluent in English. He spent several years as a military attaché in the United States and Canada, writing letters home to his wife and child, the pages filled with humorous cartoons. And he openly opposed going to war with America. The head of naval forces, Rear Admiral Toshinosuke Ichimaru, wrote poetry in Japanese and classical Chinese and was known for his calligraphy. Lieutenant Colonel Takeichi Nishi was sensitive to opportunities for fun. He was a baron, of the gossip-column-boldface variety, who won a gold medal in horse-jumping in the 1932 Los Angeles Olympics. He partied in Hollywood, had affairs with actresses, and knew Spencer Tracy. All three officers fought to the death.

Across the northern fan of Iwo Jima, a volcanic plateau is half eroded into disorderly hills. Mostly their names are nothing but their heights in feet: Hill 382, Hill 362A, and so on. Every hill caused hundreds of people to die; so did every ravine between them. Any clump of rocks providing cover to the enemy was a source of death, as were all open spaces providing no cover to the marines. About five men to an acre were killed for this island, a corpse in each subdivision house lot. On D-Day, Lieutenant Colonel Charles E. Shepard, Jr., the commander of the Third Battalion, 28th Marine Regiment, told his men that their objective was "to secure this lousy piece of real estate so we can get the hell off it."

William Manchester, in his memoir of the Pacific war, *Goodbye, darkness*, described Iwo Jima as "an ugly, smelly glob of cold lava squatting in a surly ocean."

By coincidence, just a month before, I'd been looking at other smelly globs on the far side of the same surly ocean, in the equally isolated Galápagos Islands. My fellow tourists and I ooohed at the black sands, aaahed at the sulphurous volcano vents, and told one another how beautiful the sunset was behind mounts of exactly Suribachi's shape. Iwo Jima does not have the strange life forms found in the Galápagos. But what form of life could be stranger than that which was lived on Iwo Jima from 19 February to 26 March 1945? The Galápagos Islands are internationally protected to preserve the history of biological evolution. On Iwo Jima the history of moral evolution is preserved. The litter of battle is lying where it was dropped. A seven-story Japanese fortification inside Mount Suribachi has never been re-entered.

After Iwo Jima, a few more big World War II battles took place, notably in Berlin and on Okinawa. But it wasn't long before sensitive, intelligent nations evolved beyond such things—even if Hiroshima, one of those cataclysmic events common to evolutionary history, was required to spark the progress. Since then, military hordes swarming in all-out attack and military masses falling in desperate defence have been rare. When they do happen, evolutionary throwbacks are involved—Kim Il Sung, Saddam Hussein, the Ayatollah Khomeini.

People have not gotten better, of course—just more sensitive and, maybe, intelligent. One of the things they are intelligent about is strategy. Iwo Jima is approximately 660 miles from Tokyo. At the beginning of 1945, Americans had Pacific air bases that were within range of the Japanese mainland for bombers but not for fighter escorts. If the Americans could take Iwo

Jima, B-29s would fly over Tokyo fully protected. If the Japanese could keep Iwo Jima, B-29s would not. Today 100,000 soldiers aren't thrown into one such small space on a map. There are so many other kinds of space to fight over—outer space, cyberspace, the space between most people's ears.

We gave Iwo Jima back to Japan in 1968. It is now, as it was in February of 1945, a Japanese military base. At sunset when I was there, the Japanese national anthem was played over loudspeakers near the marines' campground. Every US marine turned toward the Japanese flag, stood at attention, and saluted. A marine sergeant major of my generation, who was leading the morale-boosting trip, said under his breath, "My grandfather would be rolling over in his grave if he saw this."

Neither his grandfather nor any other American is rolling over in his grave on Iwo Jima. The American dead had been disinterred by the 1960s and returned to American soil. Their ghosts don't haunt the Iwo Jima battlefield. Nor do the ghosts of the Japanese. I don't believe in ghosts, but I'm Irish enough to be able to tell when none are around. The island is grim. Thoughts of its history are frightening. But Iwo Jima isn't spooky. I found the same opinion in James Michener's *Tales of the South Pacific*. At the end of the book, the narrator visits a military cemetery. He encounters a black sailor who has volunteered for caretaker duty.

"Isn't it strange," I asked, "for colored men to like work in a cemetery?"

My guide laughed, gently and easily. "Yes! Yes! I knows jes' what yo'-all means," he said. "All dem jokes about ghos's and cullud men. But what yo'-all doan' see," he added quietly, "is dat dey ain' no ghos's up here! . . . dey is only heroes."

Pardon, for the sake of the thought, Michener's insensitive language. He was a pre-post-modern man. And so was General Kuribayashi. In his last message to Imperial General Headquarters, he said, "Even as a ghost, I wish to be a vanguard of future Japanese operations. . . ." If so, he's haunting a Toyota factory.

General Kuribayashi sent that message from a cave in a ravine at the northwest corner of Iwo Jima, an area the Americans called "Bloody Gorge." The marines were plagued by the manifold bolt-holes, peepholes, and gunports concealed in the narrow jumble of rock and brush. I went to Kuribayashi's final redoubt with the sergeant major and a Japanese sergeant major. The sergeant majors are friends. They are authorities on the history of Iwo Jima. Together they gave lectures to the young marines and guided the hikes around the island.

I couldn't see the entrance to Kuribayashi's cave—even though his descendants had marked it with a statue of a Shinto goddess. The sergeants, on their bellies, led me inside. Kuribayashi was a wide man, five feet nine and 200 pounds. Getting him into his headquarters must have been like getting at the wine when the corkscrew is lost. Thirty feet down, the roof, walls, and floor of the cave flared like a panic attack. We stood in a large, hot, stinking chamber with dead men's belongings all over the ground.

By mid-March, Kuribayashi had only 1,500 men. They were all in one square mile around Bloody Gorge. Tens of thousands of marines were on the island. The American Pacific command declared Iwo Jima "secure" on 14 March. Yet the fighting continued for 12 more days. In the "mopping up" on Iwo Jima, 1,071 marines were killed. This is more Americans than have died in the conquest and occupation of Iraq, with its 168,000 square miles of territory and its army of half a million soldiers—although there's still time.

Maybe we're coming to the end of the long, dark modern age. Slaughters of unnumbered human beings continue but not among people who knew Spencer Tracy. Warfare persists, but the scale of battle is returning to something that Hector and Ajax would recognize. Maybe each Jessica Lynch will become a legend. Maybe everybody's death will matter.

Atlantic Monthly. 2004. June.

KEY AND DIFFICULT WORDS

Define the following, using context or other clues if possible: **post-modern, eructation, catacombs, redoubt.**

QUESTIONS

1. (a) O'Rourke uses many comparisons in his essay. Thematically, what is the most important comparison? (Hint: Consider the short first paragraph and the final paragraph). (b) What is the author's intent in comparing the movie *Sands of Iwo Jima* with the actual battle? (c) Identify one other comparison in the essay, and comment on its rhetorical purpose.

2. Like many narrative and descriptive essays, important detail in "Sulfur Island" is shown through imagery and image patterns. Find two paragraphs in which imagery (words conveying sense impressions) is prominent, and consider what images contribute to the paragraph in which they occur and the essay itself.

3. Unlike many narrative and descriptive essays, O'Rourke uses statistics extensively. What is their main function? Why does the author use them so much in paragraphs 3–6 but less often after that?

4. In addition to imagery, the writer uses many other linguistic and stylistic resources: (a) find one example of irony (in irony, there is a deeper, non-literal meaning underlying the literal meaning), and comment on its purpose; (b) find one paragraph in which sentence length is a stylistic feature, and comment on its purpose; and (c) identify one example in which the writer's use of language stands out (for example, a striking or unexpected word/phrase or the use of a sound device like alliteration, the repetition of like sounds to begin consecutive words).

5. Do you think it was a wise choice for O'Rourke to use the first-person voice ("I," "we") as much as he does? In your answer, refer to specific passages.

6. In paragraph 18, the writer says that "On Iwo Jima the history of moral evolution is preserved." What does he mean? Why is this preservation important?

7. Do you believe that O'Rourke is hopeful about the future? Why or why not?

COLLABORATIVE ACTIVITY

The nature and scope of warfare has changed greatly in the past 60 years. Discuss the validity of this statement, taking a pro or con stance. *OR* Debate another issue related to how war is conducted in the twenty-first century.

ACTIVITIES

1. The author gives a lot of historical detail about the struggle for possession of Iwo Jima. Based on this information, write a short factual account of the battle that includes the reason it was fought, its development over the course of its 36 days, its outcome, and any other important details. Write it as if you had been assigned to write a one- to two-paragraph account for a history textbook. When you are done, consider some of the main differences between the textbook version and O'Rourke's.

2. Stereotypes are rigid categories into which people and ideas can be placed. They may arise from a simplified perception or a viewpoint previously acceptable to a politically or socially dominant group. Stereotypes often denigrate minorities or severely limit their power and freedom. Cite two examples of stereotypes or stereotypical thinking in the essay. (Clichés can be considered a kind of simplified perception applied to language.) Identify examples of other collective beliefs that were once deemed truthful by a dominant group but that would be seen as damaging stereotypes today.

Why ordinary people torture enemy prisoners

Susan T. Fiske, Lasana T. Harris, and Amy J.C. Cuddy

(1,500 words)

As official investigations and courts-martial continue, we are all taking stock of the events at Abu Ghraib last year. Initial reactions were shock and disgust. How could Americans be doing this to anyone, even Iraqi prisoners of war? Some observers immediately blamed "the few bad apples" presumably responsible for the abuse. However, many social psychologists knew that it was not that simple. Society holds individuals responsible for their actions, as the military court-martial recognizes, but social psychology suggests we should also hold responsible peers and superiors who control the social context.

Social psychological evidence emphasizes the power of social context: in other words, the power of the interpersonal situation. Social psychology has accumulated a century of knowledge about how people influence each other for good or ill (*1*). Meta-analysis, the quantitative summary of findings across a variety of studies, reveals the size and consistency of such empirical results. Recent meta-analyses document reliable experimental evidence of social context effects across 25,000 studies of eight million participants (*2*). Abu Ghraib resulted in part from ordinary social processes, not just extraordinary individual evil. This Policy Forum cites meta-analyses to describe how the right (or wrong) social context can make almost anyone aggress, oppress, conform, and obey.

Virtually anyone can be aggressive if sufficiently provoked, stressed, disgruntled, or hot (*3–6*). The situation of the 800th Military Police Brigade guarding Abu Ghraib prisoners fit all the social conditions known to cause aggression. The soldiers were certainly provoked and stressed: at war, in constant danger, taunted and harassed by some of the very citizens they were sent to save, and their comrades were dying daily and unpredictably. Their morale suffered, they were untrained for the job, their command climate was lax, their return home was a year overdue, their identity as disciplined soldiers was gone, and their own amenities were scant (*7*). Heat and discomfort also doubtless contributed.

The fact that the prisoners were part of a group encountered as enemies would only exaggerate the tendency to feel spontaneous prejudice against outgroups. In this context, oppression and discrimination are synonymous. One of the most basic principles of social psychology is that people prefer their own group (*8*) and attribute bad behaviour to outgroups (*9*). Prejudice especially festers if people see the outgroup as threatening cherished values (*10–12*). This would have certainly applied to the guards viewing their prisoners at Abu Ghraib, but it also applies in more "normal" situations. A recent sample of US citizens on average viewed Muslims and Arabs as not sharing their interests

and stereotyped them as not especially sincere, honest, friendly, or warm (*13–15*).

Even more potent predictors of discrimination are the emotional prejudices ("hot" affective feelings such as disgust or contempt) that operate in parallel with cognitive processes (*16–18*). Such emotional reactions appear rapidly, even in neuroimaging of brain activations to outgroups (*19, 20*). But even they can be affected by social context. Categorization of people as interchangeable members of an outgroup promotes an amygdala response characteristic of vigilance and alarm and an insula response characteristic of disgust or arousal, depending on social context; these effects dissipate when the same people are encountered as unique individuals (*21, 22*).

According to our survey data (*13, 14*), the contemptible, disgusting kind of outgroup—low-status opponents—elicits a mix of active and passive harm: attacking and fighting, as well as excluding and demeaning. This certainly describes the Abu Ghraib abuse of captured enemies. It also fits our national sample of Americans (*14*) who reported that allegedly contemptible outgroups such as homeless people, welfare recipients, Turks, and Arabs often are attacked or excluded (*14*).

Given an environment conducive to aggression and prisoners deemed disgusting and subhuman (*23*), well-established principles of conformity to peers (*24, 25*) and obedience to authority (*26*) may account for the widespread nature of the abuse. In combat, conformity to one's unit means survival, and ostracism is death. The social context apparently reflected the phenomenon of people trying to make sense of a complex, confusing, ambiguous situation by relying on their immediate social group (*27*). People rioted at St. Paul's Church, Bristol, UK, in 1980, for example, in conformity to events they saw occurring in their immediate proximity

(*28*). Guards abuse prisoners in conformity with what other guards do in order to fulfill a potent role; this is illustrated by the Stanford Prison Study, in which ordinary college students, randomly assigned to be full-time guards and prisoners in a temporary prison, nevertheless behaved respectively as abusers and victims (*29*). Social psychology shows that, whatever their own good or bad choices, most people believe that others would do whatever they personally chose to do, a phenomenon termed false consensus (*30, 31*). Conformity to the perceived reactions of one's peers can be defined as good or bad, depending on how well the local norms fit those of larger society.

As every graduate of introductory psychology should know from the Milgram studies (*32*), ordinary people can engage in incredibly destructive behaviour if so ordered by legitimate authority. In those studies, participants acting as teachers frequently followed an experimenter's orders to punish a supposed learner (actually a confederate) with electric shock, all the way to administering lethal levels. Obedience to authority sustains every culture (*33*). Firefighters heroically rushing into the flaming World Trade Center were partly obeying their superiors, partly conforming to extraordinary group loyalty, and partly showing incredibly brave self-sacrifice. But obedience and conformity also motivated the terrorist hijackers and the Abu Ghraib guards, however much one might abhor their (vastly different) actions. Social conformity and obedience themselves are neutral, but their consequences can be heroic or evil. Torture is partly a crime of socialized obedience (*34*). Subordinates not only do what they are ordered to do but what they think their superiors would order them to do, given their understanding of the authority's overall goals. For example, lynching represented ordinary people going beyond the law to enact their view of the community's will.

Social influence starts with small, apparently trivial actions (in this case, insulting epithets), followed by more serious actions (humiliation and abuse) (*35–37*), as novices overcome their hesitancy and learn by doing (*38*). The actions are always intentional, although the perpetrator may not be aware that those actions constitute evil. In fact, perpetrators may see themselves as doing a great service by punishing and/or eliminating a group that they perceive as deserving ill-treatment (*39*).

In short, ordinary individuals under the influence of complex social forces may commit evil acts (*40*). Such actions are human behaviours that can and should be studied scientifically (*41, 42*). We need to understand more about the contexts that will promote aggression. We also need to understand the basis for exceptions—why, in the face of these social contexts, not all individuals succumb (*43*). Thus, although lay-observers may believe that explaining evil amounts to excusing it and absolving people of responsibility for their actions (*44*), in fact, explaining evils such as Abu Ghraib demonstrates scientific principles that could help to avert them.

Even one dissenting peer can undermine conformity (*24*). For example, whistle-blowers not only alert the authorities but also prevent their peers from continuing in unethical behaviour. Authorities can restructure situations to allow communication. For example, CEOs can either welcome or discourage a diversity of opinions. Contexts can undermine prejudice (*1*). Individual, extended, equal-status, constructive, cooperative contact between mutual outgroups (whether American blacks and whites in the military or American soldiers and Iraqi civilians) can improve mutual respect and even liking. It would be harder to dehumanize and abuse imprisoned Iraqis if one had friends among ordinary Iraqis. A difficult objective in wartime, but as some Iraqis work alongside their American counterparts, future abuse is less likely. The slippery slope to abuse can be avoided. The same social contexts that provoke and permit abuse can be harnessed to prevent it. To quote another report [(45), p. 94]: "All personnel who may be engaged in detention operations, from point of capture to final disposition, should participate in a professional ethics program that would equip them with a sharp moral compass for guidance in situations often riven with conflicting moral obligations."

Science. 2004. 26 November 306.

REFERENCES AND NOTES

1. S.T. Fiske, *Social Beings* (Wilcy, New York, 2004).
2. F.D. Richard, C.F. Bond, J.J. Stokes-Zoota, *Rev. Gen. Psychol.* **7**, 331 (2003).
3. B.A. Bettencourt, N. Miller, *Psychol. Bull.* **119**, 422 (1996).
4. M. Carlson, N. Miller, *Sociol. Soc. Res.* **72**, 155 (1988).
5. M. Carlson, A. Marcus-Newhall, N. Miller, *Pers. Soc. Psychol. Bull.* **15**, 377 (1989).
6. C.A. Anderson, B.J. Bushman, *Rev. Gen. Psychol.* **1**, 19 (1997).
7. A. Taguba, "Article 15-6. Investigation of the 800th Military Police Brigade," accessed 30 June 2004 from www.npr.org/iraq/2004/prison_abuse_report.pdf.
8. B. Mullen, R. Brown, C. Smith, *Eur. J. Soc. Psychol.* **22,** 103 (1992).
9. B. Mullen, C. Johnson, *Br. J. Soc. Psychol.* **29**, 11 (1990).
10. J. Duckitt, in *Advances in Experimental Social Psychology*, M.P. Zanna, Ed. (Academic Press, New York, 2001).
11. When their own mortality is salient, as in wartime, people particularly punish those from outgroups seen to threaten basic values (*12*).
12. S. Solomon, J. Greenberg, T. Pyszczynski, *Curr. Dir. Psychol. Sci.* **9**, 200 (2000).
13. S.T. Fiske, A.J. Cuddy, P. Glick, J. Xu, *J. Person. Soc. Psychol.* **82**, 878 (2002).
14. A.J. Cuddy, S.T. Fiske, P. Glick, "The BIAS map: Behaviors from intergroup affect and stereotypes," unpublished manuscript (Princeton University, Princeton, NJ, 2004).
15. L.J. Heller, thesis, Princeton University, 2002.
16. H. Schutz, B. Six, *Int. J. Intercult. Relat.* **20**, 441 (1996).
17. J.F. Dovidio *et al.*, in *Stereotypes and Stereotyping*, C.N. Macrae, C. Stangor, M. Hewstone, Ed. (Guilford, New York, 1996).
18. C.A. Talaska, S.T. Fiske, S. Chaiken, "Predicting discrimination: A meta-analysis of the racial attitudes-behavior literature," unpublished manuscript (Princeton University, Princeton, NJ, 2004).
19. A.J. Hart *et al.*, *Neuroreport* **11**, 2351 (2000).
20. E.A. Phelps *et al.*, *J. Cogn. Neurosci.* **12**. 729 (2000).
21. Neuroimaging data represent college student reactions to photographs of outgroup members. These data should not be interpreted to mean that such reactions are innate or "wired in"; they result from long-term social context (*9*) and vary depending on short-term social context (*46*).
22. M.E. Wheeler, S.T. Fiske, *Psychol. Sci.*, in press.
23. J.P. Leyens *et al.*, *Eur. J. Soc. Psychol.* **33**, 703 (2003).
24. R. Bond, P. B. Smith, *Psychol. Bull.* **119**, 111 (1996).
25. S. Tanford, S. Penrod, *Psychol. Bull.* **95**, 189 (1984).
26. J. Tata *et al.*, *J. Soc. Behav. Pers.* **11**, 739 (1996).
27. J.C. Turner, *Social Influence* (Brooks/Cole, Pacific Grove, CA, 1991).
28. S.D. Reicher, *Eur. J. Soc. Psychol.* **14**, 1 (1984).
29. C. Haney, C. Banks, P. Zimbardo, *Int. J. Criminol. Penol.* **1**, 69 (1973).

30. B. Mullen *et al.*, *J. Exp. Soc. Psychol.* **21**, 262 (1985).

31. B. Mullen, L. Hu, *Br. J. Soc. Psychol.* **27**, 333 (1988).

32. S. Milgram, *Obedience to Authority* (Harper & Row, New York, 1974).

33. T. Blass, *J. Appl. Soc. Psychol.* **29**, 955 (1999).

34. H.C. Kelman, in *The Politics of Pain: Torturers and Their Masters*, R.D. Crelinsten. A.P. Schmidt, Eds. (Univ. of Leiden, Leiden, NL, 1991).

35. A.L. Beaman *et al.*, *Pers. Soc. Psychol. Bull.* **9**, 181 (1983).

36. A.L. Dillard, J.E. Hunter, M. Burgoon, *Hum. Commun. Res.* **10**, 461 (1984).

37. E.F. Fern, K.B. Monroe, R.A. Avila, *J. Mark. Res.* **23**, 144 (1986).

38. E. Staub, *Pers. Soc. Psychol. Rev.* **3**, 179 (1999).

39. A. Bandura, *Pers. Soc. Psychol. Rev.* **3**, 193 (1999).

40. L. Berkowitz, *Pers. Soc. Psychol. Rev.* **3**, 246 (1999).

41. J.M. Darley, *Pers. Soc. Psychol. Rev.* **3**, 269 (1999).

42. A.G. Miller, Ed., *The Social Psychology of Good and Evil* (Guilford, New York, 2004).

43. Although social context matters more than most people think, individual personality also matters, in accord with most people's intuitions: Social Dominance Orientation (SDO) describes a tough-minded view that it is a zero-sum, dog-eat-dog world, where some groups justifiably dominate other groups. People who score low on SDO tend to join helping professions, be more tolerant, and endorse less aggression; they might be less inclined to abuse. People choosing to join hierarchical institutions such as the military tend to score high on SDO, in contrast (*47*). Right-Wing Authoritarianism (RWA) entails conforming to conventional values, submitting to authority, and aggressing as sanctioned by authority. People who score low on RWA would be less prone to abuse (*48*). High SDO and RWA both predict intolerance of outgroups, social groups outside one's own.

44. A.G. Miller, A.K. Gordon, A.M. Buddie, *Pers. Soc. Psychol. Rev.* **3**, 254 (1999).

45. J.R. Schlesinger, H. Brown, T.K. Fowler, C.A. Homer, J.A. Blackwell, Jr., *Final Report of the Independent Panel to Review DoD Detention Operations*, accessed 8 November 2004, from www.information clearinghouse.info/article6785.htm.

46. L.T. Harris, S.T. Fiske, unpublished data.

47. J. Sidanius, F. Pratto, *Social Dominance: An Intergroup Theory of Social Hierarchy and Oppression* (Cambridge Univ. Press, New York, 1999).

48. B. Altemeyer, *Enemies of Freedom: Understanding Right-Wing Authoritarianism* (Jossey-Bass, San Francisco, 1988).

KEY AND DIFFICULT WORDS

Define the following, using context or other clues if possible: **amygdala, insula, dissipate, ostracism, epithet.**

QUESTIONS

1. How do the authors attract the attention of their readers in the brief first paragraph?

2. Identify the essay's purpose and methodology. How is its methodology well-suited to the essay's purpose?

3. The authors of this essay back up almost every claim they make by citing a variety of studies in the field. Using the information in the "References and notes" section, identify at least three specific forms that these studies take (you will need to consider specific divisions of books, journals, and other written sources—e.g., government reports).

4. In paragraphs 7 and 8, the authors refer to two studies from the 1970s. Why do you think it was necessary to mention studies more than 30 years old? What is significant about these particular studies?

5. What do the authors mean by "[t]he slippery slope of abuse" (paragraph 11)?

6. How can the Abu Ghraib experience be used as a learning opportunity, according to the authors?

7. The primary rhetorical pattern in this essay is cause/effect (it deals with factors—causes—that make abuse of enemy prisoners more probable—effects). How is the last paragraph developed? Why is it relevant and appropriate to end the essay with a direct quote from a Department of Defense (DoD) report, the only direct quotation in the essay?

COLLABORATIVE ACTIVITIES

1. The authors of the essay refer to several studies that attempt to account for aggressive behaviour toward "outgroups." What do you believe is primarily responsible for the kind of behaviour seen at Abu Ghraib?

2. As some of the studies illustrate, "social context" or "the power of the interpersonal situation" operates in many other situations like that of Abu Ghraib. Come up with other examples in which social context appears to have played a role in aggressive or oppressive actions. These could be very specific or more general situations that seem to "bring out the worst" in groups of people.

ACTIVITY

(a) Write a 300- to 500-word summary of "The Stanford prison experiment" (1971) or Stanley Milgram's "Obedience to authority study" (1963), using at least two reliable sources, no more than one of which should be a psychology textbook (you do not need to read the original study). Provide any necessary background to the experiment, include the results, and briefly consider the controversy that has surrounded the experiment. *OR* (b) Write a 300- to 500-word critical response to one of the above studies after reading reliable sources for background information about it.

Related reading: Jenny Desai. "In the minds of men."

Moral panic and the Nasty Girl

Christie Barron and Dany Lacombe

(9,000 words)

ABSTRACT

We examine why, despite evidence to the contrary, recent incidents of female violence have been interpreted as a sign that today's girls are increasingly nasty. We argue that the Nasty Girl phenomenon is the product of a moral panic. We show that while girl violence always existed, today's discussion is dominated by the concept of risk. Reform initiatives resulting from the panic consist of disciplinary mechanisms acting on the body of the individual delinquent and techniques that regulate individuals through the fostering of a culture of risk management and security consciousness. Finally, we situate the panic in the current backlash against feminism.

Female violence became a topic of much discussion in the mid-1990s in the wake of the gruesome sexual murders of teenagers by the infamous Ontario couple Paul Bernardo and Karla Homolka. But it was the murder of Reena Virk by a group of mostly female teens, in a suburb of Victoria in November 1997, that led Canadians to believe that something had gone terribly wrong with teenage girls. The belief that girl violence is rampant is a social construction. According to Statistics Canada, the annual youth charge rate for violent crime dropped 5 per cent in 1999, signalling a decline for the fourth year in a row (Statistics Canada, 2000). Moreover, Doob and Sprott (1998) have shown that the severity of youth violence did not change in the first half of the 1990s. Questioning the federal government's concern about the increase in girls' participation in violent and gang-related activities, Reitsma-Street (1999: 350) indicates that the number of girls charged for murder and attempted murder has been constant for the past 20 years and that such charges are infrequent. Although statistics indicate a phenomenal increase in the number of young women charged with minor or moderate assault over the past 10 years (from 710 charged under the Juvenile Delinquents Act in 1980 to 4,434 under the Young Offenders Act in 1995–96), several researchers indicate that the increase is more a reflection of the youth justice system's change in policy and charging practices than a "real" change in behaviour (Doob and Sprott, 1998; Reitsma-Street, 1999). Yet the public continues to believe that youth violence, particularly girl violence, is increasing at an alarming rate and necessitates immediate attention (Chesney-Lind and Brown, 1999: 171). This perception begs the important question: Why, despite evidence to the contrary, are recent isolated incidents of female violence interpreted as a sign that today's girls have become increasingly "nasty"?

We argue that the recent alarm over girl violence is the product of a moral panic that has had a significant impact on social, educational, and legal policy-making. Drawing on the moral panic and risk society literature, as well as the work of Michel Foucault, this paper examines how the recent concern with girl violence emerged; what effects that concern has had on policy-making in particular and on society in general; and why the panic over young females is occurring today.

HOW THE NASTY GIRL EMERGED

In this paper, we refer to the anxiety over girl violence as the Nasty Girl phenomenon. The expression, Nasty Girl, is not often used in journalistic or academic discourse on young female violence. It was, however, the title of a 1997 CBC documentary (*Nasty girls*, 5 March 1997) that examined high school girls' experience of violence and incarceration (Barron, 2000: 81–85). In our brief review of the documentary, we highlight how it reflected an overall sensation that we have entered the age of the Nasty Girl.

The documentary begins with old black-and-white film footage of two charming little girls playing with dolls. "Some things are at the heart of every little girl," claims the voice-over. The next scene, a little girl ironing with her mom, is accompanied by the comment: "mother's little helper is learning to become a homemaker." This reassuring 1950s view of girls as essentially maternal and domestic is, however, shattered in the next scene. The screen goes black, and a female voice authoritatively announces the dawn of a new age: "things have changed in the 1990s." In the following scenes, we learn just how bad things have become:

> In the late 1990s, almost everything your mother taught you about polite society has disappeared from popular culture, and nowhere is this more apparent than in what is happening to our teenage girls. Once the repository of sugar and spice and every-thing nice, today young women celebrate materialism, aggressive sexuality, and nasty behaviour. . . . Canada's teenage girls are committing more violent crimes than ever before, and girl crime is growing at an even faster rate than boy crime.

The documentary proceeds to show how this metamorphosis from sweet to Nasty Girl is activated by a liking for gangsta rap music, rock videos, and teen magazines filled with scantily dressed fashion models. The disastrous effects of popular culture are illustrated by a succession of scenes of high-school girls pushing, kicking, and fighting each other, followed by scenes of incarcerated girls being searched by guards or walking behind jail fences. This imagery is interspersed with shocking newspaper headlines announcing the increase in girl violence.[1] Popular culture, the force behind the destruction of polite society, becomes the source of social decline in the 1990s. By disrupting social norms, popular culture has displaced the ideal role model of little girls—the mother/housewife—and thus produced a new species, the Nasty Girl, whose threat to the stability of our present and future society is only becoming apparent. The Nasty Girl, therefore, has become a folk devil in the 1990s.

All moral panics identify and denounce a personal agent responsible for the condition that is generating widespread public concern. As Schissel explains, "folk devils are inherently deviant and are presumed to be self-seeking, out of control and in danger of undermining the stability of society. . . ." (1997: 30). Hence, during the "warning phase" of a panic, there are, as in the documentary *Nasty girls*, predictions of impending doom, sensitization to cues of danger, frequent overreactions, and rumours speculating about what is happening or what will happen (Cohen, 1980: 144–48). Subsequently, a large part of the public becomes sensitized to the threat, and, as in the case of the Nasty Girl, when confronted with an actual act of girl violence, their perception of danger and risk solidifies.

---

[1] The headlines read: "Girl violence reported on rise," "Girls in gang," "Girl-gang violence alarms expert," "Girl-gang members more violent than boys, experts agree," and "Girl, 13, beaten by gang girls."

It is not surprising, therefore, that the beating and murder of 14-year-old Reena Virk by a group of seven girls and one boy would become the event that provided evidence that girl violence had become a significant problem in Canada. On 14 November 1997, Virk, "a pudgy East Indian girl trying desperately to fit in," (Cernetig, Laghi, Matas and McInnes, 1997: A1) was on her way back to her foster home when friends asked her to join them under the bridge, a popular hangout. According to trial testimony, an argument broke out, and accusations were directed at Virk for spreading rumours about one of the girls, talking to another's boyfriend, and rifling through the address book of another (Tafler, 1998: 20). The news that Virk was beaten to death by a youth group part of "a teen subculture where girls pretending to be members of L.A. street gangs fight each other" shocked the country. According to *The Globe and Mail*, Reena's death became: "a national tragedy" (Cernetig et al., 1997: A1).

As is often the case in a moral panic, the media distorted and exaggerated the extent of isolated acts of girl violence following Virk's death. For example, newspaper and magazine headlines associated the case with a larger trend in girl violence: "Bad girls: A brutal B.C. murder sounds an alarm about teenage violence" (Chisholm, 1997), "Spare the rod and run for cover: When students hold the cards, school violence grows, especially among the girls" (McLean, 1999), "Virk's death triggers painful questions: Girls' involvement 'exacerbates rage'" (Mitchell, 1997), and "In Reena's world, being a 'slut' can get you killed" (Anon., 1997).

Also typical of a moral panic was the media claim that girl violence today is a "new" phenomenon, stemming from an altogether different "type" of girl (e.g., Sillars, 1998; McGovern, 1999; McLean, 1999). "The girl who is charged with second-degree murder," we are told, "could

be the babysitter who minds your children" (Martin, 1998: 75). This presentation of an aggressive and murderous "girl next door" with a Jekyll-and-Hyde nature is more akin to science fiction than reality. Yet it serves to amplify an already heightened fear of crime.

Girl violence is not a new phenomenon. A glimpse at newspaper articles in 1977 reveals that acts of girl violence are not new; rather, the attention paid to them is novel. For example, one article reports a violent confrontation between a group of teenage girls who had been feuding for a week. The confrontation began after one girl told friends that two other girls had ganged up on her in a fight. "Amid the kicking and screaming, a pierced ear-ring was ripped from the lobe of one of the youthful combatants . . . the small jack-knife was plunged into the chest of another [13-year-old] girl [who] fell to the street, gasping and moaning" (Wilkes, 1977: A7). Despite a rich description of violent details, the tone of the article is non-threatening. The title, "Teenager girl in knife feud says: 'We're friends again,'" certainly prepares the reader for an account of violence but it also emphasizes the fact that the dispute has been resolved amicably. Presenting the stabbing as an act of innocent girlhood play-fighting, the author further deflates the fight by pointing out that it "wasn't a battle between warring gangs, but an argument among friends." Whereas any type of remorse is rarely documented in current accounts of girl violence, one girl in the 1977 article is quoted as saying, "everyone started crying and telling each other we were sorry." The article ends with the assurance that this violent incident is not typical of girl behaviour, a conclusion justified by the knowledge that the weapon used in the girl feud did, after all, belong to a boy. In the wake of fear created by Virk's murder, the relationship between girls and violence is presented differently.

Also central to the creation of a climate of fear is statistical manipulation of crime data to establish the amplitude of girl violence. As journalist Nolan astutely recognizes in her analysis of the media reporting of the Virk case: "'experts' and authors were appearing on TV and radio talk shows trumpeting—with the solemn self-importance that always accompanies adult laments about the various wickedness of youth—the shocking fact that, according to the Canadian Centre for Justice Statistics, crime by young girls had increased 200 per cent since 1986" (1998: 32). However, most articles failed to recognize that the increase was in reference to minor assaults, such as pushing or slapping, which did not cause serious injury. Doob and Sprott explain, "[o]ne would, we believe, have more confidence that this increase reflected a change in girls' behaviour if it were to have shown up in the 'most serious' category of assaults" (1998: 192).[2] At the time of Virk's murder, girls were still far less involved than boys in all levels of assault, and only 4.5 per cent of youths charged with a homicide offence were female (ibid.). Moreover, according to more recent official statistics, the rate of male youth crime is almost three times higher than the female rate, and in 1999 the violent crime rate dropped (-6.5 per cent) for female youths (Statistics Canada, 2000). Yet inflated statistics about girl violence are usually assumed to be factual because, as Cohen (1980) explains, they are voiced by "socially accredited experts" whose expertise alone serves to legitimize the moral panic.

It is also the experts who construct the identity of the unruly girl and establish her as a real concern for panic. Historically, as Klein (1995) details, female offenders were described by experts as masculinized monsters (Lombroso, 1920), insensitive and lacking moral values (Thomas, 1907), envious of men due to lack of a penis (Freud, 1933), psychologically maladjusted (Pollack, 1950), and promiscuous (Davis, 1961) (Madriz, 1997: 26). Moreover, conceptions of morality increasingly became central to the identification and supervision of "dangerous" females. As the legitimate guardians of the moral sphere, middle-class women, in particular, participated in social purity movements that succeeded in criminalizing females who used their sexuality to survive. The reformers' efforts to rescue "fallen women" and "delinquent girls" from the harmful effects of industrial capitalism indicate how the bourgeois preoccupation with uplifting moral standards became central to the supervision of working-class girls.

Such reform movements also led to the establishment of child welfare agencies and the creation of juvenile justice systems. The youth criminal court evolved as a judicial parent or "parens patriae" that signalled the increasing involvement of the state in regulating and rehabilitating adolescent behaviour (Geller, 1987: 116). Girls, in particular, were deemed vulnerable and were incarcerated for status offences for their own protection, both from themselves and others. In the mid-twentieth century, the popularization of psychology helped foster a shift in the understanding of unruly girls and women:

---

[2] Doob and Sprott also bring to our attention the problems associated with statistics on minor offences among youth by revealing how their increase is more related to institutional changes in reporting policies than in an actual increase in violence. For example, the Ontario Ministry of Education requested that education boards develop violence-prevention policies and implementation plans for reporting and recording violent incidents by September 1994. Increasingly, policies of "zero tolerance" of violence in the schools mandate that all cases of violence be brought to court. According to Doob and Sprott, "such policies can be expected to result in increased numbers of minor cases of violence—these are the cases that are likely to have been ignored in the past" (1998: 188).

from being inherently bad or immoral they became inherently mad (Faith and Jiwani, 2002: 87). As Myers and Sangster uncovered in their study of Canadian reform schools for girls from 1930–60, the "girl problem" was constructed by "psychologists, penal workers, administrators and nuns whose preconceived expert knowledge about the nature of young women shaped their reconstructions of delinquent girls' rebellions within a language of irrationality, incredulity and pathology" (2001: 669).

Overall, the dominant idea throughout most of the twentieth century was that females who offend are rejecting their feminine role and are emulating their male counterpart. Consequently, many criminologists feared the impact of the 1960s women's movement on the feminine role. While Thomas indicated that promiscuity among girls was increasing with women's greater participation in the workforce and Pollack anticipated that, with emancipation, female crime would become masculinized and lose its masked character (Boritch, 1997: 61), it was the media interpretation of Freda Adler's book, *Sisters in crime* (1975), that cemented the notion that the women's movement for equality had a darker side.

Adler's "emancipation hypothesis" appealed to some contemporary analysts of girl violence. In *When she was bad* (1997b), journalist Patricia Pearson mocks politically correct society by reminding us that women's equality comes at a price:

> If we concede that women are ambitious, like men, and possess a will to power as men do, then we need to concede that women, like men, are capable of injuring others who thwart them. We cannot insist on the strength and competence of women in all the traditional masculine arenas yet continue to exonerate ourselves from the consequences of

power by arguing that, where the course of it runs more darkly, we are actually power*less*. (Pearson, 1997b: 32)

Female aggression, the will to power, seems a fact of nature for Pearson. And yet she links it to the social when she argues that if they commit crimes today, it is because "Girls don't *want* to be endlessly told that they're nothing but sex objects with low self-esteem. . . ; they are rejecting victimhood" (Pearson, 1997a: D3). In the process of resisting sexism, girls have unfortunately "gotten hip" (ibid.) to their capacity for violence. In a critique of Pearson's book, Chesney-Lind (1999) notes:

> Every one of [Pearson's] discussions of women's aggression and violence, in fact, erases patriarchy as the context within which the behavior occurs. . . . She minimizes and dismisses women's victimization and its clear connection to women's violence, and then argues that such violence should be punished without regard to gender. (1999: 117–18)

Pearson's journalistic musings about the darker side of female power is appealing in the current climate of feminist backlash, but it is simplistic.

Also appealing for current media accounts of girl violence are expert opinions from professionals who tend to comprehend the issue in psychosocial terms. For example, in a draft document she prepared for the Ontario Ministry of Training and Education, Debra Pepler, a psychology professor and expert on school bullying and girl relationships, cautions the reader on the complexity of girl aggression. However, she decontextualizes the phenomenon through her emphasis on bio-psychological traits and psychosocial circumstances relating to peers, the family, and the school:

The development of aggressive behaviour is a function of individual characteristics, and social interactions with families, peers, and romantic relationships. Individual factors contributing to the development of aggression in girls include: temperament, hyperactivity, early pubertal timing, and deficits in social cognitive processing. Family factors contributing to the development of aggression include: poor attachment to a parent; poor parental monitoring of children's behaviours; many conflicts within the family; harsh parenting practices; aggressive siblings; and marital problems. Low school achievement, frequent truancy, and negative school experiences may contribute to the development of aggressive behaviour in girls. (1998: 10)

In a published document she and a colleague prepared for the Canadian government, Pepler reaffirms her position by discussing aggressive girls as suffering from problems "in the biological, family context, peer context, and psychosocial domains" (Pepler and Sedighdeilami, 1998: iii). Explanations that focus on individual circumstances—self-esteem, family life, and personal relationships—are complex, significant, and valuable, but they tend to marginalize the impact of structural factors on the life of young female offenders. The media use such explanations to reduce the complexity of the violent girl to her dysfunctional, bio-psychological self. In the Virk case, the media often presented female violence as irrational, the product of an individual pathology capable of rearing its ugly head over petty reasons, such as slights about appearance, likeability, and intelligence.

One leading authority who underscores structures of power when discussing girl violence is Sybille Artz, director of the School of Child and Youth Care at the University of Victoria. In her book, *Sex, power, and the violent school girl*

(1998), Artz clearly locates girl aggression in a culture characterized by sexism, abuse, and inequality. However, she also emphasizes psychosocial problems, such as dysfunctional families, internalization of sexist gender roles, and lack of anger management skills, as explanatory factors. For example, Artz explains that the six girls she studied:

All come from families with many generations of experience with violence, alcohol misuse, and a generalized dysfunction that has left them with a less than helpful way of constructing self and world. All have internalized notions of being female that assign low general worth to women, hold that women achieve their greatest importance when they command the attention of males, and support the entrenchment of the sexual double standard. . . . In their immediate families, and in their social circle . . . [they] have been exposed to no forms of conflict resolution other than those that settle disputes through threat, intimidation, and violence. They have internalized a way of perceiving those who displease them that shifts moral and causal responsibility for their own displeasure onto those with whom they are displeased. . . . [T]hey are quick to anger, and quick to assume that others have it in for them. (Artz, 1998: 195–96)

Those individualizing factors figure highly in the media discussion of girl crime. According to Faith and Jiwani, the media "colluded with [Artz's] emphasis of girl-on-girl violence as signifying a rising trend, with the attendant theme of family dysfunction" (2002: 90).

Lacking from media analyses of female violence is the considerable impact of structural factors, including institutional racism, and economic and social inequality in the life of young female offenders and their victims. As Faith and Jiwani contend: "Significantly absent in the range of explanations put forward by the media was Reena Virk's marginalized positioning vis-à-vis those who had beaten and killed her. The issue of race and racism was either absent from the media discourse or presented in terms of her inability to fit in" (2002: 101–02). In a re-examination of her research data, Artz (2004) draws on social interdependence theory to acknowledge the importance of social structures in girls' use of violence because they "provide us with clues as to how people may be interpreting self and world and how they may be morally positioned with regard to their actions" (Artz, 2004: 104).

In summary, we have drawn on the moral panic literature to examine the recent preoccupation with the violent girl. We argued that through distortion, exaggeration, and statistical manipulation of data, as well as expert evidence, the media was able to construct a new breed of female, the Nasty Girl, who has become one of our current folk devils. This construction is not without consequences: "We want assurances that what happened to Reena couldn't happen to anybody else," asserts the popular magazine *Chatelaine*, because "after all, next time it might be my daughter or yours who is the victim" (Martin, 1998: 71). In a climate of fear, Schissel (1997: 30) reminds us, it is easier "for average citizens to become embroiled in the alarm over [folk devils] and to call for harsh justice." Unfortunately, the reforms resorted to in a time of panic often fail to address the real source of public anxiety. It is to those reforms that we now turn.

THE EFFECTS OF THE MORAL PANIC ON POLICY-MAKING

The panic over the Nasty Girl has had a significant impact on legal, educational, and social policy in Canada. The result has been an increase in both formal and informal mechanisms of con-

trol. While proposals for legal reform mostly consist of repressive measures targeted at delinquent youths, social and educational programs contain informal mechanisms of control targeting society more generally. As we show in this section, proposals for reform are not only disciplinary mechanisms of power acting on the body of the individual delinquent, they are also part of the more recent governmental techniques of power that regulate and manage free individuals through the fostering of a culture of risk management, public safety, and security consciousness (Foucault, 1982; Cohen, 1985; O'Malley, 1996; Garland, 1997).

Following the Virk case and other high-profile youth crimes, state policies on violent youth have become punitive. The Youth Criminal Justice Act (YCJA) came into effect on 1 April 2003, and although it offers positive measures to reduce the number of youths being incarcerated, its clear distinction between "non-violent," "violent" and "serious violent" offences reflects public desire to deal harshly with violent youth. This process of labelling, as expressed by Quebec youth justice officials, ensures that "the nature of the charge, rather than the circumstances and prognosis of the youth, becomes the major governing factor in how the youth is dealt with under the Act" (Green and Healy, 2003: 191). The YCJA (sections 61 and 62) also allows for youths as young as 14 years old to be sentenced as adults, and it expands the list of offences for which these presumptive transfers apply. Public support for such branding reforms, including provisions in the YCJA that allow for publishing the names of young offenders, was echoed in the sensational media coverage one of the accused received while on trial for Virk's murder (Hall, 2000: A1). Kelly Marie Ellard, who was 15 at the time of the incident, was initially found guilty on 20 April 2000 of second-degree murder in adult court. The final outcome of her third trial is pending.

Of even more concern for girls specifically is the passage of the Secure Care Act (Bill 25) in British Columbia. Following the lead of Alberta's Protection of Children Involved in Prostitution Act (PCHIP), the Secure Care Act is intended "to provide, when other less intrusive means are unavailable or inadequate, a means of assessing and assisting children who have an emotional or behavioral condition that presents a high risk of serious harm or injury to themselves and are unable to reduce the risk. . . . These conditions may [include] severe substance misuse or addiction or the sexual exploitation of a child" (section 2 (1), cited in Busby, 2001). In essence, this legislation meant to protect children ultimately blames victims of sexual exploitation and permits the apprehension and incarceration of girls—who will be targeted more than boys due to their differential involvement in prostitution—for up to 100 days when the time for the assessment, hearing, and renewal of certificates is combined (*Justice for Girls*, 2001: 1–2). Reminiscent of the controversial nineteenth-century English Contagious Diseases Acts, which enacted a double standard into law by allowing for the forced examination and treatment of diseased prostitutes (Walkowitz, 1980), the Secure Care Act is an affront to the bodily integrity of young people (mostly girls) that authorizes medical examinations and disclosure of the results (sections 16 (1)(*b*) and 40 [Busby, 2001]). *Justice for Girls*, a Vancouver-based, non-profit organization that promotes justice and equality for street-involved or low-income girls, opposes the Secure Care Act for its lack of accountability on the part of the professionals involved and for violations of Charter rights around issues of consent and confidentiality. Moreover, they see the Act as:

> . . . a mechanism to further marginalize and institutionalize young women. Rather than addressing poverty, male violence, colonial devastation of First Nations communities, or shamefully inadequate and inappropriate voluntary services for young women, the *Secure Care Act* instead criminalizes and pathologizes young women. Ironically, young women who have actually committed a crime are entitled to greater protections under the *Charter of Rights and Freedoms* and *Young Offenders Act* than those who will be jailed under the *Secure Care Act* in the name of child protection. (*Justice for Girls*, 2001: 1)

Similar bills have been introduced in other Canadian provinces.

While harsh legal policy is aimed at incapacitating both violent boys and girls, informal mechanisms of control targeting young girls in particular have also resulted from the panic over girl violence. These mechanisms, however, did not emerge from within the centre of the criminal justice apparatus; rather, they evolved at the margins of society, through the work of social agencies, activists, and experts who helped create a consensus about the problem of girl violence. This groundwork has produced new definitions of violence and new methods of controlling both young females and society in general.

The expansion in definitions of violence is most obvious in relation to what goes on at school, a site where the threat of the violent girl is most apparent. Pepler, who was commissioned by the Ontario and Canadian governments to prepare strategies for aggressive girls, helped foster a new rationality of bullying—teasing, gossiping, and quarrelling—as an intolerable act of aggression. The new definition of aggression, which "has been expanded to include the behaviours that typically comprise girls' attacks including indirect and verbal aggression . . . , aggression directed at peer relationships . . . , and aggression directed at damaging self-esteem and/or social status . . ." is said to pose "a challenge to schools as it is difficult to observe and deal with" (Pepler, 1998: 5). Early identification of girls at risk, however, is imperative, because, as Pepler and Sedighdeilami claim, "data on the development of aggressive girls into adulthood suggests that girls who are aggressive may also constitute a significant social concern in Canada" (1998: iii). To help school officials detect girls at risk, they identify "biological and social risk" and "psychosocial difficulties" (ibid.). As Pepler's work was part of a movement to develop anti-bullying handbooks across Canada (Galt, 1998), we can only surmise how the expansive definition of aggression and call for early detection could potentially increase the surveillance of teenage girls in schoolyards and at home.

The new rationality and concern over bullying is not only targeting the aggressive girl. It also actively seeks the participation of school authorities in the informal control of girls. For example, Pepler and Sedighdeilami's caution that "[g]irls in families with violence, ineffective parenting, and high levels of conflict should be identified for supportive interventions" (ibid.) encourages school staff to observe and detect signs of risk in girls. The popular magazine *Today's Parent*, in an article entitled "When the tough get going . . . the going gets tough: How to deal with bullies," promotes parents becoming detectives through continuous observation of their children, since bullying is an "underground activity." Stuart Auty, president of the Canadian Safe School Network, is known to give parents his expert advice on how to steer children away from violence, including basic strategies such as "knowing your kid, staying connected and providing them with opportunities to develop their self-esteem, as well as establishing limits and consequences when rules are broken" (cited in Martin, 1998: 77). While it is ironic that mainstream parental and educational

advice is now repackaged as state-of-the-art technology to prevent bullying, we see in this strategy a sign of the current shift in crime control policy that Foucauldian scholars have identified as "government-at-a-distance" (Rose and Miller, 1992; Garland, 1997).

As we know from Foucault's studies of the asylum, the prison, and sexuality, power—which he also refers to as "governmentality"—is better understood as a rationality evolving from the margins of society than as one concentrated exclusively in its centre, the state. It is in the interstice between the state and the individual, that is to say, in the social field occupied by the school, the hospital, the juvenile court, and social workers' and psychologists' offices, that different forms of rationality emerge and produce their disciplinary and regulatory effects onto the social body. Diverse professionals and agencies come together to govern the behaviour and mentality of both those who pose problems, such as the violent girl, and those they can enlist in the management of the violent girl. While the strategies of power produced in those "centres of governance" (Garland, 1997: 179–80) have disciplinary effects meant to break and tame those at the receiving end, some act through the subjects for the purpose of creating a "responsibilized autonomy" in them. For example, since Virk's death, expert advice encourages parents, teachers, and youth to change their behaviour and self-image to bring them into line with socially approved desires and identities and, in the process, ensure the good functioning of the family and the school. The participation of these individuals in the management of the violent girl does not rely on force but rests instead upon an alliance with expert authorities, which is grounded in what Garland perceives as "the willingness of individuals—whether as family members, or workers, or citizens—to exercise a 'responsibilized' autonomy, and to pursue their interests and desires in ways which are socially approved and legally sanctioned" (1997: 180). This strategy of governmental power, Garland continues, characterizes most current crime control policy:

> State authorities . . . seek to enlist other agencies and individuals to form a chain of coordinated action that reaches into criminogenic situations, prompting crime-control conduct on the part of 'responsibilized' actors (see Garland, 1996). Central to this strategy is the attempt to ensure that all the agencies and individuals who are in a position to contribute to these crime-reducing ends come to see it as being in their interests to do so. "Government" is thus extended and enhanced by the creation of "governors" and "guardians" in the space between the state and the offender. (Garland, 1997: 188)

Youths are particularly targeted by this strategy of power grounded in a "responsibilized" autonomy. For example, as part of its "Taking a Stand" program, the BC government made available a toll-free, province-wide phone number to "prevent crime and violence and to offer youth a safe, confidential means to obtain information and help." The "Youth against Violence Line" wallet card distributed to schools invites young people to phone in and report incidents where they feel "scared," "threatened," or "don't know what to do." Similarly, the police force of a suburb of Victoria, BC, launched a program named "Solid Rock" in which police officers or actors perform skits to convince young people that teenagers who go to the authorities rather than putting up with bullies are not rats but exemplary, responsible citizens (McInnes, 1998: A4). We see in these well-intentioned government programs an attempt to help youth become not only law-abiding citizens but *homo*

prudens (O'Malley, 1996) too, thus enticing them in the creation of a culture of risk management in which they learn to fear youth and think of themselves as potential victims (Ericson and Haggerty, 1997). These programs illustrate the profound change in current crime control policy Garland foresaw: "the new programmes of action are directed not towards individual offenders, but towards the conduct of potential victims, to vulnerable situations, and to those routines of everyday life which create criminal opportunities as an unintended byproduct" (Garland, 1996: 451). Hence, we need to understand the moral panic about the violent girl or youth in general as a process that leads not only to the containment and transformation of violent girls and boys but also to the increased self-discipline and regulation of all youths, who learn to think of themselves as potential victims of bullying.

To summarize, the policies and programs stemming from the moral panic about violent girls include repressive measures towards violent youth that are deployed by the crime-control apparatus. They also include more informal mechanisms of crime control directed at society, which are deployed by a "government-at-a-distance." While repressive measures stem from traditional crime-control agencies, such as the police or prisons, informal control operates rather indirectly or "at a distance" by fostering the cooperation of non-state organizations and private individuals (Garland, 1997: 188). Through the actions of various experts involved in the fight against bullies, parents, teachers, young people, and, specifically, girls are encouraged to become responsible and prudent individuals. To this effect, policies and programs seek to make them recognize their responsibility in reducing crime and persuade them to change their behaviour to reduce criminal opportunities (Garland, 1996: 453).

WHY IS THE PANIC HAPPENING TODAY?

Why did the reaction to girl violence take the particular form and intensity it did during the late 1990s? The moral panic literature emphasizes that, during a panic, the anxieties the public experiences are real, but their reaction is often misplaced. Hence, the object of the panic, the violent girl, is not always the source of people's anxiety. In psychoanalytical terms, she is more likely to be the object of a projection rather than the source of concern and fear. As one media article stated, the murder of Virk resulted in "a profound self-examination and fear among Canadians that society's rules are undergoing unsettling change" (Mitchell, 1997: A1). This section attempts to situate the moral panic about girl violence in its larger social and political context in order to uncover some of the anxieties that propelled it to become symbolically attached to aggressive girls. We follow this discussion with a brief examination of the way policies aimed at violent girls could better attempt to address the problems young girls face today.

We start our attempt at contextualizing the moral panic over the violent girl by examining the larger structural forces characterizing our present. According to Young (1999), the transition from modernity (the "Golden Age" of the postwar period) to the present late modernity (late 1960s and onwards) resulted in significant structural and psychological changes that produced social anxieties. The shift primarily entailed a movement from an inclusive to an exclusive society: from a society that incorporated its members and enjoyed full (male) employment, rising affluence, stable families, and conformity to an exclusive society arising from changes in the labour force. These changes included a shift from a more social-based, communitarian labour force to one of individualism stemming from the new knowledge-based, technology society. As

late-modern society became increasingly characterized by a plurality of values, self-reflexivity, multiculturalism, and scientific and political relativism, the solid foundation of modernity began to melt. Material certainty and shared values shattered, leaving us with a heightened sense of risk and uncertainties. In such a precarious climate, crime acquires a powerful symbolic value. If we could only control crime better, we would bring safety into one aspect of our disrupted lives. It is not surprising that our quest for security often translates into a projection of our fears onto specific scapegoats, who are made responsible for our feelings of insecurity.

What social anxieties are projected onto the violent girl today? What threat to societal values has she come to represent? Acland provides direction when he argues that the fear stemming from the Virk case suggests "we are failing in the ability to reproduce our social order in the exact manner we think it ought to be done" (cited in Mitchell, 1997: A1). In our attempt to examine what transformations might account for the panic over girl violence, we are drawn back to the documentary *Nasty girls*, described at the beginning of this article, which related the problem of girl violence to the disappearance of the familial and domestic ideology of the 1950s, an ideology feminists have fought hard to challenge. Our culture associates young female offenders with feminism. As Schissel (1997) states: "[t]he 'sugar and spice' understanding of femaleness is often the standard upon which young female offenders are judged, and, in effect, the images of 'bad girls' are presented as . . . sinister products of the feminist movement" (1997: 107). Similarly, we argue that what troubles society most about the violent girl is that she has come to represent the excesses of the changed social, political, and economic status women have gained through their struggles for equality since the 1960s. The moral panic over the Nasty Girl is part of a backlash against feminism (Faludi, 1991).

In the wake of the Virk case, it was not difficult to find newspaper articles emphasizing the dangers of the rise in "Girl Power." A pullout section of the *Vancouver Province*, for example, had a picture of the petite head of the popular sitcom star Ally McBeal superimposed on the body of Rambo. While she smiles innocently at the camera, her muscular arms are holding a machine gun. The caption reads: "It's a girrrl's world: Yikes! It's only a matter of time before women take over" (Bacchus, 1998). Although Bacchus writes in a tongue-in-cheek manner, he outlines "evidence" of a shift from patriarchy to matriarchy: the Spice Girls, Buffy the Vampire Slayer, angry chanteuses like Alanis Morissette and Xena, Lilith Fair, WNBA, Martha Stewart, Rosie, and the Women's Television Network. While Bacchus quickly clarifies that women have not achieved superiority or even equality in the workplace, the evidence of the shift to matriarchy he posits is in the form of a change "in spirit." The mantra of this spirit, Bacchus claims, is "Go girl!" (ibid.).

The media sensationalized the spirit of girl power by positing it as the cause of girl violence. Showing insightful reflexivity, journalist Nolan suggests that "[f]ollowing long-standing misogynist traditions, they've made the assumption that the behaviour of a few reveals the brutality of all girls and that increased freedom for women—brought about specifically by feminism—is responsible for the supposed rise in young women's violence" (Nolan, 1998: 32). Girl power, the source of social anxieties, is the real nasty here; the moral panic over the statistically insignificant Nasty Girl is a projection of a desire to retrieve a patriarchal social order characterized by gender conformity.

While a segment of our society is increasingly worried about the ill effect of the spirit of girl power and engrossed in attacking popular culture and in developing policies to transform all girls into good girls, another segment is capitalizing on girl power to turn a profit. "Bad girls = big bucks," claims the *Vancouver Sun* (Todd, 2001: A17). It is not the first time folk devils become prey to commercial exploitation and are given a greater ethos than they originally possessed (Cohen, 1980: 140, 176). Today, young girls are implored by marketers and the media to dress like adults and to express sexual, aggressive confidence (Clark, 1999: 47). Under the headline "Hollywood discovers girl power," *USA Today* acknowledges that "where the girls are is where Hollywood wants to be" (Bacchus, 1998: B1). And whereas girls were previously sex symbols in the background of beverage advertisements, they are now staring down the camera lens as they "growl": "This is our beer" (Bacchus, 1998: B3).

The spirit of girl power is paradoxically what policies and programming for violent girls aim at transforming through the adoption of anger management skills based on a cognitive behavioural model. Programs that encourage control, empathy, self-esteem, communication, and social skills are important, yet they do little in addressing the wider social context in which girl power takes place, as well as the desire for autonomy and the consumerism it creates. These techniques assume individual pathology and are based on a punishment-correction model that has failed repeatedly to reform (Foucault, 1979). Moreover, while most current programs to curb girl violence are founded on cognitive skills training and risk technologies, we also believe there has been insufficient critical evaluation of actuarial practices with youth. As Lupton (1999: 2) argues, the technico-scientific approach to risk ignores how "risk" can be a socio-cultural phenomenon in its own right. In a study on girls incarcerated for violent offences in Saskatchewan, one of us questions if actuarial techniques depoliticize the process of social control by assisting in the efficient management of the offender rather than addressing social conditions requiring reform (Barron, forthcoming).

An alternative approach to address violence would be to focus on gender, race, and class-specific initiatives that appeal to the realities of young females. Chesney-Lind and Brown (1999) argue that because girl violence differs from boy violence in magnitude and quality, the traditional approaches to treatment and models of law enforcement are inappropriate for girls. They, and others, call for programs that recognize factors that marginalize girls, including the extensiveness of girl victimization and the complicating factors of culture, racism, and social and economic inequality, which may contribute to violent behaviour (ibid., 194; Jiwani, 1998; Jackson, 2004).

CONCLUSION

Although the moral panic framework has much utility in understanding the recent concerns about girl violence, it also has the potential to dismiss them. The framework can be used simply to deconstruct the sources of fear for the purpose of demonstrating that the societal concern is unfounded. We think, however, it should be used to uncover how the configuration of ideas surrounding a phenomenon has come into being and has moulded our life, customs, and science (Doyle and Lacombe, 2000). In this way, we would be in a better position to resist the insidious effects of a moral panic.

Secondly, it is apparent that the moral panic framework may not go far enough in addressing the effect of the panic on the "folk devils" themselves. We believe that the media caricatures of the Nasty Girl for marketing and consumer purposes provide an appealing identity. Far from implying that popular culture causes the Nasty

Girl, we suggest that the media is one venue among others that supply girls with a variety of models. What girls do with those models is a complex affair. As Young explains, "the actors can embrace these essences in order to compensate for [their marginalized position] and lack of identity. . . . We have seen how such a process of embracing the essence bestowed upon the deviant can be taken up ironically, mockingly and transformatively. But even so, it still shapes individuals' notions of themselves" (1999: 118).

Despite its potential shortcomings, the moral panic framework is useful to uncover the social construction of the violent girl and the subsequent inclusion of this construction in policy-making. Punitive proposals to contain violent youths partly resulted from the panic, as well as policies that aim at enlisting the cooperation of the general public into supporting the objectives of state authorities to create a safe and security-conscious culture. The irony is that while we conscientiously join the effort to eradicate the Nasty Girl out of a sense of responsibility, we shamelessly continue to capitalize on the marketability of the power she has come to embody.

Discussing the construction of the Nasty Girl as a moral panic should not negate a search for positive reforms or undermine the devastation resulting from rare acts of female aggression and violence. Although it can be argued that the call for gender-based programs would confirm the amplitude of girl violence, it cannot be denied that young females are incarcerated for violent acts and have different life experience and needs from those of males. Perhaps the most promising recommendations for female programming include giving girls a voice in program design, implementation, and evaluation in order to address the wider context in which violence takes place. We maintain that in addition to gender, the interlocking systems of oppression in young women's lives must be considered.

Acknowledging and responding to the connections between racism, sexism, ableism, homophobia, and economic inequality is a challenge to the philosophical underpinnings of the criminal justice and education systems.

Canadian Review of Sociology and Anthropology.
2005. February 42 (1).

REFERENCES

Acland, C.R. 1995. *Youth, Murder, Spectacle: The Cultural Politics of "Youth in Crisis."* San Francisco: Westview Press.

Alder, F. 1975. *Sisters in Crime: The Rise of the New Female Criminal.* New York: McGraw-Hill.

Anon. 1978. "16-year-old girl charged in death of taxi driver, 61." *The Globe and Mail.* 11 April, p. 5.

Anon. 1996. "When the tough get going . . . the going gets tough: How to deal with bullies." *Today's Parent*, Vol. 13, No. 7, pp. 66–70.

Anon. 1997. "In Reena's world, being a 'slut' can get you killed." *Toronto Star.* 6 December, pp. E1, E4.

Artz, S. 1998. *Sex, Power, and the Violent School Girl.* Toronto: Trifolium Books.

Artz, S. 2004. "Revisiting the moral domain: Using social interdependence theory to understand adolescent girls' perspectives on the use of violence." In *Girls and Aggression: Contributing Factors and Intervention Principles.* M. Moretti, C. Odgers and J. Jackson (eds.). New York: Kluwer Academic/Plenum Publishers, pp. 101–13.

Bacchus, C.L. 1998. "It's a girrrl's world." *Vancouver Province.* 2 August, pp. B1–B3.

Barron, C.L. 2000. *Giving Youth a Voice: A Basis for Rethinking Adolescent Violence.* Halifax: Fernwood Publishing.

Barron, C. (forthcoming). "Nasty girl: The impact of the risk society on female young offenders." Ph.D. dissertation, Burnaby, B.C.: Simon Fraser University, School of Criminology.

Boritch, H. 1997. *Fallen Women: Female Crime and Criminal Justice in Canada.* Toronto: Nelson.

Busby, K. 2001. "Protective confinement of children involved in prostitution: Compassionate response or neo-criminalization?" Notes for a presentation at the Women behind Bars Conference. University of New Brunswick, Fredericton, 9 February.

Canadian Broadcasting Corporation. 1997. *Nasty Girls.* Videotape. Broadcast 5 March.

Cernetig, M., B. Laghi, R. Matas and C. McInnes. 1997. "Reena Virk's short life and lonely death: Swept away: A 14 year-old girl beaten by the very teens she wanted as friends was left to the cold salt-water." *The Globe and Mail.* 27 November, p. A1.

Chesney-Lind, M. 1999. "When she was bad: Violent women and the myth of innocence." Book review. *Women and Criminal Justice*, Vol. 10, No. 4, pp. 113–18.

Chesney-Lind, M. and M. Brown. 1999. "Girls and violence: An overview." In *Youth Violence: Prevention, Intervention and Social Policy.* D. Flannery and C.R. Huff (eds.). Washington, DC: American Psychiatric Press.

Chisholm, P. 1997. "Bad girls: A brutal B.C. murder sounds an alarm about teenage violence." *Maclean's*, 8 December, p. 12.

Clark, A. 1999. "How teens got the power: Gen Y has the cash, the cool—and a burgeoning consumer culture." *Maclean's*, 22 March, pp. 42–49.

Cohen, S. 1980. *Folk Devils and Moral panics: The Creation of the Mods and Rockers.* New York: St. Martin's Press.

Cohen, S. 1985. *Visions of Social Control.* New York: Oxford University Press.

Doob, A. and J.B. Sprott. 1998. "Is the 'quality' of youth violence becoming more serious?"

Canadian Journal of Criminology and Criminal Justice, Vol. 40, No. 2, pp. 185–94.

Doyle, K. and D. Lacombe. 2000. "Scapegoat in risk society: The case of pedophile/child pornographer Robin Sharpe." *Studies in Law, Politics and Society*, Vol. 20, pp. 183–206.

Ericson, R. and K. Haggerty. 1997. *Policing the Risk Society*. Toronto: University of Toronto Press.

Faith, K. and Y. Jiwani. 2002. "The social construction of 'dangerous' girls and women." In *Marginality and Condemnation: An Introduction to Critical Criminology*. B. Schissel and C. Brooks (eds.). Halifax: Fernwood Publishing, pp. 83–107.

Faludi, S. 1991. *Backlash: The Undeclared War against American Women*. New York: Crown.

Foucault, M. 1979. *Discipline and Punish: The Birth of the Prison*. New York: Vintage Books.

Foucault, M. 1982. *The Subject and Power*. 2nd ed. H.L. Dreyfus and P. Rabinow (eds.). Chicago: Chicago University Press.

Galt, V. 1998. "Handbook to address bullying by girls: Recent attacks lend urgency to project." *The Globe and Mail*. 31 January, p. A3.

Garland, D. 1996. "The limits of the sovereign state: Strategies of crime control in contemporary society." *British Journal of Criminology*, Vol. 36, No. 4, pp. 445–71.

Garland, D. 1997. "'Governmentality' and the problem of crime: Foucault, criminology, sociology." *Theoretical Criminology*, Vol. 1, No. 2, pp. 173–214.

Geller, G. 1987. "Young women in conflict with the law." In *Too Few to Count: Canadian Women in Conflict with the Law*. E. Adelberg and C. Currie (eds.). Vancouver: Press Gang Publishers, pp. 113–26.

Green, R.G. and K.F. Healy. 2003. *Tough on Kids: Rethinking Approaches to Youth Justice*. Saskatoon: Purich Publishing.

Hall, N. 2000. "Slain teen's grandparents in court for 'last chapter.'" *The Vancouver Sun*. 7 March, p. A1.

Jackson, M.A. 2004. "Race, gender, and aggression: The impact of sociocultural factors on girls." In *Girls and Aggression: Contributing Factors and Intervention Principles*. M. Moretti, C. Odgers and J. Jackson (eds.). New York: Kluwer Academic/Plenum Publishers, pp. 82–99.

Jiwani, Y. 1998. *Violence against Marginalized Girls: A Review of the Current Literature*. Vancouver: The Feminist Research, Education, Development and Action Centre.

Justice for Girls. 2001. "Statement of opposition to the *Secure Care Act*." http:/www.moib.com/jfg/publications/p_sca.htm.

Lupton, D. 1999. *Risk and Sociocultural Theory: New Directions and Perspectives*. Cambridge, UK: Cambridge University Press.

Madriz, E. 1997. *Nothing Bad Happens to Good Girls*. Berkeley: University of California Press.

Martin, S. 1998. "Murder in Victoria: Why did Reena Virk die?" *Chatelaine*, May, pp. 70–77.

McGovern, C. 1999. "No feelings: Teens at the Virk trial demonstrate a chilling lack of humanity." *British Columbia Report*, Vol. 10, No. 13, pp. 42–43.

McInnes, C. 1998. "Police probe gang assault of Nanaimo teen." *The Globe and Mail*. 12 March, p. A4.

McLean, C. 1999. "Spare the rod and run for cover: When students hold the cards, school violence grows, especially among the girls." *British Columbia Report*, Vol. 10, No. 9, pp. 52–54.

Mitchell, A. 1997. "Virk's death triggers painful questions: Girls' involvement 'exacerbates rage.'" *The Globe and Mail*. 28 November, pp. A1, A8.

Myers, T. and J. Sangster. 2001. "Retorts, runaways and riots: Patterns of resistance in Canadian reform schools for girls, 1930–60." *Journal of Social History*, Vol. 34, No. 3, pp. 669–97.

Nolan, N. 1998. "Girl crazy: After the brutal murder of Reena Virk, the media whipped the country into a frenzy over a supposed 'girl crime wave.'" *This Magazine*, March/April, Vol. 31, No. 5, pp. 30–35.

O'Malley, P. 1996. "Risk and responsibility." In *Foucault and Political Reason*. A. Barry, T. Osborne and N. Rose (eds.). Chicago: University of Chicago Press, pp. 189–208.

Pearson, P. 1997a. "You're so cute when you're mad." *The Globe and Mail*. 29 November, p. D3.

Pearson, P. 1997b. *When She Was Bad: Violent Women and the Myth of Innocence*. New York: Viking.

Pepler, D.J. 1998. "Girls' aggression in schools: Scenarios and strategies." Unpublished paper. The Ministry of Training and Education, Government of Ontario.

Pepler, D.J. and F. Sedighdeilami. 1998. *Aggressive Girls in Canada*. Working Papers. Hull: Applied Research Branch, Strategic Policy, Human Resources Development Canada.

Reitsma-Street, M. 1999. "Justice for Canadian girls: A 1990s update." *Canadian Journal of Criminology and Criminal Justice*, Vol. 41, No. 3, pp. 335–64.

Rose, N. and P. Miller. 1992. "Political power beyond the state: Problematics of government." *British Journal of Sociology*, Vol. 43, No. 2, pp. 173–205.

Schissel, B. 1997. *Blaming Children: Youth Crime, Moral Panics and the Politics of Hate*. Halifax: Fernwood Publishing.

Sillars, L. 1998. "Youth murders multiply, Ottawa ponders: Five brutal teen homicides have provincial ministers demanding a tougher YOA." *Alberta Report*, Vol. 25, No. 7, pp. 45–47.

Statistics Canada. 2000. "Crime statistics." *The Daily*. 18 July. http://www.statcan/Daily/English/000718/d00718a.htm.

Tafler, S. 1998. "Who was Reena Virk?" *Saturday Night*, Vol. 113, No. 3, pp. 15–22.

Todd, D. 2001. "Bad girls = big bucks." *The Vancouver Sun*. 26 January, p. A17.

Walkowitz, J.R. 1980. *Prostitution and Victorian Society: Women, Class, and the State*. Cambridge and New York: Cambridge University Press.

Wilkes, J. 1977. "Teenage girl in knife feud says: 'We're friends again.'" *Toronto Sun*. 17 September, p. A7.

Young, J. 1999. *The Exclusive Society*. London: Sage.

KEY AND DIFFICULT WORDS

Define the following, using context or other clues if possible: **amicable, incredulity, contextualize, exonerate, pubertal, punitive, presumptive, differential, interstice, deploy, posit, misogynist, actuarial, deconstruct, configuration.**

QUESTIONS

1. Determine by context the meaning of the following phrases, all of which are important in comprehending the essay: "moral panic," "folk devil," "risk management" (each occurs at least once in the first few pages). Provide a one-sentence definition of each, using only your own words.

2. What common public perception of female violence do the authors challenge? Identify the essay plan in the introduction and any other markers throughout the essay designed to help with comprehension.

3. Name three general characteristics of moral panic.

4. What do the authors mean when they refer to "structural factors" (paragraphs 16–19) in girl violence? What factors, other than "structural" ones, has girl violence been attributed to?

5. Of the many researchers that the authors refer to in their discussion of the moral panic literature, they particularly stress the work of Debra Pepler (paragraphs 15–16, 25–6) and Sybille Artz (paragraphs 17–19). What makes them important sources for this essay? Summarize the authors' criticism of Pepler's work (paragraphs 25–6) and of the Secure Care Act (paragraph 23).

6. What is "government-at-a-distance" (paragraphs 26–9), and what is its major failing, according to the authors?

7. In the final section of the essay ("Why is the panic happening today?"), the authors contrast the postwar period with the period beginning in the late 1960s. What is their purpose in doing so? Under two headings, "postwar" and "late 1960s," list as many contrastive terms as you can (words or phrases) that define these two periods, according to the authors. Use your own words.

8. Why do the authors refer again to the CBC documentary discussed in detail in the first section ("How the Nasty Girl emerged")? Has its significance or importance to the authors' argument changed?

9. Identify one example each of a popular (newspaper or magazine) source and an academic (journal article or book) source, and show how the authors use the sources as support.

COLLABORATIVE ACTIVITY

To what extent do the authors blame the media for the misrepresentations discussed in the essay? Do you think this blame is fair? Do you believe that the "nasty girl" exists as a relatively recent phenomenon? Discuss or debate these questions.

ACTIVITIES

1. Locate at least one newspaper or magazine article dealing with the death of Reena Virk (see "References"), showing how the authors' claims about the media reporting of the occurrence are supported or not supported by the article.

2. In their conclusion, Barron and Lacombe call attention to "[t]he irony . . . that, while we conscientiously join the effort to eradicate the Nasty Girl out of a sense of responsibility, we shamelessly continue to capitalize on the marketability of the power she has come to embody." Do you agree with this assessment? Would you characterize this dual behaviour as inconsistent, paradoxical, or an example of hypocrisy? Write a 300- to 500-word response to the authors' charge in which you use either a fact-based or argument-based claim.

In the minds of men

Jenny Desai

(2,100 words)

Whether war or violent crime touches our lives directly, or whether we are subjected to it second-hand through the media, on some level we experience the connection between our own biology and our emotions each day. Anyone who's been cut off in traffic, even once, has felt the connection between that first perceived insult and the flush of anger, the spike of adrenaline, the body's fight-or-flight mechanisms that seem built into human nature.

Aggressiveness of character, early nineteenth-century phrenologists believed, could be judged by observing bumps on the skull; modern scientists peer into the brain beneath the bone. The idea that violence just might be hardwired into our genes has grown ever more acceptable as the technology, including gene mapping and brain scans, has grown more sophisticated.

By the mid-1980s, according to one study, about 40 per cent of students believed war was intrinsic to human nature. Moreover, Wesleyan University psychology professor David Adams found that these students became less likely to engage in activities for peace. To challenge the alleged biological findings being used to justify violence and war, he convened a group of scientists at the Sixth International Colloquium on Brain and Aggression held in May 1986, and together, 20 of them drafted the Seville Statement on Violence. It concluded that, "Just as 'wars begin in the minds of men,' peace also begins in our minds. The same species who invented war is capable of inventing peace. The responsibility lies with each of us." The statement was endorsed by the 65,000-member American Psychological Association at a 1987 meeting in New York, but of 400 invited reporters, only four—from the *APA Monitor*, Tass, ADN from then-East Germany, and the *People's Daily World* of the US Communist Party—showed up to cover the event.

"The myth that war is part of human nature does not appear to be so much an inherent component of 'common sense' so much as it is the end result of a campaign of psychological propaganda that has been promulgated in the mass media in order to justify political policies of militarism," Adams, the chief drafter of the document and a specialist on the brain mechanisms of aggressive behaviour and the evolution of war, would later say. The statement, he would explain, was both a response to the perceived bias toward the belief in a biological basis for violence and an appeal for "transformative tasks" to foster a culture of peace.

But because it was written after a conference and came at a good time to influence politicians, it may have been worded a bit too strongly. It was never intended as an attack on biological research but on the "misuse of biological data," Robert Hinde, another Seville signatory, claimed in an exchange with the *Human Ethology Newsletter*.

"I was not there when it was finalized, and I did not like all the details of the wording, but in group enterprises, one has to make some compromises sometimes," Hinde says today. "David Adams, who was the real architect, is sometimes over-enthusiastic. If I were redoing it now, I would recast it in very different terms."

Two decades after the Seville scientists drafted their statement, how, if at all, should it be recast? Looking at its five propositions in the slightly more rarefied scientific air of 2005, do they seem overly enthusiastic? Or have they helped us finally conclude, as Adams hoped they would, that "biology does not condemn humanity to war, and that humanity can be freed from the bondage of biological pessimism"?

Nature may be "red in tooth and claw," as English poet Alfred Tennyson wrote, but is our human nature similarly bloodied because of an inheritance from our evolutionary past? It's tempting to anthropomorphize every conflict we see on Animal Planet into a war skirmish, or to brand every chimp a war chief, but according to Richard Wrangham, a Harvard University professor of biological anthropology, war is "a political activity in which leaders direct coalitionary violence. So I don't think of 'war' as occurring in chimpanzees or other animals."

Violent behaviour abounds along our evolutionary family tree, but warlike behaviour per se does not; it begins and ends with us, he says. While humans and our closest ape relatives, the chimpanzees, "share the tendency for coalitions of related males to cooperate in defending a shared territory, and we kill our enemies," says Wrangham, the fault lies not with our shared legacy but with a shared environmental pressure to protect territory. And a shared tendency toward territorialism—a tendency we share with wolves, which are hardly our kissing cousins—is not the same as a tendency to wage war.

Slightly more nuanced than the notion that an evolutionary legacy fuels violence is the notion that violence lies somewhere in our DNA. The Seville Statement didn't claim that genes don't matter at all; the signatories allowed that genes "provide a developmental potential that can be actualized only in conjunction with the ecological and social environment."

Researchers now look for genetic defects or abnormalities that may provide links to aggressive behaviour in *individuals*—not all humankind. In 1993 one team of American and Dutch scientists reported on its study of a Dutch family in which five generations of the men had been unusually prone to aggressive and violent outbursts. These men were found to have a genetic defect that made them deficient in an enzyme that regulates the neurotransmitter serotonin. Despite cautions that the findings concerned only one family, several news stories heralded the finding of an "aggression gene"—lending some credence to Adams's claim of media bias toward biology-based violence models. Currently, the role of neurotransmitters linked to mood and emotion, including serotonin and dopamine, is being studied in several laboratories, with an eye toward locating a chromosome or brain location that might account for aggression or addiction patterns.

The willingness to be violent and to kill can be of evolutionary advantage; Wrangham speculates that chimpanzees and humans who are willing to kill fare better than those who aren't, especially when resources like space and food are limited. In an upcoming article he co-authors with University of Minnesota primatologist Michael Wilson, Wrangham argues that the ultimate example of "easy killing" among humans can be seen in street gangs, a model for human groups in general. Young men form male-male alliances (initially in adolescence or early adulthood) apparently to protect their own individual status from insults, put-downs, or physical punishment. These alliances spring from the biologically generated desire of these young males to protect their social status in relation to other males, and they are not without cost to those outside the group: street gang alliances have the byproduct of conferring power—the power to kill a lone individual rival. "It's like putting a loaded gun into the hand of a young man and sending him off to meet unarmed rivals," Wrangham says.

Wrangham conceives the evolution of war as "a recent political consequence of complex, hierarchical society that stems from an evolutionary-based tendency of men to be more concerned than women about status, and therefore to form protective alliances, and therefore to use them to their advantage when occasion arose."

Other research, however, suggests that aggression is far from advantageous. The ability to get along, to form alliances, and to bond with one's fellows isn't just the high road; it's the healthy one. Researchers Stephen C. Wright of the University of California, Santa Cruz, and Art Aron of Stony Brook University in New York have investigated the ways in which we socialize. Their findings suggest that joining and interacting with groups of others—both like and unlike ourselves—is a uniquely human need that is tied to our sense of self-esteem. Relating positively with others is valuable because it tells us who we are and who we are not. It also provides us with a feeling both of well-being and of our place in the social fabric—a fabric that cannot accommodate violent aggression without becoming damaged.

Studies funded by the Institute for Research on Unlimited Love, a centre that encourages the scientific study of altruism, suggest that we do better by doing good. Far from being a sign of evolutionary weakness, the desire and ability to be charitable and giving toward others have palpable health benefits. And when conflict does occur, it can lead to even closer relationships. "For example, chimpanzees kiss and embrace after fights, and other nonhuman primates engage in similar reconciliations," wrote Frans de Waal, director of the Living Links Center at Emory University's Yerkes Regional Primate Research Center, in the journal *Science*. Evolutionarily speaking, then, aggression isn't the only way to success, and the alliances built along the way can be of more than just material support.

Remember the movie *Falling down*, in which the actor Michael Douglas plays a desperate man pushed to his limit? Caught in one Los Angeles traffic jam too many, he snaps, jumping out of his car to wander through the rest of the movie with a loaded shotgun and a very bad attitude. Many of us have those moments, but few of us act on our impulses.

In most people, the brain can rein in overreaction to emotions like fear and anger; in normal brains, the prefrontal cortex censors inappropriate impulsive thoughts before they turn into action. But Alarik Arenander, director of the Institute of Science, Technology, and Public Policy's Brain Research Institute, believes humans *can* have a violent brain. According to a statement on the institute's website, "SPECT [single photon emission computerized tomography] images graphically reveal the presence of 'functional lesions' (areas of low-metabolic activity caused by the absence, or near absence, of neuronal firing) in the prefrontal lobes of violent children—the region of the brain that normally provides a filter against impulsive, aggressive, and violent behaviour."

Doctor Pamela Blake of Georgetown University Hospital reviewed the brain scans of 31 murderers and found 20 of them had physical evidence of frontal lobe dysfunction. University of Wisconsin-Madison psychologist Richard Davidson and his colleagues reviewed positron emission tomography scans of murderers and other people prone to violence and found that they had detectable differences in the parts of the brain that deal with emotion regulation: the orbital frontal cortex, associated with the ability to resist our physiological urges; the anterior cingulate cortex, involved in learning and pain perception; and the amygdala, linked to emotional modulation.

But is this new science or just new technology? Ever since railroad construction foreman Phineas Gage famously survived having an iron rod driven through his frontal lobe in 1848, we've been aware that damage to certain areas of the brain can affect the personality. Given what we now know about brain plasticity, it's clear the brain can change in response to experience. Recent research indicates that the combined factors of genetics and environment can lead to the specific biochemical imbalances and brain abnormalities that form the biological basis of violence.

For psychologist and Seville signatory Hinde, there's an important distinction to be made between individual and collective aggression. The howl of a hungry baby, for example, sounds aggressive because, in a sense, it is: the baby makes its hunger heard with all the outrage of a self that feels discomfort but cannot alleviate or understand its source. But war is something else, and Hinde concentrates on the vast organization and materiel needed to create the momentum to carry it out. "Modern war depends on the many incumbents of the many roles in the institution of war doing their several duties. That institution depends on many aspects of human behavior, but we have no instinct for war as such," he says. "Aggressiveness—the motivation for violence—is important in some primitive forms of warfare, but becomes less so as war becomes institutionalized." If war were instinctive, we wouldn't need to train men to overcome a natural aversion to killing, and we wouldn't have to create a sanitized military-industrial complex to wage war.

Nearly 20 years after the Seville Statement on Violence was drafted, we know more about the brain and our biology than ever before. Yet still it seems insufficient. Perhaps when we study the brain—when the brain studies itself—the Heisenberg Principle takes over: what we can know of ourselves is limited by our very study. The Seville Statement challenged the idea that our biology breeds war; today, we're still peering into the brain's depths—and still reading lurid accounts in the newspaper. We can only hope, as we know more about our own biology, we will begin to understand more about our own nature —warts and all. And maybe that understanding will be part of nurturing the transformative work begun by Adams and his colleagues all those years ago.

Science and Spirit. 2005. March/April.

KEY AND DIFFICULT WORDS
Define the following, using context or other clues if possible: **anthropomorphize, nuance, signatory, palpable, materiel.**

QUESTIONS
1. For what kind of audience was "In the minds of men" written? Give examples from the first few paragraphs of the essay to support your answer.
2. What kind of opening does Desai use (logical, dramatic, or other)? In what paragraph(s) would you locate the thesis statement?
3. How does David Adams, the "architect" of the Seville Statement on Violence in 1986, explain his controversial statement (paragraph 4)? How does Robert Hinde explain it (paragraph 5)? What accounts for the differences in their comments?
4. What inference can be drawn from the fact that only four reporters attended the endorsement of the Seville Statement in New York (paragraph 3)? Are other inferences possible?
5. Summarize the opposing views of the benefits of aggression (paragraphs 12–15). In explaining both views, Desai synthesizes the findings of experts. Which view do you find more credible and why?
6. What does Desai mean when she asks, "is this new science or just new technology?" (paragraph 19)? Using context as your guide, give a one-sentence definition of the "Heisenberg Principle" (paragraph 21) in your own words.
7. Why do you think that the author chooses to conclude the body of her essay by quoting Robert Hinde extensively? How does paragraph 20 connect with the concluding paragraph?

COLLABORATIVE ACTIVITY
Do you believe, as some of Desai's sources do, that human aggression is "hardwired?" Do you believe, as the students referred to in paragraph 3 do, that war is "intrinsic to human nature?" Discuss or debate these questions.

ACTIVITIES
1. In paragraph 4, David Adams appears to blame the "myth that war is part of human nature" on the media; in paragraph 11, the author points to news stories in which scientific findings were generalized and sensationalized. To what extent do you believe the media have helped propagate the belief that war and/or violence are a part of human nature?

2. Who was Phineas Gage, to whom the author alludes in paragraph 19? Using a reliable source, explain the allusion (an allusion is a brief outside reference to a person, place, thing, event, or idea). (One possible Internet site is www.deakin.edu.au/hbs/GAGEPAGE/.)

3. "Whether they are hawks or doves, on the political left or right, many people have come to accept war as inevitable, even 'in our genes.' The obvious problem with such fatalism is that it can become self-fulfilling. Our first step toward ending war must be to believe that we can do it"—John Horgan. Using this statement as a starting point, freewrite to uncover your opinions and feelings on this issue, or write a 300- to 500-word response to the statement, synthesizing at least two sources from "In the minds of men" in your response.

Related reading: Susan T. Fiske et al. "Why ordinary people torture enemy prisoners."

Push-me-pull-you

Susan Olding

(4,950 words)

A holiday weekend, and I am walking with my daughter to the park. She sniffs the air like a young filly and canters into a pile of leaves. "Hello!" she whinnies to every stranger we pass. "Happy Thanksgiving!" And even, "You look beautiful today!"

I set my face in what I hope is some semblance of a smile. This smile is my shield for what I know will come next: "How adorable!" "What a sweetheart!" "How old is she?" And of course, the inevitable, the ubiquitous, "You are *so* lucky!"

When we reach the park, J. wants me to push her on the swings. Her hair streams out behind, a black banner glinting with red highlights. "Now you get on, and I'll push you," she commands. At not quite five, she is strong enough to

do it too, though she forgets to get out of the swing's path on its return, and I have to stick my legs out and drag my boots in the sand so I don't slam into her. She laughs. "You stay sitting, and I'll come join you," she says. She clambers up and positions herself face to face, astride my lap. Snuggling closer, she rests her head against my shoulder. "Swing, please. Rock me." This is an old ritual of ours, one begun when she was still a baby. I croon her favourite lullaby. When she looks up into my eyes, her own eyes shine with the purest trust and affection. "You're the best mum in the whole universe," she whispers. "I love you to infinity and beyond."

I am so lucky.

That night, after I've read stories to her, brushed her teeth, cuddled under the blankets, and banished the monsters from the closet, I tuck her into bed and lean across for a goodnight kiss. But instead of the soft pressure of her lips or the butterfly's brush of her eyelashes, I feel her small hands come up around my neck. Her thumbs are at my windpipe. She squeezes. Hard. I wonder if I am imagining this, if she's really just trying to hug me in some new and original fashion. She's creative and dramatic and physical, and she likes to invent all kinds of games. Surely she's just fooling around. She doesn't really know what she is doing.

But she does know; she knows *exactly* what she is doing. She wants to choke me. To choke me.

My daughter is the human embodiment of Dr Doolittle's push-me-pull-you. Dr Doolittle is what I privately name each of the so-called experts whom I consult in search of explanations and help. These are the labels they try on and cast aside, for none of them fits exactly or covers completely:

Difficult temperament
Regulatory disorder
Sensory processing disorder
Attention deficit hyperactivity disorder
Non-verbal learning disability
Gifted, with asynchronous development
Unresolved grief or loss
Oppositional defiant disorder
Post-traumatic stress disorder
Reactive attachment disorder.

J. joined our family through adoption at the age of 10 months. Before that, she lived in a large orphanage in China. Most, if not all, of her more challenging behaviours can probably be traced in one way or another to her early experiences of abandonment and neglect, as those interact with her genetically determined sensitivities. In public, she plays two roles—the beautiful, exuberant charmer, perhaps a shade too friendly with strangers, perhaps a bit too "busy"—but precocious and delightful just the same. Her other role is the poorly governed wild child. Back at home, we see the complicated self beneath the masks. Living with J. is like living in a hurricane zone. You can't relax because you're always scanning the sky for signs of trouble. Winds are generally high, and it's hard work at the best of times to clean up the falling debris. And then the storm breaks, and you batten down; it roars and roars, and it's all you can do to keep yourself intact in the face of its fury. Unless, of course, you find yourself within its calm, still centre. The hurricane's eye surprises even the weariest with hope.

Her first year with us was relatively easy. She was active, yes—unusually so—but she liked to cuddle, made good eye contact, and grew and learned at a remarkable rate. Even during her second year, signs of trouble were subtle, mutable, and easily missed. All two-year-olds throw tantrums. Most four-year-olds don't, though, or not often. And if they do, their fury stops somewhere short of compelling them to fling chairs across the room.

She spins, hangs upside down, jumps down hard onto harder surfaces, and shows other evidence of early deprivation to her proprioceptive and vestibular systems. She suffers from subtle developmental delays; she did not establish "handedness" until she was nearly five. She struggles to sit still; she chatters and asks countless nonsense questions. Driven by impulse, she grabs and interrupts. She resists or defies almost every parental instruction, and she can be so peremptory with us that we have nicknamed her "Miss Bossypants." Yet at the same time she demands our constant attention. Until she reached the age of four, she could not bear to be in a separate room from me if we were in the same house. A recent move across the country has thrown her back to that emotional territory, and if I happen to leave her side now without repeated warnings, she screams.

And often, in the guise of seeking closeness, she aims to harm. "I'm sorry," she will say, after landing an elbow in my stomach, after leaping headlong and unannounced into my arms, after cutting me off and tripping me up on the sidewalk. "Ouch," I shout, as she plonks herself into my lap and the top of her head hits my jaw. "Oops," she says. I can't tell if that's a smirk on her face or a smile. She doesn't and yet she does want to hurt someone.

And why shouldn't she? The person she was closest to in all the world deserted her shortly after she was born. The fact that her birth-mother may have made that decision under enormous social or economic pressure, at great personal cost, and with only her baby's interests at heart is irrelevant to J. Deep in her cells, she knows only this—at the age of one week, she was left, helpless and alone. Then she was institutionalized, where she was neglected and unloved for 10 long months. Finally, she was handed off to a pair of weird-looking, strange-smelling strangers and taken a whole world away from everything known and familiar. And all this without explanation and entirely without choice. She was powerless, and being powerless felt bad, and now that she has finally gained some small measure of security and safety in our family, she never wants to feel powerless again. Hence, her constant jockeying for control. She hones her considerable charm, sharpens her wits, and strengthens her will for violence. Far below consciousness, in her primitive brain, she knows that her survival is at stake. And her anger—the anger that should rightfully be aimed at her birth-mother or at her birth-father or at the nannies at the orphan-

age or at a sexist culture or at oppressive family planning laws or at longstanding customs militating against domestic adoption in China or at the vast global network that permits middle-class Westerners like me to whisk children like her away from their countries of origin—all that anger, the full fierce force of it—she points directly at me. At the person who, however guilty I may be of participating in an ethically questionable system, am also the one who feeds her, bathes her, diapers her, teaches her how to walk, teaches her how to read, sings to her, plays with her, holds her, comforts her.

And loves her. Loves her. Loves her.

I live with a level of uncertainty about my mothering that is unusual even among the other adoptive parents I know. I am never entirely sure where I stand.

Around age two and a half, J. went through a phase of aggression towards other children. Or, more precisely, towards babies. At her pre-school, at our kinder-gym, at the park, even in our own house—whenever she saw a crawling infant, she would stomp over to him, loom above him menacingly, and then, with a glazed, cold, almost inhuman expression on her face, shove him to the ground. Snatching up the latest victim and rocking him, his mother might scold, "You need to set firmer limits. Give her some consequences!"

"There, there," others would sigh. "It's all because you are too strict with her. She needs you to be more nurturing."

"Never mind," counselled a third group. "All kids do that."

Or, in its nastier form, "What are you worrying about? She's normal. You're crazy!"

Any way you look at it, I'm to blame.

I've seen those baby books in which proud parents are supposed to record developmental milestones. First tooth, first step, first word.

The milestones I should have recorded, but didn't:

First kiss not flinched from.
First time she played for more than two minutes on her own.
First adult conversation she allowed to proceed uninterrupted.
First time she did not shriek in fury when I left the room.
First time she could engage quietly in a parallel activity in my presence.
First time she co-operated immediately with a parental request.
First time she did not explode when a parent refused a demand.
First time she truly relaxed.

Then again, maybe it's better we didn't record these. The first step and the first word are assumed to lead naturally to the next and the next and the next. A simple, reassuring linear progression. But just because J. did not explode when I disciplined her last week is no reason to think that she won't explode today. Just because she has accepted a kiss in the past is no reason to believe that she won't brush it off tonight.

At the age of four, J. told me, "I had a nightmare about a mean mummy with mustard teeth. And she was always mean to me. And I sang a happy song and put her in jail and then my nice mummy came back. But the mean mummy looked just like you except she had mustard teeth."

Normal parenting does not work, or does not work reliably. Although J. understands the relationship between cause and effect, between her actions and their repercussions, she often cannot stop herself from doing what she knows she should not. My husband, Mark, and I must become a species of super-parent, the "therapeu-

tic" parent. We're not just here to raise her, we're here to *heal* her. The Drs Doolittle agree that what children like J. need is "high structure/high nurture" parenting; sadly, they agree less on the precise meaning of that term. Consistent consequences or paradoxical reactions? Time-in or time-out? *Love and logic* or *1,2,3 magic*? Boot camp with bottle-feeding is what it sometimes feels like. What it doesn't feel like is natural. The learning curve is steep, and I don't have my climbing equipment.

I know we are not perfect. No parent is. But I know our parenting is at least as good as that of the smug know-nothings who sneer as I drag J. kicking and screaming out of the park. Because I am Caucasian and J. is Chinese, people don't always recognize immediately that I'm her mother. In the face of what the good doctors would call her "negative persistence" and the seeming absence of a parent, people sometimes feel free to treat her rudely. "Stop that," they say, in tones I know they would never use with their own children. In tones they would never *need* to use with their own children. When they learn that I'm her mother, they can barely contain their contempt. "Do you think you could do better?" I want to scream at them. "Go ahead. Give it a try. Be my guest."

I find myself a therapist. Nobody knows what to do for J., but maybe somebody can help me. The therapist asks me to find some pictures of "mothering." For a full week, despite the fact that I look and look and look, I do not see images of mothering anywhere. Or none that strikes a chord.

How can this be? My entire existence is focused on the task of parenting this child. The only other area of my life to which I have ever brought this degree of intensity and determination and pure passion is my work. And now my work is a dim second. As for my marriage—well, the less said, the better. I never expected it to be this way. Mark and I were happy. We were friends as well as lovers. Together, we'd weathered 13 years of highs and lows, 13 years of boring work and fulfilling work, 13 years of sicknesses and the return of health, 13 years of trips, and money problems, and family problems, 13 years that even included co-parenting his older children through their teenage agonies and angst. And still we had energy to spare: enough to want to raise a child from babyhood together. Now, when we're not fighting about how to handle our daughter, we lie conked out, exhausted, in the wake of her demands. I recall once hearing a friend say that her sons occupied a far bigger place in her life than her husband. At the time, I felt appalled and faintly self-satisfied. That will never happen to me, I thought. And maybe it wouldn't have, if J. had been different.

Early last summer, J. and I accompanied a friend and her daughter, E., to our local wading pool. While my friend and I sat talking under a shade tree, the girls splashed happily in the water, taking turns giving one another rides on a plastic float toy we'd brought along. Soon another girl, perhaps a year and a half younger, approached them. In the way of many three-year-olds, in the way of J. at the same age, this girl stood much too close. She tried to grab the floatie away. She tried, repeatedly, to sit on it. She wedged herself between J. and her friend and would not leave. She tugged at their bathing suits. All the while, her mother sat nearby, saying nothing.

J. "used her words." "Please. We're playing. It bothers me when you stand so close." The child ignored her. "Don't! It's my floatie!" Still, the child wouldn't go.

Finally I intervened, suggesting that maybe the other girl would cooperate better if she were given a turn. Reluctantly at first, but with increasing good grace, J. and E. agreed. "Go ahead. You can play with it for 10 minutes. Then it's our turn again."

But once the toy was hers, the girl no longer wanted it. It drifted to the pool's perimeter as, with a fixed and slightly manic smile, she chased my daughter and her friend around and around.

At last J. lost her temper. "We want to play on our own! Go away!" Not that it helped. I had her serve a time-out for rudeness and then another when she made as if to push the other child. And then another time-out and another, until she had lost a good portion of her precious play time. She accepted these consequences with relative calm, but I wondered if inside she might be feeling the way I sometimes feel in her presence, worn out by the relentlessness of her claims. What I felt now, though, was angry on her behalf. My friend and I cast hostile glances at the mother, whose only comment on the entire drama, issued with a sniff and an injured pout, was, "Those are not nice girls. Find some nice children to play with."

Suddenly, I remembered that I had seen this pair before, over a year earlier. The child, then a toddler, was playing, or rather teetering on the ledges of park equipment far too big and dangerous for her, refusing to get out of the way when older children wanted to use the slides. After asking her to move a couple of times and failing to get a response, J. simply ducked and wriggled past her. The child wailed, and the mother, until then nowhere in evidence, sprang into action, snatching her daughter away and muttering something about J.'s rudeness and my irresponsibility.

"Oh, for heaven's sake," I said. It had been a long day and this park outing was the closest I was going to get to a moment of relaxation. "Just wait until yours is three."

The woman began screaming at me then. "No wonder your daughter has such awful social skills, with you as her model! You're a terrible parent!"

It's true, I thought—though I knew, too, that the woman wasn't entirely in her right mind. No wonder her kid seemed a little "off." Who wouldn't, with a banshee like that for a mother?

Now, though, watching them again at the sun-dappled pool, it occurred to me that I might have confused the causal relationship. Because living with that child would surely drive anybody crazy.

It isn't always difficult. Whole hours, days, weeks, and even months can pass when parenting J. feels almost like parenting any other spirited and strong-willed child. And what a joy that is. During a recent car ride, she became for half an hour or so her healthiest self. On the surface, nothing had changed; she was chattering, nattering, and singing as incessantly and loudly as always. Her energy level was high, and most adults would probably consider her behaviour annoying. Yet something felt different. Something prompted Mark and me to turn to one another at the same moment, to touch one another and smile. For once, she isn't talking *at* us, I thought. For once, she isn't covertly demanding; it's enough for her to be inside her own skin. I could not believe the gift of relaxation this brought to me, the way I felt my head clear out and my heart expand in my chest.

No child could be more rewarding to parent than J. when she is thriving. She is intelligent, imaginative, active, affectionate, funny, and fun. She works hard, plays hard, and fills our lives with gusto. She is also perfectly suited to be our daughter. "She loves to eat and she loves to talk. She's come to the right family," Mark once joked. And it's true. Her passions couldn't be more similar to ours. Particularly her love of words. Her vocabulary surpasses that of some children twice her age. "I feel vulnerable," she told an adult dinner guest of ours as they walked together down a darkened hallway. "Oh, really?" said our friend. "And what does vulnerable mean?" "It means you are afraid that you aren't strong enough and that something

might hurt you," J. replied. Every night she asks me to define another word; if she hears the definition once, the word is hers. And it isn't only meaning she responds to. I have seen her shiver with pleasure at a rhyme or a new phrase. I have heard her repeat it to herself again and again, just for delight in the sounds. Hers is a poet's sensibility. I did not make her this way. She just *is*.

"Family fit" is the phrase used by adoption professionals. "There must be family fit." But our problems are not due to an absence of mystical "fit." I cannot imagine feeling closer, more akin, to any child. For better or for worse, I am J.'s mother. And she is my daughter.

When I was young, my mother and I had an intense and at times combative relationship. I recall one period, in particular, when we had just moved to an arid suburb, where our house was the very first one built in a new development. In the mornings, my father drove off to work in our VW Beetle, leaving us without a car and my mother without adult companionship. All around us stretched muddy lots and vacant skies. The nearest people lived miles away; the nearest stores were further. Mum must have gone crazy, stuck alone there with a chatty three-year-old, day after endless day. She watched the soap operas and ironed my father's shirts and the family's sheets, keeping them damp and rolled in the freezer until she was ready to begin the job. I squatted in front of her on the carpet, sometimes getting tangled in the iron's cord, often begging her to play with me or whining in a high-pitched monotone that I was bored. She used to slap me across the face and call me a brat. A selfish brat. "I hate you," I shrieked back at her. "You're an awful mummy!"

These days, J. has taken to wailing, "You don't love me," whenever her father or I tell her to stop doing something, or ask her to do something that she does not want to do. Sometimes she adds, "I don't love you!" This is painful and difficult to hear—but all part of the "normal" mother-daughter relationship, and all, to me, expected.

What I didn't expect was having to learn a safe-restraint technique before my child reached the age of five. What I didn't expect was to bear bruises and bite marks on my arms for weeks once, just for issuing a time-out. What I didn't expect was to turn around one morning as I was preparing her school lunch and find her pointing a knife at my back. A child's dull-bladed knife, true. But a knife.

At last I find an image of "mothering" that resonates for me. It's a photo taken by my husband this past summer. J. and I had just finished playing dress-up—one of the "floor time" sessions that I build in as part of my therapeutic parenting role. These are one-to-one play periods when J. directs all the action. Theory holds that allowing children a strong measure of control in their fantasy play will encourage them to relax control in other areas of their lives.

In the photo, J. and I are still in costume. We sit together on the carpet. She's cuddled in my lap, with my arms around her. In her own lap she cradles her beloved blanket—the "transitional object" that some of the Drs Doolittle see as a sign that she has internalized my love and others think ought to be wrested away from her, as a hindrance to the purity of our attachment. J. smiles sweetly at the camera; she makes a demure and delightful Bo-Peep. I, on the other hand, sport the livid green hair and the pointed black hat of the wicked witch.

J. hates it when I am sad. Sometimes she gets angry and orders me to stop crying; if especially stressed, she might even hit me. But sometimes, instead, she tries to take care of me. "See, Mum?" she says, pulling a funny face or quoting a silly riddle. "I can make you smile. Don't cry. Please don't cry."

"Boundary issues," my therapist says. "She doesn't know where you stop and she begins."

I'm not sure that I know where I stop and she begins either. Musing about that photo of J. and me, I wonder why I've chosen it. Because consider this: in the picture, the child is sweet and innocent and all good. But who or what is the mother? Is she the competent, playful and smiling one who holds the child and contains the child? Or is she really the mean witch with mustard teeth?

And as if that were not confusing enough—look again. Mummy is wearing a nametag, the kind that parents and tots are asked to put on whenever they participate in some semi-organized activity at the gym or the local library. Look; look closely. The name on this tag is not the mother's. It is the child's.

I do my best. I try to be the strong, all-loving parent that she needs. But a poor night's sleep, a skipped meal, or an annoying phone solicitation can cut my patience short; a death in the family, a conflict with a friend, or trouble in my work can draw me inward, away from her demands. "Mum, Mum, Mum, Mum, Mum," she shouts. Often, in her presence, my pulse begins to race, my breathing tightens, and my neck cramps. Her anxiety becomes my own. Vicarious trauma, this is called. And sometimes the pressure builds too high. She'll be hanging on my pant leg, chasing me into the bathroom, issuing orders in an even bossier tone than usual or shrieking at me —and I'll explode. "Go away! Leave me alone. Mum needs a time-out!"

Of course this sends her into a tailspin. Her mother, rejecting her. It is the worst thing she can imagine. Never mind "imagine." She doesn't *need* to imagine; it is the worst thing she has ever lived, and she relives it every time I walk away. Afterwards, I curse myself. I wonder if she will ever recover. I wonder if I will ever recover from the guilt. And I wonder if at bottom, her ambivalence is nothing more and nothing less than a mirror of my own.

While we're cuddling one afternoon, J. confides, "The worst day in my life was when they cut my umbilical cord. I wanted to stay inside my birth-mother forever. I was so comfortable in there." A few days later, though, I hear her on her play phone, talking to the birth-mother. "You should not have left me," she says, with sizzling indignation. "I was only a baby. That was bad of you. You were wrong!"

One night J. gives me a good night kiss that sets my eardrum ringing. "I think you did that on purpose," I say to her. "What's going on? Why do you try to hurt me when I'm about to leave your room?"

"I don't want you to go," she says. It's simple, and it's obvious, but articulating the idea seems to help her. The next night, instead of hurting me, she bars the door to my exit.

Her rages are less frequent and less violent. She is one of only two in her kindergarten class to have earned three stars for "home reading." She can focus on her drawing for half an hour. Frequently, she asks before she grabs. At day care, she is making friends. So many signs of progress.

But on our worst days, I still fear that I am raising a sociopath. At minimum, a "borderline."

> She will be pregnant, drugged, and on the streets by the age of 16.
> She will be in jail by the age of 20.
> At 30, she will ruin some psychiatrist's life with false accusations of sexual improprieties.
> At 40, she will wake up alone, with no partner and no child.
> She will never really learn how to love.
> She will never really love me.

Every night she wakes. Sometimes shrieking with fear; sometimes bellowing in rage. But tonight, she comes on quiet feet and stands silent next to our bed. I wake up and follow her back to her room. If she crawled in with us, Mark's sleep would be disturbed too; this way, at least two of us will get some rest. Three years ago, that would not have been true. Back then, she was so anxious at the intimate presence of another that she would stay awake and keep us awake all night, jumping, hitting, rolling, pulling hair. I count it as one of my incontrovertible victories over her past that now, when sharing a bed with one of us, she returns to sleep within minutes.

Under the canopy of her double bunk bed, I feel a double layer of darkness. We settle in. When she was younger and still struggling with pronoun usage, she would have barked, "Put your arm around you. Put my arm around me!" Meaning that she wanted me to hold her. Those pesky boundary issues, again. Now, instead, she gently but firmly grasps my arm and wraps it around herself, tucking it in just so. I brush her fine hair away from my chin, adjust my hand so it won't get pins and needles, inhale the scent of her apricot shampoo.

An hour or so later she cries out, thrashing and kicking and whining. She grinds her teeth with a sound like a rake on cement. A bad dream.

"Shhh, it's all right," I whisper, my promise to her a kind of prayer. "Everything will be all right. Mummy loves you. Mummy loves you."

Rolling closer, she fishes for my leg with her foot and snuggles against me. She finds my arm and drapes it across herself once more. I don't know what tomorrow will bring—whether she'll bend flexibly with the day's demands and look at me with love in her eyes, or whether she will harden herself to shield her wounds, and blindly, helplessly hurt me. But for now, her breathing calms and slows, slows and calms. She pulls me close. She does not push me away.

Prairie Fire. 2005. Summer 26 (2).

KEY AND DIFFICULT WORDS

Define the following, using context or other clues if possible: **ubiquitous, exuberant, precocious, paradoxical, demure, livid, vicarious, ambivalence, incontrovertible.**

QUESTIONS

1. What is the significance of the title? (You may have to do some research on the origins of the character mentioned in paragraph 7.)

2. Why does the author use different tenses to narrate her story? Does there seem to be a pattern in her use of the past tense? The present? Identify a paragraph in which the past predominates and one in which the present predominates, and analyze why she uses the tense she does in each.

3. What is the function of the various lists that Olding compiles in her essay (see paragraphs 7, 21, and 56)?

4. Consider the importance of mother roles and mothering in the essay. In your response, you could consider a picture of "'mothering'" that the author is asked to find (paragraph 26) and the one she eventually comes up with (paragraphs 44–9). You could also consider the vignette from her childhood with her own mother (paragraph 41).

5. What is the significance of the lengthy narrative about the child and mother at the wading pool (paragraphs 28–37)? What does it contribute to the essay as a whole?

6. Who are the "experts" whom Olding cites in her essay? Are all the experts professionals? Referring to at least two specific passages, characterize her attitude toward experts and what might account for her attitude.

7. As is true of most award-winning creative non-fiction, the author utilizes stylistic features often found in fictional works. Identify some of these features and comment on what they add to the essay; examples might include repetition, diction, metaphoric language, sentence and paragraph variety, and tone.

COLLABORATIVE ACTIVITY

Do you think that the author succeeds in portraying a balanced picture of J.? How does she accomplish this (or fail to do so)? Do you think this is primarily her aim? Why or why not?

ACTIVITY

Although personal essays like "Push-me-pull-you" focus on the memories, experiences, and perceptions of the author, they also need to be written so that they resonate with the reader and are true in some way to the experience of readers. In what ways does the essay speak to the reader—even those who cannot share her experiences of parenting, for example?

9/11: The day the world changed

Robin V. Sears

(2,500 words)

To each generation comes at least one day that changes their world: Sarajevo, Black Friday, Pearl Harbor, Hiroshima. For mine it was a cold fall day in November 1963. Bouncing down St. Clair Avenue in Toronto with friends, having finished exams and feeling pleased with ourselves and life, we were stunned by an older teen with the impossible news from Dallas. Our world did change that day, and the shocks and blows that rained down through the years that followed all seemed to have been foretold on that grey Friday afternoon.

For the generation coming of age in the new century, their day was a sparkling September morning, after which September sky took on a new meaning. An event so horrific, so unanticipated, and so stunning in the depths of the human depravity it represented that it was days before most of us could begin to digest what had happened. Some resolutely refused to "get it."

Waiting in an airport security line two days later, I watched first with bemusement and then with rage as a British Airways purser of a certain age remonstrated with a security inspector over his seizure of her enormous sterling silver corkscrew. "You insufferable young man, I have been carrying this on flights with me for 20 years. How dare you be so impertinent! Give it back!" she bellowed like a poor Hollywood parody of an English dowager. The young airport security person was deferential but resolute. Finally, an American businessman lunged out of the crowd and shouted, "Lady, have you been on another planet?! The world has changed!"

Impatient in line, we sighed in relief, and then in angst, as the implication of his reality check sank in.

Official Canada needed a reality check for the first few days too. A senior Foreign Affairs bureaucrat, recently returned from dealing with Americans at a very senior level, expressed his astonishment at the paralysis and denial of the Chrétien government in the early days. "It was as if they thought this was some sort of flood or natural disaster. That all we had to do was calculate how many blankets as opposed to tents to load on the planes." It was John Manley's one brief shining moment on the national stage. He conveyed sympathy and horror in public and raged at officials and colleagues in private, until slowly it dawned on Ottawa that the world had turned.

Ordinary Canadians, with the exception of the liberal urban upper middle class, got it immediately. Their outpouring of solidarity and determination had to be channelled by the cynics in political Ottawa, lest it get out of control. So events on Parliament Hill and New York were dutifully arranged to allow the government of Canada to appear to be leading rather than following its electorate. Not many Americans with an eye on Canada were fooled by the governmental disconnect, however.

When I bumped into the American ambassador to an important Asian country that week, we greeted each other with tears and embarrassed male hugs. After a few minutes, he asked with genuine bewilderment, "Why doesn't the Canadian government understand that we are now in a new era? What don't they get?" My humiliation was poorly covered by an incoherent response.

It sometimes takes years to recognize the days that change the world. There had after all been lots of anarchist assassinations before and after Sarajevo. The crash of the stock market was a "once a decade" event from which everyone recovered reasonably quickly—until 1929. Even Hiroshima, while an instant horror, did not reveal for decades how it would change military engagement forever. Islamic terrorists had successfully killed hundreds of civilians several times before, but the scale and audacity of 9/11 made it an epochal event with no close comparison, instantly.

Even now, it is hard to understand those who could not see.

Some weeks after the event, Janice Gross Stein of the University of Toronto's Munk Centre—Canada's grandmotherly security guru, whose gentle smile and demeanour conceal a razor-sharp analytic mind and equally hard-edged views —said that after she recovered from her horror, anger, and sadness, she was left with a feeling of great loss for her students. She recalled how strange and then electrifying it had been to teach the generation between the fall of the Berlin Wall in December of 1989 and that day in September. "I had to explain to them the burden of war, endured or simply apprehended. I struggled to give them a sense of the feeling of imminent peril that most of humanity had lived with since before time. At first I was a little jealous, and then I was uplifted, by their incredulity about such a permanently dangerous world. And then, in one day, it ended."

When the veil is lifted on a new world and we pass into an era with different rules and expectations, it quickly becomes hard to remember what life was like before. To some

one who awoke in Canada in 2006 from a coma that began in the summer five years before, it would be hard to explain why we lock citizens up without trial for years. Why we protest only mildly at the news that our governments, in league with supra-national intelligence agencies, examine our bank accounts, our phone records, and our travel patterns with impunity, or why Canadian soldiers are now fighters and not peacekeepers.

They would have awoken to a world where discussion of the start of the Third World War is greeted not as the ravings of millenarian loons but as the subject for serious academics to debate on the BBC. They would be baffled that most of us simply twitch between irritation at the impertinence at the invasions of privacy and gratitude that someone is trying to relieve some of our fears.

We watch the arrest of the children of hyphenated Canadians, teenagers from suburban Canada, apprehended trying to live adolescent male jihadi video game fantasies, and we struggle to understand how and why, and who to blame. And we see the blood, and the grief, and the helplessness of the survivors in one more soon-forgotten attack, and we become numb.

We find our commitment to a colour-blind society—one that is judgmental about no one's culture, that is respectful of even those ethnic traditions we find strange and medieval—torn by the blog ravings of young Muslim women praying for the suicide deaths of their own children.

These are indeed strange and painful days for democrats in what we curiously still call the West.

For even those most sceptical about the power of redemption, there are lessons in these world-changing days that are impossible to deny. Sarajevo launched the world's most savage and mindless war as its first impact, but it also led directly to the first—albeit ill-fated and ill-conceived—attempt to build a foundation for peace: the League of Nations. Hiroshima first begat a chilling escalation in our ability to destroy the planet, before it was the trigger for real nuclear disarmament and for multilateral control of the power to inflict nuclear horror. The collapse of the Berlin Wall delivered its redemptive message of freedom immediately. Though some still yearn for the geopolitical calm and the "balance of terror" the wall symbolized, its destruction unlocked waves of mostly successful struggles for freedom and democracy in eastern Europe, central Asia, and even Africa.

Sometimes the redemptive lesson of these generational events is more elusive. The legacy of 22 November 1963 is still the political effectiveness of assassination, made more chillingly powerful in recent years by the addition of suicide.

Still, we may hope that "in our sleep," as Aeschylus put it—and as Robert Kennedy pleaded with angry mourners to recall, on the occasion of the second bitter assassination of our generation, the murder of Martin Luther King, Jr.—"pain that cannot forget, falls drop by drop upon the heart. And in our own despair, against our will, comes wisdom to us, by the awful grace of God."

Perhaps, too, we may hope that grace grants us the wisdom to understand the legacy of that awful September morning as more than a bloody and resolute response to terror, though that must remain.

If JFK's death inspired a new generation of political assassins, 9/11 has bequeathed an even more devastating legacy, the power and political impact of modern technology deployed to kill thousands of civilians instantly. There is a direct line between the "success" of the World Trade Center attacks and the murder of hundreds of Iraqi Shiites at the Imam Ali mosque this spring, an attack that is still reverberating in the downward spiral of sectarian killing.

The jihadis who celebrated their audacious attack on American power were all Sunni, and mostly middle-class Saudis. To this day, al-Qaeda attacks its Shiite competitors for terrorist supremacy with vigour. Yet the original structure and leadership that was al-Qaeda is now a feeble shell. It is a powerful irony for the 85 per cent anti-Shia Islamic world that today it is Shiite zealotry that is the beacon of hope for their own angry Arab street.

Iran, that strange fusion of military dictatorship, racism, and theocracy, is the key beneficiary of the terrible succubus born five years ago. The mullahs and their military partners have perfected the combination of state power and religious terrorism. So far, Iran has succeeded in hiding behind a veil of denial as it has nurtured the world's most deadly networks of terror in Afghanistan, Pakistan, Iraq, Lebanon, and Palestine. (Syria is their ghoulish headwaiter, ferrying orders between the chefs in the Tehran kitchen and customers in Gaza and south Lebanon.)

The leadership of the "moderate" Arab world took a different message from 9/11: they were potential targets of terror themselves. Regimes across the region, from Libya to Saudi Arabia, began to see Osama bin Laden, the Iranian proxies, and their imitators in Madrid and London through a lens similar to ours. Sadly, until now, we and they are on the losing side of this twenty-first-century innovation in war.

Israel has once again been sucked into that swamp called Lebanon. This chapter has painfully revealed that we now face a new form of war. The Israeli invaders in 1982 were met by Lebanese and Palestinian guerrillas armed with rocket-propelled grenades, heavy machine guns, and "Stalin's pipe organ"—truck-mounted Katyusha rockets—all relatively simple weapons for a modern army to overwhelm.

Today's Israeli strategists face an enemy with the most modern communications, tracking, and monitoring capability; missiles mounted in the back of an SUV whose range made Haifa an easy target; and a network of tunnels, barracks, and missile caches hidden under dozens of mosques, schools, and hospitals. More challenging than this increased military sophistication is that Hezbollah can still play by the rules of non-state terror while Israel is held morally accountable for every accidental civilian death.

On this grim fifth anniversary, then, this is the legacy of that day: two wars being fought, in the current jargon "asymmetrically," by opponents who use the grim iconography of 9/11 as their favourite recruiting tools. The developed world struggles to find the right balance, in their own societies, between security and freedom. Citizens in Madrid, Mumbai, or Jakarta see their government incapable of protecting them from terror. They watch an imperial power incapable of defeating what started out as a trivial rebirth of an insurgency in one country, Afghanistan, and being pummelled daily by a more serious challenger in another, Iraq.

It's hard, therefore, to summon much optimism about the triumph of democratic values, let alone a victory in the "war on terror." And yet it was hard to believe Olaf Palme, Sweden's most famous prime minister, when he would declare with quiet confidence in the darkest days of racist violence and the bloody civil wars in southern Africa, "This will end in victory for the anti-apartheid movement and their regional allies sooner than anyone believes." Within five years, Nelson Mandela had begun his miraculous transformation of that shattered part of Africa.

Meeting Mikhail Gorbachev in the spring of 1985, shortly after his accession to power, a group of visitors were stunned to hear him concede in private that the days of military rivalry were over, that the Soviet Union would become a successful economic rival to the West or it would fail. He gambled and lost within only five years as well.

When we look back, the world wars that consumed the last century and even the collapse of communism seem inevitable. Some claim that this nightmare of terror was preordained, even deserved. But, of course, that is only the delusion of hindsight. Until the day that the North Korean regime collapses into history, no one will have predicted the moment. No CIA country briefing will have forewarned of the bloody insurrection that will inevitably drive another Middle East kingdom from power.

Anniversaries cause one to look forward as well as back, to muse about five years hence. So we may hope that one day soon an Iranian leader with the moral authority of a Mandela will emerge. We may pray for a Palestinian leader with the wisdom of a Rabin, and the guts of an Arafat, willing to fight for peace. Least improbably, we may hope for a return to simple competence in the White House. Any one of these would transform this generation's horizons.

Then perhaps we might hope for a less humiliating leadership of what Tom Friedman has dubbed "the world of order," allies genuinely committed to making the values of our liberal democracies as resonant to ordinary people in Arabic and in Farsi as we claim they are to us. We might hope that the world of chaos and disorder unleashed from the caves of Afghanistan five years ago, that those thousands now sucked into an ideology more horrific than all those of the twentieth century do not prevail. That the nineteenth-century dream of a brotherhood of man can be welded to a contemporary vision of a safer, fairer, interdependent world. That the witness of our living those values, not merely our technology's power to inflict ever higher levels of terror, points the way to that victory.

It seems improbable to even dream of such a transformation from the vantage point of 2006, but despair is the handmaiden of disorder and defeat. Hope is not a strategy, as the saying goes. Hope, harnessed to such a vision of a better century, with the formidable resources and capacity available to its natural allies, could be.

Policy Options. 2006. September.

KEY AND DIFFICULT WORDS

Define the following, using context or other clues if possible: **remonstrate, deferential, resolute, anarchist, epochal, incredulity, impunity, redemption, sectarian, succubus, insurgency, insurrection.**

QUESTIONS

1. What kinds of evidence does the writer rely on In paragraphs 1–6? Analyze the introduction for its effectiveness.

2. How would you characterize the author's attitude toward the Canadian government's initial response to 9/11? How does he convey this attitude?

3. Why does the author use an analogy (the hypothetical example of someone who awoke from a coma, paragraph 10) to illustrate the way the world of Canadians has changed? In two to three sentences and in your own words, summarize these kinds of changes.

4. Who is the author referring to as "we" beginning in paragraph 10? Why does Sears use this pronoun in his essay?

5. According to Sears, "world-changing" events can possess "the power of redemption" (paragraph 15). What does he mean by this phrase? What are the three events discussed in this paragraph to which he applies the phrase?

6. Does Sears see any "redemptive lesson" in the 1963 Kennedy assassination? In what sense can the "world-changing" event of Sears's generation be compared to the "world-changing" event of today's generation?

7. How does the direct quotation from a former prime minister of Sweden (paragraph 26) prepare the way for the conclusion that follows?

8. Do you think that Sears is truly hopeful that the transformation he speaks of in his conclusion will come about? Do you find his conclusion strong and rhetorically effective? Why or why not?

COLLABORATIVE ACTIVITY

In groups, discuss what you believe is the major consequence of the events of 11 September 2001. How has it changed the world? You can expand on Sears's political views if you wish or focus more on a major change that Sears does not consider.

ACTIVITIES

1. Compare Fulford's approach to history in "A box full of history" with that of Sears. A comparison could consider similarities, differences, or both. *OR* Compare O'Rourke's approach to history in "Sulfur Island" with that of Sears.

2. Using reliable biographical sources (on-line sources available at many libraries include *A dictionary of political biography* and *A dictionary of contemporary world history*, published by Oxford Reference On-line), write one- to two-sentence biographies of the following political leaders that Sears refers to in paragraph 29: Nelson Mandela, Yitzhak Rabin, and Yasser Arafat.

3. Recall your initial reaction when you found out about the events of 9/11. Freewrite for five to 10 minutes on your response. (You could begin, "When I first heard about the terrorist attacks on 11 September 2001, I...").

The Challenges of Science

The human environment

Claude A. Piantadosi

(3,370 words)

As with any other species, human survival boils down to individual survival. This is true whether people die of disease, natural disaster, or man-made holocaust. Fundamentally, survival can be defined in terms of the interactions between an individual and its natural surroundings. The surroundings determine the extent to which a person is exposed to critical changes in environment, such as temperature, water, food, or oxygen. The physical world imposes strict limits on human biology, and learning where these limits are and how to deal with them is what biologists call *limit physiology*. The principles of limit physiology can be applied to understanding human life in all extreme environments. These principles will be developed in this chapter and applied throughout the book to gain a deeper appreciation of how humans survive in extreme conditions.

THE NATURE OF HUMAN PHYSICAL BOUNDARIES

One of the most important characteristics of every living organism is its ability to maintain an active equilibrium, however brief or delicate, with its natural environment. All living beings, as integral parts of nature, can be characterized by the dynamic exchange they maintain with their physical surroundings. Being alive requires being attuned to natural change, and many organisms are exquisitely sensitive to even tiny perturbations in environmental conditions. They occupy restricted *niches*. If changes in con-ditions in the niche exceed certain limits, biological equilibrium is disrupted, and the life of the organism, or even the entire species, is threatened. Thus, all habitable environments, or *habitats*, have specific physical boundaries within which life is possible and outside which life is impossible. As an organism approaches the limits of its habitat, life is sustainable only with greater and greater effort unless the effort is sufficient for adaptation to occur. Indeed, the closer the organism approaches a tolerance limit, and the greater the stress, the more vigorous will be the attempt to compensate, and if it falls short, the shorter will be the survival time. This principle is illustrated in figure 1.1. The curve has the shape of a rectangular hyperbola, which is characteristic of many survival functions depicted throughout this book.

Human beings are among the most adaptable creatures on the planet, yet the limits of human survival are astonishingly narrow when viewed in the context of the extremes on the planet. Approximately two-thirds of the Earth's surface is covered by deep saltwater oceans, which air-breathing terrestrial mammals such as ourselves may visit briefly but are not free to inhabit. Even highly specialized diving mammals, the great cetaceans, so spectacularly adapted for life in the sea, are confined to the surface layers of the ocean. The crushing pressure of the seawater, the cold, and the darkness make the great depths of the ocean inhospitable to most marine species.

Not that life cannot exist or even thrive under such extremes, for even at the bottom of the sea super-hot water jets heated by vents in the Earth's mantle support highly sophisticated and unique forms of life, but the thought of people existing permanently in such places is unimaginable. Many species that thrive in the depths die when brought too quickly to the ocean's surface.

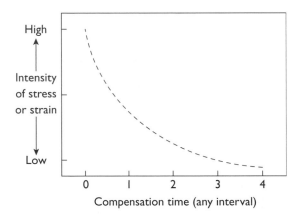

Figure 1.1. The relationship between the ability to compensate for and the severity of physiological stress or strain. X-axis indicates time to failure of functions, or in the case of survival, to death. The time scale may be in any unit, from seconds to days, depending on the nature and intensity of the stress or strain. Adaptation shifts the position of the curve to the right.

Of the land that covers the remaining third of the Earth's surface, one-fourth is permanently frozen, and one-fourth is arid desert; both are extremes that may be inhabited by humans only with arduous efforts. Add to this the high mountain ranges and the lakes and rivers that people depend on but do not routinely inhabit, and the climate and topography temperate enough for permanent habitation by humans relegates us to one-sixth of the surface of the planet. Despite the rich diversity and capacity of people to respond, adapt, or acclimatize to extreme conditions, the limits of human tolerance are remarkably narrow. Indeed, civilization's stamp has been its ability to extend an individual's tolerance to

stressful environments by making behavioural adaptations in the form of invention (Figure 1.2).

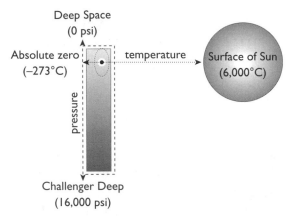

Figure 1.2. The physical environment of human beings. Natural environments are indicated on absolute temperature (X) and pressure (Y) scales. The shaded rectangle shows natural physical environments of life on Earth. The small black spot in the center indicates the range of the human natural environment, and the white circle is the region of extension of tolerance by physiological adaptation. The dotted circle indicates the range of tolerance by inventions designed to support or protect one or more critical body functions during an exposure, and the dashed line is the range of hard shell engineering, which prevents exposure to an extreme external environment. The latter two responses are forms of advanced behavioural adaptation.

The environment of human beings is constrained geographically because latitude and topography cause variations in temperature, barometric pressure, availability of food and water, and combinations of each that are critical for survival. Thus, it is no surprise that much of the world's population is perched on the brink of disaster. The loss of human life from a sudden natural disaster such as a blizzard or a flood is always appalling, but it is remarkable how well some individuals endure the most gruelling conditions, surviving prolonged immersion, high altitude, and heat or cold despite desperate thirst or impending starvation. The incredible tales of survival at sea, in the mountains, in the desert, and on the ice capture our imaginations like few others.

THE IMPORTANCE OF PREPARATION FOR EXTREME EXPOSURES

Every life-and-death struggle is influenced by intangibles, sometimes lumped under broad terms such as *survival instinct* and *will to live*. Whether an individual survives an unexpected and prolonged encounter with a potentially lethal environment, however, depends more on the equilibrium between biology and physics than on intangibles. Although much has been made of a strong will to live, this is a basic trait of the human psyche common to healthy people. Strength of spirit, motivation, and psychological factors are very important for survival but are less decisive under truly catastrophic conditions than our poets and writers would like us to believe. To state it plainly, rarely does one person survive under extreme conditions when another dies simply because the survivor has a greater will to live.

Thoughtful preparation in anticipation of extreme exposure is more important than all the fighting spirit in the world, for a naked man cannot live out a night at the South Pole. Preparation, however, requires knowledge, time, and resources. It involves allowing time to adapt, for example by gradual ascent to an altitude or by arranging resources to limit the effects of the exposure, such as by providing multiple layers of warm, dry clothing on polar expeditions. Preparation when an automobile breaks down in the desert means simply avoiding death from dehydration by having had enough foresight to carry along some water. This example implies the double failure that has killed many a bold explorer. One failure occurs before the adventure begins by counting on a single vehicle and not carrying enough water to walk out or to survive until another vehicle can come to the rescue. The second failure, engine trouble, usually nothing more than an inconvenience, proves fatal.

The double failure problem is well known to engineers who design life-support equipment such as diving gear and spacesuits. They devise diagrams to analyze potential failures or faults in systems that will affect the probability of survival in specific failure modes. These fault analysis diagrams, or trees, can become quite complex for even relatively straightforward systems. However, most of the essential information can be gleaned from simple diagrams, if properly constructed, and it is surprising how few explorers actually use this approach in planning an expedition. Fortunately, the prudent explorer appreciates the bottom line: the way to ensure safety and dependability is to build in redundancy. Deciding how much redundancy is enough is the tough part.

SOME BASIC CONCEPTS OF SURVIVAL ANALYSIS

The double failure problem and the value of redundancy can be illustrated with diagrams using a technique called nodal condensation probability. In planning an expedition, if one anticipates event A, a 1-in-1000 failure with a 99 per cent chance of survival, the probability of death is only 1 in 100,000. These odds are acceptable to most people. However, if a second independent failure possibility, B, is added to the expedition with the same probability and the same survival rate, the two probabilities must be summed, giving an expected risk of death of 1 in 50,000 for the expedition. This arrangement of events, known as a linear system, is depicted in figure 1.3.

One must also consider the effect of a rare double failure because the odds of surviving the second failure may approach zero if it occurs after the first failure. A good example is ejecting from a burning jet aircraft with a defective explosive canopy bolt. If an independent probability of 1:1000 is assigned to each event, the probability of experiencing the double failure is 1:1000 squared, or only one in a million. The chances of living through it, however, are virtually zero. Overall, the expected probability of death in this linear system is 2.1:100,000.

Start ——(a)————(b)————→ Finish

$P_a = 1{:}1{,}000$ $P_b = 1{:}1{,}000$ $P_{ab} = 1{:}1{,}000{,}000$

$P_d = 0.01$ $P_d = 0.01$ $P_d = 1.0$

$P_{d(a)} = 1{:}100{,}000$ $P_{d(b)} = 1{:}100{,}000$ $P_{d(ab)} = 1{:}1{,}000{,}000$

$P_{death(tot)} = P_{d(a)} + P_{d(b)} + P_{d(ab)}$

$= 2.1{:}100{,}000$

If a fails before start:

$P_a = 1$ $P_b = 1{:}1{,}000$

$P_d = 0$ $P_d = 1.0$

$P_{d(a)} = 0$ $P_{d(ab)} = 1{:}1{,}000$

$P_{death(tot)} = P_{d(ab)} = 1{:}1{,}000$

Figure 1.3. Survival probability by linear failure analysis. The top part of the diagram shows two independent events, **a** and **b**, in a linear arrangement. The probability (P) of each event is 1 in 1000, and the probability of death (Pd) if one event occurs is 1:100. The probability of death for each event is therefore the product of P x Pd, or 1 in 100,000. The probability of both events occurring is the product of their probabilities, or 1 in 1 million, but if both occur the probability of death is (set at) 1.0 (certainty). Therefore, the overall risk of death is the sum of the three products, or 2.1 in 100,000. The bottom part of the diagram shows two independent events, **a** and **b**, arranged in a linear system in which **a** has already occurred but has no consequences because it occurs before **b** in a different environment or location, for example, before an exposure. However, if the exposure is undertaken and **b** then occurs, the probability of death increases from 1 in 100 to 1.0 (certainty) because **a** is already in place. Therefore, failure to account for **a** fixes the probability of death at 1 in 1000, which is nearly fifty-fold higher than in the top part of the diagram. Examples are provided in the text.

Next, consider the problem of starting an expedition with a failure already in place. This is illustrated in the bottom half of figure 1.3. In the desert example above, the motorist left town without a supply of drinking water. In this case, the event, *a*, is assigned a probability of 1 because it happened, but it did not happen in the desert, and the motorist can find water anytime before departure. The probability of dying of dehydration is nil. The second failure, *b* in figure 1.3, has a probability of 1:1000, but now the probability of death is 1. This means the overall risk of dying on the expedition has gone from 2.1:100,000 to 1:1000, nearly a fifty-fold increase. These calculations give one an appreciation for why most of the deaths in mountaineering, deep sea diving, parachuting, and so on are due to double failures that involve at least one human error. The initial failure often encompasses a critical failure of preparation.

Probability calculations illustrate the value of assessing risk and preparing in advance for a trip of significant intrinsic danger. The importance of redundancy to reduce danger, although intuitive to most, can be made clear with examples. For instance, underwater divers who explore caves carry both extra lights and an independent breathing gas system. This greatly lessens the chances of double failure, such as no light and no air, and improves survival after the potentially critical failure of getting lost, for example by dropping or becoming disconnected from the lifeline.

Another example of redundancy is the use of personal flotation devices and safety harnesses on ocean-going sailing yachts. If a member of the crew falls overboard wearing a life jacket, it supports him or her until the boat comes about to make the pick up. Hence, the probability of death is quite low. However, this safety measure is not sufficient under all conditions. If the person is alone on deck and falls overboard, the probability of death is very high despite the life jacket because the boat will sail away faster than he or she can swim. Harnessing one's vest to the vessel beforehand decreases the probability of death from falling off the boat under special circumstances, such as standing watch alone at night. This principle of redundancy is illustrated in figure 1.4.

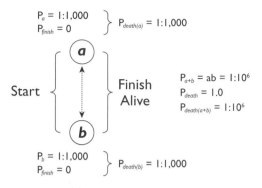

$P_a = 1:1,000$
$P_{finish} = 0$ $\}$ $P_{death(a)} = 1:1,000$

Start $\{$ $\begin{array}{c} a \\ \vdots \\ b \end{array}$ $\}$ Finish Alive

$P_{a+b} = ab = 1:10^6$
$P_{death} = 1.0$
$P_{death(a+b)} = 1:10^6$

$P_b = 1:1,000$
$P_{finish} = 0$ $\}$ $P_{death(b)} = 1:1,000$

Figure 1.4. Survival probability in a parallel system. In this diagram, events **a** and **b** are arranged in parallel. In other words, if **a** occurs, option **b** can be exercised to prevent death because of **a**, and vice versa. Thus, double failures, **a** and **b**, must occur to cause death. The risk of death during the exposure is greatly reduced, from 1 in 1000 to 1 in 1 million, by the redundancy. Examples are provided in the text.

In many extreme situations, strength and toughness may have appeared to swing the odds in favour of survival, but analysis of the events usually indicates this was because some deadly factor was held at bay by rational actions. In dramatic, highly publicized examples of survival against extreme odds, an injured party is snatched from the jaws of death in the nick of time. The would-be victim and the courage of the rescuers are applauded by all, and justifiably so, for this is the stuff of legends, yet survivors are often the best-prepared and most knowledgeable individuals in harm's way.

Whether someone lives through extreme exposure can be boiled down to a few physical and biological factors. In its minimal form, survival analysis requires an accounting of four factors, which can be defined as critical variables. The first two variables are beyond human control, while the latter two are amenable to intervention. These critical variables are as follows: (1) the physics of the environment, (2) the limits of human physiology, (3) the length of the exposure, and (4) behavioural adaptation, including what the victim understands about survival requirements and the plans made to prepare for a failure.

This approach simplifies the analysis but not greatly, because the four critical variables are complex. In other words, they are true variables, neither constants nor necessarily simple changes, and this makes survival prediction an inexact science. For instance, hostile environments do not produce "pure" physiological stresses; many places are both hot and dry, such as the Sahara, or cold and high, such as the Antarctic. This results in multiple stresses on the body that interact with one another. To further complicate the situation, human biology encompasses differences in body shape, mass, and fitness that greatly influence survival time under different conditions. This aspect of the problem, known as physical diversity, is most obvious for survival in cold water. Physical diversity implies that certain body characteristics, such as fatness, carry different degrees of importance under different conditions, such as providing temporary advantage while immersed in cold water.

As a general rule, the order in which the factors are listed above is their order of importance, even if parameters within each factor change. On the other hand, when a potentially lethal exposure is in the offing, the fourth factor, behavioural adaptation made by interventions by victim and rescuer, is the only means of producing a survivor. The principle also holds when one prepares for extreme exposure known to exceed one of the body's physiological limits. The only effective survival strategy is to use intelligence and a priori knowledge, that is, behavioural adaptation.

Some readers may take issue with this ordering of the variables or this approach in general.

Even so, it must be admitted that many places on Earth are too hot or too cold, or the pressure too high or too low, to permit unassisted human survival long enough for adaptation to occur. These places, wherever they are, define the limits. Therefore, the chapters in this book, although intended to tease out essential commonalities of human survival, are organized according to particular environments that place unusual demands on the human body.

In order to understand the limits of life in these environments, some working concepts must be provided for the biology of the human organism. This will require definition of the essential tenets of modern environmental physiology, including the concepts of homeostasis and adaptation, which will follow later. Homeostasis and adaptation also require support from the environment, such as food and water. Conditions devoid of food or water constitute special environments of hunger and thirst that lead to foraging and ultimately, if unsuccessful, to starvation or dehydration. These factors in turn impact survival in special physical environments where people encounter extremes of temperature, barometric pressure, radiation, or gravity.

CHARACTERISTICS OF LIFE-SUPPORT SYSTEMS

Survival analysis embraces the principles of life-support equipment. Life-support problems are encountered whenever physiologists and engineers collaborate to fashion systems to support human beings in extreme environments. The issues are similar for systems as simple as a diver's wet suit or as complex as the International Space Station. Not surprisingly, designs hinge on just how closely human beings should be allowed to approach a biological limit. In general, the more hostile the external environment and the closer the internal environment is kept to natural conditions, the greater the engineering requirements and the higher the cost. In considering life-support equipment, three distinct but related environments are always involved: the internal environment of the body, the environment adjacent to the body, and the external environment, that is, the environment outside the suit or system. By first principles, the objective is to maintain the internal stability and functions of the body, which means that the critical environment is immediately adjacent to the body. Thus, in deep space, where air pressure is virtually zero, a spacesuit is worthless if it cannot maintain an internal pressure compatible with physiological activity. Critical body functions will be compromised unless the pressure in the suit is equivalent to 30,000 feet of altitude or less.

To make the concepts of life support accessible, the discussions of different environments rely only sparingly on mathematics, which is limited to a few equations that offer exceptional insight into the relationships between the human body and its environment. The algebra helps add clarity to explanations of the principles of life-support technology. Many brilliant and innovative breakthroughs in life-support technology were made in the twentieth century, but mathematical models and technological subtlety are not usually critical to understanding the principles that most directly limit survival in each environment and what happens to people when equipment fails.

The principles of life support encompass many human problems, including disease, fitness, isolation and group dynamics, circadian rhythms, and sleep deprivation. These fascinating topics are important not only in extreme environments but may be crucial to life in artificial systems. They are not neglected in this book, but their effects are discussed in association with the appropriate physical environment. This approach places them in context and highlights some counter-intuitive notions, for example, that physical fitness and the ability to perform work offer a survival advantage in some environments but not in others. The ultimate extreme environment, that of space, is used to point out gaps in our knowledge of long-term human endurance and adaptation outside the confines of Earth. Throughout the book, common determinants of survival in artificial environments are highlighted as much as possible, together with their implications for the future of humankind.

In Claude A. Piantadosi. 2003. *The biology of human survival: Life and death in extreme environments*. New York, NY: Oxford University Press.

KEY AND DIFFICULT WORDS

Define the following, using context or other clues if possible: **perturbation, lethal, redundancy, amenable, circadian.**

QUESTIONS

1. Although this essay explains complex material, there are no citations. What does this tell you about its intended audience?
2. What kinds of methods and strategies does the author use to communicate technical information clearly? Come up with at least two, ensuring that you provide specific examples, and assess their usefulness.
3. Summarize the author's views concerning the "survival instinct" and "the will to live" (paragraph 6). In what kinds of scenarios might these "intangibles" actually play a role in an individual's chance of survival? In what scenarios are they unlikely to play a role?
4. What is the "double failure problem?" How is "redundancy" related to the double failure problem? What are some possible costs of too much redundancy?
5. Piantadosi uses several diagrams (figures 1.1 to 1.4) to supplement information contained in the text. Comment generally on their usefulness, then show how one of the diagrams relates to material in the text.
6. Give three examples of behavioural adaptation mentioned in the essay.
7. Why do you think the author says, "Some readers may take issue with this ordering of the [critical] variables or this approach in general" (paragraph 18)? Why might a reader challenge the ordering of the variables or the author's approach?
8. As the final paragraph makes clear, this essay was intended as a kind of introduction to the book in which it appeared. What other indications within the essay itself point to this function?

COLLABORATIVE ACTIVITY

Think up real-life examples in which "a critical failure of preparation" or the failure to build redundancy into the planning process has resulted in death or a dangerous situation. Can humans learn from such failures? Find specific examples in which such failures have led to a safer world or situation.

ACTIVITY

Do you think that this essay stresses human weakness and failure in the face of dangerous or inhospitable environments, or do you think that the emphasis is more on overcoming physical barriers and limits? Write a critical response to "The human environment" in which you address the vision of humanity's adaptability and capability in the natural world.

Related reading: Douglas W. Morris. "Enemies of biodiversity."

Enemies of biodiversity

Douglas W. Morris

(1,750 words)

One of the great commonalities that binds life together is that all species are both enemies and victims. Enemies include the obvious predators, parasites, and pathogens with their multifarious direct and indirect effects on prey and hosts. But enemies also include the not-so-obvious competitors that, in some way, either reduce or restrict access to resources. Viewed in this light, evolution by natural selection becomes a hazardous game of pursuit and escape where the winners and the losers can be one and the same. Evolution is also a ruthless game where friends are often foes and where the net effects of even the most lethal enemies may nevertheless endear them to survivors.

Thus, as Vamosi (2005) points out . . . , it is surprising that evolutionary biologists have only recently modeled the paramount roles that enemies play in the diversification of their victims. The story has numerous and delightful twists and turns driven by the inherent density and frequency dependence of enemy and victim interactions. In one scenario, disruptive selection on sympatric prey by specialized predators not only increases prey species diversity but also causes diversification and subsequent speciation in the predators. In another, adaptive divergence yields specialized prey and generalist predators. And in some models, all bets are off. Prey can diverge in anti-predator traits, converge, or change in parallel with one another.

The theories spring to life with Vamosi's (2005) examples that span not only life forms but the very history of life on Earth. We learn that predators may have been responsible for the origin of multi-cellular organisms. We learn that the diversity of Mesozoic molluscivores caused major changes in armour and habitat use by their prey. We see that predators in freshwater systems often induce character shifts among prey species. But we also discover that evidence for prey diversification is far from universal. Experiments on bacteria illustrate that divergence among allopatric populations exposed to phages is complemented by convergence within populations. Evolutionary radiations of plants with anti-herbivore adaptations are stymied when herbivores short-circuit the defences. Diversification of mimics is constrained by the variety of models. And the species richness of aposematic species that so easily capture our attention is more than equalled by their cryptic ancestors.

We might think, nevertheless, that we have the models, both theoretical and empirical, to assess the impact of the human enemy on current and future biodiversity. When we specialize on certain age or size classes, prey populations diverge from our specialization. Examples include the rapid adaptive evolution of reduced body size and altered fecundity in commercially exploited fish species (Olsen et al. 2004) and similar reductions in body mass and horn size in bighorn sheep, *Ovis canadensis* Shaw, 1804, caused by trophy hunting (Coltman et al. 2003). The evolutionary divergence of prey, as it is for natural enemies, depends on whether we choose to consume common phenotypes (disruptive selection) or whether we attempt to harvest only the most extreme individuals (directional or stabilizing selection).

We also see tacit agreement with theory when species converge in response to human effects that influence several species simultaneously. Predation on weeds by generations of farmers has produced a variety of convergent vegetative mimics on food plants, as well as seed mimics whose sizes, shapes, and masses have converged on those of numerous cereals and other seed crops (Barrett 1983). The relative strengths of directional versus stabilizing selection on weeds depend on the shape and location of the original phenotype distribution relative to the distribution of the cultivars selected by humans. Meanwhile, untold numbers of species are adapting to human-induced mortality from pests, pesticides, and antibiotics (Morris and Heidinga 1997; Palumbi 2001).

In each case that we have explored thus far, the evolutionary dynamics are determined by soft selection where survival and future reproduction depend on the victim's phenotype. For these species, the human touch on biodiversity is indeed soft. But there are many others for whom the hard selection of humanity's iron fist gives no quarter. What phenotypic adaptations must vernal wildflowers possess if they are to bloom in a city's highrise concrete forest? What traits will protect benthic invertebrates from the industrial fisher's bottom trawl? What kinds of species possess the range of tolerances that will enable some of their members to survive climate change and global warming?

We need not venture far to find the answer. Evolution by natural selection capitalizes on ecological opportunity. As we strip the opportunities for much of biodiversity, we create unparalleled options for others to profit by exploiting our domesticated plants and animals, by invading our modified habitats, and by taking advantage of an incredibly common resource, ourselves. The examples surround us: emerging diseases; novel competitors in our fields; new pests in our granaries, lakes, and cities; and old pests, weeds, and pathogens that are resistant to our controls.

Humans also destroy and disrupt native biodiversity by acting as agents of dispersal for alien species. Whether we introduce enemies by intention or accident, their impacts rival our own (e.g., Park 2004). Eradication of the invaders is sometimes effective, but there is no guarantee that native populations will recover their original abundance or distribution. Nor is there any guarantee that evolutionary adjustments to the aliens will be reversed. In each instance, we can learn from our own example. When faced with irrefutable evidence of human impact, such as through over-harvesting, intelligent managers have often "eradicated" the human predator by closing seasons, establishing reserves, and protecting endangered species. Recovery of those populations can help us assess the potential return from control measures on alien invaders. Preliminary results are not encouraging.

I searched the website of the Committee on the Status of Endangered Wildlife in Canada (COSEWIC) to determine whether listed species that had been re-evaluated were considered under more or less threat than before. Presumably, such species have witnessed some attempts at protection from negative human influences. As of November 2004, 292 species were listed as endangered or threatened (COSEWIC 2004). Of the subset whose status had been reassessed from 2000 through 2004, 63 species were placed in a higher-risk category, and only two were placed in a lower one. To be fair, the assaults on many species come from a variety of directions and involve numerous impacts. Some species do not have operating recovery plans (Anonymous 2004), and most plans that are in effect have been implemented only recently. The data are, nevertheless, a sobering reminder of how ineffective we have been thus far at rescuing threatened and endangered populations.

We are in a deadly race—not just to save species, to reduce our cumulative and interactive impacts, or to escape our enemies but to find long-term solutions while we still have time to do so. We need to engage more scientists in the study of biodiversity and its conservation. There is work for everyone. We need more theory. We need definitive experiments. We need to look carefully and creatively at the few examples where we have snatched victory from our foes. We must pay attention to the mistakes and successes of others (Diamond 2005) and make better use of adaptive management (Park 2004). We can learn from Vamosi (2005). Natural enemies are multifaceted and so too are their effects on prey. The evolutionary response of prey to their enemies depends on the direct and selective predation of certain phenotypes over others, on the indirect effects of enemies mediated through coexisting prey species, on co-evolution within and across trophic levels, and on phylogenetic constraints. But here's the rub. Success is the architect of failure. Any population freed from its enemies soon becomes an enemy unto itself.

Population growth of any species cannot be sustained. Competition from too many individuals leads to either gross inequalities in resource sharing, where the powerful and lucky survive and reproduce at the expense of their miserable conspecifics, or a shared misery by all. Why, in the face of the evidence and armed with intelligence, are we so complacent to continued growth of human populations? I suspect that we can find the answer in a well-intentioned but misunderstood interpretation of natural selection. To quote Darwin (1859):

> All that we can do, is to keep steadily in mind that each organic being is striving to increase at a geometrical ratio; that each at some period of its life, during some season of the year, during each generation or at intervals,

has to struggle for life, and to suffer great destruction. When we reflect on this struggle, we may console ourselves with the full belief, that the war of nature is not incessant, that no fear is felt, that death is generally prompt, and that the vigorous, the healthy, and the happy survive and multiply.

Oh Charles, if only it was true!

Canadian Journal of Zoology. 2005. 83.

REFERENCES

Anonymous. 2004. Species at risk. Available from http://www.speciesatrisk.gc.ca/recovery/default_e.cfm [accessed 5 January 2005].

Barrett, S.C.H. 1983. Crop mimicry in weeds. Econ. Bot. **37**: 255–282.

Coltman, D.W., O'Donoghue, P., Jorgenson, J.T., Hogg, J.T., Strobeck, C., and Festa-Bianchet, M. 2003. Undesirable evolutionary consequences of trophy hunting. Nature (Lond.), **426**: 655–658.

COSEWIC 2004. Canadian species at risk, November 2004. Available from http://www.cosewic.gc.ca [accessed 5 January 2005].

Darwin, C. 1859. On the origin of species by means of natural selection or the preservation of favoured races in the struggle for life. John Murray, London.

Diamond, J. 2005. Collapse: how societies choose to fail or succeed. Viking USA, New York.

Morris, D.W., and Heidinga, L. 1997. Balancing the books on biodiversity. Conserv. Biol. **11**: 287–289.

Olsen, E.M., Heino, M., Lilly, G.R., Morgan, M.J., Brattey, J., Ernande, B., and Dieckmann, U. 2004. Maturation trends indicative of rapid evolution preceded the collapse of northern cod. Nature (Lond.), **428**: 932–935.

Palumbi, S.R. 2001. Humans as the world's greatest evolutionary force. Science (Wash., DC), **293**: 1786–1790.

Park, K. 2004. Assessment and management of invasive alien predators. Ecology and Society [on-line], **9**(2): 12. Available from http://www.ecologyandsociety.org/vol9/iss2/art12/ [cited 5 January 2005].

Vamosi, S.M. 2005. On the role of enemies in divergence and diversification of prey: a review and synthesis. Can. J. Zool. **83**(7): 894–910.

KEY AND DIFFICULT WORDS

Define the following, using context or other clues if possible: **pathogens, multifarious, sympatric, allopatric, aposematic, cryptic, fecundity, phenotype, tacit, benthic, eradication, irrefutable, trophic, phylogenetic.**

QUESTIONS

1. "Enemies of biodiversity" was the first essay in an issue of the *Canadian Journal of Zoology*, introducing the subject of biodiversity and the 17-page essay by S.M. Vamosi that followed (see "References"). How might this special function make the essay different from more traditional science essays?

2. How much of the essay would you consider the introduction? What kind of introduction is it?

3. What does the author mean by the last sentence in paragraph 2? In paragraph 3?

4. How do the specialized usages of "mimic" and "cryptic" in paragraph 3 differ from the more general usages? (If possible, try to deduce meaning from context rather than looking up the words in a dictionary or encyclopedia of biology.)

5. Why, according to the author, might Vamosi's essay be a particularly important one for evolutionary biologists to read?

6. Which do you infer is potentially more damaging to the survival of a species: disruptive selection or directional selection? Soft selection or hard selection?

7. What is the function of the questions in paragraph 6?

8. Explain the meaning of the author's last sentence. How does it relate to the quotation from Darwin?

9. What are the greatest "enemies of biodiversity," according to Morris?

COLLABORATIVE ACTIVITY

What does Morris believe is the most critical problem facing the human population today? Do you agree with his assessment?

ACTIVITY

Write a brief (500- to 750-word) *evaluative* report (stressing your assessment of the site) or *informational* report (stressing its content) on the website of the Committee on the Status of Endangered Wildlife in Canada (COSEWIC) or a similar website (e.g., a provincial one devoted to the same concern). Organize your report by appropriate formal or descriptive categories. Formal categories could include "introduction," "methods" (basis of your evaluation), "results," and "conclusion." You could consider the website's purpose, credibility, main menu, links, navigation aids, accessibility, organization, visual appeal, quality and depth of information, use of charts to enhance understanding, and so on.

Related readings: Claude A. Piantadosi. "The human environment"; and Kevin Krajick. "In search of the ivory gull."

Bad borgs?

Andy Clark

(9,400 words)

INTRUSION

You live and work in a smart world, where your car is talking to your coffee machine (and snitching to your insurance company), and your medicine cabinet and toilet are watching your inputs and outputs (and snitching to your doctor or HMO, not to mention the drug police). Your smart badge (or maybe your cellphone) ensures that your physical movements leave a tangible trail, and your electronic trail is out there for all to see. The damn telemarketers know your soul; their machines have surfed your deepest likes and dislikes. So whatever happened to your right to a little space, some peace and privacy, a quiet affair, a little psychotropic time-out?

For my own part, I am delighted that Amazon, courtesy of some neat collaborative filtering, is able to recommend some stuff that I really do want to hear. But do I really want the government—or worse, Microsoft—to have access to all my movements, ingestions, consummations, and consumptions? The joys of the electronic trail and ubiquitous computing suddenly pale against the threats of electronic tattling and ubiquitous interference.

A few real-life horror stories can help set the scene. Consider the cookies. Cookies are electronic footprints that allow websites and advertising networks to monitor our on-line movements with granular precision. DoubleClick, a major Internet advertising company, was able to place cookies on millions of consumer hard drives. As a result, you might find yourself the target of unsolicited ads for products related to those you have most recently surfed. Innocent enough at first, but when DoubleClick acquired Abacus Direct, a huge commercial database of names, addresses, and on-line buying habits, it was able to stitch the information together to link real names and addresses to the cookie-based information about on-line use.[1] Under public and governmental pressure, the so-called profiling scheme was put on hold. But the potential is there. Amazon once deployed a system that identified the books and items most commonly purchased by people at specific major institutions and corporations, using domain names and ZIP codes to zero in. "People at Charles Schwab tend to like *Memoirs of a geisha*"—that kind of thing.

Scarier still are the GUIDs (Globally Unique Identifiers). These get pinned to you when you register for a service on-line and allow the company to link your on-line activity to your real-world details. Similarly, some Microsoft wares embed a unique identifier into each document you create, allowing it to be traced back to its real author.[2] It is well known that many companies and corporations, in blatant invasion of reasonable expectations of privacy, monitor e-mail even when it is sent from home over a company network. The trouble, as Jeffrey Rosen nicely points out, is that the more such intrusions occur and are

---

[1] This and several of the following stories are drawn from a chilling article by Jeffrey Rosen, "The Eroded Self," *New York Times Magazine*, April 30, 2000.

[2] Word 97 and Powerpoint 97 are cited by Jeffrey Rosen (see note 1 above).

not legally blocked, the lower our expectations become. The law is set up to protect our privacy in proportion to our reasonable expectations—a nasty little circle if ever you saw one. Reduce your expectations, and your rights follow suit. It is up to us, the public, to make sure that our expectations of privacy are not unreasonably eroded. We must not be browbeaten by disclaimers ("your e-mail may be monitored") whose legality is often quite untested. Correlatively, it is a matter of extreme urgency that the courts proceed with great care when making new law in this area. Privacy, once lost, is often lost forever.

Ubiquitous computing only compounds the problem. The natural support systems for information appliances and swarm intelligence equally and naturally provide for an unprecedented depth and quality of surveillance. It is one thing for your liquor cabinet to tell the store you need a new bottle of Ardbeg Single Malt, quite another when it tells your employer that you seem to be drinking more than can be good for you. The simple cellphone emits a signal that can act as a "smart badge," talking to all those semi-intelligent appliances you pass on your daily rounds. Now your friends, family, employers, lovers, and even your lovers' lovers need never be at a loss concerning your current whereabouts. Turn it off or leave it behind? Once the cellphone apparatus is lightly implanted in the skull, you won't even be able to accidentally leave it behind, though God knows, we'd better be able to turn it off. But then how does THAT look when your boss wants to find you?

Smart-badge systems, which allow the firm to track an employee's on-site movements, have already been tested at XeroxPARC, EuroPARC, and the Olivetti Research Center.[3] Really smart ones, of course, need to know who has just entered and what kinds of things they are likely to want. Worse still (but better for automatic data-mining), they need to remember exactly what previous visitors did, or bought, or accessed. In the era of ubiquitous computing and swarm intelligence, walls really *do* have ears, and memories too.

One response is just to bite the bullet—just do the calculations and decide that, on the whole, there is more good than bad in the creation of a fluid, adaptive, personalized, and rapidly responsive environment. If our health improves, or insurance costs go down, and we are always traceable in case of an emergency, who's to complain? If I am offered goods and services that I actually want, at prices that I am happy to pay, why worry? In life, there are always trade-offs, and if the price of all these benefits is a certain loss of privacy, maybe that's a price we should be prepared to pay. As Scott McNealy, CEO of SUN Microsystems, once famously remarked, "You already have zero privacy: get over it."[4]

Perhaps we can have our cake (in private) and eat it (ubiquitously, in public). To a certain extent, at least, technology itself has the potential to allow us privacy when we choose it. Wearable computing has a role to play here, as does the impressive work on public-key encryption. Wearables, as Bradley Rhodes and his colleagues point out, can help by keeping a lot of data quite literally on the person, instead of distributing it through a variety of intercommunicating fixed-

---

[3] See Bradley J. Rhodes, Nelson Minar, and Josh Weaver, "Wearable Computing Meets Ubiquitous Computing: Reaping the Best of Both Worlds," *Proceedings of the International Symposium on Wearable Computers (ISWC '99)* (October 1999); http://www.media.mit.edu/rhodes/Papers/wearhive.html; http://citeseer.nj.nec.com/rhodes99wearable.html.

[4] Said in a news conference concerning the release of Jini, a new interactive technology hailed as part of the fully networked home in which consumer appliances will communicate with each other and with outside networks (as per the vision of ubiquitous computing).

location devices.[5] The trouble, of course, is that if we *don't* allow outside agencies sufficient tracks, trails, and histories, we cannot reap the benefits of recommendation systems, personalized services and pricing, and the like. Likewise, if we don't allow the tool to know who we are, it won't be able to serve us so well. The price of any islands of privacy and disconnection is thus a reduction in the range of support and responses automatically available. Certain goods and services may also cost us more if we are unwilling to share personal information with the providers, but these trade-offs should be ours to choose. What matters most—and this is a lesson we will return to again and again in this closing chapter—is that our technologies be responsive to our individual needs, including our occasional but important need for privacy.

Encryption helps. By using clever (often *so* clever that they are currently illegal) ways of encoding digitally transmitted information, we are already able to allow outside agencies as much or as little content-access to our electronic meanderings as we choose. Public-key encryption allows you to advertise a key—a string of numbers—that anyone can use to encrypt a message to you, but the public key alone is insufficient to decrypt or decode anything. It works only in unison with another such key, the one known only to you. Using these kinds of techniques, it is simple to send secure information across the web. Freeware versions of public-key encryption systems include PGP (Pretty Good Privacy, legal *only* in the United States) and RIPEM, which is public domain software distributed by RSA.[6] Advanced cryptography applica-

tions support other useful functions, such as the so-called zero-knowledge proof.[7] This allows a merchant to bill a consumer without the merchant learning who is buying or having access to any details of the person's account.

What all this means in practice is that the user can, if she wishes, selectively opt out of some of the trailing and tracking swarm-based infrastructure. She can buy goods and services without revealing personal information and can block or filter the transmission of identity-revealing data to the various information-appliances surrounding her. Currently, the default is extreme openness to intrusive surveillance, and only the technologically sophisticated tend to take the various steps needed to protect themselves. Such users might, for example, employ advanced security tools such as Kremlin, which combine encryption capabilities with programs that are able to genuinely delete unwanted files from your hard drive.[8] This requires writing nonsense strings on top of the remaining chunks of files that standard programs simply partially delete. It helps avoid the Monica Lewinsky syndrome, where prosecutors subpoenaed her home computer and ransacked the hard drive, retrieving long-deleted and never-sent love letters to the president of the United States.[9]

Such extreme measures can smack of paranoia. As firms and legislators will inevitably argue, why worry unless you have something to hide? But worry we do. Most of us would hate to live in a state where government and employers routinely opened our physical mail. Why should we live in a state where the natural successors to such mail (e-mail and text messaging, phone calls

---

[5] Bradley Rhodes et al., "Wearable Computing Meets Ubiquitous Computing."

[6] For a lovely account, see Kevin Kelly, *Out of Control* (Reading, Mass.: Perseus Books, 1994), chap.12.

[7] Gershenfeld, *When Things Start to Think*, 94.

[8] Rosen, "The Eroded Self."

[9] Ibid. Other security measures might include the use of Atguard, a program that watches your on-line activity, alerts you to monitors and open doors, and sends cookies packing.

and faxes) lack similar protections? Moreover, the whole notion of "having nothing to hide" is fuzzy to say the least. It covers interests and activities ranging from the outright illegal to the mildly perverse to the simply socially frowned-upon to the merely eccentric. The average upstanding citizen may well have "something to hide" once this broad church is canvassed.

We live, after all, in a society where a great deal of behaviour, which is neither illegal nor harmful, might if made public impact negatively upon our lives and careers. Spare a thought for the grade school teacher who likes to cross-dress in the privacy of his own home but buys the clothes off the web and visits other sites and chat rooms to share discoveries and experiences. Or the peace campaigner with a taste for violent literature and a one-click account with Amazon. Or the Catholic priest with a nuanced love of women's lingerie. Or, to end with a real-life example from the British press, the gay police chief with a soft spot for anarchy and cannabis. I leave the reader to fill in her own special interests. The list is endless, the shades of grey innumerable.

And then there is the e-romance. Anyone foolish enough to attempt to conduct an extramarital, or otherwise unauthorized, affair using electronic media will quickly find cause to regret those tracks, trails, and incomplete deletions. They spell doom for your dreams of a private corner of cyberspace, complete with white picket fence and a full range of modern domestic appliances.

Then there are drugs. In an age when large numbers of well-informed, intelligent adults occasionally partake of recreational drugs (other than the taxed, time-honoured, and often quite lethal alcohol), it might be hoped that they will do so in as careful a manner as possible. To that end, they might visit a useful site such as Dancesafe, which offers balanced information concerning doses, effects, addictiveness, and relative toxicity. Yet if such visits are perceived as a two-edged sword, perhaps helping users avoid the worst kinds of abuse but simultaneously adding their names and details to some law enforcer's list, can we really hope for such care and caution?

All this is disturbing since it again hints at the creation of a new elite: this time, the elite subset of Internet users who stand any chance of achieving even a modicum of privacy. For every one who deploys advanced security tools such as Kremlin and public key encryption, there will be a thousand who trust to the goodwill of commerce and government. In any case, it seems unlikely that many citizens, be they ever so technologically aware, will ever win an "arms race" between users and government/employers. Encryption and firewalling is probably not the ultimate answer.

Another possibility, which I have grudgingly come to favour, involves a kind of leap of faith, or democratic optimism. As our governments, employers, colleagues, and lovers learn more and more about the typical behaviour of a wide range of valued, productive, and caring citizens, it should become clearer and clearer in what ways the goalposts of "good behaviour" must be moved. Such movement need not signal decay and decline, for only hypocrisy and more solid public/private firewalls ever kept them in place! As the lives of the populace become more visible, our work-a-day morals and expectations need to change and shift. It is time for the real world to play catch-up with our private lives, loves, and choices. As the realm of the truly private contracts, as I think it must, the public space in any truly democratic country needs to become more liberal and open-hearted. This attitude, which I am calling democratic optimism, may seem naively idealistic, but it is surely preferable to an escalation of cyber wars that the average citizen simply cannot hope to win . . .

OVERLOAD

One of the most fearsome spectres, though far less abstract and dramatic, is that of plain simple overload—the danger of slowly drowning in a sea of contact. As I write, I am painfully aware of the unread messages that will have arrived since I last logged in yesterday evening. By midday there will be around 60 new items, about 10 of which will require action. Ten more may be pure junk mail, easy to spot or filter, but it is the rest that are the real problem. These I read, only to discover they require no immediate thought or action. I call this mail e-stodge. It is filling without being necessary or nourishing, and there seems to be more of it every day.

The root cause of e-stodge, Neil Gershenfeld has suggested, is a deep but unnoticed shift in the relative costs, in terms of time and effort, of *generating* messages and of *reading* them.[10] Once upon a time, it cost much more—again in terms of time and effort—to create and send a message than to read one. Now, the situation is reversed. It is terribly easy to forward a whole screed to someone else, or to copy a message to all and sundry, just in case they happen to have an opinion or feel they should have been consulted. The length of the message grows as more and more responses get cheaply incorporated. Other forms of overload abound. The incoming messages aren't all e-mail; there are phone calls (on mobile and land lines) and text messages, even the occasional physical letter. There is the constant availability, via the Google-enhanced web, of more information about just about anything at the click of a mouse.

One cure for overload is, of course, simply to unplug. Several prominent academics have simply decided that "e-nough is e-nough" and have turned off their e-mail for good or else redirected it to assistants who sift, screen, and filter. Donald Knuth, a computer scientist who took this very step, quotes the novelist Umberto Eco, "I have reached an age where my main purpose is not to receive messages." Knuth himself asserts that "I have been a happy man ever since January 1, 1990, when I no longer had an e-mail address."[11]

We won't all be able to unplug or to avail ourselves of intelligent secretarial filters. A better solution, the one championed by Neil Gershenfeld, is to combine intelligent filtering software (to weed out junk mail) with a new kind of business etiquette. What we need is an etiquette that reflects the new cost/benefit ratio according to which the receiver is usually paying the heaviest price in the exchange. That means sparse messages, sent only when action is likely to be required and sent only to those who really need to know—a 007 principle for communication in a densely interconnected world. E-mail only what is absolutely necessary, keep it short, and send it to as few people as possible.

ALIENATION

Warwick University campus, in the English city of Coventry, was the relaxed and convivial setting for the Fourth International Conference on Cognitive Technology. The meeting took place in August 2001, and I was blessed with the task of delivering an opening keynote address. Adopting my usual upbeat approach, I spoke of a near future in which human-centred technologies progressively blur the already fuzzy boundaries between thinking systems and their tools for thought. I addressed problems and pitfalls but mostly of a technical or methodological

---

[10] Gershenfeld, *When Things Start to Think*, 121–22.

[11] Both quotes drawn from Donald Norman's discussion titled "No Moments of Silence," in D. Norman, *The Invisible Computer* (Cambridge, Mass.: MIT Press, 1999), 129.

kind. What I hadn't anticipated—especially from this well-informed, enthusiastic crowd of scientists—was the amount of real ambivalence that many felt toward a future in which so many of our interactions would be with so-called agent technologies instead of with flesh and blood humans. This, in fact, turned out to be a major discussion topic throughout the conference.

One version of this fear was articulated by John Pickering of the Warwick University Psychology Department. In a wonderful talk peppered with memorable (if sometimes disturbing) images[12] from the media, Pickering painted a worrying picture. Agent technologies, he suggested, may "harmfully degrade how people value themselves and treat each other."[13] By "agent technologies," he had in mind the kinds of long-running, potentially interactive software packages discussed in chapters 1 and 6. Examples might include a web-searching agent who seeks out the kinds of antique books and records you desire, reporting back, and bidding on your behalf; a "chat-bot" that you call up when you are feeling lonely or depressed; or a semi-intelligent interface that allows you to tell your graphics program, in plain English, what you seek to achieve and then discusses your plans in the light of its own deeper knowledge of what the underlying software can and can't do.

This kind of application is especially important because the kinds of biotechnological merger and symbiosis we have been discussing may well depend, for their ultimate success, on the creation of just such bio-friendly interfaces:

software agents that know enough about human language and human psychology to grease the wheels of human-machine interaction. Surrounded by a host of such agents, from a very early age, Pickering fears for the child's basic understanding of what it is to be human. For these "technologized social interactions" may well never be as deep, sensitive, and caring as the best of our interactions with other human beings. The software agents may mimic aspects of our social interactions, but they will do so (for the foreseeable future at least) only shallowly and imperfectly. The worry is that by exposure to such mimicry, our *own* view of ourselves and others may become warped, altered, or downgraded, and "the process of sociocultural learning in which human identity is formed will be changed as a result."[14]

The kinds of agents that Pickering is most concerned about are the learning agents: the software entities that adapt to you, learning about your likes, dislikes, tolerance for detail, best times for contact, and so on. Such agents, he thinks, will be perceived as individuals and will impact our ideas about our own "spheres of responsibility." A child who has a pet dog is already interacting with a simple form of intelligence, but a good software agent will be able to mimic more advanced aspects of human social interaction. It is this, Pickering worries, that might lead them to treat real human beings as more like software agents—to value both equally and, perhaps as a result, to "dumb down" the human-to-human interactions they engage in.

---

[12] For example, an ad for a men's fashion magazine consisting of a black-and-white commercial bar code warped open in the centre so as to resemble a vagina and accompanied by the worrying slogan "What every man wants." This image might be laid alongside the bar-coded breasts displayed in chapter 1 as a reminder of what we *don't* want to win a place in (what Donna Haraway called) "man's Family Album."

[13] John Pickering, "Human Identity in the Age of Software Agents," in *Cognitive Technology: Instruments of Mind: Proceedings of the 4th International Conference on Cognitive Technology*, ed. M. Beynon, C. Nehaniv, and K. Duatenhahn (Berlin: Springer, 2001), 450.

[14] Ibid., 446.

Kirstie Bellman of the Aerospace Corporation likened this process to the adoption of a "spell checker vocabulary" when sending messages to one another. If we know a word the spell checker doesn't but we aren't sure of the spelling, we tend not to use it. In this way, our active vocabulary for human-to-human interaction gets dragged down to the level of what the spell checker knows! Imagine, then, a scenario in which a child, interacting with a software agent that understands only a few simple emotional expressions, actually ends up limiting even her interactions with her parents to that same level of mutual understanding. This is a terrifying prospect indeed.

Pickering has a point. We really do need to pay closer attention to the many ways in which new technologies may impact our social relations and our sense of ourselves and of others. As identity becomes fluid, embodiment multiple, and presence negotiable, it is the perfect time to take a new look at who, what, and where we are. New kinds of human-machine symbiosis will, without a doubt, alter the way we see ourselves, our machines, and the world. As N. Katherine Hayles, a University of California professor, rather eloquently puts it, "When the body is integrated into a Cybernetic circuit, modification of the circuit will necessarily modify consciousness as well. Connected by multiple feedback loops to the objects it designs, the mind is also an object of design."[15]

Our redesigned minds will be distinguished by a better and more sensitive understanding of the self, of control, of the importance of the body, and of the systemic tentacles that bind brain, body, and technology into a single adaptive unit. This potential, I believe, far, far outweighs the attendant threats of desensitization, overload, and confusion. A few comments, though, on that specific worry about children's (and adult's) use of software agents.

My own reaction, at the conference, was to present a kind of benign dilemma. Either the software agents would be good enough to really engage our social skills, or they wouldn't. If the former (unlikely), then why worry? But if the latter (much more likely), then the child would still engage with her human caregivers in a visibly different way. Just as having a pet tortoise does not make a child less likely to want to play catch with her parents, having highly limited interactions with software agents won't blind her to the much wider range of interactions available with her parents.

A different kind of response came from Kirstie Bellman herself. All these worries, she suggested, actually rang *less* true to her than to her male colleagues. For Bellman is a busy working scientist who is also a mother. Even if interactions with software agents and play bots are somewhat shallow, Bellman argued, they can act as a useful supplement to the richer social interactions that are (all sides agreed) so crucially important. Busy working parents simply need all the help they can get. Just as previous generations of children loved, cared for, and talked to their dolls and pets, so new generations might add software entities to this venerable list. The kinds of fears and worries that so exercised many (predominantly male) members of the group were, she felt, a kind of luxury item freely available only to a certain professional class. This is an important point. Critics within the scientific community, such as the psychologist John Pickering of Warwick University in the UK, often fear that "enthusiasm for . . . computer-enhanced lives usually comes from a highly visible and technologically sophisticated minority [and that this] tends to conceal the more nega-

---

[15] Hayles, *How We Became Post-Human*, 115.

tive experiences and views of the less technologically adept majority."[16]

Bellman turns this on its head, pointing out that it is equally often only the lucky few who have the luxury of fearing the effects of labour-saving and opportunity-enhancing innovations such as microwaves, dishwashers, and, one day, software agents who play with the kids. What about the already real interactive toy that is designed to help children learn to share? The toy is a doll-filled castle that the child shares with a 3D computer-animated playmate whose image is projected onto a screen of the castle. The playmate tells the child stories about the dolls. But if the child makes a premature grab for a doll, the virtual playmate politely objects, reminding her that he was still playing with it. The playmate also helps structure cooperative play between many children by telling appropriate stories. Early studies suggest that children using the interactive toy learn to behave better, as a result, with their real playmates.[17] Perhaps, then, there is hope for new interactive toys that help, rather than hinder, a child's social and moral development. In the end, what really matters is that we educate ourselves and our children about *the nature and the limits of our best technologies* so that we can intelligently combine the best of the biological and engineered worlds.

The Cognitive Technology conference was also the occasion for a wonderful encounter with Steve Talbott of the Nature Institute. Steve is probably the best informed and most constructive critic of the role of advanced technologies I have ever met. He and I disagree about just about everything, but there is no better guide to the dangers of alienation inherent in the biotechnological matrix. I strongly recommend taking a look at Steve's monthly electronic publication NETFUTURE (subtitle: *Technology and Human Responsibility*). At the time of writing, NETFUTURE is well into its second hundred issues, and it covers everything from the complex issues surrounding technology for the handicapped ("Can Technology Make the Handicapped Whole?" NETFUTURE #92) to the role of computers in childhood ("Fools Gold," in #111) to the question of e-mail overload and the balance between connection and disconnection (#124). In a typically nice twist, Steve argues that technologies that enable distant communication (e-mail, cellphones, etc.) are a double-edged sword. For while they can help bring us closer together, they also create the *conditions* under which more and more of us are *willing* or required (by our firms) to move physically farther and farther apart. The simple presence of these technologies thus contributes to the generation of the very problem (frequent, easy, long-distance communication) they help to "solve." In the end, Steve's point is *not* that we should therefore give up on cellphones and e-mail accounts. Instead, he says:

> Our failure to recognize the truth about the technological forces we are dealing with . . . prevents us from bending them more effectively to our own ends. If we came to terms with the double significance of our technologies . . . we would not so routinely speak of cell phones, e-mail and the like in terms of the single virtue of connectivity. We would recognize that the underlying forces of disconnection at work in these tools are fully as powerful as the forces bringing us together.[18]

---

[16] Pickering, "Human Identity in the Age of Software Agents," 445.
[17] See report by Eugenie Samuel, "Gimme, It's Mine," *New Scientist* 2301 (July 28, 2001): 23.
[18] Both quotes from *Netfuture* 124 (October 30, 2001).

By keeping a weather eye on the darker side of our technologies and inviting us all to participate in the discussion, NETFUTURE performs an invaluable and ever more timely service. Tune in at http://www.oreilly.com/people/staff/stevet/netfuture, or just plug "netfuture" into a good search engine.

NARROWING

Consider the simple use of a software agent to suggest new books for you to read or new music for you to hear. Such an agent will make its recommendations on the basis of (*a*) its knowledge of what books or CDs you have bought before, (*b*) your feedback, if any, concerning which books or CDs you liked best, and (*c*) its knowledge—courtesy of the collaborative filtering and data-mining techniques discussed in chapter 6—of what books or CDs others, who liked the ones you liked, liked too.

This is all well and good, as far as it goes, but Patti Maes of the MIT Media lab argues that there is an attendant danger of a kind of communal tunnel vision. Such software agents will suggest more and more of what are broadly speaking "the same kinds of thing" to the same kinds of people. Choosing from these lists, these people will then confirm the software agent's "expectations" by buying (and probably even liking) many of these things. So the agents will, in effect, offer us more and more of a progressively less and less extensive band of literature, music, or whatever. The danger is of a kind of positive-feedback-driven "lock-in" following a few (perhaps ill-chosen) early purchases or decisions.

Compare this with a visit to a bookstore, where a bright jacket or a snappy title might catch your eye and where your trip to the detec-

tive fiction section takes you right past poetry and cooking. The real world, it seems, currently offers a much richer canvas for semi-random explorations than does its virtual counterpart. But a real-world bookshop, as we all know, is often less than ideal when you already know exactly what you want; stocks are limited, organization unfathomable, opening times idiosyncratic. The potential synergy between real-world browsing and on-line targeted purchasing is truly enormous. A few lucky discoveries can seed whole new areas of interest, which (once reflected in your on-line purchasing or even earlier if the cash registers talk to your software agents) will add new dimensions to your electronic profile and hence give the software agents and collaborative filters lots more avenues to explore.

The moral is simple but just about maximally important. To really make the most of the wired world, we need to understand—at least approximately—how it works. Only then can we take the measure of its weaknesses and its strengths and adjust our own role as human participants accordingly. Technological education will be crucial if human-machine cooperation is to enrich and humanize rather than restrict and alienate. Once again, the lesson seems clear: *Know Thyself: Know Thy Technologies.*

DECEIT

In 1996 there appeared an article in *Emerge* magazine called "Trashing the Information Highway: White supremacy goes hi-tech."[19] It revealed the increasing use of the Internet as a means of conducting devious smear campaigns. In one such campaign, white supremacists posing as African-Americans posted offensive calls for the legalization

---

[19] N. Sheppard, Jr., "Trashing the Information Highway: White Supremacy Goes Hi-Tech," *Emerge* (July-August 1996): 34–40. For some further discussion of related themes, see Thomas Foster, "Trapped by the Body? Telepresence Technologies and Transgendered Performances in Feminist and Lesbian Rewritings of Cyberpunk Fiction," in *The Cybercultures Reader*, ed. D. Bell and B. Kennedy (London: Routledge, 2000), 439–59.

of pedophilia. This is a pernicious abuse of the ease and anonymity of the Internet. Such abuses are fortunately uncommon and fall more or less under the authority of existing law.

More common and far less easy to control (but much harder to classify as abuse rather than innocent self-reinvention and exploration) is the use of electronic media to present a sexual or personal persona that is in some way different from the sender's biological or real-world persona. Chat rooms are full of (biological) men presenting as women, (biological) women presenting as men, (biological) older women presenting as younger women and vice versa, (biological) younger men presenting as older men and vice versa, gay (biological) men presenting as straight women, straight (biological) men presenting as gay men. The permutations seem endless, a kind of Goldberg Variations on all the rich sexual, social, and physical complexity the non-virtual world has to offer.[20] In one chat room, someone recently admitted to presenting herself as a multiple amputee even though she was biologically quite intact.

What should we make of all this? On the one hand, it seems like deceit: an impression reinforced if we view the electronic domain as a kind of hunting ground for possible real-world encounters. Those who use the media this way often resort to quick and dirty early checks, like an impromptu request for an immediate telephone conversation. But clearly, nothing is ever conclusive. Instead, the only real hope is that if it is clear that the parties concerned might want to use the net as a springboard to a real-world (and I use that term grudgingly) relationship, then they (and you) will not waste too much time presenting in ways that cannot, with a little goodwill on both sides, successfully carry over into that other context.

But what of the many folk who do not seek to cross the divide? Or those who might one day segue into a real-world meeting but believe that the real "them" is precisely the combination of a certain set of personas, some adapted to the conditions and constraints of their biological form, life situation, and previous history and others adapted to the very different conditions, constraints, and possibilities presented by these new forms of communication, contact, embodiment, and presence? Might these not be genuine, complex individuals in their own right? Who are we to insist that the real "you" is defined by some specific subset of your words, actions, and interests?

Some of the deeper issues here concern the successful integration of multiple personas, where by "integration" we can mean something quite subtle. To be integrated, in this sense, is not to have one constant persona so much as to be able to balance the needs of various personas so as to avoid compromising any one by the actions of the "others." This is, in effect, a recipe for distilling a multi-dimensional form of personal identity from a flux of potentially competing ways of presenting oneself to others and to the world.[21] This might mean, for example, being wary of the strategy of building impermeable

---

[20] I have chosen my words carefully here. Where I might have written of "men posing as women," I have written instead "(biological) men presenting as women." This is because I think (and shall argue) that it is often unclear which of the many identities and aspects available to an individual should be privileged as his/her/its "true self." Better, perhaps, to see the self as the shifting sum of multiple personas adapted to different contexts, constraints, and expectations.

[21] It would take me too far afield, and too deep into the philosophy of personhood, to pursue this much further here. But the interested reader might look at some recent treatments such as D. Dennett and N. Humphrey, "Speaking for Our Selves" in D. Dennett, *Brainchildren* (Cambridge, Mass.: MIT Press, 1998), 31–55; Carol Rovane, *The Bounds of Agency* (Princeton, N.J.: Princeton University Press, 1998); Gareth Branwyn, "Compu-Sex: Erotica for Cybernauts," in *The Cybercultures Reader*, 396–402.

firewalls between your electronic and real-world selves and instead allowing communication, overlap, and seepage. It might mean being able to be honest about your biological self and real-world situation, without taking that as devaluing these other forms of personal growth and exploration. Such an approach will become increasingly practical as more people appreciate the potential of new media to support entirely new forms of personal contact, presence, and relationship, rather than seeing them merely as imperfect attempts to recreate real-world relationships and presence at a distance.

More disturbing, in many ways, is the presence in many chat rooms of nonhuman intelligences pretending to be human. The web portal Yahoo, in 2001, was "infested by cyber-bots."[22] These were programs able to log on to the chat rooms and, posing as humans, send messages directly to other people in the chat rooms, enticing them to visit specific company websites. Free advertising, with that important personal touch. Cyber-bots can likewise pass themselves off as voters in on-line polls, or as participants in contests, or in other ways.

To prevent such abuses, researchers at Carnegie-Mellon's Aladdin Center have created what they nicely dub CAPTCHA—Completely Automated Public Turing-Test to Tell Computers and Humans Apart.[23] The test requires those seeking an account for entry to some space (say a chat room) to take a simple test to "prove" they are human.[24] A word is shown against a background that adds noise or as a distorted version of itself. The prospective account holder must identify the word. This task, simple as it sounds, currently weeds out the bots from the boys (or girls), as present-day word recognition routines cannot cope with these deviant presentations. Once again, it is simply an arms race between competing technologies, and CAPTCHA may not serve as gatekeeper for very long.

Such potential for deceit or dissimulation is balanced, however, by the very real power of new communications regimes to spread important truths quickly, without the usual impediments of censorship and bureaucracy and without regard for many of the physical, national, and social boundaries that render so much of our daily news parochial in the extreme.

A case in point is the simple e-mail sent by Tamin Ansary to some 20 friends and colleagues on the morning of 12 September 2001. Ansary was an Afghan-American living in San Francisco. The letter, which I am willing to bet nearly every reader of this book received within two or three days of the attacks on the Twin Towers, argued that any US response that involved "bombing Afghanistan back to the stone age" would be misplaced. It would be misplaced not because the crimes were not heinous but because "that's been done. The Soviets took care of it already.

---

[22] The phrase, and the account of the Carnegie-Mellon counterattack, is drawn from "Robots Help Humans Defeat Robots," which was a short news piece in the "In Brief" section of *Trends in Cognitive Sciences* 5:12 (2001): 512. The articles for that section were written by Heidi Johansen-Berg and Mark Wrexler.

[23] A. Turing, "Computing Machinery and Intelligence," *Mind* 59 (1950): 423–60; reprinted in *The Philosophy of Artificial Intelligence*, ed. M. Boden (Oxford: Oxford University Press, 1990), 40–66. The original Turing Test was named after Alan Turing, who believed that a sufficient degree of behavioural success should be allowed to establish that a candidate system, be it a human or a machine, is a genuine thinker. Turing proposed a test (today known as the Turing Test) that involved a human interrogator trying to spot—from verbal responses—whether a hidden conversant was a human or a machine. Any system capable of fooling the interrogator, Turing proposed, should be counted as a genuinely intelligent agent. Sustained, top-level verbal behaviour, if Turing is right, is a sufficient test for the presence of real intelligence.

[24] See L. von Ahn, M. Blum, and J. Langford, "Telling Humans and Computers Apart (Automatically)," Carnegie-Mellon University research paper CMU-CS-02-117. See also http://www.captcha.net.

Make the Afghans suffer? They're already suffering. Level their houses? Done. Turn their schools into piles of rubble? Done."

This message didn't need testing by gatekeepers to check its authenticity. It smelled of truth the way a diner smells of doughnuts. Those who received it saw this at once, sending it on to their own friends and colleagues. It found its way within a few days to the websites Tompaine.com and Salon.com and from that stopover conquered the world.[25] By the end of the week, the message had reached the hearts of millions upon millions of people across the globe. Ansary himself was besieged with requests for interviews, with e-mails, phone calls, and offers.

The message didn't stop the eventual bombing, but it may well have played a role in delaying, and perhaps partially reconfiguring, what was perhaps politically inevitable. At the very least, it gave millions of people new insight into the complex political and social realities upon which simplistic talk of evil and retribution is all too easily overlaid. It stands as a testimony to the power of the Internet to allow words and ideas to reach a massive audience, not because those words come with the standard trappings of authority or because they enjoy the brute force backing of standard international media, but simply in virtue of their timeliness and content. Deceit, misinformation, truth, exploration, and personal reinvention: the Internet provides for them all. As always, it is up to us, as scientists and as citizens, to guard against the worst and to create the culture and conditions most likely to favour the best. . . .

DISEMBODIMENT

I have a special stake in this one, as I have long championed the importance of the body in the sciences of the mind. One of my books even bears the subtitle "Putting brain, body, and world together again." Imagine my horror, then, to find myself suspected, in writing enthusiastically of technologies of telepresence and digital communication, of having changed sides, of now believing that the body didn't matter and the mind was something ethereal and distinct.

Far from having changed sides, however, the present work flows directly from this stress on the importance of body and world. What we have learned is that human biological brains are, in a very fundamental sense, incomplete cognitive systems. They are naturally geared to dovetail themselves, again and again, to a shifting web of surrounding structures, in the body and increasingly in the world. Minds like ours solve problems not by intellectual force majeure but by cooperating with all these other elements in a spaghetti-like matrix. Just about everything in the present treatment speaks in favour of that image, from the use of pen and paper to do complex sums to the ease with which Stelarc now deploys his "third hand," to the daily babble of cellphones and text messages with which we now coordinate our social lives, all the way to the use of mind-controlled cursors, swarm-based data-mining, and telepresence-guided house-minding devices. Moreover, as we saw in chapter 2, the intimacy of brain and body is evidenced in the very plasticity of the body-image itself. Our brains care *so much* about the fine details of our embodiment that they are ready and willing to recalibrate those details on the spot, again and again, to accommodate changes (limb growth, limb loss) and extensions (prosthesis, implants, even sports equipment). It is this tendency that allows them sometimes to be fooled by certain tricks, and it is because of this that the physical

---

[25] This account of the message's routing is based on Laura Miller's article "One E-Mail Message Can Change the World," *New York Times Magazine*, December 9, 2001.

feeling of remote presence—and even of remote embodiment—is sometimes quite easy to achieve. The brain, in all these cases, is just one player on a crowded field. Our experience of what it is to be human, and our sense of our own capacities for action and problem-solving, flows from the profile of the whole team.

Whence, then, the fears about "disembodiment"? One root of the worry is the popular image of the lonely keyboard-tapping adolescent, who prefers video games to human company, takes no interest in sports or direct-contact sex, and who identifies more closely with his or her own electronic avatar or avatars than with his or her biological body. Isolated, disconnected, disembodied, desexed. Virtues, perhaps, in a politician, but hardly what we would wish for any child of our own.

The image itself is open to empirical question. According to a University of Warwick (UK) survey, heavy Internet surfers are more likely, not less, to belong to some real-world community group and less likely to spend time passively watching TV.[26] Talking to others on the net encourages, it seems, the appreciation that we can get together with like-minded folk and actually make a difference in the world. Nonetheless, the image of the isolated key-tapper is one we seem to have indelibly added to our stock of modern-day stereotypes.

Isolation, in any case, is often a matter of perspective. The apparently isolated individual tapping away night after night is, in many cases, spending quality time in her own chosen community. These eclectic electronic communities often bring together a greater number of like-minded folk than we could ever hope to find in our hometown or even in a large city. A rather bizarre example is the on-line community of folk who gather at sites such as FurryMUCK.[27] A MUCK is a multi-user (usually role-playing) environment, and FurryMUCK caters to those whose imaginative, social, and sometimes sexual pleasure involves adopting animal personas and/or wearing furry animal costumes. This once-elusive minority now has hundreds of websites and their own (real-world) conventions and meetings. Without the distance-defying glue of electronic chat rooms and communities, it is hard to imagine such a group achieving this kind of critical mass.

There is, however, a new danger that accompanies the creation of more and more specific (often gated) electronic communities. It is one that is especially marked in the case of communities held together by shared but unusual sexual preferences or tendencies. The danger is of a new kind of marginalization. By relying upon an electronic community in which it is easy to speak of unusual needs and passions, people with special interests may find it easier to live out the rest of their lives without revealing or admitting this aspect of their identity. This could be dangerous insofar as it artificially relieves the wider society of its usual obligations of understanding and support, creating a new kind of ghetto that once again hides the group from the eyes—and protective social policies—of mainstream society.

It is a delicate matter, then, to balance this danger against the competing vision (explored a few spectres back) of new media allowing us slowly and safely to explore multiple aspects of our personal and sexual identities. Once again,

---

[26] Reported on BBC News, November 24, 2001.

[27] FurryMUCK is at www.furnation.com/fgc/. Furry newsgroups include alt.fan.furry, alt.sex.furry, and alt.sex.plushie. For a fairly detailed account, see Julene Snyder's article "Animal Magnetism," which appeared in *Life*, August 26, 1998 (and can be found on the web).

the most we can do is to be aware, as individuals and as public servants, of this danger and to make active efforts to take account of even these relatively invisible minorities in lawmaking and social policy.

A less familiar version of the more general worry about "disembodiment" takes the idea quite literally. With so much emphasis on information transmission and digital media, the physical body itself can begin to seem somewhat unnecessary. Respected scientists such as Hans Moravec speak enthusiastically of a future world in which our mental structures are somehow preserved as potentially immortal patterns of information capable of being copied from one electronic storage medium to another. In the reducing heat of such a vision, the human body (in fact, any body, biological or otherwise) quickly begins to seem disposable—"mere jelly" indeed.[28]

To be fair, Moravec himself repeatedly stresses the symbiotic nature of good forms of human-machine relationship. His vision of the self as a kind of persisting higher-order pattern is, ultimately, much more subtle and interesting than his critics allow. But what I seek to engage here is not the true vision but the popular caricature: the idea that the body and its capabilities are fundamentally irrelevant to the mind and hence the self. Nothing, absolutely nothing, in the account I have developed lends support to such a vision of essential disembodiment. In depicting the intelligent agent as a joint function of the biological brain, the rest of the human body, *and* the tangled webs of technological support, I roundly reject the vision of the self as a kind of ethereal, information-based construct. There is no informationally constituted *user* relative to whom all the rest is just *tools*. It is, as we argued in chapter 5, *tools all the way down*. We

are just the complex, shifting agglomerations of "our own" inner and outer tools for thought. We are our own best artefacts and always have been.

Some of these tools, to be sure, help constitute our conscious minds, while many operate below or beneath or otherwise outside of that domain. As we have repeatedly seen, it would be crazy to identify the physical basis of oneself solely with the machinery of the conscious goings-on. As we saw, just about everything we do and think arises from a complex interplay between the contents of conscious awareness and reflection and the more subterranean processing that throws up ideas and supports fluent real-world action. If there is any truth at all, then, in the image of the self as a kind of higher-level pattern, it is a pattern determined by the activities of multiple conscious and non-conscious elements spread across brain, body, and world.

Fine words indeed. But no consolation, one supposes, to our isolated friend, tapping away at the keyboard late at night, fearful of human contact and aroused only by the occasional warbling of "it's not my fault" emanating from the speakers as the machine crashes for the tenth time that day. While this lifestyle may have more good in it than many critics believe, it is (I submit) a vision of the past. The agenda of human-centred technology differs in just about every respect. In particular, such technologies hold out the promise of more mobility, richer interfaces, and richer interactive support. Far from being stuck in an isolated corner, our hero may find herself engulfed in a mobile, varied, and physically demanding social whirl.

First and foremost, human-centred technology aims to free the user from that whole "box on a tabletop" regime: the regime of sitting, looking at a screen, and interfacing with the digital world using the narrow and demanding channels of

---

[28] H. Moravec, *Mind Children: The Future of Robot and Human Intelligence* (Cambridge and New York: Cambridge University Press, 1998), 17.

keyboard and mouse. Wearable computers, augmented reality displays, and richer interface technologies transform this image beyond recognition. Mobile access to the web will soon be as common as mobile access to a phone line. Keyboard interfaces, of all kinds, will be augmented, and sometimes replaced, by the kinds of rich, analogue interface described in chapter 2. Instead of touching tiny and elusive keys to pull up a menu to select a favourite website, you might just move a finger to touch an icon that only you can see, hanging in the air about three inches above your eye-line. At first, such augmentations may rely on clumsy spectacle-based displays—but in the end, all the new functionality may be engineered into our eyes themselves.

As a simple taste of this kind of freedom, imagine the probable end point of the cellphone revolution. The receiver will be surgically implanted in order to make fairly direct contact with the auditory nerve or perhaps even the ventral cochlear nucleus. Alerted to an incoming call by a characteristic tingling in the fingers, you can take the call without anyone else hearing; your replies need not be spoken aloud as long as you gently simulate the correct muscle movements in your throat and larynx. Such a technology would look to us today like some kind of "telepathy." There are pros and cons to such a scenario without a doubt, but there would certainly be no feeling of being trapped, bound, or isolated, courtesy of such mobile, easy-to-use, communication-extending enhancements.

The point about mobility is probably crucial. Wearable computing and ubiquitous computing are each, in different but complementary ways, geared to freeing the user from the desktop or laptop. They are geared to *matching* the technology to a mobile, socially interactive, physically engaged human life form. The development of new and richer interfaces goes hand in hand with this. The ubiquitous devices will be more self-sufficient—more likely to monitor us than to receive deliberate commands and inputs. We will still need to communicate data and requests at times, and here the use of a variety of physical embodiment-exploiting interfaces will be crucial. The violinist Yo-Yo Ma's communications with his instrument via the bow are, we saw in chapter 2, amazingly rich and nuanced. One day soon we will see expert web-surfers and designers able to manipulate data streams and virtual objects with all the skill and subtlety of a Yo-Yo Ma. Almost certainly, they will not be using a keyboard and mouse to do so.

Where some fear disembodiment and social isolation, I anticipate *multiple* embodiment and social *complexity*. An individual may identify himself as a member of a wide variety of social groups and may (in part courtesy of the new technologies of telepresence and telerobotics) explore in each of those contexts a variety of forms of embodiment, contact, and sexuality. The feeling of disembodiment arises only when we are digitally immersed but lack the full spectrum of rich, real-time feedback that body and world provide. As feedback links become richer and more varied, our experience will rather become one of *multiple ways of being embodied*, akin, perhaps, to the way a skilled athlete feels when she exchanges tennis racket for wet suit and flippers. In these new worlds, Katherine Hayles notes, it is "not a question of leaving the body behind but rather of extending embodied awareness in highly specific local and material ways that would be impossible without electronic prostheses."[29]

In a strange way, we may even come to better appreciate the value and significance of our normal bodily presence by exploring such alternatives. Not disembodiment, then, so much as a

---

[29] N.K. Hayles, *How We Became Post-Human*, 291.

deeper understanding of why the body matters and of the space of possible bodies and perspectives. Not isolation so much as a wider and less geocentric kind of community. Not handcuffed to a desktop device in a dusty corner but walking and running out in the real world. Not mediated via the narrow and distressing bottlenecks of keyboard and screen but richly coupled via new interfaces that make the most of our biological senses and native bodily skills.

But let's not fool ourselves. The problems all too briefly scouted above are real and pressing, and the solutions I have gestured at are at best partial and often visibly inadequate. Still, there is no turning back. The drive toward biotechnological merger is deep within us—it is the direct expression of much of what is most characteristic of the human species. The task is to merge gracefully, to merge in ways that are virtuous, that bring us closer to one another, make us more tolerant, enhance understanding, celebrate embodiment, and encourage mutual respect. If we are to succeed in this important task, we must first understand ourselves and our complex relations with the technologies that surround us. We must recognize that, in a very deep sense, we were always hybrid beings, joint products of our biological nature and multi-layered linguistic, cultural, and technological webs. Only then can we confront, without fear or prejudice, the specific demons in our cyborg closets. Only then can we actively structure the kinds of world, technology, and culture that will build the kinds of *people* we choose to be.

In Andy Clark. 2004. *Natural-born cyborgs: Minds, technologies, and the future of human intelligence*. New York, NY: Oxford University Press.

KEY AND DIFFICULT WORDS

Define the following, using context or other clues if possible: **ubiquitous, correlatively, encryption, meandering, toxicity, screed, convivial, ambivalence, pedophilia, pernicious, permutation, dissimulation, parochial, recalibrate, ethereal, agglomeration.**

QUESTIONS

1. Consider the ways that the first section, "Intrusion," sets up the sections that follow: (a) by expressing the author's views and attitudes toward the general topic of biotechnology; and (b) in utilizing the kinds of evidence and the rhetorical strategies that he employs in other sections.

2. Paraphrase the final paragraph of the section titled "Intrusion." Then write a brief (150- to 250-word) critical response to it, commenting on its validity and on how it provides or does not provide a fitting conclusion to the section.

3. In "Alienation," Clark mediates a discussion at the Fourth International Conference on Cognitive Technology, summarizing the different views of conference participants. Summarize one of these viewpoints and analyze Clark's response. You could consider the following: What is his own view concerning this issue? Does he appear fair and free of bias? Does he successfully resolve the problem?

4. Do you think this book chapter is primarily designed to inform or persuade? If you believe it is to inform, summarize in two or three sentences the subject area, the significance of the subject, and the chapter's effectiveness. If you believe it is to persuade, summarize his argumentative thesis and evaluate its effectiveness as argument by considering such factors as topic, audience, purpose, and refutation strategy (if there is one).

5. How would you characterize the author's tone? Is it appropriate given the subject? Is it effective? You could consider the language level, word choice, range of emotions that the work evokes, or use of humour, pointing to specific examples.

6. Two kinds of evidence that Clark uses extensively are experts/authorities and examples. Making specific reference to at least two examples of each kind of evidence, assess their effectiveness in terms of the work as a whole.

7. Some of the longer sections could be considered mini-essays, with many, though perhaps not all, of the features of longer essays that stand on their own. Critically analyze one of these sections as a model or representative "essay," paying particular attention to its structural functions (introduction, main points with their supporting detail and development, and conclusion).

8. Explore the author's use of the first-person ("I") voice and the way it affects the work's credibility.

COLLABORATIVE ACTIVITY

In small groups (two or three members), determine what you believe are the two major problems raised by Clark. Use your own knowledge and experience to expand on some of his points, including possible ways to deal with these problems in the future. The groups can then summarize their findings and present them to the other groups.

ACTIVITIES

1. Some of the "spectres" that Clark raises are likely familiar to many computer-literate individuals in North American society today; in fact, you may well have found yourself thinking about them at one time or another. After reading a section that you find yourself relating to, such as the brief sections "Overload" or "Narrowing," freewrite on its implications as they might apply to you. If one sentence especially seems to relate to your own experience, use that sentence as a starting point for a freewriting exercise.

2. Using a dictionary and a scientific text or reliable Internet source, research the origin of the term "cyborg." What is the name of a word that is formed from two or more other words? Give a couple of examples of other words that share one of the same roots as "cyborg," and explain their meaning.

Related reading: Clive Thompson. "Game theories."

Safer injection facility use and syringe sharing in injection drug users

Thomas Kerr, Mark Tyndall, Kathy Li, Julio Montaner, and Evan Wood

(1,350 words)

Abstract: Safer injection facilities provide medical supervision for illicit drug injections. We aimed to examine factors associated with syringe sharing in a community-recruited cohort of illicit injection drug users in a setting where such a facility had recently opened. Between 1 December 2003 and 1 June 2004, of 431 active injection drug users, 49 (11.4%, 95% CI 8.5–14.3) reported syringe sharing in the past six months. In logistic regression analyses, use of the facility was independently associated with reduced syringe sharing (adjusted odds ratio 0.30, 0.11–0.82, p=0.02) after adjustment for relevant socio-demographic and drug-use characteristics. These findings could help inform discussions about the merits of such facilities.

Vancouver, Canada, like many urban centres, has been the site of continuing HIV and overdose epidemics in illicit injection drug users.[1] In response to these public health problems, health officials in Vancouver opened North America's first medically supervised safer injection facility in September 2003.[1,2] As previously described,[1] injection drug users in the facility can access sterile injecting equipment, inject pre-obtained illicit drugs under the supervision of nurses, and access nursing care and addictions counselling. Although such facilities exist in several European settings and in Sydney, Australia, few formal epidemiological analyses have been done of their effects on reported HIV risk behaviours, such as syringe sharing.[1,3,4] In Vancouver, a continuing prospective cohort study of injection drug users allowed us to examine factors associated with syringe sharing in local users after the opening of the safer injection facility.

We obtained data for these analyses from the Vancouver Injection Drug Users Study,[5] a prospective cohort that has been described previously. The study has been approved by the University of British Columbia and Providence Health Care ethics review boards, and all study participants provided written consent before enrolment. To be consistent with earlier analyses[6] and to provide sufficient statistical power, syringe sharing was defined as borrowing or lending a used syringe in the past six months. Data from participants seen between 1 December 2003 and 1 June 2004 were assessed in our study. We used univariate and multivariate statistics to determine factors associated with syringe sharing in the past six months. The associations between independent variables and the dependent variable were first analyzed by univariate logistic regression. To adjust for potential confounding between use of the safer injection facility and syringe sharing, variables that were found to be significantly associated with syringe sharing (p<0.05) were then considered in a fixed logistic regression model, which included all variables that met this criteria as well as the facility use variable. We did all statistical analyses using SAS software version 8.0 (SAS, Cary, NC, USA).

We selected socio-demographic and drug-use characteristics in these analyses on the basis of previous investigations of syringe sharing in injection drug users in Vancouver,[6,7] including: age, HIV serostatus, limited access to sterile syringes, need for help with injections, binge drug use, frequency of cocaine and heroin injection, and methadone maintenance treatment. Variable definitions were consistent with previous analyses: individuals who reported using cocaine or heroin once a day or more were defined as frequent cocaine or heroin users.[6] Bingeing was defined as periods in which drugs were used more often than usual.[6] To evaluate the effect of needle exchange program access on syringe sharing, we compared participants who did and did not report accessing sterile syringes from such a program. To consider the effect of the safer injection facility, we compared participants who reported undertaking all, most, or some of their injections at the facility with those participants who reported undertaking few or none of their injections at the facility.

431 active injection drug users were seen for follow-up during the study period, of whom 90 (20.9%, 95% CI 17.1–24.7) reported that all, most, or some of their injections were at the safer injection facility. 49 (11.4%, 8.5–14.3) individuals reported sharing syringes during this same period. Univariate analyses showed that need for help with injecting (odds ratio [OR] 2.94, 95% CI 1.59–5.42, p=0.01), bingeing (OR 2.04, 1.05–3.95, p=0.03), frequent heroin (OR 1.72, 0.95–3.13, p=0.07) or cocaine injection (OR 1.70, 0.93–3.06, p=0.08) were positively associated with syringe sharing, whereas younger age (OR 0.95 per year, 0.92–0.99, p=0.01) and use of the safer injection facility (OR 0.39, 0.15–1.03, p=0.05) were negatively associated with syringe sharing. In a logistic regression model, need for help injecting and binge drug use were positively associated with syringe sharing, whereas younger age and use of the facility were independently associated with reduced syringe sharing (table).

The protective effect of safer injection facility use remained independently associated with reduced syringe sharing when we further adjusted the model to include frequent heroin and cocaine injection (adjusted OR 0.29, 0.11–0.78, p=0.01). Although our logistic models included a small number of syringe sharing events, a goodness of fit test indicated that the estimated models fit the data.

We realized that despite multivariate adjustment, our findings could be due to residual confounding if the safer injection facility had selected injection drug users who were inherently at a lower risk of syringe sharing. To test for this, we examined the rate of syringe sharing for those who did use the facility and those who did not during their follow-up visit immediately before its opening on 22 September 2003. Rates of syringe sharing were similar in these

Table: Multivariate logistic regression of factors associated with syringe sharing.

	Adjusted odds ratio (95% CI)	p
Age (per year older)	0.95 (0.92–0.98)	0.01
Use of safer injection facility	0.30 (0.11–0.82)	0.02
Need for help injecting	2.95 (1.57–5.55)	0.01
Binge drug use	2.04 (1.02–4.08)	0.04
Intercept (constant)	(−0.79)	0.19

Model adjusted for all variables shown.

populations before the opening (X^2 0.46, 1 degree of freedom, p=0.50), and the differences only emerged during follow-up after the facility had opened.

We have shown that use of a medically supervised safer injection facility was independently associated with reduced syringe sharing in a community-recruited sample of injection drug users who had similar rates of syringe sharing before the facility's opening. Our study has several limitations. First, although previous studies have indicated that the Vancouver Injection Drug Users Study cohort is representative of local users,[6] it is not a random sample. Second, although it is highly plausible that provision of sterile injecting equipment and medical supervision of injection drug use could be causally related with reduced syringe sharing, our study is limited by its cross-sectional design, and hence we caution against inferring such a causal relation. However, our prospective approach showed that differences in the rate of syringe sharing only emerged after the facility opened. It is noteworthy that ethical issues will probably prevent interventional study designs that could completely resolve the issues of selection effects and unmeasured confounding. It should also be noted that we probably underestimated rates of syringe sharing and borrowing because of socially desirable responding, and we were forced to use a combined endpoint of lending and borrowing to obtain adequate statistical power. We have justified this approach previously, and we applied a rigorous approach in our attempts to control for potential confounders.[6] Future prospective analyses with nominal data about recent use of safer injection facilities are needed to further elucidate the relation between their use and syringe sharing. Our findings could help to inform discussions in the UK and elsewhere, where the potential public-health benefits of such facilities are of growing interest.[1,8]

CONTRIBUTORS

T Kerr and E Wood designed the study. K Li and T Kerr did statistical analyses. T Kerr drafted the report and incorporated all suggestions. J Montaner and M Tyndall contributed to conception and design of the analyses, interpretation of data, and drafting of the report, and all authors approved the version to be published.

ACKNOWLEDGEMENTS

We thank the Vancouver Injection Drug Users Study participants for their willingness to participate in the study. We also thank Bonnie Devlin, John Charette, Caitlin Johnston, Vanessa Volkommer, Steve Kain, Kathy Churchill, Dave Isham, Nancy Laliberte, and Peter Vann for administrative assistance. The study was funded by Health Canada, although the views expressed herein do not represent the official policies or perspectives of this organization. The funding source had no role in study design, data collection, data interpretation, data analysis, or writing of the report. The corresponding author had full access to all the data in the study and had final responsibility for the decision to submit for publication.

The Lancet. 2005. 23 July 366.

REFERENCES

1. Wood E, Kerr T, Montaner JS, et al. Rationale for evaluating North America's first medically supervised safer injecting facility. *Lancet Infect Dis* 2004; **4**: 301–06.

2. Wood E, Kerr T, Small W, Li K, Marsh D, Montaner JS, Tyndall MW. Changes in public order after the opening of a medically supervised safer injecting facility for illicit injection drug users. *CMAJ* 2004; **171**: 731–34.

3. Medically Supervised Injecting Centre Evaluation Committee. Final report of the Sydney medically supervised injecting centre. Sydney: MSIC Evaluation Committee, 2003.

4. Hedrich D. European report on drug consumption rooms. Lisbon: European Monitoring Centre for Drugs and Drug Addiction, 2004.

5. Kerr T, Palepu A, Barnes G, et al. Psychosocial determinants of adherence to highly active antiretroviral therapy among injection drug users in Vancouver. *Antivir Ther* 2004; **9**: 407–14.

6. Wood E, Tyndall MW, Spittal PM, et al. Unsafe injection practices in a cohort of injection drug users in Vancouver: could safer injecting rooms help? *CMAJ* 2001; **165**: 405–10.

7. Wood E, Tyndall MW, Spittal PM, et al. Factors associated with persistent high-risk syringe sharing in the presence of an established needle exchange programme. *AIDS* 2002; **16**: 941–43.

8. Wright NM, Tompkins CN. Supervised injecting centres. *BMJ* 2004; **328**: 100–02.

KEY AND DIFFICULT WORDS

Define the following, using context or other clues if possible: **illicit, cohort, epidemiological, confound.**

QUESTIONS

1. How do the authors justify the study? Why is the Vancouver site ideal for the researchers' purposes?

2. Although this essay does not employ the formal headings of many Type B essays, there are clear divisions between the different parts of the essay. Determine content categories and assign appropriate headings (e.g., abstract, introduction, method) to identify each category.

3. Why do the authors define such factors as "syringe sharing" (paragraph 2) and those mentioned in paragraph 3? Why were those particular definitions used? What is a "cohort study" (paragraph 1), and why is its existence such a vital part of Kerr et al.'s study?

4. Identify the *dependent variable* and the *independent variables* in this study (see Appendix).

5. Where in paragraph 7 do the authors summarize the results of their study? Why do they discuss their study's limitations? Do you believe they adequately address these concerns?

6. What do the authors mean by "socially desirable responding" (paragraph 7)?

7. In their acknowledgements, the authors refer to the funding for the study. What is the reason for the sentence that begins "The funding source had no role . . .?" Why might Health Canada commission such a study?

COLLABORATIVE ACTIVITY

What are the aims of safe injections sites beyond the obvious one of providing a safer environment for drug users? Do you believe that such facilities are of value in urban centres today? Discuss or debate this issue.

ACTIVITIES

1. Write a letter to the editor or an editorial in which you argue for or against the establishment of a safe injection site in your community or an urban centre near you. Refer to the study by Kerr et al. in your essay.

2. Write a formal or informal report that summarizes recent studies of the Vancouver site. Include this study, along with at least two others. Two potential studies are those numbered 1 and 2 in the references section of "Safer injection facility use and syringe sharing in injection drug users." Others include: Kerr et al. 2006. "Impact of a medically supervised safer injection facility on community drug use patterns: A before and after study." *British Medical Journal* 332:220–2; Wood et al. 2006. "Attendance at supervised injecting facilities and use of detoxification services." *New England Journal of Medicine* 354:2512–14.

Heavy drinking on Canadian campuses

Louis Gliksman, Ph.D.[1], **Edward M. Adlaf, Ph.D.**[2], **Andrée Demers, Ph.D.**[3], **Brenda Newton-Taylor, M.A.**[4]

(2,050 words)

ABSTRACT

Objective: To describe the prevalence and frequency of heavy drinking episodes among Canadian undergraduates.

Methods: Data are drawn from the Canadian Campus Survey, a national mail survey, conducted in the fall of 1998, with a random sample of 7,800 students from 16 universities.

Results: Overall, 62.7 per cent and 34.8 per cent of students reported consuming 5 or more drinks and 8 or more drinks, respectively, on a single occasion at least once during the fall semester. On average, drinkers reported having 5 or more drinks almost 5 times during the fall semester, and having 8 or more drinks almost twice during the same period. The groups reporting the highest rates of heavy drinking were males, those living in university residences, those with low academic orientation and those with high recreational orientation.

Interpretation: Generally, this study has shown that heavy drinking is highly engrained in Canadian undergraduates' drinking patterns, and is related to a number of factors. These

[1] Senior Scientist & Director, Social, Prevention & Health Policy Research, Centre for Addiction & Mental Health, and Department of Psychology, University of Western Ontario.

[2] Scientist, Centre for Addiction & Mental Health, and Department of Public Health Sciences, University of Toronto.

[3] Associate Professor, Department of Sociology, University of Montreal, and Director, Health and Prevention Social Research Group.

[4] Research Associate, Centre for Addiction & Mental Health.

Acknowledgement: This study was partially funded by the Brewer's Association of Canada.

factors can be used to develop targeted prevention efforts.

One of the most salient public health issues confronting college campuses is the consequences of heavy drinking, traditionally defined as consuming five or more drinks in a single drinking occasion.[1] In addition to alcohol intoxication, these consequences include motor vehicle crashes, high-risk sexual behaviour, and poor academic performance.[2-6] In addition, heavy drinking on campus affects non-drinkers as well as drinkers.[7,8]

The epidemiological knowledge regarding heavy drinking in the US is longstanding, but the history of such studies in Canada is recent, sparse, and regionalized,[9-12] and no study has been conducted nationally. This paper will describe the prevalence and frequency of heavy drinking among a nationally representative sample of Canadian undergraduates and assess the character of subgroup differences related to key demographic and campus lifestyle factors.

METHOD

The 1998 Canadian Campus Survey (CCS) is the first Canadian survey conducted nationally to assess alcohol and other drug use among university students.[13] The CCS employed a stratified two-stage cluster selection of undergraduates enrolled in full-time studies at accredited universities during the 1998–9 academic year. The sample was stratified equally according to five regions: British Columbia, Prairies, Ontario, Québec, and Atlantic provinces. Four universities per region were selected with probability-proportional to size (i.e., larger universities had a higher probability of selection than smaller universities) for all regions except BC, which sampled all four universities with certainty. In total, 23 universities (including three randomly selected replacements) were approached for their participation, of which 16 agreed to participate.

Within each university, 1,000 students were randomly selected with equal probability. Sixteen thousand questionnaires were mailed, of which 15,188 were deemed eligible mailings. A total of 7,800 eligible and useable completions, representing about 442,000 Canadian undergraduates, were returned, for a 51 per cent student cooperation rate. Mean student cooperation rates varied from 42 per cent to 64 per cent by university and from 46 per cent (Ontario) to 59 per cent (Québec) by region. Table I, which displays the number of respondents and the weighted percentages, also indicates that the weighted distributions closely approximate the Canadian undergraduate population for key variables.

MEASURES

Our outcome variable, heavy drinking episode, is represented by the percentage and frequency of consuming five or more drinks (*5-plus*) and eight or more drinks (*8-plus*) on a single occasion "since September," an eight to 12-week period. This timeframe was intended to capture any drinking occasions occurring on or off campus since the student began the 1998–9 academic year.

These outcomes were examined relative to seven independent variables. Sex was represented by a binary measure (male=1). The five regional categories (BC, Prairies, Ontario, Québec, and Atlantic) were represented by four effect-coded dummy variables. Living arrangement was represented by two dummy variables (university residence and off campus without parents or family) versus living at home with parents. The four categories of year of study were represented by three dummy variables (second through fourth years) versus first year. Year of study was chosen over age since it provides more campus-relevant risk factor information. Recreational orientation was based on the perceived importance of being involved in three activities (parties, athletics, and recreation), while academic orientation was

Table I: Sample characteristics

	N (unweighted)	% (weighted)
Total	7800	
Gender		
Male	2884	45.6
Female	4916	54.5
Region		
British Columbia	1795	9.8
Prairies	1467	18.4
Ontario	1277	40.5
Québec	2306	22.5
Atlantic	955	8.8
Year of study		
First	1903	25.9
Second	1910	25.3
Third	2044	25.4
Fourth	1943	23.4
Living arrangement		
University residence	1254	15.3
Off campus with parents	3433	48.0
Off campus without parents	3072	36.7

based on the importance of involvement in five activities (arts, academics, student associations, political organizations, and cultural organizations).[14] What distinguishes these groups of activities is the intellectual aspect of one versus the other. Academic hours was based on the quartile distribution of the weekly sum of hours devoted to class attendance and studying.

We first present prevalence analyses based on the total sample of students (table II) and then present multivariate logistic regression assessing the prevalence of heavy drinking among past-year drinkers (table III) and OLS regression assessing the frequency of heavy drinking among drinkers (table IV). This analysis was performed on both the raw and log-transformed data. The raw results are presented since the substantive results of the two analyses did not differ.

Because our sample design employs unequal probabilities of selection and heavy clustering,

Taylor series methods were used to estimate variances and related statistical tests. (Design effects for heavy drinking variables, which varied between two and 12, averaged 6.3.)

RESULTS

To provide some context to our results, we begin by describing the past-year drinking patterns by gender. As seen in table II, 86.6 per cent of Canadian undergraduates report consuming alcohol in the past year, and 37 per cent drank weekly. On average, students reported consuming 5.6 drinks per week (6.48 among past-year drinkers). Gender differences are also evident, with men being more likely than women to drink at least twice per week (27.0 per cent vs 15.1 per cent) and to drink in greater quantities per week (8.8 vs 4.6 drinks among past-year drinkers). The percentage reporting a *5-plus* heavy drinking episode during the past 12

Table II: Frequency of drinking, mean weekly alcohol intake, and prevalence of heavy drinking (5-plus) during the past 12 months

	Total (n=7800)		Males (n=2884)		Females (n=4916)	
Drinking frequency						
Never	13.4	(11.1–16.1)	14.6	(12.4–17.2)	12.5	(9.7–15.8)
< Once/month	22.0	(18.9–25.4)	18.0	(14.8–21.6)	25.3	(21.9–29.1)
1–3 times/month	27.7	(25.7–29.8)	22.8	(20.7–25.1)	31.8	(29.3–34.5)
1/week	16.4	(15.0–17.8)	17.6	(16.0–19.3)	15.3	(13.5–17.3)
2–3 times/week	16.0	(13.5–18.9)	20.6	(18.2–23.2)	12.2	(9.8–15.1)
4+ times/week	4.4	(3.2–4.8)	5.6	(4.4–7.1)	2.6	(2.1–3.1)
Daily	0.5	(0.3–1.0)	0.8	(0.5–1.6)	0.3	(0.1–0.6)
Mean drinks weekly						
Total sample	5.60	(4.60–6.60)	7.51	(6.50–8.52)	3.99	(3.08–4.89)
Among drinkers	6.48	(5.41–7.55)	8.80	(7.62–9.98)	4.56	(3.63–5.49)
Prevalence of 5-plus						
Total sample	62.4	(56.4–68.1)	66.9	(61.2–72.2)	58.7	(52.2–65.0)
Among drinkers	72.1	(66.8–76.9)	78.4	(73.0–82.9)	67.1	(61.5–72.2)

Gender difference: Frequency of use, Wald $F(3,33)=31.01$, $p < 0.001$; Mean drinks, total sample, Wald $F(1,11)=32.09$, $p < 0.001$; Prevalence 5-plus, total sample, Wald $F(1,11)=29.07$, $p < 0.001$; Drinkers, Wald $F(1,11)=70.90$, $p < 0.001$.

months was 62.4 per cent (72.1 per cent of drinkers) and varied significantly by gender.

More germane to the campus environment is the heavy drinking that occurs while students are enrolled in university, in our case the period since September. Table III shows the percentage of past-year drinkers consuming *5-plus* and *8-plus* drinks per occasion. In total, 62.7 per cent of the drinkers reported *5-plus* drinking, while 34.8 per cent reported *8-plus* drinking at least once. The adjusted odds ratios show that four variables—gender, residence, academic and recreational orientation—are significantly associated with both *5-plus* and *8-plus* drinking. Regarding gender, the odds of *5-plus* and *8-plus* drinking are respectively 1.75 and 2.5 times higher among men than women. Living arrangement also shows sizeable variation, with students living in residence being more likely to consume *5-plus* (OR=1.53) and *8-plus* (OR=1.77) drinks than students living with their parents.

The logit regression shows that academic and recreational orientations, as well as time devoted to academic work, were significantly associated with both *5-plus* and *8-plus* drinking. Generally, heavy drinking declined with increasing academic orientation and academic hours and increased with increasing recreational orientation. Compared to those with low academic orientation, the likelihood of *5-plus* drinking was 29 per cent lower (OR=0.71) among those with moderate academic orientation and 43 per cent lower among those with high academic orientation (OR=0.57). As well, compared to those with low recreational orientation, the likelihood of *5-plus* drinking was 1.83 times higher among those with moderate recreational orientation and 4.33 times higher among those with high recreational orientation. Similar associations were also found for *8-plus* drinking. Academic hours are generally inversely associated with both *5-plus* and *8-plus* drinking. This is especially true for *8-plus* drinking, in which the odds ratios show a clear reduction in *8-plus* drinking with every quartile increase in number of academic hours.

Table III: Percentage consuming 5-plus and 8-plus drinks on a single occasion since September, past-year drinkers

	% 5-plus since September (n=6359)			% 8-plus since September (n=6351)		
	%	(95% CI)	Adjusted odds ratio	%	(95%CI)	Adjusted odds ratio
Total sample	62.7	(55.9–69.4)	—	34.8	(29.7–39.9)	—
Gender	***		***	***		***
Female	56.1	(48.8–63.2)	—	25.2	(21.1–29.7)	—
Male	70.6	(64.0–76.5)	1.75***	46.5	(40.8–52.5)	2.50***
Region	NS		NS	NS		*
British Columbia	58.6	(49.7–67.0)	0.76	35.2	(29.1–41.8)	0.89
Prairies	69.5	(56.1–80.3)	1.26	44.6	(33.9–55.7)	1.49
Ontario	60.2	(43.5–74.8)	0.84	33.2	(22.7–45.7)	0.90
Québec	58.5	(56.3–60.7)	0.73*	27.9	(27.6–28.2)	0.65**
Atlantic	73.9	(57.1–85.8)	1.70	39.5	(26.4–54.3)	1.28
Living arrangements	*		***	**		***
University	70.3	(66.0–74.3)	1.53***	44.2	(39.8–48.8)	1.77***
Off campus w parents	59.7	(50.2–68.4)	—	32.3	(25.5–39.9)	—
Off campus no family	62.5	(55.8–68.7)	1.21	33.2	(27.7–39.3)	1.14
Year	NS		NS	NS		NS
First	65.0	(59.9–69.8)	—	35.9	(31.4–40.7)	—
Second	63.5	(56.7–69.8)	0.99	36.0	(31.1–41.1)	1.06
Third	62.0	(54.8–68.7)	0.93	33.9	(28.3–40.0)	0.97
Fourth	60.1	(49.2–70.1)	0.82	33.3	(26.5–40.8)	0.92
Academic orientation	NS		**	NS		**
Low	63.6	(55.9–70.7)	—	36.2	(29.9–43.0)	—
Medium	60.3	(55.0–65.4)	0.71**	32.3	(28.7–36.1)	0.74*
High	60.9	(50.6–70.3)	0.57**	27.3	(22.2–33.0)	0.49**
Recreational orientation	***		***	***		***
Low	54.2	(45.4–62.7)	—	27.4	(21.8–33.8)	—
Medium	67.7	(61.2–73.6)	1.83***	38.0	(33.3–42.9)	1.63***
High	83.0	(80.4–85.3)	4.33***	54.8	(50.9–58.7)	3.23***
Academic hours (weekly)	**		NS	***		***
1st quartile	66.0	(59.0–72.4)	—	40.6	(34.7–46.7)	—
2nd quartile	63.9	(55.3–71.6)	0.94	35.1	(27.2–43.9)	0.82
3rd quartile	60.9	(56.5–65.2)	0.84	31.1	(27.6–34.9)	0.71*
4th quartile	57.2	(47.9–65.9)	0.68**	27.2	(23.5–31.2)	0.53***

Notes: *$p < 0.05$; **$p < 0.01$; ***$p < 0.001$

The analysis also shows that region is significantly associated only with *8-plus* drinking. Students in Québec universities are significantly less likely to report *8-plus* drinking compared to the average student (OR=0.65). This contrast is also noticeable for *5-plus* drinking, although the overall region effect is not significant at the p<0.05 level. The only variable unrelated to both *5-plus* and *8-plus* drinking is year of study.

While most students engaged in some heavy

Table IV: Frequency of consuming five or more drinks and eight or more drinks on a single occasion since September, among past-year drinkers

	Mean 5-plus since September (n=6359)			Mean 8-plus since September (n=6351)		
	Mean	(95% CI)	b	Mean	(95% CI)	b
Total sample	4.7	(3.8–5.6)		1.9	(1.4–2.3)	
Gender			***			***
Female	3.2	(2.3–4.1)	—	1.0	(0.6–1.3)	—
Male	6.7	(5.7–7.6)	3.05***	3.0	(2.4–3.6)	1.79***
Region			0.06			0.57
British Columbia	5.2	(3.9–6.4)	–0.17	2.0	(1.3–2.8)	–0.22
Prairies	6.3	(3.7–8.8)	1.21	2.9	(1.3–4.5)	0.82
Ontario	4.4	(2.5–6.2)	–0.51	1.6	(0.8–2.4)	–0.41
Québec	3.6	(3.2–4.0)	–1.42**	1.3	(1.1–1.4)	–0.77**
Atlantic	5.7	(3.2–8.1)	0.89	2.5	(0.6–4.5)	0.59
Living arrangements			***			***
University	6.7	(5.6–7.8)	2.59***	2.8	(2.1–3.5)	1.3***
Off campus w parents	4.0	(3.0–5.0)	—	1.5	(1.1–2.0)	—
Off campus no family	4.7	(3.5–5.9)	1.01	1.9	(1.1–2.6)	0.46*
Year			NS			NS
First	5.0	(3.9–6.1)	—	1.9	(1.4–2.5)	—
Second	4.8	(3.9–5.7)	–0.01	1.9	(1.4–2.4)	–0.01
Third	4.4	(3.3–5.5)	–0.33	1.7	(1.1–2.3)	–0.16
Fourth	4.8	(3.5–6.1)	–0.08	2.0	(1.3–2.8)	0.08
Academic orientation			***			***
Low	5.0	(4.0–6.1)	—	2.0	(1.5–2.6)	—
Medium	4.2	(3.5–4.8)	–1.34**	1.6	(1.2–2.0)	–0.65**
High	3.5	(2.0–5.1)	–2.60**	1.0	(0.5–1.5)	–0.16***
Recreational orientation			***			***
Low	3.3	(2.6–4.0)	—	1.2	(0.9–1.5)	—
Medium	5.5	(4.1–6.9)	2.16***	2.2	(1.4–3.1)	1.02**
High	8.3	(7.1–9.4)	4.64***	3.7	(3.0–4.5)	2.36***
Academic hours (weekly)			***			***
1st quartile	5.9	(4.8–6.9)	—	2.5	(1.9–3.1)	—
2nd quartile	4.6	(2.8–6.4)	–1.07	1.8	(0.9–2.7)	–0.58**
3rd quartile	4.0	(3.3–4.7)	–1.50*	1.5	(1.1–1.8)	–0.84*
4th quartile	3.4	(2.9–3.9)	–2.34***	1.2	(1.0–1.4)	–1.20***

Notes: *$p < 0.05$; **$p < 0.01$; ***$p < 0.001$

drinking while in university, more compelling is the frequency of heavy drinking. As seen in table IV, on average, drinkers reported consuming *5-plus* drinks per occasion 4.7 times since September and *8-plus* drinks 1.9 times. Gener- ally, the same factors that predict prevalence of heavy drinking also predict the frequency of heavy drinking. Five variables are significantly related to the frequency of both *5-plus* and *8-plus* heavy drinking: gender, living arrangements, academic orientation, recreational orientation, and academic hours.

Males reported twice as many heavy episodic drinking occasions than did females (6.7 and 3.2 times for *5-plus* drinks and 3.0 and 1.0 times for *8-plus* drinks). For both *5-plus* and *8-plus* drinking, those living on campus reported significantly more heavy drinking than did those living with parents (6.7 vs 4.0 and 2.8 vs 1.5, respectively). As well, those living off campus without parents also reported slightly more *8-plus* drinking than did those living with parents (1.9 vs 1.5). Again, both heavy drinking measures were negatively associated with academic orientation and positively associated with recreational orientation. *Five-plus* and *8-plus* heavy drinking declined from 5.0 to 3.5 occasions and from 2.0 to 1.0, respectively, among those with low vs high academic orientation and increased from 3.3 to 8.3 and from 1.2 to 3.7, respectively, among those with low vs high recreational orientation. Also evident is a significant inverse association between heavy drinking and academic hours. *Five-plus* drinking declined from 5.9 episodes among those in the lowest quartile hours to 3.4 among those in the highest quartile, and *8-plus* drinking declined from 2.5 to 1.2 episodes. Region and year of study did not show significant group effects, although the region contrasts again showed below-average frequencies among those attending Québec universities.

DISCUSSION

Although all survey findings are bounded inherently by both sampling and non-sampling errors, we believe that our data reasonably represent Canadian undergraduates. First, although there were no means to compare respondents to non-respondents, an analysis of early versus late responders indicated no significant differences for the major demographic factors and for drinking patterns, with the exception that late respon-

ders, who had a longer exposure period, reported more heavy drinking episodes. Second, a comparison of undergraduates drawn from the 1996 National Population Health Survey revealed no significant differences for sex, age, and frequency of alcohol use. And third, the correlation between mean student completion rates by university and rates of heavy drinking was nominal and non-significant (r=-0.14; p=0.61).

This study has shown that heavy drinking is highly engrained in Canadian undergraduates' drinking patterns. Most students are drinkers, and roughly two-thirds of them reported at least one *5-plus* drinking episode and one third an *8-plus* drinking episode during the initial eight to 12-week period at school. On average, drinkers reported *5-plus* drinking roughly once every two weeks (4.7 times/8–12 weeks) and *8-plus* drinking once every month (1.9 times/8–12 weeks). Our results indicated that heavy drinking is more prevalent and more frequent among men and among students living in university residences and that heavy drinking increased with the importance attached to recreational activities and decreased when students reported being more academically oriented. However, no association between heavy drinking and year of study was evident. Finally, undergraduates in Québec were less likely to drink heavily than those in the rest of Canada.

The fact that men are more likely than women to be heavy drinkers and drink heavily more often is a recurring finding for the general population as well as for college students.[15,16] However, we must note that because our definition of heavy drinking was identical among both men and women, we might be underestimating the impact of female heavy drinking given some biological differences.[7] Thus, we should not conclude that heavy drinking among women is not a health issue worthy of concern by campus services.

Our results highlight the importance of individual experiences of university life on heavy drinking. Students who place more importance on recreational activities and those who reside in student residences are more likely to drink heavily than other students, whereas those attaching more importance to academic activities are less likely to do so. Consistent with previous results,[14,17,18] these findings suggest a pattern of social integration into university life associated with heavier alcohol intake. However, we cannot ignore the possibility of a self-selection bias in which heavy drinkers are attracted to events or locations that are heavy-drinking milieus. Longitudinal data would be needed to clarify the causal relationships of these data.

Finally, students attending university in Québec seem less likely to drink heavily, despite a higher drinking prevalence and greater availability of alcohol in Québec. This might reflect a different drinking culture or might be related to the different school system in Québec, which has CEGEP as an intermediate institution between high school and university.

The results suggest that universities may be in a position to affect the rates of heavy drinking by its students through targeted interventions. For example, by focusing on men, on students who live in residences, and by trying to get students more involved in the academic parts of the university community, heavy drinking may be decreased.

Canadian Journal of Public Health.
January/February 2003, 94 (1).

REFERENCES

1. Room R. Measuring alcohol consumption in the United States: Methods and rationales. In: Kozlowski LT, et a1. (Eds.), *Research Advances in Alcohol and Drug Problems*, Vol 10. New York, NY: Plenum, 1990;39–80.

2. Butcher AH, Manning DT, O'Neal EC. HIV-related sexual behaviors of college students. *J Am College Health* 1991;40,115–18.

3. Milgram GG. Adolescents, alcohol and aggression. *J Studies on Alcohol* 1993;54:53–61.

4. Wechsler H, Davenport A, Dowdall G, Moeykens B, Castillo S. Health and behavioral consequences of binge drinking in college: A national survey of students at 140 campuses. *JAMA* 1994;272:1672–77.

5. Johnston ID, O'Malley PM, Bachman JG. *Monitoring the Future. National Survey Results on Drug Use, 1975–1999: Volume II College Students and Adult Ages 19–40*. Washington, DC: National Institute on Drug Abuse, 2000.

6. Wechsler H, Lee JE, Kuo M, Lee H. College binge drinking in the 1990s: A continuing problem. *J Am College Health* 2000;48: 199–210.

7. Wechsler H, Dowdall GW, Davenport A, Rimm EB. A gender-specific measure of binge drinking among college students. *Am J Public Health* 1995;85:982–85.

8. Wechsler H, Lee JE, Nelson TF, Lee H. Drinking levels, alcohol problems and second-hand effects in substance-free college residences: Results of a national study. *J Studies on Alcohol* 2001;62:23–31.

9. Campbell RL, Svenson LW. Drug use among university undergraduate students. *Psychological Reports* 1992;70:1039–42.

10. Gliksman L, Newton-Taylor B, Adlaf E, Giesbrecht N. Alcohol and other drug use by Ontario university students: The roles of gender, age, year of study, academic grade, place of residence and program of study. *Drugs: Education, Prevention and Policy* 1997;4:117–29.

11. Hindmarsh KW, Gliksman L, Newton-Taylor B. Alcohol and other drug use by pharmacy students in Canadian universities. *Can Pharmaceutical J* 1993;126:358–59.

12. Spence JC, Gauvin L. Drug and alcohol use by Canadian university athletes: A national survey. *J Drug Education* 1996;26:275–87.

13. Gliksman L, Demers A, Adlaf EM, Newton-Taylor B, Schmidt K. Canadian Campus Survey 1998. Toronto, ON: Centre for Addiction and Mental Health, 2000.

14. Demers A, Kairouz S, Adlaf EM, Gliksman L, Newton-Taylor B, Marchand A. A multi-level analysis of situational drinking. *Soc Sci Med* In press.

15. Kellner F. Alcohol. In: MacNeil P, Webster I (Eds.), *Canada's Alcohol and Other Drugs Survey 1994: A Discussion of the Findings.* Ottawa: Minister of Public Works and Government Services, 1997;15–42.

16. Substance Abuse and Mental Health Services Administration: Summary of Findings from the 2000 National Household Survey on Drug Abuse. Office of Applied Statistics, NHSDA Series H-13, DHHS Publication No. (SMA) 01-3549, 2001.

17. Chaloupka FJ, Wechsler H. Binge drinking in college: The impact of price, availability and alcohol control policies. *Contemporary Economic Policy* 1996;14:112–24a.

18. Perkins HW, Wechsler H. Variation in perceived college drinking norms and its impact on alcohol abuse: A nationwide study. *J Drug Issues* 1996;26:961–74.

KEY AND DIFFICULT WORDS

Define the following, using context or other clues if possible: **epidemiological, prevalence, demographic, stratified, salient, quartile.**

QUESTIONS

1. What is the justification for the study?

2. Research studies in the sciences and social sciences are often the result of collaborative work. Note the affiliations of the authors of this study. How might they have affected the order of the authors listed? Note that the authors acknowledge the Brewers Association of Canada for its partial funding. Why might this association be interested in the study's outcome? Do you believe that this funding could affect the study's credibility in any way?

3. Although the authors state that the "epidemiological knowledge regarding heavy drinking in the US is longstanding," they do not refer further to such knowledge, nor do they compare data between the two countries. Why do you think they do not do this?

4. Tables I and II: Table I does not present any data from the questionnaire itself. Why is it important for the study's credibility? Table II summarizes students' drinking frequencies during the previous 12 months. Why did the authors include it in the study?

5. How is what is presented in table III different from what is presented in table IV (i.e., what is each intended to show)? Which table, in the words of the authors, is more "compelling" and why?

6. Which variables are significantly associated with the *prevalence* of 5-plus and 8-plus drinking? Which variables are significantly associated with the *frequency* of 5-plus and 8-plus drinking? (See Appendix.)

7. How does the authors' analysis of early versus late respondents in the "Discussion" section contribute to the study's reliability?

8. Why might heavy drinking among female undergraduates be an important concern in spite of the study's findings relative to gender? Summarize in one or two sentences.

9. In the "Discussion" section, the authors propose two hypotheses to account for the lower rate of drinking among Quebec undergraduates. Paraphrase the paragraph in which this is discussed. Suggest a hypothesis that could account for each of the following: (a) heavier drinking among students living on campus compared to those living with parents; (b) heavier drinking among students with low academic orientation compared to those with high academic orientation; and (c) heavier drinking among students with high recreational orientation compared to those with low recreational orientation. (See "Measures" for the activities on which academic orientation and recreational orientation are based.)

COLLABORATIVE ACTIVITY

In the last paragraph, the authors suggest an important use for their study: "targeted interventions" by university bodies to reduce heavy drinking. In discussion groups, brainstorm ideas to come up with an intervention strategy, specifically targeting either male students, students who live on campus, students with a high recreational orientation, or students with a low academic orientation. After each group has decided on an effective strategy, a spokesperson could outline this strategy to the class for comments and feedback.

ACTIVITY

Write a 150- to 250-word letter to the editor of a campus student newspaper in which you draw the attention of its readers to the problem of heavy drinking on campus. Refer to the study "Heavy drinking on Canadian campuses" in your letter. *OR* Write a 150- to 250-word letter to the editor of a campus publication for faculty and administration in which you draw the attention of its readers to the problem of heavy drinking on campus. Refer to and provide a bibliographically correct citation for the study "Heavy drinking on Canadian campuses" in your letter.

The poison stream: Sacrificing India's poor on the altar of modernity

Matthew Power

(9,500 words)

The months leading up to the monsoon in Kerala are drawn-out, hot, and dusty; thirst seems to become the base condition of all living things. Menace permeates casual interactions; the bartering session for an auto rickshaw or a bag of tomatoes is dreaded, seething. Stray dogs, their distended udders slack, lie as if melted next to their unconscious litters, the puppies too hot even to touch one another. Whole villages retract into the vast circles of shade cast by the absurdly pink-blossomed acacia trees, and young coconuts, hacked open with sickles and drained of milk, pile up like the severed heads of a vanquished army outside the chai stalls.

It is to this season that I arrive in Kasargod, the northernmost district of India's southwesternmost state, so close to the border with Karnataka that most of the residents speak a dialect of Kannada instead of Kerala's official Malayalam. It was a 48-hour rail journey south from Delhi, through half a dozen climatic zones and a hundred languages. An old Muslim man, prostrate across the aisle, sent evening prayers west toward Mecca. By the grass shacks of Uttar Pradesh, handmade dung-cakes were stacked in geometric perfection, drying for fuel. In the Rajasthani desert, children brought lines of cattle home along dusty roads, and women balanced water pots on their heads as bright saris billowed behind them, their camels laden with watermelons. Everywhere games of cricket were improvised: an old tire for a wicket, a ball made of scrap cloth hit with a bat pried from a fence. From a platform in Agra, an ad promoting cellphones obscured the Taj Mahal.

From the open door of the train, I had seen the vast *jhugghis* that spread out from the cities: jerry-built shacks of hammered-flat oil barrels, tattered plastic tarps, salvaged mud-bricks, and liberated billboards advertising Thums-Up or Fair & Lovely, which occupy every available inch of space for miles along the tracks. On the station platforms, mothers with full-blown AIDS reached through the bars of the second-class carriages begging alms. Old men squatted, shitting by the tracks as the train racketed by. Children salvaged scrap aluminum and plastic mineral-water bottles from rivers of sewage. Here were formerly rural people who had fallen beneath the wheels of economic progress, shut out of the "Shining India" promised them in the government's advertisements. They had fled a host of plagues to come to the cities, where at least they would not starve.

The Kasargod station platform greets me like a blast furnace. A goat walking along between tracks stoops to eat a banana peel from a stream of raw sewage. A cow, splattered with the hot-pink dye that celebrates Holi, the Hindu festival of spring, stands nearby and slowly chews a cardboard box. Even the red-shirted coolies, smoking *bidis* on a heap of onion sacks, do not jump up to offer their services. The English papers on the newsstand are full of weird, violent tales: opposition rioters in the state capital, Thiruvananthapuram, have firebombed 12 government vehicles; an entire family of elephants have been hit by a train and are to be cremated on the spot using a crude napalm of gasoline and sugar; five people were killed after drinking bootleg palm liquor spiked with pesticide. Five years of drought are followed by killing floods. Fifty perish in a bus "mishap." In a country that often seems constructed out of bizarre occurrences and unimaginable sorrows, it is difficult to shock the conscience. Many stories slip through the cracks. If I had happened to pick up a paper here in 1982, perhaps I would have come across the strange story that ultimately led to my journey 20 years later: CALVES BORN WITH WARPED LIMBS.

I have come 1,500 miles from Delhi to visit the tiny, remote hill village of Vaninagar, a place that has been devastated by a spate of mysterious illnesses over the last two decades: rare cancers, birth defects, mental retardation, miscarriages, suicides. Babies that were carried to term were sometimes born blind, or epileptic, or with deformed limbs. Children shrivelled and died from leukemia, and old women were covered with lesions that wouldn't heal. In a culture bound by notions of karmic retribution, people naturally assumed it was a curse, that they had angered their *theyyams*, or guardian spirits.

Some of the villagers, however, along with a growing number of scientists, doctors, and environmental groups, have blamed the 4,500-hectare state-owned cashew plantation, which for 20 years conducted aerial spraying of the organochlorine pesticide endosulfan over its cashew crops. The plantation borders dozens of villages and drains into the drinking water of thousands of rural people. The pesticide companies, the plantation management, and the state government have so far refused to accept any responsibility, and the matter has been swallowed up in India's infamous bureau-

cracy for more than two years. The argument over what has caused these diseases, and who is responsible, has divided Kerala politically and has pitted the purported economic interests of the state's corporations against the health of the state's citizens.

India exists in many centuries simultaneously. The glittering software capital of Bangalore is ringed with medieval slums, and blind beggars bearing smallpox scars seek alms next to Bollywood film shoots. India is home to the largest slums in Asia, and by some estimates 100 million people have been displaced by drought, hydroelectric schemes, deforestation, and sectarian violence since Independence. The vast outpouring of relief following the death of 20,000 in an earthquake in Gujarat in 2001 was followed a year later in the same state by the mass slaughter of Muslims in pogroms tacitly encouraged by the government. In Bihar "witches" are still burned to death, and Rajasthani farmers starve on grass seed, while behind barbed wire the Food Corporation of India's godowns are bursting with 60 million tons of surplus grain.

At the station I am met by my friend Vinod, a journalist and native Keralite, who has agreed to serve as a translator and guide into the hill country east of here. We negotiate a driver and Ambassador car, the ubiquitous Indian remake of a 1954 British Morris. I feel a bit like a holdover from the Raj, a mid-level bureaucrat come to inspect the coconut plantation. On the dashboard is a plastic shrine to Kali-Ma, the black goddess, tongue stuck out, wearing a necklace of severed heads. When the brakes are applied, her eyes light up red. Vinod chatters away with the driver in Malayalam, a language so rounded and elided as to sound, to a foreign ear, like the same word repeated over and over again. I watch out the window as we wind up into the hills, the temperature easing slightly from the oppressiveness of the narrow coastal plain. The parched red earth along the roadside shows the warp of the last monsoon, weathered and smooth as scar tissue.

The state of Kerala runs like a long, green snake between the cool heights of the Western Ghats and the depths of the Lakshadweep Sea on India's southwest coast. Its peculiar geography, blocked by the spine of the mountains from India's central plains and exposed to the sea along a 500-mile coastline, has set it apart from the rest of the subcontinent for millennia. Kerala was a trading stop for the Phoenicians when Bombay and Calcutta were mere fishing villages. Pepper and ivory arrived in ancient Rome via its shores. It was the point from which Chinese ideas and goods first spread west and marked landfall for Da Gama's opening of south Asia to almost five centuries of European control. Cardamom, ginger, turmeric, pepper—all brought trade here from far-off empires, which in turn introduced coffee, rubber, cocoa. And cashew. The lateritic, semiarid hills of northern Kerala are one of the best cashew-growing areas in the world.

Kerala's unique culture and its isolation have led to some striking social and political developments. Poverty is low, and the literacy rate is 90 per cent. In 1957 it voted in the world's first freely elected communist government. Political activism continues, and the state is frequently disrupted by general strikes, called *hartals*, led by whichever party happens to be in opposition. Now Kerala's chief industry is tourism. "God's Own Country" tout the brochures, luring Israeli backpackers and British package-tourists to the hypnotically swaying palm trees of its beaches. But there is a dark aspect, evident not only in the political violence that erupts periodically across the state but in the institutionalized corruption that governs almost every official interaction, from traffic tickets to the registration and use of pesticides.

We stop at a chai shop an hour up into the hills, a wooden shack with a broken table and a few wobbly benches. A group of local men stare as we walk in and order tea and *kesari*, a sweet, primary-yellow wheat pudding. A cricket game blares on a transistor radio, and I stare at Technicolor posters of Shiva and the romance of Krishna and Radha. The proprietor chats to Vinod while performing acrobatic stunts with the chai, pouring it from one container to another at full arm's length to cool it off. He tips his head toward me, asks a question. In the flow of their conversation, which has shifted to the equally unintelligible Kannada, a word I recognize pops up: endosulfan. The man quickly pours the tea, glaring at me, and turns to the other customers. Vinod just smiles and blows on his chai.

The ancient gearbox of the Ambassador protests on the rockier sections of the rutted dirt road. We pass through plantations of tall, thin areca palms, from which the dark red betel nut chewed in the mildly narcotic *paan* is harvested. To harvest areca, the pickers will bind their feet with a loop of cloth called a *thorth*, pressing their soles against the slim trunk as they inch 40 feet into the air. They keep a sprig of *thulasi*, a sacred native medicinal plant, pressed behind their ears to maintain balance. Having cut all the areca from a given tree, they shift their weight and bend the entire palm over until they can grab onto the next one, working their way down the rows without returning to the ground.

I get my first glimpse of a ripe, lipstick-red bunch of cashews hanging directly over the road, the gray seed pods hanging disembodied, like question marks, below the bulging, vaguely obscene fruit. An old woman, stooped below a huge load of firewood, stops without straightening or looking as we pass. Glancing back, I see her head tilt to the side, and a blood-red gout of *paan* spit arcs into the red dust. We pull up to the low, tree-shaded house of Sree Padre, a local farmer and activist who was one of the first to bring attention to the strange illnesses in the district. As we walk up to the shade of the porch, the stout, mustachioed Padre comes outside and extends his hand. "I got your message," he says, smiling. "I was hoping you wouldn't come."

We sit on the porch, and Padre serves us a plate of *kokum*, a fruit endemic to southwestern India that I've never seen before. It has a thick peel, which stains the fingers an indelible magenta, and inside segments of intensely tart white pulp surround large seeds. In the sun-scorched courtyard, spread-out piles of cashew, areca, and turmeric cure. I ask about the maladies that have been affecting the locals.

The first clues came in the early 1980s. Some calves in a nearby village were born with deformed limbs. Most died quickly, but one survived, and Padre wrote an article about it for a local newspaper. Other effects were slow to manifest themselves: fish, frogs, insects, honeybees, even crows vanished from the area. Then people came down with strange illnesses: warped limbs, weeping sores, cancer. The locals thought only that they were cursed, that Jatadhari, a regional deity, had been displeased with their worship. Witch doctors were hired by many villagers with diseased children to perform ritual purifications.

Padre suspected some sort of chemical poisoning, but it took years to connect the dots: the cows had grazed in the cashew plantation and drank out of the stream below it. For more than 20 years, the Plantation Corporation of Kerala (PCK) had used helicopters to spray endosulfan, two or three times a season. The cashew orchards were mostly on the hilltops, and the land was so undulating that the helicopters sprayed from far too high, causing a drift of pesticide that reached far beyond the plantation's boundaries. Five thousand people live within a stone's throw of the plantation. Disease reports have come in from 20 villages, with the majority of the victims under 25. "No one knows how many have died," Padre says.

In the late 1990s, Padre and the only local doctor, Mohan Kumar, began getting a clear picture of the region's health problems and focused on endosulfan as the probable cause. When they made enough noise about the spraying in the local press and pictures of deformed children were broadcast across the country, the slow beast of government was stirred into action. After a great deal of legal wrangling, a hold was placed on aerial spraying. Today the pesticide has been temporarily banned by Kerala's High Court, pending the release of a governmental committee's decision on its health risks. India's $850-million-a-year pesticide industry has taken great interest in the verdict.

Endosulfan is most dangerous to agricultural workers who have direct contact with it, and in the United States, the Environmental Protection Agency mandates extensive protective measures: respirators, goggles, the covering of all exposed skin. In India, as with most of the developing world, such measures are almost never put into practice. As Satish Chandra Nair, an Indian ecologist I spoke to, put it: "If you want to make a horror movie, some sort of Frankenstein or Hitchcock, come spend a few hours in Kerala. That emulsion from the spray coming down, people collecting in the evening water from the stream, carrying it home, cooking with it, bathing their babies, and using it for every domestic job. Nobody reads the skull and crossbones on the label, in five languages."

It is a tragedy that is played out in the remotest corners of the developing world, where many of the trappings of Western luxury are grown. From the flower fields of Colombia to the cocoa plantations of Ivory Coast, traditional rural populations are coming into conflict with a host of organic molecules promoted for the betterment of humanity, and the double helix wound between progress and tradition is undergoing nightmarish mutations. The World Health

Organization estimates that three million people a year, largely in the agricultural Third World, suffer the effects of pesticide poisoning and that it causes 220,000 deaths. Two boys in South Africa died last year after touching goats that had been treated with endosulfan; a few years ago, there were 37 deaths recorded in Benin among farmers who used the pesticide on their crops with no protection. Vaninagar is just one of a thousand villages around the world haunted by the spectre of slow poisoning, what came to be known among Indian environmentalists as "silent Bhopals."[1]

In a show of bureaucratic force, the central government has sent eight committees to the area to assess the situation in Kasargod. Padre is weary of seeing no lasting results, weary of people coming and leaving without doing anything to help. The web of government interests in the matter is almost impossible to unravel: endosulfan's largest manufacturer, Hindustan Insecticides Ltd., is owned by the government. The government's Central Insecticides Board is in charge of registering and approving all pesticides. The state-owned Plantation Corporation of Kerala conducted the spraying. An "expert committee" has been formed by the government to put a final verdict on endosulfan, but its capacity for objectivity has been met with deep scepticism by locals.

One of the few independent organizations to study the issue, a New Delhi-based NGO, the Centre for Science and Environment (CSE), visited the foothills in January 2001. They collected dozens of samples, including well water, soil, cow's milk, and human blood, and tested them for the presence of endosulfan residues. What they found were levels in water 50 times the MRL (the maximum residue limit, set by the US EPA), levels in soil 390 times the MRL, and levels in human blood (for which there is no MRL) up to 900 times the MRL for water. "The values were alarming," said a CSE researcher at the time. "It can hardly be doubted that this has something to do with the high incidence of disorders of the central nervous system in the village." To all appearances, this was the smoking gun: if not direct proof, then a clear indication of the cause of the health catastrophe visiting the plantation's surrounding areas.

Dr. O. P. Dubey, assistant director general of the Indian Council of Agricultural Research and a member of the Central Insecticides Board, heads the committee that will decide the fate of endosulfan. Dr. Dubey, in his cluttered office in a warren of hallways in one of the countless ministry buildings in New Delhi, derides the CSE study as flawed. "I think the CSE's results are wrong, totally wrong. You have to prove a link, and no link has been proven. The cases there reflect a political agenda, nothing else. This Kumar and Padre, they want charity, that's why they make an issue of this. Padre, with his rosy cheeks, looks as healthy as an American." Despite being appointed head of a committee to evaluate the safety of a pesticide he himself has approved and promoted, Dubey does not perceive a con-

---

[1] The train had pulled me through there, too. The platform of Bhopal station at 4 a.m. swirled with ghosts like the rush of air before an oncoming train. It was just after midnight, 13 December 1984, when an explosion at a Union Carbide pesticide plant adjacent to the station sent a cloud of vaporized methyl isocyanate, heavier than air, billowing across this very platform. Hundreds died within the station, hundreds more on an express that had pulled in to meet the cloud. Rescuers found them piled like trees felled by a hurricane: porters splayed amid mounds of luggage, chai boys next to spilled tiffins, a still-living infant suckling at its dead mother's breast. Fifteen thousand were left dead, half a million blind, mad, crippled. It was biblical; the angel of death on Pesach, but there was no way to signal one's right to be spared. The lives lost and ruined at Bhopal were casualties in the inexorable march of progress that would bring India kicking into modernity.

flict of interest. It is a healthy sign of bureaucratic transparency. When asked for an alternative theory of the illnesses in Vaninagar, he shrugs. "I think it is because these people are not taking nutritious food." This is a retreat from his earlier claim, widely reported in the Indian press, that the cause of the diseases in Kasargod district was inbreeding and the chewing of betel nut.

Dubey is fond of metaphors and uses them vigorously to defend the use of pesticides. "It is like if a train wrecks, you are compensated, people with broken limbs go to hospital, we take corrective measures. Do we stop the train running?" When it is pointed out that his committee will appear to undo "corrective measures" by recommending the endosulfan ban be lifted, he tries another metaphor. "Think of it like aspirin. Aspirin you take for a headache. If you take ten tablets, you will collapse." As Dubey sees it, it is a simple calculus: 35 per cent of crop loss is due to pests. Without chemicals, India would be unable to feed itself. India is home to more than a billion people, a vast number of whom live on less than a dollar a day, and 700 million of them depend on agriculture to survive. When he released his report last August, he recommended that endosulfan be exonerated.

Endosulfan is a neurotoxin developed in the 1950s by the German chemical giant Hoechst. It is used in the Third World as a cheap replacement for persistent organic pollutants like DDT, Heptachlor, and Dieldrin, which are widely banned. Endosulfan itself is banned or severely restricted in some 31 countries, from environmental progressives such as Germany, the UK, the Netherlands, and Sweden to developing tropical countries like Belize, Sri Lanka, Colombia, and Cambodia. The EPA classifies it as highly hazardous, due to its acute toxicity. The chemical absorbs easily through the skin, lungs, and stomach, and studies have shown that long-term exposure, even at low levels, causes damage par-

ticularly to the central nervous system, kidneys, liver, and the developing fetus. It is also suspected to be an endocrine disrupter, a molecule that by its shape mimics estrogen in the body, bringing with it a host of reproductive problems, from sterility and infertility to testicular and prostate cancer.

From the window of the Ambassador, I see the village of Vaninagar spread out beneath in a bowl of red earth. The low hills wallow to the horizon, a dusty green and undulating topography. Our driver pulls up in front of a low wooden shed, screened off in the front. A hand-painted white sign with a red cross advertises Y. Mohana Kumar, M.D. The doctor is in, attending a child, so we sit in folding chairs by the doorway. His patient is a tiny girl, perhaps five, with dark eyes. She has a wool hat on, despite the heat. Kumar listens to the child's breathing through a stethoscope, his hand spanning the width of her shoulder blades as the other presses the resonator to her chest. Everything is still for several seconds, only the faint whir of the ceiling fan and the distant pulse of insects. The doctor says a few words to the father in Tulu, a local dialect, and he takes the girl's hand as they walk off. "*Thulasi* and honey, I recommended. Excellent for colds."

He sits at his desk, which is cluttered with handwritten patients' records and medical books. Behind him is a glass cabinet of prescription medicines, and a refrigerator stocked with antibiotics and insulin hums next to it. Kumar is handsome, with a neatly trimmed mustache and a weary grin. "Three years of stress has done this," he says, tousling his graying hair. I ask him about his practice. Out of a village of 4,000, he knows perhaps half by name. He is the first doctor ever to have been born and raised in this village, and certainly no one is as familiar with the locals. While we talk, a woman comes in. She has a worried, suncreased face and speaks to him in hushed tones.

He opens the cabinet, pulls out a bottle of pills, and drops a few into a piece of newspaper, which he folds into a neat packet. She hands him a weathered 10-rupee note from a fold in her sari. She leaves, and Kumar turns to me. "Her son has epilepsy and cerebral palsy. She comes in for pills when his condition deteriorates."

It is a scene that repeats itself throughout the afternoon: villager after villager comes to the doctor's screen door displaying a catalogue of afflictions. A woman with precancerous lesions in her mouth, a mother who has two sons with mental retardation, a man with skin cancer. A pretty young woman comes in and talks to the doctor, leaves without meeting my eyes. "Issueless," he says, wobbling his head in the Indian fashion, which can mean almost anything. In this case, Kumar means she has been married a decade and has no children.

Dr. Kumar began to notice disease rates climbing in the village more than a decade ago, especially among villagers living along two streams that run through the area, the Kodenkiri and the Swarga. Swarga means "heaven" in Kannada. The streams are the lifelines of the village. People drink, bathe, and use them for cooking. In many parts of the hill country, they are the only available source of water. Unable to fly at the prescribed two-metre height above the trees, the helicopters had sprayed from much higher, and the endosulfan settled across a wide, populated area. "The law states that before aerial spraying, the PCK must cover all water sources that can be affected by the pesticide drift. You tell me," Kumar demanded, "how can you cover a stream?"

The remoteness of the area has stymied any comprehensive gathering of population and health statistics. "Nobody has done proper research, these people are spread out all over the countryside, there's no census, people don't know someone a mile away," he tells me. People in the countryside build funeral pyres for their dead on their own land. Some lives, particularly miscarriages, are never accounted for. As the only doctor in the village, he was in the best, perhaps the only, position to observe and catalogue the maladies that had descended upon the population. There were multiple cases of cancer, retardation, epilepsy, and birth defects. A six-year-old died of blood cancer. Kumar holds his hands out, as if describing the swell of a pregnant woman's belly, to show how a 50-year-old teacher in the village had been bloated before he died of liver cancer a few months earlier.

Miscarriage and infertility are rife, which in a village culture that values women foremost as procreators can mean ostracism of the victims and isolation of the village by unafflicted communities. They are afraid more than anything that it will create "matrimonial problems," as Kumar puts it, a curse whose social impact cannot be overstated in India, where 95 per cent of marriages are still arranged. A woman even thought to be infertile is unmarriageable. Even though dowry is proscribed by law, any health problem in a woman will make her family unable to afford a groom's demands. Depression and suicide have also been epidemic. Kumar had tracked at least nine suicides in the village in the past several years and suspects that clinical depression is another unstudied side effect of chronic exposure to endosulfan. I ask him what the most common means of committing suicide is in his experience. "Hanging, most often. After that, drinking the pesticide itself. It's cheap and widely available."

The villagers, he says, are more terrified of the stigma of disease than of the disease itself, deeply wary of outsiders, suspicious of anyone from the government. "They have stopped the spraying, at least temporarily, but even today they will not admit that the endosulfan caused this. They say it is from eating areca. Can you imagine? Children and pregnant women eating areca nut? They say that endosulfan is safe under laboratory conditions. But it is not used in labs; it is used in fields."

Tests of long-term endosulfan exposure on rats have shown a wide array of physiological after-effects, from reproductive damage and abnormal bone development to mutagenicity (a permanent change in genetic structure that can cause cancer and developmental disorders in subsequent generations). Mortality rates were so high in testing to determine whether it was a carcinogen that they proved inconclusive. That is, endosulfan is so toxic that it killed the rats outright before it could give them cancer. The EPA's re-registration documents, while approving the continued use of the pesticide in the United States, recommended a host of studies to determine the long-term effects of endosulfan exposure and outlined the degree to which many of these effects remain unknown.

The EPA's position highlights one of the fundamental flaws in the laboratory testing process that leads to the registration of toxic chemicals. The exposure studies done on rats were conducted over two years. The exposure at Vaninagar was over a period of decades, with unmeasurable dosages administered to unquantified people. It is a Sisyphean task even to gather census data, let alone meaningful health statistics in rural India. And the conditions under which a chemical is deemed safe in the lab often don't apply in the field. Interaction with other chemicals is not measured. Under laboratory conditions, a molecule of endosulfan has a half-life in water of one week. But in the earth, bound to soil particles, or held anaerobically in the rot of leaf litter in a streambed, unable to oxidize, it can last for years.

The government owns the cashew plantation and Hindustan Insecticides Limited and controls all regulatory bodies for both industries. The PCK and HIL were both criticized in a 2002 Greenpeace report, but as far as Kumar can see, whether due to outright corruption or bureaucratic ineptitude, they will never admit that endo-

sulfan has caused all these diseases. And they will never compensate the victims.

"Not that anything could really help," he adds. "For most, the damage is done."

He hands over a packet of photographs. Snapshot after snapshot of children with congenital abnormalities: a hand with fingers the size of pencil erasers, a young girl with a leg drawn up and twisted like a chicken's wing, a retarded boy propped against his mother, a boy with leukemia lying prostrate and withered on a bed. The worst is of a hydrocephalic infant girl, wailing, her hands clenched into fists. The head is enormous, larger than the rest of the body, inflated like a balloon about to burst. Flies crawl in the squeezed-shut corners of her eyes. "She lived for six weeks," says Kumar, shaking his head.

India is a country where the absence of a social safety net is so total that for millions of the chronically ill or physically handicapped, begging is the only means of survival, and they must promote themselves in the cities like freelance circus freaks. Nowhere is this phenomenon more striking than in Bombay, along the causeway to Haji Ali's tomb. The tomb is built several hundred yards out into the Arabian Sea, and along the paved stone jetty that reaches it lies an encyclopedia of medical horrors. Leprous stumps of hands, elephantiasis, smallpox blindness, flippers for arms, polio victims with legs like broom handles, tertiary syphilis, gigantism, goitres like tire tubes, cretinism, chemical burns. A young man smokes a cigarette casually, and through a silver-dollar-size hole in his ribcage a purplish lung is visible, pulsing behind the fogged window of his pleura. A young boy holds out his hands, chanting in English, "One rupee, one chapati, one chocolate. No mammi, no pappi." He has a black hole surrounded by pink scar tissue where his left ear was. A child mutilated in this way by his own parents functions as a retirement plan. All have laid before them a scattering of five-paise coins, a thousand to the dollar, tossed as zakat by the Muslims returning from evening prayers.

Outside Kumar's office, a group of schoolboys have abandoned their cricket match to examine the curiosity of my presence. They stand in a clutch, dust-covered, staring and as is customary in India, send forth an emissary who is to report back to the group. The boys all wear *lunghis* and collared shirts, a strange combination of Indian peasant and British public-school lad. Vinod talks to one, and he turns and reports back. Peppered in a slew of Kannada, I hear again, endosulfan, endosulfan. The boys repeat to one another, endosulfan, endosulfan. It is a visitation by the outside world, which has never taken any interest in Vaninagar until the great misfortune of its slow poisoning. Endosulfan is the name of a new deity, which, whether or not it is guilty of visiting a plague upon this village, has become for them the incarnation of the modern age and of the unfathomable mysteries of chemistry and economics that have forever altered rural life in India. And I, as an outsider, am its avatar.

We walk down the hill, led by the group of boys. The village is quiet in the late afternoon, dusty men heading home from the brick quarry, women carrying water up from the valley bottom in metal cans. Everyone stares as I walk past, trailing a swarm of ragged boys. Along the steep path, I stop to look at a cashew apple dangling over the trail. The fruit is yellow, swollen, and the nut hangs beneath it like a strange organ, or an 8-week-old fetus. I reach out and heft it, prompting one of the boys to push my hand away. It is swarming with a beneficial species of ant that according to Padre had been wiped out during the spraying. It occurs to me that India hangs just as tenuously from the vast bough of Asia, like a fruit to which a sixth of humanity clings.

Down a steep ravine, we arrive at a smooth, dry cow-dung patio where areca and pepper are spread out to dry. An ancient woman crouches on the ground, a sickle clenched beneath her splayed toes. She draws sections of dried areca leaf across the blade, slicing them up for fodder, and does not look up once. Thanoji Appe steps out from the low, thatch-roofed house to meet us. He wears a *lunghi* and a checked shirt, smiles warmly with missing teeth. The woman, his grandmother, is 98 years old. She was born here, on this same land, a few years after the death of Queen Victoria. As I talk to Appe, she continues her work, and the pile of areca strips grows beside her. Pepper, areca, and cashew dry on the smooth cow-dung-and-clay courtyard.

Behind him, through the wooden slats of the front porch, a little girl, almond-shaped eyes bright and curious, stares out at me. Her name is Sruthi, and he calls to her, tells her to come outside and say hello. She steps out shyly from the shaded porch into the afternoon sun, revealing a prosthetic leg below her school uniform, and musters all her grace to come down the steps to the courtyard. The knee is a steel hinge, the calf plastic, and the foot a brown rubber, scuffed from barefoot walking around the red-dirt paths of the village. Around the rubber ankle is a silver bangle to match the one on her other foot, and, smiling, she sits down next to us, folding her metal knee with a child's studied elegance. Her hands are like the antlers of a deer, bifurcated above the wrist into two branches, each branch with two fingers. They are shaped as popular imagination draws the hands of aliens, mutated yet somehow intelligent, capable. She sits singing quietly to herself as I talk to her father through Vinod. They speak Kannada, though Vinod is a Malayalam speaker and Appe's native language is Tulu, a regional dialect that has no written expression.

Through layers of language, Appe relates the sorrows his family has endured. He remembers the spraying, the helicopter passing right over the house, and the choking, headaches, and itching that followed for days after. They didn't know what the spray was. The Malayalam word for pesticide, *marunnu*, means medicine. That was all the explanation they were offered. It was medicine for the cashew trees. When Sruthi was born, she had an atrophied, warped leg corkscrewed like a polio victim's. The doctor had shown me a faded news clipping. Her father, before the operation, had carried her 200 yards up the hill to school every day. The 80,000-rupee operation (an amount few families make in two years) had been financed by donations from the community and a group of German documentarians who had visited the village the previous year. Now she could walk alone, was an ace student, loved school. When she was young, there was no question of an operation: her mother had stomach cancer, and her radiation treatments in Mangalore used up all the family's resources. It wasn't until she died four years ago that treatment for the girl could be considered.

Appe works as a day labourer in the plantations and farms around the village. The going rate for an eight-hour day harvesting areca or pepper, with lunch included, is about 60 rupees. It is lucky to be paid that much for a day's work, he says. They live with his new wife and their baby, who crawls around naked in the dirt, laughing, with a silver chain around his waist. The sun sinks, a dusty orange light suffuses the forest. Sruthi's stepmother carries a pail to the cow stall, and the light of a hurricane lamp casts through the slats and falls across the courtyard. It is so still I can hear jets of milk echo in the hollow of the pail like a pulse of blood into the chamber of a heart.

Thanoji Appe has a sorrow in his eyes, red from work. He does not want to be sad, he whispers, that she is a girl-child, that she won't be able to be married off. When her mother was sick, they prayed to Jatadhari, offered money at the temple. Sruthi swings her leg, sings. She'll need a new leg when she grows, her father says. I ask her a few questions. She loves Kannada, loves playing *jibly*, a local variant of hopscotch. Loves peacocks and elephants. She wasn't afraid when she went to get her leg cut off. "She was asking when it would be for months," her father says. I want to ask about her mother, if she remembers her, if she was big enough to put a stick of sandalwood in her pyre. If she is angry that she was born like this, that she was dealt such a blow from the start. But she is happy, smiles brightly, and I won't ask anything to shake her out of it. What's the use? Vinod and I walk back up in the dark under the heady scent of the overhanging mangoes, through the lamplit village to the waiting car.

Vaninagar is not the only affected area. Kumar and Padre estimate that perhaps a thousand people who live near the vast and fragmented plantation have been exposed to endosulfan. A few days later, we visit another side of the plantation, where several families of Adivasis live. These are the original inhabitants of south India, tribal forest dwellers who have been systematically relieved of their lands over the last two centuries. They are *ati sudra*, below the untouchable castes, at the bottom of the ladder by every standard. As we pull up, a group of small, intensely dark boys are playing cricket with a hand-carved bat and a coconut. The wicket is a tipped-over wheelbarrow. Seeing us, they drop their game and run off toward a low, mud-brick house. The area is flat and completely surrounded by the cashew trees of the Plantation Corporation of Kerala. A boy puts on his shirt and runs from the water pump, where a trickle peters out into a dark spot on the ground. We walk to their hut, built of bricks quarried on the site, which makes it appear like a natural extension of the red earth, thatched with palm fronds. A bright green banana plant splits the red soil. A group of men stand around with sickles tucked into their *lunghis*, arms crossed, skin almost black from the sun. On the shaded porch, a woman holds a baby wrapped up in a cloth. Vinod talks to her, talks to the men. They had thought I was a doctor. They are Mavilans, worshipers of Karinjamundi, the black fertility goddess. Their presence predates the arrival of Hinduism here by millennia. The children have never seen a white person before.

The mother's name is Sharada, and the fat little baby is named Anju. Her eyes are wide and black, emphasized by the lining of dark kohl her mother has drawn under them. Sharada moves aside the cloth covering the baby's lower half and reveals her secret. Dangling between Anju's legs, like a horrible ripe fruit, is the baby's bladder. She was born with it on the outside. A series of eight operations, none of which the family can afford or the government is willing to pay for, are necessary if the child is to survive. They remember the bad air from the helicopters, have been told that the cause might be the "medicine" that the PCK sprayed on the cashews. But the PCK had sent men to tell them that their baby's disease, and the mentally retarded infant in the house next door, was not caused by endosulfan. The swollen sun drops through the cashew trees. Some have faintly aromatic blossoms just beginning to wilt, some have fruit already swelling, strangely lobed, almost sexual in colour and shape. They are sorry they have no chairs for us. I say it is no trouble. The guest is a god, they tell Vinod.

Mr Pradeep Dave, president of the Pesticides Manufacturers and Formulators Association of India, shares Dr. Dubey's views on pesticides. He offers a number of novel theories. First, that the diseases in Kasargod are in fact caused by radioactive minerals that are naturally in the soil there and from uranium and thorium mining that has gone on nearby. Second, that this radia-

tion poisoning is compounded by intermarriage. Third, that the NGOs that are campaigning against certain pesticides are in fact being sponsored by rival pesticide manufacturers to surreptitiously promote their product. Pesticides are profoundly good, he insists, citing the millions saved in the Second World War by DDT's eradication of the Anopheles mosquito and the fact that despite five years of drought, there are 60 million tons of surplus grain in India. His metaphors are strikingly similar to Dubey's, as though they have debriefed each other: "Some farmers are using too much pesticide. It is like eating too much, or like a medicine that you take too much of. Maybe the doctor says take one tablet, and you take more and more, and instead of making you better it makes you sick." The demonization of endosulfan is just greed, Dave insists. "Fifty million litres of endosulfan are used in India every year. Why is this one village complaining? We will fight to protect our molecules. They are our babies."

In Badiadika, the nearest town of any size, we stop for lunch at a chai stall, a mountain of rice and white-hot curry served on a banana leaf. I sip chai, soaked in sweat even in the acacia shade, watching the circus of Keralite street life: near-collisions of three-wheeled auto rickshaws, bright orange trucks decorated with mirrors and Christmas lights like rolling shrines, magicians waving drug-addled cobras at their marks, elephants hauling logs, a fistfight as sudden as a cloudburst, chattering monkeys fleeing from lathi-wielding policemen. Cyclones of dust and newspaper eddy behind passing buses. Vinod disappears after lunch for half an hour, then returns, excitedly slamming a newspaper-wrapped parcel on the table.

"There is your endosulfan!" he cries, terribly pleased with himself. I unwrap the paper and look at a 100-ml bottle marked POISON in block letters. Vinod had bought it at a local farm-supply store, where the owner keeps it in the back, out of sight, because of the environmentalists and journalists. DDT was also available.

When Vinod asked if the endosulfan was dangerous, the man had said, "Don't worry, just get your workers to mix it for you."

The black market for banned pesticides in India is not measurable, but anecdotal evidence (and Vinod's foray to the farm-supply store) suggests that DDT is as easy to procure as powdered milk. "There are lots of laws in India," Vinod says, "but very little enforcement." Vast quantities are produced and supposedly severely regulated, only to be used in limited circumstances to control disease vectors. When a pneumonic-plague outbreak occurred in Gujarat in 1994, tons of DDT were shipped to control the rat flea that spread the disease. After the epidemic was brought under control, many of those stocks were sold on the black market, often repackaged as ant killer, if they were labelled at all. With endosulfan, the black market is even simpler; since it is banned only in Kerala, sellers easily can procure it in other states. I stare at the bottle. I have no idea what to do with it.

The Plantation Corporation of Kerala's Cashew Project is a massive shed in the middle of a sun-blasted, grassless expanse at the edge of the cashew groves. Men in *lunghis* hang around in the shade, boiling chai over a portable gas stove. They grumble that they have not been paid in four months despite the fact that the plantation is supposedly turning a profit. They take Vinod and me for agricultural grad students, though we do not offer this information. More chai, and Mr Roguthaman, the plantation administrator, happily launches into a lengthy discourse in Malayalam about the minutiae of plantation economics: hectares of trees planted, profits realized, labourers employed, the commodity rate per kilo

of cashew, and crop losses from the twin scourges of stem borers and tea mosquitoes, the latter of which endosulfan is meant to eradicate. It seems that despite the moratorium on spraying, the plantation has had two bumper crops in a row, though Roguthaman finds this neither remarkable nor a justification for a permanent ban.

The cashew, indigenous to northern Brazil, was brought to India in the late sixteenth century by the Portuguese, who introduced it to all their tropical colonies. The fruit was originally considered the valuable crop, and an alcoholic beverage called fenny was fermented (and still is today) from the juice of the bulbous, fibrous, astringent cashew-apple. It wasn't until the end of World War II and the rise of the cocktail-hour leisure economy that snack nuts became widely popular as a global commodity, and today cashews are second only to almonds in economic importance. The crop generates $400 million in revenue for India every year, and the PCK, which was funded by the World Bank in 1980 as a rehabilitation project, produces more than any other plantation in the country.

Roguthaman walks us out in the blinding sunlight to point out an infestation of stem borers. The cashew trees are the only green things in the landscape. Under the canopy of a large old cashew, Roguthaman peels away a slab of bark like a scab, revealing a clicking, scurrying group of enormous borers. The tree will be dead in a year. DDT and BHC, both of which are banned, are really the only things that will take care of these, he says, so for now they are absorbing their losses. As for endosulfan, he defends its use. The final verdict on the pesticide, in the form of Dubey's report, has not been returned, and he thinks that endosulfan is the cheapest and safest of the available chemicals. An alternative chemical suggested by the Ministry of Agriculture is Sevin, the very same pesticide that was manufactured at the Union Carbide plant in Bhopal before it exploded.

But what of the people who claim to have been sickened by the spray? He shrugs. Who knows? There is no proof that it's endosulfan. His workers would stir the chemical with their hands, wiping it off with grass. They would stand in the plantation during spraying with only a handkerchief over their mouths. They sprayed 3,000 litres a year. None of his labourers has become sick. He pounds his chest to demonstrate his imperviousness to a chemical a teaspoon of which would kill an elephant. Endosulfan is fine. They have barrels of the stuff in storage. Would I like to see?

My eyes adjust slowly to the darkness of the storage shed as Roguthaman slides the door open. A pile of cashews have spilled from a burlap sack across the floor. To one side are four dust-covered barrels, each containing 200 litres of endosulfan. I smell one, and there is a faint but distinct acridity coming off the barrel, something like turpentine. There is enough poison in these containers to kill 80,000 people. But of course it is not the acute poisoning that is the problem. It is the microdose, a few molecules at a time, the chronic exposure to the communities around the plantation over 20 years, that has visited upon them the wrath of a new and vengeful god. I rap my knuckles against the lid, with its skull-and-crossbones label: a dull echo. The rusting barrels in the shed are as inert as mothballed cluster-bombs, waiting only for the inconvenient ban to be lifted.

In Vaninagar I visit another small farm, 100 yards along the hillside from Appe's house, which belongs to Surender Shetty. In the front yard, under the spreading shade of a large cashew tree, is a *thulasi* plant surrounded by a cage of thorns to keep the goats away. He crushes the leaves under my nose; it gives off a sharp, lemony smell. *Thulasi* cures fevers and sore throats, and every house in the village has

one growing in its courtyard, a sacramental medicine cabinet. Shetty's 12-year-old son, Udayan, an epileptic with cerebral palsy, sits drooling on his faded Chicago Bulls T-shirt, scabby knees bent under him awkwardly. He smiles attentively, and just as quickly a spasmodic shadow crosses his face and his mind wanders elsewhere. Shetty brings chairs; they want first to know what we need, if we've had anything to drink. He brings coconuts, lopped open with a sickle, and tells me the plantation's helicopter pilot refused to drink coconuts from Vaninagar and insisted on bringing his own.

Shetty's wife rolls *bidis*. She sits cross-legged, holding in her lap a bamboo tray with a neat stack of *tendu* leaves, a pile of shredded tobacco, and thread and scissors. She cuts the leaves, rolls the tobacco, and ties them off with string. It is an unconscious process, a slavery measured out in heartbeats, but she can talk and look after her son. Working non-stop for a day, a good roller can make over 1,000, for which she will be paid 46 rupees. This is an economics to which millions of women in India are subjected. She says it would be nice if we could speak the same language, says she is blessed to have visitors. Taking care of Udayan, who frequently collapses in seizures, she can make only three or four hundred *bidis* a day. They buy Western medicines for his epilepsy from the doctor, though they use traditional cures for most things. She is the same woman who came into Kumar's office to buy epilepsy medicine with a dog-eared 10-rupee note. Her daughter, with the same aquiline features, same sorrowful eyes, collarbones as prominent as tree branches over which a sari has been hung to dry, stands beside her. I ask the mother if she is angry at what has happened to her son and her village. "What can I say? It is my fate."

Shetty works whitewashing houses, when there is work. He smells like moonshine, the country liquor also known as "sky juice" because of the custom of hanging it in jugs from the palm tops. He tells Vinod he is a competitive player of Kabbadi, a local game like capture-the-flag that involves saying "kabbadikabbadi-kabbadikabbadi" over and over when you cross into enemy territory. Twice he has made a 100-kilometre pilgrimage to a temple to shave his head as an offering to the *theyyam* Manjunatha, praying for his boy to be healed. He has prayed and made offerings to Jatadhari as well. There are more than 400 deities within the two northern districts of Kerala, and perhaps three million fill the vast Hindu pantheon across the subcontinent. People offer rupees, liquor, coconuts, chickens. In old times, they sacrificed elephants, even humans. These tributes were meant to ward off evil, cure diseases, secure blessings. Anything to influence the arbitrary wrath of the divine.

The British called these rituals black magic, but really it was the organic evolution of belief. The gods that ruled this place were natural extensions of the landscape, grew here along with the people, and followed the rhythms of plantings and monsoons, birth and death. Religion dropped roots like a banyan. The plantation economy and industrialized agriculture disrupted the pulse of life here: the monsoon grew capricious, and the jungles fell to the axe and the bulldozer. The cultivation of cash monocrops disrupted human life as completely as it upset the tropical ecology that had achieved a balance, despite Kerala's huge population density, over the course of centuries. The insatiable logic of a tropical empire created a new cycle to replace the indigenous one: deforestation in the highlands caused flooding in the plains, displacing a population that in turn knocked hungrily at the plantation gates or fled to the huge slums that now grow around every city in south Asia. The web of beneficial insects that held ecological disaster in check was unrav-

elled by vast plantings of coffee, tea, banana, and cashew. The sorcerers' apprentices concocted a host of chemicals to restore order. Consequences have been meted out over lifetimes, generations. The water was poisoned. No government committee can measure the result.

Shetty shows me his water source, a black-mouthed tunnel, called a *thuranga*, dug into the hillside. The cashew trees of the plantation are on the hill above. It is the height and shape of a man, a giant birth canal into the living earth. Stepping over the trickle of water that comes out of its mouth and collects in a pool, I walk far back into it, out of the bright tropical light and heat. A few paces and I am in almost total darkness, the entrance behind me, ringed with foliage, a window on the outer world. In the *thuranga* it is cool, the walls are covered with moss and tiny ferns, there is the sound of dripping water, and a little stream of clear water runs along the sandy floor of the cave's base. It goes 40 metres deep into the hillside, beyond the reach of light. Vinod says to be careful, some of these fork off and you'll get lost in the dark. The flashlight they've given me, dim as a lightning bug, is useless in the blackness. The *thuranga* seems haunted by restive ghosts. I imagine the endosulfan molecules, bound to soil particles, percolating down through the loamy earth, infusing the trickle of water that Shetty comes to fetch for his family, that they share with the neighbours. Incremental, tiny doses, an experiment more complicated than any ever devised in a laboratory, and more comprehensive: x factors of rain, variables of oxygen. No one to record the results, draw conclusions.

I can feel the weight of all the earth above me, the cashew roots curling like warped fingers through the soil, and the cool cave walls seem to gather closer, the moss to reach out tendrils, the ferns at the distant cave-mouth to stiffen like a dog's hackles. I turn and scramble out, a diver going up for air, clouding the stream in my panic.

Outside the *thuranga*'s mouth, we squat on our haunches, Indian-style, Shetty and Vinod and I and some local boys, as the sun drops in the red western sky over the ghats. We sit smoking *bidis*, making small talk. I don't know what to say. It is a slow disaster in a land full of disasters, where fact and myth obscure each other, where the old gods have been rendered obsolete, where millions suffer worse than this, where the chains of fate and blame are bound irrevocably around each new life.

I ask Shetty what he thinks of all these strangers coming to Vaninagar. "What can I say? These doctors come, these foreigners come, they look at Udayan like a specimen. Politicians come and say they'll consider, scientists come and draw blood, journalists come and take pictures, I parade my boy in front of them all. Nothing changes." There is quiet between us, wound through the burning-leaf smell of the *bidis* his wife has rolled and the sound of dripping water.

Vinod and I walk down a dirt path through the village to the Kodenkiri, watched by eyes from every doorway, followed by curious children. The stream runs sluggishly down from the plantation in the April heat before the arrival of the June monsoon. I watch out for cobras in the leaf litter. Upstream, women with their saris hitched up slap laundry rhythmically against the rocks, throwing off sprays of mist as they spin it in the air. Some of the stones are worn smooth from centuries of washing. A tribal boy, Ravi, red as the earth from a dollar-a-ton day in the brick quarry, washes himself, the water running out behind him like blood. He has lived here all his life. He does not know the name of the stream in which we both stand knee-deep but raises his hand above his head to show the monsoon height of the waters. He stoops and cups water to his mouth. It is the stream, he laughs, why should he know its name?

A *thumbi*, an iridescent red-eyed dragonfly, lands on a branch, wings dappled from sunlight reflecting on the water. Tiny minnows have returned, at least for now. Wild mangoes, the remnants of the vanished monsoon jungle spared for their utility, hang gnarled and enormous over the creek. Floating leaves cast amoebic shapes on the creek till, a shadow-play of mitosis. There is something primal in these expressions, an affirmation: let alone, lived with, the water will clear, the land will return.

Harper's Magazine. 2004. August.

KEY AND DIFFICULT WORDS

Define the following, using context or other clues if possible: **pogrom, lateritic, endemic, indelible, mandate (v), emulsion, avatar, astringent, sacramental, iridescent.**

QUESTIONS

1. How much of "The poison stream" would you consider the introduction? What important ideas, themes, or motifs are introduced there?

2. Throughout the essay, Power makes self-conscious references to himself as an outsider (for example, in paragraph 8, he reflects, "I feel a bit like a holdover from the Raj, a mid-level bureaucrat come to inspect the coconut plantation"). How does his role as an outsider help to make him a credible observer? Do you believe it could negatively affect his credibility in any way?

3. Referring to specific passages, discuss how the author is able to convey authentic detail about what he is observing. What effect do these kinds of details have on the reader?

4. Power intersperses the subject being investigated—the possible cause/effect relationship between the aerial spraying of the pesticide endosulfan and the incidence of diseases and deformities in the immediate area—with vignettes centring on people and places. Comment on the effectiveness of this organizational method. Was the essay ever difficult to follow?

5. What is the function of paragraph 9 in which Power gives a brief history of the state of Kerala? Can you identify later paragraphs that provide further evidence of "institutionalized corruption?"

6. What does Power suggest is the problem with using metaphors to describe the situation in and around Vaninagar (see paragraphs 23 and 47)? Referring to at least one descriptive passage, consider how Power's own metaphors and similes (for example, paragraphs 1, 13, 39, 46, and 61–2) are different from those used by Indian officials.

7. Summarize paragraphs 32 and 33 in which the author considers the problem of applying an empirical laboratory study to real-life situations.

8. In the last third of the essay, the author begins to focus more directly on the apparent victims of endosulfan. Why do you think he placed these passages here? What is his purpose, and what techniques or strategies does he use to accomplish it?

9. Power does not use direct quotations extensively in his essay, sometimes quoting only a sentence or phrase before resuming his narrative. Pointing to at least two specific examples, explain what his selective use of direct quotation contributes to the essay.

COLLABORATIVE ACTIVITY

The discussion should focus on the voice of the author. The following questions could be discussed: Is the author able to attain a basically objective voice? Is there bias in his account? If there is, where specifically does it come across? Does bias matter? Why or why not?

ACTIVITIES

1. Is "The poison stream" more like a literary journalistic essay or an investigative essay? (See pages 31–4.)

2. Explore the author's use of description and imagery in the final two paragraphs. Do they contribute to a successful and satisfying conclusion? In your view, is the ending essentially affirmative?

3. (a) Using at least two reliable sources, write a brief account (250 to 350 words) of the tragedy at Bhopal in 1984, which is cited by the author in a note. (b) Why did the author refer to this event, and how could it be connected with the issue that he is writing about (150 to 200 words)?

Kyoto: Mother of intervention

Peter Foster

(780 words)

One of the more far-fetched claims about the impact of Kyoto, which drops today on to the stable floor of history, is that it will lead to "opportunities" rather than economic destruction. This assertion was made yet again yesterday by Environment Minister Stéphane Dion in a speech at Carleton University. "Achieving our climate change goals," he declared, "provides an opportunity to transform our economy."

The notion that Kyoto might be good for business is a variant on the classic "broken window fallacy" hatched by the great French economic satirist Frederic Bastiat. The fallacy is attached to the notion that a brick through a casement window might be a stimulant to economic activity because the glass has to be replaced. Such a view ignores the fact that the glazier's benefit is the window-owner's loss. There is no net economic benefit. Moreover, an environment filled with policy brick-throwers would inevitably lead to a collapse of investment.

The allegedly more sophisticated modern version of this fallacy is Keynesianism: the belief that government can artificially stimulate the economy on an ongoing basis, and that even war might be of benefit. After all, look at all the arms manufacturing it would require and the reconstruction it would lead to. Think of radar.

The Kyoto variant is that the new technology required to meet the requirements of a carbon-constrained world will prove a great stimulus to innovative investment and may provide a net benefit for the economy. Such a suggestion is nonsensical.

Adversity has traditionally been a great stimulator of human ingenuity, but the notion that necessity—much less whimsical legislation—is the mother of invention is certainly not a law. Artificially creating a "necessity" is no guarantee that it will be successfully addressed.

One can imagine all sorts of ludicrous pieces of legislation that would undoubtedly spur innovative responses, such as the banning of wheels or food imports, or mandating 100 per cent recycling. Why do people use wheels, import food, and not recycle everything? Because it saves resources, including energy.

Businessmen and entrepreneurs almost invariably pursue least cost—that is, least resource-intensive—methods in order to maximize their profits. Increasing the efficient use of resources is not some novel notion dreamed up by policy wonks but the absolute bedrock of profitable private enterprise. Entrepreneurs and investors are perpetually on the lookout for ways to save money—that is, resources, including energy—either by improving old technologies or inventing new ones.

Perhaps with the exception of patent protection, regulation and fiscal finagling have historically not proved to be efficient promoters of innovation. Rather, they have usually led to a misallocation of resources, with bigger policy thrusts attached to bigger misallocations.

A classic example was the innovations in Arctic drilling technology encouraged by the generous government grants introduced under the Liberal government's National Energy Program a quarter century ago. Certainly, technological wonders poured forth in the shape of ice-reinforced drill ships and giant exploration platforms. But economics pulled the rug from under the entire exercise. The Arctic marvels wound up being sold off for cents on the dollar, to be adapted and used elsewhere, or sent to the scrap yard.

Truly revolutionary breakthroughs rarely come where they are expected. The current global swath of Kyoto-related subsidies are almost all directed at the same "renewable" technologies, such as photovoltaics, wind power, and fuel cells. While these are not necessarily dead-end technologies (although they may well be), they are subject to diminishing returns from a marginally economic base and suffer from fundamental flaws, which mean they can never substitute for carbon-based energy sources in many crucial uses. It is also worth remembering that the Canadian government has been subsidizing these technologies for a quarter of a century.

Climate change may indeed be coming our way, and we may be sure that human ingenuity will attempt to deal with it, but we may also be relatively certain that it has little or nothing to do with human activity.

If the Mother Necessity argument had any validity, then we should surely welcome climate change, because it would stimulate myriad investments to protect against sea level rises, resist harsher storms, and deal with a cooler climate in Europe once the Gulf Stream "collapses," not to mention lead to a boom in investment in Canadian vineyards. Strangely, however, I have never heard a government minister express such views.

The recent Asian tsunami reminds us of the horribly destructive power of nature and the contrasting concern of humanity for its own. Supporters of Kyoto effectively argue that artificial policy tsunamis will be a boon to mankind. That notion deserves to be thrown out of the broken policy window.

National Post. 2005. 16 February.

KEY AND DIFFICULT WORDS

Define the following, using context or other clues if possible: **finagle, misallocation, subsidy, myriad.**

QUESTIONS

1. What is Foster's reason for using such a direct opening? Identify his thesis statement.
2. Would you say that the author's purpose is to expose a problem, critique a position, reach a compromise, or settle an issue? What specific argumentative strategies does he use to accomplish this aim?
3. Explain the "'broken window fallacy'" in your own words. By what name does Foster later refer to this fallacy?
4. What basic economic principle does Foster rely on to counter the claim that the Kyoto Protocol will be "good for business?" What can you infer about Foster's views of Keynesian economics?

5. Foster uses direct language and even some sarcasm in criticizing the argument used by some of the government's supporters of Kyoto. Identify examples. Do you think that Foster risks his own credibility by being so direct?
6. Summarize the author's comments on alternative energy sources (paragraph 10).
7. Is Foster's conclusion successful? Analyze its effectiveness.

COLLABORATIVE ACTIVITY

Do you believe that Foster is always fair in representing the opposing viewpoint? Do you think that his editorial represents a successful and effective refutation of the Kyoto Protocol? Is it intended as a response to Kyoto in general? Discuss or debate these questions.

ACTIVITIES

1. Who is Peter Foster? Using a reliable source, write a one-paragraph biography of Foster, including any information that might be relevant to his essay on Kyoto.
2. Foster's editorial appeared in the *National Post*, 16 February 2005, the day that the Kyoto Protocol formally took effect. Many other editorials appeared in Canadian newspapers around that time. Find one editorial that clearly takes a different position from that of Foster, and write a critical response to it or a critical analysis of it. If it seems appropriate, you can mention Foster's editorial in your response/analysis.

Can science solve the riddle of existence?

John Horgan
(1,500 words)

Is science on the verge of explaining the mystery of existence once and for all? Some prominent scientists are suggesting as much. They claim that unified theories of physics, when combined with refined versions of the big bang model, will soon bequeath us a so-called "theory of everything." As described by physicists such as Stephen Hawking, a theory of everything will be a kind of mystical revelation, which permanently transforms the "Hunh?" of wonder evoked in us by our contemplation of nature into a great "Aha!"

Those who find this vision of a wonderless world chilling rather than exhilarating should be assured that it will never be fulfilled. One of the great paradoxes of modern science is that the more it tells about the origin and history of the cosmos and of life on Earth and of Homo sapiens, the more mysterious our existence becomes.

The big bang theory represents a profound insight into the history and structure of the cosmos, but it cannot tell us why creation occurred in the first place. Particle physics suggests that empty space is seething with "virtual particles," which spring into existence for an instant before vanishing; in the same way, some physicists speculate, the entire universe might have begun as a kind of virtual particle.

Honest physicists will admit that they have absolutely no idea why there is something rather than nothing. After all, what produced the quantum forces that supposedly made creation possible? "No one is certain what happened before the Big Bang, or even if the question has any meaning," the physicist and Nobel laureate Steven Weinberg writes.

Next question: Why does the universe look this way rather than some other way? Why does it adhere to these laws of nature rather than to some other laws? Altering any of the universe's fundamental parameters would have radically altered reality. For example, if the universe had been slightly more dense at its inception, it would have rapidly stopped expanding and collapsed into a black hole. If the universe had been a smidgeon less dense, it would have flown apart so rapidly that there would have been no chance for stars, galaxies, and planets to form. Cosmologists sometimes call this the fine-tuning problem, or, more colourfully, the Goldilocks dilemma: How did the density of the universe turn out not too high, or too low, but just right?

The odds that matter would have precisely its observed density, the physicist Lawrence Krauss has calculated, are as great as the odds of guessing precisely how many atoms there are in the sun. Some physicists are so troubled by the arbitrariness of the cosmos that they espouse a quasi-theological concept known as the anthropic principle. According to the anthropic principle, the universe must have the structure we observe, because otherwise we wouldn't be here to observe it.

The anthropic principle actually comes in two forms, weak and strong. The weak anthropic principle, or WAP, holds merely that any cosmic observer will observe conditions, at least locally, that make the observer's existence possible. The strong anthropic principle, SAP, insists that the universe must be constructed in such a way as to make observers possible. WAP is tautological and SAP teleological. As the physicist Tony Rothman has noted, the anthropic principle in any form is completely ridiculous and hence should be called CRAP. The anthropic principle is cosmology's version of creationism.

The next improbability is life. The evolutionary biologist Richard Dawkins opened his book *The blind watchmaker* by declaring that life "is a mystery no longer" because Darwin solved it with his theory of evolution by natural selection. Dawkins is not a silly man, but this is a silly thing to say. Life is as mysterious as ever, in spite of all the insights provided by evolutionary theory and more modern biological paradigms such as genetics and molecular biology. Neither Darwinism nor any other scientific theory tells us why life appeared on Earth in the first place or whether this event was probable or a once-in-eternity fluke.

Many scientists have argued that life must be a ubiquitous phenomenon that pervades the universe, but they can offer precious little empirical evidence to support this assertion. After decades of searching, scientists have found no signs of life elsewhere in the universe; a 1996 report of fossilized microbes in a meteorite from Mars turned out to be erroneous. Researchers still cannot make matter animate in the laboratory, even with all the tools of modern biotechnology.

In fact, the more scientists ponder life's origin, the harder it is to imagine how it occurred. Francis Crick, the co-discoverer of the double helix, once declared that "the origin of life appears to be almost a miracle, so many are the conditions which would have to be satisfied to get it going." In his book *Life itself*, Crick speculated that the seeds of life might have been planted on Earth by an alien civilization.

Once life on Earth started evolving, many scientists have contended, it was only a matter of time before natural selection produced a species as intelligent as Homo sapiens. But for more than 80 per cent of life's 3.5-billion-year history, the Earth's biota consisted entirely of single-celled organisms, such as bacteria and algae; in other words, not even the simplest multi-cellular organisms—jellyfish or sea squirts—were inevitable.

The evolutionary biologist Stephen Jay Gould estimated that if the great experiment of life were re-run a million times over, chances are that it would never again give rise to mammals, let alone mammals intelligent enough to invent negative theology and television. Similar reasoning led the evolutionary theorist Ernst Mayr to conclude that SETI—the search for extraterrestrial intelligence program, which scans the heavens for radio signals from other civilizations—is futile.

Multiply all these improbabilities and they spike to infinity. "The more the universe seems comprehensible," Steven Weinberg once wrote, "the more it seems pointless." My analysis of science suggests a corollary aphorism: The more the universe seems comprehensible, the more it seems improbable. The most wildly improbable feature of the universe is the lump of matter that can fret over its improbability.

Some researchers nonetheless insist that science will soon solve the riddle of existence, once and for all. For example, more than a decade before I argued in *The end of science* that science's grand quest to uncover the basic rules governing reality might be reaching an impasse, the British chemist Peter Atkins wrote: "Fundamental science may be almost at an end, and might be completed within a generation." But whereas I saw science leaving many riddles unresolved, Atkins envisioned science as a universal acid dissolving all mysteries, including spiritual, ethical, and philosophical ones. "Complete knowledge is just within our grasp," he intoned. "Comprehension is moving across the face of the Earth, like the sunrise."

I suspected Atkins of rhetorical excess until I met him at a reception in London in 1997. As we sipped white wine from plastic cups, Atkins assured me with almost demonic glee that science would soon provide such satisfying explanations for all of nature's mysteries—including the supreme riddle of the universe's origin—that wonder would be extinguished forever and along with it all of our silly spiritual superstitions and speculations. The world would be as solved as Fermat's last theorem: QED.

Other scientists acknowledge that science will never—can never—dispel our awe before the mystery of existence; in fact, science relies on awe for inspiration at least as much as religion does. "Our sense of wonder grows exponentially: the greater the knowledge, the deeper the mystery," wrote the evolutionary biologist Edward Wilson. "This catalytic reaction, seemingly an inborn human trait, draws us perpetually forward in a search for new places and new life."

Scientists may still go much further in plumbing nature's secrets. They may decipher the neural code, the secret language of the brain. They may arrive at a plausible explanation of how life emerged on Earth, and they may even discover life elsewhere in the universe. They may find and verify a unified theory of physics, which provides a more precise picture of the origin and history of the universe. Although there are good reasons for doubting such scientific advances, they cannot be ruled out. What can be ruled out is that science will answer the ultimate question: How did something come from nothing? Neither super-string theory nor any other of science's so-called theories of everything can resolve that mystery any more than our supernatural theologies can.

I do not believe in miracles, at least not defined in the conventional religious manner as divine disruptions of the natural order. But if a miracle is defined as an infinitely improbable phenomenon, then our existence is a miracle, which no theory natural or supernatural will ever explain.

Adbusters. 2005. March/April 13 (2).

KEY AND DIFFICULT WORDS

Define the following, using context or other clues if possible: **espouse, tautological, teleological, paradigm, ubiquitous, corollary, aphorism, QED, catalytic.**

QUESTIONS

1. What is Horgan's claim or thesis? How, primarily, does he develop this claim throughout his essay?

2. Horgan uses the "reversal" strategy in argument in which he explains an idea or builds up a concept before undercutting it. Find two examples of this strategy in his essay. Do you believe it is effective?

3. Summarize what is meant by "the fine-tuning problem" or "the Goldilocks dilemma." Why is it called "the Goldilocks dilemma?"

4. What does Horgan mean when he says he "suspected Atkins of rhetorical excess" (fourth-last paragraph)? What causes him to change his assessment?

5. What is "Fermat's last theorem?" Why is it a good analogy for Horgan to use?

6. Does the author appear to use his sources fairly? In your view, what is the strongest evidence he uses to support his claim?

7. In the final two paragraphs, the author brings science and religion together. What is his purpose in doing this?

COLLABORATIVE ACTIVITY

Do you agree that a verifiable unified theory of all matter is a worthy goal for scientists to pursue in today's world? Do you think it is attainable? Do you believe, as Horgan does, that it would produce a "wonderless world?" Discuss or debate one or more of these questions.

ACTIVITY

Using a credible source, summarize what is meant by the "theory of everything" or "TOE." Write your summary for an audience that has not heard of the "theory of everything."

On thin ice

Gordon Laird

(3,500 words)

It's February, minus 40. I'm on winter pack ice with Hans Aronsen, a hunter from Resolute Bay. It's too cold to talk—wind chill runs colder than minus 70—so all we can do is search off into the distance, the infinite white horizon of the High Arctic. And beneath our feet, the world's most northerly navigational route stretches from one side of the continent to the other. You can't tell through the snowdrifts and choppy ice, but we're standing on the legendary Northwest Passage, the world's last great unconquered shipping lane.

This is the netherworld of Canada's cryosphere—a huge constellation of glaciers, sea ice, and permafrost. It is a massive, three-season span that usually travels from the North Pole, through Canada's High Arctic Islands and across the Northwest Passage towards the edge of the continent. Lately, however, this frozen wasteland has been shrinking. Between 1978 and 2000, 1.2 million square kilometres of ice disappeared. That's an area roughly five times the size of Great Britain—and includes significant losses from the Beaufort Sea of Canada's western Arctic. Ice levels in many locales continue to run below average. In 2002 the US-based National Snow and Ice Data Center reported that summertime Arctic sea ice had reached its absolute lowest extent since the 1950s, possibly its lowest extent in several centuries. Last year NASA's Goddard Center estimated that the summertime polar cap—the permanent ice that surrounds the North Pole—could be gone by the end of the century. And by September 2003, a team of international scientists announced that the largest ice shelf in the Arctic—a seabound glacier

some 443 square kilometres in size—had fractured from the north coast of Ellesmere Island. Now floating in two pieces, this 3,000-year-old ice mass is expected to disintegrate. "We've never seen fractures like this," lamented one University of Alaska scientist in an interview with the BBC.

Southerners, even those who care nothing for the Arctic, should be concerned. About 14 to 16 million square kilometres of ice cover the Arctic in late winter. This frozen mass helps to anchor the climate of the northern hemisphere, insulating the ocean from the relentless warming rays of the sun. Once polar ice is weakened or melted completely, no one can say for sure what happens next, except that global climatic systems would be irrevocably, possibly radically, changed.

As the superhighway through our kingdom of ice, the Northwest Passage is now taking on profound commercial, environmental, and geopolitical significance. The passage was first trumpeted to European powers as the fabled shortcut to Asian spices and riches, and imperial powers have tried to commercially navigate the sea route for centuries. Until Roald Amundsen's three-year crossing in 1906, they failed, usually with tragic consequences. Now that some scientists predict an ice-free shipping lane could open up as early as 2015, the Northwest Passage will become a major prize in a world that's come to depend on global transport. An ice-free passage would save about eight days over existing Pacific-Atlantic routes, offer more protection from open-ocean storms, and even accommodate supertankers too large for the Central American canal. As a corporate-Aboriginal partnership prepares to build a new natural gas pipeline down the Mackenzie River from Canada's western Arctic, the Canadian North is opening up for resource plays that would have been unheard of a decade ago. Canada's Arctic contains roughly 40 per cent of all this country's oil and gas resources. Tomorrow's explorers will probably waste little time pushing across an ice-free Northwest Passage into the High Arctic, our continent's final frontier of onshore oil and gas reserves.

Between climate change, the accelerated shipping trade of a globalized world, and the incessant thirst for new energy sources, Canada's frozen hinterlands will experience change that is unprecedented in living memory. And yet Canada continues to display a curious ambivalence about its northern land mass—and a waning commitment to Arctic science, policy, and governance. Canada's weakened position in its own North is perhaps most vividly illustrated by the fact that Americans currently lead in Arctic research—even within Canadian territory.

What's at stake here, besides the environmental security of the hemisphere, is Canada's own fate as our North becomes the site of scientific quandaries, social change, and outright power plays over strategic territory and natural resources. Quite simply, our northern hinterlands are a portal to the future, a tomorrow-land of epic and troubling proportions.

Canada's incomplete efforts to conquer the Arctic are well remembered in Resolute Bay. Resolute and the even more northerly settlement of Grise Fiord were summarily created by the federal government in the 1950s—in reaction to the American Arctic push during the Cold War —and involuntarily populated by Inuit from communities on Baffin Island and beyond.

In Resolute, descendents of the High Arctic transfer recall happy days in camps near Pond Inlet or Igloolik, back when life was simple and free of bureaucrats. They also remember reliable seasons and steady flows of ice. "There are elders who remember seeing open sea ice once in a blue moon," says Guy D'Argencourt of the Nunavut Research Institute in Iqaluit. "But others are finding that their hunting time on the ice is getting shorter. They're very worried. The ice sets in later and breaks up earlier."

Echoing the concerns and observations of many Inuit, some scientists have even predicted an accelerated summer ice melt—and estimate that polar ice could disappear completely as early as 2050. "Considering the amount of area the polar ice cap has, it's an impressive scenario," says D'Argencourt. "Ice traffic through the passage and islands of the High Arctic has been highly variable, partially because of climatic extremes and partially because ice is clearing out of the polar cap and flushing south. So sometimes there's more ice, though not the multi-year floes that began to disappear during the late 1990s."

While the broken ice landscape of the High Arctic sometimes seems like a distant world, if the US Office of Naval Research is correct, commercial traffic could be pulling into Resolute Bay as early as 2015. Its 2002 report, "Naval operations in an ice-free Arctic," explores scenarios based on increased accessibility of Arctic waters. While the paper, declassified last December, concludes that the US Navy must rely on bilateral and multinational alliances, especially with Canada and Russia, the findings nevertheless advocate greater naval operations in the area and the creation of a new class of warships to patrol Arctic passages. The report foresees "increased economic activity with increased associated environmental protection activities. This includes both access to the region to exploit the natural resources available and access through the region to save transit time."

Ominously, it notes "potential adversaries [could] exploit the waters of the Arctic in ways that are counter to our national security."

This is particularly alarming when you consider that Canada's Arctic sovereignty question is officially unresolved, not only for shipping in the Northwest Passage but for potentially lucrative offshore oil and gas deposits in the Beaufort and currently inaccessible offshore plays that straddle the continental shelf between Russia, Canada, and Alaska. The likelihood of multilateral disputes is high: Russia and Canada claim that their northern sea routes are sovereign, while the US maintains that the waters are international.

The US Embassy in Ottawa claims that the two nations have only "agreed to disagree" on Canadian dominion in its Arctic. In other words, the whole notion of sovereignty in the Arctic is on thin ice, along with criminal laws, accountable jurisdictions, and environmental regulatory regimes common to good government. The threat, apart from illegal fishing, tourist traffic, and lawless vessels, is the sort of rule-by-force foreign policy that would see major powers jostling icebreakers in contested waters. It may not be long until American interests push northward, this time in the name of anti-terrorism, national security, or anti-drug operations.

"What a navigable Arctic means for our national security is significant," said Dennis Conlon, Arctic science program manager at the US Office of Naval Research, when the report was declassified. "Geographical boundaries, politics, and commerce changes would all become issues."

Although Americans pioneered supertanker travel in the Canadian Arctic, countries like Russia and Japan are also beginning to position themselves on the assumption that Canada, voluntarily or not, will host shipping traffic within the next few decades.

"Japan has shown considerable interest in Arctic navigation in the 1990s," reports Rob Huebert, associate director for the Centre for Military and Strategic Studies at the University of Calgary. "It was a major partner in a multi-year million-dollar study of navigation through the Russian Northern Sea Route. . . . The Japanese also were interested in buying the Canadian ice-strengthened oil tanker, *Arctic*, when the Canadian government put it up for sale. Perhaps even more telling is the amount of money that the Japanese put into polar research and development that is now substantial and continues to increase. While the Japanese have never issued a statement of their view of the status of the Northwest Passage, it is clear that they would gain if it became a functioning international strait. Oil from both Venezuela and the Gulf of Mexico would then be cheaper to ship to Japan."

Sovereignty, energy, shipping, and Arctic research are becoming inextricable. "Remember how hard President Bush pushed for the opening of the caribou lands in Alaska," says Huebert. "Well, where would you go next if you wanted to open the North? The only logical geological area is Canada's Beaufort, north of the Mackenzie Delta. You can read the writing on the wall."

It's a long, long way from that forgotten day in September of 1985, when Joe Clark, then secretary of state for external affairs, proclaimed Canadian sovereignty in the Arctic. "It embraces land, sea, and ice," he said. "It extends without interruption to the seaward-facing coasts of the Arctic islands. These islands are joined and not divided by the waters between them. They are bridged for most of the year by ice. From time immemorial Canada's Inuit people have used and occupied the ice as they have used and occupied the land."

That was probably the last mention of a comprehensive policy on the Arctic. Since then, says Huebert, we've ducked the question. "The official government position is that we wish that it would just go away and leave us alone," he says. "But these issues are slowly percolating through the system. The Northwest Passage will move because of increased shipping technology, climate, and resource capabilities. And if we lose enough of these battles, it will impact the future."

Of the five vessels that sailed through the Northwest Passage in 2000, for example, only two requested permission. Although Canada appears to have stringent shipping rules for its northern waters, compliance has been voluntary.

No matter what happens, climate change and increased shipping traffic is expected to have drastic impact on locals. "If it's going to be warmer, there will be room to pass a ship through without an icebreaker; the ice isn't setting frozen solid like before," says Guy D'Argencourt. "You're going to have communities—Pond Inlet, Arctic Bay, Resolute—exposed to international traffic. If they're going out hunting seal or narwhal and they see this big ship passing through, they're going to be concerned. Industrial shipping poses problems in environmentally sensitive communities. Lichen takes 100 years to grow in some places. Continuous traffic, that's a real issue."

And if Canada continues to muddle along on its Northwest Passage file, some Inuit organizations will simply bypass the federal government. "You'll see Nunavut and Inuit organizations heading to the United Nations," says D'Argencourt. "It'll be an interesting debate: US, France, Russia, and China—that's who has the most interest in shipping. Could be a long fight."

Some 600 metres above the pack ice near the very western edge of Ellesmere Island, a green laser searches the sky, collecting data on atmospheric chemistry, temperature trends, the position and intensity of the mysterious swirl of winds that cloak the polar cap. This is Canada's Astrolab, a high-tech launch pad for atmospheric science, known the world over for its extreme and valuable location.

At Astrolab, there is little chance of unwelcome guests or unannounced supertankers. Located 15 kilometres up a mountainside from Canada's weather station at Eureka, Astrolab is an outpost at the most northerly civilian weather station in the world. By all appearances, there seems to be no immediate threat to Canada's sovereignty around here: it's too cold, dark, and inaccessible. It's a chilly three-hour flight north from Resolute, across broken ice of the Northwest Passage, across land-fast ice and glacier of countless islands and sea passages, north even of the magnetic pole to the lonesome runway lights and metal boxes of Eureka. If minus 50 winters don't scare invaders off, summertime polar bears and boat-crushing sea ice probably will. Yet people here still talk about how the mummified forest replete with 45-million-year-old logs on Axel Heiberg Island, only a few kilometres away, was briefly taken over by an American crew in 1999. It sparked an international research battle, even as the American team systematically excavated the site and removed samples, aided by generous research budgets that afforded High Arctic base camps and helicopter travel.

In fact, foreign countries now dominate the scientific study of the Canadian Arctic. The major scientific sources on Canada's Arctic are often American—NASA, the National Oceanic and Atmospheric Association, the American Geophysical Union. Back at the weather station, budget cuts are old news: a *Globe and Mail* clipping is posted on Eureka's dining room noteboard with the following statistics twice underlined: Australia spends $2.30 per capita on Antarctic research, and the US spends $3 on Arctic science. Canada spends just 20 cents per citizen.

Canada's underfunding of Arctic research has become notorious in international circles. In Resolute and Tuktoyaktuk, Canada's Polar Continental Shelf Project, outfitter and clearinghouse for Arctic researchers, has been mostly closed in recent years. The Northern Contaminant Program, an important network of researchers who study the effect of long-distance toxins on the Arctic and Aboriginal peoples, was eliminated in 2002, although some of its projects have since found a home elsewhere. And despite broad international interest in Arctic atmosphere and ozone science, several months after my 2001 visit, Astrolab was mothballed.

The Astrolab closure was just one in a series of Arctic station and base closures since 1978. "Canadian research took a huge plunge in the 1980s," explains Kevin O'Reilly, director of research at the Canadian Arctic Resources Committee. "There have been relatively weak efforts to restore the funding, but some of the long-term research and monitoring that would assist us, we don't do anymore."

During the Mulroney era, research budgets were slashed, health and housing declined, remote outposts scaled back operations. Single initiatives like the Astrolab and the more recent creation of Nunavut were watershed moments, but the overall pattern had become clear: politicians seemed unwilling or unable to invest in a politically marginal territory.

Canadians may not realize it, but for decades we have neglected some of the biggest scientific puzzles of the twenty-first century. New, uncertain climatic cycles have manifested profoundly in Canada's Arctic. Robins can be found on Baffin Island, and ice-free waters vex Inuit hunters and elders. This zone of change is also experiencing anomalous weather events that aren't easily explained by climate science or any other science. The Arctic isn't simply warming or melting: sometimes there's too much ice, other times it's too cold, or bouts of strange weather confound observers. This past summer, irregular ice floes clogged the Northwest Passage, with some of the thickest ice seen this decade, according to the Canadian Coast Guard. Yet other parts of the circumpolar Arctic, such as Norway and Finland, reported some of the warmest weather in living memory during the summer of 2003.

The only thing that can help us parse freak occurrences from long-term trends is committed scientific study. "Trends in climate data must be carefully assessed," says Bea Alt, a long-time Arctic climatologist and independent researcher with Balanced Environment Associates. "Average trends from short station records may be misleading as a means for extrapolating to the future. Records for 100 years from the western Arctic show cycles in mean annual temperatures lasting for decades, whereas records for only the most recent 50 years tend to show only an increasing temperature trend."

While the western Arctic, especially the Mackenzie Delta, is heating up rather rapidly, Canada's eastern Arctic is considerably less consistent, with perplexing temperature variability running up and down the east coast of Baffin Island. A small part of Canada's Arctic is actually cooling. South Baffin Island, in particular, has cooled slightly in recent years despite anecdotal reports of warming. Canada's Arctic is both warming and cooling, for a whole host of possible reasons, including potential climatic dynamics that have been linked to atmospheric chain reactions as far east as Turkey.

These and other anomalies witnessed by hunters and elders are likely important clues to a global puzzle. "What the paleo-climatic record tells us is that Earth's climate system is capable of jumping from one mode of operation to another," wrote Columbia University climatologist Wally Brocker in 1999. "These modes are self-sustaining and involve major differences in mean global temperature, in rainfall pattern, and in atmospheric dustiness. In my estimation, we lack even a first-order explanation as to how the various elements of the Earth system interact to generate these alternate modes." In other words, Arctic ice has a message for us: climate change can happen swiftly and with relatively little warning. Change is non-linear and often appears within the chaos of contradictory trends.

The bottom line is that the more we know about the Arctic, the more we understand climate change. The connection between the Arctic atmosphere and ice cover has become a crucial question. For example: the damaged ozone layer from the upper atmosphere, the very target of the Astrolab's green laser, appears to be exacerbating climate change. Increased radiation from depleted ozone helps to warm an Earth that is, according to scientific consensus, retaining more terrestrial radiation than ever before.

The Astrolab was originally built to monitor the progress of the ozone layer, yet as science on the issue evolves, Canada can't keep up. As of 2000, for example, Canada's Natural Sciences and Research Council spent only $3 million, compared to $463 million spent by the US on its polar research.

What this means, apart from flimsy equipment and no-frills facilities in Arctic extremes, is that the depth of our science is sometimes lacking. Distant and remote data collection, such as relying on satellites for ozone layer monitoring or pack ice dynamics—as opposed to field deployment and hands-on science—is ultimately limiting.

As we sat in the sparse kitchen of the Astrolab's super-insulated steel hull, Yukio Makino, an eminent Japanese stratospheric scientist, explained the importance of dedicated fieldwork. During a long stay in the Antarctic, he noticed a profound difference between remote and hands-on polar science. "In the Antarctic, we received satellite images, but we always observe patterns ourselves—we could feel actual weather—and could see how the weather changed," he says, as blue twilight breaks across

the mountain slope outside. "But the person working back in Japan could never know it. On the ground we are thinking about changes, but with remote database collection many important aspects are dropped. It's our reason to be here."

Between sovereignty questions, natural resources quandaries, and natural phenomena we can't yet explain, even our best scientists are at a loss on the future. "The issues raised in the Arctic are huge," says Louis Fortier, the head of Canada's new science network, ArcticNet. "We need multidisciplinary science, big science, in the Arctic—and it's been small until now." As Fortier puts it, the most troubling questions in the Arctic—and by default those of global warming—are ones that demand an expanded frame of reference: there is no single correct explanation, just as there's no single remedy to the complex and interconnected dynamics of climate change. Piecemeal scientific efforts just won't cut it anymore.

In an effort to redeem nearly two decades of neglect, Canada launched a $66-million Arctic research program last April. While it doesn't nearly replace the lost funding and programs, ArcticNet is nevertheless tackling the great mysteries of Arctic ice, outfitted with a $27-million grant for a new icebreaker, the *Amundsen*, with science labs and hardware. With about 250 researchers from 11 different countries, the icebreaker will deploy ultramodern scientific gear until late 2004 to interpret the full annual cycle of the Beaufort Sea and Mackenzie Delta ecosystem—something that's never been done before.

It probably doesn't hurt that the *Amundsen* will also patrol some of the Arctic's most contested waters at the western mouth of the Northwest Passage, circling the resource-rich Beaufort and Mackenzie, possibly edging along the disputed offshore drilling properties near the Alaskan coast.

Fortier admits that research is inextricable from ongoing sovereignty concerns. "If there is a scientific presence, it's as good as a military presence," he says. "We hope in the next two years to become the leading supplier of Arctic research in Canada," adding "for the first time ever, we will examine the complete annual cycle of the Arctic Ocean."

It won't come too soon because Arctic ice, like other natural resources in the twenty-first century, is becoming scarce, strategic, and unpredictable. And if we're lucky, we'll grasp its significance before it's gone.

This Magazine. 2003. November/December.

KEY AND DIFFICULT WORDS
Define the following, using context or other clues if possible: **netherworld, cryosphere, ambivalence, declassify, sovereignty.**

QUESTIONS
1. What is the significance of the essay's brief title?
2. Do you believe that the author successfully attracts and maintains reader interest in the first two paragraphs? Do you think that his use of experts/authorities and of facts and figures makes the introduction more or less effective?
3. According to the author, why is an ice-free Northwest Passage important for countries like the US, Russia, and Japan? Why should it be an important concern to Canada?
4. Explain the importance of the recently declassified US report, "Naval operations in an ice-free Arctic." Why, in particular, does Laird find one of its conclusions "alarming" (paragraph 12)?
5. (a) In his essay, Laird uses many different kinds of sources, including those from the scientific, government, and academic communities. Identify at least one example of each and explain its importance to the essay. (b) Laird's sources are often quoted directly. Why do you think he uses so many direct quotations rather than summary or paraphrase?
6. Do you think Laird is more concerned with explaining or arguing? Support your answer by referring to specific statements and the language he uses.
7. Summarize the paragraphs in which the author considers how studying the Arctic can enable us to find out more about climate change (29–36).
8. In his conclusion, do you think that Laird is primarily concerned with summarizing and reinforcing his points (circular conclusion) or with leading beyond it to consider related issues (spiral conclusion)? Analyze the effectiveness of his conclusion.

ACTIVITIES

1. Like most works of investigative journalism, this essay, Marla Cone's "Dozens of words for snow, none for pollution," and Matthew Power's "The poison stream" are written to bring to public attention a little-known problem or issue. Write a 500- to 600-word critical analysis focusing on "On thin ice" and "Dozens of words for snow, none for pollution," comparing the ways they bring forward a problem that has been under-reported in the media.

2. Using at least two reliable sources, write a 400- to 500-word summary of the High Arctic relocation in mid-1950s, including the reasons given for this enforced resettlement and its consequences for the Inuit families involved. (Laird refers to the transfer in paragraphs 7–8; Matt James, in "Being stigmatized and being sorry," also cites this government action as one for which monetary reparation was made.)

Related readings: Kevin Krajick. "In search of the ivory gull"; Marla Cone. "Dozens of words for snow, none for pollution"; and Furgal and Seguin. "Climate change, health, and vulnerability in Canadian northern Aboriginal communities."

Dozens of words for snow, none for pollution

Marla Cone

(3,800 words)

On a sheet of ice where the Arctic Ocean meets the North Atlantic in the territorial waters of Greenland, Mamarut Kristiansen kneels beside the carcass of a narwhal, the elusive animal sometimes known as "the unicorn of the sea" for its spiralled ivory tusk. He slices off a piece of *mattak*, the whale's raw pink blubber and mottled gray skin, and bites into it. "*Peqqinnartoq*," he says in Greenlandic. Healthy food. Nearby, Mamarut's wife, Tukummeq Peary, a descendant of North Pole explorer Robert Peary, is boiling the main entrée on a camp stove. She, Mamarut, and his brother Gedion dip their hunting knives into the kettle and pull out steaming fibs of ringed seal.

From their home in Qaanaaq, a village in Greenland's Thule region, the Kristiansens have travelled here, to the edge of the world, by dog sledge. It took six hours to journey the 30 miles across a rugged glacier to this sapphire-hued fjord, where every summer they camp on the precarious ice awaiting their prey. The family lives much as their ancestors did thousands of years ago, relying on the bounty of the sea and skills honed by generations. Their lifestyle isn't quaint; it is a necessity in this hostile and isolated expanse. Survival here, in the northernmost civilization on earth, means living the way marine mammals live, hunting as they do, wearing their skins. No factory-engineered fleece compares to the warmth of a sealskin parka. No motorboat can sneak up on a whale like a handmade kayak lashed together with strips of hide. And no imported food nourishes the people's bodies and warms their spirits like the meat they slice from the flanks of a whale or seal.

Traditionally, this marine diet has made the people of the Arctic Circle among the world's healthiest. Beluga whale, for example, has 10 times the iron of beef, twice the protein, and five times the vitamin A. Omega-3 fatty acids in the seafood protect the indigenous people from heart disease. A 70-year-old Inuit in Greenland has coronary arteries as elastic as those of a 20-year-old Dane eating Western foods, says Dr. Gert Mulvad of the Primary Health Care Clinic in Nuuk, Greenland's capital. Some Arctic clinics do not even keep heart medications like nitroglycerin in stock. Although heart disease has appeared with the introduction of Western foods, it remains "more or less unknown," Mulvad says.

Yet the ocean diet that gives these people life and defines their culture also threatens them. Despite living amid pristine ice and glacier-carved bedrock, people like Mamarut, Tukummeq, and Gedion are more vulnerable to pollution than anyone else on earth. Mercury concentrations in Qaanaaq mothers are the highest ever recorded, 12 times greater than the level that poses neurological risks to fetuses, according to US government standards. A separate study has linked PCBs with slight effects on the intelligence of children in Qaanaaq. Although most of the village's people never leave their hunting grounds, the world travels to them, riding upon wintry winds.

The Arctic has been transformed into the planet's chemical trash can, the final destination for toxic waste that originates thousands of miles away. Atmospheric and oceanic currents conspire to send industrial chemicals, pesticides, and power-plant emissions on a journey to the Far North. Many airborne chemicals tend to migrate to, and precipitate in, cold climates, where they then endure for decades, perhaps centuries, slow to break down in the frigid temperatures and low sunlight. The Arctic Ocean is a deep-freeze archive, holding the memories of the world's past and present mistakes. Its wildlife, too, are archives, as poisonous chemicals accumulate in the fat that Arctic animals need to survive. Polar bears denning in Norway and Russia near the North Pole carry some of the highest levels of toxic compounds ever found in living animals.

Perched at the top of the Arctic food chain, eating a diet similar to a polar bear's, the Inuit also play unwilling host to some 200 toxic pesticides and industrial compounds. These include all of the "Dirty Dozen"—the 12 pollutants capable of inflicting the most damage—including PCBs and chlorinated pesticides such as chlordane, toxaphene, and DDT, long banned in most of North America and Europe. Other compounds still in use today—flame retardants in furniture and computers, insecticides, and the chemicals used to make Teflon—are growing in concentration as well.

The first evidence of alarming levels of toxic substances in the bodies of Arctic peoples came from the Canadian Inuit. In 1987 Dr. Eric Dewailly, an epidemiologist at Laval University in Quebec, was surveying contaminants in the breast milk of mothers near the industrialized, heavily polluted Gulf of St. Lawrence, when he met a midwife from Nunavik, the Inuit area of Arctic Quebec. (Across the Hudson Bay, the Inuit also have their own self-governing territory, Nunavut, or "our land.") She asked whether he wanted milk samples from Nunavik women. Dewailly reluctantly agreed, thinking they might be useful as "blanks," samples with non-detectable pollution levels.

A few months later, glass vials holding half a cup of milk from each of 24 Nunavik women arrived. Dewailly soon got a phone call from his lab director. Something was wrong with the Arctic milk. The chemical concentrations were off the charts. The peaks overloaded the lab's equipment, running off the page. The technician thought the samples must have been tainted in transit.

Upon testing more breast milk, however, the scientists realized that the readings were accurate: Arctic mothers had seven times more PCBs in their milk than mothers in Canada's biggest cities. Informed of the results, an expert in chemical safety at the World Health Organization told Dewailly that the PCB levels were the highest he had ever seen. Those women, he said, should stop breastfeeding their babies.

Dewailly hung up the phone. "Breast milk is supposed to be a gift," he says. "It isn't supposed to be a poison." And in a place as remote as Nunavik, he knew that mothers often had nothing else to feed their infants. Nearly 18 years have passed since Dewailly tested those first vials of breast milk; subsequent data has emerged to show that people, especially babies, are exposed to dangerous concentrations of contaminants all across the Arctic. The average levels of PCBs and mercury in newborn babies' cord blood and women's breast milk are a staggering 20 to 50 times higher in Greenland than in urban areas of the United States and Europe, according to a 2002 report from the Arctic Monitoring and Assessment Programme (AMAP), a project created by eight governments including the United States. Ninety-five per cent of women tested in eastern Greenland, nearly 75 per cent of women in Arctic Canada's Baffin Island, and nearly 60 per cent in Nunavik exceed Canada's "level of concern" for PCBs. Fewer measurements have been taken in Siberia, but the AMAP says contamination levels are high there as well.

In addition to their potential to cause cancer, many of the compounds found in Arctic inhabitants are capable of altering sex hormones and reproductive systems, suppressing immune systems, and obstructing brain development. Infants are the most vulnerable—subject to exposure both in utero and through breast milk, because contaminants such as PCB and DDT accumulate in the fatty nourishment—and are harmed in subtle but profound ways. Arctic babies with high PCB and DDT exposure suffer greater rates of infectious diseases. A study of such infants in Nunavik found that they have more ear and respiratory infections, a quarter of them severe enough to cause hearing loss. "Nunavik has a cluster of sick babies," says Dewailly. "They fill the waiting rooms of the clinics."

A 2003 study found that, compared to infants in lower Quebec, Nunavik infants had much higher exposure to PCBs, mercury, and lead, which resulted in lower birth weight, impaired memory skills, and difficulty in processing new information.

Excessive levels of contamination are not limited to the Arctic. People throughout the world, especially those in seafood-eating cultures, are at similar risk. In the United States, one of every six babies—about 698,000 a year—is born to a mother carrying more mercury in her body than is considered safe under federal guidelines.

The difference is that Americans and Europeans can make choices in their diets to limit their exposure, avoiding fish such as swordfish that are high on the food chain or from highly contaminated waters. For the 650,000 native people of the circumpolar North—the Inuit of Greenland and Canada, the Aleuts, Yup'ik, and Inupiat of Alaska, the Chukchi and other tribes of Siberia, the Saami of Scandinavia and western Russia—there is no real choice. Spread over three continents and speaking dozens of languages, almost all of them face the same dilemma: whether to eat traditional food and face the health risk—or abandon their food and with it their culture.

"Our foods do more than nourish our bodies," Inuit rights activist Ingmar Egede said. "When many things in our lives are changing, our foods remain the same. They make us feel the same as they have for generations. When I eat Inuit foods, I know who I am."

Known to navigators as the North Water, the ocean off Qaanaaq is a polynya, a spot that remains thawed year-round in an otherwise frozen sea. An upwelling of nutrients draws an array of marine life, and the Kristiansens and the other people of Qaanaaq, an isolated village of 860 on the slope of a granite mountain, come here to hunt seal, beluga, walrus, narwhal, even polar bear. A century ago, the famous Arctic explorers—Peary, Frederick Cook, Knud Rasmussen—learned on their expeditions through the area that eating Inuit food was key to survival.

Greenland has no trees, no grass, no fertile soil, which means no cows, no pigs, no chickens, no grains, no vegetables, no fruit. In fact, there is little need for the word "green" in Greenland. The ocean is its food basket. In the remote villages, people eat marine mammals and seabirds 36 times per month on average, consuming about a pound of seal and whale each week. One-third of their food is the meat of wild animals. The International Whaling Commission has deemed the Inuit "the most hunting-oriented of all humans." Greenland is an independently governed territory of Denmark, but 85 per cent—or 48,000—of its people are Inuit, and hunting is essential to everything in their 4,000-year-old culture: their language, their art, their clothing, their legends, their celebrations, their community ties, their economy, their spirituality.

Today, the Kristiansens are gathered on the edge of the ice, waiting to spot a whale's breath. "If only we could see one, we'd be happy," Mamarut whispers, lifting binoculars and eyeing the mirror-like water for the pale gray back of *qilalugaq*, or narwhal. "Sometimes they arrive at a certain hour of the day and then the next day, same hour, they come back."

Once, Gedion and Mamarut waited almost a month on the ice before catching a narwhal. During such vigils, hunters must remain alert for cracks or other signs that the ice beneath them is shifting. In an instant, it can break off and carry them out to sea. To Greenlanders, ice is everything—it's danger, it's the source of dinner, it's the water they drink. Their language has several dozen expressions for ice, only one for tree.

Mamarut is big, bawdy, and beefy, the elder brother and joker of the family. He celebrated his 42nd birthday on this hunting trip. Gedion is 10 years younger, lanky, quiet, the expert kayaker, wearing a National Geographic cap. The Kristiansen brothers are among the best hunters in a nation of hunters, able to sustain their families without the help of other jobs for their wives or themselves. In a good year, they can eat their fill of whale meat and earn more than $15,000 a year selling the rest to markets. In winter, they sell sealskins to a Greenlandic company marketing them in Europe. The men's hair is black, thick, and straight, cut short. Their skin is darkened by the sun, but they have no wrinkles. Their only shelter on the ice is a canvas tarp attached to their dog sledge, a makeshift tent so cramped that one person can't bend a knee or straighten an elbow without disturbing the others. A noxious oil-burning lamp is their only source of heat; the kitchen is a camp stove, used to melt ice for tea and to boil seal meat.

Hunting narwhal is a dangerous endeavour. When Gedion hears or sees them coming, he quietly climbs into his kayak with his harpoon and sealskin buoy. He must simultaneously judge the ice conditions, the current, the wind, the speed and direction of the whales. If a kayaker makes the slightest noise, a narwhal will hear it. If he throws the harpoon, the whale must be directly in front of his kayak, about 30 feet away, close but not too close—or the animal's powerful dive will submerge him and he will likely drown. Gedion, like most Greenlanders, can't swim. There's not much need to master swimming when one can't survive more than a few moments in the frigid water.

Pollution isn't the first force to disrupt local Inuit culture. A little more than a century ago, the people of Qaanaaq didn't have a written language and had scant contact with the Western world. In the 1950s, during the Cold War, their entire community was moved 70 miles to the north to make way for an American military base. The US and Danish governments built the villagers contemporary prefabricated houses—small red, green, blue, and purple chalets. Qaanaaq's population has since doubled, with people attracted by the good hunting. The move also brought liquor, television, and other distractions of modern life. Alcoholism, violence, domestic abuse, and suicide now exact a heavy toll.

Today, the people of Qaanaaq can smear imported taco sauce on their seal meat, buy dental floss and Danish porn magazines in the small local market, and watch *Nightmare on Elm Street* and *Altered States* in their living rooms on the one TV station that beams into Qaanaaq. When asked how he catches a whale, Gedion jokes that he uses a lasso like American cowboys he's seen on television.

Whatever is not hunted—from tea to bread to cheese—is imported from Denmark. Imported food is expensive, often stale, and not very tasty or nutritious. The average family income is $24,000 in Greenland's capital Nuuk, $13,000 in Qaanaaq, and though food is government-subsidized, the price of staples like milk, bread, and beef is still considerably higher than in the United States.

And so Greenland's public health officials are torn between encouraging the Inuit to keep eating their traditional foods and advising them to reduce their consumption. In part, doctors fear the Inuit will switch to processed foods loaded with carbohydrates and sugar. "The level of contamination is very high in Greenland, but there's a lot of Western food that is worse than the poisons," Dr. Mulvad says. Greenland's Home Rule government has issued no advisories, and doctors continue to tell people, even pregnant women, to eat traditional food and nurse their babies without restrictions. Jonathan Motzfeldt, who was Greenland's premier for almost 20 years and is now speaker of the Parliament, says hunting isn't sport for his people; it's survival, and the government will not discourage it. "We eat seal meat as you eat cow in your country," Motzfeldt says. "It's important for Greenlanders to have meat on the table. You don't see many vegetables in Greenland. We integrate imported foods, but hunting and eating seals as well as whales is essential for us to survive as a people."

Across the Baffin Bay, surveys show most Canadian Inuit have not altered their diet either. This is partly the result of a clash of cultures. Inuktitut, the language of Canadian Inuit, has some 50 expressions for snow and ice. *Qanniq* is falling snow. *Maujaq* is deep, soft snow. *Kinirtaq* is wet, compact snow. *Katakartanaq* is crusty snow marked by footsteps. *Uangniut* is a snowdrift made by a northwest wind. *Munnguqtuq* is compressed snow softening in spring. Yet there is no Inuktitut word for "chemical" or "pollution" or "contaminant." Over the millennia that their culture has existed, the Inuit have had no need for such words. Most have never seen soot spew from a factory smokestack, or smelled the stench of truck exhaust, or waded in an oily river. So Canadian health officials have dubbed the toxic chemicals found in native foods *sukkunartuq*—something that destroys or brings about something bad. But use of the word has made the contaminants seem lethal and mysterious, even supernatural, and that—combined with a history of government secrecy and poor communication about health risks—has left the Inuit confused, scared, and sometimes angry.

In 1985, Canadian health officials, concerned that an Arctic radar warning system might be a source of PCBs, decided to study the people of Broughton Island, a tiny hamlet in the Baffin Bay region. Government researchers, led by Dr. David Kinloch, collected blood samples and breast milk. The PCB levels were so high— much higher than what could have come from local military facilities—that the mayor of Broughton Island granted Kinloch permission to test more women. Completed in the summer of 1988, the research confirmed high concentrations of PCBs in breast milk at about the same time that Quebec's Dewailly was finding extraordinary levels of DDT, PCBs, and other toxic chemicals in the women of Nunavik. Before any of this data could be fully analyzed, and before people were notified, the discovery was leaked to the press.

On 15 December 1988, Toronto's *Globe and Mail* published a front-page story, quoting a Canadian environmental official saying that the Inuit were so contaminated that they might have to give up whale, seal, and walrus. The Inuit were terrified; some stopped eating their native foods or breastfeeding. Overnight, Arctic contaminants became a crisis for the Canadian government. Health Canada, the nation's public health agency, was paralyzed with indecision. The Nunavik and Baffin data clearly showed that most Inuit were exceeding the agency's "tolerable daily intake levels" for toxic contaminants. If the agency was to adhere to its own policies, it would have to warn the Inuit to stop eating their traditional foods. But public health officials had never encountered a problem like this before,

where the contaminated foods were so vital to a society's health, culture, and economy. On the one hand, it seemed irresponsible to advise people not to nurse their babies and eat their foods when the traditional diet had so many health benefits and alternatives were unavailable. On the other hand, if the government ignored its own toxic guidelines when it came to the Inuit, wouldn't that be discriminatory?

Crisis meetings were held in Ottawa; Aboriginal leaders begged to be included, but none were allowed to participate. It wasn't until the spring of 1989, more than a year later, that the Broughton Islanders who'd given their blood and breast milk to scientists were allowed to see the results of their own tests. It was a slap in the face that Canada's indigenous people have not forgotten.

A wide chasm has since grown between what scientists say and what native people hear, and health officials have failed to refine their message to resonate with the traditional cultures of the Arctic. As a result, at least three generations of Inuit have had little or no advice from experts on how to reduce their exposure. In the late 1990s, 42 per cent of women questioned in Nunavik said they increased their consumption of traditional foods while pregnant. Of the 12 per cent who ate less, only one of 135 said she did so to avoid contaminants. Among those who ate more native foods during pregnancy, most said they did so because they believed it would be good for their baby.

Inuit Tapiriit Kanatami, an organization that represents the Canadian Inuit, launched a project in the mid-1990s to gauge the success of authorities' efforts to inform nine Arctic communities about contaminants. The researchers found the communication so poorly handled that it caused extreme psychological distress among the Inuit. Fear, they concluded, is as dangerous a threat as the contaminants themselves.

"In every instance, there was a pervasive unease and anxiety about contaminants," the organization wrote in its 1995 report. "Whether or not individuals are exposed to . . . contaminants, the threat alone leads to anxiety, loss of familiar and staple food, loss of employment or activity, loss of confidence in the basic food source and the environment, and more generally a loss of control over one's destiny and well-being."

Lately, health officials have been doing a better job at informing the Inuit of new data. And in 2003, the Nunavik Nutrition and Health Committee, based in Kuujjuaq and composed of Inuit leaders as well as Quebec medical experts, finally took a different tack, focusing on telling people what they should eat rather than what they should not eat. Women were advised to eat Arctic char, a tasty, popular fish that has low levels of contaminants and high amounts of beneficial fatty acids; a pilot program distributed free char to three communities. The hope is that if the Inuit eat more char they will eat less beluga, the source of two-thirds of the PCBs in Nunavik residents.

The Kristiansens, like their fellow residents of Qaanaaq, learned about the contaminants from listening to the radio. But like most Greenlandic Inuit, they have not changed their diet. Virtually every day, they eat seal meat and *mattak*, and with every bite, traces of mercury, PCBs, and other chemicals amass in their bodies. "We can't avoid them," Gedion says with a shrug. "It's our food."

This hunting trip proves to be a short one, only five days, and they reap little reward for their patience. "Sometimes you have to just go back empty-handed and feed your dogs," Mamarut says. Upon returning to their village, hunters share their experiences so that everyone may benefit from them. The Kristiansen brothers learned to hunt narwhal from their father, who in turn learned from his relatives. Gedion's seven-year-old son, Rasmus, often comes along on their hunts, pretending to drive the dogs and harpoon narwhals. Soon enough, he will be paddling a kayak beside his father. Since 2500 B.C., when the forebears of the Inuit arrived in Greenland, this legacy has been passed on to generations of boys by generations of men like Gedion and Mamarut. Their ancestors' memories, as vivid as a dream, as ancient as the sea ice, mingle with their own.

"*Qaatuppunga piniartarlunga*," Mamarut says. As far back as I can remember, I hunted.

Mother Jones. 2004. January/February.

KEY AND DIFFICULT WORDS
Define the following, using context or other clues if possible: **archives, contaminant, epidemiologist.**

QUESTIONS
1. Identify the thesis statement (claim) in the introduction. (a) How does the author prepare us for the claim? (b) Rewrite the introduction to make it conform to the conventional essay pattern, omitting detail and including an expanded thesis statement/claim at the end of the introduction.

2. Looking closely at paragraph 5, show how the author's careful use of diction, rhythm, and figurative language, such as metaphors, shape reader response. Also, comment on the placement of this paragraph between two paragraphs in which statistics are used.

3. Explore the author's use of comparisons, particularly between Inuit culture and European or American culture; consider their purpose and effectiveness.

4. Summarize in a brief paragraph how a "clash of cultures" was at least partly responsible for fear and confusion experienced by the Canadian Inuit after the discovery of high levels of PCBs in blood samples and breast milk. "Clash of cultures" can be considered a neutral phrase in that it does not attribute blame. Do you think that Cone uses it in order to encourage a neutral or objective stance in her readers?

5. Analyze Cone's use of human interest throughout the essay, focusing on her use of "vignettes"—short illustrative incidents or scenes.

6. Paraphrase the fourth-last paragraph, which updates the efforts of health officials to inform Canadian Inuit about diet options.

7. How would you characterize the tone of the essay? What was the author's purpose in adopting this tone?

COLLABORATIVE ACTIVITY

Based on the information in the essay and on any other media reports you have heard about, discuss what you would consider the greatest threat to the existence of the Inuit peoples: food contamination, loss of traditional life, failure in communication, Western apathy, or something else?

ACTIVITY

Using at least one reliable source, write a short biography of Arctic explorer Robert Peary, mentioned initially in the first paragraph of Cone's essay, naming your source(s); include a summary of the controversies that surround him and his attempts to reach the North Pole in 1909. *OR* Using at least one reliable source, write a short summary of mercury contamination, including its sources and known effects on the human body.

Related readings: Gordon Laird. "On thin ice"; Kevin Krajick. "In search of the ivory gull"; and Furgal and Seguin. "Climate change, health, and vulnerability in Canadian northern Aboriginal communities."

In search of the ivory gull

Kevin Krajick

(2,000 words)

For the last two summers, Grant Gilchrist has paid $1,000 per hour for a helicopter to take him into the realm of the ivory gull: the interiors of High Arctic islands circling the pole, where the glacial terrain is too harsh for any other creatures. Gilchrist, a biologist at the Canadian Wildlife Service (CWS) in Ottawa, sought the rare, nomadic ivories at sites where researchers once reported hundreds, but he spotted only cliffs stained orange from lichens nourished by the dung of gulls past. He saw no birds and no other sign of them, not even a broken eggshell. After his rare human venture into this territory, he concludes that the gulls' numbers in Canada have plummeted 90 per cent over the past 20 years.

Ivory gulls are the ultimate survivors: They are thought to hunt largely in the dark and eat almost anything, including other gulls and the blood of wounded polar bears, and they winter on the frozen seas while other birds head south. But they are already on the Canadian list of vulnerable species and are considered uncommon in the rest of the North. Now, the birds' worldwide status seems less certain than ever. Monitoring programs in Norway and Russia—where the largest population was once thought to reside—have fallen apart, and researchers there are worried too.

Some fear that the near disappearance is a warning that climate change or other human intrusion has upset Arctic ecosystems faster than previously thought. Others hold out hope that the gulls have simply fled to secret refugia. Gilchrist sees the gulls as a possible leading indicator of the health of Arctic ecosystems, yet, he says, "I can't think of a bird we know less about."

ALONE IN THE ARCTIC

Because of the remoteness and danger of the birds' haunts, literature on the ivory gull can be as much legend as science. Early Arctic mariners viewed the graceful, pure-white birds, weighing only half a kilogram, as phantoms that soared out of nowhere with disembodied cries, then melted away. Eventually, explorers found nesting colonies on inland cliffs and plains in Russia, Norway, and east Greenland, but the Canadian breeding sites remained largely a mystery right into the 1970s and 80s, when geologists newly equipped with helicopters spotted them. The birds were nesting on nunataks—sheer-cliffed islands of rock surrounded by vast glacial icefields—up to 50 kilometres inland from the frozen seas where they scavenge carrion and hunt fish and invertebrates through cracks in the ice. Biologists have since located other Canadian colonies amid polar deserts of jumbled rock fragments just as barren as the glaciers. These hideouts apparently offer chicks protection from predators such as bears and foxes, which can't make the long trek from the sea ice.

In the few years following these finds, a brief burst of research saw hundreds of the birds banded. The total world breeding population was estimated at about 30,000, with perhaps 5,000 in Canada, 20,000 on Russian islands including the archipelago of Franz Josef Land, and smaller populations in Norway and Greenland. But many Canadian colonies were never visited again after their discovery, and no one has ever set foot on the nunataks, says Gilchrist.

Then, in 2000, Canadian Inuit hunters told researchers that they no longer saw the birds at sea or at town garbage dumps. That was ominous news, given increasing evidence that thinning sea ice from a warming climate is stressing many Arctic marine creatures, from ice-dwelling algae to polar bears (*Science*, 19 January 2001, p. 424).

Gilchrist and his colleagues scraped together money to recheck the three dozen known Canadian colonies, and in July 2002 and 2003 they flew to the sites, dodging treacherous snow and fog and landing unexpectedly more than once when visibility was lost. This summer they also searched some 7,000 square kilometres of likely habitat by plane and helicopter, including sea-ice regions where gulls once foraged. Their colleagues interviewed sailors and hunters who might have seen the birds.

"All the sources tell the same story," says Mark Mallory, a CWS biologist in Iqaluit and Gilchrist's partner. The birds are gone almost everywhere. The researchers spotted a few previously unknown nest sites, but they averaged only a few birds each. Their new estimate of the Canadian population: 500 to 700. Their preliminary work appears in this month's *Arctic*; they plan to submit their latest results to *Biological Conservation*.

Researchers suspect long-term declines in other regions too, but Russian and Norwegian fieldwork largely stopped for lack of funds in the mid-1990s. The last Russian estimate of 10,000 breeding pairs was published in 1996, but it is probably too high, says Hallvard Strøm, a marine bird biologist at the Norwegian Polar Institute who has worked in the Russian Arctic. In a 1996 survey of known nesting sites in western Franz Josef Land, a major breeding region, he could not find a single extant colony. "Now,

we hope to get back out next year, partly because of what Grant has found," he says. The 1,000 or so birds nesting in east and north Greenland appear to be stable or increasing, says Olivier Gilg, chair of the non-profit Arctic Ecology Research Group in Dijon, France, which mounted an expedition this summer that banded some 270 birds. But, he says, "we don't know too much about the movements of these birds" and whether they are related to those in other countries.

SEEKING THE SMOKING GUN

With the gulls scarce or missing, researchers are scouring the North for clues to what has happened. Climate change would seem a prime suspect, but the links may be complicated, say Gilchrist and Mallory. Some bird species that nest at the lower edges of the ice pack, such as black guillemots, have indeed seen drastic declines in recent years, apparently because their food sources have moved or died out with the melting of the ice. But ivory gulls nest at such high latitudes that they still seem to have plenty of ice for summer hunting. Instead, the researchers think the problem may be at the gulls' wintering grounds, thought to include the waters between Greenland and Canada.

There, sea ice has actually increased in extent and concentration since the 1950s, due to changed winds and water currents and a regional temperature drop, says Mads Peter Heide-Jørgensen, a senior scientist at the Greenland Institute of Natural Resources. The gulls need a delicate balance of ice and open water to get at prey, so this near-total freeze-up may be starving them, says Heide-Jørgensen, who has a paper in review at *Ambio*. In the past few years, startled amateur birders have reported hundreds of ivory gulls in Newfoundland in winter, which suggests they could be displaced southward in search of food; in 1996 one lost and exhausted-looking specimen turned up near Los

Angeles, California—the most southerly sighting recorded.

Warming could be more directly spoiling the birds' splendid isolation. Unpublished work by glaciologists Roy Koerner of the Geological Survey of Canada in Ottawa and Martin Sharp of the University of Alberta in Edmonton shows that icecaps on the Canadian islands where the gulls nest have shrunk 15 to 20 per cent since the 1960s. Some icefields are now losing up to a metre in elevation per year, says NASA's director of cryosphere sciences, Waleed Abdalati, in a paper in review at the *Journal of Geophysical Research*. As a by-product, the rugged topography of the ice around some nunataks is smoothing out, making it easier for predators to walk there. Some nunataks are ceasing to be nunataks at all, as the ice around them disappears and they rejoin the coastal bedrock. And "one fox can take out a whole colony," points out Gilchrist.

Other possibilities involve more direct human disturbance. Although the birds are not known to nest in western Greenland, they pass through in fall and spring, where they are hunted by a fast-growing Inuit population armed with long-range boats and high-powered weapons. Heide-Jørgensen thinks that shooting is helping wipe out other birds, including common eiders, king eiders, and thick-billed murres. Indeed, says Tony Gaston, a CWS ornithologist in Hull, most recoveries of banded ivory gulls have come from west Greenland hunters.

Chemical contaminants carried long distances on winds are another suspect. Five gulls shot by researchers off Canada's Ellesmere Island in 1998 carried relatively high burdens of PCBs, pesticides, and lead, says Aaron Fisk, an ecotoxicologist at the University of Georgia in Athens. He doubts that the chemicals are enough to affect the population—other birds carry similar amounts without apparent harm—but admits that the gulls' habit of scavenging carcasses, blood, and dung puts them high on the food chain and probably magnifies the effect.

A more optimistic possibility is that the birds have simply gone elsewhere. "I would like to believe in some magic refugium, and that is possible," says Keith Hobson, a CWS ornithologist in Saskatoon. Ellesmere Island alone covers 213,000 square kilometres, with uncountable nunataks. And the observations of Gilchrist and others suggest that unlike most other colonial seabirds, ivories may not use the same colonies each year, perhaps to keep predators off their trail. Biologists have actually seen a few nesting on icebergs, the ultimate temporary rookeries. "It's hard to tell if the number is changing if they don't return to where they're supposed to," says population ecologist Robert Rockwell of the American Museum of Natural History in New York City, who studies Arctic seabirds.

However, most bird species that relocate don't go more than about 200 miles, asserts Camille Parmesan, a population biologist at the University of Texas, Austin. And Gilchrist believes that the gulls' predilection for the most barren possible habitat limits their options to surprisingly few places. After the extensive recent searches, "I don't think they're hiding anywhere," he says.

Douglas Causey, an ornithologist at the Harvard Museum of Comparative Zoology, says he has observed comparable crashes in the past 20 years—the same time frame as the ivories—in two species of cormorants in the Aleutian Islands. "It's astounding and unprecedented," he says. "I believe something is going on in the environment. We just don't know what it is yet."

Gilchrist and Mallory hope to continue their studies, but the challenges are daunting. Canada's Arctic research budget has dropped since the 1980s. And the work is dangerous: Helicopters, the only way in, are a leading cause of death among Arctic scientists. In 2000 two

Canadian wildlife experts were killed when their pilot lost his orientation in snow and fog and hit the ice in the same region where Gilchrist and Mallory work.

This summer Gilchrist managed to land by helicopter a kilometre from one small ivory gull colony on a great, rolling plain of broken-up limestone on Baffin Island. Even he, a polar-travel veteran, was shocked at the utter lifelessness of the place. He picked his way through razor-sharp cobbles and spent a couple of enchanted hours watching gulls from as close as eight metres. Unfortunately, they were not alone: Just four kilometres away was a fly-in team of geologists drilling for diamonds. As northern waters grow progressively more ice-free in the summer, industrial shipping and exploration for minerals and oil are growing—bad news for a species that seems to thrive on isolation. The South African De Beers Corp. and others have recently staked out huge positions, including at one coastal base camp on Baffin near where three ivory gull colonies used to exist. There, as elsewhere this year, the gulls were nowhere to be seen.

Science. 2003. 26 September 301.

KEY AND DIFFICULT WORDS

Define the following, using context or other clues if possible: **refugia, scavenge, carrion, forage, extant, ornithologist, rookery.**

QUESTIONS

1. What is the question being asked in the essay?
2. What makes the possible disappearance of the ivory gull particularly significant?
3. Summarize the difficulties of researchers in trying to keep track of the numbers of these birds.
4. What kinds of sources does Krajick use in his essay? Referring specifically to at least three sources, address the issue of source credibility.
5. Is there a "smoking gun" that would explain the failure to find evidence of the presence of the gulls in Canada's Arctic?
6. Which hypothesis(es) among the several mentioned in "Seeking the smoking gun" do you think the author believes is the most credible? Why?
7. What is the final possibility mentioned in the essay that might account for the gulls' disappearance?
8. "In search of the ivory gull" appeared in the academic journal *Science* as a "News focus." Is it more like a Type A academic essay, a Type B academic essay, or a journalistic essay? Why?

ACTIVITY

Using the latest information from the Committee on the Status of Endangered Wildlife in Canada (COSEWIC) website or Environment Canada's Species at Risk website, write a brief (100- to 200-word) report on the most recent status of the ivory gull. Ensure that you include the reason for its current designation.

Related readings: Douglas W. Morris. "Enemies of biodiversity"; Gordon Laird. "On thin ice"; Marla Cone. "Dozens of words for snow, none for pollution"; and Furgal and Seguin. "Climate change, health, and vulnerability in Canadian northern Aboriginal communities."

Climate change, health, and vulnerability in Canadian northern Aboriginal communities

Christopher Furgal[1] **and Jacinthe Seguin**[2]

(5,300 words)

Background: Canada has recognized that Aboriginal and northern communities in the country face unique challenges and that there is a need to expand the assessment of vulnerabilities to climate change to include these communities. Evidence suggests that Canada's North is already experiencing significant changes in its climate—changes that are having negative impacts on the lives of Aboriginal people living in these regions. Research on climate change and health impacts in northern Canada thus far has brought together Aboriginal community members, government representatives, and researchers and is charting new territory.

Methods and results: In this article we review experiences from two projects that have taken a community-based dialogue approach to identifying and assessing the effects of and vulnerability to climate change and the impact on the health in two Inuit regions of the Canadian Arctic.

Conclusions: The results of the two case projects that we present argue for a multi-stakeholder, participatory framework for assessment that supports the necessary analysis, understanding, and enhancement of capabilities of local areas to respond and adapt to the health impacts at the local level.

[1] Nasivvik Centre for Inuit Health and Changing Environments, Public Health Research Unit, Centre hospitalier Universitaire du Québec—Centre hospitalier Université Laval, Department of Political Science, Laval University, Québec City, Québec, Canada.

[2] Climate Change and Health Office, Health Canada, Ottawa, Ontario, Canada.

Key words: Aboriginal, adaptive capacity, Arctic, climate change, Inuit, vulnerability.

There is strong evidence that Canada's North is already experiencing significant changes in its climate (e.g., McBean et al. 2005). The climatic and environmental changes that have been observed during the last century require greater understanding and involvement by individuals and institutions to define effective adaptation strategies. Through signing the 1992 United Nations Framework Convention on Climate Change (2006) and ratifying the Kyoto Protocol (2006), Canada has shown its commitment to the global effort to slow the rate of warming, reduce emissions, conduct research, and initiate action at the national and regional levels to develop adaptation strategies to minimize the impact throughout the country (Government of Canada 2003). Canada has recognized that Aboriginal and northern communities face unique challenges and that it is necessary to expand the assessment of vulnerabilities to effects of climate change to all areas of Canada, including the North (Government of Canada 2003). This work is essential for the development of effective adaptive strategies to protect the health of Canadians in all regions of the country.

Assessing the impacts that these climate changes are having or may have on people's lives requires a combination of disciplinary approaches and methods (Patz et al. 2000). Research on climate change and health impacts in northern Canada is in its infancy (Furgal et al. 2002). It uses and focuses particularly on indigenous knowledge and local observations of environmental change along with scientific assessments of the impacts associated with these and other forms of change. In this article, we review experiences from projects that used a community-based dialogue-oriented approach to identifying and assessing potential health impacts and vulnerabilities to climate change in two Inuit regions of Canada's North. These experiences build a strong case for a multi-stakeholder, qualitative, and participatory approach to identifying and assessing risks while enhancing the capacity of local areas to respond to the impacts of climate change.

THE CANADIAN NORTH

A common definition of Canada's North that we use here includes the three territorial administrative regions north of 60° latitude (Yukon, Northwest Territories, and Nunavut) as well as the region of Nunavik, north of 55° in the province of Québec and the Inuit settlement region of Nunatsiavut within Labrador. The latter two regions comprise communities with large Aboriginal populations and share many bio-geographic characteristics with the territorial Arctic. Together, this region covers approximately 60 per cent of Canada's land mass (figure 1).

The vast coastline, islands, and permanent multi-year ice found in Canada's North are rich in geography and biodiversity. The diversity of the regions' ecosystems, climate, and cultures forms a socio-ecologic collage across the top of the country (Canadian Arctic Contaminants Assessment Report II 2003). Communities are spread along Canada's northern coastline and interior, and the land and sea provide northern residents with a primary source of nutrition and form a central part of their livelihoods and cultures (Van Oostdam et al. 2005).

Northerners have witnessed profound environmental, social, political, and economic changes in recent decades (Damas 2002; Wonders 2003). Research on contaminants, and more recently on climate change, has uncovered what many northerners have known for some time: the Arctic environment is stressed, and irreversible changes are occurring. At the same time, many communities are transitioning economically, having become more permanent than they were 40 years ago. Many communities now have a mixed economy of traditional or land-based activities and wage employment, with many of the wage employment opportunities now associated with large-scale development of non-renewable natural resources (e.g., mining). These increases in development and cash income have resulted in changes in local economies and increased accessibility to many market items typically available in urban centres to the south. Further, dramatic political changes have resulted in Aboriginal groups in many regions now leading regionally based forms of self-government or being currently engaged in negotiations to establish such arrangements that include land claim and resource settlements. One example of this arrangement is the establishment of the Territory of Nunavut in 1999 (Indian and Northern Affairs Canada [INAC] 1993).

Just over half of the approximately 100,000 northern residents are Aboriginal and belong to distinct cultural groups, including the Yukon First Nations (Yukon), Dene, Métis, and Gwich'in (Northwest Territories), and Inuit (Nunavut, Nunavik, the new Inuit land claim area of Nunatsiavut within the region of Labrador, and the Inuvialuit Settlement Region of the Northwest Territories). Many of the communities are characterized by an increasingly young and rapidly growing population: 54 per cent of the population of Nunavut is under 15 years of age, compared with the national average of 25 per cent (Statistics Canada 2001). Many still experience lower health status than their southern counterparts. For example, life expectancy among Aboriginal people in some regions, such as Nunavik, is as much as 12 years lower than the national average for both sexes (Statistics Canada 2001). In addition, many remote communities are challenged by limited access to health services, lower average socio-economic status, crowding and poor-quality housing, and concerns regarding basic services such as drinking water quality (Statistics Canada 2001). Despite these challenges, all northern cultures retain a close relationship with the environment and a strong knowledge base of their regional surroundings. Even today, the environment and the country foods that come from the land, lakes, rivers, and sea remain central to the way of life, cultural identity, and health of northern Aboriginal people (Van Oostdam et al. 2005). More than 70 per cent of northern Aboriginal adults harvest natural resources through hunting and fishing, and of those, > 96 per cent do so for subsistence purposes (Statistics Canada 2001). This strong relationship with their environment plays a critical role in the ability of northern Aboriginal peoples to observe, detect, and anticipate changes in their natural environment.

CLIMATE CHANGE IN CANADA'S NORTH

The breadth of scientific research on the Canadian northern environment has grown significantly in recent decades. Scientific research, monitoring, and observations, and the knowledge we have acquired from Aboriginal people have resulted in an awareness that changes are taking place. Observed trends vary depending on the region and period analyzed. For example, the western and central Arctic have experienced a general warming over the past 30–50 years of approximately 2–3°C (Weller et al. 2005). This warming is more pronounced in winter months. It is not until the last 15 or so years that this same warming trend, although not to the same extent, has been observed in eastern regions of the Canadian Arctic. Observed impacts associated with these changes include a significant thinning of sea and freshwater ice, a shortening of the winter ice season, reduction in snow cover, changes in wildlife and plant species distribution, melting permafrost, and increased coastal erosion of some shorelines (Cohen 1997; Huntington and Fox 2005; Ouranos 2004; Weller et al. 2005). According to the Arctic Climate Impact Assessment (ACIA 2005) designated climate models, the predictions are for increased warming and precipitation throughout the Canadian Arctic. Annual mean warming in the west is projected to range between 3 and 4°C and upwards of 7°C in winter months. Winter warming is expected to be greatest in the more centrally located areas of southern Baffin Island and Hudson Bay (3–9°C). A 30 per cent increase in precipitation is predicted by the end of the twenty-first century, with the greatest increases occurring in areas of greatest warming (Weller et al. 2005). The predicted impacts on the environment, regional economies, and people are far-reaching. Recent research projects have begun to identify specific local vulnerabilities and risk management measures/adaptation strategies that are already in place or that can be planned (e.g., Berkes and Jolly 2002; Ford et al. 2006; Nickels et al. 2002); however, very little attention has been given to health impacts and adaptations in this region to date.

ASSESSING HEALTH IMPACTS AND VULNERABILITY

Health data series and regional scale assessments in the Canadian North are limited. However, recent qualitative studies examining the potential health impacts of environmental change provide new insights with which to focus research and proactively develop response strategies. They show the need for community participation in filling information gaps and increasing our understanding of factors that enhance or

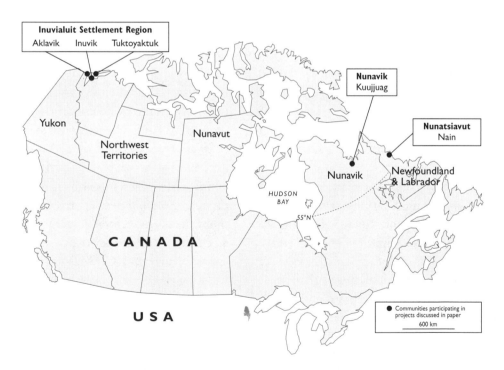

Figure 1. Map showing territories and regions of the Canadian North. Communities engaged in projects such as those discussed in Furgal et al. (2002), Nickels et al. (2002), and this present article are identified.

inhibit adaptive capabilities (Furgal et al. 2002; Nickels et al. 2002). The cases we review below present some of these experiences.

Climate change and health in Nunavik and Labrador.

The project Climate Change and Health in Nunavik and Labrador: What We Know from Science and Inuit Knowledge (Furgal et al. 2001) was conducted in the communities of Kuujjuaq, Nunavik (Québec), and Nain, Nunatsiavut (Labrador) in 2000–01. The project was initiated by members of regional Aboriginal (Inuit) agencies in charge of local environmental health issues in cooperation with a university researcher (C. Furgal, Laval University, Québec City, Québec, Canada). The project was conducted to establish a baseline understanding of the relationship between environmental changes observed in the communities and the potential impacts of these changes on health, as perceived by participants and reported in the health sciences literature.

Nunavik is home to approximately 9,000 Inuit residents living in 14 villages distributed along the coasts of Ungava Bay, Hudson Strait, and the eastern shore of Hudson Bay (figure 1). In 2005 the autonomous Inuit region of Nunatsiavut was established via a tripartite agreement between the federal and provincial governments and the Inuit of Labrador. This region is situated within the mainland boundary of the province of Newfoundland and Labrador. The region is home to approximately 4,800 Inuit living in five coastal communities (figure 1). Despite recent economic, political, and social changes in the regions of Nunavik and Nunatsiavut over the past decades, residents remain close to their traditions, and many aspects of a land-based traditional lifestyle are still commonly practised.

To identify potential impacts of observed climate-related changes on health, the project gathered information from various sources.

Investigators reviewed the available scientific literature, conducted expert consultations with northern health and environment professionals and researchers, and documented Inuit knowledge and perspectives via focus groups with 16 Inuit hunters, elders, and women in the two communities. A process of thematic content analysis was then performed on the qualitative data, and common groups or categories of environmental changes and human impacts were developed (Tesch 1990). This analysis of the collective base of information identified a series of potential direct and indirect health impacts associated with climatic changes observed in Nunavik and Nunatsiavut (table 1; Furgal et al. 2002).

Most observations and impacts were common between the two regions. For the purposes of the discussion here to present the scope of changes and impacts observed to date, the results of these two regions are combined. Participants in the two regions identified changes in climatic conditions over the past 10 years not previously experienced or reported in the region. Some changes were identified as having a direct impact on the health of individuals. Respiratory stress was reported among elderly participants and those with decreased respiratory health in association with an increase in summer temperature extremes that now exceed 30°C in both regions. The reported increase in uncharacteristic weather patterns and storm events had significant impacts on travel and hunting/fishing safety. As one focus group participant reported:

> it changes so quick now you find. Much faster than it used to . . . last winter when the teacher was caught out it was perfect in the morning . . . then it went down flat and they couldn't see anything. . . . Eighteen people were caught out then, and they almost froze, it was bitterly cold. (Nunatsiavut focus group participant, unpublished data, 2001)

Significantly more indirect associations between climate-related changes and health were reported by local residents and by northern environment and health professionals or were found in the pertinent scientific literature (table 2). For example, warming winter temperatures in the areas around both communities were reported to have changed the timing of ice freeze-up and decreased its thickness and stability. For Inuit communities, sea ice travel is critical for accessing wildlife resources and travelling between communities during winter months. There are anecdotal reports of an increase in the number of accidents and drownings associated with poor or uncharacteristic ice conditions during times of the year that are predictable and typically very safe. More events are reported each year, such as that occurring in 2003 when two young Inuit men went through the ice on their skidoos and drowned near their community as a result of a strange thinning ice phenomenon that was reported to have been "becoming more common in recent years" (Nelson 2003). With a young and increasingly sedentary population spending more time in communities engaged in wage employment and less time on the land, a combination of factors appears to make this group more vulnerable to the climate-related changes being reported in many northern regions today. Moreover, changes in the timing of the ice season are reported to impact the frequency and timing of hunting activities in communities, as indicated by the following comment:

> This year and last year, we have been stopped when we were going to go fishing. The ice broke up quickly. We would have gone fishing more in the past. (Nunavik focus group participant, unpublished data, 2001)

The implications of these changes on food security and potential implications on nutritional health among these populations, which receive significant energy and nutrient contributions to their total diet from these country foods, is only now being investigated. In fact, a number of focused research projects have been initiated with the communities involved in this present study and others in these regions. For example, work on climate and water quality, hunting behaviour, women's health, and emerging and chronic diseases in the North are currently under way.

In general, the impacts identified by local residents in this project were supported primarily by scientific evidence and the published literature, although, in some cases, the effects represented new findings. Many impacts were based on individuals' experiences in relation to observed climate-related changes in the local area. Other impacts were identified as "potential," as they were logical extrapolations for residents considering the observed patterns of change in regional climate variables and the perceived relationship between Inuit health and the environment (tables 1 and 2).

Inuit community workshops on climate change. In response to growing concern among Inuit communities about environmental changes being observed, the national Inuit organization in Canada, Inuit Tapiriit Kanatami, initiated a project in cooperation with regional Inuit organizations and Canadian research institutions to document changes and impacts experienced in communities and to discuss how communities currently are adapting or may adapt in the future. In the first series of workshops in January and February 2002, a research team involving regionally based Inuit representatives visited three of the six communities in the Inuvialuit Settlement Region of the Northwest Territories (Tuktoyaktuk, Aklavik, and Inuvik, Northwest Territories; figure 1). Community workshops occurred over two days in each community, and research team

Table 1. Summary of potential direct climate-related health impacts in Nunavik and Labrador.

Identified climate-related change	Potential direct-health impacts
Increased (magnitude and frequency) temperature extremes	Increased heat- and cold-related morbidity and mortality
Increase in frequency and intensity of extreme weather events (e.g., storms) Increase in uncharacteristic weather patterns	Increased frequency and severity of accidents while hunting and travelling, resulting in injuries, death, psychosocial stress
Increased UV-B exposure	Increased risks of skin cancers, burns, infectious diseases, eye damage (cataracts), immuno-suppression

UV-B, ultraviolet B. Adapted from Furgal et al. (2002).

Table 2. Summary of potential indirect climate-related health impacts in Nunavik and Labrador.

Identified climate-related change	Potential indirect-health impacts
Increased (magnitude and frequency) temperature	Increase in infectious disease incidence and transmission, psychosocial disruption
Decrease in ice distribution, stability, and duration of coverage	Increased frequency and severity of accidents while hunting and travelling, resulting in injuries, death, psychosocial stress Decreased access to country food items; decreased food security; erosion of social and cultural values associated with country foods preparation, sharing, and consumption
Change in snow conditions (decrease in quality of snow for igloo construction with increased humidity)	Challenges to building shelters (igloo) for safety while on the land
Increase in range and activity of existing and new infective agents (e.g., biting flies)	Increased exposure to existing and new vectorborne diseases
Change in local ecology of waterborne and foodborne agents (introduction of new parasites and perceived decrease in quality of natural drinking water sources)	Increase in incidence of diarrheal and other infectious diseases Emergence of new diseases
Increased permafrost melting, decreased structural stability	Decreased stability of public health, housing, and transportation infrastructure Psychosocial disruption associated with community relocation (partial or complete)
Sea-level rise	Psychosocial disruption associated with infrastructure damage and community relocation (partial or complete)
Changes in air pollution (contaminants, pollens, spores)	Increased incidence of respiratory and cardiovascular diseases; increased exposure to environmental contaminants and subsequent impacts on health development

Adapted from Furgal et al. (2002).

members documented Inuit residents' observations of environmental changes and the reported effects they were experiencing in association with these changes. At the same time, communities began to identify existing strategies or develop potential adaptation strategies for local-level response (table 3; Nickels et al. 2002). The processes used for the workshop drew on participatory analysis and planning techniques, including Participatory Rural Appraisal (PRA) and Objectives Oriented Project Planning (ZOPP) (Chambers 1997; Deutsche Gesellschaft für Technische Zusammenarbeit [German Agency for Technical Cooperation] 1988).

The communities of the Inuvialuit Settlement Region (ISR) have been observing changes associated with warming in their region for a longer period than those living in the eastern Arctic communities. Changes in the ISR appear more pronounced. For example, increased mean summer and winter temperatures, temperature extremes, an increase in uncharacteristic weather patterns and storm events, a decrease in precipitation, and changes in the characteristics of the ice season similar to those reported in the eastern communities (Furgal et al. 2002) were discussed in ISR community workshops (Nickels et al. 2002). These changes affect the health of individuals and communities, and in some cases communities are already beginning to respond (table 3).

For example, in association with summer warming, residents are reporting an increase in the number and species of biting flies and insects, including bees. Many residents are concerned because of the potential for spread of disease or potential allergic reactions to stings, as many of these insects have never been seen before in this region. Consequently, a public education process was recommended by workshop participants to inform people about what action could be taken to minimize the risk of being bitten and to alleviate public fear.

Currently, little information on these topics exists or is available in the communities (table 3).

Locally appropriate strategies were suggested to address climate-related impacts on animal distribution and decreased human access to important country food sources (e.g., caribou and geese). Furgal et al. (2002) reported that some people (e.g., elders and those with limited equipment and financial resources) were challenged in their access to country food species, particularly during fall and spring because of changes in ice conditions, water levels, or shifts in animal migrations. These changes were resulting in increased costs and time associated with travelling longer distances to procure these foods and a decrease in consumption of these items for some members of the community. Because of these problems, it was recommended that a community hunting and sharing program be formalized to ensure access to these foodstuffs for all (table 3).

Currently, more reactive than proactive strategies are in place to adapt to climate-related health impacts in these communities. Changes in hunting behaviour, increased investments in equipment or infrastructure (e.g., smoke houses, freezers), and the importance of increased education and information exchange were identified. As in the eastern Arctic communities, these initial workshops have led to the establishment of a variety of projects that address specific issues. Some of these projects will potentially lead to proactive primary adaptations to reduce exposure (Casimiro et al. 2001).

UNDERSTANDING THE CAPACITY OF CANADA'S NORTH FOR HEALTH ADAPTATION

A summary of examples of adaptive strategies from the work presented in table 3 is indicative of the inherently adaptive nature of Inuit society and northern Aboriginal cultures in general (Adger et al. 2003; Nickels et al. 2002; Reidlinger

Table 3. Examples of environmental changes, effects, and coping strategies/adaptations reported by community residents in the Inuvialuit Settlement Region to minimize negative health impacts of climate change.

Observation	Effect	Coping strategy/adaptation
Warmer temperatures	Not able to store country food properly while hunting; food spoils quicker; less country foods are consumed	Return to community more often in summer while hunting to store food safely (in cool temperatures) Needed: investment of more funds for hunting activities Decrease amount of future hunting and storage with fewer places to store extra meat Needed: re-investment in government-supported community freezer program
Warmer temperatures in summer	Can no longer prepare dried/smoked fish in the same way: "It gets cooked in the heat" Less dried/smoked fish eaten	Alter construction of smoke houses: build thicker roofs to regulate temperature Adapt drying and smoking techniques
Lower water levels in some areas and some brooks/creeks drying up	Decrease in sources of good natural (raw) drinking water available while on the land Increased risk of waterborne illnesses	Bottled water now purchased and taken on trips
More mosquitoes and other (new) biting insects	Increased insect bites Increasing concern about health effects of new biting insects not seen before	Use insect repellent, lotion, or sprays Use netting and screens on windows and entrances to houses Needed: information and education on insects and biting flies to address current perception/fear
Changing animal travel/migration routes	Makes hunting more difficult (requires more fuel, gear, and time) Some residents (e.g. elders) cannot afford to hunt, thus consuming less country foods	Initiation of a community program for active hunters to provide meat to others (e.g. elders) who are unable to travel/hunt under changing conditions Needed: financial and institutional support to establish program

Adapted from Nickels et al. (2002).

and Berkes 2001). However, the ability to respond varies among communities and regions and is influenced by some common critical factors. The World Health Organization framework for health adaptation (Grambsch and Menne 2003) identifies seven elements that influence vulnerability and adaptation to climate-related health impacts, many of which are applicable to the northern communities discussed here.

The ability to overcome changes in access to or availability of country food resources, which are important for nutritional and socio-cultural well-being, is significantly influenced by an individual's access to economic resources and technology. The ability to invest more in the required tools and equipment for hunting and travelling, or the access to other forms of transportation (e.g., snow machine, four-wheel all-terrain vehicle, flat-bottom or larger boat) allows individuals to adapt more easily to changing environmental conditions (Duhaime et al. 2002; Ford et al. 2006).

Similarly, the generation and sharing of local or traditional knowledge of regional environments and the relationship between the environment and humans further support this ability to adapt while on the land and safely navigate increasingly dangerous and uncharacteristic conditions. The ability to shift species, alter hunting behaviours, and read environmental cues (e.g., weather prediction, ice safety) all increase hunting and travel safety and success. The importance of this knowledge is gaining recognition among scientific and policy communities (e.g., Huntington and Fox 2005); however, its generation is being challenged locally with shifts toward a more "Western lifestyle" involving more time spent in communities engaged in indoor wage-based economic activities and less time on the land (Chapin et al. 2005).

The support provided through institutional or formal arrangements for aspects of traditional lifestyles and health may become increasingly important with climate change in Arctic regions. As many communities begin to represent more pluralistic societies in terms of livelihoods and lifestyles, establishing country food collection, storage, and distribution programs and economic support for the pursuit of traditional activities become important in reducing the vulnerabilities to and enhancing adaptive capabilities for climate-related changes. Also important is the formalization of traditional knowledge documentation and sharing mechanisms through the establishment of such things as community-based ice monitoring programs (Lafortune et al. 2004).

With warming temperatures and the potential for the introduction of new water and food-borne agents and permafrost melting, which threatens built structures in coastal communities, some basic public health infrastructures (e.g., water treatment and distribution, emergency transportation) are increasingly vulnerable. The security of basic public health infrastructure in small remote communities that are already challenged regarding provision of some basic services is a significant determinant of adaptive ability in these locations.

Finally, existing health status issues in Inuit populations (e.g., nutritional deficiencies, increasing rates of diabetes and some cancers associated with shifts toward a more "Western diet" and sedentary lifestyle, and rates of respiratory illness) appear to be further exacerbated by changes in local climate. The combination of environmental change, basic health needs, limited economic choices, and shifts in northern society and lifestyle appears to increase vulnerability and limit the ability of some Arctic communities to respond. When many of these factors overlap and the population is already facing some critical health issues, the impact of climate change is greater because of the population's vulnerability (e.g., small remote communities, with a limited natural and economic resource base).

DISCUSSION

Indigenous populations are often more vulnerable to climatic changes because of their close relationship with the environment, their reliance on the land and sea for subsistence purposes, and the fact that they are more likely to inhabit areas of more severe impact such as coastal regions, often have lower socio-economic status, are more socially marginalized, and have less access to quality health care services (Kovats et al. 2003). In the public health sector, this combination of the current exposure-response relationship, the extent of exposure, and the possible preventative measures in place creates a vulnerability baseline against which the effectiveness of future policies can be measured via changes in the burden of disease (Ebi et al. 2003). The dialogue approach we present here shows the value of establishing this baseline and engaging Arctic Aboriginal communities on these issues by a process very similar to that outlined by Ebi et al. (2006).

The findings presented in these two small studies are supported by others (e.g., Ford et al. 2006; Krupnik and Jolly 2002). A workshop with northern health professionals, community leaders, and Aboriginal representatives from across the North reported similar results (Health Canada 2002). Critical issues identified included challenges related to northern home design and a lack of ventilation causing heat stress among elderly on increasingly warm days; impacts to food security because of changes in sea-ice access routes to hunting areas or ice-road stability and effects on reliable transport of market foodstuffs; combined impacts on mental health due to reduced ability of individuals to practise aspects of traditional lifestyles; and impacts to infrastructure and threats of community disruption or relocation (Health Canada 2002).

Although a regionally based analysis was not possible with the data available, variations in vulnerabilities and adaptive abilities appear to exist between and within regions on the basis of a number of common factors (see "Understanding the capacity of Canada's North for health adaptation"; Grambsch and Menne 2003). Similarly, both projects were conducted with Inuit communities, and hence, differences between Arctic cultural groups were not identified. However, as each Aboriginal group is uniquely adapted to its geography and local ecology, it is reasonable to speculate that each group's socio-ecologic resilience and adaptive capacity

for health issues is similarly unique. Observed climate changes, impacts, and response abilities of Yukon First Nations living in the interior of the western Arctic likely are very different from those of the Inuit communities presented here. It is therefore critical to conduct such assessments locally.

As in other regions of the world, enhancing adaptive capacity can be regarded as a "no regrets" option in the North, as it not only reduces vulnerability but also improves immediate resilience to current-day stresses (Yohe and Tol 2002). Strengthening access and availability to country foods throughout the year for communities or increasing public health education associated with environmental causes of disease are such examples. Establishing community freezer and distribution plans will help in addressing current nutritional and other food issues as well as increase the capability of an individual to access safe and healthy foods in the face of environmental changes. Increased knowledge and awareness of environmental causes of disease will address perceived risks and provide valuable information to empower individuals to continue to make healthy decisions.

Both the Nunavik-Nunatsiavut (Labrador) project and the workshops in the ISR are starting points in the collection of information to support community, regional, national, and international processes on climate change. Many new projects have since begun on components of the climate-health relationship in northern communities, and many of these are taking a similarly participatory approach (e.g., ArcticNet 2004). Arctic indigenous peoples have also participated in the international assessment of climate change impacts through their involvement in the ACIA with academic and government researchers (ACIA 2004). This level of engagement and contribution is a significant advance in environmental health impact and vulnerability research.

Despite these advances, research on climate and health in northern Aboriginal populations is sparse (Berner and Furgal 2005), and the identification of the impacts on local populations and community adaptations is still in its infancy and requires continued effort, with attention to thresholds and limits to adaptation (Berkes and Jolly 2002).

The studies presented here on populations in Canada's North and a review of other recent research in this region (e.g., ACIA 2005; Ford et al. 2006; Health Canada 2003) identify data gaps that we need to fill and methods that we need to use to increase our understanding of climate and health assessment, vulnerability, and the capacity to adapt in northern Aboriginal communities. They include the following:

Multiple-scale research and data. Community-based assessments and systematic research must be conducted on the issues of climate change impacts in the North and elsewhere in Canada. Local, regional, and national levels are interconnected in supporting and facilitating action on climate change; thus, data at multiple levels and research that link scales to understand these relationships are needed. Fine-scale meteorologic data is required in many northern regions and must be collected in a way that allows the data to be linked to existing and future health data sets. Models of change and impact must be linked with currently used global change scenarios.

Quality, comparable, standardized data. Innovative approaches to health and climate assessment are needed and should consider the role of socio-cultural diversity present among Arctic communities. This requires both qualitative and quantitative data and the collection of long-term data sets on standard health outcomes at comparable temporal and spatial levels. These

data must include local observations and knowledge collected using reliable and standardized methods.

Integrated, interdisciplinary approaches to assessment. Assessments that take a multidisciplinary approach bringing together health scientists, climatologists, biologists, ecologists, social and behavioural scientists, and policy researchers and include demographic, socio-economic, and health and environmental data are required to develop an adequate understanding of impacts, vulnerabilities, and capabilities in Arctic communities.

Increased analysis of historical data. Historical data (climate, health, social, economic) from appropriate locations with climate systems similar to those projected for Canadian northern regions must be used for integrated and geographic analyses of the spread of disease relative to climate variables. These analyses would make efficient use of existing information and increase our understanding of these issues and their interconnected nature.

Improvement of scenarios and models for health assessment. Developing and improving regional scenarios is needed for areas projected to experience significant impacts, such as the western Arctic. Socio-economic scenarios to model and project impacts and changes within northern indigenous populations are needed. Such scenarios are currently sparse, poorly developed, and inadequate.

Conceptual and analytical understanding of vulnerability and capacity. Work is needed at both the conceptual and analytical levels to define and increase our understanding of vulnerability and community health, how best to measure these concepts, and the use of these concepts in making decisions about the health of the community and in risk management. This work should include local knowledge and informal institutions (e.g., cultural sharing networks) to best understand these concepts in Aboriginal communities.

Enhancement of local capacities to identify, conduct, and analyze data related to climate change and the impacts on health. To ensure success and sustainability of adaptation strategies, development of local and regional monitoring, analytical, and decision-making capabilities are needed to support cooperative and empowering approaches to research and action.

CONCLUSIONS

In the Canadian North, the debate is no longer solely about identifying and predicting effects of climatic change but rather about what can and should be done to adapt, as some communities are already reporting impacts. This research focuses on improving the understanding of the magnitude and timing of the impacts of climate change, how individuals and communities cope with current and predicted changes, and what public institutions should do to actively support adaptation.

There is currently sparse information on the effectiveness of any current strategies for dealing with climate-related or environmental risks to health in the locations described here and in other areas of the country. This lack of information is an important gap in our understanding and ability to assess which, where, and when Canadians may be vulnerable to the effects of climate change. A significant component is the lack of an assessment of the Canadian health sector's ability at various levels and in various locations to cope with and plan for the impacts of climate change. The cooperative planning,

development, and conduct of projects in Inuit communities bringing together scientists, northern environment and health professionals, and community residents and experts, as presented here, has been essential to the success of the projects described in this article. The community-based, dialogue-focused approach has proven valuable in engaging communities and establishing a local baseline for understanding the changes, impacts, vulnerabilities, and ability to respond at the local scale. Such an approach may very well prove useful in establishing this baseline in other regions.

This article is part of the mini-monograph *Climate change and human health: National assessments of impacts and adaptation.*

We acknowledge the participation and contribution made by northern residents and organizations to this work to date. C.F. acknowledges Canadian Institutes of Health Research—Institute for Aboriginal Peoples' Health for support to his work provided through a grant to the Nasivvik Centre. Thanks are also extended to three anonymous reviews for their comments.

Environmental Health Perspectives.
2006. December 114 (12).

REFERENCES

ACIA. 2004. Arctic Climate Impact Assessment. Overview Report. Cambridge, UK: Cambridge University Press.

ACIA. 2005. Arctic Climate Impact Assessment. Scientific Report. Cambridge, UK: Cambridge University Press.

Adger WN, Huq S, Brown K, Conway D, Hulme M. 2003. Adaptation to climate change in the developing world. Prog Dev Stud 3(3):179–195.

ArcticNet. 2004. Network Centres of Excellence. Available: http://www.arcticnet.ulaval.ca [accessed 15 June 2006].

Berkes F, Jolly D. 2002. Adapting to climate change: social-ecological resilience in a Canadian western Arctic community. Conserv Ecol 5(2):18. Available: http://www.consecol.org/vol5/iss2/art18 [accessed 3 July 2006].

Berner J, Furgal C. 2005. Human health. In: Arctic Climate Impact Assessment (ACIA). Cambridge, UK: Cambridge University Press, 863–906.

Canadian Arctic Contaminants Assessment Report II. 2003. Canadian Arctic Contaminants Assessment Report II (Health, Biotic, Abiotic and Knowledge in Action). Ottawa, Ontario, CN: Northern Contaminants Program, Department of Indian and Northern Affairs.

Casimiro E, Calheiros JM, Dessai S. 2001. Human health. In: Climate Change in Portugal: Scenarios, Impacts and Adaptation Measures (Santos FD, Forbes K, Moita R, eds). Lisbon: Scenarios, Impacts and Adaptation Measures.

Chambers R. 1997. Whose Reality Counts? Putting the First Last. London: Intermediate Technology Publications.

Chapin FS. 2005. Polar systems. In: Millenium Ecosystem Assessment. Available: http://www.millenniumassessment.org/en/products.aspx [accessed 15 June 2006].

Cohen SJ. 1997. Mackenzie Basin Impact Study. Final Report. Ottawa, Ontario, CN: Environment Canada.

Damas D. 2002. Arctic Migrants/Arctic Villagers. Montréal, Québec, CN: McGill-Queen's University Press.

Deutsche Gesellschalt für Technische Zusammenarbeit (German Agency for Technical Cooperation). 1988. ZOPP (Objectives Oriented Project Planning: An Introduction to the Method). Eschborn, Germany: Deutsche Gesellschalt für Technische Zusammenarbeit.

Duhaime G, Chabot M and Gaudreault M. 2002. Food consumption patterns and socioeconomic factors among the Inuit of Nunavik. Ecol Food Nutr 41:91–118.

Ebi KL, Kovats RS, Menne B. 2006. An approach for assessing human health vulnerability and public health interventions to adapt to climate change. Environ Health Perspect 114:1930–1934.

Ebi KL, Mearns O, Nyenzi B. 2003. Weather and climate: changing human exposures. In: Climate Change and Health: Risks and Responses (McMichael AJ, Campbell-Lendrum OH, Corvalan CF, Ebi KL, Githeko A, et al., eds). Geneva: World Health Organization.

Ford JD, Smit B, Wandel J. 2006. Vulnerability to climate change in the Arctic: a case study from Arctic Bay, Canada. Global Environ Change 16:145–160.

Furgal C, Martin D, Gosselin P. 2002. Climate change and health in Nunavik and Labrador: lessons from Inuit knowledge. In: The Earth is Faster Now: Indigenous Observations of Arctic Environmental Change (Krupnik I, Jolly D, eds). Washington, DC: Arctic Research Consortium of the United States, Arctic Studies Center, Smithsonian Institute, 266–300.

Furgal C, Martin D, Gosselin P, Viau A, Labrador Inuit Association (LIA), Nunavik Regional Board of Health and Social Services (NRBHSS). 2001. Climate change in Nunavik and Labrador: what we know from science and Inuit ecological knowledge. Final Project Report prepared for Climate Change Action Fund. Beauport, Québec, CN: Centre hospitalier Universitaire du Québec Pavillon Centre hospitalier Université Laval.

Government of Canada. 2003. Climate Change Impacts and Adaptation: A Canadian Perspective. Available: http://www.adaptation. nrcan.gc.ca/perspective_e.asp [accessed 15 June 2006].

Grambsch A, and Menne B. 2003. Adaptation and adaptive capacity in the public health context. In: Climate Change and Health: Risks and Responses (McMichael AJ, Campbell-Lendrum DH, Corvalan CF, Ebi KL, Githeko A, Scheraga JD, et al., eds). Geneva: World Health Organization, 220–236.

Health Canada. 2002. Climate Change and Health and Well-Being in Canada's North. Report on the Public Health Planning Workshop on Climate Change and Health and Well-Being in the North, 6–7 July 2002, Yellowknife, Northwest Territories. Ottawa, Ontario, CN: Health Canada.

Health Canada. 2003. Climate Change and Health: Assessing Canada's Capacity to Address the Health Impacts of Climate Change. Prepared for the Expert Advisory Workshop on Adaptive Capacity, 27–28 November 2003, Mont Tremblant, Québec, CN. Ottawa, Ontario, CN: Climate Change and Health Office, Safe Environments Program, Health Environments and Consumer Safety Branch, Health Canada.

Huntington H, Fox S. 2005. The changing Arctic: indigenous perspectives. In: Arctic Climate Impact Assessment. Cambridge, UK: Cambridge University Press, 61–98.

Indian and Northern Affairs Canada (INAC). 1993. Agreement between the Inuit of the Nunavut Settlement Area and Her Majesty the Queen in Right of Canada. Ottawa, Ontario, CN: Indian Affairs and Northern Development Canada and the Tunngavik Federation of Nunavut.

Kovats S, Ebi KL, Menne B. 2003. Methods of assessing human health vulnerability and public health adaptation to climate change. In: Health and Global Environmental Change, Series no 1. Copenhagen: World Health Organization, World Meteorological Organization, Health Canada, United Nations Environment Programme.

Krupnik I, Jolly D. 2002. The Earth Is Faster Now: Indigenous Observations of Climate Change. Fairbanks, AK: Arctic Research Consortium of the United States.

Kyoto Protocol. 2006. Home Page. Available: http://unfccc.int/kyoto_protocol/items/2830. php [accessed 7 November 2006].

Lafortune V, Furgal C, Drouin J, Annanack T, Einish N, Etidloie B, et al. 2004. Climate Change in Northern Quebec: Access to Land and Resource Issues. Project report. Kuujjuaq, Québec, CN: Kativik Regional Government.

McBean G, Alekssev GV, Chen D, Forland E, Fyfe J, Groisman PY, et al. 2005. Arctic climate: past and present. In: Arctic Climate Impact Assessment. Cambridge, UK: Cambridge University Press, 21–60.

Nelson O. 2003. Two men drown in Inukjuak: snowmobile crashes through thin ice. Nunatsiaq News, 31 January 2003. Available: http://www.nunatsiaq.com/archives/nunavut 030131/news/nuunavik/30131_02.html [accessed 3 July 2006].

Nickels S, Furgal C, Castleden J, Moss-Davies P, Buell M, Armstrong B, et al. 2002. Putting the human face on climate change through community workshops: Inuit knowledge, partnerships, and research. In: The Earth is Faster Now: Indigenous Observations of Arctic Environmental Change (Krupnik I, Jolly D, eds). Washington, DC: Arctic Research Consortium of the United States, Arctic Studies Center, Smithsonian Institute, 300–344.

Ouranos. 2004. S'adapter aux changements climatiques. Bibliothèque nationale du Québec.

Montréal, Québec, CN: Ouranos Climate Change Consortium.

Patz JA, Engelberg D, Last J. 2000. The effects of changing weather on public health. Annu Rev Public Health 21:271–307.

Reidlinger D, Berkes F. 2001. Responding to climate change in northern communities: impacts and adaptations. Arctic 54(1):96–98.

Statistics Canada. 2001. Aboriginal People's Survey 2001—Initial Findings: Well-Being of the Non-Reserve Aboriginal Population. Catalogue no. 89-589-XIE. Ottawa, Ontario, CN: Statistics Canada.

Tesch R. 1990. Qualitative research: analysis types and software tools. New York: Falmer.

United Nations Framework Convention on Climate Change. 2006. Home Page. Available: http://unfccc.int/2860.php [accessed 7 November 2006].

Van Oostdam J, Donaldson SG, Feeley M, Arnold D, Ayotte P, Bondy G, et al. 2005. Human health implications of environmental contaminants in Arctic Canada: a review. Sci Total Environ 351–352:165–246.

Weller G, Bush E, Callaghan TV, Corell R, Fox S, Furgal C, et al. 2005. Summary and Synthesis of the ACIA. In: Arctic Climate Impact Assessment. Cambridge, UK: Cambridge University Press, 989–1020.

Wonders W, ed. 2003. Canada's Changing North. Revised ed. Montréal: McGill-Queen's University Press.

Yohe G, Tol RSJ. 2002. Indicators for social and economic coping capacity—moving toward a working definition of adaptive capacity. Global Environ Change Hum Policy Dimen 12:25–40.

KEY AND DIFFICULT WORDS
Define the following, using context or other clues if possible: **autonomous, tripartite, anecdotal, extrapolation, alleviate, pluralistic, subsistence, resilience.**

QUESTIONS
1. Identify the essay plan. What could account for the absence of a separate literature review section?
2. What is the function of the section "The Canadian North?" What is meant by the phrase "a socio-ecologic collage" (paragraph 4)?
3. In two to three sentences for each study, summarize the purpose and methodology used in the two major studies that the authors focus on in this essay (under "methodology," consider the participants in the study and the methods used to collect and measure data—see, in particular, paragraphs 9–11 and 14).
4. How do "qualitative studies" differ from the "quantitative studies" that typify methods of evidence-gathering and presentation in Type B essays (see pages 22–4)? Why have qualitative methods been used so extensively to assess the impact of climate change in northern Aboriginal communities?

5. (a) Identify which paragraph(s) focus on the material presented in table 1; identify which paragraph(s) focus on the material presented in table 2. Is the more complete picture conveyed through the tables or through the corresponding sections of text? Explain why this might be the case by discussing the different functions of tables and text in this essay. (b) How is the focus of table 3 different from that of tables 1 and 2? What accounts for the differing focus?

6. Explain the differences between "reactive" and "proactive" strategies (paragraph 18). In the long term, which could be considered more important?

7. Identify two general factors that can affect the capacity for health adaptation to climate change. Why is it important to establish a "vulnerability baseline" for Aboriginal groups experiencing the effects of climate change? For what other kinds of groups might it also be important?

8. What is the purpose of the list of "data gaps" mentioned in the "Discussion" section? Paraphrase one of the items in the list.

COLLABORATIVE ACTIVITY

As a follow-up to question 4, discuss the pros and cons of using qualitative methods to investigate a problem or study a phenomenon (you could consider using qualitative methods only or combining them with quantitative ones—the "mixed method" approach). Then come up with one specific situation in which qualitative methods might be useful as a means of investigating a phenomenon. This could be a situation that exists at your university/college or within a particular student group. Along with describing the specific situation, identify which specific approach(es) or method(s) would be the most useful or appropriate (e.g., roundtable discussion, focus groups, workshops, direct observation, unstructured interview).

ACTIVITIES

1. The authors mention the value of knowledge-sharing among members of groups or cultures who want to maintain a traditional lifestyle (paragraph 21) but state that the generation of this knowledge "is being challenged locally with shifts toward a more 'Western lifestyle.'" Write a response (300 to 500 words) that addresses central issues around the maintenance of traditional lifestyles in the face of cultural pressures to conform to mainstream values or practices. Note: This activity could also be used for Marla Cone's "Dozens of words for snow, none for pollution."

2. Write a brief (500- to 750-word) *evaluative* report (stressing assessment) or *informational* report (stressing content) on a website dedicated to the study of climate change in the Canadian Arctic. One such site mentioned in the article

is ArcticNet; this site also contains links to similar sites that you could consider. Organize your report by appropriate formal or descriptive categories. Formal categories could include introduction, methods (basis of your evaluation), results, and conclusion. You could consider the website's purpose, credibility, main menu, links, navigation aids, accessibility, organization, visual appeal, quality and depth of information, use of charts to enhance understanding, and so on.

Related readings: Claude A. Piantadosi. "The human environment"; Gordon Laird. "On thin ice"; Marla Cone. "Dozens of words for snow, none for pollution"; and Kevin Krajick. "In search of the ivory gull."

Appendix

The Active Voice
What Do Students Need to Know about Statistics?

There are two main types of research: **qualitative** and **quantitative**. Both types help us to describe or explain a phenomenon (e.g., the experience of war veterans); however, each method goes about describing the situation in very different ways. Qualitative research uses non-numerical data, such as words or pictures, in order to describe a phenomenon. In-depth interviews and/or extensive observations are typically used in order to collect this type of data. An interview with a war veteran about his experience during the war is an example of a qualitative research approach. Quantitative research, on the other hand, uses numbers in order to describe or explain a phenomenon and typically investigates the relationship between variables (e.g., the relationship between war veterans and depression). Quantitative research typically includes questionnaires with large samples of participants and uses a strict methodology in order to control all factors that are related to the data and therefore may affect the interpretation of that data. A questionnaire mailed out to a random sample of 500 male war veterans across Canada between the ages of 65 and 85 who have no family history of depression is an example of a quantitative research approach.

The decision to use qualitative versus quantitative methods depends on the research question that you ask and the type of information you want to obtain. Qualitative research provides rich and detailed words to describe a phenomenon, but the data is situation- and context-specific. By contrast, quantitative research provides numerical data to describe the relationship between variables, and these relationships may be generalized to the population as a whole. In this essay, we will describe why and how quantitative research methods may be used to answer a research question.

In the social sciences, we conduct research because we are interested in better understanding human behaviour (e.g., frequency of drinking, reaction time, level of intelligence). Most of the time, however, we do not limit ourselves to describing just that behaviour but we also want to know whether it is related (and how) to some other feature of the person or the situation. For example, suppose you are interested in studying the level of intelligence (IQ) of undergraduate students in Linguistics. You might be wondering whether female and male students will have, on average, the same IQ or whether it varies depending on gender. That is, do female students have higher or lower IQ than males? In this case, IQ is what we call the **dependent variable**, and the feature in your study that you think has an influence on it—gender—is the **independent variable**.

Mean and variance: Now suppose you recruit 10 male and 10 female students from one of your classes to answer this question. After administering an intelligence test to your 20 participants (N=20), you realize that each has a different IQ level. For some participants, their IQ value is 100, for others 130, and for still others 110. Because you want to compare the IQ of two groups (females vs. males), you need a unique value, representative of each group, that would allow you to make this comparison. The best way to create that value is by averaging the individual IQ values within each group, creating the **mean** IQ for each group.

Because the mean is only an average of individual IQ values, it will not tell us much about each value from which it was calculated. For example, suppose the mean IQ of both the male and female groups is the same (e.g., 115). The single values used to compute those means could nonetheless be very different. Some males, for example, may have values of 90 and others 130, averaging out to 100, whereas the IQ values of females may be in general closer to the mean (e.g., some 115 and others 120) but also averaging out to 100. In other words, the group of males may have more variation in their IQ values than the group of females.

As you can probably infer by now, the mean becomes less trustworthy as an estimate of the group's IQ when the variation is greater. Therefore, it is useful to have information about how much the single values used to calculate the mean differ from this mean (i.e., a general measure of how spread these values are from the mean). You can obtain this information by calculating the **variance**.

Once you have the information about the mean IQ and the variance for each of your groups, you can use a statistical test of inference to determine whether the means of the two groups are actually different from each other. Recall that you were interested in determining whether, on average, females in your class have higher or lower IQ than males. If the mean IQ for males and females is exactly the same, you would intuitively conclude that females and males are equally smart (as measured by IQ). If they differ by one or two points, your conclusion would probably be the same, because you would consider those one or two points to be random and unimportant. However, what would you conclude if the two means differed by 10 points? How would you determine whether the two means are meaningfully different and that their difference is not just due to chance?

Researchers consider two means to be **significantly different** when there is a very small probability (less than 0.05 or less than five in 100 times) that these two means are different only by chance. In order to determine this probability there are a number of statistical tests you can use (see below, "Correlation and prediction"). Returning to our example, if the mean IQ for female students was 130 and the mean IQ for male students was 120, and if the test you used indicated that there was less than a five in 100 probability that these two values differed by chance, then you could (sadly or happily) say that the girls in your class have a significantly higher IQ value than the boys. The standard of five in 100 for "statistical significance" is an arbitrary but useful convention in research. It does not refer to the social or practical significance of the result, because that is not a statistical issue.

If you had obtained the 20 participants from your class (i.e., your sample) using a random procedure, you could generalize the results of your study to your entire class (in this case, your **population**). However, notice that very rarely do researchers randomly select subjects to participate in their studies and, instead, the selection depends on other factors (e.g., those people who agree to participate in the study).

Correlation and prediction: Say we want to know the relationship between high school GPA and college GPA. Our research question could be, What is the relationship between GPA in high school and GPA in college? A simple **bivariate correlation** can be used to answer this question. Correlations describe the extent to which two variables co-vary (e.g., as high school GPA goes up, so does college GPA).

However, say we determine that mothers' college GPA, fathers' college GPA, age, gender, and parents' income are also related (correlated) to GPA, and we want to know which factors influence college GPA the most. We can use **multiple regression** to answer this question. In multiple regression, all of the variables are entered into a regression (mathematical) equation, which then determines which factors most strongly influence college GPA when controlling for all other factors that were entered into the equation. Let's say fathers' college GPA and mothers' college GPA are revealed as the strongest factors influencing a college GPA. We can then use this information to screen and/or predict who will do the best in college based on their scores on the predictor variables. For example, if a student's mother and father had a high college GPA, we would predict that the student would have a high college GPA.

Another common statistical procedure is called an **ANOVA** (analysis of variance), which allows us to compare groups. Say we want to compare basketball players, volleyball players, and soccer players on their GPA. A **t-test** can be used to compare two groups (e.g., basketball players and volleyball players); however, an ANOVA will allow us to compare 2+ groups (e.g., basketball, volleyball, and soccer players).

For many people, statistics seem intimidating and overwhelming. However, the importance of statistics cannot be understated. At the most basic level of statistics, there are means, medians, modes, and percentages that tell us basic descriptive information (e.g., can describe the current situation). At the more complex level of statistical analysis used by most researchers, statistics allow us to answer some very interesting questions and to make important predictions about human behaviour.

Rachel Dean, Ph.D., and Agustin Del Vento, M.Sc.
Department of Psychology, University of Victoria

Credits

BARRON, Christie, and Dany LACOMBE. "Moral panic and the Nasty Girl." *Canadian Review of Sociology & Anthropology* 42.1 (2005): 51–69. By permission of CSAA/SCSA.

BINKLEY, Peter. "Wikipedia grows up." Originally published in *Feliciter* (April 2006), 52(2) the magazine of the Canadian Library Association.

BRYSON, Mary, Stephen PETRINA, Marcia BRAUNDY, and Suzanne DE CASTELL. "Conditions for success? Gender in technology-intensive courses in British Columbia secondary schools." *Canadian Journal of Science, Mathematics and Technology Education* (www.utpjournals.com/cjsmte).

CLARK, Andy. "Bad borgs?" From *Natural-Born Cyborgs* (2005). Reproduced by permission of Oxford University Press, Inc.

CONE, Marla. "Dozens of words for snow, none for pollution." Reprinted with permission from *Mother Jones* (Jan./Feb. 2005), © 2005, Foundation for National Progress.

DESAI, Jenny. "In the minds of men." *Science & Spirit* (March/April 2005). Reprinted with permission of the Helen Swight Reid Educational Foundation. Published by Heldref Publications, 1319 18th Street, NW, Washington, DC 20036-1802. www.heldref.org. Copyright © 2005.

EKMAN, Paul, Richard J. DAVIDSON, Matthieu RICARD, and B. Alan WALLACE. "Buddhist and psychological perspectives on emotions and well-being." *CDIR Current Directions in Psychological Science*, 24.2 (2005), pp. 59–63. By permission of Blackwell Publishing.

FERGUSON, Sue. "How computers make our kids stupid." *Maclean's*. Reprinted by permission of the publisher.

FISKE, Susan T., Lasana T. HARRIS, and Amy J.C. CUDDY. "Why ordinary people torture enemy prisoners." *Science* 306: 1482–83 (2004). Copyright 2004 AAAS. Reprinted with permission of AAAS.

FOSTER, Peter. "Kyoto: Mother of intervention." *The National Post* (16 Feb. 2005). Reprinted by permission of the author.

FULFORD, Robert. "A box full of history: TV and our sense of the past." *Queen's Quarterly* 112.1 (2005): 89–97. Reprinted by permission of the author.

FURGAL, Christopher, and Jacinthe SEGUIN. "Climate change, health, and vulnerability in Canadian northern Aboriginal communities." *Environmental Health Perspectives*, vol. 114 (12). (Dec. 2006).

GIDENGIL, Elisabeth, André BLAIS, Richard NADEAU, and Neil NEVITTE. "Enhancing democratic citizenship." Reprinted by permission of the publisher from *Citizens* by Elisabeth Gidengil et al. © University of British Columbia Press 2004. All rights reserved by the Publisher.

GLIKSMAN, Louis, E. ADLAF, A. DEMERS, and B. NEWTON-TAYLOR. "Heavy drinking on Canadian campuses." *Canadian Journal of Public Health* 2003, 94(1): 17–21. Reprinted with permission of the Canadian Public Health Association.

HENIGHAN, Stephen. "White curtains." *Geist* 13.55 (Winter 2004), pp. 69–70. Used by permission of Stephen Henighan.

HORGAN, John. "Can science solve the riddle of existence?" Adbusters 13.2. Reprinted by permission of the author.

IYER, Pico. "Canada: Global citizen." *Canadian Geographic* 124.6 (2004). © Pico Iyer. Used by permission of the author.

JAMES, Matt. "Being stigmatized and being sorry: Past injustices and contemporary citizenship." From *Passions for Identity, Canadian Studies for the 21st Century*, 4th edition by TARAS/RASPORICH. 2001. Reprinted with permission of Nelson, a division of Thomson Learning: www.thomsonrights.com.

KERR, Thomas, Mark TYNDALL, Kathy LI, Julio MONTANER, and Evan WOOD. "Safer injection facility use and syringe sharing in injection drug users." Reprinted from *The Lancet*, vol. 366, pp. 316–18. Copyright © 2005, with permission from Elsevier.

KRAJICK, Kevin. "In search of the ivory gull." *Science* 301: 1840–1 (2003). Copyright 2003 AAAS. Reprinted by permission.

LAIRD, Gordon. "On thin ice." *This* (2003): 32–7. Gordon Laird is a Calgary writer and author of *Power* and *Slamming It at the Rodeo*. www.gordonlaird.com. Reprinted by permission of the author.

MORRIS, Douglas W. "Enemies of biodiversity." *Canadian Journal of Zoology* 83.7 (2005): 891–3. Reproduced with permission of the National Research Council Press © 2005.

NIEDZVIECKI, Hal. "The future's books from nowhere." *The Globe and Mail*, 13 Oct. 2005.

NUNGAK, Zebedee. "Qallunology: An introduction to the Inuit study of white people." Used by permission of Zebedee Nungak, Inuit writer and commentator: Kangirsuk, Nunavik, Quebec.

OLDING, Susan. "Push-me-pull-you." *Prairie Fire* (2005). Summer 26(2). Reprinted by permission of the author.

O'ROURKE, P.J. "Sulfur Island." *Atlantic Monthly.* (June 2004). Used by permission of the author.

PIANTADOSI, Claude A. "The human environment." In Claude A. Piantadosi, *The Biology of Human Survival: Life and Death in Extreme Environments* (2003). Reproduced by permission of Oxford University Press, Inc.

POPLAK, Richard. "Fear and loathing in Toontown." *This* 38.6 (2005): 39–40.

POSNER, Michael. "Image world." *Queen's Quarterly* (2003). Reprinted by permission of the author.

POWER, Matthew. "The poison stream." *Harper's Magazine.* Reprinted by permission of International Creative Management, Inc. Copyright © Matthew Power.

ROBIDOUX, Michael A. "Imagining a Canadian identity through sport: A historical interpretation of lacrosse and hockey." *Journal of American Folklore* 115.456 (2002), pp. 209–25. Reprinted by permission of the American Folklore Society, www.afsnet.org.

SAUL, John Ralston. From *Reflections of a Siamese Twin: Canada At the End of the Twentieth Century* by John Ralston Saul © John Ralston Saul 1997. Reprinted by permission of the author and Penguin Group (Canada), a Division of Pearson Canada Inc.

SCHWARTZ, Marlene B., Jennifer J. THOMAS, Kristin M. BOHAN, and Lenny R. VARTANIAN. "Intended and unintended effects of an eating disorder educational program: Impact of presenter identity." *International Journal of Eating Disorders* (2007) 40(2).

SEARS, Robin V. "9/11: The day the world changed." (September 2006). *Policy Options*, Institute for Research on Public Policy. Reproduced with permission of IRPP @ www.IRPP.org.

THOMPSON, Clive. "Game theories." First appeared in *The Walrus*. Reprinted by permission of the author and Featurewell.

TITCHKOSKY, Tanya. "Situating disability: Mapping the outer limits" from *Disability, Self & Society*. University of Toronto Press, pp. 46–63. Reprinted by permission of the publisher.

UNWIN, Peter. "Dead cooks & clinking sandwiches." *The Beaver* 84.5 (2004). Copyright © 2004 Peter Unwin. With permission of the author.

WOHLGEMUT, Joel Pauls. "AIDS, Africa and indifference: A confession." Reprinted from *CMAJ* 03-Sept-02, 167(5), pp. 485–7 by permission of the publisher. © 2002 CMA Media Inc.

YOUNG, Simon N. "Universities, governments and industry: Can the essential nature of universities survive the drive to commercialize?" Reprinted from *JPN* May 2005; 30 (3), pp. 160–3 by permission of the publisher. © 2002 CMA Media Inc.

Index